Cassell's Dictionary of Proverbs

Cassell's Dictionary of Proverbs

DAVID PICKERING

CASSELL&CO

This edition first published in the UK 2001

First published 1997 by
Cassell & Co.
Orion House, 5 Upper St Martins Lane, London WC2H 9EA

Distributed in the United States by
Sterling Publishing Company Co. Inc.
387 Park Avenue South, New York NY 10016–8810

British Library Cataloguing-in-Publication Data
A catalogue record for this book is available from the British Library

ISBN 0-304-35738-3

Designed by Gwyn Lewis
Printed and bound in Finland by WS Bookwell

Contents

Preface

Dictionary definitions of the word 'proverb' vary considerably and it is inevitable that reference sources should differ when it comes to deciding what should qualify for inclusion and what should not. In compiling this revised and enlarged edition of *Cassell's Dictionary of Proverbs*, possible inclusions have been judged on the following grounds. To be included, a proverb had – in most cases, at least – to be concise, memorable (usually traditional) and expressive of a commonplace truth or perceived fact of experience.

The best proverbs, most readers will agree, are short, pithy, often allegorical sayings that are redolent of vanished eras, but that still have something to communicate to the contemporary age. A good proverb neatly summarizes what might otherwise be difficult to express and is immediately understood by the person to whom it is addressed (regardless of whether he or she agrees with it or not). Proverbs represent a shorthand route in conversation – an invaluable tool in this modern era of sound-bites and linguistic functionality. This does not mean, however, that defunct proverbs of purely historical interest have been neglected – they have not, unless they are so obscure that their meaning has long since been lost. This considerably expanded version of the original text includes greatly improved coverage of less familiar proverbs of both English and foreign-language origin, with the accent as always strongly placed upon the most striking and colourful sayings and saws. Many of the most diverting entries added for this edition are for sayings that are known only in specific localities or that are now very rarely encountered, either because they depend upon familiarity with the everyday vocabulary and practices of a vanished rural society or with widely shared knowledge of traditional trades and crafts that have been in decline for many decades.

Dictionaries of proverbs may be divided into those that adopt a wholly alphabetical approach and those that rely solely on thematic organization. Some consist of little more than lists of citations, while others go into such detail on a small number of proverbs that relatively few are covered. *Cassell's Dictionary of Proverbs* attempts to combine elements of both approaches, gathering often large numbers of related proverbs around key headwords and incorporating within the entries copious cross-references (indicated by small capitals) to associated sayings, all within a strict alphabetical framework. Thus, the reader benefits from the convenience of an easily accessible source of reference while still enjoying the opportunity to read in some detail about a particular proverb's origins or history. The addition with this edition of a substantial index, arranged by theme, is designed to provide the reader with an alternative route into the body of the text. It is hoped that this index will prove particularly useful to the author, the speechmaker, the researcher, or any other reader in search of proverbs relating to a particular subject, providing links between proverbs expressing both similar and opposing sentiments.

With around 3000 entries, every attempt has been made to ensure a high degree of comprehensiveness, with proverbs being gleaned from a wide range of cultures and all periods of history, including our own. Where possible, some indication has been given of the actual country of origin (though this may sometimes reflect only a proverb's earliest known history rather than its actual beginnings). Meanings are fully explained and are supported by information about early usage, variant forms and equivalents in other languages, together with cross-references to related entries and, in many cases, examples of usage (with full citations).

It would be both churlish and unrealistic to contemplate the compilation of a new dictionary of proverbs without acknowledging that it will, by necessity, build upon the knowledge amassed in other celebrated collections over the years.

Notable authorities to which all modern collections must inevitably owe a debt include: R. Taverner's *Proverbs or Adages with New Additions, gathered out of the Chiliades of Erasmus* (1539), John Heywood's *A Dialogue containing ... the Proverbs in the English Tongue* (1546), Randle Cotgrave's *A Dictionary of the French and English Tongues* (1611), T. Draxe's *Bibliotheca Scholastica* (1616), J. Clarke's *Paroemiographia Anglo-Latina* (1639), George Herbert's *Outlandish Proverbs* (1640), John Ray's *A Collection of English Proverbs* (1670), James Kelly's *A Complete Collection of Scotish Proverbs* (1721), Thomas Fuller's *Gnomologia* (1732), Benjamin Franklin's *Poor Richard's Almanack* (1733), W.C. Hazlitt's *English Proverbs* (1869), and *The Oxford Dictionary of English Proverbs* (1935 and later editions). Among more recent publications of note are *Dictionary of Proverbs and their Origins* (1993) by Linda and Roger Flavell, *Dictionary of Proverbs* (1993) by G.L. Apperson, and *The Multicultural Dictionary of Proverbs* (1997) by Harold V. Cordry.

This volume in its turn humbly adds to the common store a modest number of 'new' proverbs, renders some old ones in forms now current, and in some instances casts a new light on the history, meaning and origins of already collected sayings.

Finally, thanks are also due to the editors and production staff at Cassell & Co. for their assistance and, as ever, to Jan, Edward and Charles.

DAVID PICKERING

Note on the use of the Dictionary

Keywords and location of proverbs

The main substance of *Cassell's Dictionary of Proverbs* is an alphabetical list of proverbs accompanied by their definitions and related information. For ease of access the proverbs are listed not necessarily under their first word but under their first 'significant' word, i.e. the first word which is intrinsic to the meaning of the proverb. This word will usually be a noun, a verb, an adjective, or an adverb, but occasionally prepositions have been used for this purpose if they appear to be particularly emphatic or meaningful.

> For example: **an angry man is not fit to pray** is listed under its first significant word **angry** (its 'keyword') rather than under its first word **an**.

For simplicity's sake these 'keywords' are given in their 'basic' form, i.e. singular in the case of nouns, infinitive in the case of verbs and positive (as opposed to comparative or superlative) in the case of adjectives. Thus a single keyword may introduce a list of proverbs in which it features in various forms.

> For example: the keyword **apple** governs both **an apple a day keeps the doctor away** and **apples, pears and nuts spoil the voice**.

The keyword appears, in enlarged font, at the head of one or more proverbs of which it is the first significant word. Proverbs whose first word is also their first significant word and which do not share this word with any other proverbs are not listed under a keyword, but have the first word enlarged so that the alphabetical ordering can be easily followed. The following demonstrates an instance in the Dictionary where both forms of presentation are used.

> **generous. a generous confession disarms slander** (*English*) Those who confess their faults freely and sincerely deprive their enemies of the opportunity to spread slander about them. Thomas Fuller, *Gnomologia*, 1732.
> ~ *See also* be JUST before you're generous.
>
> **genius is an infinite capacity for taking pains** (*English*) Genius is not a natural gift, but the result of diligent hard work ...

Some verbs, though in theory constituting a proverb's first significant word, are *not* used as keywords in the Dictionary simply because the list they would otherwise generate would be impractically large. The verbs in question are **be**, **be able** (i.e. **can, cannot**), **come**, **do**, **get**, **go**, **have**, **let**, **make**, **put**, **take**. Thus the proverb **as you make your bed, so you must lie in it** is listed not under **make**, but under **bed**.

Cross-references

To assist the reader each proverb is provided with cross-references at all significant words subsequent to the keyword.

> For example: **apples, pears and nuts spoil the voice** is cross-referenced at **pear**, **nut**, **spoil** and **voice**.

The words **thing** and **man**, though used as keywords for the purposes of presenting proverbs and some cross-references do not generate a full list of cross-references for all proverbs in which they appear. Again such a list for either word would be unwieldy. Instead cross-references are presented for those proverbs in which these words appear to be particularly emphatic.

> For example: **a bad woman is worse than a bad man** is listed under the keyword **man**, whereas **the hasty man never wants woe** is not since in this instance the word 'man' is used in a generic sense and stands for the word 'person'.

THE DICTIONARY

abhor. *See* NATURE abhors a vacuum.

abide. *See* PRIDE must abide.

a-borrowing. he that goes a-borrowing, goes a-sorrowing (*English*) Those who borrow are fated to regret doing so. Wright and Halliwell, *Reliquiae Antiquae*, *c.*1470. *See also* NEITHER a borrower nor a lender be.

> Ah, him that goes a borrowin' goes a sorrowin'! ... An' there isn't hardly a neighbour in the whole street that hasn't lent him money on the strength of what he was going to get.
>
> Sean O'Casey, *Juno and the Paycock*, 1924

above. that which cometh from above let no man question (*Spanish*) It is unwise to question what has been ordered by higher authorities. Thomas Fuller, *Gnomologia*, 1732.

Abraham. *See* there's no LEAPING from Delilah's lap into Abraham's bosom.

abroad. go abroad and you'll hear news of home (*English*) When far afield the traveller is sure to hear news from home. John Ray, *A Collection of English Proverbs*, 1678.

> You must go into the country to hear what news at London.
>
> John Ray, *A Collection of English Proverbs*, 1678

~ *See also* an ARGUS abroad but a mole at home; DRY bread at home is better than roast meat abroad; RICHES are like muck, which stink in a heap, but spread abroad make the earth fruitful; what CHILDREN hear at home soon flies abroad.

absence. absence makes the heart grow fonder (*English*) Separation from a loved one serves only to intensify the feelings of one partner for another. In this form the sentiment was first expressed *c.*1830 in the song 'Isle of Beauty', written by Thomas Haynes Bayly (1797–1839). It has been suggested, however, that the identical line appeared as the opening of an anonymous poem published in 1602, and certainly the same feeling was expressed in a range of variant forms in various seventeenth-century literary works. Other variants in which it appeared included 'absence sharpens love, presence strengthens it' and 'absence works wonders'. The French, meanwhile, know the proverb in the form 'a little absence does much good'. A less well-known proverb suggests that the effect of absence depends largely on the quality of the relationship involved, advising that 'absence diminishes little passions and increases great ones', quoted by La Rochefoucauld in the form *L'absence diminue les médiocres passions et augmente les grandes, comme le vent éteint les bougies et allume le feu*. This notion is sometimes succinctly expressed in the form 'far from eye, far from heart'. Admiral Horatio Nelson (1758–1805), whose voyages took him and his crews far from home for long periods, came up with his own observation on the effect of long absences upon love: 'salt water and absence wash away love.' Another variant runs 'absence is a shrew'. *See also* OUT of sight, out of mind.

> I dote upon his very absence.
>
> William Shakespeare, *Othello*, *c.*1602

~ *See also* SALT water and absence wash away love.

absent. the absent are always wrong (*French*) It is easy to lay the blame on others not present to defend themselves. John Lydgate, *The Fall of Princes*, *c.*1440. Originally known in the French version *les absents ont toujours tort*.

> The absent are never without fault, nor the present without excuse.
> Benjamin Franklin, 1736

~ *See also* LONG absent, soon forgotten.

abundance, like want, ruins many (*Chinese*) Too much of good things can be as damaging as not enough. *Goody Two-Shoes*, 1766 (originally a saying of Confucius). Related proverbs include 'the abundance of money ruins youth' and 'abundance of things ingendereth disdainfulness'. The French, however, insist that 'abundance is no fault' (also found as 'abundance of a thing does no harm'), and the Japanese compare an abundance of good things to having 'flowers in both hands', while all are agreed that 'one can never have too much of a good thing'. *See also* you can have too MUCH of a good thing.

abuse. *See* the BEST things may be abused; an OLD cart, well used, may last out a new one abused.

accidents will happen in the best regulated families (*English*) Misfortunes may befall anyone, regardless of conduct, station or family background. George Colman, *The Deuce is in Him*, 1763. In common currency by the mid-eighteenth century, when it was frequently applied in the discussion of such domestic disasters as unwanted pregnancies or scandalous romantic liaisons among the most upstanding in society, the proverb is now often heard in the truncated form 'accidents will happen' (in which form George Colman rendered it in *The Deuce is in Him*). Variants have included the waggish 'actresses will happen in the best regulated families'.

> 'Copperfield,' said Mr Micawber, 'accidents will occur in the best-regulated families; and in families not regulated by … the influence of Woman, in the lofty character of Wife, they must be expected with confidence, and must be borne with philosophy.'
> Charles Dickens, *David Copperfield*, 1850

accompany. *See* ARTFUL speech and an ingratiating demeanour rarely accompany virtue.

accomplish. *See* he who BEGINS too much accomplishes little.

accord. *See* there is no GOOD accord where every man would be a lord.

according. *See* CUT your coat according to your cloth.

account (noun). *See* HAPPINESS takes no account of time.

account (verb). **there is no accounting for tastes** (*English*) There is no explaining divergence of taste. J. Minsheu, *A Spanish Grammar*, 1599. Originally given in the Latin form *De gustibus non est disputandum* (there is no disputing about tastes). Variants include 'all meat is not the same in every man's mouth'. *See also* ONE man's meat is another man's poison.

> De gustibus non est disputandum; men may be convinced, but they cannot be pleased, against their will.
> Samuel Johnson, *Lives of the Poets*, 1781

accuse. accusing the times is but excusing ourselves (*English*) It is no excuse to blame the times in which one lives rather than one's own failings when things go wrong. Thomas Fuller, *Gnomologia*, 1732.

~ *See also* he who EXCUSES himself, accuses himself.

accuser. *See* a GUILTY conscience needs no accuser.

ace. *See* BATE me an ace, quoth Bolton.

ache. *See* the COMFORTER's head never aches; EVERY heart hath its own ache; NEVER tell thy foe that thy foot acheth; the TONGUE ever turns to the aching tooth; when the HEAD acheth all the body is the worse.

acolyte. the acolyte at the gate reads scriptures he has never learned (*Japanese*) Those anxious to please will profess all manner of things they do not really believe.

acorns. *See* GREAT oaks from little acorns grow.

acre. *See* ONE acre of performance is worth twenty of the Land of Promise.

act (noun). *See* you cannot make people HONEST by Act of Parliament.

act (verb). **act quickly, think slowly** (*Greek*) Be decisive in action, but think carefully before acting.

action. actions speak louder than words (*US*) A person may be judged more tellingly by their deeds than by their words. *Melancholy State of Province*, 1736, in A.M. Davis, *Colonial Currency*, 1911. Although popularized in this form initially in the United States, much the same sentiments have been expressed in different words through the centuries, as far back as the Roman poet Ovid (43BC–AD17), who wrote, 'no need of words, trust deeds'. In 1659 James Howell, in *English Proverbs*, gave the version 'a man of words and not of deeds, is like a garden full of weeds'. *See also* FINE words butter no parsnips; HANDSOME is as handsome does; PRACTISE what you preach.

> 'Actions speak louder than words' is the maxim;
> and, if true, the South now distinctly says to
> the North, 'Give us the measures, and you take
> the men.'
>
> Abraham Lincoln, 1856, quoted in *Works*, 1953

~ *See also* ONE mad action is not enough to prove a man mad.

Adam. Adam's ale is the best brew (*English*) The best drink of all is water, the only drink available to the biblical Adam. The Scottish sometimes refer to water as 'Adam's wine'.

when Adam delved and Eve span, who was then the gentleman? (*English*) When only Adam and Eve populated the world, what meaning then had class and rank? Richard Rolle of Hampole, *c.*1340 (quoted in G.G. Perry, *Religious Pieces*). According to the fifteenth-century writer Thomas Walsingham, in his *Historia Anglicana*, this argument was employed by John Ball when he delivered a famous speech at Blackheath during the Peasants' Revolt of 1381.

> When Adam dalfe and Eve spanne
> To spire of thou may spede,
> Where was then the pride of man,
> That now marres his meed?
>
> Richard Rolle of Hampole, *c.*1340, quoted in G.G. Perry, *Religious Pieces*

adder. if the adder could hear and the blindworm could see, neither man nor beast would ever go free (*English*) If circumstances were different, the overall situation would be much altered. *Notes & Queries*, 1856. In former times rural folklore had it that the markings on the belly of an adder (once believed to be deaf because of the creature's lack of obvious ears) could be interpreted as spelling out: 'if I could hear as well as see, no mortal man should master me.' Variants include 'if the adder could hear and the blindworm could see, no poor man's children could go their way free'.

addle. *See* but ONE egg and that addled too.

ad infinitum. *See* BIG fleas have little fleas upon their backs to bite them, and little fleas have lesser fleas, and so *ad infinitum*.

admiration is the daughter of ignorance (*US*) People tend to admire individuals and things of which they have incomplete knowledge. Benjamin Franklin, *Poor Richard's Almanack*, 1733–58. Also found as 'things not understood are admired'. Alexander Pope produced his own version of this idea in the form 'fools admire, but men of sense approve'.

admonish your friends in private, praise them in public (*Roman*) A wise person reserves criticism of his friends until they are in private together. Robert Burton, *Anatomy of Melancholy*, 1621.

a-doing. *See* HAPPY is the wooing that is not long a-doing.

adventures are to the adventurous (*English*) Only those who show some daring are likely to have exciting, adventurous lives. Benjamin Disraeli, *Coningsby*, 1844. A Spanish proverb, quoted by Cervantes, warns however that 'those who seek adventures do not always find happy ones', a notion supported by the French expression, 'who seeks adventure finds blows'.

> 'I fear that the age of adventures is past. … Adventures are to the adventurous,' said the stranger.
>
> Benjamin Disraeli, *Coningsby*, 1844

adverb. *See* GOD is better pleased with adverbs than with nouns.

adversity makes strange bedfellows (*English*) Circumstances sometimes oblige a person to forge unlikely alliances. William Shakespeare, *The Tempest*, *c.*1610. The proverb is variously applied to politics and poverty, among other contexts. Other proverbs concerning adversity include 'adversity flattereth no man', 'adversity makes a man wise, though not rich', 'adversity is the trial of courage', 'adversity makes a great man', 'adversity tries virtue' and 'he that has no cross will have no crown'. The Chinese offer consolation to those faced with struggle in the form of the proverb 'a gem is not polished without friction, nor a man perfected without trials', which may have inspired the English equivalent, 'adversity is the diamond dust heaven polishes its jewels with'. For those who find little comfort in these sayings and feel the whole world is against them, the Hindus observe sympathetically 'when an elephant is in trouble, even a frog will kick him'.

> Misery acquaints a man with strange bedfellows.
> William Shakespeare, *The Tempest*, *c.*1610

advertise. *See* it PAYS to advertise.

advice. advice should be viewed from behind (*Swedish*) Quality of advice will become apparent in after days. This is perhaps an echo of a Roman saying, quoted by Cicero, which runs 'advice is judged by results, not by intentions'. Related proverbs in other cultures include the US 'counsel after action is like rain after harvest'.

~ *See also* when a THING is done, advice comes too late.

afar. *See* WATER afar quencheth not fire.

affirmative. *See* TWO negatives make an affirmative.

afford. *See* LEND only that which you can afford to lose.

afraid. *See* he who RIDES a tiger is afraid to dismount.

Africa. *See* ALWAYS something new out of Africa.

after. after a famine in the stall comes a famine in the hall (*English*) A bad crop of hay (which is used as food for animals) tends to be followed by a poor harvest of corn (which is used for human foodstuffs). John Ray, *A Collection of English Proverbs*, 1678.

after a storm comes a calm (*English*) Peace inevitably follows trouble. *Ancrene Riwle*, 1250. Related proverbs include 'always a calm before a storm'.

> The mingled, mingling threads of life are woven
> by warp and woof – calms crossed by storms, a
> storm for every calm.
> Herman Melville, *Moby-Dick*, 1851

after death the doctor (*French*) Help, like the doctor, always seems to come when it is too late. Geoffrey Chaucer, *Troilus and Criseyde*, *c.*1385–90.

> All his tricks founder, and he brings his physic
> After his patient's death: the King already
> Hath married the fair lady.
> William Shakespeare, *Henry VIII*, 1612–13

after dinner rest a while, after supper walk a mile (*English*) For the sake of good health, the diner is recommended to take things easy after a large dinner but to take a walk to aid the digestion after taking supper. Cogan, *Haven of Health*, 1588.

> As the proverb says, for health sake, after dinner,
> or rather after supper, willingly then I'll walk a
> mile to hear thee.
> Philip Massinger, *The Unnatural Combat*, 1639

after drought cometh rain (*English*) Even the most long-lasting periods of hardship or adversity will eventually come to an end. *Reliquae Antiquae*, fifteenth century.

after rain comes sunshine (*English*) Fine weather often follows quickly on a shower. William Caxton, *Aesop's Fables*, 1484. Not unrelated are the proverbs 'a little rain stills a great wind', 'a sunshiny shower won't last half an hour', 'plenty rain, plenty sunshine' and the sailors' saying 'more rain, more rest'. Gardeners are similarly advised that rain will not necessarily last, via the proverb 'although it rain, throw not away thy watering-pot'. *See also* EVERY cloud has a silver lining.

after wit comes too late (*English*) It is too late to think up a witty reply after the opportunity to use it has passed. William Shakespeare, *King Lear*, 1594. Also found as 'after wit is not the best'. Related proverbs include 'the afterthought is good for nought, except it be to catch blind horses'.

~ *See also* it is EASY to be wise after the event.

after-love. *See* SCORN at first makes after-love the more.

afternoon. *See* CLOUDY mornings turn to clear afternoons; a GAUDY morning bodes a wet afternoon.

Agamemnon. *See* BRAVE men lived before Agamemnon.

age. age and wedlock bring a man to his nightcap (*English*) Men are tamed by age and marriage. William Shakespeare, *The Taming of the Shrew*, *c.*1592. Sometimes encountered (as in *The Taming of the Shrew*) with reference to winter rather than age and wedlock. Related proverbs include 'age and wedlock tame man and beast', 'marriage and want of sleep tame both men and beast' and 'age and wedlock we all desire and repent of'.

> But, thou knowest, winter tames man, woman
> and beast.
>
> William Shakespeare, *The Taming of the Shrew*, *c.*1592

age can be a bad travelling companion (*English*) Many ills are attendant on old age. Similar sentiments are implicit in the saying 'age breeds aches'.

age does not give sense – it only makes one go slowly (*Finnish*) Wisdom does not necessarily come with experience.

the age of miracles is past (*English*) Miracles are unlikely to happen and belong to the long-distant, legendary, past. William Shakespeare, *Henry V*, *c.*1598. In more recent years the proverb has been reworked into the facetious 'the age of miracles is not past', often quoted sarcastically when something unexpected (but long overdue) actually happens. For those who regret the lack of miracles in modern living the Russians offer the consolatory 'even miracles become boring in the end'.

> It must be so; for miracles are ceas'd;
> And therefore we must needs admit the means
> How things are perfected.
>
> William Shakespeare, *Henry V*, *c.*1598

~ *See also* the GOLDEN age never was the present age; an HOUR may destroy what an age was a building; an IDLE youth, a needy age; make a PAGE of your own age; RULE youth well, for age will rule itself; where OLD age is evil, youth can learn no good; YOUTH and old age will never agree.

agley. *See* the BEST laid schemes of mice and men gang oft agley.

agree. agree, for the law is costly (*English*) It is better to settle a dispute before going to court, to save on legal bills. William Camden, *Remains Concerning Britain*, 1605. Frequently repeated in the seventeenth and eighteenth centuries. Variants along the same lines include 'a bad agreement is better than a good lawsuit' and the Italian 'a lean agreement is better than a fat sentence'.

> Come to a composition with him, Turfe, the law
> is costly.
>
> Ben Jonson, *A Tale of a Tub*, 1633

~ *See also* BEAUTY and honesty seldom agree; BIRDS in their little nests agree; NAMES and natures do often agree; NOTHING agreeth worse than a lady's heart and a beggar's purse; a PROUD heart and a beggar's purse agree not well together; TWO cats and a mouse, two wives in one house, two dogs and a bone, never agree in one; TWO of a trade never agree; YOUTH and old age will never agree.

agreement. *See* an ILL agreement is better than a good judgement.

agues come on horseback but go away on foot (*English*) Fevers and other minor ailments develop suddenly, but fade away slowly. Randle Cotgrave, *A Dictionary of the French and English Tongues*, 1611.

ahead. *See* QUIT while you are ahead.

aim. *See* he will SHOOT higher who shoots at the moon than he who aims at a tree.

akin. *See* PITY is akin to love.

alarm. *See* whom a SERPENT has bitten, a lizard alarms.

ale. ale in, wit out. *See* when the DRINK is in, the wit is out; when the WINE is in, the wit is out.

~ *See also* ADAM's ale is the best brew; GOOD ale is meat, drink and cloth.

alehouse. *See* EVERYONE has a penny to spend at a new alehouse; in SETTLING an island, the first building erected by a Spaniard will be a church; by a

Frenchman, a fort; by a Dutchman, a warehouse; and by an Englishman, an alehouse.

ale-sellers should not be tale-tellers (*English*) A good landlord keeps to himself the secrets that his customers disclose when they are drunk. James Kelly, *A Complete Collection of Scottish Proverbs*, 1721.

alike. *See* GREAT minds think alike; SHARE and share alike; the WAY to heaven is alike in every place; we shall LIE all alike in our graves.

all. all are not merry that dance (*English*) Appearances of jollity can be deceptive. Geoffrey Chaucer, *The Parlement of Foules*, 1374–81. Also found as 'all are not merry that dance lightly'.

> Daunseth he murye that is myrtheles?
>
> Geoffrey Chaucer, *The Parlement of Foules*, 1374–81

all are not saints that go to church (*English*) Those who attend church regularly are not necessarily morally any better than those who do not. L. Evans, *Withals Dictionary Revised*, 1586. Equivalent proverbs include 'all are not saints that use holy water'.

all are not thieves that dogs bark at (*English*) It does not follow that a person is guilty of something just because everyone says they are. Henry Peacham, *The Garden of Eloquence*, 1577. *See also* GIVE a dog a bad name and hang him.

all cats are grey in the dark (*English*) When matters are obscured (as at night) or confused, it is impossible to tell one thing from another. John Heywood, *A Dialogue containing ... the Proverbs in the English Tongue*, *c.*1549.

> He knew not which was which; and, as the saying is, all cats in the dark are grey.
>
> Tobias Smollett, *Humphry Clinker*, 1771

all cats love fish but fear to wet their paws (*English*) There are those who desire something but are not prepared to endure the discomfort or risk required to obtain it. *Trinity MS*, *c.*1225.

> Letting 'I dare not' wait upon 'I would', like the poor cat i' the adage.
>
> William Shakespeare, *Macbeth*, *c.*1604

all countries stand in need of Britain (*English*) Britain provides what the rest of the world needs. W. Harrison, *Description of England*, 1577. Also found in the fuller, even more overtly patriotic form, 'all countries stand in need of Britain, and Britain of none'.

all fellows at football (*English*) All footballers are (or should be) friends on the field of play. *Sir John Oldcastle*, 1600.

all fish are not caught with flies (*English*) Sometimes different methods from the obvious must be used to achieve a particular end. John Lyly, *Euphues and His England*, 1580.

all flesh is not venison (*English*) There are many different kinds of meat, some better than others. Wodroephe, *Spared Houres*, 1623.

all geese are swans (*English*) Spoken about a person who tends to exaggerate the quality of what he or she owns. John Skelton, *Magnyfycence*, 1529.

> Taylor, who praised every thing of his own to excess ... 'whose geese were all swans' ... expatiated on ... his bull-dog.
>
> James Boswell, *Johnson*, 1777

all good things must come to an end (*English*) No pleasure lasts for ever. Originally the proverb, recorded as early as the mid-fifteenth century, omitted the word 'good'. *See also* EVERYTHING has an end.

> All things have an end, and a pudden [type of sausage] has two.
>
> Jonathan Swift, *Polite Conversation*, 1738

all is fish that comes to the net (*English*) The best should be made of any benefit that happens to fall into a person's hands, regardless of what it is (sometimes heard in sarcastic reference to another's unscrupulous readiness to make use of any opportunity). *c.*1520, published in *Ballads from MSS*, 1868–72. *See also* ALL is grist that comes to the mill.

> Black, brown, fair, or tawny, 'tis all fish that comes in your net.
>
> Richard Cumberland, *The Brothers*, 1769

all is grist that comes to the mill (*English*) Anything that comes along can be made use of. Thomas Fuller, *Church History of Britain*, 1655. Grist was the name formerly given to corn when it was first brought to the mill for grinding. The proverb appears to have developed from the earlier phrase 'to bring grist to the mill', which signified the getting of some benefit or other. *See also* ALL is fish that comes to the net.

> Well, let them go on, it brings grist to our mill: for whilst both the sexes stick firm to their honour, we shall never want business.
>
> Samuel Foote, *The Lame Lover*, 1770

all is lost that is put into a riven dish (*English*) Anything that is entrusted to the care of an unreliable person or object risks being lost. Thomas Middleton, *The Roaring Girl*, 1611.

all lay loads on a willing horse (*English*) The gullible and acquiescent will always be taken advantage of. John Heywood, *A Dialogue containing ... the Proverbs in the English Tongue*, 1546. Variants include 'the willing horse is always most ridden'.

all men are mortal (*English*) All men must die. Geoffrey Chaucer, *The Canterbury Tales*, *c.*1387.

all publicity is good publicity (*English*) It does not matter what kind of publicity you get, because publicity of any kind gets your name or product known. P. Cave, *The Dirtiest Picture Postcard*, 1974. Also encountered in the form 'any publicity is good publicity'.

all roads lead to Rome (*Italian*) All alternative courses or lines of thought lead to the same destination or conclusion. Geoffrey Chaucer, *A Treatise on the Astrolabe*, 1391–2. The saying recalls the prime of Imperial Rome, when much of Europe was linked by the unparalleled Roman road system and when Rome dominated all cultural matters. The idea that Rome was the centre of the human universe was kept alive after the collapse of the Empire through the Roman Catholic Church, which sited its headquarters at the Vatican and thus endowed the city with the claim of being the spiritual centre of the civilized world. Similar proverbs may be found in many other cultures, including Chinese (where all roads lead to Peking) and Japan (where they lead to the palace of the Mikado).

> Every one soon or late comes round by Rome.
>
> Robert Browning, *The Ring and the Book*, 1869

all's fair in love and war (*English*) All strategies are forgivable in love or war, no matter how underhand or unprincipled they may be. T. Shelton, *Cervantes' Don Quixote*, 1620. *See also* the END justifies the means.

> All stratagems in love, and that the sharpest war, are lawful.
>
> Beaumont and Fletcher, *Lovers' Progress*, *c.*1630

all's for the best in the best of all possible worlds (*French*) Everything that happens is for a purpose, namely the ultimate good of the world. Voltaire, *Candide*, translated by W. Rider, 1759.

> Pangloss would sometimes say to Candidus: 'All Events are linked together in this best of all possible Worlds.'
>
> Voltaire, *Candide*, translated by W. Rider, 1759

all Stuarts are not sib (*Scottish*) People who share the same surname are not necessarily related. James Kelly, *A Complete Collection of Scotish Proverbs*, 1721. The proverb was quoted originally with reference to the royal Stuart family, to which many Scots liked to claim a link.

all's well that ends well (*English*) If something comes out right at the end then this justifies or compensates for all actions taken or sacrifices made to achieve this end result. *Proverbs of Hending*, *c.*1250. The phrase is most familiar as the title of one of William Shakespeare's comedies, written in 1602. One version of the proverb extends it thus: 'all's well that ends well, as the peacock said when he looked at his tail.' *See also* the END justifies the means.

> All's well that ends well: still the fine's the crown.
>
> William Shakespeare, *All's Well That Ends Well*, *c.*1602

all that breed in the mud are not eels (*English*) Where one particular thing may be found other kinds of things may also be found. John Lyly, *Euphues and his England*, 1580.

all that glitters is not gold (*Roman*) Not everything that appears valuable or desirable is in fact worth anything. *Hali Meidenhad*, *c.*1220. The original Latin version was *non omne quod nitet aurum est* (not all that shines is gold). For a long time 'glisters' was the common form, but this was generally replaced by 'glitters' after David Garrick introduced it in the Prologue to Oliver Goldsmith's play *She Stoops to Conquer* in 1773. Equivalents in other European languages include the Italian 'every glow-worm is not a fire'. *See also* APPEARANCES are deceptive.

> All that glisters is not gold,
> Often have you heard that told.
>
> William Shakespeare, *The Merchant of Venice*, *c.*1596

all the keys hang not at one man's girdle (*English*) What one person refuses another person may provide (usually delivered as a retort when someone has turned down a plea for help or a request for a favour of some kind). John Heywood, *A Dialogue containing ... the Proverbs in the English Tongue*, 1546.

all things are difficult before they are easy (*English*) Nothing is easy at first (spoken as encouragement to those who are having trouble doing something unfamiliar). Thomas Fuller, *Gnomologia*, 1732. A Chinese equivalent runs 'he who accounts all things easy will have many difficulties'.

all things are obedient to money (*Roman*) There is no limit to the influence of money in earthly affairs. Geoffrey Chaucer, *The Canterbury Tales*, *c.*1387 (also quoted by Horace). Related proverbs include 'what will not money do?' and 'money answers all things'.

> All the world to gold obeieth.
>
> John Gower, *Confessio Amantis*, *c.*1390

all things are possible with God (*Hebrew*) With God's assistance there is no limit to what can be achieved. Bible, Matthew 19:26 (also quoted by Homer).

> Jesus ... said unto them, With men this is unpossible, but with God all things are possible.
>
> Matthew 19:26

all things come to those who wait (*English*) Patience will be rewarded. Alexander Barclay, *Eclogues*, 1530. *See also* EVERYTHING comes to him who waits.

> I have got it at last, everything comes if a man will only wait.
>
> Benjamin Disraeli, *Tancred*, 1847

all things grow with time, except grief (*Yiddish*) Grief will lessen with the passage of time. A Latin proverb on similar lines runs 'time tames the strongest grief'. *See also* TIME heals all wounds.

all work and no play makes Jack a dull boy (*English*) Those who spend all their time working and allow no time for other interests make dull company. J. Howell, *Proverbs*, 1659.

> 'All work and no play makes Jack a dull boy'; but all play and no work makes him something greatly worse.
>
> Samuel Smiles, *Self-Help*, 1859

do not all you can, spend not all you have, believe not all you hear, and tell not all you know (*English*) It is sensible to keep something back in one's dealings with the world. H.G. Bohn, *A Handbook of Proverbs*, 1855.

don't put all your eggs in one basket (*Italian / Spanish*) Don't place all your hopes on one thing alone (lest an accident result in the destruction of all of them). Miguel de Cervantes, *Don Quixote de la Mancha*, 1605. The proverb largely replaced the English equivalent 'don't venture all your goods in one bottom' ('bottom' here meaning 'ship'), which was descended from a much older Greek saying. Other largely archaic versions include 'do not hang all your bells upon one horse' (usually referring to a decision not to leave all one's riches to just one child). It is often heard in the context of business discussions, recommending the spreading of risk.

> It was odd how, with all this ingrained care for moderation and secure investment, Soames never put his emotional eggs into one basket. First Irene – now Fleur.
>
> John Galsworthy, *To Let*, 1921

it takes all sorts to make a world (*Spanish*) The mass of humanity includes characters of all shades and humours, who should be tolerated for their apparent eccentricities. T. Shelton, *Cervantes' Don Quixote*, 1620.

> In the world there must be of all sorts.
>
> Miguel de Cervantes, *Don Quixote*, 1615

it will all be one in a hundred years' time (*English*) Nothing we do now will make any difference to how things are in a hundred years' time. Randle Cotgrave, *A Dictionary of the French and English Tongues*, 1611.

when all fruit falls, welcome haws (*English*) When nothing better is available, what is less than perfect will be warmly welcomed. James Kelly, *A Complete Collection of Scotish Proverbs*, 1721. Often quoted in relation to what may be judged less than ideal partners in love.

> When all Fruit's fa's welcome ha's ... Spoken when we take up with what's coarse, when the good is spent.
>
> James Kelly, *A Complete Collection of Scotish Proverbs*, 1721

~ *See also* CONSCIENCE makes cowards of us all; do not HANG all your bells upon one horse; a FRIEND to all is a friend to none; GOD's in his heaven, all's right with the world; GRASP all, lose all; HEAR all, see all, say nowt; he has not LOST all who has one cast left; if a MAN once fall, all will tread on him; LOVE conquers all; one is not SMELT where all stink; PARDON all but thyself; VENTURE not all in one bottom; who GIVES to all denies all; you can't WIN them all; you may FOOL all of the people some of the time, some of the people all of the time, but not all of the people all of the time.

allow. *See* EVERY dog is allowed one bite.

allure. *See* EMPTY hands no hawks allure.

almost was never hanged (*English*) No person can be condemned for something they might have considered doing but never actually committed. J. Clarke, *Paroemiographia Anglo-Latina*, 1639. Related proverbs include 'almost and hard by save many a lie'.

alms quencheth sin (*Hebrew*) Those who give to the poor atone for any sins they have committed. Bible, Ecclesiastes 3:30. Another proverb emphasizing the beneficial aspect of giving alms reminds the giver that 'alms never make poor', while another has it that 'great almsgiving lessens no man's living'.

> Alms-giving never made any man poor, nor robbery rich, nor prosperity wise.
> H.G. Bohn, *A Handbook of Proverbs*, 1855

alone. *See* EAGLES fly alone; he TRAVELS fastest who travels alone; LAUGH and the world laughs with you, weep and you weep alone; LEAVE well alone; let WELL alone; MAN cannot live by bread alone; WELCOME evil, if thou comest alone; a WISE man is never less alone than when he is alone.

aloof. *See* on PAINTING and fighting look aloof.

alter. *See* the CASE is altered; CIRCUMSTANCES alter cases.

although. although the sun shine, leave not thy cloak at home (*English*) Do not trust the weather to stay fine just because the sun is shining at the present. George Herbert, *Outlandish Proverbs*, 1640.

always. always look on the bright side (*English*) Always maintain an optimistic outlook, even when things seem to be going against you. James Payn, *Lost Sir Massingberd*, 1864. *See also* where there's LIFE there's hope.

always something new out of Africa (*Greek*) Africa may be depended upon as a rich source of new sights and discoveries. Aristotle, *De Anima*, fourth century BC. The original Greek proverb was quoted in Pliny's *Natural History*, in the form *Africa semper aliquid novi afferre*, and was probably inspired by the commonly held notion that Africa was the haunt of monsters.

> Out of Africa.
> Film title, 1985

one has always strength enough to bear the misfortunes of one's friends (*English*) It is human nature to gain secret comfort from the misfortunes of others. Oliver Goldsmith, *She Stoops to Conquer*, 1773.

> Ay, people are generally calm at the misfortunes of others.
> Oliver Goldsmith, *She Stoops to Conquer*, 1773

that is not always good in the maw that is sweet in the mouth (*English*) Things that taste sweet are not necessarily good for the digestion. John Lyly, *Euphues*, 1579.

> Things sweet to taste prove in digestion sour.
> William Shakespeare, *Richard II*, *c.*1594

there is always room at the top (*English*) There will always be opportunities for the ambitious to reach the upper echelons. Attributed to the nineteenth-century US politician Daniel Webster. The story goes that Webster quoted the line when it was suggested to him that he should abandon his plans to become a lawyer, as the profession was already overcrowded.

> You're the sort of young man we want. There's always room at the top.
> John Braine, *Room at the Top*, 1957

~ *See also* the ABSENT are always wrong; a BAD penny always turns up; a BULLY is always a coward; BUSY folks are always meddling; CLERGYMEN's sons always turn out badly; the CUSTOMER is always right; a DEAF husband and a blind wife are always a happy couple; the DEVIL always leaves a stink behind him; a DOG's nose and a maid's knees are always cold; the FISH always stinks from the head downwards; FRIENDSHIP cannot stand always on one side; GOD is always on the side of the big battalions; the GRASS is always greener on the other side of the fence; HELL and Chancery are always open; he who has ONCE burnt his mouth always blows his soup; the HUSBAND is always the last to know; KEEP a thing seven years and you'll always find a use for it; the LEAST boy always carries the greatest fiddle; LOSERS are always in the wrong; a MAN's destiny is always dark;

MEN's years and their faults are always more than they are willing to own; the MILL that is always going grinds coarse and fine; ONCE a priest, always a priest; ONCE a thief, always a thief; ONCE a whore, always a whore; PAUL's will not always stand; put an IRISHMAN on the spit and you can always get another Irishman to baste him; the SHOEMAKER's son always goes barefoot; SORROW is always dry; the TIDE never goes out so far but it always comes in again; TRUTH and sweet oil always come to the top; TRUTH should not always be revealed; the UNEXPECTED always happens; a USED key is always bright; the WEST wind always brings wet weather, the east wind wet and cold together, the south wind surely brings us rain, the north wind blows it back again.

amiss. *See* GOOD counsel never comes amiss; he that THINKS amiss concludes worse.

an. 'IF' and 'an' spoils many a good charter.

anchor. *See* GOOD riding at two anchors.

ancient. with the ancient is wisdom, and in the length of days understanding (*Hebrew*) Wisdom comes with experience. One of many proverbs taken from the Bible, this time Job 12:12.

~*See also* CUSTOM without reason is but ancient error.

and. *See* if IFS and ands were pots and pans, there'd be no work for tinkers' hands.

angel. *See* FOOLS rush in where angels fear to tread; a PHYSICIAN is an angel when employed but a devil when one must pay him; a WOMAN is an angel at ten, a saint at fifteen, a devil at forty and a witch at fourscore.

anger. anger can be an expensive luxury (*Italian*) Outbursts of anger can cost dear. Variations include 'anger and haste hinder good counsel' and 'anger punishes itself'. The Chinese warn that 'the fire you kindle for your enemy often burns yourself more than him'.

anger without power is folly (*German*) Unless one can act on them, displays of anger are always a mistake. A Chinese equivalent takes the form 'anger is as useless as the waves of the ocean without wind'.

~*See also* KEEP yourself from the anger of a great man, from the tumult of a mob, from a man of ill fame, from a widow that has been thrice married, from a wind that comes in at a hole, and from a reconciled enemy; like ICE, anger passes away; when MEAT is in anger is out.

angered. I was angered, for I had no shoes – then I met a man who had no feet (*Chinese*) Keep your own problems in perspective and count your blessings. Attributed to Confucius.

angler. an angler eats more than he gets (*Spanish*) Some work-shy people accept relatively unexacting work paying low wages in order to avoid more strenuous employment. J. Collins, *A Dictionary of Spanish Proverbs*, 1823.

angry. an angry man is not fit to pray (*Yiddish*) A man in the heat of anger is incapable of rational thought and in a wrong frame of mind to come before his God. A US proverb similarly links anger and religion in the form 'anger begins with folly and ends with prayer', while another interprets anger as an affront to Paradise: 'who spits against heaven, it falls in his face.'

angry men make themselves beds of nettles (*English*) People with angry natures will find they rarely rest easy. T. Draxe, *Bibliotheca Scholastica*, 1616. Variants include 'he that is angry is seldom at ease' and 'angry men seldom want woe'.

he who has been angry becomes cool again (*Greek*) Anger is a temporary state and will eventually subside. Other proverbs on similar lines include 'anger dieth quickly with a good man', 'anger is a short madness' and the Roman 'like ice anger passes away'. Another warns that 'anger is a brief madness but it can do damage that lasts forever'.

~ *See also* a HUNGRY man is an angry man; no MAN is angry that feels not himself hurt; SHORT folk are soon angry; TWO things a man should never be angry at: what he can help and what he cannot help.

animal. *See* never WORK with children or animals.

Anne. *See* QUEEN Anne is dead.

annuity. *See* GIVE a man an annuity and he'll live for ever.

another. another course would have done it (*English*) A little more would have completed the job. This proverb has its origins in a celebrated story concerning some Yorkshire peasants who attempted to trap a cuckoo by building a wall around it (thinking that by so doing they would enjoy eternal spring). The cuckoo escaped by simply flying over the top of the wall, prompting one of the disappointed workers to comment 'another course would have done it'. Ever since, the phrase has been applied to any ridiculous project that no sensible person would undertake.

let another's shipwreck be your sea-mark (*English*) Learn from others' mistakes in order to avoid repeating them. Thomas Fuller, *The History of the Worthies of England*, 1662.

> I am your sea-mark; and, though wrecked and lost,
> My ruin stands to warn you from the coast.
> John Dryden, *The Conquest of Granada*, 1670

put another man's child in your bosom and he'll creep out at your elbow (*English*) Adopted children rarely return the love of those who adopt them. John Ray, *A Collection of English Proverbs*, 1670.

~ *See also* do not make FISH of one and flesh of another; have a HORSE of your own and then you may borrow another's; he PULLS with a long rope that waits for another's death; he that HURTS another hurts himself; he that TELLS a secret is another's servant; if ONE will not another will; ONE beggar does not hate another as much as one doctor hates another; ONE business begets another; ONE good turn deserves another; ONE grief drives out another; ONE ill word asketh another; ONE love expels another; ONE man may steal a horse, while another may not look over a hedge; ONE man's loss is another man's gain; ONE man's meat is another man's poison; ONE mule doth scrub another; ONE potter envies another; ONE shoulder of mutton draws down another; ONE sword keeps another in the scabbard; ONE thief robs another; ONE thing thinketh the horse, and another he that saddles him; ONE wedding brings another; put an IRISHMAN on the spit and you can always get another Irishman to baste him; the RISING of one man is the falling of another; SAYING is one thing, and doing another; SCALD not your lips in another man's pottage; the SMOKE of a man's own country is better than the fire of another's; there's ONE law for the rich and another for the poor; THREE helping one another bear the burthen of six; TOMORROW is another day; WHAT one day gives us, another takes away from us; when ONE door shuts, another opens.

answer. *See* ASK a silly question and you'll get a silly answer; FOOLS ask questions that wise men cannot answer; the SHORTEST answer is doing; a SOFT answer turneth away wrath; who UNDERSTANDS ill answers ill.

ant. an ant hole may collapse an embankment (*Japanese*) An apparently insignificant event may have important repercussions.

in the ants' house the dew is a flood (*Persian*) What might seem an insignificant event to one person might be crucial to someone in a more vulnerable position. Another proverb observes that when ants are unusually busy with building walls then rain is imminent: 'if ants their walls do frequent build, rain will from the clouds be spilled.'

anticipate. *See* that which one MOST anticipates soonest comes to pass.

anvil. *See* the CHURCH is an anvil which has worn out many hammers.

any. any port in a storm (*English*) Any shelter will do if the situation is desperate enough. J. Cleland, *Memoirs of a Woman of Pleasure*, 1749. Occasionally encountered in the form 'sailors have a port in every storm'.

> As the Scotsman's howf lies right under your lee,
> why, take any port in a storm.
> Walter Scott, *The Pirate*, 1821

what may be done at any time will be done at no time (*English*) Things that can be put off end up never being done at all. James Kelly, *A Complete Collection of Scotish Proverbs*, 1721.

anyone can kill a trussed foe (*Turkish*) There is no glory in accomplishing an easy task.

anything. anything may be spoken if it be under the rose (*English*) You may speak without fear of your confidences being betrayed. This old English proverb, often rendered in the form *sub rosa* (under the rose), may have originated in the classical myth in which Cupid bribed Harpocrates, the god of silence, with the gift of a rose so that he would not speak of Venus's love affairs. The rose subsequently came to symbolize silence, and in Tudor times the rose, also a symbol of kingship, was carved on the ceilings of banqueting halls, confessionals and other meeting-places to remind those present of their duty not to reveal what they heard in confidence.

anything will fit a naked man (*Irish*) In extreme necessity, any aid should be gratefully accepted. *See also* BEGGARS can't be choosers.

if anything can go wrong, it will (*US*) 'Murphy's law', concerning the inevitability of disaster, was promulgated by George Nichols, a project manager working for the Northrop aircraft company, in 1949. Murphy was Captain E. Murphy, an employee of the Wright Field-Aircraft Laboratory, with whom Nichols worked. The celebrated observation was first expressed in *Aviation Mechanics Bulletin*, May-June 11, 1955, thus: 'Murphy's Law: If an aircraft part can be installed incorrectly, someone will install it that way.' Subsequent decades have dubbed the same principle 'sod's law'.

~ *See also* if you don't make MISTAKES you don't make anything.

apace. *See* ILL weeds grow apace.

ape. an ape's an ape, a varlet's a varlet, though they be clad in silk or scarlet (*Greek*) Dressing up in fine clothes will not disguise baseness of character. The proverb was quoted by the ancient Greek satirist Lucian in the first century AD in the form 'an ape is an ape ... even if it has gold insignia'. According to other proverbs, 'an ape is never so like an ape as when he wears a doctor's cap' and 'apes are never more beasts than when they wear men's clothes'. Other equivalents include the Scottish 'bonny feathers dinna aye make bonny birds' and 'no fine clothes can hide the clown'. *See also* the HIGHER the monkey climbs the more he shows his tail.

~ *See also* OLD maids lead apes in hell.

apparel makes the man (*English*) A man may be judged by the clothes he wears. John Florio, *Second Fruites*, 1591. There are equivalent proverbs in many other cultures, among them the Chinese 'a man is estimated by his clothes and a horse by its saddle', the Danish 'a smart coat is a good letter of introduction', the Irish 'he who wears a ten-bob suit must needs have a ten-bob mind', and the Spanish 'a stick dressed up does not look like a stick', 'dress a little toad and it will look pretty' and 'that which covers thee discovers thee'. For those who feel they must accordingly renew the contents of their wardrobe, an Iraqi proverb offers the advice that 'silk goes with everything'. *See also* NINE tailors make a man.

> For the apparel oft proclaims the man.
> William Shakespeare, *Hamlet*, *c.*1600

appear. *See* TALK of the devil and he is bound to appear; what's done by NIGHT appears by day; when a NEW book appears, read an old one.

appearance. appearances are deceptive (*Greek*) Trust should not be placed on superficial appearances, because the underlying reality might be quite different. G. Torriano, *Italian Proverbs*, 1666. Known to the ancient Greeks, it was not commonly encountered in England before the eighteenth century. It is often heard in the United States in the form 'appearances are deceiving'. *See also* ALL that glitters is not gold; BEAUTY is only skin deep; the COWL does not make the monk; never JUDGE by appearances; STILL waters run deep.

> Egad, appearances are very deceitful.
> Tobias Smollett, *Gil Blas*, 1750

~ *See* NEVER judge by appearances.

appetite. appetite comes with eating (*French*) The more one indulges in something, the more one wants to continue to indulge. Rabelais, *Gargantua*, 1534. The proverb was originally almost exclusively applied to the consumption of food, but has since been applied to greed for conquest and for sex, among other cravings. An Arabic equivalent runs 'taste, and you will feed'. *See also* HUNGER is the best sauce.

> Why, she would hang on him,
> As if increase of appetite had grown
> By what it fed on.
> William Shakespeare, *Hamlet*, *c.*1600

~ *See also* NEW meat begets a new appetite.

apple. an apple a day keeps the doctor away (*English*) Consuming an apple every day will improve the health and ward off illness. *Notes & Queries*, 1866. Although the apple has long been considered magically potent, being employed in a variety of ways in love magic and divination, this proverb is of relatively recent coinage. Modern science approves the sentiment because apples contain vitamins, fibre and boron and, by aiding absorption of calcium, promote strong teeth and healthy bones. Variants include 'eat an apple on going to bed, and you'll keep the doctor from earning his bread' (also found as 'eat an apple going to bed, make the doctor beg his bread').

the apple never falls far from the tree (*German*) Children will inevitably echo their parents in traits, appearance, interests and so forth and will, in all likelihood, never stray far from the parents. Ralph Waldo Emerson, letter, 22 December 1839. Possibly of Eastern origin, although first recorded in Germany in the sixteenth century. *See also* like FATHER, like son.

> As men say the apple never falls far from the stem, I shall hope that another year will draw your eyes and steps to this old dear odious haunt of the race.
>
> Ralph Waldo Emerson, letter, 22 December 1839

apples, pears and nuts spoil the voice (*Italian*) Those who wish to preserve their voice should avoid apples, pears and nuts. J. Howell, *Paroemiographia*, 1659.

apples taste sweetest when they are going (*Roman*) Apples (and many other foodstuffs and pleasures) are best enjoyed at the moment of greatest ripeness, just before they go rotten.

how we apples swim (*Greek*) How well you think you've done – an expression intended to deflate someone who boasts unwontedly of their achievements. J. Withals, *A Short Dictionary in Latin and English*, 1586. The origins of the proverb, now little heard, are indicated by the fuller form in which it was formerly known: 'see how we apples swim!, quoth the horse-turd.' According to Aesop's *Fables*, some lumps of horse dung were washed into a stream by heavy rain and found themselves floating among apples, prompting them to congratulate themselves with the line 'how we apples swim!'

> And even this, little as it is, gives him so much self-importance in his own eyes that he assumes a consequential air, sets his arms akimbo, and, strutting among the historical artists, cries, 'How we apples swim!'
>
> William Hogarth, *Works*, 1768

if apples bloom in March, in vain for them you'll search; if apples bloom in April, then they'll be plentiful; if apples bloom in May, you may eat them night and day (*English*) A traditional saying linking the time when apple trees blossom with the size of the crop that will follow later in the year. *Notes & Queries*, 1883.

~ *See also* GOOD apple on a sour stock; the ROTTEN apple injures its neighbours; there is SMALL choice in rotten apples; your NEIGHBOUR's apples are the sweetest.

April. April showers bring forth May flowers (*English*) A wet April promises a good show of flowers the following month. T. Wright, *Songs and Ballads*, *c.*1560. This piece of horticultural wisdom dates from the sixteenth century or earlier, but it is not, according to the experts, always borne out by experience. This is but one of a series of similar rural traditions. If it rains on Saint Paul's Day (25 January) there will be a poor harvest of corn; if it rains at Easter the grass will grow lush but there will be little hay; if it rains on Saint Peter's Day (29 June) there will be a good crop of apples. The proverb is also encountered in the longer form 'March winds and April showers bring forth May flowers'. Other sayings linking the weather in April with the harvest to come include 'a flood in April, a flood in May and a flood to take away the hay', 'a raggy April and a raw May, prudent farmers ettle out their hay', 'when April blows his horn it's good for hay and corn' (a reference to thunder) and 'a sharp April kills the pig'. *See also* SAINT Swithin's day, if thou dost rain, for forty days it will remain; Saint Swithin's Day, if thou be fair, for forty days 'twill rain no more.

> I believe, if showers fall in April, that we shall have flowers in May.
>
> Walter Scott, *Kenilworth*, 1821

~ *See also* a COLD April the barn will fill; the CUCKOO comes in April, and stays the month of May, sings a song at midsummer, and then goes away; if APPLES bloom in March, in vain for them you'll search; if apples bloom in April, then they'll be plentiful; if apples bloom in May, you may eat them night and day.

apt. *See* a MAN apt to promise is apt to forget.

architect. *See* EVERY man is the architect of his own fortune.

are. *See* BE.

Argus. an Argus abroad but a mole at home (*English*) Some people can discern distant things clearly but miss the obvious closer to home (a reference to the mythological Argus, who had a hundred watchful eyes, and to the weak eyesight of the mole). Thomas Fuller, *Gnomologia*, 1732. Sometimes found with the elements transposed, as 'an Argus at home but a mole abroad'.

arm. *See* GREEDY folks have long arms; KINGS have long arms; STRETCH your arm no further than your sleeve will reach; YORKSHIRE born and Yorkshire bred, strong in the arm and weak in the head.

armed. *See* HALF warned, half armed.

army. an army marches on its stomach (*French*) The progress of an army depends directly on the quality and quantity of its provisions. *Windsor Magazine*, January 1904. This military maxim has been variously attributed to both Napoleon and Frederick the Great. Also found as 'an army, like a serpent, goes on its belly'. Another French proverb advises that 'the broth makes the soldier'.

~ *See also* SKILL and confidence are an unconquered army.

arrant. *See* TWO daughters and a back door are three arrant thieves.

arrive. *See* by the STREET of by and by one arrives at the house of never; it is BETTER to travel hopefully than to arrive.

arrow. *See* DRAW not your bow till your arrow is fixed.

art. art consists in concealing art (*Roman*) The true artist conceals the technique by which he gets his effects. B. Melbancke, *Philotimus*, 1583. This old adage, sometimes rendered in Latin as *ars est celare artem*, has been heard less frequently in the twentieth century with the new emphasis on deliberate deconstruction of technique in full public view, to the point where exploration of technique and materials and so on becomes the whole point of the work in question. Variants include the Roman 'it is the perfection of art when no trace of the artist appears' and 'art must be deluded by art'.

> In oratory the greatest art is to hide art.
> Jonathan Swift, *The Faculty of the Mind*, 1707

art has no enemy but ignorance (*Roman*) Only the ill-educated fail to appreciate art. Ben Jonson, *Every Man Out of His Humour*, 1599.

> Arte hath an enemy cal'd Ignorance.
> Ben Jonson, *Every Man Out of His Humour*, induction, 1599

art helps nature, and experience art (*English*) Art can improve on nature and is itself improved by experience. R. Rainoldes, *Foundation of Rhetoric*, 1563. Also given as 'art improves nature'. Rather the opposite view is, however, expressed in such proverbs as 'he who paints the flower cannot paint its fragrance' and 'nature without an effort surpasses art'.

art is long, life is short (*Greek*) A lifetime is too short to achieve a mastery of art. Geoffrey Chaucer, *The Parlement of Foules*, 1374–81. Often given in its Latin form *ars longa, vita brevis*, a reworking of Seneca's *vita brevis est, ars longa*, this proverb provided the basis of the Hippocratic oath that is sworn by members of the modern medical profession. It was the ancient Greek physician Hippocrates himself who first applied the saying to the medical profession, lamenting that, when it came to learning medicine: 'life is short, the art long, opportunity fleeting, experience treacherous, judgement difficult.' The expression made its first appearance in English as early as the fourteenth century, and it has since been applied to many other forms of art than medicine (although often somewhat inaccurately conveying the idea that it is about the survival of artistic works beyond the lifetimes of their creators).

> The lyf so short, the craft so long to lerne,
> Th'assay so hard, so sharp the conqueriynge.
> Geoffrey Chaucer, *The Parlement of Foules*, 1374–81

artful speech and an ingratiating demeanour rarely accompany virtue (*Chinese*) The silver-tongued and the charming are not necessarily to be trusted. Attributed to Confucius.

Arthur. Arthur could not tame a woman's tongue (*English*) Even King Arthur himself could not curb a woman's sharp tongue (apparently a reference to the legend of the scolding a disguised Arthur received from a peasant woman after he absent-mindedly let her cakes burn). J. Howell, *Paroemiographia*, 1659.

Arthur was not but whilst he was (*English*) Even the greatest of men cannot outlive their own lifetime. J. Howell, *Paroemiographia*, 1659.

artist. an artist lives everywhere (*Greek*) An artist or other skilled person can draw on his skills to make a living wherever he finds himself. Francis Bacon, *Catechism*, 1560. A Spanish equivalent runs 'he who has learned any art may live in any place', while the Italians have 'it is a poor art that does not maintain the artisan.'

> Nero … replied to his censurers by the Greek proverb, 'An artist lives every where.'
> Isaac D'Israeli, *Curiosities of Literature*, 1823

ascend. *See* it is EASIER to descend than to ascend; STEP after step the ladder is ascended.

ash. *See* BEWARE of the oak, it draws the stroke; avoid the ash, it courts the flash; when the OAK is before the ash, then you will get only a splash.

ask. ask a silly question and you'll get a silly answer (*English*) Stupid questions deserve meaningless answers. Related proverbs include the Italian 'ask the host if he has good wine'.

ask much to have a little (*English*) Ask for more than you need and you stand a chance of getting sufficient. R. Taverner, *Proverbs or Adages with New Additions, gathered out of the Chiliades of Erasmus*, 1545. An Italian equivalent is 'he who wants a great deal must not ask for a little'. Other proverbs advise 'nothing ask, nothing have', 'many things are lost for want of asking' and 'ask but enough and you may lower the price as you list'.

ask no favour during the solano (*Spanish*) Do not ask for favours in troubled times. *Brewer's Phrase and Fable*, 1959. The *solano* is a hot, dusty wind that blows through Spain from the southeast, causing much discomfort to those caught in it.

ask no questions and hear no lies (*English*) To make enquiries is an invitation to deceit. Oliver Goldsmith, *She Stoops to Conquer*, 1773. Related proverbs include 'he that asketh nothing, nothing learneth' and the rather more forbidding 'he that cannot ask cannot live'. Another warns that 'he that asketh faintly beggeth a denial'.

> Ask me no questions and I'll tell you no fibs.
> Oliver Goldsmith, *She Stoops to Conquer*, 1773

you must ask your neighbour if you shall live in peace (*English*) A person will not enjoy a harmonious home life if he does not have the goodwill of his neighbours. J. Clarke, *Paroemiologia Anglo-Latina*, 1639. The Romans acknowledged this truth with their proverb 'a bad neighbour brings bad luck', while more modern variants include the Swedish 'no one's house is so big that he does not need good neighbours', the US 'a good neighbour is a precious thing', the Italian 'he who has a good neighbour has a good morning', the Chinese 'live in harmony with your neighbours', the Greek 'love thy neighbour', the Maltese 'love your neighbour, but don't let him in your house', and the Arabic 'distance from people is great booty'.

> Nobody can live longer in peace than his neighbour pleases.
> H.G. Bohn, *A Handbook of Proverbs*, 1855

~ *See also* FOOLS ask questions that wise men cannot answer; GIVE neither counsel nor salt till you are asked for it; he that will THRIVE must first ask his wife; LOSE nothing for asking; an OLD sack asketh much patching; ONE ill word asketh another.

asleep. *See* when SORROW is asleep wake it not.

a-sorrowing. *See* he that goes A-BORROWING, goes a-sorrowing.

ass. the ass loaded with gold still eats thistles (*Roman*) A fool is a fool, no matter now rich he may be. George Chapman, *The Widow's Tears*, 1612. Possibly German in origin, although a similar sentiment was recorded in the writings of Plutarch. Variants include 'an ass is but an ass, though laden with gold'. Other proverbs observe that 'an ass laden with gold will go lightly uphill' and 'an ass loaded with gold climbs to the top of a castle', the way ahead being cleared by virtue of the wealth it carries.

> Or wilt thou, being keeper of the cash, like an ass that carries dainties, feed on thistles?
>
> Philip Massinger, *The City Madam*, 1632

he that makes himself an ass must not take it ill if men ride him (*English*) A man who freely allows others to take advantage of him must not complain when such advantage is taken. Thomas Fuller, *Gnomologia*, 1732. Those who seek to make asses of others, however, are warned: 'jest with an ass and he will flap you in the face with his tail.'

> We may make ourselves asses, and then everybody will ride us.
>
> Charles Spurgeon, *John Ploughman's Talk*, 1869

when an ass climbs a ladder we may find wisdom in women (*English*) Only when an ass climbs a ladder will women be presumed clever, and not before. John Ray, *A Collection of English Proverbs*, 1678. This inflammatory saying is unsurprisingly little heard today; the root of it ('when the ass climbs to the tiles') was known to the Romans.

~ *See also* the DEVIL is an ass; EVERY ass loves to hear himself bray; the HORSES of hope gallop, but the asses of experience go slowly; a KING without learning is but a crowned ass; the LAW is an ass; a THISTLE is a fat salad for an ass's mouth.

assault. *See* it is EASY to keep a castle that was never assaulted.

ate. *See* EAT.

atheist. an atheist is one point beyond the devil (*English*) An atheist is worse than the devil himself, because the devil at least believes in God. T. Adams, *Sermons*, 1629.

there are no atheists in foxholes (*US*) When under extreme threat to life and limb, many professed non-believers will suddenly rediscover their religious faith. This rather cynical observation was first voiced in a sermon delivered by Father W.T. Cummings, a US Army chaplain stationed in Bataan during the Second World War.

attack is the best form of defence (*US*) If threatened, it is best to attack rather than to wait passively to be attacked. W.H. Drayton, 1775 (quoted in R.W. Gibbes, *Documentary History of the American Revolution*, 1855). This militaristic slogan was heard with increasing frequency after the American War of Independence (1776–83), when its adherents included the US commander George Washington.

> Make them believe, that offensive operations, often times, is the surest, if not the only ... means of defence.
>
> George Washington, *Writings*, 1799 (published 1940)

August. as August so the next February (*English*) A warm August is an indication that the following winter will be mild. R. Inwards, *Weather Lore*, 1893. A contradictory point of view is suggested in the proverb 'if the first week in August is unusually warm, the winter will be white and long'. Other August-related proverbs include 'dry August and warm doth harvest no harm' and 'if the twenty-fourth of August be fair and clear, then hope for a prosperous autumn that year', and 'so many August fogs, so many winter mists'.

aunt. if my aunt had been a man, she'd have been my uncle (*English*) If circumstances were otherwise it would be pointless having the discussion in progress, as the causes that gave rise to it would not have existed. It is said in response to anyone who, in the course of an argument, postulates what might happen in a different situation. John Ray, *A Collection of English Proverbs*, 1813.

~ *See also* VISIT your aunt, but not every day of the year.

authority. *See* he who has no BREAD has no authority; SOLDIERS and travellers may lie by authority; a TRAVELLER may lie with authority.

autumn. *See* CLEAR autumn, windy winter; warm autumn, long winter.

available. *See* WORK expands so as to fill the time available.

avoid. *See* BEWARE of the oak, it draws the stroke; avoid the ash, it courts the flash; a DANGER foreseen is half avoided.

avoidance is the only remedy (*English*) Some problems have no solution, and the only way to overcome them is to avoid them in the first place. Geoffrey Chaucer, *Minor Poems*, *c.*1380.

away. away goes the devil when he finds the door shut against him (*English*) Those who intend evil will achieve nothing when others refuse all temptations they offer. James Howell, *Paroemiographia*, 1659.

~ *See also* an APPLE a day keeps the doctor away; the BEST throw of the dice is to throw them away; READY money will away; when the CAT's away, the mice will play.

awhile. *See* LAD's love's a busk of broom, hot awhile and soon done; SIT awhile and go a mile.

axe. *See* the PINE wishes herself a shrub when the axe is at her root.

axletree. *See* the FLY sat upon the axletree of the chariot-wheel and said, what a dust do I raise!

aye. *See* he that would LIVE for aye must eat sage in May.

B

babe. *See* out of the MOUTHS of babes and sucklings.

baby. the baby comes out of the parsley bed (*English*) Babies are born in beds of parsley. R. Brome, *Antipodes*, 1640. Curious children were formerly told by their parents that baby girls issued from parsley beds, while baby boys were found under gooseberry bushes or in beds of nettles.

~ *See also* don't THROW the baby out with the bathwater.

Bacchus hath drowned more men than Neptune (*English*) More people die from alcohol than are drowned at sea. Thomas Fuller, *Gnomologia*, 1732.

bachelor. bachelors' wives and maids' children be well taught (*English*) Those who do not have wives and children of their own envisage the ones they might have as perfect in every regard. John Heywood, *A Dialogue containing … the Proverbs in the English Tongue*, 1546. Another proverb, however, insists that 'he that has not got a wife is not yet a complete man'.

> What a pity it is that nobody knows how to
> manage a wife, but a batchelor.
> George Colman, *The Jealous Wife*, 1761

~ *See also* a LEWD bachelor makes a jealous husband.

back. the back door robs the house (*English*) It is through the unobserved back door that one's possessions tend to disappear, in the hands of servants and family members and so on. Thomas Fuller, *Gnomologia*, 1732.

~ *See also* BIG fleas have little fleas upon their backs to bite them, and little fleas have lesser fleas, and so *ad infinitum*; GOD makes the back to the burden; it is the LAST straw that breaks the camel's back; a NICE wife and a back door will soon make a rich man poor; TWO daughters and a back door are three arrant thieves; what is GOT over the devil's back is spent under his belly; you may BREAK a horse's back, be he never so strong; you SCRATCH my back, and I'll scratch yours.

backward. See go FORWARD and fall, go backward and mar all.

bacon. *See* CHILD's pig but father's bacon.

bad. a bad bush is better than an open field (*French*) Meagre possessions are better than nothing at all (just as the shelter of a sparse bush is better than none at all). 1300 or earlier.

> These evil showers make the low bush better
> than no bield.
> Walter Scott, *The Monastery*, 1820

a bad custom is like a good cake, better broken than kept (*English*) Rules and habits that are unhelpful should be discarded. Randle Cotgrave, *A Dictionary of the French and English Tongues*, 1611.

a bad excuse is better than none (*English*) In the absence of a better reason, a poor excuse may serve better than none at all. Nicholas Udall, *Ralph Roister Doister*, *c.*1550. Also found as 'a bad shift is better than none'.

Yea Custance, better (they say) a badde scuse
than none.
Nicholas Udall, *Ralph Roister Doister*, *c.*1550

bad is the best (*English*) In some circumstances, something that is bad is the best that can be hoped for. W. Bullein, *Dialogue*, 1564. A German proverb claims that 'there is nothing so bad but may be of some use'.

Bad is the best (this English is flat).
Edmund Spenser, *The Shepheardes Calendar*, 1579

bad luck is fertile (*Russian*) Misfortunes breed more quickly than blessings.

bad money drives out good (*English*) When good and bad currencies mix, the bad currency will prevail. V.S. Lean, *Collecteana*, 1902–4. Known as Gresham's law, this principle was first voiced by Sir Thomas Gresham (*c.*1519–79), founder of the Royal Exchange, when he wrote to Elizabeth I in 1558 to stress the need to defend the purity of the coinage at a time when much debased currency was in circulation. The proverb has since been applied in many fields other than finance.

bad news travels fast (*Greek*) News of disasters or other setbacks spreads much faster than any other kind of news. Thomas Kyd, *The Spanish Tragedy*, 1592 (also found in essence in the writings of Plutarch). Also encountered in the form 'ill news comes apace'.

Evil news flies faster still than good.
Thomas Kyd, *The Spanish Tragedy*, 1592

a bad padlock invites a picklock (*English*) Those who do not take care of their own possessions and interests will find themselves robbed. Thomas Fuller, *Gnomologia*, 1732.

a bad penny always turns up (*English*) Unwelcome people have a tendency to turn up time and time again. Early nineteenth century. Originally, the proverb referred to miscreants who attempted to pass counterfeit money, warning them that their debased coinage was sure to find its way back to them, to their own detriment.

She had not seen him for thirty-six years. He must be over seventy years of age, and he had turned up again like a bad penny, doubtless a disgrace!
Arnold Bennett, *The Old Wives' Tale*, 1908

a bad woman is worse than a bad man (*English*) A woman given to wickedness will prove far more evil than any male counterpart. Henry Liddon, *Sermons*, 1893. Another proverb along the same lines runs 'a wicked woman and an evil is three halfpence worse than the devil'.

a bad workman blames his tools (*English/French*) A slipshod worker will seek to avoid culpability for bungled work by blaming it on the tools or some other interfering factor. Randle Cotgrave, *A Dictionary of the French and English Tongues*, 1611. Also encountered in the form 'an ill workman quarrels with his tools' and, in agricultural circles, as 'a bad shearer never had a good sickle'.

Never had ill workman good tools.
George Herbert, *Outlandish Proverbs*, 1640

it is a bad cause that none dare speak in (*English*) If no one will speak in defence of something then it can only be assumed that it has nothing at all to recommend it. J. Clarke, *Paroemiologia Anglo-Latina*, 1639.

it is never a bad day that hath a good night (*English*) Any enterprise that ends well cannot be considered a failure. John Denison, *Three-fold Resolution*, 1608.

They had never an ill day that had a good evening.
David Fergusson, *Scottish Proverbs*, 1641

no bad deed goes unpunished (*English*) Anyone guilty of an evil act will get their comeuppance eventually. A cynical modern reworking of this rather moralistic proverb runs 'no good deed goes unpunished'.

who is bad to his own is bad to himself (*English*) Those who treat others close to them badly will find their own interests damaged. H.G. Bohn, *A Handbook of Proverbs*, 1855.

~ *See also* AGE can be a bad travelling companion; the BEST go first, the bad remain to mend; CLERGYMEN's sons always turn out badly; FIRE and water are good servants but bad masters; GIVE a dog a bad name and hang him; a GOOD hay year a bad fog year; a GOOD horse cannot be of a bad colour; a GOOD lawyer makes a bad neighbour; a GOOD salad may be the prologue to a bad supper; HARD cases make bad law; HOPE is a good breakfast but a bad supper; into the MOUTH of a bad dog often falls a good bone; it is NEVER a bad day that hath a good night; KEEP bad men company and you'll soon be of their number; LITERATURE is a good staff but a bad crutch; make the BEST of a bad bargain; the MONTH that comes in good will go out bad; NOTHING so bad but it might have been worse; ONE bad general is better than two good ones; PRAISE makes good men better and bad men worse; there is but an HOUR in a day between a good housewife and a bad; THREE removals are as bad as a fire; while the THUNDER lasted two bad men were friends.

bag. *See* there's MANY a good cock come out of a tattered bag.

baggage. *See* RICHES are but the baggage of fortune.

bagpipe. he is like a bagpipe: he never talks till his belly be full (*English*) He does not speak until he has been fed (just as a bagpipe will not sound until the bag is filled with air). T. Draxe, *Bibliotheca Scholastica*, 1616.

> A baggepipe will not lightly speake, untill his
> belly be full.
> T. Draxe, *Bibliotheca Scholastica*, 1616

bairn. *See* FOOLS and bairns should never see half-done work; IDLE bairns are the devil's workhouses.

bait. the bait hides the hook (*English*) Fair appearances conceal a hidden threat. John Lyly, *Euphues: The Anatomy of Wit*, 1578. Another proverb offers the cautionary advice 'better shun the bait than struggle on the hook'.

> Beauty ... was a deceitful bayte with a deadly
> hooke.
> John Lyly, *Euphues: The Anatomy of Wit*, 1578

~ *See also* the FISH will soon be caught that nibbles at every bait; it is a SILLY fish that is caught twice with the same bait; when the WIND is in the south it blows the bait into the fish's mouth.

bake. as you bake, so shall you brew (*Roman*) The better something is prepared, the better it will turn out. Edward Hall, *Hall's Chronicle*, 1542 (also quoted by Terence in *Phormio*). *See also* as you BREW, so shall you bake; as you make your BED, so you must lie in it; as you SOW, so shall you reap.

> As they bake they shall brew.
> Old Nick and his crew.
> David Garrick, *May-Day*, 1775

baker. be not a baker if your head be of butter (*English*) It is foolish to undertake work to which one is unsuited. George Herbert, *Outlandish Proverbs*, 1640.

> Don't turn baker, if your head be made of butter.
> Thomas Fuller, *Gnomologia*, 1732

~ *See also* the OWL was a baker's daughter; PULL devil, pull baker.

bald. a bald head is soon shaven (*English*) It takes little time to complete the task when there is little to be done. *Reliquae Antiquae*, *c.*1450.

~ *See also* EXPERIENCE is a comb which nature gives us when we are bald.

bale. when bale is highest, boot is nighest (*Icelandic*) When evil (bale) does its worst, help (boot) is most likely to be at hand. *The Owl and the Nightingale*, 1250.

> Did you never hear, that when the need is
> highest the help is nighest?
> Sir Walter Scott, *Nigel*, 1822

balm. is there no balm in Gilead? (*Hebrew*) Is there no remedy? A reference, first given in this form in the Geneva Bible of 1560, to the gold-coloured resin 'balm of Gilead', the glutinous substance exuded by the mastic tree, *Pistacia lentiscus*, which was supposed to have medicinal properties.

> There are two guineas to buy a new frock. Come,
> Cary, never fear: we'll find balm in Gilead.
> Charlotte Brontë, *Shirley*, 1849

barber. a barber learns to shave by shaving fools (*English*) Only fools volunteer themselves to be shaved by inexperienced barbers. Randle Cotgrave, *A Dictionary of the French and English Tongues*, 1611.

> He is a fool that will suffer a young beginner to
> practise first upon him.
> John Ray, *A Collection of English Proverbs*, 1670

bare. bare words are no good bargain (*English*) Verbal agreements have no legal validity. *Politeuphuia*, 1597, attributed to J. Bodenham. Related proverbs include 'bare words buy no barley'.

~ *See also* HAIR and hair makes the carle's head bare;

it is too LATE to spare when the bottom is bare; there goes MORE to marriage than four bare legs in a bed.

barefoot. he that goes barefoot must not plant thorns (*English*) Those who are vulnerable themselves should not set traps into which they themselves might fall. S. Daniel, *Philotas*, 1605.

> He that scatters thorns let him not go barefoot.
> Benjamin Franklin, *Poor Richard's Almanack*, October 1736

~ *See also* the SHOEMAKER's son always goes barefoot.

bargain. a bargain is a bargain (*English*) Once a bargain has been made there is no going back on it. T. Wilson, *The Arte of Rhetorique*, 1553. A cautionary note is sounded by related proverbs in several other languages, including the Yiddish 'a bargain is always dear', the Japanese 'cheap purchase is money lost' and the Italian 'on a good bargain think twice'.

> However ... 'tis ill luck to go back upon a bargain.
> Charles Reade, *The Cloister and the Hearth*, 1860

the bargain is ill made where neither party gains (*Roman*) A bargain by virtue of which nobody gains anything is of no use to anyone. *c.*1597, A. Douglas, quoted in *Notes & Queries*.

~ *See also* at a GOOD bargain, make a pause; BARE words are no good bargain; if you BUY the cow, take the tail into the bargain; it takes TWO to make a bargain; make the BEST of a bad bargain; on a GOOD bargain, think twice.

bark (noun). *See* put not thy HAND between the bark and the tree.

bark (verb). **a barking dog never bites** (*English*) A dog that barks at strangers is unlikely to attack them. *Proverbs of Alfred*, *c.*1275 (also recorded in thirteenth-century France). The proverb is frequently applied not to dogs, but to people, implying that the most vociferous individuals are, in fact, often quite harmless. Also known in the forms 'great barkers are no biters' and 'his bark is worse than his bite', it may be found in Latin, French, Italian, German and sundry other languages.

> A barking dog doth seldom strangers bite.
> *Locrine*, 1595

~ *See also* ALL are not thieves that dogs bark at; CRACK was a good dog but he got hung for barking; DOGS bark as they are bred; the DOGS bark but the caravan goes on; the DOG that is idle barks at his fleas, but he that is hunting feels them not; a DOG will bark ere he bite; if the OLD dog bark, he gives counsel; the MOON does not heed the barking of dogs; why KEEP a dog and bark yourself?

barley-corn. a barley-corn is better than a diamond to a cock (*English*) Only fools prefer worthless things to more valuable objects. Robert Greene, *Euphues his Censure*, 1587.

> We catch at barley-grains, while pearls stand by
> Despis'd; such very fools art thou and I.
> Francis Quarles, *Divine Emblems*, 1635

barn. *See* a COLD April the barn will fill; if the ROBIN sings in the bush then the weather will be coarse; but if the robin sings in the barn then the weather will be warm.

Barnaby bright, Barnaby bright, the longest day and the shortest night (*English*) Traditionally, according to the Old Style calendar, the longest day of the year was held to be Saint Barnabas Day (11 June). Edmund Spenser, *Epithalamion*, 1595. The rhyme fell into disuse after the adoption of the New Style calendar in 1752.

> Barnaby bright all day and no night.
> Edith Holden, *The Country Diary of an Edwardian Lady* (published 1977)

barrel. *See* you cannot KNOW wine by the barrel.

bashfulness is an enemy to poverty (*Greek*) Those who are in need cannot afford to be bashful. John Ray, *A Collection of English Proverbs*, 1670 (quoting Homer). Another proverb of Greek origin observes that 'bashfulness is an ornament to youth, but a reproach to old age'. Equivalents in other languages include the Roman 'bashfulness will not avail a beggar' and the Dutch 'bashfulness is of no use to the needy'.

basin. *See* there is no DIFFERENCE of bloods in a basin.

basket. *See* don't put ALL your eggs in one basket.

bastard. *See* the MORE hazelnuts, the more bastard children.

baste. *See* put an IRISHMAN on the spit and you can always get another Irishman to baste him.

bate me an ace, quoth Bolton (*English*) Allow me some advantage. Richard Edwards, *The Excellent Comedie of Damon and Pithias*, 1571. The Bolton in the proverb was John Bolton, a courtier who once played cards and dice with Henry VIII. By asking the king to deal him an ace, Bolton played the monarch a deft compliment, in effect asking for an advantage to counter the king's implied greater playing skills. The proverb acquired a new interpretation, however, in the reign of Elizabeth I, after the queen was presented with a new collection of proverbs with the boast that it included all the proverbs in the language. The queen replied only with 'bate me an ace, quoth Bolton', which had been omitted by the author. From then on the proverb was also used to imply that it is wise to exercise caution before making brash boasts.

bathe. he who bathes in May will soon be laid in clay, he who bathes in June, will sing a merry tune, he who bathes in July, will dance like a fly (*English*) Those who bathe in May (with its uncertain weather) will soon perish, while those who bathe in the warmer months of June and July will flourish. William Hone, *Table-Book*, 1827. *See also* MARRY in May and rue the day; ne'er CAST a clout till May be out; a SWARM of bees in May is worth a load of hay.

bathwater. *See* don't THROW the baby out with the bathwater.

baton. *See* EVERY soldier has the baton of a field-marshal in his knapsack.

battalion. *See* GOD is always on the side of the big battalions.

Battersea. go to Battersea to get your simples cut (*English*) You are so foolish you should go to Battersea for a cure. F. Grose, *A Provincial Glossary*, 1787. Battersea was where market gardeners grew medicinal herbs ('simples') for the London apothecaries, who were quick to sell them to their more gullible customers. Also found as 'go to Battersea to be cut for the simples'.

battle. *See* the FIRST blow is half the battle; the RACE is not to the swift, nor the battle to the strong.

be. be as be may (*English*) Accept things as they are. Geoffrey Chaucer, 'The Monk's Tale', *The Canterbury Tales*, *c.*1387. Also encountered in the fuller form 'be as be may is no banning'.

> Be it so, is no banning. Spoken when we unwillingly give our consent to a thing.
>
> James Kelly, *A Complete Collection of Scotish Proverbs*, 1721

be what you would seem to be (*English*) Be true to your nature. W. Baldwin, *Treatise of Moral Philosophy*, 1547. The proverb echoes the biblical injunction 'I am what I am'. Variant forms include 'be what thou wouldst be called'.

> It's a vegetable. It doesn't look like one, but it is ... the moral of that is – 'Be what you would seem to be'.
>
> Lewis Carroll, *Alice's Adventures in Wonderland*, 1865

you are what you eat (*German*) The state of a person's character and physical being is closely associated with their diet. Anthelme Brillat-Savarin, *La Physiologie du goût*, 1825. The saying was revived in the 1960s, when it became a slogan of a new health-conscious generation (it was used as the title of a US health film shown in 1969). Variants include the French 'tell me what you eat and I will tell you what you are'.

bean. *See* CANDLEMAS day, put beans in the clay, put candles and candlesticks away; DUNDER do gally the beans; he KNOWS how many beans make five.

bear (noun)**. as a bear has no tail, for a lion he'll fail** (*English*) One cannot aspire to greatness if one lacks the essential qualities necessary (applied against those who aspire to stations beyond their natural reach). Thomas Fuller, *The History of the Worthies of England*, 1662. The story goes that the ambitious Robert Dudley, Earl of Leicester, who sought dominion over the Netherlands in 1585, claimed descent from the noble Warwick family and accordingly exchanged his own crest, featuring a two-tailed lion, for the bear and ragged staff of the Warwicks. When his crest was set up in public, a wag scrawled beneath it: 'Your bear for lion needs must fail, because your true bears have no tail.'

~ *See also* CALL the bear 'uncle' till you are safe across the bridge; he must have IRON nails that scratches a bear.

bear (verb). **bear and forbear** (*Greek*) Endure with patience. J. Sandford, *Hours of Recreation*, 1576. The so-called 'golden rule' of Epictetus.

> You must take two bears to live with you – Bear and Forbear.
>
> H.W. Thompson, *Body, Boots and Britches*, 1940

bear wealth, poverty will bear itself (*French*) It is more difficult to cope with wealth, because of the temptations it brings with it, than it is to adjust to poverty. David Fergusson, *Scottish Proverbs*, 1641.

bear with evil and expect good (*French*) Endure the bad and hope for better things to come. George Herbert, *Outlandish Proverbs*, 1640.

he may bear a bull that hath borne a calf (*Greek*) Those who are used to coping with relatively small challenges will progress to coping with greater things. R. Taverner, *Proverbs or Adages with New Additions, gathered out of the Chiliades of Erasmus*, 1539.

~ *See also* be it for BETTER, be it for worse, do you after him that beareth the purse; BEWARE of Greeks bearing gifts; the BOUGHS that bear most hang lowest; a CLEAR conscience can bear any trouble; he that BLOWS best bears away the horn; if the ICE will bear a man before Christmas, it will not bear a duck after; it is a PROUD horse that will not bear his own provender; the OLDER the crab-tree the more crabs it bears; one has ALWAYS strength enough to bear the misfortunes of one's friends; only an ELEPHANT can bear an elephant's load; PLANT the crab-tree where you will, it will never bear pippins; so we get the CHINK, we'll bear with the stink; THREE helping one another bear the burthen of six; where no one else will, the DEVIL must bear the cross.

beard. if the beard were all, the goat might preach (*Greek*) If physical appearances were all-determining, the most dimwitted might aspire to greatness. Thomas Fuller, *The History of the Worthies of England*, 1662.

it is not the beard that makes the philosopher (*English*) A learned appearance does not necessarily reflect a learned mind. E. Gayton, *Festivious Notes on Don Quixote*, 1654. *See also* APPEARANCES are deceptive; never JUDGE by appearances.

~ *See also* HARES may pull dead lions by the beard; 'tis MERRY in hall when beards wag all.

beast. *See* if the ADDER could hear and the blind-worm could see, neither man nor beast would ever go free; it is not the BURDEN but the overburden that kills the beast; when the WIND is in the east, 'tis neither good for man nor beast.

beat. beat the dog before the lion (*English*) By punishing a lesser person a more powerful enemy may be cowed. *Douce MS*, *c.*1350.

> Even so as one would beat his offenceless dog to affright an imperious lion.
>
> William Shakespeare, *Othello*, 1604–05

if you can't beat 'em, join 'em (*US*) If one's opponents are invincible, it is advisable to change sides or to adopt a similar position to theirs. Quentin Reynolds, *The Wounded Don't Cry*, 1941. Often heard in the United States in the form 'if you can't lick 'em, join 'em'.

one beats the bush, another takes the bird (*English*) One man does the work, while his master takes the profit. *Ipomadon*, *c.*1300.

> And while I at length debate and beate the bushe, there shall steppe in other men, and catche the burdes.
>
> John Heywood, *A Dialogue containing the Proverbs in the English Tongue*, 1546

~ *See also* the ENGLISH never know when they are beaten; GIVE a slave a rod and he'll beat his master; it is EASY to find a stick to beat a dog; a MAN surprised is half beaten; ONE Englishman can beat three Frenchmen; when it RAINS and the sun shines at the same time the devil is beating his wife; where DRUMS beat, laws are silent; a WOMAN, a dog and a walnut tree, the more you beat them the better they be.

beautiful. *See* BIG is beautiful; SMALL is beautiful.

beauty. beauty and honesty seldom agree (*English*) A woman who is both beautiful and honest is very rare, because beauty invites temptation. John Lyly, *Euphues and His England*, 1580. Related proverbs include 'a beauty's smile covers a multitude of sins' and 'rare is the union of beauty and modesty', in which form it was quoted by Juvenal.

Beawtie and honesty seldome agree, for of beautie comes temptation, of temptation dishonour.
John Florio, *Second Fruites*, 1591

beauty draws more than oxen (*English*) Beauty attracts all to itself. John Florio, *Second Frutes*, 1591. A German equivalent runs 'one hair of a woman draws more than a bell-rope'.

And beauty draws us with a single hair.
Alexander Pope, *The Rape of the Lock*, 1712

beauty is but a blossom (*English*) Beauty does not last long. T. Draxe, *Bibliotheca Scholastica*, 1616. Variants include 'beauty is soon blasted'.

beauty is in the eye of the beholder (*English*) The judgement of beauty is subjective and not likely to be the same between one individual and another. F. Brooke, *History of Emily Montague*, 1769. Recorded in this form for the first time towards the close of the nineteenth century, but known in variant forms for some 200 years previously. A Chinese variant, attributed to Confucius, runs 'everything has its beauty but not everyone sees it'. *See also* ONE man's meat is another man's poison.

Most true is it that 'beauty is in the eye of the gazer'.
Charlotte Brontë, *Jane Eyre*, 1847

beauty is no inheritance (*English*) Beauty is not necessarily passed from one generation to the next. T. Draxe, *Bibliotheca Scholastica*, 1633.

beauty is only skin deep (*English*) Physical beauty is in the final analysis superficial and cannot be relied upon as an indication of underlying character. First recorded in English in the poem 'A Wife' by Sir Thomas Overbury in 1613 but also found in classical literature, including the works of Virgil. Authorities observe that it is an expression most often heard on the lips of those who are not themselves outwardly beautiful. Variants include 'beauty is only skin deep, but ugly goes to the bone', 'beauty may have fair leaves yet bitter fruit' and the Japanese 'beauty is only one layer'. *See also* APPEARANCES are deceptive; HANDSOME is as handsome does; NEVER judge by appearances.

I'm tired of all this nonsense about beauty being only skin-deep. That's deep enough. What do you want – an adorable pancreas?
Jean Kerr, *The Snake Has All the Lines*, 1960

beauty is potent, but money is omnipotent (*English*) Money exerts more power than beauty. John Ray, *A Collection of English Proverbs*, 1670.

beauty provoketh thieves sooner than gold (*English*) Beauty has a greater lure than things of purely monetary value. William Shakespeare, *As You Like It*, *c.*1599.

beauty without virtue is a flower without perfume (*French*) Good looks are worthless if unsupported by good character.

~ *See also* FANCY passes beauty; GRACE will last, beauty will blast; TELL a woman she's a beauty and the devil will tell her so fifty times.

because is a woman's reason (*English*) Referring to an opinion that is illogically held without any supporting argument and purely from personal prejudice. William Shakespeare, *The Two Gentlemen of Verona*, *c.*1594.

I have no other but a woman's reason: I think him so because I think him so.
William Shakespeare, *The Two Gentlemen of Verona*, *c.*1594

bed. as you make your bed, so you must lie in it (*English*) A person must bear the consequences of his or her own actions. G. Harvey, *Marginalia*, *c.*1590. Similar sentiments were expressed in the classical world, Terence, for instance, observing in his *Phormio* (161BC) that 'you have mixed the mess and you must eat it'. *See also* as you BAKE, so shall you brew; as you BREW, so shall you bake; as you SOW, so shall you reap.

As you make your bed, so you lye down. According to your Conditions you have your Bargain.
*c.*1590, quoted in James Kelly, *A Complete Collection of Scotish Proverbs*, 1721

bed is the poor man's opera (*Italian*) The poor man cannot afford to go to the opera, so finds a parallel passion in his sex life.

'Bed,' as the Italian proverb succinctly puts it, 'is the poor man's opera.'
Aldous Huxley, *Heaven and Hell*, 1956

go to bed with the lamb and rise with the lark (*English*) Go to sleep early and get up early. Wright, *Songs*, *c.*1555. Another proverb cautions 'too much bed makes a dull head'. *See also* the EARLY bird catches the worm.

> We were compelled to rise, having been perhaps not above four hours in bed – (for we were no go-to-beds with the lamb, though we anticipated the lark oft times in her rising).
>
> Charles Lamb, *The Last Essays of Elia*, 1833

he that goes to bed thirsty riseth healthy (*English*) It is bad for the health to drink too much before going to bed. George Herbert, *Outlandish Proverbs*, 1640.

~ *See also* ANGRY men make themselves beds of nettles; DRY feet, warm head, bring safe to bed; EARLY to bed and early to rise, makes a man healthy, wealthy and wise; a GREAT dowry is a bed full of brambles; if the COCK crows on going to bed, he's sure to rise with a watery head; it is a DANGEROUS fire begins in the bed straw; there goes MORE to marriage than four bare legs in a bed; TURNIPS like a dry bed but a wet head; the WEST wind is a gentleman and goes to bed.

bedfellow. *See* ADVERSITY makes strange bedfellows; HONOUR and ease are seldom bedfellows; POLITICS makes strange bedfellows.

bee. bees that have honey in their mouths have stings in their tails (*English*) Something may be desirable, but carries with it the risk of an unpleasant surprise. *Passe forth, pilgrime*, *c.*1440.

> There are some things which are pleasant but not good, as youthful lusts and worldly delights. These bees carry honey in their mouths, but they have a sting in their tails.
>
> W. Secker, *Nonsuch Professor*, 1660

where the bee sucks honey the spider sucks poison (*English*) Some will find good things while others find only bad from the same source. G. Harvey, *Letter-book*, 1573.

> Sweet poetry's a flower, where men, like bees and spiders, may bear poison, or else sweets and wax away.
>
> Francis Beaumont and John Fletcher, *Four Plays* (published 1905), 1614

~ *See also* the CALF, the goose, the bee: the world is ruled by these three; a DEAD bee will make no honey; OLD bees yield no honey; a SWARM of bees in May is worth a load of hay.

beef. *See* HONOUR buys no beef; SYMPATHY without relief is like mustard without beef.

beer. *See* LIFE isn't all beer and skittles; NEW beer, new bread and green wood will make a man's hair grow through his hood; there is no such THING as good small beer, good brown bread, or a good old woman; TURKEY, heresy, hops and beer came into England all in one year.

befall. *See* our WORST misfortunes are those which never befall us.

beg. beg from beggars and you'll never be rich (*English*) Those who seek to get what others have themselves got from begging will never prosper. James Kelly, *A Complete Collection of Scotish Proverbs*, 1721. Related proverbs include 'neither beg of him who has been a beggar nor serve him who has been a servant'.

~ *See also* GIVE a loaf and beg a slice; ILL egging makes ill begging; a MAN of many trades begs his bread on Sunday.

beget. *See* LENGTH begets loathing; LOVE begets love; MONEY begets money; NEW meat begets a new appetite; ONE business begets another.

beggar. a beggar is never out of his way (*English*) A beggar has no reason to be in one place rather than another, as he may pursue his way of life anywhere. T. Adams, *Works*, 1630.

a beggar may sing before a pickpocket (*Roman*) A beggar need not worry about pickpockets, because he has nothing in his pocket to be stolen. Juvenal, *Satires*, first century AD. Also found in the form 'a beggar may sing before a thief'.

> The last prerogative of beggary, which entitled him to laugh at the risk of robbery.
>
> Walter Scott, quoted in Lockhart's *Life*, 1829

beggars breed and rich men feed (*English*) The offspring of beggars find work as servants of the rich. John Ray, *A Collection of English Proverbs*, 1670.

> Poor people's children find a support in the service of the rich and great.
>
> James Kelly, *A Complete Collection of Scotish Proverbs*, 1721

beggars can't be choosers (*English*) Those in need cannot afford to question what is offered to them, even if it is not quite what they hoped for. John Heywood, *A Dialogue containing … the Proverbs in the English Tongue*, 1546. The date of the proverb suggests it might have arisen in connection with the huge increase in vagrancy that occurred in sixteenth-century England, when social and economic changes, coupled with the decline of the medieval feudal system, forced many people into a condition of indigence. *See also* NEEDS must when the devil drives; never LOOK a gift horse in the mouth.

> For all this we were to pay at a high rate; but beggars cannot be choosers.
>
> Robert Louis Stevenson, *The Master of Ballantrae*, 1889

a beggar's purse is bottomless (*English*) No amount of wealth will satisfy some people. R. Taverner, *Proverbs or Adages with New Additions, gathered out of the Chiliades of Erasmus*, 1539.

~ *See also* BEG from beggars and you'll never be rich; EAT peas with the king and cherries with the beggar; if WISHES were horses, beggars would ride; it is BETTER to be born a beggar than a fool; NOTHING agreeth worse than a lady's heart and a beggar's purse; ONE beggar does not hate another as much as one doctor hates another; a PROUD heart and a beggar's purse agree not well together; SET a beggar on horseback, and he'll ride to the devil; SIT a beggar at your table, and he will soon put his feet on it; SUE a beggar and get a louse; who DAINTIES love shall beggars prove.

beggary. *See* TRASH and trumpery is the highway to beggary.

begin. he begins to die that quits his desires (*English*) Any person who abandons all ambitions and hopes for the future might as well be dead. Randle Cotgrave, *A Dictionary of the French and English Tongues*, 1611.

he who begins too much accomplishes little (*German*) Those who set their sights too high may end up achieving nothing.

~ *See also* as SOON as man is born he begins to die; CHARITY begins at home; DOGS begin in jest and end in earnest; he that would the DAUGHTER win, must with the mother first begin; it is a DANGEROUS fire begins in the bed straw; LIFE begins at forty; a MAN has choice to begin love but not to end it; NEEDLES and pins, needles and pins, when a man marries his trouble begins; on the FIRST of March, the crows begin to search; THINK on the end before you begin; WELL begun is half done; when THINGS are at the worst they soon begin to mend; when WAR begins hell opens.

beginning. such beginning, such end (*English*) Projects tend to end as they began. John Heywood, *A Dialogue containing … the Proverbs in the English Tongue*, 1546. Variants include 'as you begin the year so you'll end it', 'good to begin well, better to end well' and the German 'beginning hot, middle lukewarm, ending cold'.

~ *See also* EATING and scratching wants but a beginning; the FIRST breath is the beginning of death; a GOOD beginning makes a good ending; what the FOOL does in the end, the wise man does at the beginning.

beguile. *See* they that THINK none ill are soonest beguiled.

behind. behind the horseman sits black care (*Greek*) Worry will continue to dog those who try to run away from it. John Florio, *Montaigne*, 1603 (quoting Horace).

~ *See also* ADVICE should be viewed from behind; the DEVIL's behind the glass; FAR behind must follow the faster; the FURTHER you go, the further behind.

beholder. *See* BEAUTY is in the eye of the beholder.

belfry. *See* the DEVIL gets up to the belfry by the vicar's skirts.

believe. believe nothing of what you hear, and only half of what you see (*English*) Question the truth of everything you learn. Layamon, *Brut*, *c.*1205. In the simplified form 'don't believe all you hear' it was recorded well before 1300 and has even been attributed to King Alfred the Great himself. Another proverb observes that 'we are prone to believe what we don't understand'. A twentieth-century gloss on the original proverb produced 'believe nothing until it has been officially denied'. A contrasting proverb runs 'believe well and have well', while another insists that 'he that believes all, misseth; he that believes nothing, misseth'.

~ *See also* do not ALL you can, spend not all you have, believe not all you hear, and tell not all you know; he whose BELLY is full believes not him who is fasting; a LIAR is not believed when he speaks the truth; SEEING is believing; we SOON believe what we desire.

bell. bells call others but themselves enter not into the church (*English*) Some people summon others to their duty, which they cannot fulfil themselves. H. Smith, *Sermons*, 1591.

~ *See also* a CRACKED bell can never sound well; do not HANG all your bells upon one horse.

bellowing. a bellowing cow soon forgets her calf (*English*) Exaggerated displays of grief soon subside. T. Wilson, *The Art of Rhetoric*, 1553.

> When a woman, newly widowed, had tried to throw herself into her husband's grave at his funeral ... some one ... said drily ... 'Ah, you wait. The bellowing cow's always the first to forget its calf.'
>
> Flora Thompson, *Lark Rise to Candleford*, 1945

belly. the belly carries the legs and not the legs the belly (*English*) A person must be well fed before they can hope to walk far or meet demanding physical challenges. T. Shelton, *Cervantes' Don Quixote*, 1620.
a belly full of gluttony will never study willingly (*English*) The student works best on an empty stomach. George Pettie, *Guazzo*, 1586.
the belly hath no ears (*English*) No amount of words will make a hungry man forget he is hungry. R. Taverner, *Proverbs or Adages with New Additions, gathered out of the Chiliades of Erasmus*, 1539. Another related proverb runs 'the belly is not filled with fair words'.
he whose belly is full believes not him who is fasting (*English*) It is hard to put oneself in the position of those whose circumstances are radically different. J. Sandford, *The Garden of Pleasure*, 1573.
when the belly is full the mind is among the maids (*English*) When a man's appetite for food is satisfied, his mind turns inevitably to sex. H. Estienne, *World of Wonders*, 1607.

> When the belly is full, the breech would be frigging.
>
> Randle Cotgrave, *A Dictionary of the French and English Tongues*, 1611

~ *See also* the EYE is bigger than the belly; FULL bellies make empty skulls; GRAIN by grain the hen fills her belly; a GROWING youth has a wolf in his belly; he is like a BAGPIPE: he never talks till his belly be full; he was CURSED in his mother's belly that was killed by a cannon; HUNGRY bellies have no ears; what is GOT over the devil's back is spent under his belly.

belong. what belongs to everybody belongs to nobody (*Spanish*) No one can claim ownership of something that is common property.

bemire. *See* a HOG that's bemired endeavours to bemire others.

bench. *See* HALL benches are slippery.

bend. *See* BETTER bend than break.

benefit. *See* the LAST benefit is most remembered.

bent. *See* as the TWIG is bent, so is the tree inclined; a BOW long bent at last waxeth weak.

Bernard. *See* the GOOD Bernard does not see everything.

berry. *See* there is a DEVIL in every berry of the grape.

best. the best cart may overthrow (*English*) Accidents may befall the best people or things just as easily as they befall the less perfect. John Heywood, *A Dialogue containing ... the Proverbs in the English Tongue*, 1546.
the best doctors are Dr Diet, Dr Quiet and Dr Merryman (*English*) Rest, a sensible diet and a cheerful outlook are the best treatment for many ailments. W. Bullein, *Government of Health*, 1558.
the best fish swim near the bottom (*English*) The most valuable things can be gained only through the taking of some trouble or effort. Nicholas Breton, *Proverbs*, 1616.

> The best fish swim deep.
>
> Thomas Fuller, *Gnomologia*, 1732

the best go first, the bad remain to mend (*English*) It is always those of better character who perish first, leaving behind lesser men. John Donne, 'Sonnet on Death', 1631. *See also* only the GOOD die young; whom the GODS love die young.

And soonest our best men with thee doe goe.
John Donne, 'Sonnet on Death', 1631

the best is the enemy of the good (*English*) The exceptional eclipses what is merely very good. William Shakespeare, *King Lear*, 1605. *See also* the GOOD is the enemy of the best.

the best laid schemes of mice and men gang oft agley (*Scottish*) The most carefully prepared plans all too often turn out not as intended. Robert Burns, *Poems*, 1786. *See also* the BEST cart may overthrow.

I am sorry the book-binding has gone pop. But there 'The best laid schemes' etc. etc.
D.H. Lawrence, letter, 1911

the best manure is under the farmer's foot (*English*) It is human nature to reserve the best of something for yourself.

the best mirror is an old friend (*Spanish*) Old friends can be relied on to give the truest accounts of how you look or are behaving. George Herbert, *Outlandish Proverbs*, 1640.

the best of friends must part (*English*) All friendships come to an end. Geoffrey Chaucer, *Troilus and Criseyde*, *c*.1385–90.

Friends must part, we came not all together, and we must not goe all together.
George Chapman, *May-Day*, 1611

the best of men are but men at best (*English*) Even the greatest of men have human failings. John Aubrey, letter, 15 June 1680. *See also* even HOMER sometimes nods.

I remember one sayeing of Generall Lambert's, that 'the best of men are but men at best'.
John Aubrey, letter, 15 June 1680

the best remedy against an ill man is much ground between (*English*) The best way to cope with an unpleasant or hostile person is to stay as far away from him or her as possible. George Herbert, *Outlandish Proverbs*, 1640. The same thinking underlies the proverb 'the remedy for love is land between'.

the best smell is bread, the best savour salt, the best love that of children (*English*) Nothing is superior to the smell of newly baked bread, to the taste of salt and to the love of children. George Herbert, *Outlandish Proverbs*, 1640.

the best things are worst to come by (*English*) The most desirable things in life are usually the most difficult to obtain. J. Clarke, *Paroemiologia Anglo-Latina*, 1639.

the best things come in small packages (*English*) The modest size of the package does not necessarily reflect the value of what is inside. J. Howell, *Paroemiographia*, 1659.

the best things in life are free (*English*) The greatest pleasures in life are not to be bought for money, but are freely available to all. Popularized by the song 'The best things in life are free', written by B.G. De Silva in 1927. Related proverbs include 'best is best cheap'.

the best things may be abused (*English*) Even the best things may be wasted or turned to ill advantage. John Lyly, *Euphues*, 1579.

Nor aught so good but strain'd from that fair use
Revolts from true birth, stumbling on abuse.
William Shakespeare, *Romeo and Juliet*, 1594–5

the best throw of the dice is to throw them away (*English*) A wise man will have nothing to do with gambling. Henry Smith, *Sermons*, 1591.

the best wine comes out of an old vessel (*English*) The best advice comes from those who have the experience of age. Robert Burton, *Anatomy of Melancholy*, 1621.

he is the best general who makes the fewest mistakes (*English*) The most successful leaders are those who make the fewest errors of judgement. Sir I. Hamilton, *Staff Officer's Scrap-Book*, 1907.

it is best to be on the safe side (*English*) Caution is the best policy. John Dryden and William Cavendish, Duke of Newcastle, *Sir Martin Mar-all*, 1668. Related proverbs include 'safe is the word'. *See also* BETTER safe than sorry.

Determining to be on the safe side, he made his apology in form as soon as he could say any thing.
Jane Austen, *Sense and Sensibility*, 1811

it is the best swimmers who drown (*English*) Those who are overconfident in what they do are the most likely to come to grief. V.S. Lean, *Collecteana*, 1902.

make the best of a bad bargain (*English*) Those who are obliged to agree to a disadvantageous bargain must make the best they can of it. Samuel Pepys, *Diary*, 14 August 1663. Also encountered in the form 'make the best of a bad market'.

Matters have not been carried on with due secrecy; however, we must make the best of a bad bargain.
John Arbuthnot, *John Bull*, 1712

~ *See also* ACCIDENTS will happen in the best regulated families; ADAM's ale is the best brew; ALL's for the best in the best of all possible worlds; ATTACK is the best form of defence; BAD is the best; BOUGHT wit is best; CORRUPTION of the best becomes the worst; DEEM the best till the truth be tried; EAST, west, home's best; ELBOW-GREASE gives the best polish; EXPERIENCE is the best teacher; FEW words are best; a GOOD example is the best sermon; the GOOD is the enemy of the best; a GOOD wife and health is a man's best wealth; the GREATEST crabs be not all the best meat; a HEARTY welcome is the best cheer; he KNOWS best what good is that has endured evil; he that BLOWS best bears away the horn; HONESTY is the best policy; HOPE for the best and prepare for the worst; HUNGER is the best sauce; in the DEEPEST water is the best fishing; KITCHEN physic is the best physic; LAUGHTER is the best medicine; LEAVE a jest when it pleases you best; a MAN's best friend is his dog; NEXT to no wife, a good wife is best; of SOUP and love the first is the best; OLD fish and young flesh feed men best; OLD friends and old wine are best; an OLD poacher makes the best gamekeeper; PROVIDE for the worst, the best will save itself; QUIETNESS is best; REVENGE is a dish that is best eaten cold; the ROUGH net is not the best catcher of birds; SECOND thoughts are best; she SMELLS best that smells of nothing; SILENCE is a woman's best garment; TEMPERANCE is the best physic; TRUTH's best ornament is nakedness; WEALTH is best known by want; when the WIND is in the west the weather is at the best; whom we LOVE best, to them we can say least; why should the DEVIL have all the best tunes?

bestow. *See* KINDNESS is lost that is bestowed on children and old folks.

betide. *See* if SAINT Paul's Day be fair and clear, it will betide a happy year; SOUND travelling far and wide a stormy day will betide.

betimes. *See* he that will DECEIVE the fox must rise betimes; he that would be WELL old must be old betimes.

betrothed. the betrothed of good is evil, the betrothed of life is death, the betrothed of love is divorce (*Malay*) Every good thing in life has its undesirable but inseparable counterpart.

better. be it for better, be it for worse, do you after him that beareth the purse (*English*) It is good policy to obey those who have the money, whether they be right or wrong. *Douce MS*, *c.*1350.

My puir mither used aye to tell me, Be it better, be it worse, Be ruled by him that has the purse.
Sir Walter Scott, *Rob Roy*, 1818

better a clout than a hole out (*English*) It is better to accept a possibly unsightly repair than to risk more serious damage to something. William Camden, *Remains concerning Britain*, 1605.

better a dinner of herbs than a stalled ox where hate is (*Hebrew*) It is preferable to dine off modest fare in friendly company than to feast in a hostile atmosphere. Proverbs 15:17. The fuller form of the proverb, as given in the 1560 translation of the Bible, runs: 'better is a dinner of grene herbes where love is, then a stalled oxe and hatred therewith.' A 'stalled ox' is an ox fattened in a stall and ready for slaughter.

better a good cow than a cow of a good kind (*English/Scottish*) A proven good personal reputation is better than a good family background. John Buchan, *Huntingtower*, 1922.

better a little fire to warm us than a great one to burn us (*Scottish*) A minor benefit that carries with it no danger is preferable to a much greater one that carries with it much risk. James Kelly, *A Complete Collection of Scotish Proverbs*, 1721. Related proverbs in other languages include the Italian saying 'the fire that does not warm me shall never scorch me'.

better a louse in the pot than no flesh at all (*English*) It is better to have something, however negligible, than nothing whatsoever. J. Clarke, *Paroemiologia Anglo-Latina*, 1639.

better a mischief than an inconvenience (*English*) It is better to put up with some small nuisance in order to avoid some greater problem. T. Wilson, *Discourse upon Usury*, 1572.

better an egg today than a chicken tomorrow (*English*) A small benefit that can be enjoyed at once is better than the uncertain promise of something better that may be enjoyed at some future date.

J. Howell, *Paroemiographia*, 1659. *See also* a BIRD in the hand is worth two in the bush; don't COUNT your chickens before they are hatched.

better be a fool than a knave (*English*) It is more defensible to be naturally stupid than it is to be deliberately wicked. T. Lodge, *A Fig for Momus*, 1595.

> 'Tis better be a foole then be a fox.
>
> Thomas Lodge, *A Fig for Momus*, 1595

better be an old man's darling than a young man's slave (*English*) The wife of an old man enjoys an easier life than the wife of a younger man, who will make more demands on her. John Heywood, *A Dialogue containing ... the Proverbs in the English Tongue*, 1546.

better be envied than pitied (*Greek*) It is better to inspire jealousy than have people feeling sorry for you. John Heywood, *A Dialogue containing ... the Proverbs in the English Tongue*, 1546 (also found in the writings of Pindar and Herodotus among other classical authors). The Greeks similarly advise that 'he who goes unenvied shall not be admired'.

> Men say, and truly, that they better be which
> be envyed then pittied.
>
> John Donne, *Poems*, 1631

better be first in a village than second at Rome (*Roman*) It is better to be in a position to exercise unchallenged power in a small community or organization than to play second fiddle to someone else in a grander situation. Nicholas Udall, *Apothegms of Erasmus*, 1542 (also found in Plutarch's *Caesar*). Tradition has it that Julius Caesar quoted the proverb when opting to rule Gaul rather than share power in Rome.

> Caesar, when he went first into Gaul, made no scruple to profess *That he had rather be first in a village than second at Rome.*
>
> Francis Bacon, *The Advancement of Learning*, 1605

better be happy than wise (*English*) Happiness is preferable to wisdom. Francis Bacon, *Promus*, *c.*1594. Related proverbs include the Italian 'a happy heart is better than a full purse'.

better bend than break (*English*) It is better to compromise than to be defeated utterly because one will not yield ground. Geoffrey Chaucer, *Troilus and Criseyde*, *c.*1385–90.

> I have had ... sorrows ... but I have borne them ill.
> I have broken where I should have bent.
>
> Charles Dickens, *Barnaby Rudge*, 1840

better be out of the world than out of fashion (*English*) It is preferable to be dead than to be seen to be out of touch with what is modish or fashionable. J. Clarke, *Paroemiologia Anglo-Latina*, 1639.

> 'Why, Tom, you are high in the Mode.' ... 'It is better to be out of the World, than out of the Fashion.'
>
> Jonathan Swift, *Polite Conversation*, 1738

the better gamester the worser man (*English*) Gambling corrupts all those who dabble in it. J. Clarke, *Paroemiologia Anglo-Latina*, 1639. Another proverb cautions that 'gamesters and racehorses never last long'.

better give a penny than lend twenty (*Italian*) It is preferable to make a gift of a single penny, knowing that it will never be repaid, than to lend a larger amount, as the latter may never be repaid.

better late than never (*Roman*) Doing something late is better than not doing it at all. *Ancrene Riwle*, *c.*1200 (also quoted by Livy *c.*10BC). Ambrose Bierce added his own lighthearted version of the proverb, writing 'better late than before anybody has invited you'.

> Oh, Mr Dexter, we have been so anxious, but better late than never. Let me introduce you to Miss Wilbraham and Gräfin von Meyersdorf.
>
> Graham Greene, *The Third Man*, 1950

better lost than found (*English*) Sometimes it is better to have mislaid something or someone that will only be a source of greater grief if found again. G. Pettie, *Petite Pallace*, 1576.

> He is gone to seek my young mistress; and I think she is better lost than found.
>
> Porter, *The Angry Woman of Abingdon*, 1599

better no doctor at all than three (*Polish*) Doctors can always be relied on to give contrary advice about a person's condition and treatment, so the fewer consulted the better. Related proverbs include the Czech saying 'many doctors, death accomplished'.

better no ring than a ring of rush (*English*) If a thing has no real value it is better not to display it at all. William Shakespeare, *All's Well That Ends Well*, 1602–3.

better one house spoiled than two (*English*) It is preferable for two argumentative or otherwise undesirable people to be married to each other than for them to marry elsewhere and thus blight the lives of other partners. T.B. de la Primaudaye's *French Academy*, 1586. Also encountered in the form 'better one house troubled than two' and 'better one house filled than two spilled'.

> Where the old proverb is fulfild, better one house troubled then two.
>
> Robert Greene, *Penelope's Web*, 1587

better safe than sorry (*English*) Don't take unnecessary risks. S. Lover, *Rory O'More*, 1837.

better say nothing than nothing to the purpose (*English*) If you have nothing worthwhile to add, then it is better not to say anything at all. J. Chamberlain, *Letters*, 1605. Related proverbs include 'say well or be still'.

better sit idly than work for nothing (*English*) There is no point working if you are not going to be paid. D. Rogers, *Matrimonial Honour*, 1642. Related proverbs include 'better sit still than rise up and fall'.

the better the day, the better the deed (*English*) Work done on a Sunday or other holy day will be doubly blessed. Thomas Middleton, *Michaelmas Term*, 1607. Also recorded in similar form in French in the early fourteenth century.

> Ask Mr Landless to dinner on Christmas Eve (the better the day the better the deed).
>
> Charles Dickens, *The Mystery of Edwin Drood*, 1870

better the devil you know than the devil you don't know (*English*) When faced with a choice between a known evil and an unknown evil, most people will settle for the evil that is at least familiar. Anthony Trollope, *Barchester Towers*, 1857 (although also recorded in variant forms in writings of the classical authors). In the sixth century Aesop illustrated the proverb in a fable about some frogs. These frogs asked Jupiter for a king but were given a lump of wood, and when they scorned the log and asked for a new king from Jupiter, he sent them a frog-eating water snake. The moral of the story was rendered as 'likewise, you must bear the evil that you have, lest a greater one befall you'. *See also* of TWO evils choose the lesser.

> The dread of something after death ... makes us rather bear those ills we have, Than fly to others that we know not of.
>
> William Shakespeare, *Hamlet*, *c.*1600

the better, the worse (*Greek*) The better a person is at something undesirable or wicked, the worse it is. Nicholas Udall, *Apothegms of Erasmus*, 1542 (quoting Diogenes).

better to hang than to hold (*English*) It is better to hang some people (the sick, the old and so forth) than bother to feed them. T. Brewer, *A Knot of Fools*, 1624.

better untaught than ill taught (*English*) It is better to remain in ignorance than to be taught things that are wrong. John Ray, *A Collection of English Proverbs*, 1670.

better wed over the mixen than over the moor (*English/Scottish*) It is safer to marry someone from your own neighbourhood than someone from farther afield, of whom you inevitably know less. 1628, quoted in M.L. Anderson, *Proverbs in Scots*, 1957. 'Mixen' signifies midden or dunghill.

> He might hae dune waur than married me ...
> Better wed over the mixen as over the moor, as they say in Yorkshire.
>
> Walter Scott, *The Heart of Midlothian*, 1818

it is better to be a cuckold and not know it, than be none and everybody say so (*English*) Bearing the reputation of having a faithless wife, even when the rumour is false, is worse than actually having a faithless wife and not knowing about it. J. Howell, *Paroemiographia*, 1659. Another proverb comments 'to be a cuckold and know it not is no more than to drink with a fly in the cup and see it not'.

it is better to be born a beggar than a fool (*Spanish*) It is better to be born poor than stupid. R. Percyvall, *A Spanish Grammar*, 1599.

> It is better to be a beggar than an Ignoramus.
>
> G. Torriano, *Select Italian Proverbs*, 1642

it is better to be born lucky than rich (*English*) Good luck is of more value than mere riches. J. Clarke, *Paroemiologia Anglo-Latina*, 1639.

it is better to conceal one's knowledge than to reveal one's ignorance (*Spanish*) In attempting to demonstrate one's knowledge one may reveal only how little one really knows.

it is better to give than to receive (*Hebrew*) Those who give are more blessed in the eyes of heaven than those who receive. Bible, Acts 20:35. Another, concise, proverb backs up the sentiment with 'give and be blessed'.

it is better to marry a shrew than a sheep (*English*) It is better to marry a lively, shrewish woman than a dull, beautiful one. T. Tusser, *Five Hundred Points of Good Husbandry*, 1573. Related proverbs include 'a shrew profitable may serve a man reasonable'.

> It is an olde saying, one shrew is worth two sheep.
>
> George Gascoigne, *The Glasse of Government*, 1573

it is better to travel hopefully than to arrive (*English*) It is often better to have something to aim for than actually to achieve it. Robert Louis Stevenson, *Virginibus Puerisque*, 1881.

> To travel hopefully is a better thing than to arrive, and the true success is to labour.
>
> Robert Louis Stevenson, *Virginibus Puerisque*, 1881

it is better to wear out than to rust out (*English*) It is better to die sooner after a busy life than to decay gradually with nothing to do. The proverb is usually ascribed to Bishop Cumberland around 1700, when he quoted the line to a friend who suggested that he was wearing himself out through overwork. Similar sentiments are to be found in a number of other European languages; centuries before Bishop Cumberland coined the English version Martin Luther included among his favourite quips, 'If I rest, I rust'.

> If ye will needs say I am an old man, you should give me rest ... I were better to be eaten to death with a rust than to be scoured to nothing with perpetual motion.
>
> William Shakespeare, *Henry IV, Part 2*, c.1598

'tis better to have loved and lost than never to have loved at all (*English*) Any experience of love, whether happy or not, is better than no experience of it at all. William Congreve, *The Way of the World*, 1700.

> Say what you will, 'tis better to be left, than never to have lov'd.
>
> William Congreve, *The Way of the World*, 1700

you had better be drunk than drowned (*English*) It is better to indulge occasionally in strong alcohol than frequently in weaker brews. R. Forby, *The Vocabulary of East Anglia*, 1830.

~ *See also* a BAD bush is better than an open field; a BAD custom is like a good cake, better broken than kept; a BAD excuse is better than none; a BARLEYCORN is better than a diamond to a cock; be not too BOLD with your biggers or betters; BRAG is a good dog, but Holdfast is better; the CAT and dog may kiss, yet are none the better friends; CREDITORS have better memories than debtors; DISCRETION is the better part of valour; DRY bread at home is better than roast meat abroad; EXAMPLE is better than precept; a FOE is better than a dissembling friend; FORECAST is better than work hard; a FRIEND in court is better than a penny in purse; GOD is better pleased with adverbs than with nouns; a GOOD name is better than a good girdle; the GREY mare is the better horse; HALF a loaf is better than no bread; the HALF is better than the whole; HEALTH is better than wealth; he that SERVES God for money will serve the devil for better wages; an ILL agreement is better than a good judgement; a JUST war is better than an unjust peace; LEAN liberty is better than fat slavery; LEARNING is better than house and land; LEARNING makes a good man better and an ill man worse; a LEG of a lark is better than the body of a kite; a LIVE dog is better than a dead lion; the MORE a fox is cursed, the better he fares; the MORE knave, the better luck; a NEAR friend is better than a far-dwelling kinsman; a NIMBLE ninepence is better than a slow shilling; an OLD wise man's shadow is better than a young buzzard's sword; ONE bad general is better than two good ones; PRAISE makes good men better and bad men worse; PREVENTION is better than cure; PROSPECT is often better than possession; the SMOKE of a man's own country is better than the fire of another's; SOMETHING is better than nothing; SUBTLETY is better than force; there may be BLUE and better blue; TWO heads are better than one; an UNLAWFUL oath is better broken than kept; a WOMAN, a dog and a walnut tree, the more you beat them the better they be.

between. between two stools you fall to the ground (*Roman*) He who hesitates between two choices may miss the chance of either. Seneca, *Controversia*, first century AD.

> While the two stools her sitting-part confound, between 'em both fall squat upon the ground.
>
> Henry Fielding, *Tom Thumb*, 1730

~ *See also* it's ILL speaking between a full man and a fasting.

bewail. *See* CARRION crows bewail the dead sheep and then eat them.

beware. beware of a silent dog and still water (*Roman*) Silent dogs (or men) and still water are the most dangerous. H.G. Bohn, *A Handbook of Proverbs*, 1855.

beware of Greeks bearing gifts (*Roman*) Be suspicious of those who curry favour with presents and favours. Virgil, *Aeneid*, 19BC. The proverb is an allusion to the legend of the wooden horse, by means of which Greek soldiers were smuggled into the midst of their enemies, the Trojans. Rendered in Latin as *timeo Danaos et dona ferentes* (I fear the Greeks even when they bring gifts).

> Tell Mrs Boswell that I shall taste her marmalade cautiously at first. *Timeo Danaos et dona ferentes.*
> Samuel Johnson, letter, 3 May 1777

beware of 'had I wist' (*English*) It is pointless speculating on what might have been if a person had known something much earlier. *Douce MS*, *c.*1350. Variants on the theme include 'had I wist, was a fool', 'had I wist comes too late', 'had I fish, is good without mustard' and 'had I fish, was never good with garlic'.

> And that deliberation doth men assist,
> Before they wed, to beware of
> Had I wist.
> John Heywood, *A Dialogue containing … the Proverbs in the English Tongue*, 1546

beware of the forepart of a woman, the hind part of a mule and all sides of a priest (*English*) Exercise caution in the presence of women, mules and, above all, priests. John Florio, *Second Frutes*, 1591.

> Beware of a mule's hind foot, a dog's tooth, and a woman's tongue.
> Charles Spurgeon, *Ploughman's Pictures*, 1880

beware of the oak, it draws the stroke; avoid the ash, it courts the flash (*English*) To evade lightning during a thunderstorm, it is best not to seek shelter under oak or ash trees. *Folk-Lore Record*, 1878. In its fullest form, the proverb advises: 'creep under the thorn, it can save you from harm.' Other trees and plants recommended by superstition as places of safety during storms include the beech, walnut, bay, laurel, elder, holly and mistletoe. Somewhat perversely, many householders in past centuries kept boughs of oak in the house in the belief that they would protect the building from lightning strike (to this day window-blinds and lights often have pulls in the shape of an oak acorn). *See also* LIGHTNING never strikes the same place twice.

~ *See also* let the BUYER beware; when EASTER falls in our Lady's lap, then let England beware of a rap; when our LADY falls in our Lord's lap, then let England beware a sad clap.

beyond. *See* an ATHEIST is one point beyond the devil; POLICY goes beyond strength.

bid. *See* a MAN that breaks his word bids others be false to him; a PENNY in purse will bid me drink when all the friends I have will not.

bide. *See* the DEVIL bides his day.

big. big fish eat little fish (*English*) It is part of the natural order of things that the strong prey on those weaker than themselves. *Old English Homilies*, 1200.

> *Third Fisherman* Master, I marvel how the fishes live in the sea.
> *First Fisherman* Why, as men do a-land; the great ones eat up the little ones.
> William Shakespeare, *Pericles*, *c.*1608

big fleas have little fleas upon their backs to bite them, and little fleas have lesser fleas, and so *ad infinitum* (*English*) Those who prey upon others are themselves preyed upon. Jonathan Swift, *Poems*, 1733.

the bigger they are, the harder they fall (*English*) The more powerful an opponent, the greater the impact when overthrown. H. Parker, *Dives and Pauper*, 1493. Popularized around 1900 after it was used by the boxer Robert Fitzsimmons in discussing a forthcoming bout. Variants include 'the highest tree hath the greatest fall' and 'the bigger the man, the better the mark'.

big is beautiful (*US*) The bigger something is, the greater the advantages. Commonly applied in discussion of large business enterprises. *See also* SMALL is beautiful.

however big the whale may be, the tiny harpoon can rob him of life (*Malay*) The largest opponent or hardest task may still be overcome by an apparently insignificant effort.

~ *See also* be not too BOLD with your biggers and betters; the EYE is bigger than the belly; GOD is always on the side of the big battalions; LITTLE pitchers have big ears; the MOTHER of mischief is no bigger than a midge's wing; SPEAK softly and carry a big stick.

billet. *See* EVERY bullet has its billet.

bind. bind the sack before it be full (*English*) Do not tax a person or thing to the absolute limit. David Fergusson, *Scottish Proverbs*, 1641.

~ *See also* FAST bind, fast find; SAFE bind, safe find.

bird. a bird in the hand is worth two in the bush (*Greek*) Something of modest value but securely held is more valuable than something of potentially greater worth that has yet to be firmly seized. *Harleian MS*, *c.*1470 (also quoted by Theocritus). The sentiment of the proverb was commonly expressed in various forms as far back as ancient Greece, when Aesop used it as the basis of several of his fables. It has since been recorded in a host of European languages, including French ('a bird in the hand is worth two in the hedge') and Italian ('better a sparrow in the pan than a hundred chickens in the priest's yard'). Other European variants include 'a sparrow in the hand is worth a pheasant that flyeth by', which was recorded in England in 1732, 'a pullet in the pen is worth an hundred in the fen' and 'a pound in the purse is worth two in the book'.

> That proverb, *A bird in the hand is worth two in the bush*, is of more authority with them than are all … testimonies of the good of the world to come.
>
> John Bunyan, *Pilgrim's Progress*, 1678

a bird never flew on one wing (*Scottish*) One should always take a balanced view of things (often used as a justification for taking a second drink). James Kelly, *A Complete Collection of Scotish Proverbs*, 1721. Sometimes formerly given as 'the bird must flighter [flutter] that flies with one wing'.

birds in their little nests agree (*English*) People sharing confined quarters should not argue among themselves. I. Watts, *Divine Songs*, 1715.

> 'Birds in their little nests agree,' she said, smiling … She knew nothing at all about birds.
>
> Laura Ingalls Wilder, *Little Town on the Prairie*, 1941

birds of a feather flock together (*Greek*) People of similar character tend to come together. W. Turner, *Rescuing of the Romish Fox*, 1545 (also quoted by Homer and Cicero). Commonly heard since the sixteenth century; usually said disparagingly of more dubious sorts, typically the criminal classes. *See also* a man is KNOWN by the company he keeps.

> Clifford and the haught Northumberland, and of their feather many more proud birds.
>
> William Shakespeare, *Henry VI, Part 3*, *c.*1591

there are no birds in last year's nest (*English*) Things change as time passes, just as each season the birds build new nests rather than re-use those of the previous year. T. Shelton, *Cervantes' Don Quixote*, 1620. Sometimes quoted in reference to those who are of advanced years and cannot be expected to come out with new ideas or physical feats (as an old man, Winston Churchill quoted it on one occasion when someone pointed out that he had absentmindedly forgotten to do up his flies). Also encountered in the form 'there are no birds of this year in last year's nest'.

~ *See also* by LITTLE and little the bird makes his nest; the CROW thinks her own birds fairest; DESTROY the nests and the birds will fly away; EACH bird loves to hear himself sing; the EARLY bird catches the worm; FAR shooting never killed bird; FINE feathers make fine birds; an ILL bird lays an ill egg; in VAIN the net is spread in the sight of the bird; it's an ILL bird that fouls its own nest; the JAY bird don't rob his own nest; LITTLE birds that can sing and won't sing must be made to sing; one BEATS the bush, another takes the bird; the ROUGH net is not the best catcher of birds; SMALL birds must have meat; you cannot CATCH old birds with chaff.

birth. birth is much but breeding more (*English*) A person's character is partly inherited, but the influences to which they are exposed in childhood will ultimately have the greater impact. John Clarke, *Paroemiologia Anglo-Latina*, 1639.

~ *See also* BREEDING rather than birth.

bishop. *See* the DEVIL is a busy bishop in his own diocese.

bit. *See* BITE.

bitch. *See* the HASTY bitch bringeth forth blind whelps; whom GOD loves, his bitch brings forth pigs.

bite (noun). *See* a BLEATING sheep loses a bite; EVERY dog is allowed one bite.

bite (verb). **don't bite the hand that feeds you** (*English*) It is foolhardy, as well as ungrateful, to attack a person or organization on whom you are dependent.
he who has been bitten by a snake fears a piece of string (*Persian*) Bitter experience can cause a person to hesitate in the future, even when there is no real risk. John Ray, *Adages of the Hebrews*, 1678. *See also* whom a SERPENT has bitten, a lizard alarms.
if you cannot bite, never show your teeth (*English*) Never threaten to act unless you are prepared to follow the threat through. Thomas Fuller, *The History of the Holy War*, 1639.

~ *See also* a BARKING dog never bites; BIG fleas have little fleas upon their backs to bite them, and little fleas have lesser fleas, and so *ad infinitum*; the BITER is sometimes bit; DEAD men don't bite; a DOG will bark ere he bite; he that SLEEPS bites no body; HUNGRY flies bite sore; a MOUSE in time may bite in two a cable; ONCE bitten, twice shy; take the HAIR of the dog that bit you; whom a SERPENT has bitten, a lizard alarms.

biter. the biter is sometimes bit (*Greek*) Those who criticize or attack others must expect to be attacked in return on occasion. Thomas D'Urfey, *The Richmond Heiress*, 1693 (also quoted by Lucian).

bitten. *See* BITE.

bitter pills may have blessed effects (*English*) Hard lessons, like sour medicines, may yield the best results. Geoffrey Chaucer, *Troilus and Criseyde*, *c.*1385–90. A proverb related to the principle 'the more desperate the disease, the more desperate the remedy'. Variants include 'bitter pills may have wholesome effects'.

> The medicine, the more bitter it is, the more better it is in working.
> John Lyly, *Euphues: The Anatomy of Wit*, 1578

black. the black ox treads on one's foot (*English*) Misfortune (typically in the shape of age, adversity or care in general) has an influence on one's life. John Heywood, *A Dialogue containing ... the Proverbs in the English Tongue*, 1546.

> Now crowes foote is on her eye, and the black oxe hath trod on her foot.
> John Lyly, *Sapho and Phao*, 1584

black will take no other hue (*Roman*) Some people are so wicked that nothing will change their perverse natures. John Heywood, *A Dialogue containing ... the Proverbs in the English Tongue*, 1546 (quoting Pliny). Related proverbs include 'above black there is no colour and above salt no savour'.
there's a black sheep in every family (*English*) Every family has its rebel, whose conduct is a cause of disgrace and regret. Walter Scott, *Old Mortality*, 1816. Originally often given in the form 'there are black sheep in every flock/fold'. Superstition had it that if the first lamb born into a flock in the spring was black, this brought bad luck to the owner (although in other circumstances the presence of a black sheep promoted the luck of the flock). The birth of twin black sheep was considered particularly ominous as regards the luck of the shepherd. In practical terms, the birth of a black sheep was unwelcome because its fleece could not be dyed, thus rendering the creature relatively worthless.

> I suppose every family has a black sheep. Tom had been a sore trial to his for twenty years.
> W. Somerset Maugham, *Cosmopolitans*, 'The Ant and the Grasshopper', 1926

~ *See also* BEHIND the horseman sits black care; the DEVIL is not as black as he is painted; EVERY white hath its black and every sweet its sour; it is ILL to drive black hogs in the dark; the POT calls the kettle black; a SHUT mouth never fills a black coffin; those that EAT black pudding will dream of the devil; TWO blacks don't make a white.

blacken. *See* no WOOL is so white that a dyer cannot blacken it.

blame. do not blame God for having created the tiger, but thank him for not having given it wings (*Indian*) Rather than complain about something, it is better to console oneself with the thought that it might have been much worse.
he that blames would buy (*English*) Those who decry the value of what is on offer are the most likely to buy it. George Herbert, *Outlandish Proverbs*, 1640 (based on a biblical quotation).

~ *See also* a BAD workman blames his tools.

blast. *See* GRACE will last, beauty will blast.

bleat. a bleating sheep loses a bite (*English*) Time wasted in talking could be better used. J. Minsheu, *Dialogues in Spanish*, 1599.

> He said something about a bleating sheep losing a bite; but I should think this young man is not much of a talker.
>
> Thomas Hughes, *Tom Brown at Oxford*, 1861

blessed. blessed are the dead that the rain rains on (*English*) If it rains at a funeral this is a portent that the angels are mourning the passing of the deceased and further constitutes a sign that he or she has been allowed entry into heaven. *The Puritan*, 1607. *See also* HAPPY is the bride the sun shines on.

> I could only remember, without resentment, that Daisy hadn't sent a message or a flower. Dimly I heard someone murmur, 'Blessed are the dead that the rain falls on'.
>
> F. Scott Fitzgerald, *The Great Gatsby*, 1925

blessed is he who expects nothing, for he shall never be disappointed (*English*) Those who adopt a pessimistic outlook to life thus safeguard themselves from disappointment of their hopes. Alexander Pope, letter, 6 October 1727.

~ *See also* BITTER pills may have blessed effects; GIVE and be blessed.

blessing. blessings are not valued until they are gone (*English*) Good things are only appreciated after they are gone. Thomas Fuller, *Gnomologia*, 1732.

blessings brighten as they take their flight (*English*) It is only when some benefit is gone that its full worth is appreciated. Thomas Fuller, *Gnomologia*, 1732. Also heard as 'blessings are not valued till they are gone'.

> How blessings brighten as they take their flight.
>
> Edward Young, *Night Thoughts*, 1742

~ *See also* a CHILD may have too much of his mother's blessing.

blind. as the blind man catches the hare (*English*) Sometimes a person can succeed against the odds by luck or good fortune. P. Stubbes, *Anatomy of Abuses*, 1583. Also found in the form 'as the blind man starts the hare'.

a blind man cannot judge colours (*Roman*) Someone who is ignorant of a subject should not be expected to understand it. Geoffrey Chaucer, *Troilus and Criseyde*, *c.*1385–90. Related proverbs include 'a pebble and a diamond are alike to a blind man'.

> A blind man can nat juggen wel in hewis.
>
> Geoffrey Chaucer, *Troilus and Criseyde*, *c.*1385–90

a blind man's wife needs no paint (*Spanish*) It is pointless and even suspicious if a person goes to some trouble that in normal circumstances will not be appreciated (in this case, a blind man's wife putting on make-up, presumably in order to impress someone other than her husband). *c.*1627, quoted in Correas, *Vocabulary*, 1906.

> For whom does the blind man's wife paint herself?
>
> Thomas Fuller, *Gnomologia*, 1732

if the blind lead the blind, both shall fall into the ditch (*Hebrew*) Disaster will befall those who put their faith in the leadership of others who know no better than themselves. *Anglo-Saxon Gospel*, AD995 (also quoted in the Bible, Luke 6:39). Also found in numerous variants in classical literature. The French, meanwhile, know it in the form 'when the blind man carries the banner, woe to those who follow'. Hieronymus Bosch, Breughel the Elder and Breughel the Younger are among the artists to have produced celebrated works of art on the theme of the blind leading the blind. Now often heard in the shortened form 'the blind leading the blind'. British theatre critic Kenneth Tynan produced his own variation of the proverb when about to join the *New Yorker* magazine in 1958: 'They say the *New Yorker* is the bland leading the bland.'

> When the blind leads the blind, no wonder they both fall into – matrimony.
>
> George Farquhar, *Love and a Bottle*, 1699

~ *See also* in the COUNTRY of the blind, the one-eyed man is king; a DEAF husband and a blind wife are always a happy couple; FORTUNE is blind; the HASTY bitch bringeth forth blind whelps; LOVE is blind; MASTERS should be sometimes blind, and sometimes deaf; MEN are blind in their own cause; METTLE is dangerous in a blind horse; a NOD is as good as a wink to a blind horse; NOTHING so bold as a blind mare; there are NONE so blind as those who will not see; though the CAT winks a while, yet sure she is not blind.

blindworm. *See* if the ADDER could hear and the blindworm could see, neither man nor beast would ever go free.

bliss. *See* IGNORANCE is bliss.

blister. a blister will rise upon one's tongue that tells a lie (*English*) A lie is betrayed by blisters upon the tongue, or by some other telling sign. John Lyly, *Sapho and Phao*, 1584.

I have a blister on my tongue; yet I don't remember I told a lie.

Jonathan Swift, *A Complete Collection of Polite and Ingenious Conversation*, 1738

block. *See* a BOOK that is shut is but a block; if the COCK moult before the hen we shall have weather thick and thin, but if the hen moult before the cock we shall have weather hard as a block.

blood. blood is thicker than water (*German*) Loyalty felt to one's blood relations will always outweigh loyalty to friends. John Ray, *A Collection of English Proverbs*, 1813.

Weel – blude's thicker than water – she's welcome to the cheeses.

Walter Scott, *Guy Mannering*, 1815

the blood of the martyrs is the seed of the Church (*Roman*) The persecution of Christian martyrs through the ages inspired the growth of the Church. T. Adams, *Works*, 1630 (also quoted by Tertullian in *Apologeticus* in the second century AD).

And hanged he had been, had not Harry Marteyn told them that *sanguis martyrum est semen ecclesiae*, and that way would do them more mischief.

John Aubrey, *Brief Lives*, 1697

blood will have blood (*English*) Violence begets violence. *Mirror for Magistrates*, 1559. *See also* an EYE for an eye, and a tooth for a tooth.

It will have blood; they say blood will have blood.

William Shakespeare, *Macbeth*, *c*.1604

blood will tell (*English*) Individuals inherit certain traits of character from their ancestors, and these will inevitably show themselves. G.H. Boker, *World a Mask*, 1850.

you cannot get blood from a stone (*Roman*) There is no point trying to extract some benefit where there is no benefit to be had. John Lyly, *Euphues and His England*, 1580 (also quoted by Plautus). Originally, the word 'water' often appeared in the place of 'blood', and the 'stone' might be given as 'pummice' or 'flint'.

Blood cannot be obtained from a stone, neither can anything on account be obtained … from Mr Micawber.

Charles Dickens, *David Copperfield*, 1850

~ *See also* GOOD wine engendreth good blood; there is no DIFFERENCE of bloods in a basin; where the DEER is slain, some of her blood will lie.

bloom. *See* if APPLES bloom in March, in vain for them you'll search; if apples bloom in April, then they'll be plentiful; if apples bloom in May, you may eat them night and day; when the FURZE is in bloom, my love's in tune; when the GORSE is out of bloom, kissing's out of fashion.

blossom. *See* BEAUTY is but a blossom; GREY hairs are death's blossoms.

blot. a blot is not blot unless it be hit (*English*) A stain on one's honour is no stain until it is discovered (originally a reference to backgammon, in which a 'blot' is an exposed piece in danger of being captured). J. Wilson, *The Cheats*, 1664.

But then a blot is not a blot till hit.

Sir Walter Scott, *Family Letters*, 1820

~ *See also* the FAIRER the paper, the fouler the blot; PENS may blot but they cannot blush.

blow (noun). *See* the FIRST blow is half the battle; the SECOND blow makes the fray; the TREE falls not at the first blow.

blow (verb). **he that blows best bears away the horn** (*Scottish*) Those who do best win the top prize. David Fergusson, *Scottish Proverbs*, 1641.

~ *See also* he who has ONCE burnt his mouth always blows his soup; HIGH winds blow on high hills; it's an ILL wind that blows nobody any good; the NORTH wind doth blow and we shall have snow; a PALE moon doth rain, a red moon doth blow; a white moon doth neither rain nor snow; SEPTEMBER blow soft, till the fruit's in the loft; STRAWS tell which way the wind blows; the WEST wind always brings wet weather, the east wind wet and cold together, the south wind surely brings us rain, the north wind blows it back again; when the WIND is in the south it blows the bait into the fish's mouth.

blue. blue are the hills that are far away (*Scottish*) Some things look better at a distance than they do at close quarters. T.H. Hall Caine, *Deemster*, 1887. *See also* DISTANCE lends enchantment to the view.

there may be blue and better blue (*English*) There may be subtle differences between people or objects superficially belonging to the same group, class and so forth. James Kelly, *A Complete Collection of Scottish Proverbs*, 1721.

~ *See also* TRUE blue will never stain.

blush. blushing is a sign of grace (*English*) Only those with finer feelings will have the sensitivity to blush when they are embarrassed, and a blush may thus be taken as a sign of nobility of character. *A Quest of Enquirie*, 1595. Variants include 'blushing is virtue's colour'. The Italians, however, warn that a blush may be interpreted as a sign of a guilty conscience, as illustrated by the saying 'the blush is beautiful but it is sometimes inconvenient'.

> Well, however, blushing is some sign of grace.
> Jonathan Swift, *Polite Conversation*, 1738

~ *See also* PENS may blot but they cannot blush.

blustering. a blustering night, a fair day follows (*Spanish*) A stormy night presages a fine day. George Herbert, *Outlandish Proverbs*, 1640.

boaster. a boaster and a liar are all one (*English*) There is no difference in morality between a boast and a lie. Geoffrey Chaucer, *Troilus and Criseyde*, *c.*1385–90. Also encountered as 'a boaster and a liar are cousins'.

boat. *See* too MANY boatmen will run the boat up to the top of the mountain.

boatman. *See* too MANY boatmen will run the boat up to the top of the mountain.

bode. *See* a GAUDY morning bodes a wet afternoon.

body. *See* CORPORATIONS have neither bodies to be punished nor souls to be damned; GREAT bodies move slowly; he that SLEEPS bites no body; a LEG of a lark is better than the body of a kite; a LITTLE body often harbours a great soul; when the HEAD acheth all the body is the worse.

boil. boil stones in butter and you may sup the broth (*English*) By adding other good ingredients even the most unpromising meat may be turned into an appetizing meal. James Kelly, *A Complete Collection of Scotish Proverbs*, 1721.

~ *See also* take HEED of reconciled enemies and of meat twice boiled; a WATCHED pot never boils.

boisterous. a boisterous horse must have a rough bridle (*English*) Those with wild, untamed temperaments require stern handling. R. Taverner, *Proverbs or Adages with New Additions, gathered out of the Chiliades of Erasmus*, 1539.

bold. be not too bold with your biggers or betters (*English*) It is foolish to risk antagonizing those who are more powerful than you. J. Howell, *Paroemiographia*, 1659.

> Be bold but not too bold.
> H.G. Bohn, *A Handbook of Proverbs*, 1855

he was a bold man that first ate an oyster (*English*) It takes courage to be the first to do something that, lacking the knowledge of hindsight, appears to be very risky. Thomas Fuller, *The History of the Worthies of England*, 1662.

> King James was wont to say, 'he was a very valiant man who first adventured on eating of oysters'.
> Thomas Fuller, *The History of the Worthies of England*, 1662

it is a bold mouse that breeds in the cat's ear (*English*) To survive in a position of potential danger requires much cunning and wariness. John Lydgate, *Minor Poems*, *c.*1430. Variants include 'it is a wily mouse that nestles in the cat's ear'.

> Let Philautus behave himself never so craftely,
> he shal know that it must be a wyly Mouse that
> shall breede in the Cats eare.
> John Lyly, *Euphues: The Anatomy of Wit*, 1578

~ *See also* FORTUNE favours the bold; NOTHING so bold as a blind mare.

boldness in business is the first, second and third thing (*English*) A determined, resolute approach is the one essential in all business matters. Thomas Fuller, *Gnomologia*, 1732. A Greek proverb cautions that 'boldness leads a man to heaven and to hell'.

bolt (noun). *See* a FOOL's bolt is soon shot.

bolt (verb). *See* it is too LATE to shut the stable door after the horse has bolted.

Bolton. *See* BATE me an ace, quoth Bolton.

bond. *See* an ENGLISHMAN's word is his bond.

bone. bones bring meat to town (*English*) It is sometimes necessary to accept something inconvenient or undesirable along with what is desirable. *Berkeley MSS*, 1639.

> The bones bear the beef home. An answer to them that complain that there are so many bones in the meat that they are buying.
>
> James Kelly, *A Complete Collection of Scottish Proverbs*, 1721

~ *See also* BROKEN bones well set become stronger; CAST a bone in the devil's teeth; the DOG that trots about finds a bone; a DOG that will fetch a bone will carry a bone; FAIR words break no bones; GNAW the bone which is fallen to thy lot; a GOOD dog deserves a good bone; HARD words break no bones; into the MOUTH of a bad dog often falls a good bone; a JOKE breaks no bones; let not a CHILD sleep upon bones; the NEARER the bone, the sweeter the flesh; STICKS and stones may break my bones, but names will never hurt me; TWO cats and a mouse, two wives in one house, two dogs and a bone, never agree in one; TWO dogs fight for a bone, and a third runs away with it; what's BRED in the bone will come out in the flesh; you BUY land you buy stones, you buy meat you buy bones.

bonny. a bonny bride is soon buskit and a short horse is soon wispit (*Scottish*) A pretty woman is soon dressed (as she needs little to adorn her beauty), just as a small horse is soon 'wispit' (brushed). David Fergusson, *Scottish Proverbs*, 1641.

book. a book that is shut is but a block (*English*) A book is a useless item unless it is read. Thomas Fuller, *Gnomologia*, 1732.

books and friends should be few and good (*Spanish*) One should be selective in both one's reading and in one's friends. Related proverbs include 'a good book is your best friend'.

~ *See also* CARDS are the devil's books; a GREAT book is a great evil; PICTURES are the books of the unlearned; when a new BOOK appears, read an old one; YEARS know more than books; you can't JUDGE a book by its cover.

boot. *See* a LIE travels around the world while truth is putting on her boots; when BALE is highest, boot is nighest.

born. if you're born to be hanged then you'll never be drowned (*French*) A lucky escape may simply be a sign that one is destined for a worse fate later on. Alexander Barclay, translation of *Gringore's Castle of Labour*, *c.*1503.

> Go, go; begone to save your ship from wreck,
> Which cannot perish, having thee aboard,
> Being destined to a drier death on shore.
>
> William Shakespeare, *The Two Gentlemen of Verona*, *c.*1594

we are born crying, live complaining and die disappointed (*English*) It is man's lot to suffer at all stages of life. Thomas Fuller, *Gnomologia*, 1732.

~ *See also* as SOON as man is born he begins to die; FIRST born, first fed; it is as NATURAL to die as to be born; it is BETTER to be born a beggar than a fool; it is BETTER to be born lucky than rich; the MAN who is born in a stable is a horse; a POET is born not made; YORKSHIRE born and Yorkshire bred, strong in the arm and weak in the head.

borne. *See* BEAR (verb).

borrow. borrowed garments never fit well (*English*) The clothes, position or responsibilities of one person will never fit another person perfectly. Thomas Fuller, *Gnomologia*, 1732. Equivalents in other languages include the Arabic proverb 'a borrowed cloak does not keep one warm'.

he that borrows must pay again with shame or loss (*English*) Those who borrow money must pay it back later, either in shame because they have not met the full amount or suffering a loss because they have had to pay back more than they borrowed in the first place. J. Clarke, *Paroemiologia Anglo-Latina*, 1639.

who would borrow when he hath not, let him borrow when he hath (*English*) It is easier to borrow money when one has some money already than when one has nothing. N.R., *Proverbs English, French, Dutch, etc.*, 1659.

~ *See also* the EARLY man never borrows from the late man; have a HORSE of your own and then you may borrow another's; he that goes A-BORROWING, goes a sorrowing.

borrower. *See* NEITHER a borrower nor a lender be.

bosom. *See* put ANOTHER man's child in your bosom and he'll creep out at your elbow; there's no LEAPING from Delilah's lap into Abraham's bosom.

both. you can't have it both ways (*English*) In some circumstances choosing to enjoy one particular benefit necessarily precludes a person from enjoying an alternative one. *See also* you can't have your CAKE and eat it.

~ *See also* you cannot BURN the candle at both ends.

bottle. *See* a THOUSAND pounds and a bottle of hay is all one thing at doomsday; you can't put NEW wine in old bottles.

bottom. *See* the BEST fish swim near the bottom; EVERY tub must stand on its own bottom; it is too LATE to spare when the bottom is bare; no MISCHIEF but a woman or a priest is at the bottom of it; TRUTH lies at the bottom of a well; VENTURE not all in one bottom.

bottomless. *See* a BEGGAR's purse is bottomless; the LAW is a bottomless pit.

bough. the boughs that bear most hang lowest (*English*) The truly great are often the most humble in discussing their achievements. Thomas Fuller, *Church History of Britain*, 1655.

> The vines that bear much fruit are proud to stoop with it.
>
> Elizabeth Barrett Browning, *Aurora*, 1856

~ *See also* CUT not the bough that thou standest upon.

bought. *See* BUY.

bound. the bound must obey (*English*) Those who have no other choice are obliged to do what is demanded of them. Layamon, *Brut*, 1205. Related proverbs include 'bound is he that takes gifts'.

> Wo is hym that is bun, ffor he must abyde.
>
> *Towneley Plays*, *c.*1410

~ *See also* if you LEAP into a well providence is not bound to fetch you out; TALK of the devil and he is bound to appear.

bow. a bow long bent at last waxeth weak (*English*) Something that is regularly used will eventually wear out. John Heywood, *A Dialogue containing ... the Proverbs in the English Tongue*, 1550.

~ *See also* DRAW not your bow till your arrow is fixed; MANY talk of Robin Hood who never shot with his bow.

Bowden. *See* not EVERY man can be vicar of Bowden.

bowl. *See* LIFE is just a bowl of cherries; those who PLAY at bowls must look out for rubbers.

boy. boys will be boys (*Roman*) It is in the nature of young boys to be at times boisterous and mischievous, and such behaviour should therefore be excused. W. Robertson, *Phraseology Generalis*, 1681. The proverb was known to the Romans in the form *pueri sunt pueri, pueri puerilia tractant* (children are children and employ themselves with childish things), and it has been suggested that the modern form of the proverb limited to boys alone may have arisen from a mistranslation of the Latin *pueri*, which actually signified children of both sexes. Variants include 'boys will be men' (meaning, all boys will grow to manhood, with all its responsibilities, in time).

> Would old Anstruther consider an outrage perpetrated on the person of Bertram Wooster a crime sufficiently black to cause him to rule Thos out of the race? Or would he just give a senile chuckle and mumble?
>
> P. G. Woodhouse, *Very Good Jeeves!*, 1930

~ *See also* ALL work and no play makes Jack a dull boy; if the LAIRD slight the lady, so will all the kitchen boys; if you PLAY with boys you must take boys' play; the LEAST boy always carries the greatest fiddle; ONE for sorrow, two for joy; three for a girl, four for a boy; five for silver, six for gold; seven for a secret, never to be told; eight for heaven, nine for hell; and ten for the devil's own self; a SMILING boy seldom proves a good servant; TWO boys are half a boy, and three boys are no boy at all; an UNTOWARD boy may make a good man.

brae. *See* put a STOUT heart to a stey brae.

brag. Brag is a good dog, but Holdfast is better (*English*) Quietly determined action counts for more than boastful and conceited talk. A. Munday, *Zelanto*, 1580. Not unrelated is the proverb of seventeenth-century origins, 'Brag's a good dog but dares not bite', which underlines the idea that some people make threats or boasts that they are not brave or resolute enough to carry through. Other variants include 'Brag's a good dog but that he hath lost his tail', 'Brag is a good dog but dares not bite' and 'Brag's a good dog if he be well set on'. *See also* they BRAG most that can do least.

> When I envied the finery of any of my neighbours, [my mother] told me, that 'brag was a good dog, but holdfast was a better'.
>
> Samuel Johnson, *The Rambler*, 4 February 1752

they brag most that can do least (*English*) Those who boast loudest of their powers are the least likely to possess them. R. Taverner, *Proverbs or Adages with New Additions, gathered out of the Chiliades of Erasmus*, 1545. *See also* BRAG is a good dog, but Holdfast is better.

brain. if the brain sows not corn, it plants thistles (*English*) Minds that are not occupied with good thoughts inevitably turn to bad thoughts. George Herbert, *Outlandish Proverbs*, 1640.

~ *See also* an IDLE brain is the devil's workshop; the MOB has many heads but no brains.

bramble. *See* a GREAT dowry is a bed full of brambles.

Bran. if not Bran, it is Bran's brother (*English*) A compliment that suggests that someone or something is so good as to be indistinguishable from an original of fabled excellence. Walter Scott, *Waverley*, 1814. Bran was the celebrated dog belonging to Fingal, the hero of Gaelic legend.

> '*Mar e Bran, is e a brathair*, if it be not Bran, it is Bran's brother,' was the proverbial reply of Maccombich.
>
> Walter Scott, *Waverley*, 1814

brass. *See* the EARTHEN pot must keep clear of the brass kettle.

brave (adj.). **brave men lived before Agamemnon** (*Roman*) Our own age should not be accepted as the only time when great men and women lived and great things were done (as the ancient Greeks might have been tempted to do). Horace, *Odes*, first century BC. It is often quoted as 'there were brave men before Agamemnon'. In Horace the proverb appears in the form *vixere fortes ante Agamemnon*; it was later famously reworked by Byron. In 1902 Dean Hole contributed '*vixere fortes ante Agamemnon* – there was splendid cricket before Grace'.

> Brave men were living before Agamemnon
> And since, exceeding valorous and sage,
> A good deal like him too, though quite the same
> none:
> But then they shone not on the poet's page,
> And so have been forgotten.
>
> George Gordon, Lord Byron, *Don Juan*, 1819

~ *See also* NONE but the brave deserve the fair.

brave (verb). *See* ROBIN HOOD could brave all weathers but a thaw wind.

brawling curs never want sore ears (*English*) Those who are quick to pick quarrels with others will find they are frequently at the receiving end of others' wrath. Randle Cotgrave, *A Dictionary of the French and English Tongues*, 1611. Also recorded in the now archaic form 'babbling curs never want sore ears'.

> Come, come, sir, babling curs never want sore ears.
>
> Thomas D'Urfey, *Quixote*, 1694

Bray (noun). *See* the VICAR of Bray will be vicar of Bray still.

bray (verb). *See* EVERY ass loves to hear himself bray.

bread. bread and cheese be two targets against death (*English*) Eating bread and cheese preserves good health. T. Muffet, *Healths Improvement*, 1655.

bread is the staff of life (*English*) Bread has a unique value, being a staple food of life. Jonathan Swift, *Tale of a Tub*, 1704. Another proverb goes a little further: 'bread is the staff of life, but beer's life itself'.

> 'Bread,' says he, 'dear brothers, is the staff of life.'
>
> Jonathan Swift, *Tale of a Tub*, 1704

the bread never falls but on the buttered side (*English*) When things go awry, ill luck will ensure that the worst happens. John Ray, *A Collection of English Proverbs*, 1678. Originated in the north of England. *See also* if ANYTHING can go wrong, it will.

We express the completeness of ill-luck by saying 'the bread never falls but on its buttered side'.
John Lockwood Kipling, *Man and Beast in India*, 1891

he who has no bread has no authority (*Turkish*) Only those who have something to offer can hope to enjoy influence over others.

~ See the BEST smell is bread, the best savour salt, the best love that of children; DRY bread at home is better than roast meat abroad; EATEN bread is soon forgotten; HALF a loaf is better than no bread; it is a GOOD thing to eat your brown bread first; it is HARD to pay for bread that has been eaten; MAN cannot live by bread alone; a MAN of many trades begs his bread on Sunday; NEW beer, new bread and green wood will make a man's hair grow through his hood; no BUTTER will stick to his bread; the SAME knife cuts bread and fingers; there is no such THING as good small beer, good brown bread, or a good old woman; who hath no MORE bread than need must not keep a dog.

break. you may break a horse's back, be he never so strong (*English*) Everyone has their breaking point, no matter how strong they are. J. Clarke, *Paroemiologia Anglo-Latina*, 1639.

~ *See also* a BAD custom is like a good cake, better broken than kept; BETTER bend than break; a COLT you may break, but an old horse you never can; the CORD breaketh at the last by the weakest pull; FAIR words break no bones; HARD words break no bones; HUNGER breaks through stone walls; if it were not for HOPE, the heart would break; if the LAD go to the well against his will, either the can will break or the water will spill; it is the LAST straw that breaks the camel's back; a JOKE breaks no bones; a MAN that breaks his word bids others be false to him; NEVER give a sucker an even break; STICKS and stones may break my bones, but names will never hurt me; the THREAD breaks where it is weakest; the WORST spoke in a cart breaks first; you cannot make an OMELETTE without breaking eggs.

breaker. *See* LAW makers should not be law breakers.

breakfast. *See* HOPE is a good breakfast but a bad supper; LAUGH before breakfast, you'll cry before supper; a NOD from a lord is a breakfast for a fool.

breast. *See* HOPE springs eternal in the human breast.

breath. *See* FAME is but the breath of the people; the FIRST breath is the beginning of death; SAVE your breath to cool your porridge.

bred. *See* BREED.

breeches. *See* WINE wears no breeches.

breed. what's bred in the bone will come out in the flesh (*English*) A person's true character, inherited traits or long-ingrained habits will inevitably reveal themselves. William Caxton, *Reynard*, 1481. The proverb has undergone a gradual change from its original form, which suggested something slightly different: 'what's bred in the bone will not out of the flesh.' In this earlier form, the proverb implies rather that there is no faking the kind of qualities with which one is born.

Sir Launcelot smyled and said hard hit is to take oute of the flesshe that is bred in the bone.
Thomas Malory, *Morte d'Arthur*, 1485

~ *See also* ALL that breed in the mud are not eels; BEGGARS breed and rich men feed; FAMILIARITY breeds contempt; DOGS bark as they are bred; DROUGHT never bred dearth in England; it is a BOLD mouse that breeds in the cat's ear; LIKE breeds like; LOOKS breed love; POVERTY breeds strife; YORKSHIRE born and Yorkshire bred, strong in the arm and weak in the head.

breeding. breeding rather than birth (*Japanese*) Upbringing is more important than ancestry. Related proverbs include the English 'breed is stronger than pasture'.

~ *See also* BIRTH is much but breeding more.

brevity is the soul of wit (*English*) Wit is best when pithy and concise. William Shakespeare, *Hamlet*, *c.*1600 (much the same sentiment was expressed by many writers of the classical world, among them Plautus and Horace). In Shakespeare's time the word 'wit' did not necessarily imply humour, but understanding of all kinds. Equivalents in other languages include 'few words are best', the Roman 'brevity is pleasing' and the Scottish 'few words sufficeth to a wise man', although Yoruban tradition provides 'contraction of words conceals the sense'. To US wit Dorothy Parker (1893–1967) is attributed the *bon mot* 'brevity is the soul of lingerie'.

> Since brevity is the soul of wit – I will be brief.
> Your noble son is mad.
> William Shakespeare, *Hamlet*, *c.*1600

brew. as you brew, so shall you bake (*English*) In due course you will have to accept the consequences of your actions, good and bad. 1264, quoted in C. Brown, *English Lyrics of the XIIIth Century*, 1932. Variants include 'as you brew, so drink'. *See also* as you BAKE, so shall you brew; as you make your BED, so you must lie in it; as you SOW, so shall you reap.

> Bot we must drynk as we brew
> And that is bot reson.
> *Towneley Play of the Second Shepherd*, *c.*1450

~ *See also* ADAM's ale is the best brew.

bribe. a bribe will enter without knocking (*English*) Through bribery a person may gain immediate access where a more honest approach would be of no avail. B. Rich, *Irish Hubbub*, 1619. Also encountered in the form 'a bribe entereth everywhere'. Equivalents in other languages include the Roman 'bribes buy both gods and men' and the Spanish 'no lock will hold against the power of gold'.

~ *See also* he that SHOWS his purse bribes the thief.

brick. you can't make bricks without straw (*English*) The right materials (or knowledge etc.) must be acquired before certain tasks can be successfully accomplished. Robert Burton, *The Anatomy of Melancholy*, 1624. The proverb is loosely derived from a passage in Exodus 5:7, which runs 'yee shall no more give the people straw to make bricke, as heretofore: let them goe and gather straw for themselves'. The background to this passage was that the Israelites, then under the Egyptians, asked for time off to make a pilgrimage into the desert; the Egyptians, impressed by the fact that their slaves now dared to ask for time off, decided they were not being kept busy enough and so ordered that as well as making bricks as before the Israelites would also have to collect the straw for them themselves.

> You can only acquire really useful general ideas by first acquiring particular ideas ... you cannot make bricks without straw.
> Arnold Bennett, *Literary Taste*, 1909

bride. the bride goes to her marriage-bed but knows not what shall happen to her (*English*) It is foolish to speculate on how something will turn out when one has no previous experience of it. Jeremy Taylor, *Holy Dying*, 1651. Not entirely unrelated is the Spanish proverb 'at the wedding feast the least eater is the bride' (presumably because she is nervous about what lies ahead).

~ *See also* a BONNY bride is soon buskit and a short horse is soon wispit; HAPPY is the bride the sun shines on.

bridge. *See* CALL the bear 'uncle' till you are safe across the bridge; don't CROSS the bridge until you get to it; it is GOOD to make a bridge of gold to a flying enemy; it is HARD to turn tack upon a narrow bridge; let EVERY man praise the bridge he goes over.

bridle. a bridle for the tongue is a necessary piece of furniture (*English*) Wise people refrain from speaking too freely. Thomas Fuller, *Gnomologia*, 1732.

~ *See also* a BOISTEROUS horse must have a rough bridle; a MAN without religion is like a horse without a bridle; PROSPERITY lets go the bridle.

bright. bright rain makes fools fain (*English*) When rain clouds are broken by a little sunshine only fools imagine the weather will stay fine. W. Roper, *Weather Sayings*, 1883.

~ *See also* ALWAYS look on the bright side; BARNABY bright, Barnaby bright, the longest day and the shortest night; if CANDLEMAS Day be sunny and bright winter will have another flight; if Candlemas Day be cloudy with rain, winter is gone and won't come again; a USED key is always bright.

brighten. *See* BLESSINGS brighten as they take their flight.

bring. bring a cow to the hall and she'll run to the byre (*Scottish*) People promoted above their natural station will long for their former condition (just as a cow brought into a hall will yearn to be back in the cowshed). David Fergusson, *Scottish Proverbs*, 1641.

he that bringeth himself into needless dangers dieth the devil's martyr (*Dutch*) It is foolish to expose oneself needlessly to danger. Thomas Fuller, *The History of the Holy War*, 1639.

> Who perisheth in needless danger is the devil's martyr.
>
> John Ray, *A Collection of English Proverbs*, 1678

he that brings good news knocks hard (*English*) Those who bring good news are not reticent in announcing their arrival, as someone bringing bad news might be. J. Wodroephe, *The Spared Houres of a Soldier in His Travels*, 1623.

he who would bring home the wealth of the Indies, must carry the wealth of the Indies with him (*Spanish*) To attract wealth, one must be wealthy in the first place. James Boswell, *Life of Johnson*, 1791. The proverb had its roots in the days when Spanish adventurers sought to make their fortune in the West Indies, though success depended largely upon substantial financial backing for their voyages.

~ *See also* AGE and wedlock bring a man to his nightcap; APRIL showers bring forth May flowers; BONES bring meat to town; CARE and diligence bring luck; DRY feet, warm head, bring safe to bed; the EVENING brings all home; EVERY sin brings its punishment with it; the FULL moon brings fair weather; a GOOD tree brings forth good fruit; a GOOD winter brings a good summer; HAIL brings frost in the tail; the HASTY bitch bringeth forth blind whelps; if you would have FRUIT, you must bring the leaf to the grave; a MAN must take such as he finds, or such as he brings; MIST from the hill brings water to the mill; MISUNDERSTANDING brings lies to town; ONE wedding brings another; take what you FIND or what you bring; the WEST wind always brings wet weather, the east wind wet and cold together, the south wind surely brings us rain, the north wind blows it back again; a WET May brings plenty of hay; what a DAY may bring a day may take away; what MAINTAINS one vice would bring up two children; when a COUPLE are newly married the first month is honeymoon, or smick smack; the second is hither and thither; the third is thwick thwack; the fourth the devil take them that brought thee and I together; whom GOD loves, his bitch brings forth pigs; the WORTH of a thing is what it will bring.

Britain. *See* ALL countries stand in need of Britain.

brittle. *See* GLASSES and lasses are brittle ware.

broad. *See* make not thy TAIL broader than thy wings; the MORE you tramp on a turd the broader it grows.

broaden. *See* TRAVEL broadens the mind.

broken. a broken leg is not healed by a silk stocking (*English*) When things are wrong trying to disguise the fact will not do anything to put them right. A.B. Cheales, *Proverbial Folklore*, 1875.

broken bones well set become stronger (*English*) Relationships that are well repaired are often stronger than they were originally. John Lyly, *Euphues*, 1579. Another proverb, however, warns that 'a broken friendship may be soldered but will never be sound'.

> As broken bones well set become stronger, so Sir Henry Wotton did not only recover, but was much more confirmed in his Majesty's estimation.
>
> Izaak Walton, *Lives*, 1651

if it ain't broke, don't fix it (*US*) If something is working perfectly well it should not be interfered with just for the sake of change. Tim Rice, quoted in the *Independent*, 12 November 1988. There seems to be no record of this proverb before 1977, when President Carter's Director of Management and Budget, Bert Lance, apparently said it when discussing the possibility of governmental reform.

~ *See also* the PITCHER goes so often to the well that it is broken at last; PROMISES, like pie-crust, are made to be broken; an UNLAWFUL oath is better broken than kept.

broker. *See* a CRAFTY knave needs no broker.

broom. *See* LAD's love's a busk of broom, hot awhile and soon done; let EVERY man sweep the ice with his own broom; a NEW broom sweeps clean.

broth. *See* BOIL stones in butter and you may sup the broth; EVERY cook praises his own broth; GOOD broth may be made in an old pot; too MANY cooks spoil the broth.

brother. *See* the COFFIN is the brother of the cradle; if not BRAN, it is Bran's brother; SLEEP is the brother of death.

brought. *See* BRING

brown. *See* it is a GOOD thing to eat your brown bread first; there is no such THING as good small beer, good brown bread, or a good old woman.

browse. *See* the GOAT must browse where she is tied.

bubble. *See* MAN is a bubble.

build. building and marrying of children are great wasters (*English*) It is possible to waste huge sums of money on building and on marrying off one's children. Randle Cotgrave, *A Dictionary of the French and English Tongues*, 1611. Related proverbs include 'building is a sweet impoverishing', the Italian 'who builds cleans out his purse' and the Roman 'those who love building will soon ruin themselves and need no other enemies', in which form it was quoted by Marcus Crassus.

~ *See also* FOOLS build houses and wise men live in them; it is EASIER to build two chimneys than to maintain one; it is EASIER to pull down than to build up; LAWYERS' houses are built on the heads of fools; ROME was not built in a day; where GOD builds a church, the devil will build a chapel.

building. *See* a HIGH building, a low foundation; an HOUR may destroy what an age was a building; in SETTLING an island, the first building erected by a Spaniard will be a church; by a Frenchman, a fort; by a Dutchman, a warehouse; and by an Englishman, an alehouse; no GOOD building without a good foundation.

bull. *See* he may BEAR a bull that hath borne a calf.

bullet. *See* EVERY bullet has its billet.

bully. a bully is always a coward (*English*) Those who use others cruelly usually lack courage themselves. Maria Edgeworth, *Harrington and Ormond*, 1817. Related proverbs include 'the bully bags a lion at a distance but runs when a mule starts kicking', which is of US origin.

> Mrs M'Crule, who like all other bullies was a coward, lowered her voice.
> Maria Edgeworth, *Harrington and Ormond*, 1817

bung-hole. *See* SPARE at the spigot, and let out at the bung-hole.

burden. it is not the burden but the overburden that kills the beast (*Spanish*) Take care not to overburden pack animals, employees and the like beyond their capacity. J. Collins, *A Dictionary of Spanish Proverbs*, 1823.

~ *See also* CUNNING is no burden; GOD makes the back to the burden; LIGHT burdens far heavy.

burdensome. *See* NOTHING is burdensome as a secret.

burn. burn not your house to fright away the mice (*English*) In coping with a minor nuisance do not create an even bigger problem for oneself. Thomas Fuller, *Gnomologia*, 1732. Related proverbs include 'he that burns his house warms himself for once'.

> But ye needna burn the hoose to rid the rottans [rats].
> G. MacDonald, *Alec Forbes*, 1865

a burnt child dreads the fire (*Roman*) We learn from experience to avoid that which harms us. *Proverbs of Hending*, *c.*1250 (also quoted by Cicero). Parallel proverbs in other languages include the French 'a scalded dog fears cold water', the Italian 'a dog which has been beaten with a stick fears its own shadow' and the Jewish 'one bitten by a serpent is afraid of a rope's end'. *See also* he who has been BITTEN by a snake fears a piece of string; once BITTEN, twice shy; he who has once BURNT his mouth always blows his soup; a SCALDED cat fears cold water.

> The burnt child fears the fire, and bitter experience had taught Pongo Twistleton to view with concern the presence in his midst of Ickenham's fifth earl.
> P.G. Wodehouse, *Uncle Dynamite*, 1948

you cannot burn the candle at both ends (*English*) If a person works too hard or too long at something they will have no energy (or health) left to apply to anything else. Francis Bacon, *Promus*, 1592.

> By sitting up till two in the morning, and rising again at six … Frank Headley burnt the candle of life at both ends.
> Charles Kingsley, *Two Years Ago*, 1857

~ *See also* BETTER a little fire to warm us than a great one to burn us; he who has ONCE burnt his mouth always blows his soup; if you PLAY with fire you get burnt; if your EAR burns someone is thinking about you; a LITTLE fire burns up a great deal of corn; WOOD half burnt is easily kindled.

burthen. *See* THREE helping one another bear the burthen of six.

bury. *See* it takes a GOOD many shovelfuls of earth to bury the truth; let the DEAD bury the dead.

bush. *See* a BAD bush is better than an open field; a BIRD in the hand is worth two in the bush; GOOD wine needs no bush; if the ROBIN sings in the bush then the weather will be coarse; but if the robin sings in the barn then the weather will be warm; one BEATS the bush, another takes the bird; the THIEF doth fear each bush an officer.

bushel. *See* don't HIDE your light under a bushel; don't MEASURE other people's corn by one's own bushel; GENTRY sent to market will not buy one bushel of corn.

busiest. *See* BUSY.

business. business before pleasure (*French*) Business matters should be dealt with before one turns to pleasure. *Grobiana's Nuptials*, *c*.1640. The wisdom of the proverb was underlined in ancient times when news of a plot to murder him was brought to the Spartan garrison commander Archias at Thebes: Archias, who was in the midst of a banquet, put the message under a cushion with the words 'business tomorrow', without reading it. Before the next day dawned he was dead.

business is business (*English*) Business should be tackled in a businesslike way, without sentiment or emotion. William Thackeray, *The Virginians*, 1857. Another proverb advises that 'business is the salt of life'.

> Business is business, my dear young sir.
>
> William Thackeray, *The Virginians*, 1857

business makes a man as well as tries him (*English*) A life in business builds and tests character. H.G. Bohn, *A Handbook of Proverbs*, 1855.

without business, debauchery (*English*) Those who have nothing to do tend to fall into debauched ways. George Herbert, *Outlandish Proverbs*, 1640.

~ *See also* BOLDNESS in business is the first, second and third thing; DRIVE your business, do not let it drive you; EVERYBODY's business is nobody's business; he that hath a WIFE and children wants not business; MIND your own business; ONE business begets another; PUNCTUALITY is the soul of business; who LIKES not his business, his business likes not him.

busk. *See* LAD's love's a busk of broom, hot awhile and soon done.

buskit. *See* a BONNY bride is soon buskit and a short horse is soon wispit.

busy. the busiest men have the most leisure (*English*) Those whose lives are the fullest are often also those who find the most time for pleasure (presumably because they are obliged by necessity to keep their affairs in good order). S. Smiles, *Self-Help*, 1866. Not unrelated was the now neglected proverb 'who is more busy than he that hath least to do?' *See also* IDLE people have the least leisure.

busy folks are always meddling (*English*) People who like to be busy often interfere in what does not really concern them. James Kelly, *A Complete Collection of Scotish Proverbs*, 1721. Another proverb warns that 'to be too busy gets contempt'. Those who find themselves continually interrupted by busy people are advised that the 'busy will have bands' (suggesting that the only way to keep busy people at bay is to tie them up or restrain them some other way).

the busy man has few idle visitors (*US*) Idle people find little attraction in people who are always busy. Benjamin Franklin, *Poor Richard's Almanack*, 1733–58. Equivalents include 'to the boiling pot the flies come not'.

he that is busy is tempted but by one devil, he that is idle by a legion (*Italian*) Those who are idle are easily distracted. Variants include 'he that is busy is tempted but by one devil, he that is idle by a thousand.'

~ *See also* the DEVIL is a busy bishop in his own diocese.

butcher. *See* ONE butcher does not fear many sheep.

butter. butter is mad twice a year (*English*) Some things, though usually reliable, may be counted on to go awry at certain times or under certain circumstance (just as butter made in July was supposed to be too thin and butter made in December too hard). Ben Jonson, *Staple of News*, 1625. Another proverb exploring the mutable nature of butter runs 'butter is gold in the morning, silver at noon, lead at night'.

> Butter is said to be mad twice a year; once in summer … when it is too thin and fluid; and once in winter … when it is too hard and difficult to spread.
>
> John Ray, *A Collection of English Proverbs*, 1678

butter is once a year in the cow's horn (*English*) It is inevitable that every now and again a cow will give no milk (typically when it is in calf). J. Howell, *Paroemiographia*, 1659.

no butter will stick to his bread (*English*) Every method a person adopts in order to advance himself seems doomed to failure. John Heywood, *A Dialogue containing … the Proverbs in the English Tongue*, 1546.

~ *See also* be not a BAKER if your head be of butter; BOIL stones in butter and you may sup the broth; the BREAD never falls but on the buttered side; FINE words butter no parsnips; there are MORE ways of killing a dog than choking it with butter.

button up to the chin till May comes in (*English*) Do not discard winter clothing before the month of May. *See also* ne'er CAST a clout till May be out.

buy. bought wit is the best (*English*) Knowledge is of any worth only if someone else is prepared to pay for it. H. Medwall, *Nature*, *c.*1490. Also encountered in the forms 'bought wit is dear', 'wit once bought is the best' and 'wit is never good till it be bought'.

> We say, Wisdom is not good till it is bought; and he that buys it … usually smarts for it.
>
> John Bunyan, *Accept Sacrifice*, 1688

buy in the cheapest market and sell in the dearest (*English*) In business there are profits to be made by buying merchandise at a low price and selling it for more. T. Lodge, *A Fig for Momus*, 1595. Related proverbs include 'buy at a fair, but sell at home' and 'he that buys dearly must sell dearly'.

> Buy in the cheapest market? – yes; but what made your market cheap? … Sell in the dearest? … but what made your market dear?
>
> John Ruskin, *Unto this Last*, 1862

if you buy the cow, take the tail into the bargain (*English*) If you take on a large project it is churlish to leave a minor part of it undone. James Kelly, *A Complete Collection of Scotish Proverbs*, 1721.

why buy a cow when milk is so cheap? (*English*) It is illogical to go to great lengths to enjoy something that is readily available without such trouble. J. Howell, *Proverbs*, 1659. Often quoted by those opposed to marriage, on the grounds that sex is easily obtainable elsewhere.

> Who would keep a Cow of their own, that can have a quart of milk for a penny? Meaning, Who would be at the charge to have a Wife, that can have a Whore when he listeth?
>
> John Bunyan, *Mr Badman*, 1680

you buy land you buy stones, you buy meat you buy bones (*English*) Many purchases necessitate acquiring things one does not want because they are inseparable from what is desired. John Ray, *A Collection of English Proverbs*, 1670. A variant runs: 'he that buys land buys many stones; he that buys flesh buys many bones; he that buys eggs buys many shells; but he that buys good ale buys nothing else.'

> He that buys Land, buys Stones; He that buys Nuts, buys shells: He that buys good Ale, buys nought else.
>
> James Kelly, *A Complete Collection of Scotish Proverbs*, 1721

~ *See also* GENTRY sent to market will not buy one bushel of corn; GOLD may be bought too dear; he is WELL worth sorrow that buys it with silver; he that BLAMES would buy; HONEY is dear bought if licked off thorns; HONOUR buys no beef; an INCH of gold will not buy an inch of time; the PLEASURES of the rich are bought with the tears of the poor; while the DUST is on your feet, sell what you have bought; a WILLOW will buy a horse before an oak will pay for a saddle.

buyer. let the buyer beware (*Roman*) It is the buyer's responsibility to make sure that he does not allow himself to be duped in a business transaction. J. Fitzherbert, *Husbandry*, 1523. Often quoted in the Latin form, *caveat emptor*. The fullest form of the maxim runs *caveat emptor, quia ignorare non debuit quod ius* *alineum emit* (let the buyer beware, for he ought not to be ignorant of the nature of the property which he is buying from another). Modern consumer law provides some protection for the purchaser by insisting that any item offered for sale should be of a quality 'proper for the purposes for which it is required'.

the buyer has need of a hundred eyes, the seller of but one (*Italian*) In business, it is the purchaser rather than the vendor who runs all the risks and has the most need of vigilance. George Herbert, *Outlandish Proverbs*, 1640.

> He taught him … to get … from customers by taking advantage of their ignorance … He often repeated … 'The buyer has need of a hundred eyes; the seller has need of but one.'
> Maria Edgeworth, *The Parent's Assistant*, 1800

buzzard. *See* an OLD wise man's shadow is better than a young buzzard's sword; you can't make a SPARROW-HAWK of a buzzard.

bygones. let bygones be bygones (*Greek*) Past arguments with others should be consigned to history. John Heywood, *A Dialogue containing … the Proverbs in the English Tongue*, 1546 (similar sentiments may be found in various forms in the writings of Epictetus, Homer and other classical authors). *See also* FORGIVE and forget.

> Let us adopt a Scotch proverb … 'Let bygones be bygones, and fair play for the future'.
> Walter Scott, *Guy Mannering*, 1815

byre. *See* BRING a cow to the hall and she'll run to the byre.

C

cabbage twice cooked is death (*Greek*) Some things, like cabbage, should be discarded if not consumed or otherwise dealt with at once. R. Taverner, *Proverbs or Adages with New Additions, gathered out of the Chiliades of Erasmus*, 1545 (also quoted by Juvenal).

> Which I must omitte, least I set before you, colewortes twice sodden.
> John Lyly, *Euphues: The Anatomy of Wit*, 1578

cable. *See* a MOUSE in time may bite in two a cable.

cackle. *See* he that would have EGGS must endure the cackling of hens.

Caesar. Caesar's wife must be above suspicion (*Roman*) The spouses of those in the public eye need to preserve untarnished reputations. Plutarch, *Lives*, first century AD. The proverb refers to Pompeia, the wife of Roman dictator Julius Caesar, who became embroiled in a scandal involving Publius Clodius, a notorious libertine, who was supposed to have seduced her after gaining entrance to the all-female Feast of the Great Goddess disguised as a woman. Although Caesar declared himself to be convinced of his wife's innocence, he went ahead and divorced her, explaining that even the taint of suspicion rendered her position as his wife untenable: 'I will not, sayd he, that my wife be so much as suspected'.

> Your moral character must be not only pure, but, like Caesar's wife, unsuspected.
> Lord Chesterfield, *Letters*, 1774

~ *See also* RENDER unto Caesar that which is Caesar's.

cage. *See* a NIGHTINGALE cannot sing in a cage; we must not LOOK for a golden life in an iron cage.

cake. you can't have your cake and eat it (*English*) In certain circumstances one must make a choice between two benefits, because they are mutually incompatible (for example, saving one's money and at the same time spending it). John Heywood, *A Dialogue containing … the Proverbs in the English Tongue*, 1546. Variants in other languages include the French proverb 'you can't have the cloth and keep the money' and the Italian proverb 'do you want to eat your cake and still have it in your pocket?' *See also* you can't have it BOTH ways.

> She was handsome in her Time; but she cannot eat her Cake, and have her Cake.
> Jonathan Swift, *Polite Conversation*, 1738

~ *See also* a BAD custom is like a good cake, better broken than kept; EVERY cake hath its make.

calendar. *See* DEATH keeps no calendar.

calf. calf love, half love, old love, cold love (*English*) Love that comes too early or too late in life is unlikely to prosper. R.D. Blackmore, *Cripps*, 1876.

the calf, the goose, the bee: the world is ruled by these three (*English*) The world is ruled by parchment, the pen and wax. J. Howell, letter, 3 July 1635.

~ *See also* a BELLOWING cow soon forgets her calf; CHANGE of pasture makes fat calves; the GREATEST calf is not the sweetest veal; he may BEAR a bull that hath borne a calf; MANY a good cow hath an evil calf; there are many WAYS of dressing a calf's head.

call. call a man a thief and he will steal (*English*) Give a person a bad reputation and they will be inclined to live up to it. Thomas Carlyle, *Sartor Resartus*, 1838.

In a very plain sense the proverb says, Call one a thief, and he will steal.

Thomas Carlyle, *Sartor Resartus*, 1838

call a spade a spade (*English*) Call things by their proper names, so that their real nature is revealed. William Rastell, *The Four Elements*, 1519 (also quoted by Erasmus).

call no man happy till he dies (*Greek*) A life that ends badly cannot be called happy, however good it may have been up to that point. R. Taverner *Proverbs or Adages with New Additions, gathered out of the Chiliades of Erasmus*, 1545 (also quoted by Sophocles in *Oedipus Rex*, fifth century BC, by Herodotus, by Aristotle and by Ovid in *Metamorphoses*).

'Call no man happy until he is dead' ... He was seventy-two, and yet there was still time for this dream ... to change to a nightmare.

C.S. Forester, *Hornblower and Crisis*, 1967

call the bear 'uncle' till you are safe across the bridge (*Turkish*) Do not provoke those who can harm you until you are safe from any retaliation on their part. *Times Weekly*, 12 April 1912. *See also* don't HALLOO till you are out of the wood.

I wouldn't call the king my cousin (*English*) I am content with things as they are (and would be no better off even if related to the monarch himself). James Kelly, *A Complete Collection of Scotish Proverbs*, 1721.

Added when we say, Had I such a thing, could I get such a place, or effect such a project: I would think myself so happy, that I would flatter no body.

James Kelly, *A Complete Collection of Scotish Proverbs*, 1721

~ *See also* BELLS call others but themselves enter not into the church; he who PAYS the piper calls the tune; the HOLE calls the thief; NOBODY calls himself rogue; the POT calls the kettle black; YESTERDAY will not be called again.

calm. calm weather in June sets corn in tune (*English*) Fine weather in June bodes well for a good harvest of corn. T. Tusser, *Five Hundred Points of Good Husbandry*, 1573.

in a calm sea every man is a pilot (*Roman*) When there is no threat or challenge to test one's skills, any man may claim mastery of a subject safe in the knowledge that it will not be challenged. John Ray, *A Collection of English Proverbs*, 1670 (also quoted by Seneca in his *Epistles*). Variants include 'in a calm sea every passenger is a pilot'. Also recorded in Spanish and several other European languages.

In a calm sea everyone can steer.

Thomas Fuller, *Gnomologia*, 1732

the calmest husbands make the stormiest wives (*English*) Women married to patient husbands are liable to find their forbearance provoking. Isaac D'Israeli, *Curiosities of Literature*, 1823. Variants in other languages include the Roman 'the better the man, the less good will he get out of his wife'. A Scottish proverb, however, insists that 'a gude man maks a gude wife'.

~ *See also* AFTER a storm comes a calm; VOWS made in storms are forgotten in calms.

camel. *See* it is EASIER for a camel to go through the eye of a needle than it is for a rich man to enter into the kingdom of heaven; it is the LAST straw that breaks the camel's back.

camomile. *See* the MORE camomile is trodden on, the faster it grows.

can (noun). *See* if the LAD go to the well against his will, either the can will break or the water will spill.

can (verb). **he who can does, he who cannot teaches** (*English*) Only those who have failed to realize their ambitions of practising an art or craft themselves end up teaching it to others. George Bernard Shaw, *Maxims for Revolutionaries*, 1903.

candle. a candle lights others and consumes itself (*English*) Some people sacrifice themselves in inspiring others. J. Minsheu, *A Spanish Grammar, now augmented ... by J. Minsheu*, 1599.

The painful preacher, like a candle bright, consumes himself in giving others light.

Benjamin Franklin, *Poor Richard's Almanack*, 1742

~ *See also* CANDLEMAS Day, put beans in the clay, put candles and candlesticks away; he that WORST may shall hold the candle; TACE is Latin for candle; the WAY to see divine light is to put out thine own candle; you cannot BURN the candle at both ends.

candlelight. *See* NEVER choose your women or your linen by candlelight.

Candlemas. Candlemas Day, put beans in the clay, put candles and candlesticks away (*English*) Candlemas Day (the festival of the Virgin Mary, 2 February), traditionally the halfway point through the winter, marks the date on which candles and candlesticks used in religious services should be put away and the first planting of broad beans should take place. John Ray, *A Collection of English Proverbs*, 1678. The proverb dictates that on this day, the anniversary of Christ's first visit to the Temple with his mother, candles and candlesticks used in services of vespers and litanies should be put away until the following All Hallow's Mass in October. Candles blessed on Candlemas Day were formerly particularly valued as protectives against witchcraft.

> Broad beans were planted ... on Candlemas Day. *Candlemas Day, stick beans in the clay, Throw candle and candlestick right away*, they would quote.
> Flora Thompson, *Still Glides the Stream*, 1948

if Candlemas Day be sunny and bright, winter will have another flight; if Candlemas Day be cloudy with rain, winter is gone, and won't come again (*English*) The weather on Candlemas Day (2 February) may be interpreted to foretell what weather is in store. John Skelton, *Works*, 1523. The wording of the proverb varies from one source to another. Variants include 'if Candlemas Day be fair and fine, half the winter is left behind; if Candlemas Day be dull and gloom, half the winter is yet to come' and 'if Candlemas Day be cloudy and black, 'twill carry cold winter away on its back; but if Candlemas Day be fine and clear, then half the winter's to come this year'. A starker version insists 'on Candlemas Day, if the sun shines clear, the shepherd had rather see his wife on the bier'. In practical terms, farmers tended to regard Candlemas Day as marking the halfway point through the winter, and would husband their livestock rations so that there was still at least half left at this date. This piece of folk wisdom was rendered in proverb form as 'on Candlemas Day, you must have half your straw and half your hay'. Other proverbs offer more detail about the weather to come: 'as much ground as is covered with snow on Candlemas Day will be covered with snow before Lady-Day', alternatively: 'when the wind's in the east on Candlemas Day, there it will stick to the second of May'. *See also* SAINT Swithin's Day, if thou dost rain, for forty days it will remain; Saint Swithin's Day, if thou be fair, for forty days 'twill rain no more.

> If Candlemas Day be fair and bright Winter will have another flight but if Candlemas Day be clouds and rain Winter is gone and will not come again.
> Edith Holden, *The Country Diary of an Edwardian Lady*, 1906

candlestick. *See* CANDLEMAS Day, put beans in the clay, put candles and candlesticks away.

cannon. *See* DOUBLE charge will rive a cannon; he was CURSED in his mother's belly that was killed by a cannon.

canoe. *See* PADDLE your own canoe.

cap. if the cap fits, wear it (*English*) If you are guilty of some act of blame or folly, then you should acknowledge it. N. Breton, *Pasquil's Fools-Cap*, 1600. The proverb has its origins in the fool's cap (often adorned with bells) that was worn in medieval times by fools and jesters as a symbol of their craft. The last fools disappeared in the early eighteenth century, but the fool's cap is still remembered as a symbol of stupidity or folly. In former times anyone who became the butt of a company's jokes might be said to be 'wearing the cap and bells'. The proverb is usually quoted in an aggressive context, suggesting to the recipient of the remark that they should recognize their own foolishness.

> If indeed thou findest ... that the cap fits thy own head, why then ... e'en take and clap it on.
> Samuel Richardson, *Clarissa*, 1748

capacity. *See* GENIUS is an infinite capacity for taking pains.

caravan. *See* the DOGS bark but the caravan goes on.

carcass. where the carcass is, there shall the eagles be gathered together (*Hebrew*) The wicked and the avaricious will gather where circumstances allow them to prosper. Bible, Matthew 24:28. The meaning of the proverb becomes clearer when it is appreciated that in the original Hebrew 'eagles' could signify vultures. Also found in the form 'where the carcass is, the ravens will gather'. *See also* BIRDS of a feather flock together.

Where carcasses are, eagles will gather, And where good laws are, much people flock thither.
Benjamin Franklin, *Poor Richard's Almanack*, 1734

card. cards are the devil's books (*English*) Those who indulge in gambling lay themselves open to all manner of evil. *Poor Robin's Almanack*, 1676. The phrase was much used by Presbyterian opponents of card-playing and similar trivial 'ungodly' pastimes, partly in response to the older name for a pack of cards – 'the king's books' (derived from the French *livre des quatre rois*, the book of the four kings). Alternatively, a deck of cards might be referred to on occasion as the 'devil's Bible'. Particularly ominous among gamblers is the four of clubs, which is dubbed the devil's bedpost (any hand including this card is called the devil's four-poster).

He thought that cards had not without reason been called the Devil's Books.
Robert Southey, *The Doctor*, 1834

~ *See also* LUCKY at cards, unlucky in love; there is no PACK of cards without a knave.

care (noun). **care and diligence bring luck** (*English*) Good fortune is the product of hard work and careful attention. R. Taverner, *Flores aliquot sententiarum*, 1540.

Diligence is the mother of good fortune.
W. Stepney, *The Spanish Schoolmaster*, 1591

care is no cure (*English*) Kindness and good intentions cannot cure all ills. William Shakespeare, *Henry VI, Part 1*, *c.*1590.

Care is no cure, but rather corrosive, for things that are not to be remedied.
William Shakespeare, *Henry VI, Part 1*, *c.*1590

care killed the cat (*English*) Excessive worrying or anxiety is self-defeating, particularly if one is set on enjoying oneself. William Shakespeare, *Much Ado About Nothing*, *c.*1598. A fuller Scottish version of the proverb runs 'care will kill a cat, but ye canna live without it'. *See also* CURIOSITY killed the cat.

What, courage, man! What though care killed a cat.
William Shakespeare, *Much Ado About Nothing*, *c.*1598

~ *See also* as your WEDDING ring wears, your cares will wear away; BEHIND the horseman sits black care; CHILDREN are certain cares but uncertain comforts; LIGHT cares speak, great ones are dumb; LITTLE gear, less care; MUCH coin, much care; PAINS to get, care to keep, fear to lose; PAST cure, past care; a POUND of care will not pay an ounce of debt; WANT of care does us more damage than want of knowledge.

care (verb). **care not would have it** (*English*) Those who say they do not care if they have a thing are often those who want it most. John Ray, *A Collection of English Proverbs*, 1670.

he cares not whose child cry so his laugh (*English*) Selfish people will ignore the unhappiness of others as long as their own interests are being served. *Shirburn Ballads*, 1585–1616.

careful. *See* if you can't be GOOD, be careful.

careless. a careless hussy makes many thieves (*Scottish*) A negligent housewife makes thieves by giving them too many opportunities to steal. P. Stampoy, *A Collection of Scotch Proverbs*, 1663.

carle. *See* HAIR and hair makes the carle's head bare.

carpenter. a carpenter is known by his chips (*English*) The best craftsmen may be distinguished by the small amount of waste they leave as they work. Thomas Coryat, *Coryats Crudities*, 1611.

They say a carpenter's known by his chips.
Jonathan Swift, *Polite Conversation*, 1738

~ *See also* QUININE is made of the sweat of ship carpenters.

carries. *See* CARRY.

carrion crows bewail the dead sheep and then eat them (*English*) The hypocritical bemoan the fate of others, then set about profiting from their misfortune. George Herbert, *Outlandish Proverbs*, 1640.

carry. he carries fire in one hand and water in the other (*Roman*) Spoken of a person who says one thing but means another (usually deceiving others for his own nefarious ends). John Lydgate, *Troy Book*, 1412–20 (also recorded in Plautus).

Whatsoever I speake to men, the same also I speake to women, I meane not … to carye fire in the one hand and water in the other.
John Lyly, *Euphues: The Anatomy of Wit*, 1578

~ *See also* the BELLY carries the legs and not the legs the belly; a DOG that will fetch a bone will carry a bone; he who would BRING home the wealth of the Indies must carry the wealth of the Indies with him; it is a SHAME to steal but a worse to carry home; the LEAST boy always carries the greatest fiddle; MACKEREL sky and mares' tails make lofty ships carry low sails; SPEAK softly and carry a big stick.

cart. don't put the cart before the horse (*Greek*) Don't do things in the wrong order. Sir Thomas More, *Works*, 1528 (also quoted by Lucian). A variant warns of the dangers of putting the plough before the oxen.

> Excuse me, that the Muses force the cart to stand before the horse.
>
> Edward Ward, *Hudibras Redivivus*, 1705

~ *See also* the BEST cart may overthrow; an OLD cart, well used, may last out a new one abused; an UNHAPPY man's cart is eith to tumble; the WORST spoke in a cart breaks first.

case. the case is altered (*English*) The situation has changed. Robert Greene, *Looking-Glass*, 1594. Sometimes encountered in the fuller version 'the case is altered, quoth Plowden' – an obscure reference to Edmund Plowden (1518–85), a famous English lawyer.

> I have betrayed myself with my own tongue;
> The case is altered.
>
> Ben Jonson, *The Case is Altered*, 1609.

~ *See also* CIRCUMSTANCES alter cases; HARD cases make bad law.

cask. the cask savours of the first fill (*Roman*) A person or project begun badly will never be rid of the taint of that first evil (just as a wine cask will preserve an echo of the wine it first contained). Horace, *Epistles*, *c.*AD19. Variants include 'every cask smells of the wine it contains'.

> With what the maiden vessel is season'd first – you understand the proverb.
>
> Beaumont and Fletcher, *The Custom of the Country*, *c.*1615

~ *See also* WINE savours of the cask.

casket. *See* NONE can guess the jewel by the casket.

cast (noun). *See* he has not LOST all who has one cast left.

cast (verb). **cast a bone in the devil's teeth** (*English*) When harassed by someone one option is to distract their attention by tossing them something they would like. James Kelly, *A Complete Collection of Scottish Proverbs*, 1721.

don't cast your pearls before swine (*Hebrew*) Don't bestow valuable things on those who will not appreciate them. Bible, Matthew 7:6. It has been suggested that 'pearls' in the original biblical context was a mistranslation for 'crumbs'. A Chinese equivalent is 'don't play the lute before a donkey'.

> Give not that which is holy unto the dogs, neither cast your pearls before swine, lest they trample them under their feet and turn again and rend you.
>
> Matthew 7:6

ne'er cast a clout till May be out (*English*) Do not discard winter clothing until after the month of May, because the weather may still turn wintry. J. Stevens, *Spanish and English Dictionary*, 1706 (also recorded in Spanish, *c.*1627). 'Clout' here signifies a rag or patch of material, hence clothing. Less well-known proverbs expressing similar sentiments include 'who doffs his coat on a winter's day will gladly put it on in May'. May is traditionally considered the unluckiest of all the months and the worst possible time to come down with a cold due to chilly weather. The notion that the proverb refers to hawthorn blossom (often called may), suggesting that not till the blossoms are over is it safe to wear less, is probably erroneous. In much the same vein in many areas it was considered unwise even to bathe the body in the month of May, as the loss of a protective coat of grime acquired over the winter would render the person concerned vulnerable to sudden cold snaps. *See also* BUTTON up to the chin till May comes in; he who BATHES in May will soon be laid in clay; MARRY in May and rue the day; a SWARM of bees in May is worth a load of hay.

> The wind at North and East
> Was never good for man nor beast,
> So never think to cast a clout
> Until the month of May be out.
>
> F.K. Robinson, *Whitby Glossary*, 1855

though you cast out nature with a fork, it will still return (*Roman*) Any attempt to deny the true nature of something or someone is futile, as underlying character will always reveal itself. Horace, *Epistles*, fifth century BC. *See also* TRUTH will out.

> Mr Crotchet ... seemed ... to settle down ... into an English country gentleman ... but, though, you expel nature with a pitchfork, she will always come back.
>
> Thomas Love Peacock, *Crotchet Castle*, 1831

~ *See also* COMING events cast their shadows before; it is in VAIN to cast your net where there is no fish; OLD sins cast long shadows.

castle. a castle that speaketh is near a surrender (*English*) If one party is prepared to negotiate, this may be taken as a sign that it may soon come to terms. John Lyly, *Euphues and His England*, 1580. The proverb was formerly commonly quoted in reference to the courting of women, suggesting that any woman who allowed herself to engage in wordplay with a suitor would soon surrender to his advances.

~ *See also* an ENGLISHMAN's home is his castle; it is EASY to keep a castle that was never assaulted.

cat. the cat and dog may kiss, yet are none the better friends (*English*) A public show of friendship does not necessarily reflect genuine feelings. *Trinity MS*, *c.*1225.

a cat has nine lives (*Indian*) Some people seem to lead charmed lives, just as cats are supposed to die only after they have survived the threat of imminent death nine times (a notion probably inspired by the cat's ability to survive falls from considerable heights). 'The Greedy and Ambitious Cat', *Fables of Pilpay* (first recorded in English by John Heywood in *A Dialogue containing ... the Proverbs in the English Tongue*, 1546). As a child the philosopher and statesman Francis Bacon tried to test the superstition that cats have nine lives by tossing cats from an upper-storey window (history does not record what became of them). In former times the sentiment was often expressed of cats and women together. *See also* he is like a CAT; fling him which way you will, he'll light on his legs.

> A cat has nine lives, and a woman has nine cats' lives.
>
> Thomas Fuller, *Gnomologia*, 1732

a cat in gloves catches no mice (*French/Italian*) A person who holds back will not gain his objective (said particularly of those who do their work in gloves in order to keep their hands clean). J. Sandford, *The Garden of Pleasure*, 1572 (recorded in France in the fourteenth century). Variant forms include the words 'gloved', 'muffled' and 'muzzled'. Known in Italian as *gatta guantata non piglia sorce*.

> A muffled cat was never good mouser.
>
> William Camden, *Remains concerning Britain*, 1623

the cat knows whose lips she licks (*English*) Some people reserve their affections or praise for those from whom they might expect some benefit. Wright, *Essays on the Middle Ages*, *c.*1210. Also found in the form 'the cat knows whose beard she licks'.

> But the cat knoweth whose lips she lickth well enough.
>
> John Heywood, *A Dialogue containing ... the Proverbs in the English Tongue*, 1550

a cat may look at a king (*English/French/German*) Matters of rank and status are irrelevant in some circumstances (a humble cat has no regard for human rank and may cast its gaze as readily upon a king as on any less distinguished person). John Heywood, *A Dialogue containing ... the Proverbs in the English Tongue*, 1546. Usually said in retaliation to someone who assumes a superior air to his or her supposed inferiors or in circumstances where a person is accused of showing a lack of deference or respect. A famous political pamphlet was published with this title in 1652. An equivalent proverb in French runs *un chien regarde bien un évêque* (even a dog may look at a bishop). This is said to hark back to a decree of the sixth century AD, under which bishops were prohibited from keeping dogs, so that petitioners might not be bitten. In Germany this proverb also exists in the form *Darf doch die Katze den Kaiser ansehen*' (even a cat may look at an emperor). The tradition is that when Maximilian I paid a visit to a woodcarver's workshop the man's cat stared openly at the monarch, regardless of his high standing.

> A cat may look at a king, and so may I at her.
>
> Thomas Heywood, *The Wise Woman of Hogsdon*, 1638

cats eat what hussies spare (*English*) What a person tries to keep back through meanness is just as likely to be wasted anyway. J. Clarke, *Paroemiologia Anglo-Latina*, 1639.

> The things that wives hains, cats eat.
>
> James Kelly, *A Complete Collection of Scottish Proverbs*, 1721

cats hide their claws (*English*) Those who plan to prey on others conceal their intentions until the right time. Thomas Fuller, *Gnomologia*, 1732.

the cat shuts its eyes while it steals cream (*English*) People tend to ignore the fact that they are doing wrong as they go about their misdeeds. R.C. Trench, *On the Lessons in Proverbs*, 1853.

the Cat, the Rat and Lovell our Dog rule all England under an Hog (*English*) Historical reference to the three advisers (Sir William Catesby, Sir Richard Ratcliffe and Lord Lovell) who exercised power under Richard III (whose emblem was a wild boar). R. Holinshed, *Chronicles*, 1577. The original author of the rhyme was a man named Collingbourne, who was executed on the orders of the king for his presumption.

cat will to kind (*English*) People will always revert to their true natures. G. Harvey, *Letterbook*, *c.*1580. Related proverbs include 'that cat is out of kind that sweet milk will not lap'.

> If the cat will after kind,
> So be sure will Rosalind.
> William Shakespeare, *As You Like It*, 1601

he is like a cat: fling him which way you will, he'll light on his legs (*English*) Some people will always emerge unscathed from the most perilous adventures, just as cats always land on their feet after a fall. Horman, *Vulgaria*, 1519.

> Not hurt him,
> He pitcht upon his legs like a cat.
> Beaumont and Fletcher, *Monsieur Thomas*, 1616

let the cat wink and let the mouse run (*English*) Allow others to do what they want without interference. John Heywood, *A Dialogue containing ... the Proverbs in the English Tongue*, 1546.

though the cat winks a while, yet sure she is not blind (*English*) Because someone chooses to ignore something this does not necessarily mean that they do not know what is going on. John Ray, *A Collection of English Proverbs*, 1678.

when the cat's away, the mice will play (*English*) When authority is absent, others will engage in mischief. *Harley MS*, *c.*1470. Similar sentiments are found in many other languages. The French version may be translated as 'when the cat runs on the roofs, the mice dance on the floors'. The Spanish and Italians know the proverb in the form 'when the cat is not in the house, the mice dance', while the Germans have 'cat outside the house, repose for the mouse'.

> So it is, and such is life. The cat's away, and the mice they play.
> Charles Dickens, *Bleak House*, 1852

~ *See also* ALL cats are grey in the dark; ALL cats love fish but fear to wet their paws; it is a BOLD mouse that breeds in the cat's ear; CARE killed the cat; CURIOSITY killed the cat; he that PLAYS with cats must expect to be scratched; KEEP no more cats than will catch mice; an OLD cat sports not with her prey; a SCALDED cat fears cold water; take the CHESTNUTS out of the fire with the cat's paw; there are MORE ways of killing a cat than choking it with cream; TWO cats and a mouse, two wives in one house, two dogs and a bone, never agree in one; WANTON kittens make sober cats; you can have no MORE of a cat than her skin.

catch. catching fish is not the whole of fishing (*English*) There is more to fishing (and many other pursuits and enterprises) than simply the climactic moment of final success. *Times Literary Supplement*, 1913.

catch not at the shadow and lose the substance (*English*) In concentrating on something trivial you might neglect what is more important. John Lyly, *Euphues: The Anatomy of Wit*, 1578.

> Like the dog in the fable, to throw away the substance in catching at the shadow.
> Thomas Love Peacock, *Nightmare Abbey*, 1818

he that will catch eels must disturb the flood (*Greek*) Sometimes a person must create some disturbance in order to get what they want. *Lingua*, 1607 (quoting Aristophanes). Variants include 'to catch gudgeons you must stir up the mud'.

you cannot catch old birds with chaff (*English*) The experienced and the wily are not easily deceived (just as birds will not be deceived if they are thrown chaff rather than birdseed). William Caxton, *Reynard the Fox*, 1481.

> Tis well – an olde birde is not caught with chaffe.
> William Shakespeare, *Timon of Athens*, *c.*1607

~ *See also* ALL fish are not caught with flies; as the BLIND man catches the hare; a CAT in gloves catches no mice; a CLOSE mouth catches no flies; EAGLES don't catch flies; the EARLY bird catches the worm; FIRST catch your hare; the FISH will soon be caught that nibbles at every bait; HARM watch, harm catch; he that MISCHIEF hatcheth, mischief catcheth; HONEY catches more flies than vinegar; a HOOK is well lost to catch a salmon; if the SKY falls we shall catch larks; if you RUN after two hares you will catch neither; if you SWEAR you will catch no fish; it is a SILLY fish that is caught twice with the same bait; KEEP no more cats than will catch mice; MOCKING is catching; NEVER catch at a falling knife or friend; NEVER let the plough stand to catch a mouse; SET a thief to catch a thief; SILENCE catches a mouse; the SLEEPING fox catches no poultry; SOFTLY, softly, catchee monkey; THROW out a sprat to catch a mackerel.

catcher. *See* the ROUGH net is not the best catcher of birds.

caught. *See* CATCH.

cause (noun). **take away the cause and the effect must cease** (*Spanish*) The best way to tackle something undesirable is to remove the cause. R. Percyvall, *A Spanish Grammar, now augmented ... by J. Minsheu*, 1599. Earlier equivalents include the Roman 'the cause ceasing, the effect ceases also'.

~ *See also* it is a BAD cause that none dare speak in; it is not the SUFFERING but the cause which makes a martyr; a MAN is a lion in his own cause; MEN are blind in their own cause; no one should be JUDGE in his own cause.

cause (verb). *See* that which a MAN causes to be done, he does himself.

cease. *See* take away the CAUSE and the effect will cease; WONDERS will never cease.

ce n'est que le premier pas qui coûte (*French*) It is only the first step that costs anything (meaning, it is the first step that is remarkable). Attributed to Madame du Deffand (1697–1780) when told the miracle of Saint Denys, who is supposed to have walked some distance after he was beheaded. *See also* it is the FIRST step that is difficult.

certain. *See* CHILDREN are certain cares but uncertain comforts; NOTHING is certain but death and taxes; NOTHING is certain but the unforeseen.

certainty. *See* NEVER quit certainty for hope.

chaff. *See* you cannot CATCH old birds with chaff.

chain. a chain is no stronger than its weakest link (*English*) A single flaw may compromise the strength of the whole. Charles Kingsley, letter, 1856. *See also* the THREAD breaks where it is weakest.

chamber. the chamber of sickness is the chapel of devotion (*English*) Those who are ill are prone to turn to religion for comfort, regardless of any previous lack of conviction. T. Draxe, *Bibliotheca Scholastica*, 1616. *See also* the DEVIL sick would be a monk.

chance (noun). *See* LOOK to the main chance.

chance (verb). **it chanceth in an hour that happeneth not in seven years** (*English*) Things can happen straightaway that have not happened in many years. *Douce MS*, *c.*1350.

> Yet somtyme it shal fallen on a day
> That falleth nat eft withinne a thousand yeer.
> Geoffrey Chaucer, 'The Knight's Tale', *The Canterbury Tales*, *c.*1387

Chancery. *See* HELL and Chancery are always open.

change (noun). **a change is as good as a rest** (*English*) Doing something different can be as therapeutic as doing nothing at all. J. Thomas, *Randigal Rhymes*, 1895. Variants include 'a change of work is as good as touch-pipe', a 'touch-pipe' signifying a short period of rest.

change of pasture makes fat calves (*English*) A change of surroundings can promote well-being. John Heywood, *A Dialogue containing ... the Proverbs in the English Tongue*, 1546.

change of weather is the discourse of fools (*English*) Only fools pass the time talking about the weather. J. Howell, *Paroemiographia*, 1659.

change (verb). **don't change horses in midstream** (*US*) Don't switch allegiances halfway through whatever you are doing. Abraham Lincoln, 1864 (quoted in *Collected Works*, 1953). Lincoln himself, who is largely responsible for popularizing the proverb, claimed to be quoting an old Dutch farmer. He quoted the proverb on 9 June 1864 while explaining his reasons for accepting renomination as president of the United States despite doubts voiced by others about his handling of the Civil War.

> Don't change horses in midstream ... if we think it necessary to make changes, we must choose the right moment to make them.
>
> Ridout and Witting, *English Proverbs Explained*, 1967

to change the name and not the letter, is a change for the worse, and not for the better (*English*) Any woman who marries a man whose surname begins with the same letter as her maiden name will experience bad luck in her married life. Chambers, *Book of Days*, 1862. Conversely, a woman who marries a man who happens to share the same surname as her own will be blessed with powers of healing (according to Cheshire superstition).

~ *See also* HONOURS change manners; a LEOPARD can't change its spots; a MAN will never change his mind if he has no mind to change; only FOOLS exult when governments change; PLUS ça change, plus c'est la même chose; TIMES change and we with time; TRAVELLERS change climates not conditions; a WISE man changes his mind, a fool never will.

chapel. *See* the CHAMBER of sickness is the chapel of devotion; where GOD builds a church, the devil will build a chapel.

chaplain. *See* he that PREACHES war is the devil's chaplain.

character. *See* a MAN's studies pass into his character.

charge. *See* DOUBLE charge will rive a cannon.

chariot-wheel. *See* the FLY sat upon the axletree of the chariot-wheel and said, what a dust do I raise!

charity. charity and pride do both feed the poor (*English*) Acts of generosity to the deserving may be variously inspired by charity or vanity. *Politeuphuia*, 1597, attributed to J. Bodenham.

charity begins at home (*Greek*) Those keen to do good works should begin by doing what they can to improve the circumstances of those immediately around them. John Wycliffe, *Of Prelates*, *c.*1380 (also quoted by Theocritus and Terence). A possible origin of the proverb may be the biblical passage in Timothy 5:4: 'Let them learn first to show piety at home, and to requite their parents.' In modern times this somewhat overused proverb has assumed a cynical overtone and is often used in reference to those who, eschewing acts of charity towards strangers, have directed their largesse towards their friends and business acquaintances, perhaps in the hope of promoting some self-interest. A French gloss on the original proverb advises 'charity begins at home, but should not end there'.

> But charity begins at home, and justice begins next door.
>
> Charles Dickens, *Martin Chuzzlewit*, 1850

charity covers a multitude of sins (*Hebrew*) Those who perform generous acts may be compensating for evil acts that they have committed. Bible, Peter 4:8. In the original context 'charity' signified Christian love rather than acts of generosity to others.

> Ah, you always were one for a pretty face, weren't you? Covers a multitude is what I always say.
>
> Kingsley Amis, *Lucky Jim*, 1954

charm. *See* MUSIC hath charms.

charter. *See* 'IF' and 'an' spoils many a good charter.

chase (noun). *See* a STERN chase is a long chase.

chase (verb). *See* LOSE an hour in the morning, chase it all day.

chasten. he that chastens one chastens twenty (*English*) When a person scolds someone their words will chasten many others guilty of the same faults. George Herbert, *Outlandish Proverbs*, 1640. Also found as 'he that chastiseth one chastiseth twenty' and 'he that chastiseth one amendeth many'.

cheap. it is as cheap sitting as standing (*English*) An invitation to sit. G. Torriano, *Italian Proverbs*, 1666.

~ *See also* BUY in the cheapest market and sell in the dearest; GOOD cheap is dear; why BUY a cow when milk is so cheap?

cheat (noun). **cheats never prosper** (*English*) Those who cheat will not profit by their dishonesty in the long run. John Harington, *Epigrams*, 1612. Related proverbs on the subject of cheating include 'he that cheateth in small things is a fool, but in great things is a rogue'.

cheat (verb). **he that will cheat at play will cheat you anyway** (*English*) A person who disobeys the rules in trivial matters should not be trusted to behave honourably in more serious contexts. James Kelly, *A Complete Collection of Scottish Proverbs*, 1721.

~ *See also* FAIR words and foul deeds cheat wise men as well as fools.

cheek. *See* he that WIPES the child's nose kisseth the mother's cheek.

cheep. *See* MAY chickens come cheeping.

cheer. *See* a HEARTY welcome is the best cheer; when GOOD cheer is lacking, our friends will be packing.

cheerful. a cheerful look makes a dish a feast (*English*) A meal, no matter how modest, that is eaten in jovial company will be much more enjoyable than one eaten in an atmosphere of gloom. George Herbert, *Outlandish Proverbs*, 1640.

cheese. cheese digests all things but itself (*English*) The consumption of cheese at the end of the meal aids the digestion of the previous courses, but may prove indigestible itself. John Lyly, *Sapho and Phao*, 1584.

> They say, cheese digests everything but itself.
> Jonathan Swift, *Polite Conversation*, 1738

~ *See also* BREAD and cheese be two targets against death; 'tis an OLD rat that won't eat cheese.

cherry. a cherry year, a merry year; a plum year, a dumb year (*English*) A good show of cherry blossom (or a good crop of cherries) bodes well for the coming months, while plentiful plum blossom (or fruits) bodes ill. John Ray, *A Collection of English Proverbs*, 1678.

~ *See also* EAT peas with the king and cherries with the beggar; LIFE is just a bowl of cherries; a WOMAN and a cherry are painted for their own harm.

chestnut. take the chestnuts out of the fire with the cat's paw (*French*) Use an unwitting partner to gain some benefit for yourself, thus avoiding any risk involved. G. Whitney, *Emblems*, 1586. The proverb is illustrated by a fable told by La Fontaine in which a monkey, taking a fancy to a chestnut roasting in a fire, uses a cat's paw to retrieve the morsel, thus escaping injury to itself (regardless of damage to the cat). The proverb is sometimes given with a dog rather than a cat being thus abused.

> He makes her … become herself the cat's paw
> to help him to the ready roasted chestnuts.
> Samuel Richardson, *Sir Charles Grandison*, 1753

chicken. *See* BETTER an egg today than a chicken tomorrow; CHILDREN and chicken must always be pickin'; CURSES, like chickens, come home to roost; don't COUNT your chickens before they are hatched; MAY chickens come cheeping.

chief. *See* when the DEVIL is dead, he never lacks a chief mourner.

child. the child is the father of the man (*English*) A persons's character is determined while they are still very young. William Wordsworth, 'My heart leaps up', *Poems*, 1807.

a child may have too much of his mother's blessing (*English*) A child may easily be spoiled by an over-indulgent mother. John Clarke, *Paroemiologia Anglo-Latina*, 1639.

> Mothers are oftentimes too tender and fond of
> their children. Who are ruined and spoiled by
> their cockering and indulgence.
> John Ray, *A Collection of English Proverbs*, 1670

children and chicken must always be pickin' (*English*) Children and chicken alike are always hungry. T. Tusser, *Five Hundred Points of Good Husbandry*, 1573.

children and fools have merry lives (*English*) Children and fools are always happy, because they are interested only in the present rather than in what has passed or in what may be to come. J. Clarke, *Paroemiologia Anglo-Latina*, 1639. *See also* CHILDREN and fools tell the truth.

children and fools must not play with edged tools (*English*) The young and the mad should not be allowed to tamper with anything that is potentially dangerous. Roger Ascham, *The Scholemaster*, 1570.

'Oh dear, what an edged tool you are!' 'Don't play with me then,' said Ralph impatiently, 'You know the proverb.'

Charles Dickens, *Nicholas Nickleby*, 1839

children and fools tell the truth (*English*) The young (or in some versions drunkards) and the mad are incapable of telling untruths. R. Taverner, *Proverbs or Adages with New Additions, gathered out of the Chiliades of Erasmus*, 1545. *See also* CHILDREN and fools have merry lives; FOOLS and madmen speak the truth.

Fools and children always speak truth, they say.

George Colman, *Man and Wyfe*, 1769

children are certain cares but uncertain comforts (*English*) Children are bound to cause their parents heartache, but will not necessarily provide compensating pleasure. *How the Good Wyfe*, *c.*1460.

children are poor men's riches (*English*) The poor man might consider himself rich because he has children. Randle Cotgrave, *A Dictionary of the French and English Tongues*, 1611. Also encountered in the form 'children are the parents' riches'.

They say barnes are blessings.

William Shakespeare, *All's Well That Ends Well*, *c.*1602

children are to be deceived with comfits and men with oaths (*Greek*) Sweets will distract children and promises will satisfy men, no matter how hollow they are. Plutarch, *Lysander*, first century AD.

That other principle of Lysander, That children are to be deceived with comfits, and men with oaths: and the like evil and corrupt positions.

Francis Bacon, *The Advancement of Learning*, 1605

children have wide ears and long tongues (*English*) The young have a habit of hearing all manner of things they perhaps should not hear and then repeating them. Thomas Fuller, *Gnomologia*, 1732. Equivalent proverbs include 'children pick up words as pigeons pease, and utter them again as God shall please'.

children should be seen and not heard (*Greek*) Well-behaved children should refrain from making noise in the presence of adults. George Bernard Shaw, *Misalliance*, 1914 (also quoted by Aristophanes in *The Clouds* in 423BC). In its original English form, first recorded in the fourteenth century, the proverb was often directed at 'maidens' rather than 'children' (the more common form from the mid-nineteenth century). *See also* SPEAK when you are spoken to.

Father heard the children scream,
So he threw them in the stream,
Saying as he drowned the third,
'Children should be seen, not heard!'

Harry Graham, *Ruthless Rhymes for Heartless Homes*, 1899

children suck the mother when they are young, and the father when they are old (*English*) In their infancy children rely on mother's milk for sustenance, but when they are older they are inclined to dip into their father's wallet for maintenance. John Ray, *A Collection of English Proverbs*, 1678.

child's pig but father's bacon (*English*) What one person may like to consider their pet or plaything may be regarded as a business opportunity by another and a possible source of profit. *Douce MS*, *c.*1350.

Child's pig, but father's bacon. Parents usually tell their children, this pig or this lamb is thine, but when they come to be grown up and sold, parents themselves take the money for them.

John Ray, *A Collection of English Proverbs*, 1678

he that has no children knows not what is love (*Italian*) Only parents know the meaning of true love. G. Torriano, *Select Italian Proverbs*, 1642.

he that hath no children feedeth them fat (*English*) Those who have no children themselves imagine that if they did they would bring them up very well. R. Sandford, *The Garden of Pleasure*, 1573.

let not a child sleep upon bones (*English*) Do not allow your children to sleep in the nurse's lap. John Ray, *A Collection of English Proverbs*, 1678.

there are no children nowadays (*French*) Children grow up much more quickly than they used to. V.S. Lean, *Collecteana*, 1902–4 (tracing it back 200 years to Molière's play *Le Malade imaginaire*).

what children hear at home soon flies abroad (*English*) Children who overhear private conversations at home are likely to repeat them elsewhere. Randle Cotgrave, *A Dictionary of the French and English Tongues*, 1611. Variants include 'the child says nothing but what it heard by the fire'.

Children pick up words as pigeons peas,
And utter them again as God shall please.

John Ray, *A Collection of English Proverbs*, 1670

when children stand still they have done some ill (*English*) Uncharacteristic quiet in a child is ominous, as it may signify that the child in question is up to no good. George Herbert, *Outlandish Proverbs*, 1640. Another proverb emphasizing the capacity of children to do ill runs 'the devil could not be everywhere so he made children'.

> I remember a wise old gentleman who used to say, 'when children are doing nothing, they are doing mischief.'
>
> Henry Fielding, *Tom Jones*, 1749

~ *See also* BACHELORS' wives and maids' children be well taught; the BEST smell is bread, the best savour salt, the best love that of children; BUILDING and marrying of children are great wasters; a BURNT child dreads the fire; he CARES not whose child cry so his laugh; the DEVIL's children have the devil's luck; GIVE a child all he shall crave and a dog while his tail doth wave and you'll have a fair dog and a foul knave; GIVE me a child for the first seven years, and you may do what you like with him afterwards; HAPPY is he that is happy in his children; HEAVEN protects children, sailors, and drunken men; he that hath a WIFE and children hath given hostages to fortune; he that hath a WIFE and children wants not business; he that MARRIES a widow and three children marries four thieves; he that WIPES the child's nose kisseth the mother's cheek; it is a WISE child that knows its own father; KINDNESS is lost that is bestowed on children and old folks; LATE children, early orphans; MANY kiss the child for the nurse's sake; MONDAY's child is fair of face; the MORE hazelnuts, the more bastard children; NEVER work with children or animals; OLD men are twice children; OLD men will die and children soon forget; ONE father can support ten children; ten children cannot support one father; PRAISE the child, and you make love to the mother; put ANOTHER man's child in your bosom and he'll creep out at your elbow; SPARE the rod and spoil the child; a TRULY great man never puts away the simplicity of a child; what MAINTAINS one vice would bring up two children.

chimney. *See* it is EASIER to build two chimneys than to maintain one; SILKS and satins put out the fire in the chimney; SOLDIERS in peace are like chimneys in summer.

chin. *See* BUTTON up to the chin till May comes in.

chink. so we get the chink, we'll bear with the stink (*Roman*) Providing we get paid, we will put up with any accompanying taint. Sir John Harington, *The Metamorphosis of Ajax*, 1596 (also quoted by Suetonius in *Vespasian* in the second century AD). According to Suetonius, the Emperor Vespasian made the remark *Non olet* (it does not smell) when taking receipt of his taxes on urine.

> But the gain smells not of the excrement.
>
> John Dryden, *To Mr Southern*, 1692

no chink, no drink (*English*) If a person does not have the money for a drink they cannot expect to be served one. T. Pecke, *Parnassi Puerperum*, 1659.

chip. *See* a CARPENTER is known by his chips; he that HEWS too high may get a chip in his eye.

choice. *See* a MAN has choice to begin love but not to end it; there is SMALL choice in rotten apples; you PAYS your money and you takes your choice.

choke. *See* he that EATS the king's goose shall be choked with his feathers; it is IDLE to swallow the cow and choke on the tail; there are MORE ways of killing a cat than choking it with cream; there are MORE ways of killing a dog than choking it with butter.

choleric. from a choleric man withdraw a little, from him that says nothing for ever (*English*) Retreat temporarily from those who are openly angry, but permanently avoid those who remain silent in their anger, for their enmity is much more dangerous. James Mabbe, *Celestina*, 1631.

choose. choose a horse made and a wife to make (*English*) It is best for a man to choose a horse that has already been broken in, but a wife who has yet to be moulded. Randle Cotgrave, *A Dictionary of the French and English Tongues*, 1611. Related proverbs include 'the best horse needs breaking and the aptest child needs teaching'. Another, however, warns that 'he that hath a white horse and a fair wife is never without trouble'.

choose not a house near an inn or in a corner (*English*) It is foolish to choose a house near an inn (because it will be noisy) or in a corner (because the filth of the street will be trapped there). George Herbert, *Outlandish Proverbs*, 1640.

~ *See also* go down the LADDER when thou marriest a wife, go up when thou choosest a friend; NEVER choose your women or your linen by candlelight; of TWO evils choose the lesser.

chooser. *See* BEGGARS can't be choosers.

chose. *See* PLUS ça change, plus c'est la même chose.

Christian. *See* the JEWS spend at Easter, the Moors at marriages, the Christians in suits.

Christmas. Christmas comes but once a year (*English*) Christmas coming only once in the year should be enjoyed to the fullest (often spoken to justify some act of supposed extravagance or self-indulgence). T. Tusser, *Five Hundred Points of Good Husbandry*, 1573.
if at Christmas ice hangs on the willow, clover may be cut at Easter (*English*) Frozen conditions at Christmas are a signal that the spring will be warm and early. Ralph Inwards, *Weather Lore*, 1893.

~ *See also* the DEVIL makes his Christmas pies of lawyers' tongues and clerks' fingers; EASTER in snow, Christmas in mud; Christmas in snow, Easter in mud; if the ICE will bear a man before Christmas, it will not bear a duck after.

church. the church is an anvil which has worn out many hammers (*English*) The Church, though attacked from many quarters, has outlasted its many enemies. Alexander MacLaren, *Acts of the Apostles*, 1908.
church work goes on slowly (*English*) Projects connected with the Church, especially building, always proceed at a notoriously slow pace. Thomas Fuller, *Holy War*, 1639.

> The fifty new churches will ... mend the prospect; but church-work is slow!
>
> Joseph Addison, *Spectator*, 1712

let the church stand in the churchyard (*English*) Leave everything in its proper place. John Ray, *A Collection of English Proverbs*, 1678.

~ *See also* ALL are not saints that go to church; BELLS call others but themselves enter not into the church; the BLOOD of the martyrs is the seed of the Church; he is a GOOD dog who goes to church; in SETTLING an island, the first building erected by a Spaniard will be a church; by a Frenchman, a fort; by a Dutchman, a warehouse; and by an Englishman, an alehouse; the NEARER the church, the further from God; NEW church, old steeple, poor town and proud people; the POORER the church, the purer the church; where GOD builds a church, the devil will build a chapel; WOMEN are saints in church.

church-going. *See* a HOUSE-GOING parson makes a church-going people.

churchyard. *See* a GREEN winter makes a fat churchyard; let the CHURCH stand in the churchyard; a PIECE of a churchyard fits everybody; a YOUNG physician fattens the churchyard.

cider is treacherous because it smiles in the face and then cuts the throat (*English*) Cider tastes pleasant and innocuous in the mouth, but when swallowed quickly overcomes the drinker with its alcoholic power. T. Adams, *Works*, 1653.

circumstances alter cases (*English*) Different decisions may be necessitated by changed circumstances. Thomas Rymer, *The Tragedies of the Last Age*, 1678.

> It is undoubtedly true that circumstances alter cases. I do feel ... that in the present circumstances decisions may have to be reconsidered.
>
> Agatha Christie, *Appointment with Death*, 1938

circus. *See* if you can't RIDE two horses at once, you shouldn't be in the circus.

city. cities are taken by the ears (*English*) The populace of cities are easily swayed by propaganda. George Herbert, *Outlandish Proverbs*, 1640.

~ *See also* if EVERY man would sweep his own doorstep the city would soon be clean; it is the MEN who make a city.

civility. civility costs nothing (*English*) Good manners and politeness cost nothing. J. Stevens, *Spanish and English Dictionary*, 1706. Equivalents in other languages include the Spanish 'there is nothing that costs less than civility'.

~ *See also* there is NOTHING lost by civility.

clad. *See* an APE's an ape, a varlet's a varlet, though they be clad in silk or scarlet; the SLUGGARD must be clad in rags.

clap. *See* when our LADY falls in our Lord's lap, then let England beware a sad clap.

clarty. the clartier the cosier (*Scottish*) The dirtier the quarters, the more comfortable they are likely to prove. Walter Scott, *Antiquities*, 1816.

> There was dirt good store. Yet ... an appearance of ... comfort, that seemed to warrant their old sluttish proverb, 'The clartier the cosier'.
>
> Walter Scott, *Antiquities*, 1816

claw (noun). *See* CATS hide their claws; don't let your JAWS outrun your claws; a GOOSE quill is more dangerous than a lion's claw.

claw (verb). **claw me and I'll claw thee** (*English*) You treat me well, and I will treat you well. J. Palsgrave, *L'Éclaircissement de la langue française*, 1530.

clay. *See* CANDLEMAS Day, put beans in the clay, put candles and candlesticks away; he who BATHES in May will soon be laid in clay, he who bathes in June will sing a merry tune, he who bathes in July will dance like a fly; the SAME heat that melts the wax will harden the clay.

clean. clean heels, light meals (*English*) Cows reared on clay, which promotes the growth of lush grass, will yield more milk than cows reared on lighter sandy soils. R. Holland, *Cheshire Glossary*, 1886.

~ *See also* DIRTY hands make clean money; if EVERY man would sweep his own doorstep the city would soon be clean; a NEW broom sweeps clean.

cleanliness is next to godliness (*Roman*) Keeping the body pure and living life in a blameless fashion are sure to win the approval of heaven. Francis Bacon, *The Advancement of Learning*, 1605. The origins of the proverb have been traced back to the writings of the ancient rabbi Phinehas ben Yair. Acceptance of this notion has been so widespread that at times in the past some religious figures, such as Christian Scientist Mary Baker Eddy, have sought to play down the link between cleanliness and godliness because of their worry that members of their flocks would consider a quick wash alone sufficient to restore their spiritual health.

> Slovenliness is no part of religion; neither this, nor any text of Scripture, condemns neatness of apparel. Certainly this is a duty, not a sin; 'cleanliness is indeed next to godliness'.
>
> John Wesley, *Sermons: On Dress*, *c.*1780

clear. clear autumn, windy winter; warm autumn, long winter (*English*) A fair autumn is a sign of a hard winter to come. R. Inwards, *Weather Lore*, 1893.
a clear conscience can bear any trouble (*English*) Those who are without guilt can withstand trouble better than those whose consciences are uneasy. Thomas Fuller, *Gnomologia*, 1732. Related proverbs include 'a clear conscience is a sure card', 'a good conscience is a soft pillow', 'a clear conscience laughs at false accusations' and the Roman 'a clear conscience is a wall of brass'.

~ *See also* CLOUDY mornings turn to clear afternoons; the EARTHEN pot must keep clear of the brass kettle; if SAINT Paul's Day be fair and clear, it will betide a happy year; no DAY so clear but hath dark clouds; a STRANGER's eye sees clearest.

clergyman. clergymen's sons always turn out badly (*English*) Those brought up by strict religious rules are certain to rebel against them. E.J. Hardy, *How to be Happy though Married*, 1885.

clerk. the clerk makes the justice (*English*) It is often the humble clerk or assistant who does the real work, rather than his master. A. Brome, 'The Leveller', 1660.

> So makeing good the old proverb that the clark makes the justice, while the master does just nothing.
>
> Daniel Defoe, *The Complete Gentleman*, 1729

~ *See also* the CLOCK goes as it pleases the clerk; the DEVIL makes his Christmas pies of lawyers' tongues and clerks' fingers; the GREATEST clerks be not the wisest men; a LEAN fee is a fit reward for a lazy clerk; the PRIEST forgets that he was clerk.

client. *See* a MAN who is his own lawyer has a fool for his client.

climate. *See* TRAVELLERS change climates not conditions.

climb. *See* he that NEVER climbed never fell; he that would EAT the fruit must climb the tree; the HIGHER the monkey climbs the more he shows his tail; when an ASS climbs a ladder we may find wisdom in women.

climber. *See* HASTY climbers have sudden falls.

cloak. *See* ALTHOUGH the sun shine, leave not thy cloak at home; HYPOCRISY can find out a cloak for every rain; it is GOOD to have a cloak for the rain; PRIDE may lurk under a threadbare cloak.

clock. the clock goes as it pleases the clerk (*English*) Bureaucrats often determine how time is to be governed and spent, following their own inclination. John Ray, *A Collection of English Proverbs*, 1678.

~ *See also* KNAVES and whores go by the clock.

clogs. from clogs to clogs is only three generations (*English*) A newly rich family can all too easily be reduced to poverty within the space of three generations. *Notes & Queries*, 1871. This salutary proverb, perhaps meant to console those not newly rich, is thought to have arisen in Lancashire, where clogs were worn by factory and manual workers. Also found as 'twice clogs, once boots'. An alternative Lancashire saying runs 'rags to riches to rags'. *See also* from SHIRTSLEEVES to shirtsleeves in three generations.

cloister. *See* a MONK out of his cloister is like a fish out of water.

close. a close mouth catches no flies (*Italian*) Those who keep their own counsel will not experience unpleasant consequences. J. Minsheu, *A Spanish Grammar, now augmented … by J. Minsheu*, 1599. Variants include 'a close mouth makes a wise head'.

> Not flattering lies shall soothe me more to sing
> with winking eyes,
> And open mouth, for fear of catching flies.
> John Dryden, *Fables*, 1700

cloth. *See* CUT your coat according to your cloth; GOOD ale is meat, drink and cloth; he that DINES and leaves lays the cloth twice; THREE ills come from the north: a cold wind, a shrinking cloth and a dissembling man.

clothe. *See* VICE is often clothed in virtue's habit.

clothes. *See* at EASTER let your clothes be new, or else be sure you will it rue; CRAFT must have clothes but truth loves to go naked; GOOD clothes open all doors.

cloud. when the clouds go up the hills, they'll come down by the mills (*English*) Rain will quickly follow after clouds gather round hilltops. John Ray, *A Collection of English Proverbs*, 1678. Also found as 'when the clouds are upon the hills, they'll come down by the mills' and in the form 'a round-topped cloud, with flattened base, carries rainfall in its face'.

~ *See also* EVERY cloud has a silver lining; no DAY so clear but hath dark clouds; ONE cloud is enough to eclipse all the sun.

cloudy mornings turn to clear afternoons (*English*) A dull morning promises a brighter afternoon (or, alternatively, evening). *Ancrene Riwle*, *c.*1200. Equivalents include 'a misty morning may prove a good day' and 'after clouds, clear weather'.

> Thus cloudy mornynges turne to cleere after
> noones.
> John Heywood, *A Dialogue containing … the Proverbs in the English Tongue*, 1546

~ *See also* if CANDLEMAS Day be sunny and bright winter will have another flight; if Candlemas Day be cloudy with rain, winter is gone and won't come again.

clout. *See* BETTER a clout than a hole out; ne'er CAST a clout till May be out.

cloven. *See* EVERY devil has not a cloven hoof.

clover. *See* if at CHRISTMAS ice hangs on the willow, clover may be cut at Easter.

clown. *See* GIVE a clown a finger and he will take your hand.

clubs are trumps (*English*) Force of arms will overwhelm all opposition. Robert Greene, *Pandosto*, 1588.

> Taking up a cudgel … sware solemnly that she
> would make clubs trump if hee brought any
> bastard brat within her dores.
> Robert Greene, *Pandosto*, 1588

clutch. *See* a DROWNING man will clutch at a straw.

coal. *See* GLOWING coals sparkle oft.

coarse. *See* if the ROBIN sings in the bush then the weather will be coarse; but if the robin sings in the barn then the weather will be warm; the MILL that is always going grinds coarse and fine.

coat. *See* CUT your coat according to your cloth; he who has but ONE coat cannot lend it; it is not the GAY coat that makes the gentleman; NEAR is my coat but nearer my skin; QUARRELSOME dogs get dirty coats.

cob. *See* GIVE a cob a hat and a pair of shoes and he'll last for ever.

cobbler. let the cobbler stick to his last (*Greek*) One should confine one's opinions to what one actually knows about (just as a cobbler should restrict his views to business connected with his last, the foot-shaped wooden or metal device around which he builds his shoes). Pliny, *Natural History*, first century AD (first recorded in English literature in the sixteenth century). The proverb is traditionally ascribed to the Greek painter Apelles, a friend of Alexander the Great, who lived in the fourth century BC. The story goes that a cobbler, unaware of the painter's presence, found fault with one of his portraits, criticizing the execution of a shoe – the artist acted on the man's comments and altered the shoe accordingly, but when the cobbler ventured to criticize the painting of a leg he refused to countenance the artisan's opinion on the grounds it was beyond the province of his expertise (none of his paintings survive). Variants of the proverb run 'the shoemaker must not go above his latchet, nor the hedger meddle with anything but his bill' and 'the cobbler to his last and the gunner to his linstock' (a linstock being the staff that musketeers formerly used to steady their guns in battle).

> Let not the shoemaker go beyond hys shoe.
> R. Taverner, *Proverbs or Adages with New Additions, gathered out of the Chiliades of Erasmus*, 1539

cobweb. where cobwebs are plenty, kisses are scarce (*English*) No one loves a slovenly housewife. *Notes & Queries*, 1864.

cock. if the cock crows on going to bed, he's sure to rise with a watery head (*English*) If a cock crows in the evening, it will rain the following morning. M.A. Denham, *A Collection of Proverbs ... relating to the Weather*, 1846.

if the cock moult before the hen we shall have weather thick and thin, but if the hen moult before the cock we shall have weather hard as a block (*English*) The character of the weather to come may be discerned by observation of the moulting of cocks and hens. John Ray, *A Collection of English Proverbs*, 1670.

~ *See also* a BARLEY-CORN is better than a diamond to a cock; EVERY cock crows on his own dunghill; it is a SAD house where the hen crows louder than the cock; the ROBIN and the wren are God's cock and hen; a SERVANT and a cock should be kept but a year; there's MANY a good cock come out of a tattered bag; the YOUNG cock crows as he heard the old one.

coffin. the coffin is the brother of the cradle (*German*) Death is as much a part of life as birth is.

~ *See also* a SHUT mouth never fills a black coffin.

coin. *See* MUCH coin, much care.

cold. a cold April the barn will fill (*English*) Cold weather in April is a sign of a good harvest to come. J. Howell, *Paroemiographia*, 1659. Another proverb, however, warns that 'a sharp April kills the pig'. Also found as 'April cold and wet fills barn and barrel'.

cold hands, warm heart (*English*) Those who keep their feelings to themselves may turn out to be the most passionate of all (just as a lover with cold hands may well harbour the sincerest love). V.S. Lean, *Collecteana*, 1903. Related proverbs include 'cold of complexion, good of condition'.

> I knew you would be on my side ... cold hand – warm heart. That is the saying, isn't it?
> J.M. Barrie, *Shall We Join the Ladies?*, 1927

cold pudding will settle your love (*English*) A helping of cold pudding will calm the wits and settle the emotions. Samuel Wesley, *Maggots*, 1685.

in the coldest flint there is hot fire (*English*) Even the calmest people can explode with emotion, given sufficient cause. John Lyly, *Euphues*, 1579.

> It lies as coldly in him as fire in a flint, which will not show without knocking.
> William Shakespeare, *Troilus and Cressida*, 1601–2

~ *See also* after a WET year a cold one; as the DAY lengthens, so the cold strengthens; CALF love, half love, old love, cold love; a DOG's nose and a maid's knees are always cold; FEED a cold and starve a fever; HASTY love is soon hot and soon cold; HOT love is soon cold; HUNGER and cold deliver a man up to his enemy; if on the TREES the leaves still hold, the coming winter will be cold; LONGEST at the fire soonest finds cold; REVENGE is a dish that is best eaten cold; a SCALDED cat fears cold water; SOON hot, soon cold; THREE ills come from the north: a cold wind, a shrinking cloth and a dissembling man; the WEST wind always brings wet weather, the east wind wet and cold together, the south wind surely brings us rain, the north wind blows it back again.

collapse. *See* an ANT hole may collapse an embankment.

colour. *See* a BLIND man cannot judge colours; a GOOD horse cannot be of a bad colour.

colt. a colt you may break, but an old horse you never can (*English*) It is possible to train the young, but impossible to change the ways of the old. Thomas Fuller, *Gnomologia*, 1732.

~ *See* a RAGGED colt may make a good horse.

comb. *See* EXPERIENCE is a comb which nature gives us when we are bald.

come. coming events cast their shadows before (*English*) The imminence of change often inspires change itself. T. Campbell, *Lochiel's Warning*, 1802.

> 'Tis the sunset of life gives me mystical love,
> And coming events cast their shadows before.
> T. Campbell, *Lochiel's Warning*, 1802

comfit. *See* CHILDREN are to be deceived with comfits and men with oaths.

comfort. *See* CHILDREN are certain cares but uncertain comforts.

comforter. the comforter's head never aches (*English*) Though others may offer sympathy for the afflicted, they can never actually share the grief or pain that the real sufferer is experiencing. George Herbert, *Outlandish Proverbs*, 1640.

coming. *See* COME.

command. the command of custom is great (*English*) The influence of habit or tradition is not easily ignored. George Herbert, *Outlandish Proverbs*, 1640.

command your man and do it yourself (*English*) A person will always defend their own interests better than another person would. G. Torriano, *Select Italian Proverbs*, 1642.

~ *See also* he is not FIT to command others that cannot command himself; PAY well, command well, hang well; RICHES serve a wise man but command a fool.

commence. he who commences many things finishes but a few (*Italian*) Those who embark on more than one project at a time are unlikely to finish everything they begin. H.G. Bohn, *A Handbook of Proverbs*, 1855.

commend. commend not your wife, wine, nor house (*Italian*) It is immodest to boast of one's own possessions. G. Torriano, *Select Italian Proverbs*, 1642. *See also* SELF-PRAISE is no recommendation.

~ *See also* who ERRS and mends to God himself commends.

comment. *See* don't JUDGE a man by the words of his mother, listen to the comments of his neighbours.

commit. *See* the FIRST faults are theirs that commit them, the second theirs that permit them.

commodious. *See* WATER is as dangerous as commodious.

common. common fame is a common liar (*English*) Rumours are often based on falsehoods. B. Rich, *Faultes*, 1606. Another proverb, however, insists 'common fame is seldom to blame'.

> But common fame, Magnus considered, was a common liar.
> Walter Scott, *The Pirate*, 1821

a common servant is no man's servant (*English*) A servant who answers to several masters is not at the sole command of any of them. J. Sandford, *The Garden of Pleasure*, 1573.

~ *See also* when TWO friends have a common purse one sings and the other weeps.

communication. *See* EVIL communications corrupt good manners.

companion. *See* AGE can be a bad travelling companion; he is an ILL companion that has a good memory; the HUNCHBACK does not see his own hump, but sees his companion's; a MAN knows his companion in a long journey and a little inn.

company. the company makes the feast (*English*) An enjoyable meal with others depends primarily upon who one's fellow-guests are, rather than upon the fare on offer. Izaak Walton, *The Compleat Angler*, 1653.

> 'Tis the company and not the charge that makes the feast.
> Izaak Walton, *The Compleat Angler*, 1653

~ *See also* a CROWD is not company; DESERT and reward seldom keep company; GOOD company is the shortest cut; it is GOOD to have company in misery; KEEP bad men company and you'll soon be of their number; a MAN is known by the company he keeps; MERRY is the company till the reckoning comes; MISERY loves company; SEVEN may be company but nine are confusion; TWO's company, three's a crowd; who KEEPS company with the wolf will learn how to howl.

comparisons are odious (*French/English*) Comparing one thing or person with another is not necessarily helpful and may cause offence. John Lydgate, *Debate Between the Hors, Shepe and Ghoos*, *c.*1430 (also recorded in French in the thirteenth century and found in other European languages). In 1598 Shakespeare turned the proverb into a joke in *Much Ado About Nothing*, with Dogberry delivering it as the malapropism 'comparisons are odorous'. Related proverbs include 'it is comparison that makes men happy or miserable' and 'comparisons make enemies of our friends'.

> But comparisons are odious; another man may write as well as he.
> Henry Fielding, *An Apology for the Life of Mrs Shamela Andrews*, 1742

compel. *See* LOVE cannot be compelled.

complain. he complains wrongfully on the sea who twice suffers shipwreck (*English*) Anyone who suffers a setback has only themselves to blame if they risk a repetition of that same setback. Edmund Spenser, *The Shepheardes Calendar*, 1579 (also recorded in the writings of Publius Syrus). Variants include 'he who is shipwrecked the second time cannot lay the blame on Neptune'. *See also* let another's SHIPWRECK be your sea-mark.

> The Soveraigne of the Seas he blames in vain
> That, once sea-beate, will to sea again.
> Edmund Spenser, *The Shepheardes Calendar*, 1579

~ *See* we are BORN crying, live complaining and die disappointed.

complimenting is lying (*English*) Compliments are rarely truthful. Jonathan Swift, *Polite Conversation*, 1738.

comply. he that complies against his will is of his own opinion still (*English*) A person obliged to cooperate against his will should not be assumed thereby to have given up their former views. Samuel Butler, *Hudibras*, 1678.

> No one should submit their mind to another mind: He that complies against his will is of his own opinion still – that's *my* motto. I won't be brainwashed.
> Muriel Spark, *Mandelbaum Gate*, 1965

conclude. *See* he that THINKS amiss concludes worse.

conceal. *See* ART consists in concealing art; DRUNKENNESS reveals what soberness conceals; it is BETTER to conceal one's knowledge than to reveal one's ignorance.

conceive. *See* a GOOD judge conceives quickly, judges slowly.

condition. *See* TRAVELLERS change climates not conditions.

confess. confess and be hanged (*English*) A man may be hanged on the strength of his own confession. 'Misophonus', *De Caede Gallorum*, 1589.

> Handkerchief – confessions – handkerchief! To confess, and be hanged for his labour.
> William Shakespeare, *Othello*, *c.*1602

~ *See also* a FAULT confessed is half redressed.

confession. *See* a GENEROUS confession disarms slander; OPEN confession is good for the soul.

confidence. confidence is a plant of slow growth (*English*) It takes time to build up confidence. Earl of Chatham, speech, 14 January 1776. Variants include 'confidence is wont to come slowly in matters of great moment', in which form it was quoted by the Roman writer Livy.

~ *See also* SKILL and confidence are an unconquered army.

confusion. *See* SEVEN may be company but nine are confusion.

conquer. *See* LOVE conquers all.

conscience. conscience is a cut-throat (*English*) Conscience is merciless to those who have done wrong. J. Withals, *A Short Dictionary in Latin and English*, 1616. Related proverbs include 'an evil conscience breaks many a man's neck' and 'conscience is the avenging angel in the mind'.

conscience makes cowards of us all (*English*) Those with something to hide are less likely to take risks. William Shakespeare, *Richard III*, *c.*1592.

> Where's thy conscience now? – I'll not meddle with it – it makes a man a coward.
> William Shakespeare, *Richard III*, *c.*1592

~ *See also* a CLEAR conscience can bear any trouble; a GOOD conscience is a continual feast; a GUILTY conscience needs no accuser; he that has no SHAME has no conscience; a QUIET conscience sleeps in thunder.

consent. *See* SILENCE means consent.

consist. *See* ART consists in concealing art.

constant. constant dropping wears away the stone (*Roman*) Perseverance and patient effort will achieve their object in the end, no matter how puny the effort might seem when considered singly (just as a stone will be gradually worn away by dripping water). Ovid, *Epistolae ex Ponto*, first century AD (also found in the writings of Choerilus of Samos). *See also* SLOW but sure wins the race.

> Time's office is to ... waste huge stones with little water-drops.
> William Shakespeare, *The Rape of Lucrece*, *c.*1594

a constant guest is never welcome (*English*) A visitor who keeps on returning will soon outstay his welcome. Thomas Fuller, *Gnomologia*, 1732. Similar sentiments may be found in many other languages, including the Indian 'the first day a guest, the second day a guest, the third day a calamity' and the Chinese 'the guest who outstays his fellow-guests loses his overcoat'. A Spanish version runs 'a guest and a fish stink on the third day', while a saying of US origin observes that 'after three days men grow weary of a wench, a guest, and rainy weather'. The Swedish dourly remind visitors that 'guests should not forget to go home'. *See also* FISH and guests stink after three days.

consume. *See* a CANDLE lights others and consumes itself.

contempt. contempt will sooner kill an injury than revenge (*English*) Contempt for an enemy is more effective than any other kind of revenge. H.G. Bohn, *A Handbook of Proverbs*, 1855. Related proverbs include 'contempt pierces even through the shell of the tortoise'.

~ *See also* FAMILIARITY breeds contempt.

contend. *See* not even HERCULES could contend against two.

content. content is more than a kingdom (*English*) A person with a contented mind has more riches than any monarch possesses. John Clarke, *Paroemiologia Anglo-Latina*, 1639. Variants include 'content is happiness', 'content is worth a crown', 'content is all' and 'content is the philosopher's stone that turns all it touches to gold'.

he who is content in his poverty is wonderfully rich (*English*) Those who can reconcile themselves to what they lack are guaranteed to be happy. R. Dallington, *Aphorisms*, 1613. Related proverbs include 'contentment is the greatest wealth' and the French 'content surpasses wealth'.

~ *See also* he that hath a GOOD harvest may be content with some thistles.

contented. a contented mind is a continual feast (*English*) Those who find content in themselves will find interest in many things. Miles Coverdale, Bible,

Proverbs, 1535. *See also* a GOOD conscience is a continual feast.

> A quiet heart is a continual feast.
> Miles Coverdale, Bible, Proverbs, 1535

continual. *See* a CONTENTED mind is a continual feast; a GOOD conscience is a continual feast.

contrary. *See* DREAMS go by contraries.

convent. *See* a RUNAWAY monk never praises his convent.

conversation. *See* although there EXIST many thousand subjects for elegant conversation, there are persons who cannot meet a cripple without talking about feet.

cook (noun). **a cook is known by his knife** (*English*) A cook's most important possession is his knife. Thomas Fuller, *Gnomologia*, 1732.

~ *See also* EVERY cook praises his own broth; GOD sends meat, but the devil sends cooks; he is a POOR cook that cannot lick his own fingers; too MANY cooks spoil the broth.

cook (verb). *See* CABBAGE twice cooked is death.

cool (adj.). *See* he who has been ANGRY becomes cool again.

cool (verb). *See* MANY irons in the fire, some must cool; SAVE your breath to cool your porridge.

cord. the cord breaketh at the last by the weakest pull (*Spanish*) When something is already greatly weakened, it takes only a slight effort to complete its destruction. Francis Bacon, *Essays*, 1625. *See also* it is the LAST straw breaks the camel's back.

Corinth. *See* it is not GIVEN to every man to go to Corinth.

corn. there is corn in Egypt (*Hebrew*) There is a plentiful supply of something. Charles Lamb, *Letters*, 1834. The proverb is derived from the biblical story of Joseph in Egypt (Genesis 43:2).

> There is corn in Egypt while there is cash at Leadenhall.
> Charles Lamb, *Letters*, 1834

up corn, down horn (*English*) If corn prices go up, then the price of beef will come down (because people will have less money to spend on it and demand will be reduced). A contrasting proverb (first recorded by John Ray in *A Collection of English Proverbs* in 1678) runs 'corn and horn go together', suggesting that the prices of the two commodities rise and fall together.

~ *See also* CALM weather in June sets corn in tune; don't MEASURE other people's corn by one's own bushel; GENTRY sent to market will not buy one bushel of corn; if the BRAIN sows not corn, it plants thistles; a LITTLE fire burns up a great deal of corn; the WEEDS overgrow the corn.

corner. See CHOOSE not a house near an inn or in a corner.

corporations have neither bodies to be punished nor souls to be damned (*English*) Large organizations are impervious to the threat of physical punishment or the dictates of morality, in contrast to individuals. E. Bulstrode, *Reports*, 1658.

corrupt. *See* EVIL communications corrupt good manners; POWER corrupts.

corruption of the best becomes the worst (*Roman*) The corruption of the best is the worst kind of corruption. William Shakespeare, *Sonnets*, 1609. Also encountered in the form 'the best things corrupted become the worst'.

cost (noun). *See* he that COUNTS all costs will never put plough in the earth; it is GOOD to learn at other men's cost; the MORE cost, the more honour.

cost (verb). *See* CIVILITY costs nothing; NOTHING costs so much as what is given us.

costly. *See* AGREE, for the law is costly.

cosy. *See* the CLARTIER, the cosier.

cottage. *See* LOVE lives in cottages as well as in courts.

cough. *See* a DRY cough is the trumpeter of death; if you DRINK in your pottage, you'll cough in your grave; LOVE and a cough cannot be hid.

councils of war never fight (*English*) Committees (especially councils of war) typically fail to commit themselves to battle – or any other course of action – as promptly as individuals might. H.W. Halleck, telegram, 1863 (popularly attributed originally to Solomon).

> Act upon your own judgment and make your Generals execute your orders. Call no counsel of war. It is proverbial that counsels of war never fight.
>
> Henry Wager Halleck, telegram, 13 July 1863

counsel (noun). **come not to counsel uncalled** (*English*) Do not offer advice unless it is asked for. R. Taverner, *Proverbs or Adages with New Additions, gathered out of the Chiliades of Erasmus*, 1539. Related proverbs include 'he who comes uncalled sits unserved'.

if the counsel be good, no matter who gave it (*English*) Good advice should be welcome, regardless of what quarter it comes from. Thomas Fuller, *Gnomologia*, 1732. Variants include 'good counsel never comes amiss' and 'good counsel does no harm'. Another proverb rather sourly observes 'good counsel is lacking when most needed'.

~ *See also* a FOOL may give a wise man counsel; GIVE neither counsel nor salt till you are asked for it; GOOD counsel never comes amiss; if the OLD dog bark, he gives counsel; NIGHT is the mother of counsel; SHORT counsel is good counsel; WINE counsels seldom prosper.

counsel (verb). **he that will not be counselled cannot be helped** (*English*) There is no helping those who will not listen to advice. J. Clarke, *Paroemiologia Anglo-Latina*, 1639.

count. don't count your chickens before they are hatched (*Greek*) Never presume that something will turn out well before it has actually happened. T. Howell, *New Sonnets*, *c.*1570 (also quoted by Philemon). The sentiment behind the proverb was the subject of 'The Milkmaid and the Pail', one of Aesop's *Fables* of the sixth century BC. In this tale a milkmaid, walking along with her pail of milk balanced on her head, daydreams about the eggs she will buy with the money she gets for the butter she is going to make with the milk; how she will sell the chickens these hatch into to buy a pretty dress; and how, with this, she will attract the attention of well-heeled young men. These, she fancies, she will be in a position to reject, on the basis of her new-found wealth as a raiser of chickens. Unfortunately, in practising the flounce with which she will turn down all but the most desirable suitors, she loses her balance and the pail of milk falls to the ground. According to Walter Scott, in his journal for 20 May 1829, it is foolhardy to presume one's 'chickens' will hatch out as intended, 'even though they are chipping the shell now'. A related Dutch proverb runs 'you can't hatch chickens from fried eggs'. Other equivalents in English advise 'make not your sauce before you have caught the fish' and 'don't sell the bear's skin before the bear has been caught'. *See also* don't HALLOO till you are out of the wood; FIRST catch your hare; GUT no fish till you get them; there's MANY a slip 'twixt cup and lip.

> To swallow Gudgeons ere th'are catch'd, And
> count their Chickens ere th'are hatch'd.
>
> Samuel Butler, *Hudibras*, 1664

he that counts all costs will never put plough in the earth (*Scottish*) A person who worries too much about what might go wrong will never get anything done. David Fergusson, *Scottish Proverbs*, 1641.

~ *See also* MEN count up the faults of those who keep them waiting.

country. in the country of the blind, the one-eyed man is king (*English*) When all others are totally ignorant (or foolish), a man who possesses even slight knowledge (or slight cunning) may claim precedence. Erasmus, *Adagia*, 1536. Also found in several other languages in addition to English. H.G. Wells wrote a short story on the theme suggested by the proverb, under the title 'The Country of the Blind' (1911).

> A man were better be half blind than have both
> his eyes out.
>
> John Ray, *A Collection of English Proverbs*, 1678

our country, right or wrong (*English*) Expressing unswerving support for one's native country, regardless of whether that country is in the right or not. S. Decatur, *Toast*, 1816. Also encountered in the form 'my wife, right or wrong'.

~ *See also* ALL countries stand in need of Britain; GOD made the country, and man made the town; HAPPY is the country which has no history; a PROPHET is not without honour save in his own country; the SMOKE of a man's own country is better than the fire of another's; so MANY countries, so many customs; there's ONE good wife in the country, and every man thinks he hath her.

couple. when a couple are newly married the first month is honeymoon, or smick smack; the second is hither and thither; the third is thwick thwack; the fourth the devil take them that brought thee and I together (*English*) It takes just four months for the relationships of newly wed couples to degenerate from complete happiness to total hostility. John Ray, *A Collection of English Proverbs*, 1670.

~ *See also* a DEAF husband and a blind wife are always a happy couple.

courage. *See* DESPAIR gives courage to a coward.

course. the course of true love never did run smooth (*English*) Love affairs are typically tempestuous and likely to encounter difficulty. William Shakespeare, *A Midsummer Night's Dream*, *c*.1596.

> Ay me! for aught that I could ever read,
> Could ever hear by tale or history,
> The course of true love never did run smooth.
> William Shakespeare, *A Midsummer Night's Dream*, *c*.1596

~ *See also* ANOTHER course would have done it; DISEASE will have its course; HORSES for courses; NATURE will have its course.

court (noun). *See* a FRIEND in court is better than a penny in purse; HOME is home, as the devil said when he found himself in the Court of Session; LOVE lives in cottages as well as in courts.

court (verb). *See* BEWARE of the oak, it draws the stroke; avoid the ash, it courts the flash.

courtesy. courtesy on one side never lasts long (*French*) Politeness that is not returned will not last. George Herbert, *Outlandish Proverbs*, 1640.

~ *See also* FULL of courtesy, full of craft; LESS of your courtesy and more of your purse.

cousin. *See* I wouldn't CALL the king my cousin.

coûte. *See* CE n'est que le premier pas qui coûte.

cover (noun). *See* you can't JUDGE a book by its cover.

cover (verb). *See* CHARITY covers a multitude of sins; an HONEST look covereth many faults.

coverlet. *See* EVERYONE stretches his legs according to the length of his coverlet.

cow. the cow gives good milk but kicks over the pail (*English*) Some people undo all the work they do through temperamental outbursts. John Heywood, *A Dialogue containing … the Proverbs in the English Tongue*, 1546.

the cow knows not the worth of her tail till she loses it (*English*) The value of some things is apparent only when they are gone. George Herbert, *Outlandish Proverbs*, 1640. Another proverb runs 'if you buy the cow, take the tail into the bargain'.

the cow that's first up gets the first of the dew (*English*) Those who rise early get the greatest benefit. James Kelly, *A Complete Collection of Scottish Proverbs*, 1721.

~ *See also* a BELLOWING cow soon forgets her calf; BETTER a good cow than a cow of a good kind; BRING a cow to the hall and she'll run to the byre; BUTTER is once a year in the cow's horn; a CURST cow has short horns; if you BUY the cow, take the tail into the bargain; it is IDLE to swallow the cow and choke on the tail; MANY a good cow hath an evil calf; THREE things are not to be trusted: a cow's horn, a dog's tooth and a horse's hoof; why BUY a cow when milk is so cheap?; you cannot SELL the cow and sup the milk.

coward. cowards are cruel (*English*) Those who are afraid are inclined to show little mercy to others. Sir Thomas Malory, *Le Morte d'Arthur*, 1485. Related proverbs include 'cruelty is a tyrant that's always attended with fear'.

> The magistrates are … frightened, and, like all cowards, show a tendency to be cruel.
> Charlotte Brontë, *Shirley*, 1849

cowards die many times before their death (*English*) Those who lack courage imagine the terror of death often before they actually experience it. William Shakespeare, *Julius Caesar*, 1599 (also found, as 'every houre he dyes, which ever feares', in Michael Drayton's *Mortimeriados* in 1596). Also found as 'cowards die often' and as 'cowards die daily, the brave but once'.

> Cowards die many times before their deaths:
> The valiant never taste of death but once.
> William Shakespeare, *Julius Caesar*, 1599

put a coward to his mettle and he'll fight the devil (*English*) In the last resort cowards will fight as desperately as any other person. Robert Herrick, *Hesperides*, 1648. Variants include 'a coward's fear can make a coward valiant'.

~ *See also* a BULLY is always a coward; CONSCIENCE makes cowards of us all; DESPAIR gives courage to a coward; NECESSITY and opportunity may make a coward valiant.

cowl. the cowl does not make the monk (*French*) Do not rely upon appearances as an indication of character. *Ayenbite of Inwit*, 1340. Also found as 'the habit does not make the monk' and 'the hood does not make the monk'. *See also* APPEARANCES are deceptive.

> Such impostures are sure of support from the sort of people ... who think that it is the cowl that makes the monk.
> George Bernard Shaw, *Music in London*, 1891

cow-turd. *See* a HUMBLE-BEE in a cow-turd thinks himself a king.

crab. *See* the GREATEST crabs be not all the best meat; the OLDER the crab-tree the more crabs it bears.

crab-tree. *See* HANG a dog on a crab-tree and he'll never love verjuice; the OLDER the crab-tree the more crabs it bears; PLANT the crab-tree where you will, it will never bear pippins.

crack (noun). **Crack was a good dog but he got hung for barking** (*English*) Those who are given to boasting will inevitably come to a bad end. S.O. Addy, *Sheffield Glossary Supplement*, 1891.

crack (verb). **a cracked bell can never sound well** (*English*) Underlying weaknesses will always reveal themselves eventually (often referring to people of weak or impaired intellect). T. Adams, *Sermons*, 1629. Also encountered in the form 'a cracked bell is never sound'.

cradle. *See* the COFFIN is the brother of the cradle; the HAND that rocks the cradle rules the world.

craft. craft must have clothes but truth loves to go naked (*English*) Cunning must be disguised, whereas the truth needs no concealing. *Politeuphuia*, 1597, attributed to J Bodenham.

~ *See also* FULL of courtesy, full of craft.

crafty. a crafty fellow never has any peace (*English*) Those who rely on their cunning cannot afford to relax for a moment. Thomas Fuller, *Gnomologia*, 1732.

a crafty knave needs no broker (*English*) Cunning people do not need someone else to act on their behalf. John Heywood, *A Dialogue containing ... the Proverbs in the English Tongue*, 1546.

> That cannot be, if the proverb hold; for a crafty knave needs no broker.
> Ben Jonson, *Every Man in his Humour*, 1598

crane. *See* as SORE fight wrens as cranes.

crave. *See* GIVE a child all he shall crave and a dog while his tail doth wave and you'll have a fair dog and a foul knave.

creak. creaking doors hang the longest (*English*) Those who long suffer ill health often outlive those who are in apparently rude health. T. Coggan, *John Buncle, Junior*, 1776. Alternative versions run 'cracked pots last longest' and 'a creaking cart goes long on the wheels'.

cream. *See* the CAT shuts its eyes while it steals cream; there are MORE ways of killing a cat than choking it with cream.

create. *See* do not BLAME God for having created the tiger, but thank him for not having given it wings.

credit (noun). *See* GIVE credit where credit is due.

credit (verb). *See* THREE things are not to be credited.

creditors have better memories than debtors (*Spanish*) It is easier to forget what one owes than what one is owed. J. Howell, *Paroemiographia*, 1659.

> When you have got your bargain; you may, perhaps, think little of payment, but ... Creditors ... have better memories than Debtors.
> Benjamin Franklin, *English Garner*, 1758

creep. *See* LOVE will creep where it cannot go; put

ANOTHER man's child in your bosom and he'll creep out at your elbow.

cries. *See* CRY.

crime. *See* POVERTY is not a crime.

criminal. *See* MERCY to the criminal may be cruelty to the people.

cripple. *See* although there EXIST many thousand subjects for elegant conversation, there are persons who cannot meet a cripple without talking about feet; it is HARD halting before a cripple.

crooked logs make straight fires (*English*) In some circumstances it makes no difference whether a person or object has some flaw or other, because the end result will be the same. Randle Cotgrave, *A Dictionary of the French and English Tongues*, 1611.

crop. *See* GOOD seed makes a good crop.

cross (noun). **crosses are ladders that lead to heaven** (*English*) It is through coping with troubles and suffering that a person may prove his worth and finally earn his heavenly reward. T. Draxe, *Adages*, 1616.
no cross, no crown (*English*) There is no enjoying the prize without some effort or sacrifice first. Francis Quarles, *Ester*, 1621.

~ *See also* the DEVIL lurks behind the cross; EACH cross hath its inscription; where no one else will, the DEVIL must bear the cross.

cross (verb). **cross the stream where it is ebbest** (*English*) It is sensible to take the easiest course (ebbest signifying 'shallowest'). Philemon Holland, *Plutarch's Morals*, 1603.
don't cross the bridge until you get to it (*English*) Don't worry about possible future problems until they actually arise. Henry Wadsworth Longfellow, *Journal*, 29 April 1850. Earlier variants of the proverb include 'you must not leape over the stile before you come to it', recorded in Henry Porter's *The Two Angrie Women* in 1599. *See also* SUFFICIENT unto the day is the evil thereof.

crow (noun). **a crow on the thatch, soon death lifts the latch** (*English*) If a crow (or raven) perches on the roof of a house then a member of the household will soon die. M'Crie, *Scotch Church History*, 1841. This time-honoured superstition, dating back to classical times, has its origins in the notion that all black birds are portents of evil. It is also supposed to be ominous if a crow taps at the windowpane or settles in the churchyard. A counter-charm recorded in northern England runs 'crow, crow, get out of my sight, or else I'll eat thy liver and thy lights'.

> By the will of the Fates ... your respective lots have been assigned ... to the raven prophecy, unfavourable omens to the crow.
> Phaedrus, *Fables*, AD35

the crow thinks her own birds fairest (*English*) Every mother thinks her own offspring the most beautiful of all, regardless of how others may see them. Gavin Douglas, *Aeneis*, 1513. Also encountered in the form 'the crow thinks her own bird whitest'.

> You think you never heard of this wonderful son of mine, Miss Hale. You think I'm an old woman whose ... own crow is the whitest ever seen.
> Elizabeth Gaskell, *North and South*, 1855

~ *See also* CARRION crows bewail the dead sheep and then eat them; ONE for the mouse, one for the crow, one to rot, one to grow; on the FIRST of March, the crows begin to search.

crow (verb). *See* EVERY cock crows on his own dunghill; if the COCK crows on going to bed, he's sure to rise with a watery head; it is a SAD house where the hen crows louder than the cock; a WHISTLING woman and a crowing hen are neither fit for God nor men; the YOUNG cock crows as he heard the old one.

crowd. a crowd is not company (*English*) A person can feel lonely even within a crowd of strangers. Francis Bacon, *Essays*, 1625.

~ *See also* TWO's company, three's a crowd.

crown. a crown is no cure for the headache (*English*) Even monarchs are subject to ordinary physical ailments. Joseph Hall, *Contemplations*, 1612–15.

> The royal crown cures not the headache.
> Benjamin Franklin, *Poor Richard's Almanack*, August 1757

~ *See also* the END crowns the work; the EVENING crowns the day; no CROSS, no crown; a KING without learning is but a crowned ass.

cruel. you've got to be cruel to be kind (*French*) In some circumstances it is necessary to act in what appears to be a harsh manner in order to save another from greater harm in the long run. Early variants of the proverb include the Italian saying 'sometimes clemency is cruelty and cruelty is clemency'. Similar sentiments were expressed by writers as far back as the classical world, with Sophocles quoting something along similar lines in 409BC. Legend has it that in 1572 Catherine de' Medici quoted the proverb on the eve of Saint Bartholomew's Day (24 August) to justify her son Charles IX's massacre of the French Huguenots, which led to some 50,000 deaths. *See also* SPARE the rod and spoil the child.

> I must be cruel, only to be kind.
> William Shakespeare, *Hamlet*, c.1600

~ *See also* COWARDS are cruel.

cruelty. *See* MERCY to the criminal may be cruelty to the people.

crust. *See* it's an ILL dog that deserves not a crust.

crutch. *See* LITERATURE is a good staff but a bad crutch.

cry. *See* he CARES not whose child cry so his laugh; it's no USE crying over spilt milk; the LAPWING cries farthest from her nest; LAUGH before breakfast, you'll cry before supper; MUCH cry and little wool; no MAN cries stinking fish; we are BORN crying, live complaining and die disappointed; we must not LIE down and cry God help us.

cuckold. *See* in RAIN and sunshine cuckolds go to heaven; it is BETTER to be a cuckold and not know it, than be none and everybody say so.

cuckoo. the cuckoo comes in April, and stays the month of May, sings a song at midsummer, and then goes away (*English*) Traditional rhyme delineating the months in which the cuckoo may be found in England. W.C. Hazlitt, *English Proverbs*, 1869. One variant runs 'the cuckoo comes in mid-March, sings in mid-April, struts in mid-May and in mid-June flies away', while yet another insists that 'in April, come he will; in May, he sings all day; in June he alters his tune; in July, he prepares to fly; in August, go he must; if he stay till September, 'tis as much as the oldest man can ever remember'.

when the cuckoo comes he eats up all the dirt (*English*) The first call of the cuckoo signals the end of wet winter weather (and the consequent drying of mud). *Yea and Nay Almanack*, April 1680.

~ *See also* the NIGHTINGALE and cuckoo sing both in one month.

cudgel. *See* REASON governs the wise man and cudgels the fool.

cunning is no burden (*German*) It is no hardship to be skilled at something. R. Taverner, *Proverbs or Adages with New Additions, gathered out of the Chiliades of Erasmus*, 1539.

> Skill is no burthen.
> Thomas Fuller, *Gnomologia*, 1732

cup. *See* FULL cup, steady hand; the LAST drop makes the cup run over; POISON is poison though it comes in a golden cup; there's MANY a slip 'twixt cup and lip.

Cupar. he that will to Cupar maun to Cupar (*Scottish*) Obstinate persons cannot be dissuaded from pursuing their course, however misguided it may be. Walter Scott, *Rob Roy*, 1818. The proverb has its origins in the historical fact that the Fife Courts of Justice were formerly sited at Cupar, a town in Fife, which thus became a risky place to be.

> The Heccate ... ejaculated, 'A wilfu' man will hae his way: them that will to Cupar maun to Cupar!'
> Walter Scott, *Rob Roy*, 1818

cupboard. *See* EVERY family has a skeleton in the cupboard.

cur. *See* BRAWLING curs never want sore ears; YELPING curs will raise mastiffs.

cure (noun). *See* CARE is no cure; a CROWN is no cure for the headache; PAST cure, past care; PREVENTION is better than cure; that SICK man is not to be pitied who hath his cure in his sleeve.

cure (verb). **what can't be cured must be endured** (*English*) What cannot be changed must be put up with. William Langland, *Piers Plowman*, 1377.

What was over couldn't be begun, and what couldn't be cured must be endured.
Charles Dickens, *Pickwick Papers*, 1837

~ *See also* DIET cures more than doctors; a DISEASE known is half cured; he is a GOOD physician who cures himself; if the DOCTOR cures, the sun sees it, but if he kills, the earth hides it; LIKE cures like; no HERB will cure love; PITY cureth envy.

curiosity killed the cat (*English*) There are risks in being too inquisitive. Eugene O'Neill, *Diff'rent*, 1921. The origins of this proverb are obscure, although there is clearly a reference to the natural curiosity for which cats are notorious (though one variant replaces the cat with a monkey). Complementary proverbs include 'curiosity is ill manners in another's house' (first recorded in 1622) and 'curiosity is endless, restless, and useless'. *See also* CARE killed the cat.

curry. *See* a SHORT horse is soon curried.

curse (noun)**. curses, like chickens, come home to roost** (*English*) Those who wish ill on others will only find their malice eventually rebounds on them (just as chickens return to their roosts at the end of the day). Robert Southey, *Curse of Kehama*, 1809 (also found in an early form in Geoffrey Chaucer's 'The Parson's Tale', *The Canterbury Tales*, *c.*1387). Some variants have the curses, like arrows or stones, rising into the air and then falling back down on to the head of the person who uttered them: 'I have heard a good man say, that a curse was like a stone flung up to the heavens, and maist like to return on the head that sent it' (Walter Scott, *Old Mortality*, 1816).

Curses, like rookses, flies home to nest in bosomses and barnses.
Stella Gibbons, *Cold Comfort Farm*, 1932

curse (verb)**. he was cursed in his mother's belly that was killed by a cannon** (*English*) Those who are killed by cannon shot must have been cursed since even before their birth (an allusion to the bad luck associated with any death resulting from cannon fire, which was formerly wildly inaccurate). William Camden, *Remains concerning Britain*, 1614.

Yet do I not believe what soldiers commonly say, 'that he was cursed in his mother's belly, who is killed with a cannon'.
Thomas Fuller, *Gnomologia*, 1732

~ *See also* the MORE a fox is cursed, the better he fares.

curst. a curst cow has short horns (*English*) Vengeful persons are rarely in a position to do as much mischief as they would like. Geoffrey Chaucer, *Eight Goodly Questions*, 1375. Sometimes encountered in Latin, as *Dat Deus immiti cornua curta bovi*.

A curst cow hath oftentimes short hornes, and a willing minde but a weake arm.
Robert Greene, *Pandosto*, 1588

custom. custom is a second nature (*Roman*) Things done by long habit can become part of a person's character. John Gower, *Confessio Amantis*, *c.*1390 (quoting Cicero). Another Roman proverb, however, insists that 'never can custom conquer nature'.

Habit and use, as we read, are second nature.
Mrs Henry Wood, *Trevlyn Hold*, 1864

custom without reason is but ancient error (*English*) Those who do things purely out of habit rather than reason are merely repeating the same mistake. *Politeuphuia*, 1597, attributed to J Bodenham. Variants include 'custom is a master that makes a slave of reason' and 'custom is the reason of fools'. A Scottish proverb advises 'break the legs o' an ill custom'.

~ *See also* a BAD custom is like a good cake, better broken than kept; the COMMAND of custom is great; so MANY countries, so many customs.

customer. the customer is always right (*English/US*) In business, the wishes of the customer must always be paramount. Carl Sandburg, *Good Morning, America*, 1928. There is much debate over who coined this business axiom, with authorities arguing both British and US claims for the honour. Those credited with coining it include the business tycoon H. Gordon Selfridge (*c.*1864–1947), who was born in the USA but later took British citizenship and who adopted the proverb as the motto for his Selfridges retail store. It has also been attributed to US retailer John Wanamaker (1838–1922), whose stores bear his name.

cut (noun)**.** *See* GOOD company is the shortest cut; the SHORT cut is often the longest way round.

cut (verb)**. cut not the bough that thou standest upon** (*English*) Do not act against your own interests by damaging something you depend on (often addressed to people in positions of power who ride roughshod over the wishes of the populace in general). William Tyndale, *The Obedience of a Christian Man*, 1528.

cut your coat according to your cloth (*English*) Compromise according to what is reasonable, bearing in mind your resources (financial or otherwise). John Heywood, *A Dialogue Containing … the Proverbs in the English Tongue*, 1546. Historically, the proverb may well reflect the laws that governed the amount of cloth that English citizens were permitted to wear (laid down according to social rank by an Act of Parliament passed in 1533). These laws were introduced in the wake of the Black Death, as a result of which surviving labourers had been able to demand higher wages and thus pay for better clothes, thereby obscuring class distinctions (which the higher classes naturally wished to retain).

> I love your wit well, sir; but I must cut my coat according to my cloth.
>
> John Dryden, *The Wild Gallant*, 1669

don't cut off your nose to spite your face (*French*) Do not indulge in petty or more serious acts of malice that will ultimately result only in harm to yourself. *Deceit of Women*, *c.*1560 (also recorded in the writings of Peter of Blois, 1200, and in variant forms in the works of Roman authors). Other versions include 'he that biteth his nose off, shameth his face', and Chinese equivalents include 'don't burn down your house even to annoy your chief wife's mother' and 'don't thrust your fingers through your own lantern'.

> He cut off his nose to be revenged of his face, said of one who, to be revenged of his neighbour, has materially injured himself.
>
> Francis Grose, *Dictionary of the Vulgar Tongue*, 1788

~ *See also* CIDER is treacherous because it smiles in the face and then cuts the throat; DIAMOND cuts diamond; a FOOL's tongue is long enough to cut his own throat; go to BATTERSEA to get your simples cut; if at CHRISTMAS ice hangs on the willow, clover may be cut at Easter; let not your TONGUE cut your throat; MEASURE thrice and cut once; MEN cut large thongs of other men's leather; the SAME knife cuts bread and fingers; SAVE a thief from the gallows and he shall cut your throat; SCORE twice before you cut once; a SLICE off a cut loaf isn't missed; the TAILOR must cut three sleeves to every woman's gown; the TONGUE is not steel yet it cuts.

cut-throat. *See* CONSCIENCE is a cut-throat.

D

dainty. who dainties love, shall beggars prove (*English*) Those with expensive tastes will soon be reduced to penury. T. Tusser, *Five Hundred Points of Good Husbandry*, 1573. On similar lines are 'dainty makes dearth', 'dear bought and far fetched are dainties for ladies' and 'the dainties of the great are the tears of the poor'.

> You know the proverb – those that are dainty …
> Hannah Cowley, *More Ways Than One*, 1783

daisy. *See* it is not SPRING until you can plant your foot upon twelve daisies.

dally not with women or money (*English*) It is dangerous to trifle with either women or money. George Herbert, *Outlandish Proverbs*, 1640.

dam. where the dam leaps over, the kid follows (*English*) The young or inexperienced will follow the example of their peers. Thomas Fuller, *Gnomologia*, 1732.

damage. *See* WANT of care does us more damage than want of knowledge.

damn. *See* CORPORATIONS have neither bodies to be punished nor souls to be damned.

dance. they that dance must pay the fiddler (*US*) Those who want to enjoy themselves must be prepared to pay for their enjoyment themselves. J. Taylor, *Taylor's Feast*, 1638. Related proverbs include 'he'll dance to nothing but his own pipe', 'he dances well to whom fortune pipes' and 'those who dance are thought mad by those who hear not the music'. *See also* he who PAYS the piper calls the tune.

> I am decidedly opposed to the people's money being used to pay the fiddler. It is an old maxim and a very sound one, that he that dances should always pay the fiddler.
> Abraham Lincoln, speech, 11 January 1837

when you go to dance take heed whom you take by the hand (*English*) How well one dances depends on one's choice of partner (usually addressed to those who are suspected of having been imprudent in their choice of partner in some enterprise). J. Clarke, *Paroemiologia Anglo-Latina*, 1639.

~ *See also* ALL are not merry that dance; the DEVIL dances in an empty pocket; he that LIVES in hope dances to an ill tune; he who BATHES in May will soon be laid in clay, he who bathes in June will sing a merry tune, he who bathes in July will dance like a fly.

danger. a danger foreseen is half avoided (*English*) Knowledge of a threat goes a long way to enabling a person to escape it. R. Franck, *Northern Memoirs*, 1658. The Spanish, however, have the contrasting saying 'he who sees danger perishes in it'.

danger is next neighbour to security (*English*) Those who have great faith in the security of their own position are often thereby those who are most open to danger. James Kelly, *A Complete Collection of Scottish Proverbs*, 1721.

the danger past and God forgotten (*English*) Those in trouble may call on God to help them, but neglect to show any gratitude afterwards or to remember any promises made. Randle Cotgrave, *A Dictionary of the French and English Tongues,* 1611.

Proverbs on similar lines include 'danger is sauce for prayers' (recorded by Benjamin Franklin). *See also* the DEVIL sick would be a monk.

> In time of danger and affliction men will address themselves earnestly to God for relief.
>
> James Kelly, *A Complete Collection of Scottish Proverbs*, 1721

dangers are overcome by dangers (*Roman*) It is sometimes only through taking further risks that risk may be overcome. George Herbert, *Outlandish Proverbs*, 1651. Also encountered in the form 'without danger we cannot get beyond danger'. Other variants include 'danger itself the best remedy for danger', 'a danger is never overcome without danger', and 'without danger we cannot be beyond danger'.

~ *See also* he that BRINGETH himself into needless dangers dieth the devil's martyr; the MORE danger, the more honour; NOUGHT is never in danger; out of DEBT, out of danger; out of OFFICE, out of danger; the POST of honour is the post of danger; SNEEZE on a Monday, you sneeze for danger; when we have GOLD we are in fear, when we have none we are in danger.

dangerous. it is a dangerous fire begins in the bed straw (*English*) Marital discord is often the most damaging. Geoffrey Chaucer, 'The Merchant's Tale', *The Canterbury Tales*, *c.*1387.

~ *See also* DELAYS are dangerous; a GOOSE quill is more dangerous than a lion's claw; a LITTLE learning is a dangerous thing; METTLE is dangerous in a blind horse; WATER is as dangerous as commodious.

dare. *See* it is a BAD cause that none dare speak in; one may THINK that dares not speak.

dark. the darkest hour is just before the dawn (*English*) Things may seem their worst just before they get better. Thomas Fuller, *A Pisgah-Sight of Palestine*, 1650. The same sentiment may be found in various forms in numerous other languages, including, to take just one example, Persian: 'it is at the narrowest part of the defile that the valley begins to open'. *See also* when BALE is highest, boot is nighest; HOPE springs eternal in the human breast; never SAY die.

> It is usually darkest before day break. You shall shortly find pardon.
>
> John Wesley, *Journal*, 1760

~ *See also* ALL cats are grey in the dark; he that GIVES to be seen will relieve none in the dark; he that GROPES in the dark finds that he would not; it is ILL to drive black hogs in the dark; JOAN is as good as my lady in the dark; a MAN's destiny is always dark; no DAY so clear but hath dark clouds.

darling. *See* BETTER be an old man's darling than a young man's slave.

dash. *See* FOLLOW not truth too near the heels, lest it dash out thy teeth.

daughter. daughters and dead fish are no keeping wares (*English*) Daughters, like the flesh of caught fish, do not improve with long keeping, but need to be disposed of (through marriage) while still at their best. Thomas Fuller, *Gnomologia*, 1732. Variants include the Welsh proverb 'the worst store is a maid unbestowed'.

he that would the daughter win, must with the mother first begin (*English*) To court a girl successfully, a young man does well to win the approval of her mother first. John Ray, *A Collection of English Proverbs*, 1670. *See also* PRAISE the child and you make love to the mother.

~ *See also* ADMIRATION is the daughter of ignorance; a LIGHT heeled mother makes a heavy heeled daughter; like MOTHER, like daughter; my SON is my son till he gets him a wife, but my daughter's my daughter all the days of her life; the OWL was a baker's daughter; TWO daughters and a back door are three arrant thieves; WONDER is the daughter of ignorance.

dawb. *See* DRINK washes off the dawb and discovers the man.

dawn. *See* the DARKEST hour is just before the dawn.

day. as the day lengthens, so the cold strengthens (*English*) The weather at the start of the year, when the days are growing longer, is often colder than the weather before the New Year. E. Pellham, *God's Power*, 1631. Another proverb advises 'as the days grow longer, the storms grow stronger', while another claims 'as the days begin to shorten, the heat begins to scorch them'.

> At the time of writing we have just enjoyed a virtually

frost-free January, and it was followed by two mild winter months and then heat-waves and drought in April, May and June. *As the day lengthens, so the cold strengthens* is usually correct, however.

Ralph Whitlock, *March Winds and April Showers*, 1993

be the day never so long, at length cometh evensong (*English*) Even the longest day must come to an end eventually. John Gower, *Confessio Amantis*, *c.*1390.

Yet is he sure be the daie neuer so long,
Evermore at laste they ryng to euensong.

John Heywood, *A Dialogue containing ... the Proverbs in the English Tongue*, 1546

come day, go day, God send Sunday (*English*) May the working week pass quickly until Sunday (the traditional pay-day for servants) arrives. T. Draxe, *Bibliotheca Scholastica*, 1616.

Spoken to lazy, unconscionable servants, who only mind to serve out their time, and get their wages.

James Kelly, *A Complete Collection of Scotish Proverbs*, 1721

the day is short and the work is long (*English*) A man's life is short and there is a great deal he must do in the time he has been allotted. *Beryn*, *c.*1400. Also found in the form 'the day is short and the work is much'.

no day passeth without some grief (*English*) Each day brings its share of misfortune. R. Codrington, *The Second Part of Youth's Behaviour*, 1664. Related proverbs include 'no day so clear but hath dark clouds'.

no day so clear but hath dark clouds (*English*) Difficulties always arise, even when things are generally going well. George Herbert, *Outlandish Proverbs*, 1651.

no day without a line (*Roman*) Each day has its work to be done. John Lyly, *Euphues: The Anatomy of Wit*, 1578. Lyly attributed it to the classical painter Apelles, who never let a day pass without doing some work on his paintings. Sometimes encountered in its Latin form, as *nulla dies sine linea*.

Nulla dies sine linea. But never a being, from my infancy upwards, hated task-work as I hate it.

Walter Scott, *Journal*, 1 December 1825

what a day may bring a day may take away (*English*) What may come to a person one day can easily be taken away from him or her the next day. George Herbert, *Outlandish Proverbs*, 1651.

~ *See also* an APPLE a day keeps the doctor away; BARNABY bright, Barnaby bright, the longest day and the shortest night; the BETTER the day, the better the deed; a BLUSTERING night, a fair day follows; the DEVIL bides his day; DRUNKEN days have all their tomorrows; EASTER so longed for is gone in a day; an ENGLISH summer, three hot days and a thunderstorm; the EVENING crowns the day; EVERY dog has his day; FAIR and soft goes far in a day; a FAIR day in winter is the mother of a storm; FISH and guests stink after three days; FOG on the hill, water to the mill; fog in the hollow, fine day to follow; he is a FOOL that is not melancholy once a day; a FOUL morning may turn to a fair day; get a NAME to rise early, and you may lie all day; he that RISETH late must trot all day; he who FIGHTS and runs away, lives to fight another day; an HOUR of pain is as long as a day of pleasure; if APPLES bloom in March, in vain for them you'll search; if apples bloom in April, then they'll be plentiful; if apples bloom in May, you may eat them night and day; if SAINT Paul's Day be fair and clear, it will betide a happy year; it is never a BAD day that hath a good night; the LONGEST day must have an end; LOSE an hour in the morning, chase it all day; MARRY in May and rue the day; MERRY nights make sorry days; a MISTY morning may have a fine day; my SON is my son till he gets him a wife, but my daughter's my daughter all the days of her life; NEVER offer your hen for sale on a rainy day; not a LONG day but a good heart rids work; ONE of these days is none of these days; a PIN a day is a groat a year; ROME was not built in a day; SAINT Swithin's Day, if thou dost rain, for forty days it will remain; Saint Swithin's Day, if thou be fair, for forty days 'twill rain no more; SAVE something for a rainy day; SEE a pin and pick it up, all the day you'll have good luck; SOUND travelling far and wide a stormy day will betide; SUFFICIENT unto the day is the evil thereof; there are only TWENTY-FOUR hours in the day; there is but an HOUR in a day between a good housewife and a bad; TOMORROW is another day; what ONE day gives us, another takes away from us; VISIT your aunt, but not every day of the year; what's done by NIGHT appears by day; with the ANCIENT is wisdom, and in the length of days understanding; you cannot have TWO forenoons in the same day.

dead. a dead bee will make no honey (*English*) You cannot expect someone who is dead or otherwise defunct to produce what you want. John Florio, *First*

Fruites, 1578. Related proverbs include 'when bees are old they yield no honey'.

dead folks are past fooling (*English*) There is no deceiving the dead. Thomas Fuller, *Gnomologia*, 1732. Other proverbs dwelling on the unresponsiveness of the dead include 'a dead mouse feels no cold'.

the dead have few friends (*English*) The dead have no legal rights and few defenders once they have passed away. Robert Mannyng, *Handlynge Synne*, *c.*1303.

dead men don't bite (*English*) There is nothing to be feared from a corpse. Edward Hall, *Hall's Chronicle*, 1542 (also found in the writings of Erasmus). Also encountered as 'dead dogs bark not' and 'dead dogs bite not'.

> Yet am I glad he's quiet, where I hope He will not bite again.
>
> Beaumont and Fletcher, *The Knight of the Burning Pestle*, 1611

dead men tell no tales (*English*) Secrets are never divulged by the dead. John Wilson, *Andronicus Commenius*, 1663.

> Where are the stories of those who have not risen – ... who have ended in desperation? ... Dead men tell no tales.
>
> Charles Kingsley, *Alton Locke*, 1850

let the dead bury the dead (*Hebrew*) There comes a point when the living should forsake the dead, in order to get on with their own lives. Bible, Matthew 8:22.

> Jesus said unto him, Follow me, and let the dead, bury their dead.
>
> Matthew 8:22

~ *See also* BLESSED are the dead that the rain rains on; CARRION crows bewail the dead sheep and then eat them; DAUGHTERS and dead fish are no keeping wares; EARLY wed, early dead; GIVING is dead and restoring very sick; HARES may pull dead lions by the beard; he that GAPETH until he be fed, well may he gape until he be dead; it's ILL waiting for dead men's shoes; a LIVE dog is better than a dead lion; NEVER speak ill of the dead; the only GOOD Indian is a dead one; PRAISE no man till he is dead; QUEEN Anne is dead; there is but ONE good mother-in-law, and she is dead; THREE may keep a secret, if two of them are dead; when the DEVIL is dead, he never lacks a chief mourner.

deadly. *See* the FEMALE of the species is more deadly than the male.

deaf. a deaf husband and a blind wife are always a happy couple (*English*) Those who are unconscious of the failings of their spouse or partner will enjoy a peaceful life together. John Florio, *First Fruits*, 1578.

~ *See also* MASTERS should be sometimes blind, and sometimes deaf; there are NONE so deaf as those who will not hear.

deal (noun). *See* a LITTLE fire burns up a great deal of corn.

deal (verb). **they that deal with the devil get a dear pennyworth** (*Scottish*) Those who adopt evil ways are likely to have to pay for it later. A. Hislop, *The Proverbs of Scotland*, 1862. Related proverbs include 'he that deals in dirt has aye foul fingers' and 'if thou dealest with a fox think of his tricks'.

dealing. *See* PLAIN dealing is a jewel.

dear. *See* BUY in the cheapest market and sell in the dearest; EXPERIENCE keeps a dear school; GOLD may be bought too dear; GOOD cheap is dear; they that DEAL with the devil get a dear pennyworth.

dear-bought. *See* FAR-FETCHED and dear-bought is good for ladies; HONEY is dear-bought if licked off thorns.

dearly. *See* WEIGH justly and sell dearly.

dearth. *See* DROUGHT never bred dearth in England.

death. death defies the doctor (*English*) Death eventually must overwhelm all the efforts of doctors and physicians to keep the patient alive. James Kelly, *A Complete Collection of Scotish Proverbs*, 1721. Related proverbs include 'a deadly disease neither physician nor physic can ease' and 'death when it comes will have no denial'.

death devours lambs as well as sheep (*English*) Death claims with equal impartiality the young and the innocent as well as the older and more worldly wise. T. Shelton, *Don Quixote*, 1620.

death is the great leveller (*Roman*) Death erases all marks of distinction between classes, races, sexes and so on. T. Shelton, *Don Quixote*, 1620 (also quoted by Claudian in *De Raptu Proserpinae* in the fourth century AD). Also found as 'death is the grand leveller'. Variants on much the same theme include the Roman 'death brings to a level spades and sceptres'.

> Death is the grand leveller.
>
> Thomas Fuller, *Gnomologia*, 1732

death keeps no calendar (*English*) Death strikes regardless of the date or of the age of the victim. George Herbert, *Outlandish Proverbs*, 1640. A Yiddish version of the proverb runs 'no one needs a calendar to die'.

death pays all debts (*English*) All financial obligations to others cease at death. William Shakespeare, *The Tempest*, *c.*1610. Also encountered as 'death squares all accounts', in which form it was quoted by Shirley in *Cupid and Death* in 1653. Another proverb claims 'death cancels everything but truth'.

> The Laird's dead – aweel, death pays a' scores.
>
> Walter Scott, *Guy Mannering*, 1815

~ *See also* AFTER death the doctor; the BETROTHED of good is evil, the betrothed of life is death, the betrothed of love is divorce; BREAD and cheese be two targets against death; CABBAGE twice cooked is death; COWARDS die many times before their death; a CROW on the thatch, soon death lifts the latch; a DRY cough is the trumpeter of death; a FAIR death honours the whole life; the FIRST breath is the beginning of death; GREY hairs are death's blossoms; he PULLS with a long rope that waits for another's death; NOTHING is certain but death and taxes; OLD men go to death, death comes to young men; SLEEP is the brother of death; there is a REMEDY for everything except death; there is no MEDICINE against death.

debauchery. *See* without BUSINESS, debauchery.

debt. out of debt, out of danger (*English*) Those who owe nothing to anyone may be judged safe from all threat or from the temptation to do wrong. J. Clarke, *Paroemiologia Anglo-Latina*, 1639. Related proverbs include 'out of debt out of deadly sin', 'he that gets out of debt grows rich' and 'he who oweth is in all the wrong.'

> Out of Debt out of Danger ... A Man in Debt is a Slave, and can't act with Liberty.
>
> S. Palmer, *Proverbs*, 1710

~ *See also* DEATH pays all debts; a HUNDRED pounds of sorrow pays not one ounce of debt; a POUND of care will not pay an ounce of debt; PROMISE is debt; SPEAK not of my debts unless you mean to pay them.

debtor. debtors are liars (*English*) Those who are in debt are virtually obliged to tell lies. George Herbert, *Outlandish Proverbs*, 1640.

> Debtors can hardly help being liars.
>
> Charles Spurgeon, *John Ploughman's Talk*, 1869

~ *See also* CREDITORS have better memories than debtors.

deceit. *See* to DECEIVE a deceiver is no deceit; TRUST is the mother of deceit.

deceive. he that will deceive the fox must rise betimes (*English*) Those who try to fool others as crafty as themselves must keep their wits about them. George Herbert, *Outlandish Proverbs*, 1640.

to deceive a deceiver is no deceit (*English*) It is no sin to pull the wool over the eyes of someone who is seeking to deceive others. Fulwell, *Ars Adulandi*, *c.*1580.

~ *See also* CHILDREN are to be deceived with comfits and men with oaths; if a MAN deceive me once, shame on him, but if he deceive me twice, shame on me.

deceiver. *See* to DECEIVE a deceiver is no deceit.

deceptive. *See* APPEARANCES are deceptive.

decide. *See* the DIFFERENCE is wide that the sheets will not decide.

deed. deeds are fruits, words are but leaves (*English*) It is not words but deeds that count. T. Draxe, *Bibliotheca Scholastica*, 1633. Equivalents sayings include 'deeds are males, words are females' and 'deeds not words'.

~ *See also* the BETTER the day, the better the deed; FAIR words and foul deeds cheat wise men as well as fools; ITALIANS are wise before the deed, the Germans in the deed, the French after the deed; a MAN of words and not of deeds is like a garden full of weeds; no BAD deed goes unpunished.

deem the best till the truth be tried (*English*) Reserve judgement until the truth is known. John Heywood, *A Dialogue containing ... the Proverbs in the English Tongue*, 1546.

Judge nothing till the end be seene.
John Florio, *Second Frutes*, 1591

deep. the deeper the sweeter (*English*) The further a person probes into something they enjoy, the more pleasure they will get from it. Ben Jonson, *Every Man in His Humour*, 1596.

Stir it up with the spoon, miss; for the deeper the sweeter.
Jonathan Swift, *Polite Conversation*, 1738

in the deepest water is the best fishing (*English*) The biggest fish are caught where the water is deepest. T. Draxe, *Bibliotheca Scholastica*, 1616.

~ *See also* BEAUTY is only skin deep; STILL waters run deep.

deer. where the deer is slain, some of her blood will lie (*English*) There is always some evidence left behind at the scene where something is done. James Kelly, *A Complete Collection of Scotish Proverbs*, 1721.

defence. *See* ATTACK is the best form of defence.

defend. *See* GOD defend me from my friends; from my enemies I can defend myself.

defer. *See* HOPE deferred makes the heart sick.

defies. *See* DEFY.

defile. *See* he that TOUCHES pitch shall be defiled.

defy. *See* DEATH defies the doctor; FEED by measure and defy the physician.

delay. delays are dangerous (*English*) Putting something off allows more time for something to go wrong. John Lyly, *Euphues: The Anatomy of Wit*, 1578. Similar sentiments were expressed by Geoffrey Chaucer in *Troilus and Criseyde*, *c.*1385–90: 'That peril is with dreeching in y-drawe'. The proverb appears in Shakespeare in the guise of 'defer no time; delays have dangerous ends'. A saying of US origin is less adamant, advising 'delays are dangerous but they make things sure'. *See also* PROCRASTINATION is the thief of time.

Delay, they say, begetteth peril.
Robert Louis Stevenson, *The Black Arrow*, 1888

delays are not denials (*English*) The fact that a response is delayed does not necessarily mean that it constitutes a denial. W.H.G. Thomas, *Commentary on Genesis*, 1907.

~ *See also* DESIRES are nourished by delays.

delight. *See* a RAINBOW in the morning is the shepherd's warning; a rainbow at night is the shepherd's delight; RED sky at night, shepherd's delight; red sky in the morning, shepherd's warning.

Delilah. *See* there's no LEAPING from Delilah's lap into Abraham's bosom.

deliver. *See* from HELL, Hull and Halifax, Good Lord deliver us; HUNGER and cold deliver a man up to his enemy.

delve. *See* when ADAM delved and Eve span, who was then the gentleman?

demand (noun). **when the demand is a jest, the answer is a scoff** (*English*) If one is faced with a ludicrous request the only possible response is to mock what has been suggested. John Clarke, *Paroemiologia Anglo-Latina*, 1639.

demand (verb). *See* a MAN may lose his goods for want of demanding them.

demeanour. *See* ARTFUL speech and an ingratiating demeanour rarely accompany virtue.

denial. *See* DELAYS are not denials.

deny. denying a fault doubles it (*English*) Refusing to recognize your own misdeeds only makes them worse. *Politeuphuia*, 1597, attributed to J. Bodenham.

~ *See also* who GIVES to all denies all.

depend. he who depends on another dines ill and sups worse (*English*) Those who depend on others for their maintenance will find their fare may be less satisfactory than they might hope for. John Ray, *A Collection of English Proverbs*, 1813. Another proverb remarks 'dependence is a poor trade'.

descend. *See* it is EASIER to descend than to ascend.

desert (noun). **desert and reward seldom keep company** (*English*) Hard work is not necessarily rewarded. J. Davies, *The Scourge of Folly*, 1611. Also encountered in the form 'desert and reward be ever far odd'. A Latin variant runs 'riches fall not always to the lot of the most deserving'.

desert (verb). *See* RATS desert a sinking ship.

deserve. he deserves not the sweet that will not taste the sour (*English*) Those who are not prepared to put up with bad things do not deserve good things. R. Taverner, *Proverbs or Adages with New Additions, gathered out of the Chiliades of Erasmus*, 1539.

~ *See also* a FORCED kindness deserves no thanks; a GOOD dog deserves a good bone; it's an ILL dog that deserves not a crust; NONE but the brave deserve the fair; ONE good turn deserves another.

desire (noun). **desire hath no rest** (*English*) Passion allows no peace for those afflicted by it. W. Baldwin, *Beware the Cat*, 1551.

> A true saying it is, desire hath no rest.
> Robert Burton, *Anatomy of Melancholy*, 1621

desires are nourished by delays (*English*) The longer a person must wait for something the more intensely they long for it. T. Draxe, *Bibliotheca Scholastica*, 1616.

~ *See also* he BEGINS to die that quits his desires; HUMBLE hearts have humble desires.

desire (verb). **he that desires honour is not worthy** (*English*) Those who value fame and glory for their own sake are thereby less deserving of such recognition. William Shakespeare, *Henry V*, *c.*1598.

> But if it be a sin to covet honour, I am the most offending soul alive.
> William Shakespeare, *Henry V*, *c.*1598

~ *See also* he is not POOR that hath little, but he that desireth much; we SOON believe what we desire.

despair gives courage to a coward (*English*) Even the most timorous person will find courage when a situation looks entirely hopeless. Thomas Fuller, *Gnomologia*, 1732.

desperate diseases call for desperate remedies (*English*) The worse a problem is the more radical the solution must be. R. Taverner, *Proverbs or Adages with New Additions, gathered out of the Chiliades of Erasmus*, 1539 (also recorded in the form of a maxim in the *Aphorisms* of the Greek physician Hippocrates around 400BC). In historical terms, quack doctors, witches and other practitioners of folk medicine learned to recommend cures for physical ailments that incorporated all manner of unusual and even revolting ingredients, knowing that the more outlandish the remedy was the more impressed the patient would be and thus more likely to agree to pay a high price for it. Tradition has it that Guy Fawkes quoted the proverb to James I on 6 November 1605 to explain his motives on his arrest following the failed Gunpowder Plot. Variants include 'desperate cuts must have desperate cures'.

> Diseases desperate grown by desperate appliance are reliev'd, or not at all.
> William Shakespeare, *Hamlet*, *c.*1600

despise. he that despises his own life is soon master of another's (*Roman*) Those who care little for their own safety or reputation are thus able to exert power over those who are less abandoned. Robert Burton, *Anatomy of Melancholy*, 1621.

> He that hath neither reputation nor bread hath very little to lose, and hath therefore as little to fear … 'Who ever values not his own life, is master of another man's' …
> Jonathan Swift, *Remarks upon 'Rights of Church'*, 1708

destiny. *See* HANGING and wiving go by destiny; a MAN's destiny is always dark.

destroy. destroy the lion while he is yet but a whelp (*English*) It is best to dispose of rivals or other potential threats before they have reached the point where they are invincible. Thomas Fuller, *Gnomologia*, 1732.

destroy the nests and the birds will fly away (*English*) Destroy the places where your enemies lurk and they will move elsewhere. Thomas Fuller, *The Church History of Britain*, 1655.

~ *See also* an HOUR may destroy what an age was a building; whom the GODS would destroy, they first make mad.

devil. the devil always leaves a stink behind him (*English*) Wickedness always leaves its taint behind. Henry Smith, *Sermons*, 1591. Superstition had it that when the devil materialized at witches' covens he often took the form of a rank-smelling male goat.

the devil bides his day (*Scottish*) Those who demand debts, wages and the like before they are due should copy the devil, who waits patiently for the death of those who have signed a covenant with him in order to claim their souls. James Kelly, *A Complete Collection of Scotish Proverbs*, 1721.

the devil can quote scripture for his own purpose (*English*) The ill-intentioned can easily turn well-meaning maxims and writings to their own evil or unworthy ends. William Shakespeare, *The Merchant of Venice*, *c.*1596. The proverb has its origins in the biblical story of the temptation of Christ, although Shakespeare may also have been influenced by a line in Christopher Marlowe's *The Jew of Malta* (*c.*1592): 'What, bring you scripture to confirm your wrongs.' Related proverbs include 'the devil sometimes speaks the truth'.

> Does anyone doubt the old saw, that the Devil (being a layman) quotes Scripture for his own ends?
>
> Charles Dickens, *Martin Chuzzlewit*, 1850

the devil dances in an empty pocket (*English*) Those who have no money are vulnerable to temptation. Thomas Hoccleve, *The Regiment of Princes*, 1412. Related proverbs include 'the devil's mouth is a miser's purse'.

> The devil sleeps in my pocket; I have no cross [with which coins were once marked] to drive him from it.
>
> Philip Massinger, *The Bashful Lover*, 1636

the devil finds work for idle hands (*English*) Those with nothing better to do will soon be tempted to mischief. Isaac Watts, *Divine Songs*, 1715 (a similar sentiment is expressed in the letters of Saint Jerome). Also encountered in the form 'if the devil find a man idle, he'll set him to work'. *See also* an IDLE brain is the devil's workshop; IDLENESS is the root of all evil.

> If the Devil find a man idle, he'll set him to work.
>
> Thomas Fuller, *Gnomologia*, 1732

the devil gets up to the belfry by the vicar's skirts (*English*) The wicked may work hand in hand with the good in order to achieve their evil aims. J. Howell, *Paroemiographia*, 1659. Related proverbs include 'the devil lurks behind the cross'. A Scottish proverb along similar lines runs: 'the devil and the dean begin with a letter; when the devil gets the dean, the kirk will be the better.'

the devil goes shares in gaming (*English*) Gambling of all kinds provokes evil and temptation. J. Mapletoft, *Select Proverbs*, 1707.

the devil is a busy bishop in his own diocese (*English*) Acts of evil multiply where men are disposed to wickedness. Hugh Latimer, *Sermon on Ploughers*, 1549.

the devil is an ass (*English*) Although evil, the devil is easily duped by those more cunning than he. Ben Jonson, *The Devil is an Ass*, 1616. Among other proverbs emphasizing the limitations of the devil's influence are 'the devil has no power over a drunkard' and 'the devil dares not peep under a maid's coat'.

the devil is at home (*English*) The source of much wickedness is often to be found in the home. Thomas Middleton, *Works*, 1620. Another proverb warns 'the devil is never far off'.

> A foolish proverb says, 'The devil's at home'.
>
> George Crabbe, *The Borough*, 1810

the devil is not as black as he is painted (*English*) Some people (or things) are not as bad as is commonly believed. Thomas More, *Dialogue of Comfort*, 1535. Also encountered in the form 'the devil is not so ill as he's called'. *See also* GIVE the devil his due.

> Fear kills more people than the yellow fever ... The devil's not half so black as he's painted – nor the yellow fever half so yellow, I presume.
>
> Captain Frederick Marryat, *Peter Simple*, 1834

the devil looks after his own (*English*) The devil protects those who have devoted themselves to mischief and evil. J. Day, *Isle of Gulls*, 1606. Also encountered in the form 'the devil is kind to his own'.

> The Dee'ls ay good to his own ... Spoken when they whom we affect not, thrive and prosper in the World; as if they had their Prosperity from the Devil.
>
> James Kelly, *A Complete Collection of Scotish Proverbs*, 1721

the devil lurks behind the cross (*English*) Evil attends closely upon religion, awaiting opportunities. T. Shelton, *Don Quixote*, 1612. Another proverb has it that 'the devil has a chapel wherever God has a church', although another warns that 'when the devil preaches, the world's near an end'.

the devil makes his Christmas-pies of lawyers' tongues and clerks' fingers (*Italian*) Evil prospers through the immorality and cunning of lawyers and the corruption of clerks. John Florio, *Second Fruits*, 1578.

> Sir Robert Pye, attorney of the court of wards, ... happened to die on Christmas day: the news being

> brought to the serjeant, said he 'The devil has a Christmas pie'.
>
> John Aubrey, *Brief Lives*, 1669–96

the devil rides upon a fiddlestick (*English*) Sometimes a great deal of fuss and trouble may arise from the most trivial grounds. William Shakespeare, *Henry IV, Part 1*, *c.*1597.

> Heigh, heigh! The Devil rides upon a fiddlestick: what's the matter?
>
> William Shakespeare, *Henry IV, Part 1*, *c.*1597

the devil's behind the glass (*English*) Those who are given to admiring themselves too long in the mirror are likely to fall prey to vanity and other evils. H.G. Bohn, *A Handbook of Proverbs*, 1855.

the devil's children have the devil's luck (*English*) It is often those least deserving of good fortune who seem to enjoy the best luck, as if the devil himself is helping them. John Ray, *A Collection of English Proverbs*, 1678.

> The Dee'ls Bairns have Dee'ls luck. Spoken enviously when ill People prosper.
>
> James Kelly, *A Complete Collection of Scotish Proverbs*, 1721

the devil sick would be a monk (*English*) Ill health or other adverse circumstances prompt many people to make rash promises to reform that are forgotten as soon as their health or fortunes are restored. L. Evans, *Withals Dictionary Revised*, 1586. Also encountered in the form 'the devil was sick, the devil a saint would be; the devil was well, the devil a saint was he!' or, more concisely, 'the devil was sick'. Equivalent proverbs may be found in many other European languages and even in Chinese ('when times are easy we do not burn incense, but when trouble comes we embrace the feet of Buddha'). *See also* the CHAMBER of sickness is the chapel of devotion; the DANGER past and God forgotten.

> The old, the irrepressible adage … was to live again between them: 'When the devil was sick the devil a saint would be; when the devil was well the devil a saint was he!'
>
> Henry James, *A Small Boy and Others*, 1913

the devil's mouth is a miser's purse (*English*) Money handed over to a miser will not be used for good. L. Wright, *A Summons for Sleepers*, 1589. Related proverbs include 'the devil lies brooding in the miser's chest'.

the devil to pay and no pitch hot (*English*) Trouble looms, and there seems no immediate way to counter it. *c.*1400, published in *Reliquae Antiquae*, 1841. The proverb alludes to the business of sealing ('paying') with pitch the seam (the 'devil') between the outboard plank and waterways of a ship – a particularly awkward operation.

> If they hurt but one hair of Cleveland's head, there will be the devil to pay, and no pitch hot.
>
> Walter Scott, *The Pirate*, 1821

there is a devil in every berry of the grape (*English*) Alcohol brings with it opportunities for evil and temptation. J. Howell, *Letters*, 1647 (sometimes attributed to a Turkish original).

when the devil is dead, he never lacks a chief mourner (*English*) When some nefarious practice is brought to an end there is always someone who will regret it, because they profited by it. R.C. Trench, *On the Lessons in Proverbs*, 1853.

where no one else will, the devil must bear the cross (*English*) If no one better is available, tasks that must be done have to be entrusted to those one would not normally select. John Lyly, *Euphues: The Anatomy of Wit*, 1578.

> Where none will, the Divell himselfe must beare the crosse.
>
> John Lyly, *Euphues: The Anatomy of Wit*, 1578

where the devil cannot come, he will send (*English*) Where the devil cannot exert influence over a person directly he will send temptations to lure them into evil. R.C. Trench, *On the Lessons in Proverbs*, 1853.

why should the devil have all the best tunes? (*English*) Why should music and other amusements (together with other attractions of the secular world) be reserved for the wicked alone? W. Chappell, *Popular Music*, 1859. The phrase is often quoted in discussion of church music set to popular secular tunes (as controversially espoused by the early Methodists) and may have first been used by evangelist and hymn-writer Rowland Hill (according to his biographer E.W. Broome) in reference to Charles Wesley, who adapted popular tap-room tunes for his songs. Later, the proverb was quoted by General Booth, founder of the Salvation Army, when he borrowed the tunes of many well-known music-hall songs to accompany religious lyrics.

~ *See also* an ATHEIST is one point beyond the devil; AWAY goes the devil when he finds the door shut against him; BETTER the devil you know than the devil you don't know; CARDS are the devil's books; CAST a bone in the devil's teeth; EVERY devil has not a cloven hoof; EVERY man for himself, and the devil take the hindmost; FRIDAY's hair and Sunday's horn go to the devil on Monday morn; GIVE the devil his due; GOD sends meat, but the devil sends cooks; HASTE is from the devil; he that BRINGETH himself into needless dangers dieth the devil's martyr; he that is BUSY is tempted but by one devil, he that is idle by a legion; he that PREACHES war is the devil's chaplain; he that SERVES God for money will serve the devil for better wages; he who SUPS with the devil should have a long spoon; HOME is home, as the devil said when he found himself in the Court of Session; IDLE bairns are the devil's workhouses; an IDLE brain is the devil's workshop; it is a SIN to lie against the devil; it is EASIER to raise the devil than to lay him; NEEDS must when the devil drives; ONE for sorrow, two for joy; three for a girl, four for a boy; five for silver, six for gold; seven for a secret, never to be told; eight for heaven, nine for hell; and ten for the devil's own self; PARSLEY seed goes nine times to the devil; a PHYSICIAN is an angel when employed but a devil when one must pay him; PULL devil, pull baker; put a COWARD to his mettle and he'll fight the devil; SET a beggar on horseback, and he'll ride to the devil; TALK of the devil and he is bound to appear; TELL a woman she's a beauty and the devil will tell her so fifty times; TELL the truth and shame the devil; there are GOD's poor and the devil's poor; they that DEAL with the devil get a dear pennyworth; those that EAT black pudding will dream of the devil; to GIVE a thing, and take a thing, is to wear the devil's gold ring; what is GOT over the devil's back is spent under his belly; when a COUPLE are newly married the first month is honeymoon, or smick smack; the second is hither and thither; the third is thwick thwack; the fourth the devil take them that brought thee and I together; when it RAINS and the sun shines at the same time the devil is beating his wife; where GOD builds a church, the devil will build a chapel; a WOMAN is an angel at ten, a saint at fifteen, a devil at forty and a witch at fourscore; YOUNG saint old devil.

devotion. *See* the CHAMBER of sickness is the chapel of devotion; IGNORANCE is the mother of devotion; a SHARP stomach makes short devotion.

devour. *See* DEATH devours lambs as well as sheep; TIME devours all things.

dew. *See* in the ANTS' house the dew is a flood; the COW that's first up gets the first of the dew.

diamond. diamond cuts diamond (*English*) Cunning can outwit cunning, denoting a clash between two equally acute minds. John Marston, *The Malcontent*, 1604. Because diamonds are so hard, only by rubbing one against another will the stones be scratched.

> Wit must be foiled by wit; cut a diamond with a diamond.
>
> William Congreve, *The Double Dealer*, 1693

~ *See also* a BARLEY-CORN is better than a diamond to a cock.

dice. *See* the BEST throw of the dice is to throw them away.

die. they die well that live well (*English*) Those who have led good, worthwhile lives die more peacefully than those who have wasted their lives. J. Clarke, *Paroemiologia Anglo-Latina*, 1639. Variants include 'he dies like a beast who has done no good while he lived'. *See also* who LIVES well dies well.

~ *See also* as a MAN lives so shall he die; as SOON as man is born he begins to die; CALL no man happy till he dies; COWARDS die many times before their death; ENVY never dies; he BEGINS to die that quits his desires; he that BRINGETH himself into needless dangers dieth the devil's martyr; he that WEDS before he's wise shall die before he thrive; he who LIVES by the sword dies by the sword; if you TRUST before you try, you may repent before you die; it is as NATURAL to die as to be born; a MAN can die but once; NEVER say die; OLD habits die hard; OLD men will die and children soon forget; OLD praise dies unless you feed it; OLD soldiers never die, they simply fade away; only the GOOD die young; PRETTINESS dies first; REMOVE an old tree and it will die; SEE a pin and let it lie, you'll want a pin before you die; SEE Naples and die; we are BORN crying, live complaining and die disappointed; who LIVES well dies well; whom the GODS love die young; you cannot SHIFT an old tree without it dying; YOUNG men may die, but old men must die; you've got to EAT a peck of dirt before you die.

diet. diet cures more than doctors (*English*) A sensible diet does more to protect the health than any amount of medical attention. A.B. Cheales, *Proverbs*, 1875. A variant runs 'diet cures more than the lancet'. Related proverbs include 'whatsoever was the father of disease, ill diet was mother'.

~ *See also* the BEST doctors are Dr Diet, Dr Quiet and Dr Merryman.

differ. *See* TASTES differ.

difference. the difference is wide that the sheets will not decide (*English*) Most disagreements between lovers and married couples can be reconciled in bed. John Ray, *A Collection of English Proverbs*, 1678.

there is no difference of bloods in a basin (*English*) Differences in class have no physical reality. T. Becon, *Works*, 1560.

> You talke of your birth, when I knoew there is no difference of blouds in a basen.
>
> John Lyly, *Euphues*, 1580

difficult. the difficult we do at once, the impossible takes a little longer (*English/French*) Nothing is impossible, but some things will take longer to achieve (often delivered sarcastically when requested to perform an impossible task). Anthony Trollope, *Phineas Redux*, 1873. Formerly often repeated in military and naval circles.

~ *See also* ALL things are difficult before they are easy; it is the FIRST step that is difficult.

difficulty. *See* ENGLAND's difficulty is Ireland's opportunity.

digest. *See* CHEESE digests all things but itself.

diligence. *See* CARE and diligence bring luck.

din. *See* SHALLOW streams make most din.

dine. he that dines and leaves lays the cloth twice (*English*) The guest who does not overstay his welcome is likely to be invited back in the future. George Herbert, *Outlandish Proverbs*, 1640.

~ *See also* he who DEPENDS on another dines ill and sups worse.

dinner. *See* AFTER dinner rest a while, after supper walk a mile; BETTER a dinner of herbs than a stalled ox where hate is; HALF an hour is soon lost at dinner.

diocese. *See* the DEVIL is a busy bishop in his own diocese.

dirt. *See* FLING enough dirt and some will stick; he that FALLS in the dirt, the longer he stays there the fouler he is; when the CUCKOO comes he eats up all the dirt; you've got to EAT a peck of dirt before you die.

dirty. dirty hands make clean money (*English*) Money gained through hard work is honestly earned. W. C. Hazlitt, *English Proverbs*, 1869.

dirty water will quench fire (*English*) Certain desires – especially sexual ones – are readily sated by less than what might be ideally hoped for (for instance, through the use of an ugly prostitute in the place of an idealized lover). John Heywood, *A Dialogue containing … the Proverbs in the English Tongue*, 1546.

> As this proverbe saieth, for quenchyng hot desire,
> Foul water as soone as fayre, wyl quenche hot fire.
>
> John Heywood, *A Dialogue containing … the Proverbs in the English Tongue*, 1546

~ *See also* don't THROW out your dirty water until you get in fresh; don't WASH your dirty linen in public; QUARRELSOME dogs get dirty coats; SCORNFUL dogs will eat dirty puddings.

disappoint. *See* BLESSED is he who expects nothing, for he shall never be disappointed; we are BORN crying, live complaining and die disappointed.

disarm. *See* a GENEROUS confession disarms slander.

discourse. *See* CHANGE of weather is the discourse of fools.

discover. *See* DRINK washes off the dawb and discovers the man; the FILTH under the white snow the sun discovers.

discretion is the better part of valour (*English*) It is sometimes wiser to back down than to risk a course of action in which one may come off worst. William Caxton, *Jason*, *c.*1477 (also recorded in the writings of Euripides and other classical authors). It has been suggested that originally 'discretion' signified tactics or strategy, throwing a rather different light upon the meaning. *See also* he who FIGHTS and runs away, lives to fight another day.

The better part of valour is discretion: in the which better part, I have saved my life.
William Shakespeare, *Henry IV, Part 1*, c.1597

disease. a disease known is half cured (*English*) By recognition of the nature of a disease, or some other problem, one is halfway to curing it. James Wright, *Country Contentments*, 1694. Equivalents in other cultures include the Spanish 'the beginning of health is to know the disease'.

diseases are the price for ill pleasures (*English*) Diseases are provoked by overindulgence in vice. John Ray, *A Collection of English Proverbs*, 1670.

disease will have its course (*English*) Some diseases must run their full course before there can be any hope of effecting a recovery. T. Muffett, *Healths Improvement*, 1655.

~ *See also* DESPERATE diseases call for desperate remedies; the DOCTOR is often more to be feared than the disease; MANY dishes make many diseases; the REMEDY may be worse than the disease.

disgrace. *See* POVERTY is no disgrace, but it is a great inconvenience.

dish. *See* ALL is lost that is put into a riven dish; a CHEERFUL look makes a dish a feast; the FIRST dish pleaseth all; MANY dishes make many diseases; REVENGE is a dish that is best eaten cold; WISHES won't wash dishes.

dismount. *See* he who RIDES a tiger is afraid to dismount.

dispose. *See* MAN proposes, but God disposes.

disputant. *See* of TWO disputants the warmer is generally in the wrong.

dispute. *See* in too MUCH dispute truth is lost.

dissemble. dissembled sin is double wickedness (*English*) Those who try to conceal their wicked natures are doubly guilty. T. Draxe, *Bibliotheca Scholastica*, 1633.

~ *See also* a FOE is better than a dissembling friend; THREE ills come from the north: a cold wind, a shrinking cloth and a dissembling man.

distance lends enchantment to the view (*English*) Some situations or things look better when considered from a detached position. T. Campbell, *Pleasure of Hope*, 1799. A French variant runs 'from a distance it is something; nearby it is nothing'. *See also* BLUE are the hills that are far away.

distress. *See* TWO in distress makes sorrow less.

distrust. when distrust enters in at the foregate, love goes out at the postern (*English*) Friendship withers when trust no longer exists between the parties concerned. J. Howell, *Letters*, 1645. *See also* when PASSION entereth at the foregate, wisdom goeth out of the postern.

disturb. *See* he that will CATCH eels must disturb the flood.

ditch. *See* if the BLIND lead the blind, both shall fall into the ditch.

divide. divide and rule (*Roman*) By setting your opponents against each other you can establish your own supremacy over both. Phineas Fletcher, *Purple Island*, 1633. Rendered in Latin as *divide et impera*.

As Machiavel taught 'em, divide and ye govern.
Jonathan Swift, *Poems*, 1732

~ *See* a HOUSE divided against itself cannot stand; KNAVES and fools divide the world; UNITED we stand, divided we fall.

divine. *See* on SAINT Thomas the Divine kill all turkeys, geese and swine; to ERR is human, to forgive divine; the WAY to see divine light is to put out thine own candle.

divorce. *See* the BETROTHED of good is evil, the betrothed of life is death, the betrothed of love is divorce.

do. do as I say, not as I do (*Hebrew*) Do as I advise, but do not expect me to be restrained by the same rules myself. Bible, Matthew, 23:3. Often delivered sarcastically in reference to those who hypocritically fail to live up the standards they espouse. Variants include 'do as the friar saith, not as he doth'. A defence available to those who find themselves incapable of realizing these ideals is offered in the proverb 'he that may not do as he would, must do as he may'.

It is as folke dooe, and not as folke say.

John Heywood, *A Dialogue containing ... the Proverbs in the English Tongue*, 1546

do as you would be done by (*Hebrew/Chinese/Hindu*) Treat others as you would like to be treated yourself. A. Munday and others, *Sir Thomas More*, *c.*1596 (also attributed to Confucius and as the 'Golden Rule' a maxim of the Hindu, Judaic and Christian religions). The version given in Matthew 7:12 runs 'therefore all things whatsoever ye would that men should do to you, do ye even so to them: for this is the law and the prophets'. Luke 6:31 has 'as yee would that men should doe to you, doe yee also to them likewise'. Sometimes encountered in the form 'do unto others as you would they should do unto you'. Charles Kingsley introduced the characters Mrs Doasyouwouldbedoneby and Mrs Bedonebyasyoudid in *The Water Babies*, 1863. In 1898, in *David Harum*, Edward N. Westcott added his own variation on the theme: 'Do unto the other feller the way he'd like to do unto you an' do it fust.'

'Do as you would be done by', is the surest method that I know of pleasing.

Lord Chesterfield, letter, 16 October 1747

we must do as we may, if we can't do as we would (*Roman*) Where it is impossible for a person to do everything as they would ideally like they should at least do what they can. T. Draxe, *Bibliotheca Scholastica*, 1633. Variants include 'he that may not do as he would must do as he may'.

what's done cannot be undone (*Greek*) There is no changing past deeds. Geoffrey Chaucer, *The Book of the Duchess*, 1368 (also found, as 'things could not now be otherwise' in Sophocles). *See also* THINGS done cannot be undone.

Things without all remedy
Should be without regard: what's done is done.

William Shakespeare, *Macbeth*, *c.*1604

dock. in dock, out nettle (*English*) Originally a charm based on a traditional cure for nettle stings (involving rubbing the site with a dock leaf), since used as a condemnation of a fickle or inconstant character. Geoffrey Chaucer, *Troilus and Criseyde*, *c.*1385–90.

Waveryng as the wynde, in docke out nettle.

John Heywood, *A Dialogue containing ... the Proverbs in the English Tongue*, 1546

doctor. the doctor is often more to be feared than the disease (*English*) The courses of treatment recommended by doctors may be more harmful than the diseases they are meant to cure. Robert Burton, *Anatomy of Melancholy*, 1621. By the same token another proverb runs 'one doctor makes work for another'.

Paupers got sick and got well as Nature pleased;
but woe betided the rich in an age when, for one
Mr Malady killed three fell by Dr Remedy.

Charles Reade, *The Cloister and the Hearth*, 1861

if the doctor cures, the sun sees it, but if he kills, the earth hides it (*French*) Doctors bury their mistakes because their patients die. James Kelly, *A Complete Collection of Scottish Proverbs*, 1721.

~ *See also* AFTER death the doctor; an APPLE a day keeps the doctor away; the BEST doctors are Dr Diet, Dr Quiet and Dr Merryman; BETTER no doctor at all than three; DEATH defies the doctor; DIET cures more than doctors; ONE beggar does not hate another as much as one doctor hates another; there are MORE old drunkards than old doctors; where the SUN enters the doctor does not.

doer. *See* EVIL doers are evil dreaders; the GREATEST talkers are the least doers; ILL doers are ill dreaders.

does. *See* DO.

dog. dog does not eat dog (*Roman*) Like does not attack like (just as animals of the same species rarely attack one another). W. Turner, *The Hunting of the Romish Fox*, 1543 (similar sentiments may be found in the writings of Juvenal and Shakespeare, among others). Also found in the form 'wolf does not eat wolf'. *See also* there is HONOUR among thieves.

Dogs are hard drove, when they eat dogs.
It is an hard Winter, when Dogs eat Dogs.

Thomas Fuller, *Gnomologia*, 1732

the dog returns to its vomit (*Hebrew*) The wicked and the foolish often return to the scene of their past misdeeds. *Romaunce of the Rose*, *c.*1400 (also quoted in the Bible, in Proverbs 26:11).

Le chien est retourné à son propre vomissement.

William Shakespeare, *Henry IV, Part 2*, *c.*1598

dogs bark as they are bred (*English*) The way people behave depends on the kind of upbringing they have had. James Kelly, *A Complete Collection of Scotish Proverbs*, 1721. Variants include 'as the old dog barks, so the young one'. Another proverb observes that 'like dogs, when one barks all bark'.

the dogs bark but the caravan goes on (*Arabian*) Protests about something may be made, but will not last long (just as the barking of dogs at the passing of a caravan of travellers in the desert soon dies away). Marcel Proust, *A l'Ombre des Jeunes Filles en Fleurs*, 1918. A favourite saying of South African politician Jan Smuts, it was also quoted – in the form 'the dogs bark, but the caravan passes by' – by British theatre director Sir Peter Hall in response to his critics in the 1970s.

> In the words of a fine Arab proverb, 'The dogs may bark; the caravan goes on!'
>
> Marcel Proust, *A l'Ombre des Jeunes Filles en Fleurs*, 1918; translated as *Within a Budding Grove*, 1924, by C.K. Scott Moncrieff

dogs begin in jest and end in earnest (*English*) Disputations that may begin in a spirit of fun can easily develop into something more serious. Bishop Hall, *Contemplations*, 1612–15. Sometimes found in the form 'fools begin in jest and end in earnest'.

a dog's nose and a maid's knees are always cold (*English*) A dog's nose and a girl's knees are never warm. J. Clarke, *Paroemiologia Anglo-Latina*, 1639.

the dog that is idle barks at his fleas, but he that is hunting feels them not (*English*) Those who are busily engaged tend not to notice the trivial discomforts that trouble the idle. Dean Hole, *More Memories*, 1894.

the dog that trots about finds a bone (*English*) Those who wander about or go to some effort are more likely to receive rewards than those who do nothing. George Borrow, *The Bible in Spain*, 1843. Often quoted in connection with the roaming lifestyle of gypsies.

a dog that will fetch a bone will carry a bone (*English*) A gossip who shares others' confidences with you is in turn equally likely to divulge your own confidences to others. R. Forby, *Vocabulary of East Anglia*, 1830.

> So Nellie twisted what you said and told it to Miss Wilder … 'A dog that will fetch a bone, will carry a bone'.
>
> Laura Ingalls Wilder, *Little Town on the Prairie*, 1941

a dog will bark ere he bite (*English*) A dog will give a warning before it attacks. John Heywood, *A Dialogue containing … the Proverbs in the English Tongue*, 1550.

~ *See also* ALL are not thieves that dogs bark at; a BARKING dog never bites; BEAT the dog before the lion; BEWARE of a silent dog and still water; BRAG is a good dog, but Holdfast is better; the CAT and dog may kiss, yet are none the better friends; the CAT, the Rat and Lovell our Dog rule all England under an Hog; CRACK was a good dog but he got hung for barking; EVERY dog has his day; EVERY dog is a lion at home; EVERY dog is allowed one bite; GIVE a child all he shall crave and a dog while his tail doth wave and you'll have a fair dog and a foul knave; GIVE a dog a bad name and hang him; a GOOD dog deserves a good bone; HANG a dog on a crab-tree and he'll never love verjuice; he is a GOOD dog who goes to church; he that would HANG his dog gives out first that he is mad; if the OLD dog bark, he gives counsel; if you LIE down with dogs, you will get up with fleas; into the MOUTH of a bad dog often falls a good bone; it is a POOR dog that is not worth whistling for; it is EASY to find a stick to beat a dog; it's an ILL dog that deserves not a crust; a LEAN dog to get through the hedge; let SLEEPING dogs lie; a LIVE dog is better than a dead lion; LOVE me, love my dog; a MAN's best friend is his dog; MESSMATE before a shipmate, shipmate before a stranger, stranger before a dog; take the HAIR of the dog that bit you; the MOON does not heed the barking of dogs; QUARRELSOME dogs get dirty coats; SCORNFUL dogs will eat dirty puddings; there are MORE ways of killing a dog than choking it with butter; there are MORE ways of killing a dog than hanging it; THREE things are not to be trusted: a cow's horn, a dog's tooth and a horse's hoof; TWO cats and a mouse, two wives in one house, two dogs and a bone, never agree in one; TWO dogs fight for a bone, and a third runs away with it; who hath no MORE bread than need must not keep a dog; why KEEP a dog and bark yourself?; a WOMAN, a dog and a walnut tree, the more you beat them the better they be; you can't TEACH an old dog new tricks.

dogged. it's dogged as does it (*English*) Perseverance pays off in the end. M.B. Chesnut, *Diary*, 6 August 1864.

> There ain't nowt a man can't bear if he'll only be dogged ... It's dogged as does it. It's not thinking about it.
>
> Anthony Trollope, *The Last Chronicle of Barset*, 1867

done. *See* DO.

doomsday. *See* a THOUSAND pounds and a bottle of hay is all one thing at doomsday.

door. a door must either be shut or open (*French*) It must be one way or the other (there is no third option). Brueys and Palaprat, *Le Grondeur*, 1691. Rendered in French as *il faut qu'une porte soit ouverte ou fermée*. In the original play a servant is scolded for leaving the door open, on which he complains bitterly that last time, when he closed the door, he had also been scolded.

> There are but the two ways; the door must either be shut, or it must be open.
>
> Oliver Goldsmith, *Citizen of the World*, 1762

~ *See also* AWAY goes the devil when he finds the door shut against him; the BACK door robs the house; CREAKING doors hang the longest; a GOLDEN key can open any door; GOOD clothes open all doors; it is too LATE to shut the stable door after the horse has bolted; JEALOUSY shuts one door and opens two; JOY and sorrow are next door neighbours; a NICE wife and a back door will soon make a rich man poor; an OPEN door may tempt a saint; OPPORTUNITY seldom knocks twice at any man's door; a POSTERN door makes a thief; TWO daughters and a back door are three arrant thieves; when ONE door shuts, another opens; when POVERTY comes in at the door, love flies out of the window.

doorstep. *See* if EVERY man would sweep his own doorstep the city would soon be clean.

double (adj.). **double charge will rive a cannon** (*English*) Put too much powder in the cannon and it will explode (usually quoted by a person declining offers of further food or drink on the grounds that they are already full). James Kelly, *A Complete Collection of Scotish Proverbs*, 1721.

~ *See also* DISSEMBLED sin is double wickedness; SUSPICION has double eyes.

double (verb). *See* DENYING a fault doubles it; MARRIAGE halves our griefs, doubles our joys, and quadruples our expenses.

doubt (noun). **when in doubt, do nowt** (*English*) When uncertain what course to take, the best policy is to do nothing. G. Weatherly, *'Little Folks' Proverb Painting Book*, 1884. An equivalent of US origin runs 'when in doubt leave it out'. *See also* NOTHING ventured, nothing gained.

doubt (verb). *See* he that KNOWS nothing, doubts nothing.

doubtful. *See* the PERSUASION of the fortunate sways the doubtful.

down. he that is down, down with him (*English*) When a person is down on their luck their friends tend to desert them, while their enemies wish them further down still. *Pepysian Garland*, *c.*1632.

~ *See also* he that is FALLEN cannot help him that is down; what goes UP must come down.

dowry. *See* a GREAT dowry is a bed full of brambles.

draw. draw not your bow till your arrow is fixed (*English*) Do not start doing something until the necessary first steps have been made. *See also* don't put the CART before the horse.

whosoever draws his sword against the prince must throw the scabbard away (*English*) Those who lead rebellions against established powers will never be able to relax their constant vigilance against attack themselves. R. Dallington, *View of France*, 1604.

> Hampden ... was for vigorous and decisive measures. When he drew the sword, as Clarendon has well said, he threw away the scabbard.
>
> Thomas Macaulay, *Hampden*, 1843

~ *See also* BEAUTY draws more than oxen; BEWARE of the oak, it draws the stroke; avoid the ash, it courts the flash; ONE hair of a woman draws more than a team of oxen; ONE shoulder of mutton draws down another.

dread. *See* a BURNT child dreads the fire; EVIL doers are evil dreaders; ILL doers are ill dreaders.

dream (noun). **dreams go by contraries** (*English*) In the interpretation of dreams, the opposite of what is dreamed may be expected to come true. *Tale of Beryn*, *c.*1400 (also found in the first century AD writings of Apuleius). *See also* DREAM of a funeral and you hear of a marriage.

> I took your letter last night to bed with me. In the morning I found your name on the sealing wax obliterated. I was startled at the bad omen till I recollected that it must have happened in my dreams, and they you know fall out by contraries.
>
> John Keats, letter to Fanny Brawne, 15 July 1819

~ *See also* FRIDAY night's dream on the Saturday told, is sure to come true be it never so old; MORNING dreams come true.

dream (verb). **dream of a funeral and you hear of a marriage** (*English*) Dreams of death presage good events (typically news of a wedding) in one's waking life. John Clarke, *Paroemiologia Anglo-Latina*, 1639. Sometimes encountered in the reverse form. *See also* DREAMS go by contraries.

> My wife had the most lucky dreams in the world ... It was one night a coffin and cross-bones, the sign of an approaching wedding.
>
> Oliver Goldsmith, *The Vicar of Wakefield*, 1766

~ *See also* those that EAT black pudding will dream of the devil.

dress. *See* there are MANY ways of dressing a calf's head.

drill. *See* no NAMES, no pack drill.

drink (noun). **drink washes off the dawb and discovers the man** (*English*) When a person drinks he or she reveals their true character. Thomas Fuller, *Gnomologia*, 1732.

when the drink is in, the wit is out (*Roman*) The more a person has to drink, the less quick-witted they are and the less subtle and clever their sense of humour becomes. John Gower, *Confessio Amantis*, *c.*1390 (also quoted by Pliny). Also encountered in the form 'drink in, wit out'. Warburton, Bishop of Gloucester in the eighteenth century, offered an alternative version with his own 'those who drink beer will think beer' (to which a resentful drinker replied 'and those that drink water will think water'). *See also* when the WINE is in, the wit is out.

> But after dinner is after dinner – an old saying and a true, 'much drinking, little thinking'.
>
> Jonathan Swift, *Journal to Stella*, 1712

~ *See also* GOOD ale is meat, drink and cloth; he was HANGED that left his drink behind; no CHINK, no drink.

drink (verb). **drink wine and have the gout, drink no wine and have the gout too** (*English*) It makes no difference to one's health whether one drinks alcohol or not. John Ray, *A Collection of English Proverbs*, 1670. By way of contrast, another proverb advises the health-conscious that the best policy is to 'drink less and go home by daylight'. Another recommends nettle juice rather than alcohol, insisting 'if they would drink nettles in March and eat mugwort in May, so many fine maidens wouldn't go to the clay'.

he that drinketh well sleepeth well, and he that sleepeth well thinketh no harm (*English*) Alcohol promotes sleep and through healthy sleep generosity of spirit. J. Palsgrave, *L'Éclaircissement de la langue française*, 1530.

> He that eateth well, drinketh well, he that drinketh well, sleepeth well, he that sleepeth well sinneth not, and he that sinneth not goeth straight through Purgatory to Paradise.
>
> William Lithgow, *Rare Adventures*, 1632

if you drink in your pottage, you'll cough in your grave (*English*) Those who drink while eating (or just having eaten) soup will find their health suffers as a result. John Ray, *A Collection of English Proverbs*, 1670.

~ *See also* EAT at pleasure, drink by measure; EATING and drinking takes away one's stomach; GARLIC makes a man wink, drink and stink; a MAN cannot whistle and drink at the same time; the MORE one drinks the more one may; a PENNY in purse will bid me drink when all the friends I have will not; WALK groundly, talk profoundly, drink roundly, sleep soundly; you can LEAD a horse to water, but you can't make him drink

drip. a dripping June sets all in tune (*English*) Wet weather in June promises well for crops and flowers later in the season. *Agreeable Companion*, 1742. Also encountered as 'a dry May and a dripping June bringeth all things into tune' and (from the Isle of Man) 'a dry May and a leaking June makes the farmer whistle a merry tune'.

drive. drive gently over the stones (*English*) Take things slowly and carefully when troubled times loom. Jonathan Swift, letter, 30 June 1711. Originally a piece of advice to riders, but later applied in other contexts.

drive your business, do not let it drive you (*English*) Do not let your work overtake your life. R. Codrington, *The Second Part of Youth's Behaviour*, 1672.

~ *See also* BAD money drives out good; FATE leads the willing but drives the stubborn; FIRE drives out fire; HUNGER drives the wolf out of the wood; it is ILL to drive black hogs in the dark; NAIL drives out nail; NEEDS must when the devil drives; ONE grief drives out another; THREE things drive a man out of his house: smoke, rain and a scolding wife.

drop (noun). *See* the LAST drop makes the cup run over; MANY drops make a shower.

drop (verb). *See* CONSTANT dropping wears away the stone.

drought. drought never bred dearth in England (*English*) Lack of rain never brought famine in England. John Heywood, *Play of Weather*, 1533. The sentiment is supported by another proverb, which runs 'a dry year never starves itself'.

> Drought never brought dearth.
>
> George Herbert, *Outlandish Proverbs*, 1640

~ *See also* AFTER drought cometh rain.

drown. a drowning man will clutch at a straw (*English*) When in desperate straits a person will grasp at any hope of relief, no matter how slim. Thomas More, *Dialogue of Comfort*, 1534. The proverb, or variants of it, is known in many languages. The Italian version has the drowning man clutching at razors.

> We drift down time, clutching at straws. But what good's a brick to a drowning man?
>
> Tom Stoppard, *Rosencrantz and Guildenstern are Dead*, 1966

~ *See also* BACCHUS hath drowned more men than Neptune; a FOOL will laugh when he is drowning; if you're BORN to be hanged then you'll never be drowned; it is the BEST swimmers who drown; POUR not water on a drowned mouse; WINE hath drowned more men than the sea; you had BETTER be drunk than drowned.

drum. where drums beat, laws are silent (*Roman*) When a country is torn by warfare, the normal safeguards of the civil law no longer apply in practical terms. Cicero, *Pro Milone*, first century BC.

> For the laws are dumb in the midst of arms.
>
> Cicero, *Pro Milone*, first century BC

drunk. drunken days have all their tomorrows (*English*) The morning after always comes round after a bout of drunkenness. Samuel Smiles, *Thrift*, 1875. Related proverbs include 'a drunken night makes a cloudy morning'.

he that is drunk is as great as a king (*English*) Drunkards believe they are more capable and more powerful than they really are. *Westminster Drollery*, 1672. Another proverb warns, however, that 'what you do when you are drunk you must pay for when you are dry'.

~ *See also* EVER drunk, ever dry; HEAVEN protects children, sailors and drunken men; he that KILLETH a man when he is drunk shall be hanged when he is sober; you had BETTER be drunk than drowned.

drunkard. *See* there are MORE old drunkards than old doctors.

drunkenness reveals what soberness conceals (*Roman*) What sober men keep secret is revealed when they are drunk. Geoffrey Chaucer, *The Canterbury Tales*, c.1387 (also quoted by Horace).

> It is an old proverbe, whatsoever is in the heart of the sober man, is in the mouth of the drunkarde.
>
> John Lyly, *Euphues: The Anatomy of Wit*, 1578

dry (adj.). **a dry cough is the trumpeter of death** (*Turkish*) A dry, hacking cough may be a symptom of approaching death for someone in poor health. John Ray, *A Collection of English Proverbs*, 1670.

dry bread at home is better than roast meat abroad (*English*) Something modest but certainly held is preferable to something better but still to be secured. George Herbert, *Jacula Prudentum*, 1651. *See also* a BIRD in the hand is worth two in the bush.

dry feet, warm head, bring safe to bed (*English*) In cold, wet weather it is important to keep the feet dry and the head warm in order to preserve the health. George Herbert, *Outlandish Proverbs*, 1640.

~ *See also* EVER drunk, ever dry; no coming to HEAVEN with dry eyes; put your TRUST in God and keep your powder dry; SORROW is always dry; SOW dry and set wet; TURNIPS like a dry bed but a wet head; we NEVER know the worth of water till the well is dry; you NEVER miss the water till the well runs dry.

dry (verb). *See* NOTHING dries sooner than a tear.

duck. *See* if it LOOKS like a duck, walks like a duck and quacks like a duck, it's a duck; if the ICE will bear a man before Christmas, it will not bear a duck after.

due. *See* GIVE credit where credit is due; GIVE the devil his due.

dull. *See* ALL work and no play makes Jack a dull boy.

dumb. the dumb man gets no land (*English*) A person who is not prepared to stand up for his own interests cannot expect to gain reward. John Gower, *Confession Amantis*, *c.*1390.

> The proverbe is 'the doumb man no lond getith'.
> Thomas Hoccleve, 'La Male Règle', 1406

~ *See also* a CHERRY year, a merry year; a plum year, a dumb year; LIGHT cares speak, great ones are dumb.

dunder do gally the beans (*English*) Beans grow faster after a thunderstorm. John Ray, *A Collection of English Proverbs*, 1678.

dunghill. *See* EVERY cock crows on his own dunghill.

dure. *See* the MIRTH of the world dureth but a while.

dust. while the dust is on your feet, sell what you have bought (*English*) It is good business practice to sell on stock you have acquired as quickly as possible (before even brushing away the dust of the journey taken to get the goods). John Ray, *A Collection of English Proverbs*, 1678.

> The meaning is that we should sell quickly (though with light gaines) that we may trade for more.
> John Ray, *A Collection of English Proverbs*, 1678

~ *See also* the FLY sat upon the axletree of the chariot-wheel and said, what a dust do I raise!; a PECK of March dust is worth a king's ransom.

Dutchman. *See* in SETTLING an island, the first building erected by a Spaniard will be a church; by a Frenchman, a fort; by a Dutchman, a warehouse; and by an Englishman, an alehouse.

duty. *See* the FIRST duty of a soldier is obedience; PROPERTY has its duties as well as its rights.

dwarf. a dwarf on a giant's shoulders sees further of the two (*Roman*) By taking advantage of the achievements or knowledge of great men, a lesser person may surpass them. Robert Burton, *Anatomy of Melancholy*, 1621.

> I say with Didacus Stella 'A dwarf standing on the shoulders of a giant may see farther than a giant himself' ...
> Robert Burton, *Anatomy of Melancholy*, 1621

dwell. *See* PRIDE and grace dwell never in one place.

dyer. *See* no WOOL is so white that a dyer cannot blacken it.

dyke. *See* if ONE sheep leap o'er the dyke, all the rest will follow.

each. each bird loves to hear himself sing (*English*) People love the sound of their voices. J. Howell, *Paroemiographia*, 1659. A related proverb runs 'a bird is known by its note and a man by his talk'.

each cross hath its inscription (*English*) Providence imposes hardships upon specific individuals as a punishment for what they have done wrong. J. Clarke, *Paroemiologia Anglo-Latina*, 1639.

eagle. eagles don't catch flies (*English*) The great are not interested in trifles. *Mirror for Magistrates*, 1563 (also found in the writings of Erasmus). Also related, and indicative of the forbearance of the great towards the humble and lowly, is 'the eagle suffers little birds to sing'.

> With regard to slight insults ... 'They sting one (says he) but as a fly stings a horse; and the eagle will not catch flies.'
>
> Hester Piozzi, *Anecdotes of Johnson*, 1786

eagles fly alone (*English*) People with inner strength and self-confidence tend to remain independent of others, pursuing their course alone. J. Clarke, *Paroemiographia Anglo-Latina*, 1639.

> Eagles commonly fly alone: they are crows, daws, and starlings that flock together.
>
> John Webster, *The Duchess of Malfi*, 1623

~ *See also* a GOOD surgeon must have an eagle's eye, a lion's heart and a lady's hand; where the CARCASS is, there shall the eagles be gathered together.

ear. if your ear burns someone is thinking about you (*Roman*) A tingling sensation in the ear is a sure sign that someone is thinking or talking about you. Geoffrey Chaucer, *Troilus and Criseyde*, *c.*1385–90. Also found as 'if your ear glows someone is thinking about you'.

> What fire is in my ears? Can this be true?
>
> William Shakespeare, *Much Ado About Nothing*, 1599

~ *See also* the BELLY hath no ears; BRAWLING curs never want sore ears; CHILDREN have wide ears and long tongues; CITIES are taken by the ears; FIELDS have eyes, and woods have ears; he that goes to LAW holds a wolf by the ears; HUNGRY bellies have no ears; it is a BOLD mouse that breeds in the cat's ear; LITTLE pitchers have big ears; SPIES are the ears and eyes of princes; WALLS have ears; WIDE ears and a short tongue; you can't make a SILK purse out of a sow's ear.

early. the early bird catches the worm (*English*) Those who set about their work promptly will prosper most. William Camden, *Remains concerning Britain*, 1605. Related proverbs include 'the early bird gets the late one's breakfast'. An Indian variant noted by Rudyard Kipling runs 'who sleeps late gets the bull-calf, he who rises early the cow-calf' – the cow-calf being preferable. Other proverbs on similar lines include the Scottish 'the cow that's first up gets the first of the dew' and the Danish 'the first bird gets the first grain'.

> And it's the early bird, as the saying goes, that gets the rations.
>
> Robert Louis Stevenson, *Treasure Island*, 1883

the early man never borrows from the late man (*English*) Those who get their work done promptly will never have need to borrow from those who do not. J. Howell, *Proverbs*, 1659.

Oats, too, benefit from early sowing ... Another agricultural proverb ... declares that, 'the early man never borrows from the late man'.

Ralph Whitlock, *Calendar of Country Customs*, 1978

early master, long knave (*English*) A youth who becomes his own master at too young an age will quickly go wrong and end up servant to someone else. James Kelly, *A Complete Collection of Scotish Proverbs*, 1721. Also found as 'early master, soon knave'.

early sow, early mow (*English*) The sooner you start on something, the sooner you will see results from your efforts. J. Clarke, *Paroemiographia Anglo-Latina*, 1639. Confirming the notion that the early sower does best comes another proverb, 'the early sower never borrows of the late'.

early thunder, early spring (*English*) If there is thunder early in the year spring will come early too. R. Inwards, *Weather Lore*, 1893. Another proverb advises that 'thunder in spring cold will bring', while another claims that 'the first thunder of the year awakes all the frogs and all the snakes'.

early to bed and early to rise, makes a man healthy, wealthy and wise (*German*) Those who avoid late nights and get up at an early hour will benefit in all ways. *Treatise of Fishing with Angle*, 1496. The sentiment did not find favour with US humorist James Thurber who, in *Fables for Our Time*, 1940, coined his own version of it: 'early to rise and early to bed makes a male healthy and wealthy and dead.' The saying would appear to have its roots in the Roman proverb 'to rise betimes makes one healthy, virtuous, and rich'. Other variants around the world include the Yiddish 'early to bed and early to get married', the Spanish 'he who does not rise with the sun does not enjoy the day', the Wolof 'he who rises early finds the way short' and the English 'God helps the early riser'.

Early to bed and early to rise being among Mr Sponge's maxims, he was enjoying the view ... shortly after daylight.

Robert Smith Surtees, *Sponge's Sport*, 1853

early wed, early dead (*English*) Those who marry young are fated to die prematurely. *Notes & Queries*, 1895.

it early pricks that will be a thorn (*English*) A child that is destined to turn out badly will show early signs of bad behaviour. *Coventry Plays*, *c.*1450.

It early pricks that will be a thorn. Children soon shew their propensities and inclinations.

James Kelly, *A Complete Collection of Scotish Proverbs*, 1721

~ *See also* get a NAME to rise early, and you may lie all day; LATE children, early orphans.

earn. *See* a PENNY saved is a penny earned.

earnest. *See* DOGS begin in jest and end in earnest.

earth. earth must to earth (*English*) All living things (including men and animals as well as plants, literally born of the earth) are fated to return to earth when they die. *c.*1480, *Early Miscellany*, 1855. A less concise version of the proverb runs 'the earth produces all things and receives all again'.

An old said saw, earth must to earth.

George Peele, *Edward I*, 1593

~ *See also* he that COUNTS all costs will never put plough in the earth; if the DOCTOR cures, the sun sees it, but if he kills, the earth hides it; it takes a GOOD many shovelfuls of earth to bury the truth; RICHES are like muck, which stink in a heap, but spread abroad make the earth fruitful; SIX feet of earth make all men equal.

earthen. the earthen pot must keep clear of the brass kettle (*Hebrew*) Weaker persons (or states and so on) should avoid clashing with those who are stronger. Thomas Fuller, *Gnomologia*, 1732 (also quoted in the Apocrypha, Ecclesiasticus 13).

Buckingham is Lord of the Ascendant ... you are the vase of earth; beware of knocking yourself against the vase of iron.

Walter Scott, *The Fortunes of Nigel*, 1822

ease. he is at ease who has enough (*English*) Those who have all they need can afford to relax. George Herbert, *Outlandish Proverbs*, 1640. Related proverbs include 'ease and success are fellows' and 'he that is at ease seeks dainties'. The Irish, however, warn that 'a life of ease is the most unpleasant thing in the world'.

~ *See also* HONOUR and ease are seldom bedfellows; ITCH and ease can no man please; of SUFFERANCE cometh ease.

easier. *See* EASY.

easily. *See* a LOW hedge is easily leaped over; the MOUSE that has only one hole is easily taken; an OLD fox is not easily snared; WOOD half burnt is easily kindled.

east. east, west, home's best (*English*) No matter how far you may go, you will never find a place preferable to home. W.K. Kelly, *Proverbs of all Nations*, 1859.

~ *See also* if it RAINS when the wind is in the east, it will rain for twenty-four hours at least; the WEST wind always brings wet weather, the east wind wet and cold together, the south wind surely brings us rain, the north wind blows it back again; when the WIND is in the east, 'tis neither good for man nor beast.

Easter. at Easter let your clothes be new, or else be sure you will it rue (*English*) Always wear new clothes at Easter, or suffer the consequences. William Shakespeare, *Romeo and Juliet*, *c.*1593. Superstition claims that ill luck will befall any person who does not wear some new item of clothing on Easter Sunday. Those who fail to observe this tradition will suffer, among possible misfortunes, birds' droppings falling on them. It was said in Hampshire that even the dogs would spit at someone who did not wear new clothing on Easter Sunday; in Ireland it was believed that crows would peck out the person's eyes.

> Didst thou not fall out with a tailor for wearing
> his new doublet before Easter?
>
> William Shakespeare, *Romeo and Juliet*, *c.*1593

Easter in snow, Christmas in mud; Christmas in snow, Easter in mud (*English*) A cold spring precedes a wet winter, while a cold winter precedes a wet spring. R. Inwards, *Weather Lore*, 1893. Other proverbs on the subject of Easter weather include 'if the sun shines on Easter Day, it shines on Whit Sunday', 'such weather as there is on Easter Day there will be at harvest' and 'late Easter, long cold spring'.

Easter so longed for is gone in a day (*Italian*) Things long awaited are often over all too quickly. G. Torriano, *Select Italian Proverbs*, 1642.

when Easter falls in our Lady's lap, then let England beware of a rap (*English*) It is ominous for the nation if Good Friday happens to fall on the same date as Lady Day. 1648, quoted in Rollins, *Cavalier and Puritan*, 1923. *See also* when our LADY falls in our Lord's lap, then let England beware a sad clap.

~ *See also* if at CHRISTMAS ice hangs on the willow, clover may be cut at Easter; the JEWS spend at Easter, the Moors at marriages, the Christians in suits.

easy. easier said than done (*Roman*) It is sometimes easier to discuss doing something than it is to get it done. *Religious and Love Poems*, *c.*1450 (also recorded in the writings of Plautus and Livy). Also found as 'sooner said than done'.

> That is (quoth she) sooner said then doone,
> I dreede.
>
> John Heywood, *A Dialogue containing … the Proverbs in the English Tongue*, 1546

easy come, easy go (*English*) What has been acquired without much trouble is easily parted with (usually quoted in relation to money). John Arbuthnot, *John Bull*, 1712. Also encountered in former times with 'easy' replaced by 'lightly' or 'quickly'. *See also* a FOOL and his money are soon parted; here TODAY, gone tomorrow.

> A thriftless wretch, spending the goods and gear
> that his forefathers won with the sweat of their
> brows; light come, light go.
>
> John Arbuthnot, *John Bull*, 1712

easy does it (*English*) A reminder that some tasks require gentle, unhurried handling. Tom Taylor, *The Ticket-of-Leave Man*, 1863. Also found as 'gently does it'.

> Important to build bridges … between the faiths.
> Gently does it.
>
> Salman Rushdie, *Midnight's Children*, 1981

it is easier for a camel to go through the eye of a needle than it is for a rich man to enter into the kingdom of heaven (*Hebrew*) The lowly and humble are favoured in the eyes of heaven, whereas the wealthy will find it more difficult to prove their worth. Bible, Matthew 19:24 and Mark 10:25. The proverb is also to be found in the Koran: 'the impious shall find the gates of heaven shut; nor shall he enter till a camel shall pass through the eye of a needle'.

it is easier to build two chimneys than to maintain one (*English*) It can be harder to maintain something than it is to build it (or otherwise set it up) in the first place. George Herbert, *Outlandish Proverbs*, 1640.

It is easier to build two chimneys than to keep one in fuel.

Benjamin Franklin, *The Way to Wealth*, 1736

it is easier to descend than to ascend (*English*) It is harder to go up in the world than it is to go down. Jan Gruter, *Florilegium Ethicopoliticum*, 1611. Related proverbs include the Roman 'the descent to Avernus is easy'.

it is easier to pull down than to build up (*English*) Destroying things is easier than creating them. R. Stanyhurst, *History of Ireland*, 1577.

it is easier to raise the devil than to lay him (*English*) It is easier to start trouble than it is to restore peace once more. Thomas Fuller, *The Church History of Britain*, 1655. Related proverbs include 'raise no more spirits than you can conjure down'.

Alas! the Devil's sooner raised than laid.

David Garrick, prologue to Sheridan's *The School for Scandal*, 1777

it is easy to be wise after the event (*English*) It is easy to see things more clearly with the benefit of hindsight. G. Harvey, *Marginalia*, *c.*1590.

Away, thou strange justifier of thy selfe, to bee wiser then thou wert, by the event.

Ben Jonson, *Epicoene*, 1616

it is easy to fall into a trap but hard to get out again (*English*) It is easy to make a mistake, but it may be more difficult to escape the consequences of it. John Lyly, *Euphues and his England*, 1580. Also found as 'it is easy to fall into a net but hard to get out again'.

it is easy to find a stick to beat a dog (*English*) It is no difficult task to find some way of attacking or criticizing an enemy if you are set on such action. T. Becon, *Early Works*, 1563.

A staff is quickly found to beat a dog.

William Shakespeare, *Henry VI, Part 2*, *c.*1591

it is easy to keep a castle that was never assaulted (*English*) It is not hard to resist when no one is attacking. Sir John Harington, *Orlando Furioso*, 1591.

it is easy to rob an orchard when none keeps it (*English*) It is easy to steal something when no one is keeping an eye on it. John Ray, *A Collection of English Proverbs*, 1670.

~ *See also* ALL things are difficult before they are easy; GEAR is easier gained than guided; a GENTLE heart is tied with an easy thread.

eat. eat at pleasure, drink by measure (*English*) Wise people eat as much as they like, but limit how much alcohol they drink. Randle Cotgrave, *A Dictionary of the French and English Tongues*, 1611. Related proverbs on the subject include 'eat enough and it will make you wise' and 'eat less and drink less and buy a knife at Michaelmas'.

eaten bread is soon forgotten (*English*) A consumed meal (or other pleasure or favour) is quickly forgotten when the time for the next meal arrives. J. Minsheu, *A Spanish Grammar*, 1599. *See also* it is HARD to pay for bread that has been eaten.

eating and drinking takes away one's stomach (*English*) Eating and drinking satisfies a person's appetite. Randle Cotgrave, *A Dictionary of the French and English Tongues*, 1611.

eating and scratching wants but a beginning (*English*) Once started, a person may eat more or scratch more than they originally thought they would. James Kelly, *A Complete Collection of Scotish Proverbs*, 1721.

They say, eating and scratching wants but a beginning ... I'll help myself to ... veal.

Jonathan Swift, *Dialogues*, 1738

eat peas with the king and cherries with the beggar (*English*) Choose inferior fare when dining (or otherwise dealing) with your betters, for they are sure to choose the best things, leaving other diners with the dregs. James Kelly, *A Complete Collection of Scotish Proverbs*, 1721.

eat till you sweat and work till you freeze (*English*) Exhortation to the lazy to work harder. J. Lyly, *Euphues*, 1579.

he that eats the king's goose shall be choked with his feathers (*English*) Those who accept favours from their betters must expect to have favours asked of them in return in the future. Randle Cotgrave, *A Dictionary of the French and English Tongues*, 1611. Variants include 'he that eats the king's goose doth void fethers an hundred yeares after.'

Often have I thought of that excellent old adage;
He that eats the King's goose shall be choaked with his feathers.

Samuel Richardson, *Clarissa*, 1748

he that would eat the fruit must climb the tree (*English*) Those who hope to enjoy benefits must work for them. James Kelly, *A Complete Collection of Scotish Proverbs*, 1721. Equivalents include 'he that will eat the kernel must crack the nut'.

those that eat black pudding will dream of the devil (*English*) Those who eat black pudding will suffer nightmares. Jonathan Swift, *Polite Conversation*, 1738.

we must eat to live and not live to eat (*Greek*) A person should eat enough to maintain his physical health, without surrendering himself to gluttony. J. Trevisa, *Higden's Polychronicon*, 1387. The saying is attributed to Socrates, who is said to have uttered it on declining an invitation to live in luxury at the Athenian court of King Archelaus. According to Plutarch, Socrates actually said 'bad men live that they may eat and drink, whereas good men eat and drink that they may live'. Related proverbs include 'eat enough and it will make you wise', 'eat when you're hungry and drink when you're dry' and 'eat at pleasure, drink by measure'. Anyone who fails to follow the advice of such proverbs and overindulges in the pleasures of the table may consult another saying to aid recovery: 'he that eats till he is sick must fast till he is well.' *See also* the EYE is bigger than the belly.

> I shall eat sufficient ... But I eat to live; I don't live to eat.
>
> Sir Arthur Wing Pinero, *Preserving Mr Panmure*, 1912

you've got to eat a peck of dirt before you die (*English*) Everyone must expect to suffer a certain amount of hardship and disappointment in their lives (just as everyone must accept that there will be small amounts of dirt in their food). J. Clarke, *Paroemiographia Anglo-Latina*, 1639. Also encountered with 'ashes' or 'salt' in the place of 'dirt'. A warning note is sounded, however, by a proverb of US origin that runs 'bad meals kill more than the best doctors ever cured' and another, of Danish origin, that runs 'more people are killed by supper than by the sword'.

~ *See also* an ANGLER eats more than he gets; APPETITE comes with eating; the ASS loaded with gold still eats thistles; BIG fish eat little fish; CARRION crows bewail the dead sheep and then eat them; CATS eat what hussies spare; DOG does not eat dog; he that would LIVE for aye must eat sage in May; he was a BOLD man that first ate an oyster; if APPLES bloom in March, in vain for them you'll search; if apples bloom in April, then they'll be plentiful; if apples bloom in May, you may eat them night and day; if you won't WORK you shan't eat; it is a GOOD thing to eat your brown bread first; it is HARD to pay for bread that has been eaten; a JADE eats as much as a good horse; NEVER eat an oyster unless there is an R in the month; the PROOF of the pudding is in the eating; REVENGE is a dish that is best eaten cold; SCORNFUL dogs will eat dirty puddings; 'tis an OLD rat that won't eat cheese; when the CUCKOO comes he eats up all the dirt; you ARE what you eat; you can't have your CAKE and eat it.

ebb. *See* CROSS the stream where it is ebbest; EVERY flow hath its ebb; the HIGHEST flood has the lowest ebb.

eclipse. *See* ONE cloud is enough to eclipse all the sun.

edge. *See* IDLENESS turns the edge of wit.

edged. *See* CHILDREN and fools must not play with edged tools; it is ILL jesting with edged tools.

eel. *See also* ALL that breed in the mud are not eels; he that will CATCH eels must disturb the flood.

effect. the effect speaks, the tongue needs not (*English*) There is no need to say anything when events speak for themselves. George Herbert, *Outlandish Proverbs*, 1640.

~ *See also* BITTER pills may have blessed effects; take away the CAUSE and the effect must cease.

egg. he that would have eggs must endure the cackling of hens (*English*) Sometimes a person must put up with inconvenience in order to get what they desire. John Ray, *A Collection of English Proverbs*, 1670.

> I would not have your trouble and noise for all the advantage you bring me.
>
> James Kelly, *A Complete Collection of Scotish Proverbs*, 1721

~ *See also* BETTER an egg today than a chicken tomorrow; but ONE egg and that addled too; don't put ALL your eggs in one basket; don't TEACH your grandmother to suck eggs; an ILL bird lays an ill egg;

ILL egging makes ill begging; KILL not the goose that lays the golden egg; there is REASON in the roasting of eggs; a WILD goose never lays a tame egg; you cannot make an OMELETTE without breaking eggs.

Egypt. *See* there is CORN in Egypt.

eight. *See* ONE for sorrow, two for joy; three for a girl, four for a boy; five for silver, six for gold; seven for a secret, never to be told; eight for heaven, nine for hell; and ten for the devil's own self; SIX hours' sleep for a man, seven for a woman and eight for a fool.

elbow. *See* put ANOTHER man's child in your bosom and he'll creep out at your elbow; you should NEVER touch your eye but with your elbow.

elbow-grease gives the best polish (*English*) There is no substitute for application and diligent hard work when it comes to getting a good result. Andrew Marvell, *The Rehearsal Transpros'd*, 1672.

> Two or three brawny fellows in a corner with meer ink and elbow-grease, do more harm than ...
> Andrew Marvell, *The Rehearsal Transpros'd*, 1672

elegant. *See* although there EXIST many thousand subjects for elegant conversation, there are persons who cannot meet a cripple without talking about feet.

elephant. an elephant never forgets (*English*) Some people will never forget wrongs or injuries done to them (just as elephants are reputed to do). Saki, *Reginald: Reginald on Besetting Sins*, 1910. The proverb is of ancient origin, being known to the Greeks – except that, until the early twentieth century, it was always the camel rather than the elephant that never forgot: 'the camel never forgets an injury'. Elephants owe their reputation for long memories to the ability of working elephants in India to remember the many varied instructions of their handlers.

only an elephant can bear an elephant's load (*Indian*) Only someone remarkable can achieve remarkable things. Sometimes given in the form of an apology when finding oneself incapable of doing something.

eleven. *See* RAIN before seven, fine before eleven.

ell. See ILL comes in by ells and goes out by inches.

elm. *See* EVERY elm has its man.

embankment. *See* an ANT hole may collapse an embankment.

embitter. *See* a LITTLE poison embitters much sweetness.

embrace. *See* when FORTUNE smiles, embrace her.

employ. *See* a PHYSICIAN is an angel when employed but a devil when one must pay him.

empty. empty hands no hawks allure (*English*) Those who have nothing to offer cannot expect to attract much interest. John of Salisbury, *Polycraticus*, *c.*1175.

> 'Tis god must such an instrument procure; with empty fist no man doth falcons lure.
> John Webster, *The White Devil*, 1612

an empty purse fills the face with wrinkles (*English*) The poor age quickly because of worry about their finances. T. Draxe, *Bibliotheca Scholastica*, 1616. Related proverbs include 'an empty purse causes a full heart', 'an empty purse is the devil' and 'an empty purse frights away friends'. *See also* WRINKLED purses make wrinkled faces.

empty sacks will never stand upright (*Italian*) Without sustenance it is impossible to function. G. Torriano, *Select Italian Proverbs*, 1642. Often quoted to excuse petty acts of gluttony.

> Poverty often deprives a Man of all Spirit and Virtue; 'Tis hard for an empty Bag to stand upright.
> Benjamin Franklin, *Poor Richard's Almanack*, 1758

empty vessels make the most sound (*Roman*) Those who have least of value to impart often have the loudest voices. John Lydgate, *Pilgrimage of Man*, 1430. Variants in other languages include the Russian 'there is plenty of sound in an empty barrel' and the Scottish 'toom [empty] bags rattle'.

> I did never know so full a voice issue from so empty a heart: but the saying is true – The empty vessel makes the greatest sound.
> William Shakespeare, *Henry V*, *c.*1598

~ *See also* the DEVIL dances in an empty pocket; FULL bellies make empty skulls; WINE and wenches empty men's purses.

enchantment. *See* DISTANCE lends enchantment to the view.

end (noun). **the end crowns the work** (*Roman*) It is by the end result that effort should be judged. H. Watson, *The Ship of Fools*, 1509. Another proverb claims that 'the end tries all', similarly suggesting that it is by the result that a course of action will be assessed. Other sayings along similar lines include the English 'at the end of the work you may judge of the workmen' and the French 'in everything consider the end'. *See also* the PROOF of the pudding is in the eating.

> Proof must be built up stone by stone ... As I say, the end crowns the work.
>
> Charles Dickens, *The Mystery of Edwin Drood*, 1870

the end justifies the means (*Roman*) Any course of action is permissible as long as the desired end is achieved; it is often quoted in defence of morally dubious deeds. G. Babington, *Exposition of the Commandments*, 1583 (also found in Ovid's *Heroides*, first century AD). A succinct German proverb suggesting much the same thing runs 'end good, all good'. Other related proverbs from around the world include the English 'by fair means or foul', the Irish 'where you cannot climb over you must crawl under', and the Scottish 'a good day's work may be done with a dirty spade', although the Italians observe that 'dirty water does not wash clean'. *See also* ALL's fair in love and war; ALL's well that ends well.

> The End must justifie the means;
> He only sins who Ill intends;
> Since therefore 'tis to combat Evil;
> 'Tis lawful to employ the Devil.
>
> Matthew Prior, 'Hans Carvel', 1701

~ *See also* ALL good things must come to an end; EVERYTHING has an end; he who WILLS the end, wills the means; the LAME foot overtakes the swift one in the end; the LONGEST day must have an end; LOOK to the end; such BEGINNING, such end; there was NEVER a good town but had a mire at one end of it; the THIN end of the wedge is to be feared; THINK on the end before you begin; what the FOOL does in the end, the wise man does at the beginning; you cannot BURN the candle at both ends.

end (verb). *See* ALL's well that ends well; DOGS begin in jest and end in earnest; either MEND or end; FROST and fraud both end in foul; a MAN has choice to begin love but not to end it.

endeavour. *See* a HOG that's bemired endeavours to bemire others.

ending. *See* a GOOD beginning makes a good ending.

endure. he that endures is not overcome (*Roman*) Any person who quietly puts up with hardship or cruelty without breaking is thereby unconquered. George Herbert, *Outlandish Proverbs*, 1640 (also quoted by Virgil). A biblical version of the same thought runs 'he that shall endure unto the end, the same shall be saved'. Related proverbs on the subject of endurance include 'he that can quietly endure overcometh', 'he that will not endure labour in this world, let him not be born', the Roman 'every trial is to be overcome by endurance', the Yiddish 'he that can't endure the bad will not live to see the good', the Japanese 'to endure what is unendurable is true endurance' and the US 'there is no greater misfortune than not to be able to endure misfortune'.

> Men seyn 'the suffrant overcom'th', parde.
>
> Geoffrey Chaucer, *Troilus and Criseyde*, c.1385–90

~ *See also* he KNOWS best what good is that has endured evil; he that would have EGGS must endure the cackling of hens; what can't be CURED must be endured.

enemy. *See* ART has no enemy but ignorance; BASHFULNESS is an enemy to poverty; the BEST is the enemy of the good; GOD defend me from my friends; from my enemies I can defend myself; the GOOD is the enemy of the best; HUNGER and cold deliver a man up to his enemy; it is GOOD to make a bridge of gold to a flying enemy; a JOKE never gains over an enemy, but often loseth a friend; KEEP yourself from the anger of a great man, from the tumult of a mob, from a man of ill fame, from a widow that has been thrice married, from a wind that comes in at a hole, and from a reconciled enemy; MONEY makes friends enemies; ONE enemy is too much; take HEED of reconciled enemies and of meat twice boiled; there is no LITTLE enemy; TRUST not a new friend nor an old enemy; WEALTH is enemy to health.

engender. *See* GOOD wine engendreth good blood.

England. England is the paradise of women, the hell of horses and the purgatory of servants (*English*) The English treat women well, but are cruel both to their animals and especially to their servants. John Florio, *Second Fruits*, 1591.

> 'England is the paradise of women, hell for horses, purgatory of servants.' For the first, *bilia vera* … For the next, … *Ignoramus* … For the last, … we cast it forth as full of falsehood.
>
> Thomas Fuller, *The History of the Worthies of England*, 1662

England's difficulty is Ireland's opportunity (*Irish*) When England is distracted by trouble of some kind Ireland has the chance to gain some advantage. *Tribune*, 19 January 1856. Another proverb, identifying Ireland as the vulnerable target for invaders, claims 'he that England will win must with Ireland begin'.

~ *See also* the CAT, the Rat and Lovell our Dog rule all England under an Hog; DROUGHT never bred dearth in England; TURKEY, heresy, hops and beer came into England all in one year; what MANCHESTER says today, the rest of England says tomorrow; when EASTER falls in our Lady's lap, then let England beware of a rap; when HEMPE is spun, England is done; when our LADY falls in our Lord's lap, then let England beware a sad clap.

English. the English are a nation of shopkeepers (*French*) The English have the character and aspirations of an uncultured and unimaginative middle-class merchant (and should be treated as such). Adam Smith, *The Wealth of Nations*, 1776. The saying is popularly attributed (by the English) to the French Emperor Napoleon, although the idea had been voiced in so many words by several English writers decades before the Napoleonic wars. Other proverbs allege that the English are 'the swearing nation' and 'the Frenchmen's apes'.

> To found a great empire for the sole purpose of raising up a people of customers, may at first sight appear a project fit only for a nation of shopkeepers.
>
> Adam Smith, *The Wealth of Nations*, 1776

the English never know when they are beaten (*French*) It is part of the English national character never to admit defeat. G.J. Whyte-Melville, *Digby Dand*, 1853 (attributed originally to Napoleon Bonaparte).

an English summer, three hot days and a thunderstorm (*English*) English summers are rarely hot and when they are do not last long. Robert Smith Surtees, *Handley Cross*, 1854.

Englishman. an Englishman's home is his castle (*English*) Every Englishman considers himself safe from the law and from interference from his neighbours when safe in his own home. H. Étienne, *Stage of Popish Toys*, 1581. In reality, various authorities are entitled to force entry into an Englishman's home under certain conditions (for instance, in pursuit of arrest or search warrants or to enforce a compulsory purchase order). In the past, some commentators have expanded the terms of reference of the proverb, maintaining that it applies equally to the Englishman's conscience, the home of his soul, as much as to his physical residence.

> Some people maintain that an Englishman's house is his castle. That's gammon.
>
> Charles Dickens, *The Pickwick Papers*, 1836–7

an Englishman's word is his bond (*English*) A promise made by an Englishman will always be kept, as a matter of honour. G. Benham, *Book of Quotations*, 1924. Also encountered centuries earlier in the forms 'a king's word should be a king's word' and 'an honest man's word is his bond'.

> O kingis word shuld be o kingis bonde.
>
> *Lancelot of the Lake*, *c.*1500

~ *See also* in SETTLING an island, the first building erected by a Spaniard will be a church; by a Frenchman, a fort; by a Dutchman, a warehouse; and by an Englishman, an alehouse; ONE Englishman can beat three Frenchmen; SCRATCH an Englishman and you'll find a seaman.

enjoy. if you would enjoy the fruit, pluck not the flower (*English*) If you wish to enjoy a particular benefit take care not to stifle or destroy the source from which it may emerge. H.G. Bohn, *A Handbook of Proverbs*, 1855. Another proverb advises 'he that would enjoy the fruit must climb the tree'.

enough. enough is as good as a feast (*Greek*) Having sufficient of something is as satisfying as over-indulgence in it. John Lydgate, *Assembly of the Gods*, *c.*1420 (also quoted by Euripides in *Suppliants*, *c.*421BC). Originally applied largely to gluttony, but now used in many other contexts. *See also* you can have too MUCH of a good thing.

> A little dish oft furnishes enough: And sure enough is equal to a feast.
> Henry Fielding, *Covent Garden Tragedy*, 1732

enough is enough (*Roman*) Sufficient of something should be enough for anyone. John Heywood, *A Dialogue containing ... the Proverbs in the English Tongue*, 1546 (also found in various forms in the writings of the classical authors). Rendered in other European languages as *assai basta, e troppo guasta* (Italian), *mieux vaut assez que trop* (French) and *genoeg is meer dan overvloed* (Dutch). Related proverbs include 'he hath enough who is contented with a little'. As regards those who seem never to have enough, an English proverb warns 'he will have enough one day when his mouth is full of mould' (in other words, when the person concerned is dead).

> As for money, enough is enough; no man can enjoy more.
> Robert Southey, *The Doctor*, 1834

~ *See also* FLING enough dirt and some will stick; a FOOL's tongue is long enough to cut his own throat; GIVE a man enough rope and he will hang himself; GOD send you joy, for sorrow will come fast enough; HAP and halfpenny goods enough; he is at EASE who has enough; he is RICH enough that wants nothing; it is MISERY enough to have been once happy; MORE than enough is too much; ONE cloud is enough to eclipse all the sun; one has ALWAYS strength enough to bear the misfortunes of one's friends; ONE mad action is not enough to prove a man mad; SOON enough if well enough; there will be SLEEPING enough in the grave; what is WELL done is done soon enough; a WORD to the wise is enough.

enrich. *See* ENVY never enriched any man.

enter. *See* BELLS call others but themselves enter not into the church; a BRIBE will enter without knocking; GIFTS enter without knocking; it is EASIER for a camel to go through the eye of a needle than it is for a rich man to enter into the kingdom of heaven; when DISTRUST enters in at the foregate, love goes out at the postern; when PASSION entereth at the foregate, wisdom goeth out of the postern; where the SUN enters the doctor does not.

envy (noun). **envy never dies** (*English*) Envy does not diminish with the passage of time, as other emotions do. John Berners, *Froissart*, 1523–5. Variants include the Roman 'envy has no holidays', the Arabic 'envy never rests', and the French 'the envious die but envy never'.

> Hatred hath an end, envy never ceaseth.
> Robert Burton, *Anatomy of Melancholy*, 1624

envy never enriched any man (*English*) No one ever profited through envy of others. T. Draxe, *Bibliotheca Scholastica*, 1616. Related proverbs include 'a wise man cares not for what he cannot have', 'the envious man shall never want woe', 'the envious heart fretteth itself', 'envy shoots at others and wounds herself' and 'as rust corrupts iron so envy corrupts man'.

~ *See also* PITY cureth envy.

envy (verb). *See* BETTER be envied than pitied; ONE potter envies another.

equal. *See* on the TURF all men are equal, and under it; SIX feet of earth make all men equal.

erect. *See* in SETTLING an island, the first building erected by a Spaniard will be a church; by a Frenchman, a fort; by a Dutchman, a warehouse; and by an Englishman, an alehouse.

err. to err is human, to forgive divine (*Roman/Greek*) One should forgive others for their mistakes, as all men make them. Henry Wotton, *J. Yver's Courtly Controversy*, 1578 (similar sentiments were also expressed by Menander and Seneca). Equivalents in other languages include the French 'love truth but pardon error.' The fact that there may be limits to such forbearance is hinted at in the Spanish proverb 'him who errs forgive once but never twice'.

> Good-Nature and Good-Sense must ever join; To Err is Humane; to Forgive, Divine.
> Alexander Pope, *Essay on Criticism*, 1711

who errs and mends to God himself commends (*Spanish*) A person who repents or attempts to make up for past mistakes thereby wins divine favour. Thomas Shelton, *Don Quixote*, 1616.

error. *See* CUSTOM without reason is but ancient error.

escape. *See* LITTLE thieves are hanged, but great ones escape.

estate. *See* a GENTLEMAN without an estate is a pudding without suet.

eternal. *See* HOPE springs eternal in the human breast; the PRICE of liberty is eternal vigilance.

Eve. *See* when ADAM delved and Eve span, who was then the gentleman?

even. even reckoning makes long friends (*English*) Those who deal fairly towards others lay the foundation of lasting friendships. John Heywood, *A Dialogue containing ... the Proverbs in the English Tongue*, 1546. *See also* SHORT reckonings make long friends.

> Right reckoning makes long friends, you know.
> George Colman, *Polly Honeycombe*, 1760

~ *See also* NEVER give a sucker an even break.

evening. the evening brings all home (*Greek*) As a person grows older their views tend to become less intolerant. Quoted by Sappho.

the evening crowns the day (*English*) A satisfactory conclusion rounds off what has gone before. R. Taverner, *Proverbs or Adages with New Additions, gathered out of the Chiliades of Erasmus*, 1545. Related proverbs include 'the evening praises the day' and 'a joyful evening may follow a sorrowful morning'.

> 'Tis matter of humanity ... to be tender one of another: for no man living knows his end, and 'tis the evening crowns the day.
> Roger L'Estrange, *Aesop's Fables*, 1692

evening red and morning grey help the traveller on his way (*English*) Good weather will follow a red sky in the evening and a grey morning. L. Evans, *Withals Dictionary Revised*, 1586. The fuller version of the proverb runs 'evening red and morning grey help the traveller on his way; evening grey and morning red bring down rain upon his head'.

> An evening red and a morning gray, are sure signs of a fair day.
> John Clarke, *Paroemiologia Anglo-Latina*, 1639

evensong. *See* be the DAY never so long, at length cometh evensong.

event. *See* COMING events cast their shadows before; it is EASY to be wise after the event.

ever. ever drunk, ever dry (*English*) Habitual drunkards are always thirsty. Alexander Barclay, *Ship of Fools*, 1509.

> He that's most drunken may soonest be athirst.
> Chapman, Jonson, and Marston, *Eastward Ho*, 1605

~ *See also* GIVE a cob a hat and a pair of shoes and he'll last for ever; GIVE a man an annuity and he'll live for ever; he that ONCE hits will be ever shooting; if the ADDER could hear and the blindworm could see, neither man nor beast would ever go free; MILLS and wives are ever wanting; the TONGUE ever turns to the aching tooth.

every. every ass loves to hear himself bray (*English*) A fool loves the sound of his own voice. Thomas Fuller, *Gnomologia*, 1732. Related proverbs add 'the ass brays when he pleases', 'the ass that brays most eats least' and 'the ass knows well in whose face he brays.'

every bullet has its billet (*English*) Fate dictates all things, including whether a bullet will strike its target or not (in other words, whether a person is killed or survives). George Gascoigne, *Fruits of War*, 1575. Tradition ascribes the proverb to William of Orange (although there is some doubt as to which particular William of Orange is meant, with William III of England being a favourite contender for the honour). The same notion inspired the fanciful belief that a person would die by shooting only if a particular bullet 'had his name' on it. Napoleon often repeated the idea, boasting that the bullet that would kill him had yet to be cast.

> He never received one wound. So true is the odd saying of King William, that 'every bullet has its billet'.
> John Wesley, *Journal*, 6 June 1765

every cake hath its make (*English*) There are few things that do not have their match or equal elsewhere in the world. David Fergusson, *Scottish Proverbs*, 1641. Related proverbs include 'every cake hath its make, but a scrape cake hath two' (the import of which is that everyone has their match in the world, if they can but find that person, but also that the commonest or dirtiest of people have more than one match).

> There's no cake, but there's another of the same make.
>
> Tobias Smollett, *Sir Launcelote Greaves*, 1762

every cloud has a silver lining (*English*) There is no situation so lamentable that it does not offer some consoling hope for the future (just as the sun or the moon behind a rain cloud will give it a striking silver edge). John Milton, *Comus*, 1634. Equivalents from other parts of the world include the Indian saying 'there is no evil without its advantages'. *See also* always LOOK on the bright side; HOPE springs eternal in the human breast; where there's LIFE there's hope.

> Don't let's be downhearted. There's a silver lining to every cloud.
>
> W.S. Gilbert, *The Mikado*, 1885

every cock crows on his own dunghill (*Roman*) Any man may be tempted to arrogance on what he feels is his home ground, where he is unlikely to be challenged. *Ancrene Riwle*, *c.*1225 (also quoted by Seneca in *Ludus de Morte Claudii* in AD55). Also encountered as 'every cock is bold on his own dunghill' and recorded in parallel forms in other European languages.

> Cock of the dunghill. He's got to be cock – even if it's only of the tiniest Fabian dunghill. Poor old Mark! What an agony when he can't get to the top of his dunghill!
>
> Aldous Huxley, *Eyeless in Gaza*, 1936

every cook praises his own broth (*English*) Any worker may be expected to praise his own achievements. Gerbier, *Counsel*, 1663.

every devil has not a cloven hoof (*English*) It is not always obvious from superficial appearances that a person is evil-minded. Daniel Defoe, *The History of the Devil*, 1726.

every dog has his day (*Roman*) Although currently oppressed, even the lowliest and most humble will eventually get their chance to enjoy a moment of glory (typically by avenging wrongs done to them). R. Taverner, *Proverbs or Adages with New Additions, gathered out of the Chiliades of Erasmus*, 1546. Erasmus traced the saying back to the death of the Greek playwright Euripides, who is reputed to have been mauled to death by dogs set on him by his rivals Arrhidaeus and Crateuas. It was often given in Latin as *hodie mihi, cras tibi* (today to me, tomorrow to thee). A variation recorded in Essex in 1864 runs 'every dog has his day, and a cat has two Sundays'.

> Let Hercules himself do what he may, the cat will mew, and dog will have his day.
>
> William Shakespeare, *Hamlet*, *c.*1600

every dog is a lion at home (*English*) Many people who brag of their courage while safe at home find their courage deserts them when in public. N.R. Gent, *Proverbs English, French, Dutch etc*, 1659. Variants include 'every dog is valiant at his own door'.

every dog is allowed one bite (*English*) Every person should be allowed to make one mistake before any action is taken in retribution. V.S. Lean, *Collecteana*, 1902–4. The proverb harks back to the common law maxim that no action should be taken against those who keep domestic animals that are accused of biting someone, unless it is at least a second offence.

every elm has its man (*English*) Elm trees, being more likely than other trees to break in a high wind and cause injuries, are supposedly destined by fate to fall on certain people. Rudyard Kipling, *Puck of Pook's Hill*, 1906. *See also* EVERY bullet has its billet.

every family has a skeleton in the cupboard (*English*) Every family has shameful secrets that are kept carefully hidden from public view. William Thackeray, *The Newcomes*, 1855. A Chinese equivalent is 'nobody's family can hang up the sign "nothing the matter here"'.

every flow hath its ebb (*English*) After things reach a climactic peak, no matter how great and unprecedented, sooner or later they inevitably fall back (just as the tide turns after reaching its high point). John Lydgate, *Troy Book*, *c.*1420.

> There is a time when families, and single persons thrive, and there is a time when they go backward.
>
> James Kelly, *A Complete Collection of Scotish Proverbs*, 1721

every heart hath its own ache (*English*) Everyone has their own private sorrow. Thomas Fuller, *Gnomologia*, 1732. Equivalents include the biblical quotation 'the heart knoweth its own bitterness'. A German proverb, meanwhile, observes that 'a wounded heart is hard to cure'.

every herring must hang by its own gill (*English*) It is up to each individual to account for his own actions. S. Harward, *MS*, 1609. Another saying connected with herrings claims 'of all the fish in the sea, the herring is the king'.

Na, na! let every herring hing by its ain head, and every sheep by its ain shank.

Walter Scott, *Rob Roy*, 1817

every honest miller has a thumb of gold (*English*) Even the most honest millers make illegal money by cheating their customers by virtue of the flour that sticks to their thumb. Geoffrey Chaucer, *The Canterbury Tales*, *c.*1387. If thus accused of having a 'golden thumb', many a miller in former times would retort that only a cuckold could see it. Other proverbs questioning the honesty of millers include 'many a miller many a thief' and 'put a miller, a tailor and a weaver into one bag, and shake them, the first that comes out will be a thief'.

Wel koude he stelen corn and tollen thries,
And yet he hadde a thombe of gold pardee.

Geoffrey Chaucer, *The Canterbury Tales*, *c.*1387

every Jack has his Jill (*English*) For every man there is a woman who will be for him an ideal match. John Skelton, *Magnyfycence*, 1529. Often quoted to reassure those who despair of ever finding a mate. Also found as 'never a Jack but there's a Jill'. Equivalents include 'every pot has its lid'. *See also* a GOOD Jack makes a good Jill; MARRIAGES are made in heaven.

Jack shall have Jill;
Nought shall go ill.

William Shakespeare, *A Midsummer Night's Dream*, *c.*1596

every land has its own law (*Scottish*) Each nation has it own legal codes, with its own peculiar emphases. J. Carmichaell, *Proverbs in Scots*, 1628.

Every land hath its own Laugh, and every Corn its own Caff. Every Country hath its own Laws, Customs and Usages.

James Kelly, *A Complete Collection of Scotish Proverbs*, 1721

every little helps (*French*) Even the smallest contributions help to increase the total. Variants include 'little and often fills the purse'. *See also* LOOK after the pennies and the pounds will look after themselves; MANY a mickle makes a muckle.

Every little helps, said the ant, weeing in the sea at the height of midday.

Gabriel Meurier, *Trésor des Sentences*, 1590

every man after his fashion (*English*) Each individual must follow his or her own inclination. John Heywood, *A Dialogue containing … the Proverbs in the English Tongue*, 1546.

Every man after his fashen.

Francis Bacon, *Promus*, *c.*1594

every man can rule a shrew but he who has her (*English*) Everyone believes they would know what to do with an unruly wife, except those who are actually married to one. John Heywood, *A Dialogue containing … the Proverbs in the English Tongue*, 1546.

every man for himself and the devil take the hindmost (*Spanish*) Those who finish last must look after themselves. Beaumont and Fletcher, *Philaster*, 1620 (also recorded in variant forms in the writings of Horace). Legend has it that devotees of the devil at Toledo, or Salamanca, were forced to run the length of a subterranean hall, the devil snatching the man who came last and making him his imp. The line is shouted out in a traditional children's chasing game. Originally found in the shorter form 'devil take the hindmost'.

every man has his hobby-horse (*English*) Every person has their own pet passion, interest or line of argument. Sir Matthew Hale, *Contemplations*, 1676. A hobby-horse, in Middle English, signified a small or medium-sized horse.

Nay, if you come to that, Sir, have not the wisest of men in all ages, not excepting Solomon himself, – have they not had their Hobby-Horses; – their running horses, – their coins and their cockle-shells, their drums and their trumpets, their fiddles, their pallets, – their maggots and their butterflies? – and so long as a man rides his Hobby-Horse peaceably and quietly along the King's highway, and neither compels you or me to get up behind him, – pray, Sir, what have either you or I to do with it?

Laurence Sterne, *Tristram Shandy*, 1759–67

every man has his price (*English*) Every person will betray his principles if offered a big enough reward. The proverb is often attributed to Sir Robert Walpole, though it seems that in reality it was his political rival Sir William Wyndham who coined it in the course of a speech attacking Walpole that he gave in the House of Commons on 13 March 1734. Sir

William himself denied he had originated the phrase and claimed it was already old when he used it (it may tentatively be derived from the writings of Epictetus as far back as the first century AD).

every man hath his weak side (*English*) Everyone has their weaknesses. Roger L'Estrange, *Aesop's Fables*, 1692.

every man is the architect of his own fortune (*Roman*) It is up to each individual to create their own good fortune in life. R. Taverner, *Proverbs or Adages with New Additions, gathered out of the Chiliades of Erasmus*, 1539 (also quoted by Juvenal and others).

> Architects of their own happiness.
>
> John Milton, *Eikonoklastes*, 1649

every man is the son of his own works (*English*) A person's character and worth may be judged from the things they do. Thomas Shelton, *Don Quixote*, 1620.

every man to his trade (*English*) Each individual should be allowed to practise the trade in which they have been trained. R. Taverner, *Proverbs or Adages with New Additions, gathered out of the Chiliades of Erasmus*, 1539.

> Every man to his craft, says the proverb, the parson to the prayer-book, and the groom to the curry-comb.
>
> Walter Scott, *Kenilworth*, 1821

every medal hath its reverse (*Italian*) There are two sides to every coin. John Florio, *Montaigne*, 1603.

every mile is two in winter (*English*) Travel can be much harder in the winter than in the summer. George Herbert, *Outlandish Proverbs*, 1640.

every path hath a puddle (*English*) There is no easy path to success. George Herbert, *Outlandish Proverbs*, 1640.

> But ilka bean has its black, and ilka path has its puddle.
>
> Walter Scott, *Rob Roy*, 1817

every picture tells a story (*English*) Much may be read into superficial images. Charlotte Bıontë, *Jane Eyre*, 1847. The phrase enjoyed a revival in the early twentieth century when it was adopted as a slogan for Doane's Backache Kidney Pills.

every shoe fits not every foot (*English*) Circumstances that suit one person will not necessarily suit another. B. Rich, *Looking Glasse*, 1616.

every sin brings its punishment with it (*English*) Those who do wrong lay themselves open to the consequences of their actions. T. Draxe, *Bibliotheca Scholastica*, 1616. A related proverb warns that 'sin and sorrow are inseparable', while another cautions that 'sin is the seed and death is the punishment'.

> That is the punishment of making free with the bottle ... but if it is an offence, then it carries its own punishment.
>
> Captain Frederick Marryat, *Jacob Faithful*, 1824

every soldier has the baton of a field-marshal in his knapsack (*French*) Any soldier, however humble, may aspire to the rank of commander. Usually attributed to Napoleon Bonaparte, although also to Louis XVIII. First recorded in English in 1840.

every tub must stand on its own bottom (*English*) Every person must defend their own independence and stand on their own merits (just as the most humble tub must rest on its own bottom). W. Bullein, *Dialogue against Fever*, 1564.

> I have nothing to do with that ... Let every Tub stand on its own Bottom.
>
> Colley Cibber, *The Refusal*, 1721

every white hath its black and every sweet its sour (*English*) Strokes of good fortune are invariably accompanied by, or sooner or later followed by, misfortune. *Beryn*, *c.*1400.

every why hath its wherefore (*English*) There is a reason behind everything. George Gascoigne, *Supposes*, 1566.

> For they say every why hath a wherefore.
>
> William Shakespeare, *The Comedy of Errors*, *c.*1593

if every man would sweep his own doorstep the city would soon be clean (*English*) Great things would be accomplished if individuals could be persuaded to play their part (typically by living their lives honestly and decently). T. Adams, *The Temple*, 1624. The usual implication when the proverb is quoted is that it is only rarely that the mass of people are willing to sacrifice their own self-interest in order to promote a common cause.

let every man praise the bridge he goes over (*English*) All men should acknowledge services done for them by others. John Ray, *A Collection of English Proverbs*, 1678. Sometimes heard in the form 'everyone speaks well of the bridge which carries him over'. Other variants include 'it is not good praising a ford till a man be over'.

Well, praise the bridge that carried you over.

George Colman the Younger, *The Heir-at-Law*, 1797

let every man sweep the ice with his own broom (*Scottish*) Some tasks are the responsibility of the individual, who must not expect others to do them for him. Also rendered in the dialect form 'let ilka man soop the ice with his ain besom' and in such variants as 'let ilka ane soop before their ain door'.

not every man can be vicar of Bowden (*English*) It is impossible for all men to occupy the best positions. John Ray, *A Collection of English Proverbs*, 1678. Bowden was celebrated as one of the best livings in Cheshire. See also the VICAR of Bray will be vicar of Bray still.

~ *See also* the FISH will soon be caught that nibbles at every bait; FORTUNE knocks once at least at every man's gate; had I REVENGED every wrong, I had not worn my skirts so long; HYPOCRISY can find out a cloak for every rain; it is not GIVEN to every man to go to Corinth; the TAILOR must cut three sleeves to every woman's gown; there are TRICKS in every trade; there are TWO sides to every question; there is a DEVIL in every berry of the grape; there is an EXCEPTION to every rule; there is a SCORPION under every stone; there is no GOOD accord where every man would be a lord; there's a BLACK sheep in every family; there's a SALVE for every sore; there's ONE good wife in the country, and every man thinks he hath her; VISIT your aunt, but not every day of the year; the WAY to heaven is alike in every place.

everybody. everybody loves a lord (*English*) All men respect rank. F.J. Furnivall, in *Queen Elizabeth's Academy*, 1869.

everybody's business is nobody's business (*English*) When something is the responsibility of many people, nobody can be found who is willing to take personal responsibility for it. Randle Cotgrave, *A Dictionary of the French and English Tongues*, 1611. Aristotle voiced similar sentiments in *Politics* and Daniel Defoe wrote an essay under the same title in 1725.

I remember that a wise friend of mine did usually say, 'That which is everybody's business is nobody's business'.

Izaak Walton, *The Compleat Angler*, 1653

what everybody says must be true (*English*) If something is generally believed, the implication is that it must be accurate. *Legends of the Saints*, 1400. *See also* there's no SMOKE without fire.

~ *See also* he that has a GREAT nose thinks everybody is speaking of it; it is BETTER to be a cuckold and not know it, than be none and everybody say so; a PIECE of a churchyard fits everybody; what BELONGS to everybody belongs to nobody.

everyone. everyone has a penny to spend at a new alehouse (*English*) New enterprises always attract interest. John Ray, *A Collection of English Proverbs*, 1678.

everyone is innocent until proved guilty (*English*) No one should be presumed guilty until actually proved to be so. *Spectator*, 6 August 1910. Another proverb, however, warns that 'innocence is no protection'.

everyone stretches his legs according to the length of his coverlet (*English*) The sensible person adjusts his or her needs according to the resources available. Walter of Henley, *Husbandry*, 1300. Also encountered in the form 'whoso stretcheth his foot beyond the blanket, shall stretch it in the straw'. *See also* CUT your coat according to your cloth.

everyone to his taste (*French*) Questions of taste are personal and vary from one person to another. John Lyly, *Euphues and His England*, 1580. Given in French as *chacun à son goût*, which is often quoted by English speakers. Equivalent proverbs include 'tastes differ', 'everyone after his fashion', 'each to his own', 'all feet tread not in one shoe', 'some prefer turnips and others pears' and the Scottish saying 'every man as he loveth, quoth the good man when he kissed his cow'. *See also* there is no ACCOUNTING for tastes.

I own I never could envy Didius in these kinds of fancies of his: – But every man to his own taste.

Laurence Sterne, *Tristram Shandy*, 1759

~ *See also* you can't PLEASE everyone.

everything. everything comes to him who waits (*English*) Patience will be rewarded in the long run. Alexander Barclay, *Eclogues*, *c.*1514. A French equivalent quoted by Rabelais runs 'he who has patience may accomplish anything'. *See also* ALL things come to those who wait.

All things come round to him who will but wait.

Henry Wadsworth Longfellow, *Tales of a Wayside Inn*, 1863

everything has an end (*English*) Nothing lasts for ever. Geoffrey Chaucer, *Troilus and Criseyde*, *c.*1385–90. In its fullest form the proverb runs 'everything has an end, and a pudding has two'. Other proverbs claim 'everything hath a beginning' and 'everything hath its time'. *See also* ALL good things must come to an end.

Everything has an end. Even young ladies in love cannot read their letters for ever.

Charles Dickens, *Barnaby Rudge*, 1841

everything is good in its season (*English*) All things (especially foodstuffs) are best enjoyed when in prime condition. W. Stepney, *The Spanish Schoolmaster*, 1591.

everything tastes of porridge (*English*) All our attempts to deceive ourselves will fail ultimately to mask the unpalatable truth. *Brewer's Phrase and Fable*, 1959.

~ *See also* the GOOD Bernard does not see everything; LOVE does much, money does everything; MONEY isn't everything; a PLACE for everything and everything in its place; there is a REMEDY for everything except death; there is a TIME for everything.

everywhere. *See* an ARTIST lives everywhere.

evil. evil be to him who thinks it (*English*) May ill luck befall those who wish ill on others. Geoffrey Chaucer, *The Canterbury Tales*, *c.*1387. A Spanish proverbs warns those tempted to evil that 'the evil which issues from thy mouth falls into thy bosom'.

Now the evyl which men wysshe to other cometh to hym whiche wyssheth hit.

William Caxton, *Aesop's Fables*, 1484

evil communications corrupt good manners (*Hebrew*) The influence of those who hold wicked opinions ruins those of good character. J. Palsgrave, *L'Éclaircissement de la langue française*, 1530 (also found in the Bible, Corinthians 15:33, quoted by Saint Paul, although the same saying is also found in Menander's *Thaïs*). *See also* he that TOUCHES pitch shall be defiled; ONE scabbed sheep infects the whole flock; the ROTTEN apple injures its neighbours.

Gude forgie me for swearing – but evil communication corrupteth good manners.

Walter Scott, *The Pirate*, 1821

evil doers are evil dreaders (*English*) Those who act wickedly are often those who most fear suffering from wickedness themselves. Roger Ascham, *The Scholemaster*, 1570. *See also* ILL doers are ill dreaders.

If you were more trustful, it would better befit your time of life ... We have a proverb ... that evil doers are aye evil-dreaders.

Robert Louis Stevenson, *Kidnapped*, 1886

an evil lesson is soon learned (*English*) It takes little time and effort to learn how to do mischief. J. Clarke, *Paroemiologia Anglo-Latina*, 1639. Related proverbs include the Roman 'a strong remedy for evils is ignorance of them'.

~ *See also* BEAR with evil and expect good; the BETROTHED of good is evil, the betrothed of life is death, the betrothed of love is divorce; a GREAT book is a great evil; he KNOWS best what good is that has endured evil; IDLENESS is the root of all evil; the LOVE of money is the root of all evil; MANY a good cow hath an evil calf; of TWO evils choose the lesser; PUT off the evil hour as long as you can; SEE no evil, hear no evil, speak no evil; SUFFICIENT unto the day is the evil thereof; that which is GOOD for the head is evil for the neck and the shoulders; WELCOME evil, if thou comest alone; where OLD age is evil, youth can learn no good.

example. example is better than precept (*English*) Men learn quicker from practical example than from spoken advice. J. Mirk, *Festial*, *c.*1400. Variants include the Roman 'precepts lead, examples draw', 'precepts invite but examples drag us to conclusions' and 'the path of precept is long, that of example short', and the French 'precept begins, example accomplishes'.

It is a trite but true observation, that examples work more forcibly on the mind than precepts.

Henry Fielding, *The Adventures of Joseph Andrews*, 1742

~ *See also* a GOOD example is the best sermon.

exceeding. *See* the MILLS of God grind slowly, yet they grind exceeding small.

except. *See* ALL things grow with time, except grief; GOLD goes in at any gate except heaven's; there is a REMEDY for everything except death.

exception. the exception proves the rule (*Roman*) If something is described as an exception, then it follows that there is a rule that covers all other cases. G. Watts, *Bacon's Advancement of Learning*, 1640 (also encountered in variant forms in the Bible and in classical writings). In modern usage the proverb is usually quoted to justify the exceptional case, although originally the idea was that it was by the exception that a rule might be tested. *See also* there is an EXCEPTION to every rule.

> They serve only as exceptions; which, in the grammarian's phrase, confirm and prove a general canon.
>
> Tobias Smollett, *Humphry Clinker*, 1771

there is an exception to every rule (*English*) No rule applies in a hundred per cent of cases. T.F., *News from the North*, 1579. *See also* the EXCEPTION proves the rule.

exchange. *See* FAIR exchange is no robbery.

excuse (noun). *See* a BAD excuse is better than none; IDLE people lack no excuses; IGNORANCE of the law is no excuse.

excuse (verb). **he who excuses himself, accuses himself** (*French*) Those who seek to excuse themselves sometimes end up only attracting blame to themselves. Randle Cotgrave, *A Dictionary of the French and English Tongues*, 1611. Rendered in French as *qui s'excuse, s'accuse*. The Romans had it that 'an excuse which was uncalled for becomes an obvious accusation'.

~ *See also* ACCUSING the times is but excusing ourselves.

executor. *See* FAT housekeepers make lean executors.

exist. although there exist many thousand subjects for elegant conversation, there are persons who cannot meet a cripple without talking about feet (*Chinese*) Some people lack any sense of tact in sensitive situations.

expand. *See* WORK expands so as to fill the time available.

expect. what can you expect from a pig but a grunt? (*English*) Poor behaviour is only to be expected from someone of no refinement. Benjamin Franklin, *Poor Robin's Almanack*, 1732. Related proverbs include 'what can you expect of a hog but his bristles'.

> If he had not ... been but a Dumfriesshire hog ... he would have spoken more like a gentleman, but you cannot have more of a sow than a grumph.
>
> Walter Scott, *The Two Drovers*, 1827

~ *See also* BEAR with evil and expect good; BLESSED is he who expects nothing, for he shall never be disappointed; he that PLAYS with cats must expect to be scratched.

expel. *See* ONE love expels another.

expense. *See* MARRIAGE halves our griefs, doubles our joys, and quadruples our expenses.

expensive. *See* ANGER can be an expensive luxury.

experience. experience is a comb which nature gives us when we are bald (*Chinese*) By the time a person has acquired a lifetime's knowledge it is too late to use it.

experience is the best teacher (*Roman*) People learn quickest from practical experience. M.L. Weems, letter, 12 November 1803. Originally known in the form of the Latin tag *experientia docet* (experience teaches). The proverb is known in several languages, including Spanish, in which it is rendered as 'experience is not always the kindest of teachers, but it is surely the best'. Oscar Wilde's reply to the proverb was 'experience is the name everyone gives to his own mistakes'.

experience is the mother of wisdom (*Greek*) Knowledge comes from experience. R. Taverner, *The Garden of Wisdom*, 1539 (also found in the writings of the seventh-century BC Greek lyric poet Alcman). Sometimes encountered as 'experience is the father of wisdom' and in its fullest form as 'experience is the father of wisdom, and memory the mother'.

experience is the teacher of fools (*Roman*) Stupid people have no option but to learn by making mistakes. Roger Ascham, *The Scholemaster*, 1570 (also found in Livy's *History of Rome*, *c.*10BC). Also encountered in the form 'experience is the mistress of fools' (possibly a reference to sixteenth-century dame schools for English children).

Experience is the mistress of knaves as well as of fools.

Roger L'Estrange, *Aesop*, 1692

experience keeps a dear school (*US*) Learning by one's mistakes may prove very costly and painful. Benjamin Franklin, *Poor Richard's Almanack*, 1743. A fuller version of the proverb, recorded by Benjamin Franklin, is 'experience keeps a dear school, yet fools will learn in no other'. Another proverb concurs: 'experience is good, if not bought too dear', while another of US origin runs that 'experience bought by suffering teaches wisdom'. Others, however, warn that 'experience is sometimes dangerous' and that 'by falling we learn to go safely'.

Experience keeps a dear school, but Fools will learn in no other.

Benjamin Franklin, *Poor Richard's Almanack*, 1743

~ *See also* ART helps nature, and experience art; the HORSES of hope gallop, but the asses of experience go slowly.

explain. *See* a JUDGE knows nothing unless it has been explained to him three times.

extinguish. *See* KINDLE not a fire that you cannot extinguish.

extremes meet (*French*) Similarities may often be identified in apparently opposing standpoints, characters, situations and so forth. Blaise Pascal, *Pensées*, 1662.

That dead time of the dawn, when (as extremes meet) the rake ... and the hard-handed artizan ... jostle ... for the honours of the pavement.

Charles Lamb, *Essays of Elia*, 1822

extremity. *See* MAN's extremity is God's opportunity.

exult. *See* only FOOLS exult when governments change.

eye. an eye for eye, and a tooth for a tooth (*Hebrew*) Those who inflict harm on others should have to suffer the same harm themselves. Bible, Exodus 21:24. Leviticus 24:20 confirms divine authority for such revenge-taking – 'breach for breach, eye for eye, tooth for tooth: as he hath caused blemish in a man, so shall it be done to him again' – but in the Sermon on the Mount Jesus tempers this, suggesting 'turning the other cheek' when under attack from another. Sometimes encountered in the longer form 'an eye for an eye, a tooth for a tooth, a hand for a hand, a foot for a foot'. Equivalent proverbs include the Lebanese 'if someone steps on your foot, step on his neck'. A Maltese saying reflecting upon the consequences of such retribution goes 'I gave him the plague, he gave me pneumonia'. *See also* BLOOD will have blood; KA me, ka thee.

From the continued existence of the old theory, 'an eye for an eye' condemned to death over nineteen hundred years ago, but still dying very hard in this Christian country.

John Galsworthy, *The Spirit of Punishment*, 1910

the eye is bigger than the belly (*English*) Greed encourages a person to take more than they will be able to cope with (usually quoted in relation to food). John Lyly, *Euphues and His England*, 1580. Also found as 'your eyes are bigger than your stomach'. Related proverbs include the Scottish 'a greedy eye never got a full wame [belly]', the Yiddish 'the eye is bigger than the mouth', and the French 'the belly overreaches the head'.

A person is said to have his 'eyes bigger than his belly' who takes more food upon his plate than he can eat.

Thomas Love Peacock, *Manley*, 1889

the eye of the master does more work than both his hands (*English*) Through the supervision of others, a person may achieve more than he or she could by doing the work personally. Benjamin Franklin, *The Way to Wealth*, 1736. Related proverbs include 'the eye of the master sees more than ten of the servants'.

But continual vigilance, rigorous method, what we call 'the eye of the master', work wonders.

Thomas Carlyle, *Past and Present*, 1843

the eyes are the window of the soul (*Roman*) A study of a person's eyes will reveal what they are secretly thinking. T. Phaer, *Regiment of Life*, 1545 (the proverb is also found in the writings of Cicero). There is some practical truth in the notion in so far as the pupils dilate when a person is happy or looking at something of which they approve, but shrink when they are displeased by something. Also found as 'the eye is the mirror of the soul'. *See also* the FACE is the index of the mind.

what the eye does not see, the heart does not grieve over (*English*) What a person does not know cannot worry him (often said to justify keeping a secret from someone). R. Taverner, *Proverbs or Adages with New Additions, gathered out of the Chiliades of Erasmus*, 1539. Related proverbs include 'what the eye sees not, the heart craves not', meaning that a person cannot yearn for something of which he is unaware. *See also* IGNORANCE is bliss.

> I never desire or find fault with that I see not:
> that proverb is verifies in me; What eye seeth
> not, the heart rueth not.
>
> John Florio, *Montaigne*, 1603

~ *See also* BEAUTY is in the eye of the beholder; the BUYER has need of a hundred eyes, the seller of but one; the CAT shuts its eyes while it steals cream; FIELDS have eyes, and woods have ears; FOUR eyes see more than two; a GOOD surgeon must have an eagle's eye, a lion's heart and a lady's hand; HAWKS will not pick out hawks' eyes; he that HEWS too high may get a chip in his eye; it is EASIER for a camel to go through the eye of a needle than it is for a rich man to enter into the kingdom of heaven; KEEP your mouth shut and your eyes open; the MASTER's eye maketh the horse fat; no coming to HEAVEN with dry eyes; PLEASE your eye and plague your heart; SPIES are the ears and eyes of princes; a STRANGER's eye sees clearest; SUSPICION has double eyes; to the JAUNDICED eye all things look yellow; who hath a FAIR wife needs more than two eyes; you should NEVER touch your eye but with your elbow.

face. face to face the truth comes out (*English*) People find it harder to hide the truth when they are questioned face to face. Thomas Fuller, *Gnomologia*, 1732. Also encountered in the form 'face to face truth comes out apace'.

the face is the index of the mind (*Roman*) A person's character is revealed in his or her face. J. Pilkington, *Nehemiah*, 1575 (also found in the writings of Cicero). The notion that all is revealed in the face was the basis of the pseudo-science of physiognomy, in which examination of every feature allowed an insight into inner character. Short noses, for instance, indicated a lazy nature, while joined eyebrows were a sign that someone was a witch, and fat cheeks suggested greed and sensuality. Also encountered in the variant form 'the face is the index of the heart' and in the contrary version 'the face is no index to the heart'. *See also* the EYES are the window of the soul.

> You have not to learn that the face is the outward index of the mind within.
>
> Mrs Henry Wood, *Trevlyn Hold*, 1864

~ *See also* CIDER is treacherous because it smiles in the face and then cuts the throat; don't CUT off your nose to spite your face; an EMPTY purse fills the face with wrinkles; FAIR face and a foul heart; a GOOD face is a letter of recommendation; the JOY of the heart makes the face merry; MONDAY's child is fair of face, Tuesday's child is full of grace; Wednesday's child is full of woe, Thursday's child has far to go; Friday's child is loving and giving, Saturday's child works hard for its living; and the child that's born on the Sabbath day, is fair and wise and good and gay; a PROUD look makes foul work in a fine face; TRUTH has a scratched face; who SPITS against heaven it falls in his face; WRINKLED purses make wrinkled faces.

fact. fact is stranger than fiction (*English*) What happens in real life is often much stranger than anything someone might invent. Lord Byron, *Don Juan*, 1823. A Roman proverb on the same theme advises writers of fiction that 'fiction intended to please should resemble truth as much as possible'. *See also* TRUTH is stranger than fiction.

> 'Tis strange – but true; for truth is always strange, –
> Stranger than fiction.
>
> Lord Byron, *Don Juan*, 1823

facts are stubborn things (*English*) Reality can be inconvenient and hard to control. E. Budgell, *Liberty and Progress*, 1732.

> Facts, however, are stubborn things, and will not even make a bow to the sweetest of young ladies.
>
> R.D. Blackmore, *Cradock Nowell*, 1866

fade. *See* OLD soldiers never die, they simply fade away.

fail. *See* as a BEAR has no tail, as a lion he'll fail; he who NEVER fails will never grow rich.

fain. *See* BRIGHT rain makes fools fain.

faint heart ne'er won fair lady (*English*) There is no place for timidity in romance. R. Taverner, *Proverbs or Adages with New Additions, gathered out of the Chiliades of Erasmus*, 1546.

> But 'faint heart never won fair lady,' so I made bold to speak to Rose.
>
> Maria Edgeworth, *Irish Bulls*, 1802

fair. fair and soft goes far in a day (*English*) Those who take things gently and in even temper will do better than those who allow themselves to be overcome by their emotions. *Douce MS*, *c.*1350. Related proverbs include the rather cynical 'fair and softly, as lawyers go to heaven'.

> Fair and softly goes far in a day ... He that spurs on too fast at first setting out, tires before he comes to his journeys end.
>
> John Ray, *A Collection of English Proverbs*, 1670

a fair day in winter is the mother of a storm (*English*) An unseasonably warm day in winter is a warning of bad weather to come. John Clarke, *Paroemiologia Anglo-Latina*, 1639.

a fair death honours the whole life (*English*) A person who dies well will be remembered with respect. George Herbert, *Outlandish Proverbs*, 1640.

the fairer the hostess, the fouler the reckoning (*English*) The more attractive the host, the more a customer or client is likely to have to pay for their services, company, etc. J. Howell, *Paroemiographia*, 1659.

the fairer the paper, the fouler the blot (*English*) Mistakes or blemishes look worst when they happen in otherwise untainted circumstances. Thomas Fuller, *Gnomologia*, 1732. Related proverbs include 'the fairest silk is soonest stained'.

the fairest rose at last is withered (*English*) Even the most beautiful will eventually lose their looks. John Florio, *Second Fruites*, 1591. Related proverbs include 'the finest flower will soonest fade', 'the finest lawn soonest stains' and 'the fairest silk is soonest stained'.

the fairest silk is soonest stained (*English*) The most beautiful women are the most open to temptation (just as the finest silk is the most vulnerable to damage). John Lyly, *Euphues*, 1579.

fair exchange is no robbery (*English*) No one is worse off when goods or services of equal value are exchanged. John Heywood, *A Dialogue containing ... the Proverbs in the English Tongue*, 1546.

> Fair Exchange is no Rob'ry. Spoken when we take up one Thing, and lay down another.
>
> James Kelly, *A Complete Collection of Scotish Proverbs*, 1721

fair face and a foul heart (*English*) A pretty appearance often conceals a vicious nature. Ben Jonson, *Every Man in His Humour*, 1598. Variants include 'fair without, false within'. Another proverb, 'a fair face cannot have a crabbed heart' disputes this notion, but others that support it include 'fair and foolish' and 'a fair face may be a foul bargain'. *See also* APPEARANCES are deceptive.

> I have known fair hides have foul hearts ere now, sister.
>
> Ben Jonson, *Every Man in His Humour*, 1598

fair play is a jewel (*US*) Nothing is more precious than honesty in dealings with others. Washington Irving, *The History of New York*, 1809. One historical extension of the proverb, now little heard, runs 'fair play is a jewel – let go my hair' (sometimes, 'Lucy, let go my hair'). Related proverbs include 'fair play is good play' and 'fair is fair, work or play'.

> Well, fair play's a jewel. But I've got the lead of you, old fellow.
>
> James Fenimore Cooper, *The Pioneers*, 1823

fair words and foul deeds cheat wise men as well as fools (*English*) The wise can be deceived as well as fools by those who disguise their wickedness with fair words. J. Sandford, *The Garden of Pleasure*, 1573. Variants include 'fair words and foul play cheat both young and old' and 'fair words make fools fain'.

> Faire words brake never bane, foule words breaks many ane.
>
> David Fergusson, *Scottish Proverbs*, 1641

fair words break no bones (*English*) Those who speak kindly and softly of others run little risk of causing anyone hurt. *How the Good Wyfe*, *c.*1460. Other proverbs along similar lines include 'fair words cost nothing', 'fair words slake wrath' and 'fair words hurt not the tongue', though a contrasting view is expressed in 'fair words fill not the belly' and 'fair words will not make the pot boil'. Equally cynical are 'he who gives fair words feeds you with an empty spoon' and 'fair words make me look to my purse'. A Swahili variant on the same basic theme of fair words runs 'fair speech turns elephants away from the garden path'. *See also* STICKS and stones may break my bones, but names will never hurt me.

in fair weather prepare for foul (*English*) Good times (like good weather) do not go on for ever and thus it is wise to make preparations for bad times ahead. Thomas Fuller, *Gnomologia*, 1732. Related proverbs include 'to a fair day open the window, but make you ready as to a foul'.

who hath a fair wife needs more than two eyes (*English*) A man who is married to a pretty wife needs to keep vigilant for the rivals she will attract. R. Codrington, *The Second Part of Youth's Behaviour*, 1664. Related proverbs emphasizing the negative aspects of a good-looking wife include 'a fair wife, a wide house, and a back door will quickly make a rich man poor' and 'a fair wife and a frontier castle breed quarrels'.

~ *See also* ALL's fair in love and war; a BLUSTERING night, a fair day follows; the CROW thinks her own birds fairest; FAINT heart ne'er won fair lady; a FOUL morning may turn to a fair day; the FULL moon brings fair weather; GIVE a child all he shall crave and a dog while his tail doth wave and you'll have a fair dog and a foul knave; GIVE and take is fair play; he that hath a WHITE horse and a fair wife is never without trouble; HOIST your sail when the wind is fair; if SAINT Paul's Day be fair and clear, it will betide a happy year; LEARN young, learn fair; MONDAY's child is fair of face, Tuesday's child is full of grace; Wednesday's child is full of woe, Thursday's child has far to go; Friday's child is loving and giving, Saturday's child works hard for its living; and the child that's born on the Sabbath day, is fair and wise and good and gay; NEW things are fair; NONE but the brave deserve the fair; the PEACOCK hath fair feathers, but foul feet; QUESTION for question is all fair; SAINT Swithin's Day, if thou dost rain, for forty days it will remain; Saint Swithin's Day, if thou be fair, for forty days 'twill rain no more; the SMOKE follows the fairest; SOFT and fair goes far; SPEAK fair and think what you will; take HEED is a fair thing; TURN about is fair play.

faith will move mountains (*Hebrew*) Those who have true belief in something (typically in God) will have the confidence to attempt the seemingly impossible. Bible, Matthew 17:20. *See also* if the MOUNTAIN will not go to Mahomet, Mahomet must go to the mountain.

> As faith can move mountains, so nothing was impossible to Holy Church.
>
> John Betjeman, *Ghastly Good Taste*, 1933

fall. a falling master makes a standing servant (*English*) When one person comes down in the world their place may be taken by someone who was formerly their servant or employee. James Kelly, *A Complete Collection of Scottish Proverbs*, 1721.

the falling out of friends is the renewal of love (*Roman*) When friends quarrel there is every chance that when they make up their friendship will be all the closer. *Parade of Dainty Devices*, 1576 (also quoted by Terence). Also found as 'the falling out of lovers is the renewing of love'. Other proverbs recommending the renewal of friendship include the cautionary 'fall not out with a friend for a trifle'. *See also* the QUARREL of lovers is the renewal of love.

> Old Terence has taken notice of that; and observes upon it, That lovers falling-out occasions lovers falling-in.
>
> Samuel Richardson, *Clarissa*, 1748

he that falls in the dirt, the longer he stays there the fouler he is (*English*) The longer rumours about a person persist the harder it is to refute them. George Herbert, *Outlandish Proverbs*, 1640.

he that falls today may rise tomorrow (*English*) Those whose fortunes are low at the present may enjoy an improvement in their luck in the future. Thomas Fuller, *Gnomologia*, 1732. Other proverbs on a similar consolatory theme include 'he falls low that cannot rise again'.

he that is fallen cannot help him that is down (*English*) Those who have themselves fallen on hard times are not well placed to help others in the same situation. George Herbert, *Outlandish Proverbs*, 1640.

~ *See also* the APPLE never falls far from the tree; as a TREE falls, so shall it lie; BETWEEN two stools you fall to the ground; the BIGGER they are, the harder they fall; the BREAD never falls but on the buttered side; GNAW the bone which is fallen to thy lot; go FORWARD and fall, go backward and mar all; HASTY climbers have sudden falls; he RIDES well that never falls; he that LIES upon the ground can fall no lower; he that NEVER climbed never fell; if a MAN once fall, all will tread on him; if the BLIND lead the blind, both shall fall into the ditch; if the SKY falls we shall catch larks; into the MOUTH of a bad dog often falls a good bone; it is EASY to fall into a trap but hard to get out again; LOOK high and fall low; a MAN of gladness seldom falls into madness; NEVER catch at a falling knife or friend; PRIDE goes before a fall; a REED before the wind lives on, while mighty oaks do fall; the RISING of one man is the falling of another; a STUMBLE may prevent a fall; a SUDDEN rising hath a sudden fall; the TREE falls not at the first blow; UNITED we stand, divided we fall; when ALL fruit falls, welcome haws; when EASTER falls in our Lady's lap, then let England beware of a rap; when our LADY falls in our Lord's lap, then let England beware a sad clap; when the TREE is fallen, all go with their hatchet; when THIEVES fall out honest men come by their own; who SPITS against heaven it falls in his face.

false. a false tongue hardly speaks truth (*English*) Dishonest people cannot be expected to tell the truth. T. Draxe, *Bibliotheca Scholastica*, 1616. Related proverbs include 'false with one can be false with two'.

~ *See also* a MAN that breaks his word bids others be false to him.

fame. fame is a magnifying glass (*English*) People who are famous will find all their doings are subject to public scrutiny. Thomas Fuller, *Gnomologia*, 1732. **fame is but the breath of the people** (*English*) Fame has no substance. Coryat, *Crudities*, 1611. Variants include 'all fame is dangerous', 'fame, like a river, is narrowed at its source and broadest afar off' and 'fame to infamy is a beaten road'. A Burmese proverb on the same subject runs 'the top of a pinnacle now, firewood soon'.

~ *See also* COMMON fame is a common liar; KEEP yourself from the anger of a great man, from the tumult of a mob, from a man of ill fame, from a widow that has been thrice married, from a wind that comes in at a hole, and from a reconciled enemy.

familiarity breeds contempt (*Roman*) Respect for someone or something tends to diminish as familiarity increases. Alanus de Insulis, *Satires*, *c.*1160 (also found in Livy and in Publilius Syrus, *Sententiae*, *c.*43BC). Aesop illustrated the proverb in his fable of 'The Fox and the Lion', in which the fox quickly loses his fear of the lion after several meetings. Variants on the same theme include the Scottish 'a maid aft seen and a gown aft worn are disesteemed and held in scorn', the French 'a thing too much seen is little prized' and the Spanish 'a rose too often smelled loses its fragrance'. Mark Twain, meanwhile, took the original and added his own touch: 'familiarity breeds contempt – and children.' *See also* no man is a HERO to his valet.

> Men seyne that 'over-greet hoomlynesse
> engendreth dispreisynge'.
>
> Geoffrey Chaucer, 'The Tale of Melibee', *The Canterbury Tales*, *c.*1387

family. the family that prays together stays together (*US*) Families that share acts of religious worship are less likely to disintegrate. Father Patrick Peyton, *All for Her*, 1967. Father Peyton invented the slogan for the Roman Catholic Family Rosary Crusade, and it was first heard in a radio broadcast in 1947. This proverbial phrase is now usually heard in a number of variations, the most common of which includes 'the family that plays together stays together'.

~ *See* ACCIDENTS will happen in the best regulated families; EVERY family has a skeleton in the cupboard; it is a POOR family that has neither a whore nor a thief in it; there's a BLACK sheep in every family.

famine. *See* AFTER a famine in the stall comes a famine in the hall.

fan (noun). **there are no fans in hell** (*Arabic*) Those who follow wicked lives cannot expect any mercy when their souls are cast into the fires of hell. R.C. Trench, *On the Lessons in Proverbs*, 1853.

fan (verb). **fanned fires and forced love never did well yet** (*English*) Relationships that arise naturally do much better than relationships that have been in some way forced upon those concerned. James Kelly, *A Complete Collection of Scotish Proverbs*, 1721.

fancy (noun). **fancy passes beauty** (*English*) Liking is more persuasive than beauty. John Ray, *A Collection of English Proverbs*, 1678. Related proverbs include 'fancy flees before the wind', 'fancy may bolt bran and think it flour', and 'fancy may kill or cure'.

fancy (verb). *See* a LITTLE of what you fancy does you good.

far. far behind must follow the faster (*Scottish*) Those who have fallen behind must work all the harder in order to catch up. James Kelly, *A Complete Collection of Scottish Proverbs*, 1721. Related proverbs include 'they are far behind that may not follow' (meaning that those left behind still have a chance to catch up if they work hard enough).

far folks fare well (*English*) People tend to boast of the wealth and achievements of friends who live far away (and whose real condition cannot be checked). John Ray, *A Collection of English Proverbs*, 1678. A fuller version of the proverb runs 'far folks fare well and fair children die' (suggesting that some people will even boast of the well-being and achievements of their absent friends' dead children). Variants include 'far fowls have fair feathers'.

far shooting never killed bird (*English*) To be really effective, an attack should be carried through at close quarters. George Herbert, *Outlandish Proverbs*, 1640.

he goes far that never returns (*English*) The chances are that those who stray from the straight and narrow will attempt to retrace their steps at some point in the future. R. Taverner, *Proverbs or Adages with New Additions, gathered out of the Chiliades of Erasmus*, 1545.

> 'But they go far who turn not again'; and in
> him the proverb was verified, 'Naughty boys
> sometimes make good men'.
>
> Thomas Fuller, *The History of the Worthies of England*, 1662

further than the wall we cannot go (*English*) Sometimes circumstances prevent us from doing anything further. Thomas More, *Works*, 1528.

the further you go, the further behind (*English*) A person who goes in the wrong direction goes further out of his way with every step. J. Palsgrave, *L'Éclaircissement de la langue française*, 1530.

> Ye maie walke this waie, but sure ye shall fynde,
> The further ye go, the further behynde.
>
> J. Heywood, *A Dialogue containing … the Proverbs in the English Tongue*, 1546

~ *See also* BLUE are hills that are far away; a DWARF on a giant's shoulders sees further of the two; FAIR and soft goes far in a day; the FOX preys furthest from his hole; GOD comes at last when we think he is furthest off; the LAPWING cries farthest from her nest; LIGHT burdens far heavy; MONDAY's child is fair of face, Tuesday's child is full of grace; Wednesday's child is full of woe, Thursday's child has far to go; Friday's child is loving and giving, Saturday's child works hard for its living; and the child that's born on the Sabbath day, is fair and wise and good and gay; the NEARER the church, the further from God; SOFT and fair goes far; SOFT pace goes far; SOUND travelling far and wide a stormy day will betide; THINKING is very far from knowing; the TIDE never goes out so far but it always comes in again.

far-dwelling. *See* a NEAR friend is better than a far-dwelling kinsman.

fare. *See* FAR folks fare well; the MORE a fox is cursed, the better he fares.

far-fetched and dear-bought is good for ladies (*English*) Women are most likely to be pleased with gifts that are both expensive and difficult to obtain. *Douce MS*, *c.*1350.

> But you know, far-fetch'd and dear-bought is fit
> for Ladies. I warrant, this cost your Father Two
> pence half-penny.
>
> Jonathan Swift, *Polite Conversation*, 1738

farmer. *See* the BEST manure is under the farmer's foot.

farthest. *See* FAR.

fashion. *See* BETTER be out of the world than out of fashion; EVERY man after his fashion; TAILORS and writers must mind the fashion; when the GORSE is out of bloom, kissing's out of fashion.

fast. fast bind, fast find (*English*) If things are made secure, there is less chance that they will be lost when the owner returns for them (usually quoted when locking doors). William Caxton, *Aesop's Fables*, 1484. *See also* SAFE bind, safe find.

> 'Fast bind, safe find,' is an excellent proverb. I'll
> e'en lock her up with the rest.
>
> Beaumont and Fletcher, *The Spanish Curate*, 1622

~ *See also* BAD news travels fast; FAR behind must follow the faster; GOD send you joy, for sorrow will come fast enough; LAST make fast; the MORE camomile is trodden on, the faster it grows; he TRAVELS fastest who travels alone; a MONEYLESS man goes fast through the market; when the MISTRESS is the master, parsley grows the faster.

fasting. *See* he whose BELLY is full believes not him who is fasting; it's ILL speaking between a full man and a fasting.

fat. fat housekeepers make lean executors (*English*) Those who spend lavishly in their lifetime leave little wealth to be distributed by their executors after their death. Randle Cotgrave, *A Dictionary of the French and English Tongues*, 1611. Also encountered in the form 'a fat kitchen makes a lean will'.

fat paunches make lean pates (*Greek*) Fat people tend to be less intelligent than others. B. Young, translation of Guazzo's *Civil Conversation*, 1586.

> Fat paunches have lean pates, and dainty bits
> Make rich the ribs, but bankrupt quite the wits.
> William Shakespeare, *Love's Labour's Lost*, 1594–5

~ *See also* CHANGE of pasture makes fat calves; a GREEN winter makes a fat churchyard; he that hath no CHILDREN feedeth them fat; LAUGH and grow fat; LEAN liberty is better than fat slavery; LITTLE knoweth the fat man what the lean man thinketh; the MASTER's eye maketh the horse fat; the OPERA isn't over till the fat lady sings; a THISTLE is a fat salad for an ass's mouth.

fatten. *See* a YOUNG physician fattens the churchyard.

fate leads the willing but drives the stubborn (*Greek*) It is better to obey the dictates of fate willingly, as there is no alternative. T. Adams, *Sermons*, 1629. Related proverbs upon the theme of the inevitability of fate include the Scottish 'nae fleeing frae fate', the Russian 'you cannot avoid your fate, even by getting up early' and the Yiddish 'if you're fated to be drowned, you'll drown in a spoonful of water'.

father. he whose father is judge goes safe to his trial (*Spanish*) Those with personal connections among those who judge them may be sure of a favourable response. Thomas Fuller, *Gnomologia*, 1732.

like father, like son (*English*) Children take after their parents. William Langland, *Piers Plowman*, 1362. Sometimes encountered in its Latin form, *qualis pater, talis filius*. Variants include 'like hen, like chicken', 'like cow, like calf' and 'like crow, like egg'. *See also* LIKE breeds like; like MOTHER, like daughter; MANY a good cow hath an evil calf.

> An olde proverbe hath longe agone be sayde That
> oft the sone in maners lyke wyll be unto the father.
> Alexander Barclay, *The Ship of Fools*, 1509

~ *See also* the CHILD is the father of the man; CHILD's pig but father's bacon; CHILDREN suck the mother when they are young and the father when they are old; it is a WISE child that knows its own father; ONE father can support ten children; ten children cannot support one father; ONE father is more than a hundred schoolmasters; TELL money after your own father; the WISH is father to the thought.

fault. a fault confessed is half redressed (*English*) Admitting one's mistakes is a good step towards atoning for them. *Interlude of Wealth and Health*, 1558. The sentiment is reinforced by another proverb, 'a fault once denied is twice committed'.

> A fault confessed is more than half amends, but
> men of such ill spirite as your selfe Worke crosses
> and debates twixt man and wife.
> *Arden of Feversham*, 1592

faults are thick where love is thin (*Welsh*) People who dislike one another are quick to find fault with each other. T. Draxe, *Bibliotheca Scholastica*, 1616.

~ *See also* DENYING a fault doubles it; the FIRST faults are theirs that commit them, the second theirs that permit them; GREAT men have great faults; an HONEST look covereth many faults; LOVE your friend with his fault; MEN count up the faults of those who keep them waiting; MEN's years and their faults are always more than they are willing to own; WINK at small faults; WISE men learn by others' faults, fools by their own.

faultless. *See* he is LIFELESS that is faultless.

favour (noun). *See* ASK no favour during the solano; KISSING goes by favour.

favour (verb). *See* FORTUNE favours fools; FORTUNE favours the bold.

fear (noun). **fear lends wings** (*French*) Through terror a person acquires a new turn of speed when it comes to escaping what they are terrified of. Philip Sidney, *Arcadia*, 1580. Less well-known, but related, proverbs include 'fear causeth a man to cast beyond the moon' and 'fear hath a quick ear'. Some, however, contend that fear can have the opposite effect, as in the Russian proverb 'fear has lead in its feet'.

> Therto fear gave her wings.
>
> Edmund Spenser, *The Faerie Queene*, 1590

~ *See also* LOVE is full of fear; when we have GOLD we are in fear, when we have none we are in danger.

fear (verb). *See* ALL cats love fish but fear to wet their paws; the DOCTOR is often more to be feared than the disease; do RIGHT and fear no man; FOOLS rush in where angels fear to tread; he who has been BITTEN by a snake fears a piece of string; ONE butcher does not fear many sheep; PAINS to get, care to keep, fear to lose; a SCALDED cat fears cold water; SHIPS fear fire more than water; the THIEF doth fear each bush an officer; the THIN end of the wedge is to be feared; 'tis TIME to fear when tyrants seem to kiss; TRUTH fears no trial; who hath SKIRTS of straw needs fear the fire.

feast. *See* a CHEERFUL look makes a dish a feast; the COMPANY makes the feast; a CONTENTED mind is a continual feast; ENOUGH is as good as a feast; FLIES come to feasts unasked; a GOOD conscience is a continual feast.

feather. feather by feather the goose is plucked (*Italian*) Step by step a task is completed. G. Torriano, *Select Italian Proverbs*, 1642.

~ *See also* BIRDS of a feather flock together; FINE feathers make fine birds; he that EATS the king's goose shall be choked with his feathers; the PEACOCK hath fair feathers, but foul feet.

February. if in February there be no rain, 'tis neither good for hay nor grain (*English*) A dry February bodes ill for hay and grain harvests later in the year. John Ray, *A Collection of English Proverbs*, 1670. In agreement with this saying, other proverbs claim 'if it rains in February every day, in June you're sure of plenty of hay', 'February's rain fills the barn', 'a February spring is not worth a pin', 'if February give much snow, a fine summer it doth foreshow' and 'February fill ditch, black or white, don't care which' ('black' being rain and 'white' being snow). Yet another runs 'February, if ye be foul, the sheep will die in every pool'. Another is blunter still, claiming that 'a Welshman had rather see his dam on her bier than see a fair Februeer'. *See also* CANDLEMAS Day, put beans in the clay, put candles and candlesticks away; if CANDLEMAS Day be sunny and bright, winter will have another flight; if Candlemas Day be cloudy with rain, winter is gone, and won't come again.

> All the moneths in the year curse a fair Februeer.
>
> John Ray, *A Collection of English Proverbs*, 1670

~ *See also* as AUGUST so the next February.

fed. *See* FEED.

fee. *See* a LEAN fee is a fit reward for a lazy clerk.

feed. feed a cold and starve a fever (*English*) Patients with colds should be encouraged to eat healthily, while those with fevers should be denied sustenance. Edward Fitzgerald, *Polonius: A Collection of Wise Saws and Modern Instances*, 1852. In times gone by superstition offered various things a feverish patient might take. These included rolled-up cobwebs, spiders and live insects eaten in slices of apple or with jam or treacle. It has been suggested that the proverb was originally intended to be a warning to the effect that any person who attempted to control a cold by overeating could expect to suffer a fever as a consequence. Modern medical opinion agrees that a sensible, healthy diet will help to fight a cold, while those suffering from fevers are best sustained with drinks only (they will in any case be disinclined to eat).

> Edwin's cold was now fully developed; and
> Maggie had told him to feed it.
>
> Arnold Bennett, *Clayhanger*, 1910

feed by measure and defy the physician (*English*) The best recipe for good health is a sensible, moderate diet. John Heywood, *A Dialogue containing … the Proverbs in the English Tongue*, 1550.

> Live in measure, and laugh at the mediciners.
>
> James Kelly, *A Complete Collection of Scotish Proverbs*, 1721

~ *See also* BEGGARS breed and rich men feed; don't BITE the hand that feeds you; CHARITY and pride do both feed the poor; FIRST born, first fed; he that GAPETH until he be fed, well may he gape until he be dead; he that hath no CHILDREN feedeth them fat; OLD fish and young flesh feed men best; OLD praise dies unless you feed it.

feel. *See* the DOG that is idle barks at his fleas, but he that is hunting feels them not; a MAN is as old as he feels, and a woman as old as she looks; no man is ANGRY that feels not himself hurt; PRIDE feels no pain.

feeling hath no fellow (*English*) Having a gut feeling about something or someone is a more reliable guide than the evidence of the other senses. John Ray, *A Collection of English Proverbs*, 1678.

feet. *See* FOOT.

fell. *See* LITTLE strokes fell great oaks; an OAK is not felled at one stroke.

fellow. *See* ALL fellows at football; a CRAFTY fellow never has any peace; FEELING hath no fellow; STONE-dead hath no fellow.

female. the female of the species is more deadly than the male (*English*) Women can prove more ruthless and without mercy than their male counterparts (just as the female spider is more to be feared than its mate). Rudyard Kipling, *Morning Post*, 20 October 1911.

fence. no fence against ill fortune (*English*) There is no way to protect oneself effectively from bad luck. W. Camden, *Remains concerning Britain*, 1614. Equivalents include 'no fence against a flail'.

> Some evils and calamities assault so violently, that there is no resisting of them.
>
> John Ray, *A Collection of English Proverbs*, 1670

~ *See also* GOOD fences make good neighbours; the GRASS is always greener on the other side of the fence

fertile. *See* BAD luck is fertile.

festina lente. *See* make HASTE slowly.

fetch. *See* a DOG that will fetch a bone will carry a bone; if you LEAP into a well providence is not bound to fetch you out.

fever. *See* FEED a cold and starve a fever.

few. few words are best (*English*) A few well-chosen words are better than a long rambling speech. *Roxborough Ballads*, *c.*1600. Related proverbs include 'few words and many deeds' and 'few words to the wise suffice'.

> I wonder what the devil possessed me – but few words are best.
>
> Tobias Smollett, *Humphry Clinker*, 1771

~ *See also* BOOKS and friends should be few and good; the BUSY man has few idle visitors; the DEAD have few friends; he is the BEST general who makes the fewest mistakes; he who COMMENCES many things finishes but a few; you WIN a few, you lose a few.

fiction. *See* FACT is stranger than fiction; TRUTH is stranger than fiction.

fiddle. *See* the LEAST boy always carries the greatest fiddle; there's MANY a good tune played on an old fiddle.

fiddler. *See* they that DANCE must pay the fiddler.

fiddlestick. *See* the DEVIL rides upon a fiddlestick.

field. fields have eyes, and woods have ears (*English*) Secrets will always leak out, even when there seems to be no one else around. *Trinity MS*, *c.*1225. *See also* WALLS have ears.

> Woods have their eares, and fields their eyes, everie thing hath some instrument of, or helpe for, discoverie.
>
> Randle Cotgrave, *A Dictionary of the French and English Tongues*, 1611

~ *See also* a BAD bush is better than an open field; a LAMB in the house, a lion in the field.

field-marshal. *See* EVERY soldier has the baton of a field-marshal in his knapsack.

fierce. *See* the LION is not so fierce as he is painted.

fifteen. *See* a WOMAN is an angel at ten, a saint at fifteen, a devil at forty and a witch at fourscore.

fifty. *See* he that is not HANDSOME at twenty, wise at forty and rich at fifty, will never be rich, wise or handsome; ONE reason is as good as fifty; TELL a woman she's a beauty and the devil will tell her so fifty times.

fight. fight fire with fire (*English*) Employ the same methods that are used against you when retaliating.

William Shakespeare, *Coriolanus*, *c.*1608. Another proverb insists 'fire drives out fire'.

he who fights and runs away, lives to fight another day (*Greek*) It is sometimes wisest to back down from a fight, so that one may return to the fray at a later date. *The Owl and the Nightingale*, 1250 (also found in the writings of Menander). Legend has it that the line was spoken by Demosthenes as he fled from Philip of Macedon at Chaeronea. *See also* DISCRETION is the better part of valour.

For, those that fly, may fight againe,
Which he can never do that's slain.
Samuel Butler, *Hudibras*, 1678

~ *See also* as SORE fight wrens as cranes; COUNCILS of war never fight; put a COWARD to his mettle and he'll fight the devil; TWO dogs fight for a bone, and a third runs away with it.

fighting. *See* on PAINTING and fighting look aloof.

fill (noun). *See* the CASK savours of the first fill.

fill (verb). *See* a COLD April the barn will fill; an EMPTY purse fills the face with wrinkles; GRAIN by grain the hen fills her belly; LITTLE and good fills the trencher; a LITTLE house well filled, a little land well tilled, and a little wife well willed; the NET fills though the fisherman sleeps; a SHUT mouth never fills a black coffin; WORK expands so as to fill the time available.

filth. the filth under the white snow the sun discovers (*English*) Underlying corruption is soon exposed. George Herbert, *Outlandish Proverbs*, 1640.

~ *See also* STANDING pools gather filth.

find. take what you find or what you bring (*English*) Those who do not like what they are offered must settle for what they have brought themselves. Geoffrey Chaucer, 'The Reeve's Tale', *The Canterbury Tales*, *c.*1387. *See also* a MAN must take such as he finds, or such as he brings.

If this like you not, take that you finde, or that
you bring, for me.
Robert Greene, *George a Greene*, 1599

~ *See also* AWAY goes the devil when he finds the door shut against him; BETTER lost than found; the DEVIL finds work for idle hands; the DOG that trots about finds a bone; FAST bind, fast find; GOOD finds good; he that GROPES in the dark finds that he would not; he that LOOKS not before finds himself behind; HOME is home, as the devil said when he found himself in the Court of Session; HYPOCRISY can find out a cloak for every rain; ILL luck is worse than found money; it is EASY to find a stick to beat a dog; KEEP a thing seven years and you'll always find a use for it; LONGEST at the fire soonest finds cold; LOST time is never found again; LOVE will find a way; a MAN must take such as he finds, or such as he brings; SAFE bind, safe find; SCRATCH an Englishman and you'll find a seaman; SCRATCH a Russian and you find a Tartar; SEEK and ye shall find; those who HIDE can find; when an ASS climbs a ladder we may find wisdom in women; who HOLDS his peace and gathers stones will find a time to throw them; WINTER finds out what summer lays up.

finders keepers, losers weepers (*Roman*) Anyone who finds something is entitled to it, while the person who has lost it must reconcile himself to the loss. J.T. Brockett, *Glossary of North Country Words*, 1825 (variants are also found in the writings of Plautus). The notion encapsulated in the proverb is supported by the law only in certain very limited circumstances. Also encountered in the form 'finding's keepings'.

fine. fine feathers make fine birds (*French*) Fine clothes lend distinction to the wearer. G. Delamothe, *French Alphabet*, 1592. *See also* APPEARANCES are deceptive.

As everybody knows, fine feathers make fine birds.
Thomas Hardy, *Tess of the D'Urbervilles*, 1891

fine words butter no parsnips (*English*) Nothing is actually achieved by talk alone. J. Clarke, *Paroemiologia Anglo-Latina*, 1639. Parsnips are traditionally served with melted butter (words clearly being a poor substitute). Also encountered in the form 'fair words butter no parsnips'. On the other hand, another proverb suggests that 'fine words dress ill deeds'.

Who ... said that 'fine words butter no parsnips'?
Half the parsnips of society are served and rendered palatable with no other sauce.
William Thackeray, *Vanity Fair*, 1848

~ *See also* FOG on the hill, water to the mill; fog in the hollow, fine day to follow; the MILL that is always going grinds coarse and fine; a MISTY morning may have a fine day; a PROUD look makes foul work in a fine face; RAIN before seven, fine before eleven.

finger. fingers were made before forks and hands before knives (*English*) Before the invention of cutlery people used their hands to eat with (quoted as an excuse for using the fingers to eat with). *Loseley MSS*, 1567. The fork was first introduced, in Venetian society, in the early sixteenth century, although John the Good, Duke of Burgundy (1286–1341), allegedly used two forks to eat with as early as the fourteenth century. It was not until the eighteenth century that the use of knives and forks became widespread in British society. The proverb is sometimes quoted in other contexts in reference to the employment of less refined methods. A Cornish proverb dating from the nineteenth century or earlier recommends 'fingers for fish, prongs for meat'.

> Miss Thorne ... was always glad to revert to anything and ... would doubtless in time have reflected that fingers were made before forks, and have reverted accordingly.
>
> Anthony Trollope, *Barchester Towers*, 1857

~ *See also* the DEVIL makes his Christmas pies of lawyers' tongues and clerks' fingers; GIVE a clown a finger and he will take your hand; he is a POOR cook that cannot lick his own fingers; he that HANDLES thorns shall prick his fingers; the SAME knife cuts bread and fingers.

finish. *See* he who COMMENCES many things finishes but a few; NICE guys finish last.

fire. fire and water are good servants but bad masters (*English*) Fire and water are useful in various ways but are dangerous if allowed to get out of control. W. Bullein, *Bulwarke of Defence*, 1562. Also encountered as 'fire is a good friend, but a bad enemy' and 'fire is as hurtful as healthful'. Another proverb claims 'water is as dangerous as commodious' and the two elements are brought together in 'fire and water have no mercy' and 'fire is love and water sorrow'.

> Fire, the saying goes, is a good servant but a bad master.
>
> Charles Dickens, *Barnaby Rudge*, 1841

fire drives out fire (*English*) One passion or sensation will be eclipsed by another. William Shakespeare, *Romeo and Juliet*, *c.*1593.

> Tut, man, one fire burns out another's burning.
>
> William Shakespeare, *Romeo and Juliet*, *c.*1593

~ *See also* BETTER a little fire to warm us than a great one to burn us; a BURNT child dreads the fire; CROOKED logs make straight fires; DIRTY water will quench fire; FANNED fires and forced love never did well yet; FIGHT fire with fire; he CARRIES fire in one hand and water in the other; if you PLAY with fire you get burnt; in the COLDEST flint there is hot fire; it is a DANGEROUS fire begins in the bed straw; KINDLE not a fire that you cannot extinguish; a LITTLE fire burns up a great deal of corn; LONGEST at the fire soonest finds cold; LOOK to thyself when thy neighbour's house is on fire; MANY irons in the fire, some must cool; MUCH smoke, little fire; out of the FRYING-PAN into the fire; SHIPS fear fire more than water; SILKS and satins put out the fire in the chimney; a SMALL spark makes a great fire; the SMOKE of a man's own country is better than the fire of another's; a SOFT fire makes a sweet malt; take the CHESTNUTS out of the fire with the cat's paw; there's no SMOKE without fire; THREE removals are as bad as a fire; WATER afar quencheth not fire; WATER, fire and soldiers quickly make room; when the HEART is a fire some sparks will fly out of the mouth; who hath SKIRTS of straw needs fear the fire; you should KNOW a man seven years before you stir his fire.

first. the first blow is half the battle (*Greek*) He who begins well will find half his work already done. George Herbert, *Outlandish Proverbs*, 1640 (also quoted by Pythagoras, sixth century BC). Related proverbs include 'the first blow is as much as two' and 'the first blow makes the wrong, but the second makes the fray'. *See also* WELL begun is half done.

> The beginning is half the whole.
>
> Pythagoras, sixth century BC

first born, first fed (*English*) The oldest child generally takes first place in the pecking order among his or her siblings. T. Draxe, *Bibliotheca Scholastica*, 1616.

the first breath is the beginning of death (*English*) All living things begin the journey to death from the moment they first draw breath. Thomas Fuller, *Gnomologia*, 1732.

first catch your hare (*English*) Do not forget to take the essential first step before embarking on some project or enterprise (often said as a word of warning to those whose enthusiasm for a project tempts them to forget what they must do first before they can proceed). William Thackeray, *The Rose and the Ring*, 1855. The proverb is often inaccurately attributed to Hannah Glasse, in her *The Art of Cookery made Plain and Easy*, 1747, or else to Mrs Beeton, in her *Book of Household Management*, 1851, in neither of which does it appear in precisely this form (Hannah Glasse's authorship of *The Art of Cookery* itself is also open to question). Although Glasse's apparent use of the phrase made it famous, it had, in fact, been in common parlance for many years beforehand, a variant of it (mentioning deer rather than hares) being quoted, for instance, by Henry de Bracton in his *De Legibus Angliae* in the thirteenth century: 'it is a common saying that it is best first to catch the stag, and afterwards, when he has been caught, to skin him.' Equivalent proverbs to much the same effect include 'catch your bear before you sell its skin'. *See also* don't COUNT your chickens before they are hatched; don't HALLOO till you are out of the wood.

> Take your hare when it is cased [skinned], and make a pudding …
>
> Hannah Glasse, *The Art of Cookery made Plain and Easy*, 1747

first come, first served (*English/French*) Those who arrive promptly will get first choice of what is on offer and have the least time to wait. Geoffrey Chaucer, *The Canterbury Tales*, *c.*1387.

> He found the sexton … making nine graves … and whoso dies next, first comes, first served.
>
> Robert Armin, *A Nest of Ninnies*, 1608

the first dish pleaseth all (*English*) The first course of a meal is always well received by those who are hungry. George Herbert, *Outlandish Proverbs*, 1640.

the first duty of a soldier is obedience (*English*) Above all else, a soldier is required to obey the orders of his superiors. J. Grant, *The Romance of War*, 1847.

the first faults are theirs that commit them, the second theirs that permit them (*English*) Those who do nothing to prevent some offence being committed are almost as guilty of it as the actual perpetrators. Thomas Fuller, *Gnomologia*, 1732.

the first glass for thirst, the second for nourishment, the third for pleasure, and the fourth for madness (*Greek*) Each successive glass of wine that a person drinks has a different effect.

> The first pot quencheth thirst (so Panyasis the poet determines in Athenaeus): *secunda Gratiis, Horis, et Dionysis* – the second makes merry: the third for pleasure: *quarta ad insanium*, the fourth makes them mad.
>
> Robert Burton, *Anatomy of Melancholy*, 1621

first impressions are the most lasting (*English*) The impression a person makes on first acquaintance has a lasting impact. William Congreve, *The Way of the World*, 1700. Jane Austen's novel *Pride and Prejudice*, 1796–7, was originally entitled *First Impressions*.

> First impressions, you know, often go a long way, and last a long time.
>
> Charles Dickens, *Martin Chuzzlewit*, 1843–4

the first seven years are the hardest (*English*) Things get easier after the difficult initial stages (usually quoted in reference to marriages and new jobs). The saying probably arose during the First World War, when service in the regular army was set at seven years. As far back as the fourteenth century, however, a seven-year period was regarded as significant (superstition, for instance, claimed that children's characters changed every seven years).

first things first (*English*) Tackle things in the correct order (typically in order of importance). G. Jackson, *First Things First*, 1894.

first thrive and then wive (*English*) A wise man establishes himself in his business before he acquires a wife. William Shakespeare, *Pericles*, 1608–9.

first try and then trust (*English*) It is best to test a person's loyalty or reliability before accepting that person as a friend, ally, partner and the like. J. Clarke, *Paroemiographia Anglo-Latina*, 1639.

he that comes first to the hill may sit where he will (*Scottish*) Those who arrive first may take first choice. David Fergusson, *Scottish Proverbs*, 1641. *See also* FIRST come, first served.

> He that is first on the midding [dunghill], may sit where he will.
>
> James Kelly, *A Complete Collection of Scotish Proverbs*, 1721

if at first you don't succeed, try, try, try again (*English*) Do not be discouraged by early failure at something.

T.H. Palmer, *Teacher's Manual*, 1840. The proverb was popularized on both sides of the Atlantic in a poem, 'Try (try) again', part of W.E. Hickson's *Moral Songs*, 1857.

it is the first step that is difficult (*French*) In many enterprises, it is the first stage that presents the biggest challenge. A. Munday and others, *Sir Thomas More*, *c.*1596. The proverb has its origins in the legend of Saint Denys, who was beheaded by his enemies but then picked up his head and walked six miles with it. A wise man commented of the story: 'the distance ... is not important. It was the first step that was difficult.' *See also* CE n'est que le premier pas qui coûte.

on the first of March, the crows begin to search (*English*) The first day of March signals the start of the mating season for crows. M.A. Denham, *Proverbs Relating to the Seasons*, 1846. Medieval superstition placed the beginning of the mating season for birds on 14 February, Saint Valentine's Day.

> By the first of March the crows begin to search,
> By the first of April they are sitting still,
> By the first of May they are flown away,
> Creeping greedy back again
> With October wind and rain.
>
> Edith Holden, *The Country Diary of an Edwardian Lady*, 1906

~ *See also* the BEST go first, the bad remain to mend; BETTER be first in a village than second at Rome; BOLDNESS in business is the first, second and third thing; the CASK savours of the first fill; the COW that's first up gets the first of the dew; GIVE me a child for the first seven years, and you may do what you like with him afterwards; he is not LAUGHED at that laughs at himself first; he that will THRIVE must first ask his wife; he that would HANG his dog gives out first that he is mad; he that would the DAUGHTER win, must with the mother first begin; he was a BOLD man that first ate an oyster; in SETTLING an island, the first building erected by a Spaniard will be a church; by a Frenchman, a fort; by a Dutchman, a warehouse; and by an Englishman, an alehouse; it is a GOOD thing to eat your brown bread first; no MAN can be a good ruler unless he hath first been ruled; no one LIKES to be the first to step on the ice; of SOUP and love the first is the best; ORDER is heaven's first law; PRETTINESS dies first; SAFETY first; SELF-PRESERVATION is the first law of nature; THINK first and speak afterwards; the TREE falls not at the first blow; TRY your skill in gilt first and then in gold; when a COUPLE are newly married the first month is honeymoon, or smick smack; the second is hither and thither; the third is thwick thwack; the fourth the devil take them that brought thee and I together; whom the GODS would destroy they first make mad; the WORST spoke in a cart breaks first.

fish (noun). **do not make fish of one and flesh of another** (*English*) Treat others equally, with impartiality. J. Clarke, *Paroemiologia Anglo-Latina*, 1639. Also encountered as 'do not make fish of one and fowl of another'.

> The complaints alleged against the maids are ... very applicable to our gentleman's gentlemen; I would, therefore, have them under the very same regulations, and ... would not make fish of one and flesh of the other.
>
> Daniel Defoe, *Everybody's Business*, 1725

the fish always stinks from the head downwards (*Greek*) Corruption always starts at the top (often quoted in discussion of political corruption). George Pettie, *Guazzo's Civil Conversation*, 1581.

> Teste, Fish ever begins to taint at the head; the first thing that's deprav'd in man's his wit.
>
> Randle Cotgrave, *A Dictionary of the French and English Tongues*, 1611

fish and guests stink after three days (*English*) Three days are enough to make the presence of any guest irksome (just as a fish will start to go off in that time). John Lyly, *Euphues and His England*, 1580 (a variant may also be found in the writings of Plautus). Also found as 'fish and company stink in three days'. *See also* a CONSTANT guest is never welcome.

> Fish and visitors smell in three days.
>
> Benjamin Franklin, *Works*, *c.*1736

fish must swim thrice (*English*) Fish should swim first in water and then in butter or sauce (while being cooked) and finally in wine (in the stomach after being eaten). Randle Cotgrave, *A Dictionary of the French and English Tongues*, 1611.

the fish will soon be caught that nibbles at every bait (*English*) Those who recklessly accept any offer that is presented to them without considering the possible pitfalls will soon find themselves in trouble. Thomas Fuller, *Gnomologia*, 1732.

~ *See also* ALL cats love fish but fear to wet their paws; ALL fish are not caught with flies; ALL is fish that comes to the net; the BEST fish swim near the bottom; BIG fish eat little fish; CATCHING fish is not the whole of fishing; DAUGHTERS and dead fish are no keeping wares; GUT no fish till you get them; if you SWEAR you will catch no fish; it is a SILLY fish that is caught twice with the same bait; it is in VAIN to cast your net where there is no fish; LITTLE fish are sweet; LITTLE fishes slip through nets but great fishes are taken; a MONK out of his cloister is like a fish out of water; no MAN cries stinking fish; OLD fish and young flesh feed men best; there are PLENTY more fish in the sea; when the WIND is in the south it blows the bait into the fish's mouth.

fish (verb). *See* CATCHING fish is not the whole of fishing; in the DEEPEST water is the best fishing; it is GOOD fishing in troubled waters; it is ILL fishing before the net.

fisherman. *See* the NET fills though the fisherman sleeps.

fit (verb). **you can't fit a quart into a pint pot** (*US/English*) Some things are impossible to achieve due to shortage of space, time or other resources. Charlotte Gilman, *The Living of Charlotte Perkins Gilman*, 1935. Also encountered with pint bottle, pint mug and pint cup.

~ *See also* ANYTHING will fit a naked man; BORROWED garments never fit well; EVERY shoe fits not every foot; if the CAP fits, wear it; a PIECE of a churchyard fits everybody.

fit (adj.). **he is not fit to command others that cannot command himself** (*English*) No one should assume control over others when incapable of controlling their own behaviour. J. Stanbridge, *Vulgaria*, *c.*1510. Related proverbs include 'he that commands well shall be obeyed well'.

> Cato ... would say, 'No man is fit to command another, that cannot command himself'.
> William Penn, *No Cross, No Crown*, 1669

~ *See also* an ANGRY man is not fit to pray; a LEAN fee is a fit reward for a lazy clerk; a WHISTLING woman and a crowing hen is neither fit for God nor men.

five. *See* he KNOWS how many beans make five; he that will THRIVE must rise at five; ONE for sorrow, two for joy; three for a girl, four for a boy; five for silver, six for gold; seven for a secret, never to be told; eight for heaven, nine for hell; and ten for the devil's own self.

fix. *See* DRAW not your bow till your arrow is fixed; if it ain't BROKE, don't fix it.

flag. *See* TRADE follows the flag.

flame. *See* take away FUEL, take away flame.

flash. *See* BEWARE of the oak, it draws the stroke; avoid the ash, it courts the flash.

flatterer. there is no such flatterer as a man's self (*English*) No one can flatter a person as well as the person themself. Thomas Fuller, *Gnomologia*, 1732. Other proverbs on the subject of flatterers include the Italian 'a flatterer's throat is an open sepulchre', 'when flatterers meet the devil goes to dinner' and 'no foe to a flatterer'.

flattery. *See* IMITATION is the sincerest form of flattery.

flaunt. *See* if you've GOT it, flaunt it.

flea. *See* BIG fleas have little fleas upon their backs to bite them, and little fleas have lesser fleas, and so *ad infinitum*; the DOG that is idle barks at his fleas, but he that is hunting feels them not; if you LIE down with dogs, you will get up with fleas; NOTHING should be done in haste but gripping a flea.

flee. *See* FOLLOW love and it will flee thee; flee love and it will follow thee.

flesh. *See* ALL flesh is not venison; BETTER a louse in the pot than no flesh at all; do not make FISH of one and flesh of another; the NEARER the bone, the sweeter the flesh; OLD fish and young flesh feed men best; the SPIRIT is willing but the flesh is weak; what's BRED in the bone will come out in the flesh.

flew. *See* FLY (verb).

flies. *See* FLY.

flight. *See* BLESSINGS brighten as they take their

flight; if CANDLEMAS Day be sunny and bright winter will have another flight; if Candlemas Day be cloudy with rain, winter is gone and won't come again.

fling. fling enough dirt and some will stick (*Roman*) Heaping allegations of misdoings and so forth on an opponent is a good policy, because some at least are bound to be believed. Francis Bacon, *De Dignitate et Augmentis Scientiarum*, 1623 (quoting Latin sources). The practice was originally associated with Medius, a courtier in the time of Alexander the Great, who favoured such tactics against his enemies. The word 'mud' often replaces 'dirt' (hence the coinage 'mud-slinging'). *See also* GIVE a dog a bad name and hang him; SLANDER leaves a scar behind it.

> Scurrility's a useful trick,
> Approv'd by the most politic;
> Fling dirt enough, and some will stick.
> Edward Ward, *Hudibras Redivivus*, 1706

~ *See also* he is like a CAT: fling him which way you will, he'll light on his legs.

flint. *See* in the COLDEST flint there is hot fire.

flit. *See* SATURDAY's flit will never sit.

flock (noun). *See* ONE scabbed sheep infects the whole flock.

flock (verb). *See* BIRDS of a feather flock together.

flood. *See* he that will CATCH eels must disturb the flood; the HIGHEST flood has the lowest ebb; in the ANTS' house the dew is a flood.

flourish. *See* where ROSEMARY flourishes the lady rules.

flow. *See* EVERY flow hath its ebb.

flower. *See* APRIL showers bring forth May flowers; BEAUTY without virtue is a flower without perfume; if you would ENJOY the fruit, pluck not the flower.

fly (noun). **flies come to feasts unasked** (*English*) Parasites and other undesirables gather where there is hope of some benefit, regardless of whether their presence has been requested. *Sphere*, 27 September 1924.

the fly sat upon the axletree of the chariot-wheel and said, what a dust do I raise! (*Greek*) Said when a person boasts of their influence upon the world, when the reality is that they are deluding themselves about their importance. Francis Bacon, *Essays*, 1612 (referring to a fable by Aesop in which the image was first devised).

> The fly on the cart-wheel might as well have claimed not only that it was raising all the dust, but that it had built the cart.
> *Observer*, 5 March 1922

~ *See also* ALL fish are not caught with flies; a CLOSE mouth catches no flies; do not REMOVE a fly from your friend's forehead with a hatchet; EAGLES don't catch flies; he who BATHES in May will soon be laid in clay, he who bathes in June will sing a merry tune, he who bathes in July will dance like a fly; HONEY catches more flies than vinegar; HUNGRY flies bite sore.

fly (verb). **fly the pleasure which paineth afterward** (*English*) Refrain from indulging in pleasures that are likely to lead a person to feel regret later. R. Sandford, *The Garden of Pleasure*, 1573. Also encountered in the form 'fly that pleasure which bites tomorrow'.

no flying without wings (*Roman*) It is impossible to do something without the necessary equipment, training and so on. George Chapman, Ben Jonson, and John Marston, *Eastward Ho* 1605 (quoting Plautus).

> No flying without wings. He would fain fly, but he wants feathers ...
> John Ray, *A Collection of English Proverbs*, 1670

~ *See also* a BIRD never flew on one wing; DESTROY the nests and the birds will fly away; EAGLES fly alone; it is GOOD to make a bridge of gold to a flying enemy; PIGS might fly, if they had wings; TIME flies; what CHILDREN hear at home soon flies abroad; when POVERTY comes in at the door, love flies out of the window; when the HEART is a fire some sparks will fly out of the mouth.

foe. a foe is better than a dissembling friend (*Greek*) An open enemy is less of a threat than a friend of whose devotion you are not entirely sure. Briant, *Dis-*

praise of the Life of a Courtier, 1548. The proverb is attributed originally to Alexander the Great.

~ *See also* ANYONE can kill a trussed foe; NEVER tell thy foe that thy foot acheth; WOES unite foes.

fog. fog on the hill, water to the mill; fog in the hollow, fine day to follow (*English*) When the fog settles on the hills, rain will follow; when it lies low on the ground good weather will follow. *Spectator*, 3 November 1928. Related proverbs include 'a fog from the sea brings honey to the bee; a fog from the hills brings corn to the mills'.

~ *See also* a GOOD hay year a bad fog year.

folk. *See* BUSY folks are always meddling; DEAD folks are past fooling; FAR folks fare well; GREEDY folks have long arms; he KENS his groats among other folk's kail; KINDNESS is lost that is bestowed on children and old folks; LAZY folk take the most pains; RICH folk have many friends; SHORT folk are soon angry; there's NOWT so queer as folk; YOUNG folks think old folks to be fools, but old folks know young folks to be fools.

follow. follow love and it will flee thee; flee love and it will follow thee (*English*) Those who pursue love will be disappointed, while those who try to escape it will find it comes to them. *Romaunce of the Rose*, *c.*1400. Also encountered in the form 'follow pleasure and it will flee thee; flee pleasure and it will follow thee'.

follow not truth too near the heels, lest it dash out thy teeth (*English*) Historians and others who write about recent events risk provoking those involved. Sir Walter Raleigh, *History of the World*, 1614.

> I know how dangerous it is to follow truth too near to the heels; yet better it is that the teeth of an historian be struck out of his head for writing the truth, than that they ... rot in his jaws, by feeding ... on the sweetmeats of flattery.
>
> Thomas Fuller, *Church History*, 1655

follow the river and you'll get to the sea (*English*) All rivers lead eventually to the sea. *Edward III*, 1595.

~ *See also* as NOVEMBER so the following March; a BLUSTERING night, a fair day follows; FAR behind must follow the faster; FOG on the hill, water to the mill; fog in the hollow, fine day to follow; if ONE sheep leap o'er the dyke, all the rest will follow; PAIN is forgotten where gain follows; the SMOKE follows the fairest; TRADE follows the flag.

folly. folly grows without watering (*English*) Folly needs little encouragement to multiply. George Herbert, *Outlandish Proverbs*, 1640. Variants include 'fools grow without watering'.

~ *See also* ANGER without power is folly; there is no JOLLITY but hath a smack of folly; ZEAL without knowledge is the sister of folly.

fond. *See* ABSENCE makes the heart grow fonder.

fool (noun)**. a fool and his money are soon parted** (*English*) Those who are incapable of looking after their own money will soon be deprived of it by sharper minds. Thomas Tusser, *Five Hundred Pointes of Good Husbandrie*, 1573. The story goes that the proverb was first quoted by the historian George Buchanan, a tutor to James VI of Scotland, who easily won a wager with another courtier as to which of them could produce the coarsest passage of verse. Centuries later Carolyn Wells came up with a humorous variant on the old original: 'a fool and his money are soon married.'

> She tossed her nose in distain, saying, she supposed her brother had taken him into favour ... that a fool and his money were soon parted.
>
> Tobias Smollett, *Humphry Clinker*, 1771

a fool at forty is a fool indeed (*English*) By the time a person reaches the age of forty, he should possess some knowledge of the way the world works; if he does not he must be irredeemably stupid. Edward Young, *The Love of Fame, the Universal Passion*, 1725. Another proverb claims 'every man is a fool or a physician at forty' (sometimes 'thirty'), meaning that by that age a man of any sense has a fairly clear idea of his own constitution. According to Plutarch, this last proverb was a favourite saying of the Emperor Tiberius. *See also* there's no FOOL like an old fool.

> Be wise with speed; A fool at forty is a fool indeed.
>
> Edward Young, *The Love of Fame, the Universal Passion*, 1725

a fool may give a wise man counsel (*Greek*) Even the wisest person may learn something he or she did not know from a fool (sometimes spoken in self-deprecation by a person offering a supposedly cleverer person advice). *Ywain and Gawain*, 1350. Another proverb reminds that 'a fool may sometimes speak to the purpose'.

> A Fool may give a wise Man counsel by a time. An Apology of those who offer their Advice to them, who may be supposed to excel them in Parts and Sense.
>
> James Kelly, *A Complete Collection of Scotish Proverbs*, 1721

fools and bairns should never see half-done work (*Scottish*) Fools and children should not be shown incomplete work, as they will be tempted to judge the finished article from what they are shown. Robert Burton, *Anatomy of Melancholy*, 1621.

> It is not fit to be shown to 'bairns and fools,' who, according to our old canny proverb, should never see half done work.
>
> Walter Scott, quoted in Lockhart's *Life*, 1818

fools and madmen speak the truth (*English*) Fools and madmen may be forgiven for speaking the truth where others might not. Thomas Dekker, *Satiromastix*, 1602. *See also* CHILDREN and fools tell the truth.

fools ask questions that wise men cannot answer (*English*) Sometimes the slow-witted ask so many questions, or ones of such insight, that even the most intelligent are unable to answer. G. Torriano, *Italian Proverbs*, 1666. Also encountered in the form 'a fool may ask more questions in an hour than a wise man can answer in seven years'.

> Bryce Snaelsfoot is a cautious man ... He knows a fool may ask more questions than a wise man cares to answer.
>
> Walter Scott, *The Pirate*, 1821

a fool's bolt is soon shot (*English*) Those who act without taking the time to think first waste their efforts (just as a marksman who fires his crossbow too quickly is liable to miss his target). *Proverbs of Alfred*, *c.*1320. Another proverb, however, cautions that 'a fool's bolt may sometimes hit the mark'.

> 'Zounds, I have done,' said he. 'Your bolt is soon shot, according to the old proverb,' said she.
>
> Tobias Smollett, *Roderick Random*, 1748

fools build houses, and wise men live in them (*English*) Stupid people do all the work, while the more intelligent enjoy the results. John Ray, *A Collection of English Proverbs*, 1670. Equivalent sayings include 'fools make feasts and wise men eat them' and 'fools may invent fashions that wise men will wear'.

> Fools [build] Big Houses and wise Men buy them. I knew a Gentleman buy 2000 l. worth of Land, build a House upon it, and sell both House and Land to pay the Expences of his building.
>
> James Kelly, *A Complete Collection of Scotish Proverbs*, 1721

fools for luck (*English*) Stupid or mentally retarded people are often held to be the luckiest. Ben Jonson, *Bartholomew Fair*, 1631. The fullest version of the proverb runs 'a fool for luck, and a poor man for children'. Fools and the mad have always been considered lucky, and time was when communities took special care of such people in order to benefit from the luck they brought with them. Fishermen believed that meeting a madman in the street guaranteed a good catch that day, while others insisted that the saliva of a madman had special healing powers. *See also* FORTUNE favours fools.

fools rush in where angels fear to tread (*English*) Where the more intelligent hesitate to venture, some reckless souls rush in regardless of the risks. Alexander Pope, *Essay on Criticism*, 1711. In Pope's essay, from which the proverb arose, the poet was discussing those critics who express views more thoughtful readers would hesitate to share. Variants include 'a fool always rushes to the fore'.

a fool's tongue is long enough to cut his own throat (*English*) Fools say things that will damage their own interests. Thomas Fuller, *Gnomologia*, 1732. Another proverb advises that 'a fool's heart is in his tongue', while the Danish have 'a fool is like other men as long as he is silent'.

a fool thinks himself wise (*English*) Foolish people have an inflated idea of themselves. Sir Thomas North, *The Diall of Princes*, 1557. A fuller version of the proverb runs 'the fool doth think he is wise, but the wise man knows himself to be a fool'.

> I do now remember a saying, 'the fool doth think he is wise, but the wise man knows himself to be a fool'.
>
> William Shakespeare, *As You Like It*, *c.*1599

a fool will laugh when he is drowning (*English*) Fools may behave with inappropriate optimism when they are in fact in the deepest trouble. *Misogonus*, 1577.

he is a fool that is not melancholy once a day (*English*) Intelligent people are not cheerful all the time. John Ray, *A Collection of English Proverbs*, 1678.

only fools exult when governments change (*English*) Only fools believe that a change of government will make any real difference. *Times*, 19 November 1928.

there's no fool like an old fool (*English*) Those who cling stubbornly to foolish opions even into old age are doubly culpable. John Heywood, *A Dialogue containing ... the Proverbs in the English Tongue*, 1546.

> And troth he might hae ta'en warning, but there's nae fule like an ould fule.
>
> Walter Scott, *Waverley*, 1814

what the fool does in the end, the wise man does at the beginning (*English*) Fools put off doing what wise people do straightaway. R.C. Trench, *On the Lessons in Proverbs*, 1853. Another proverb warns 'fools are known by their babbling'.

> 'It's a fool's trick,' answered the stranger ... 'to put off what you must do at last.'
>
> Charles Kingsley, *Hereward the Wake*, 1866

~ *See also* a BARBER learns to shave by shaving fools; BETTER be a fool than a knave; BRIGHT rain makes fools fain; CHANGE of weather is the discourse of fools; CHILDREN and fools have merry lives; CHILDREN and fools must not play with edged tools; CHILDREN and fools tell the truth; EXPERIENCE is the teacher of fools; FAIR words and foul deeds cheat wise men as well as fools; FORTUNE favours fools; he is not a WISE man who cannot play the fool on occasion; he that TALKS to himself talks to a fool; he that TEACHES himself has a fool for his master; it is BETTER to be born a beggar than a fool; KNAVES and fools divide the world; LAWYERS' houses are built on the heads of fools; a MAN at thirty must be either a fool or a physician; a MAN who is his own lawyer has a fool for a client; MORE people know Tom Fool than Tom Fool knows; a NOD from a lord is a breakfast for a fool; REASON governs the wise man and cudgels the fool; RICHES serve a wise man but command a fool; SEND a fool to market and a fool he'll return; SIX hours' sleep for a man, seven for a woman, and eight for a fool; SUCCESS makes a fool seem wise; TWO fools in a house are too many; a WHITE wall is a fool's paper; a WISE man changes his mind, a fool never will; WISE men learn by others' faults, fools by their own; a WISE woman is twice a fool; YOUNG folks think old folks to be fools, but old folks know young folks to be fools.

fool (verb). **you may fool all of the people some of the time, some of the people all of the time, but not all of the people all of the time** (*US*) No one is clever enough to succeed in deceiving everyone consistently without eventually being discovered. Abraham Lincoln, speech, Bloomington, Illinois, 29 May 1856. Another source alleges that Lincoln coined the slogan while in conference with a visitor at the White House. In either event, Lincoln's version echoed similar statements by, among others, Pliny the Younger, Benjamin Franklin, La Rochefoucauld and English essayist John Sterling.

> One may be more clever than another, but not more clever than all the others.
>
> La Rochefoucauld, *Maximes*, 1665

~ *See also* DEAD folks are past fooling.

foolish. *See* PENNY wise, pound foolish.

foot. *See* AGUES come on horseback but go away on foot; although there EXIST many thousand subjects for elegant conversation, there are persons who cannot meet a cripple without talking about feet; the BEST manure is under the farmer's foot; the BLACK ox treads on one's foot; DRY feet, warm head, bring safe to bed; EVERY shoe fits not every foot; it is not SPRING until you can plant your foot upon twelve daisies; I was ANGERED, for I had no shoes – then I met a man who had no feet; KEEP something for the sore foot; the LAME foot overtakes the swift one in the end; NEVER tell thy foe that thy foot acheth; the PEACOCK hath fair feathers, but foul feet; SICKNESS comes on horseback, but goeth away on foot; SIT a beggar at your table, and he will soon put his feet on it; SIX feet of earth make all men equal; while the DUST is on your feet, sell what you have bought; a WILLING mind makes a light foot.

football. *See* ALL fellows at football.

forbear. *See* BEAR and forbear; that may be LAWFULLY done which cannot be forborne.

forbidden fruit tastes sweetest (*English*) There is more enjoyment, allegedly, to be had from something one is not entitled to than from those things one has a legitimate claim to. T. Adams, *The Devil's Banquet*, 1614. The popularity of the proverb was doubtless much reinforced by the tale of the forbidden fruit in the Garden of Eden, and a passage in the Old Testament book of Proverbs further advises that 'stolen waters are sweet and bread eaten in secret is pleasant'. Variants include 'stolen fruit is sweet', 'stolen kisses are always sweeter' and 'forbid a thing and that we will do'. A French equivalent runs 'stolen bread stirs the appetite'. *See also* the GRASS is always greener on the other side of the fence.

> Stolen sweets are sweeter;
> Stolen kisses much completer;
> Stolen looks are nice in chapels;
> Stolen, stolen be your apples.
> Thomas Randolph, *Song of Fairies*, c.1635

forborne. *See* FORBEAR.

force. a forced kindness deserves no thanks (*English*) There is no obligation to thank someone for a favour that was not done voluntarily. Thomas Fuller, *Gnomologia*, 1732.

~ *See also* FANNED fires and forced loves never did well yet; SUBTLETY is better than force.

ford. *See* NEVER praise a ford till you get over.

forearm. *See* FOREWARNED is forearmed.

forecast is better than work hard (*English*) Forethought can be more valuable than mere labour. George Chapman, *Widow's Tears*, 1612. Related proverbs on the theme of foresight include 'one good forewit is worth two afterwits', the Chinese 'dig a well before you are thirsty', the Arabic 'light your lamp before it becomes dark' and the Scottish 'a wise man carries his cloak in fair weather, and a fool wants his in rain'.

> Force, without forecast, is little worth. Strength, unless guided by skill and discretion, will avail but little.
> James Kelly, *A Complete Collection of Scottish Proverbs*, 1721

foregate. *See* when DISTRUST enters in at the foregate, love goes out at the postern; when PASSION entereth at the foregate, wisdom goeth out of the postern.

forehead. *See* do not REMOVE a fly from your friend's forehead with a hatchet.

forelock. *See* take TIME by the forelock.

forenoon. *See* you cannot have TWO forenoons in the same day.

forepart. *See* BEWARE of the forepart of a woman, the hind part of a mule and all sides of a priest.

foretold. *See* LONG foretold long last, short notice soon past.

forewarned is forearmed (*Roman*) Having foreknowledge of something puts a person at a big advantage. J. Arderne, *Treatises of Fistula*, c.1425 (also quoted by Plautus).

> I now knew the ground which I stood upon; and forewarned was being forearmed.
> Captain Frederick Marryat, *Peter Simple*, 1834

foresee. *See* a DANGER foreseen is half avoided.

forget. *See* a BELLOWING cow soon forgets her calf; the DANGER past and God forgotten; EATEN bread is soon forgotten; an ELEPHANT never forgets; FORGIVE and forget; LONG absent, soon forgotten; a MAN apt to promise is apt to forget; OLD love will not be forgotten; OLD men will die and children soon forget; PAIN is forgotten where gain follows; the PRIEST forgets that he was clerk; the RIVER passed and God forgotten; SELDOM seen, soon forgotten; SOON learnt, soon forgotten; SOUND love is not soon forgotten; VOWS made in storms are forgotten in calms.

forgive. forgive and forget (*English*) Do not harbour resentment against those who have committed offences against you. *Ancrene Riwle*, c.1200 (also found in the writings of Philo De Josepho around AD40). Another proverb advises 'revenge a wrong by forgiving it', but another consoles the naturally resentful thus: 'if we are bound to forgive an enemy, we are not bound to trust him.' *See also* let BYGONES be bygones.

> All our great fraie ... Is forgiven and forgotten betwene us quight.
> John Heywood, *A Dialogue containing ... the Proverbs in the English Tongue*, 1546

~ *See also* he that does you an ILL turn will never forgive you; the NOBLEST vengeance is to forgive; to ERR is human, to forgive divine.

forgotten. *See* FORGET.

fork. *See* FINGERS were made before forks and hands before knives; though you CAST out nature with a fork, it will still return; what the RAKE gathers, the fork scatters.

form. *See* ATTACK is the best form of defence; IMITATION is the sincerest form of flattery.

fort. *See* in SETTLING an island, the first building erected by a Spaniard will be a church; by a Frenchman, a fort; by a Dutchman, a warehouse; and by an Englishman, an alehouse.

fortunate. *See* the MORE wicked, the more fortunate; the PERSUASION of the fortunate sways the doubtful.

fortune. fortune favours fools (*Roman*) The simple-minded often seem to be protected by their own streak of luck. L. Wager, *The Longer thou Livest*, *c.*1560. *See also* FOOLS for luck.

> 'Tis a gross error, held in schools, that Fortune
> always favours fools.
> John Gay, *Fables*, 1737

fortune favours the bold (*Roman*) The courageous and bold may often enjoy the best luck. Geoffrey Chaucer, *Troilus and Criseyde*, *c.*1385–90 (the phrase is also found in Terence and Virgil). Also found in the form 'fortune favours the brave'.

> Who had been often told
> That fortune still assists the bold.
> Jonathan Swift, *Strephon and Chloe*, 1731

fortune helps those who help themselves (*English*) Luck attends those who work at promoting their own interests. Randle Cotgrave, *A Dictionary of the French and English Tongues*, 1611. *See also* GOD helps those who help themselves.

fortune is blind (*English*) Fortune bestows favours or disappointments without distinction. Robert Greene, *Pandosto*, 1588.

> All human business fortune doth command
> without all order; and with her blind hand, she,
> blind, bestows blind gifts.
> Ben Jonson, *Poetaster*, 1601

fortune knocks once at least at every man's gate (*English*) All people can expect to enjoy a stroke of good fortune on at least one occasion in their life. W.F. Butler, *C.G. Gordon*, 1889.

when fortune smiles, embrace her (*English*) When luck turns your way, take full advantage of it. John Ray, *A Collection of English Proverbs*, 1670. Related proverbs include 'when fortune knocks, open the door'.

~ *See also* EVERY man is the architect of his own fortune; a GREAT fortune is a great slavery; he that hath a WIFE and children hath given hostages to fortune; INDUSTRY is fortune's right hand, and frugality her left; no FENCE against ill fortune; RICHES are but the baggage of fortune.

forty. *See* a FOOL at forty is a fool indeed; he that is not HANDSOME at twenty, wise at forty and rich at fifty, will never be rich, wise or handsome; LIFE begins at forty; SAINT Swithin's Day, if thou dost rain, for forty days it will remain; Saint Swithin's Day, if thou be fair, for forty days 'twill rain no more; a WOMAN is an angel at ten, a saint at fifteen, a devil at forty and a witch at fourscore.

forward. go forward and fall, go backward and mar all (*English*) It is better to falter while pushing ahead than to retreat and fail completely. J. Clarke, *Paroemiologia Anglo-Latina*, 1639.

foul (verb). *See* it's an ILL bird that fouls its own nest.

foul (adj.). **a foul morning may turn to a fair day** (*English*) Bad weather early in the day may be replaced by better weather later. Robert Burton, *Anatomy of Melancholy*, 1624. *See also* CLOUDY mornings turn to clear afternoons; a GAUDY morning bodes a wet afternoon.

~ *See also* the FAIRER the hostess, the fouler the reckoning; the FAIRER the paper, the fouler the blot; FAIR face and a foul heart; FAIR words and foul deeds cheat wise men as well as fools; FROST and fraud both end in foul; GIVE a child all he shall crave and a dog while his tail doth wave and you'll have a fair dog and a foul knave; he that FALLS in the dirt, the longer he stays there the fouler he is; in FAIR weather prepare for foul; the PEACOCK hath fair feathers, but foul feet; a PROUD look makes foul work in a fine face.

found. See FIND.

foundation. *See* a HIGH building, a low foundation; no GOOD building without a good foundation.

four. four eyes see more than two (*Roman*) More may be discovered by two people working together than by one alone. A. Colynet, *True History of the Civil Wars in France*, 1591. *See also* TWO heads are better than one.

> Matters of inferiour consequence he will communicate to a fast friend, and crave his advice; for two eyes see more than one.
> Thomas Fuller, *Holy State*, 1642

~ *See also* he that MARRIES a widow and three children marries four thieves; ONE for sorrow, two for joy; three for a girl, four for a boy; five for silver, six for gold; seven for a secret, never to be told; eight for heaven, nine for hell; and ten for the devil's own self; there goes MORE to marriage than four bare legs in a bed; TWO and two make four.

fourscore. *See* a WOMAN is an angel at ten, a saint at fifteen, a devil at forty and a witch at fourscore

fourth. *See* the FIRST glass for thirst, the second for nourishment, the third for pleasure, and the fourth for madness; when a COUPLE are newly married the first month is honeymoon, or smick smack; the second is hither and thither; the third is thwick thwack; the fourth the devil take them that brought thee and I together.

fox. the fox preys furthest from his hole (*English*) Anyone who engages in criminal or otherwise dubious business is best advised to pursue it away from his home territory, so as not to be easily identified as the perpetrator. T. Adams, *Sermons*, 1629. J. Clarke, in *Paroemiologia Anglo-Latina* in 1639, quoted it in the form 'a crafty fox never preyeth neare his den'. Another proverb to the same effect insists 'a wise fox will never rob his neighbour's henroost'.

~ *See also* he that will DECEIVE the fox must rise betimes; if the LION's skin cannot, the fox's shall; the MORE a fox is cursed, the better he fares; an OLD fox is not easily snared; the SLEEPING fox catches no poultry; you can have no MORE of a fox than the skin.

foxhole. *See* there are no ATHEISTS in foxholes.

fraud. *See* FROST and fraud both end in foul.

fray. *See* the SECOND blow makes the fray.

free. *See* the BEST things in life are free; if the ADDER could hear and the blindworm could see, neither man nor beast would ever go free; LOVE is free; there is no such THING as a free lunch; THOUGHT is free.

freeze. *See* EAT till you sweat and work till you freeze.

French. *See* ITALIANS are wise before the deed, the Germans in the deed, the French after the deed; JACK would be a gentleman if he could speak French.

Frenchman. *See* in SETTLING an island, the first building erected by a Spaniard will be a church; by a Frenchman, a fort; by a Dutchman, a warehouse; and by an Englishman, an alehouse; ONE Englishman can beat three Frenchmen.

fresh. *See* don't THROW out your dirty water until you get in fresh.

Friday. as the Friday, so the Sunday (*English*) Whatever the weather is like on a Friday dictates what it will be like on the Sunday. *Notes & Queries*, 1853. An extension of the proverb indicates that whatever the weather is like on the Sunday dictates what the rest of the week will be like: 'as the Friday, so the Sunday, as the Sunday, so the week.' Another version runs 'if on Friday it rain, 'twill on Sunday again; if Friday be clear, have for Sunday no fear'.

Friday night's dream on the Saturday told, is sure to come true be it never so old (*English*) Anyone who shares a Friday night's dream the following day is sure to see it come to pass. Thomas Overbury, *Characters*, 1626.

> A Frydayes dreame is all her superstition: that shee conceales for feare of anger.
> Sir Thomas Overbury, *Characters*, 1626

Friday's hair and Sunday's horn go to the devil on Monday morn (*English*) It is unlucky to cut the hair on a Friday (the day of the Crucifixion) or to trim the fingernails on a Sunday (also a sacred day to Christians). Thomas Middleton, *Any Thing for a Quiet Life*, 1621.

~ *See also* MONDAY's child is fair of face, Tuesday's child is full of grace; Wednesday's child is full of woe, Thursday's child has far to go; Friday's child is loving and giving, Saturday's child works hard for its living; and the child that's born on the Sabbath day, is fair and wise and good and gay.

friend. a friend in court is better than a penny in purse (*English*) Personal contacts within the law will prove more beneficial than mere wealth. *Romaunce of the Rose*, *c.*1400. Related proverbs include 'a friend in the market is better than money in the chest'.

I shouldn't wonder – friends at court you know ...
Charles Dickens, *Dombey and Son*, 1848

a friend in need is a friend indeed (*Roman*) A friend who remains constant in time of trouble may be considered true. *Durham Proverbs*, *c.*1035 (variants may be found in Ennius and in *Epidicus*, written by Plautus in 200BC). Alternative versions include 'a good friend is never known till a man have need'. A French equivalent runs 'prosperity gives friends, adversity proves them'. A Swedish proverb states 'one should go invited to a friend in good fortune, and uninvited in misfortune'. Lord Samuel rather cynically advised 'a friend in need is a friend to be avoided'. Another proverb warns that 'it is good to have friends but bad to need them', while another cautions those who draw heavily upon friendship that 'friends are like fiddle-strings, they must not be screwed too tight'. *See also* never CATCH at a falling knife or friend.

A freende is never knowen tyll a man have neede. Before I had neede, my most present foes Semed my most freends, but thus the world goes.
John Heywood, *A Dialogue containing ... the Proverbs in the English Tongue*, 1546

a friend is not so soon gotten as lost (*English*) It is easier to lose a friend than gain one. John Lyly, *Euphues*, 1580. Another proverb warns that 'the best of friends must part'. The Germans, meanwhile, have 'a lost friendship is an enmity won'.

They that study man say of a friend, There's nothing in the world that's harder found, Nor sooner lost.
William Rowley and John Webster, *A Cure for a Cuckold*, *c.*1625

a friend to all is a friend to none (*Greek*) A person who makes friends with all and sundry will find no one values his or her friendship. Wodroephe, *Spared Houres*, 1623 (also quoted by Diogenes Laertius and attributed ultimately to Aristotle). The notion that it is best to restrict the number of your friends is supported by another proverb, which runs 'have but few friends though much acquaintance'. An extreme viewpoint is represented by the saying 'if you have one true friend, you have more than your share'.

~ *See also* ADMONISH your friends in private, praise them in public; the BEST mirror is an old friend; the BEST of friends must part; BOOKS and friends should be few and good; the CAT and dog may kiss, yet are none the better friends; the DEAD have few friends; do not REMOVE a fly from your friend's forehead with a hatchet; EVEN reckoning makes long friends; the FALLING out of friends is the renewal of love; a FOE is better than a dissembling friend; GOD defend me from my friends; from my enemies I can defend myself; go down the LADDER when thou marriest a wife, go up when thou choosest a friend; he that doth LEND doth lose his money and friend; it is MERRY when friends meet; a JOKE never gains over an enemy, but often loseth a friend; LEND your money and lose your friend; LOVE your friend with his fault; a MAN's best friend is his dog; MONEY makes friends enemies; a NEAR friend is better than a far-dwelling kinsman; NEVER catch at a falling knife or friend; the NIGHT is no man's friend; OLD friends and old wine are best; one has ALWAYS strength enough to bear the misfortunes of one's friends; a PENNY in purse will bid me drink when all the friends I have will not; PROVE thy friend ere thou have need; RICH folk have many friends; SHORT reckonings make long friends; SHORT visits make long friends; TRUST not a new friend nor an old enemy; when GOOD cheer is lacking, our friends will be packing; when TWO friends have a common purse one sings and the other weeps; while the THUNDER lasted two bad men were friends.

friendship. friendship cannot stand always on one side (*Scottish*) True friendship involves generosity from both parties. David Fergusson, *Scottish Proverbs*, 1641.

~ *See also* a HEDGE between keeps friendship green;

SUDDEN friendship, sure repentance; when LOVE puts in, friendship is gone.

frighten. *See* BURN not your house to fright away the mice; he that has NOTHING is frightened of nothing; I have LIVED too near a wood to be frightened by owls.

frost. frost and fraud both end in foul (*English*) Lies are (like frost) bound to have undesirable consequences. W. Camden, *Remains concerning Britain*, 1614. Also found as 'frost and fraud have always foul ends'.

> Frost and falsehood has ay a foul hinder end.
> James Kelly, *A Complete Collection of Scotish Proverbs*, 1721

~ *See also* HAIL brings frost in the tail; they must HUNGER in frost that will not work in heat; MANY hips and haws, many frosts and snaws; so MANY mists in March, so many frosts in May.

frugality. *See* INDUSTRY is fortune's right hand, and frugality her left.

fruit. fruit out of season, sorrow out of reason (*English*) It is an ominous sign of trouble in store when fruits develop out of their proper season. H. Friend, *Flowers and Flower Lore*, 1884.

if you would have fruit, you must bring the leaf to the grave (*English*) The best time to transplant fruit trees is in the autumn, when the leaves drop. John Ray, *A Collection of English Proverbs*, 1678.

~ *See also* DEEDS are fruits, words are but leaves; FORBIDDEN fruit tastes sweetest; a GOOD tree brings forth good fruit; he that would EAT the fruit must climb the tree; if you would ENJOY the fruit, pluck not the flower; like TREE, like fruit; SEPTEMBER blow soft, till the fruit's in the loft; the TREE is known by its fruit; when ALL fruit falls, welcome haws.

fruitful. *See* RICHES are like muck, which stink in a heap, but spread abroad make the earth fruitful.

frying-pan. out of the frying-pan into the fire (*Greek*) Escaping one danger only to be exposed to an even worse one. Alexander Barclay, *Eclogues*, 1514 (also found in the writings of Plato and Lucian). The original Greek saying was 'out of the smoke into the flame', while the French render it as *tomber de la poêle dans la braise*. The fuller, little heard, version of the proverb runs 'like the flounder, out of the frying-pan into the fire'.

> But I was sav'd, as is the flounder, when
> He leapeth from the dish into the fire.
> Sir John Harington, *Orlando Furioso*, 1591

fuel. take away fuel, take away flame (*English*) No fire will continue to burn for long if deprived of fuel (often quoted with reference to scandals arising from gossip and rumour). J. Clarke, *Paroemiologia Anglo-Latina*, 1639.

full. full bellies make empty skulls (*English*) Those who are well fed are less inclined to enterprising thought. Thomas Fuller, *Gnomologia*, 1732. Further proverbs insist 'full bowls make empty brains' and 'a full belly neither fights nor flies well'. On rather different lines, another proverb runs 'he's so full of himself that he is quite empty'.

full cup, steady hand (*English*) Those who have much to lose should tread carefully, lest they lose what they have. *Durham Proverbs*, *c.*1025. Variants include 'a full cup must be carried steadily'.

> When the Cup's full carry it even. When you have arrived at Power and Wealth, take a care of Insolence, Pride, and Oppression.
> James Kelly, *A Complete Collection of Scotish Proverbs*, 1721

full of courtesy, full of craft (*English*) The most polite and tactful people are often the least trustworthy, whereas honest men tend to talk bluntly and simply. Thomas Nashe, *The Unfortunate Traveller*, 1594.

> Sincere and true hearted persons are least given to compliment and ceremony. It's suspicious he hath some design upon me, who courts and flatters me.
> John Ray, *A Collection of English Proverbs*, 1670

the full moon brings fair weather (*English*) The appearance of a full moon is usually followed by a period of fine weather. H.G. Bohn, *A Handbook of Proverbs*, 1855. Other proverbs making links between the moon and the weather include 'the full moon eats clouds', 'a dry moon is far north and soon seen', 'if the full moon rise red expect wind', 'if the moon show a silver shield, be not afraid to reap your field; but if she rises haloed round, soon we'll tread on deluged ground', 'pale moon doth rain, red moon doth blow, white moon doth neither rain nor snow', 'the moon on her back holds water' and 'two full moons in a month bring on a flood'.

~ *See also* a BELLY full of gluttony will never study willingly; BIND the sack before it be full; a GREAT dowry is a bed full of brambles; he is like a BAGPIPE: he never talks till his belly be full; he whose BELLY is full believes not him who is fasting; it's ILL speaking between a full man and a fasting; LOVE is full of fear; a MAN of words and not of deeds is like a garden full of weeds; MONDAY's child is fair of face, Tuesday's child is full of grace; Wednesday's child is full of woe, Thursday's child has far to go; Friday's child is loving and giving, Saturday's child works hard for its living; and the child that's born on the Sabbath day, is fair and wise and good and gay; when the BELLY is full the mind is among the maids; when the WELL is full it will run over.

funeral. *See* DREAM of a funeral and you hear of a marriage; ONE funeral makes many.

furniture. *See* a BRIDLE for the tongue is a necessary piece of furniture.

furrow. *See* an OLD ox makes a straight furrow.

further, furthest. *See* FAR.

fury. *See* HELL hath no fury like a woman scorned.

furze. when the furze is in bloom, my love's in tune (*English*) When the gorse is in flower, it is the season for love (gorse, or furze, flowers virtually throughout the year). Benjamin Franklin, *Poor Robin's Almanack*, 1752. Another related proverb runs 'under the furze is hunger and cold; under the broom is silver and gold'. *See also* when the GORSE is out of bloom, kissing's out of fashion.

> Dog-days are in he'll say's the reason Why kissing now is out of season: but Joan says furze in bloom still, and she'll be kiss'd if she's her will.
>
> Benjamin Franklin, *Poor Robin's Almanack*, 1752

G

gain (noun). **no gains without pains** (*English*) Hard work and self-sacrifice are usually necessary to secure some benefit. J. Grange, *Golden Aphroditis*, 1577. The saying has become a slogan of health and fitness experts, usually in the form 'no pain, no gain'. Related proverbs include 'pain is forgotten where gain follows' and 'great pain and little gain make a man soon weary'.

> Who will the fruyte that harvest yeeldes, must take the payne.
>
> J. Grange, *Golden Aphroditis*, 1577

~ *See also* if you LOSE your time you cannot get money or gain; ILL-GOTTEN gains seldom prosper; LIGHT gains make heavy purses; ONE man's loss is another man's gain; PAIN is forgotten where gain follows; PAIN is gain; there's no GREAT loss without some gain.

gain (verb). **he that gains time gains all things** (*English*) There is nothing more valuable to a person than time. S. Palmer, *Moral Essays on Proverbs*, 1710.

~ *See also* the BARGAIN is ill made where neither party gains; GEAR is easier gained than guided; a JOKE never gains over an enemy, but often loseth a friend; a MERCHANT that gains not, loseth; NOTHING ventured, nothing gained; what you LOSE on the swings you gain on the roundabouts.

gallop. *See* the HORSES of hope gallop, but the asses of experience go slowly.

gallows. *See* SAVE a thief from the gallows and he shall cut your throat; the SEA and the gallows refuse none.

gally. *See* DUNDER do gally the beans.

game. *See* LOOKERS-ON see most of the game; PERSEVERANCE kills the game; PLAY the game.

gamekeeper. *See* an OLD poacher makes the best gamekeeper.

gamester. *See* the BETTER gamester the worser man.

gaming. *See* the DEVIL goes shares in gaming.

gander. *See* what's SAUCE for the goose is sauce for the gander.

gang. *See* the BEST laid schemes of mice and men gang oft agley.

gape. he that gapeth until he be fed, well may he gape until he be dead (*English*) Those who wait passively for others to provide for them may find that their needs are never met. John Heywood, *A Dialogue containing ... the Proverbs in the English Tongue*, 1550. Related proverbs include 'you may gape long enough ere a bird fall in your mouth'.

> Gape while you get it. Spoken to those who expect a thing without reason.
>
> James Kelly, *A Complete Collection of Scotish Proverbs*, 1721

garbage in, garbage out (*US*) What you get out of something depends upon what you put into it (usually quoted in reference to computers). *CIS Glossary of Automated Typesetting and Related Computer Terms*, 1964. Sometimes encountered in the abbreviated form GIGO.

garden. no garden without its weeds (*English*) It is inevitable that the occasional bad element will crop up among even the best people, situations, organizations etc. John Lyly, *Euphues*, 1579.

> The divel ... will never suffer the church to be quiet or at rest: no garden so well tilled but some noxious weedes grow up in it.
>
> Robert Burton, *Anatomy of Melancholy*, 1621

~ *See also* as is the GARDENER, so is the garden; if you would be HAPPY for a week take a wife; if you would be happy for a month kill a pig; but if you would be happy all your life plant a garden; a MAN of words and not of deeds is like a garden full of weeds.

gardener. as is the gardener, so is the garden (*English*) The quality of a gardener (or any other worker) may be judged by the results of his or her work. Thomas Fuller, *Gnomologia*, 1732.

garlic makes a man wink, drink and stink (*English*) The consumption of garlic promotes a tendency to lust, heavy drinking and foul breath. Thomas Nashe, *The Unfortunate Traveller*, 1594.

garment. *See* BORROWED garments never fit well; our LAST garment is made without pockets; SILENCE is a woman's best garment.

gate. *See* the ACOLYTE at the gate reads scriptures he has never learned; FORTUNE knocks once at least at every man's gate; GOLD goes in at any gate except heaven's.

Gath. *See* TELL it not in Gath.

gather. gather ye rosebuds while ye may (*English*) Make the most of things while they are available to you. Robert Herrick, 'To the Virgins, to Make Much of Time', *Hesperides*, 1648. *See also* make HAY while the sun shines.

> Gather ye rosebuds while ye may,
> Old time is still a-flying:
> And this same flower which smiles today
> Tomorrow will be dying.
>
> Robert Herrick, 'To the Virgins, to Make Much of Time', *Hesperides*, 1648

~ *See also* the HAND that gives, gathers; a ROLLING stone gathers no moss; STANDING pools gather filth; what the RAKE gathers, the fork scatters; where the CARCASS is, there shall the eagles be gathered together; who HOLDS his peace and gathers stones will find a time to throw them.

gaudy. a gaudy morning bodes a wet afternoon (*English*) A bright morning is often followed by a rainy afternoon. *Edward III*, 1595. *See also* CLOUDY mornings turn to clear afternoons; a FOUL morning may turn to a fair day.

> A fair morning turns to a lowring afternoone.
>
> Robert Burton, *Anatomy of Melancholy*, 1624

gay. it is not the gay coat that makes the gentleman (*English*) There is more to gentility than a fine appearance. W. Goddard, *Nest of Wasps*, 1615.

gear. gear is easier gained than guided (*Scottish*) It is easier to obtain wealth or property than it is to use it properly. James Kelly, *A Complete Collection of Scotish Proverbs*, 1721.

~ *See also* LITTLE gear, less care.

geese. *See* GOOSE.

general. *See* he is the BEST general who makes the fewest mistakes; ONE bad general is better than two good ones.

generally. *See* of TWO disputants the warmer is generally in the wrong.

generation. *See* from CLOGS to clogs is only three generations; from SHIRTSLEEVES to shirtsleeves in three generations; it takes THREE generations to make a gentleman.

generous. a generous confession disarms slander (*English*) Those who confess their faults freely and sincerely deprive their enemies of the opportunity to spread slander about them. Thomas Fuller, *Gnomologia*, 1732.

~ *See also* be JUST before you're generous.

genius is an infinite capacity for taking pains (*English*) Genius is not a natural gift, but the result of diligent hard work. Thomas Carlyle, *Frederick the Great*, 1858. Equivalent proverbs in other languages include the French 'genius is patience'.

> 'Genius' ... means transcendent capacity of taking trouble, first of all.
>
> Thomas Carlyle, *Frederick the Great*, 1858

gentle. a gentle heart is tied with an easy thread (*English*) A timid person is easily manipulated. George Herbert, *The Glimpse*, 1633. Variants in other cultures include the Persian 'a gentle hand may lead the elephant with a hair'.

a gentle housewife mars the household (*English*) A housewife who fails to control her household properly fails in her work. Randle Cotgrave, *A Dictionary of the French and English Tongues*, 1611.

gentle is that gentle does (*English*) A gentleman may be judged by his actions. Geoffrey Chaucer, 'The Wife of Bath's Tale', *The Canterbury Tales*, *c.*1387. Related proverbs include 'a gentleman will do like a gentleman'.

gentleman. a gentleman without an estate is a pudding without suet (*English*) A gentleman is not a proper gentleman without money or property. J. Howell, *Paroemiographia*, 1659. Related proverbs include 'a gentleman should have more in his pocket than on his back'.

gentlemen and rich men are venison in heaven (*English*) The rich and high-born are rarely destined for heaven. J. Northbrooke, *Treatise against Dicing*, *c.*1577.

> A wealthy and great man, served up to Gods
> table in his kingdome, is as rare as Venison at
> our Boardes on earth.
>
> T. Adams, *Gallant's Burden*, 1616

~ *See also* it is not the GAY coat that makes the gentleman; it takes THREE generations to make a gentleman; JACK would be a gentleman if he could speak French; the KING can make a knight, but not a gentleman; PRESBYTERIANISM is no religion for a gentleman; the WEST wind is a gentleman and goes to bed; when ADAM delved and Eve span, who was then the gentleman?

gently. if you gently touch a nettle it'll sting you for your pains (*English*) In certain circumstances bold action is the only alternative, as anything less will result in harm being suffered. John Lyly, *Euphues: The Anatomy of Wit*, 1578. The fullest version of the proverb runs 'if you gently touch a nettle it'll sting you for your pains; grasp it like a lad of mettle, and it soft as silk remains'. Another proverb relating to nettles advises 'nettles don't sting in the month of May'.

> Hee which toucheth the nettle tenderly, is
> soonest stoung.
>
> John Lyly, *Euphues: The Anatomy of Wit*, 1578

~ *See also* DRIVE gently over the stones.

gentry sent to market will not buy one bushel of corn (*English*) Gentility of birth is of little real value in the practical world. Thomas Fuller, *The History of the Worthies of England*, 1662. Variants include 'gentility, sent to market, will not buy a peck of meal'.

> Gentility is all very well to talk about, but it
> gets you nothin' at the market.
>
> Robert Smith Surtees, *Ask Mamma*, 1858

German. *See* ITALIANS are wise before the deed, the Germans in the deed, the French after the deed.

get. he who gets doth much, but he who keeps doth more (*English*) A person achieves more by preserving what he or she has obtained than by obtaining it in the first place. J. Mapletoft, *Select Proverbs*, 1707.

giant. *See* a DWARF on a giant's shoulders sees further of the two.

gift. a gift long waited for is sold not given (*English*) A gift that is long in coming will not be regarded as freely given. George Herbert, *Outlandish Proverbs*, 1640. Also found in the form 'a gift much expected is paid, not given'. Other proverbs making much the same point include the Roman sayings 'he gives too late who waits to be asked', 'a gift in season is a double favour to the needy' and 'a gift in time of need is most acceptable'.

gifts enter without knocking (*English*) Those coming with gifts or bribes are rarely refused entry. T. Draxe, *Bibliotheca Scholastica*, 1616. Also encountered in the form 'gifts enter everywhere without a wimble'. Another proverb emphasizing the power of gifts runs 'gifts break a rock'.

~ *See also* BEWARE of Greeks bearing gifts; NEVER look a gift horse in the mouth.

gild. *See* if the PILLS were pleasant they would not want gilding.

Gilead. *See* is there no BALM in Gilead?

gill. *See* EVERY herring must hang by its own gill.

gilt. gilt spurs do not make the knight (*English*) A noble character depends on more than appearance. J. Bossewell, *Workes of Armorie*, 1572.

~ *See also* TRY your skill in gilt first and then in gold.

girdle. *See* ALL the keys hang not at one man's girdle; a GOOD name is better than a good girdle.

girl. *See* ONE for sorrow, two for joy; three for a girl, four for a boy; five for silver, six for gold; seven for a secret, never to be told; eight for heaven, nine for hell; and ten for the devil's own self.

gist. the gist of a lady's letter is in the postscript (*English*) Female correspondents communicate the most important things in their letters in the postscript, almost as an afterthought. Maria Edgeworth, *Belinda*, 1801.

> Watching ... the last communication of the sun, and his postscript (which, like a lady's, is the gist of what he means).
> R.D. Blackmore, *Springhaven*, 1887

give. give a child all he shall crave and a dog while his tail doth wave and you'll have a fair dog and a foul knave (*English*) Children who are allowed everything they want will develop into bad men. Thomas Fuller, *Gnomologia*, 1732.

> Yet remember if you give a child his will and a whelp his fill, both will surely turn out ill.
> Charles Spurgeon, *Ploughman's Pictures*, 1880

give a clown a finger and he will take your hand (*Italian*) Fools latch on to those who show them kindness. George Herbert, *Outlandish Proverbs*, 1640. A Spanish equivalent runs 'give a clown your foot and he will take your hand'.

give a cob a hat and a pair of shoes and he'll last for ever (*English*) A properly made mud wall (a cob) with a slate coping and stone foundation will last for many years. W.C. Hazlitt, *English Proverbs*, 1869.

give a dog a bad name and hang him (*English*) A person may be damned by a poor reputation, whether or not it is deserved. J. Stevens, *Spanish and English Dictionary*, 1706. *See also* he that has an ILL name is half hanged.

> The Liberal impulse is almost always to give a dog a bad name and hang him: that is, to denounce the menaced proprietors as enemies of mankind, and ruin them in a transport of virtuous indignation.
> George Bernard Shaw, *The Intelligent Woman's Guide to Socialism*, 1928

give a loaf and beg a slice (*English*) A person who is over-generous will end up begging for themselves. John Ray, *A Collection of English Proverbs*, 1678. Also encountered in the form 'give a loaf and beg a shive'.

give a man an annuity and he'll live for ever (*English*) Agree to pay a man an income until he dies, and he will live much longer than originally envisaged. Lord Byron, *Don Juan*, 1824.

> 'Tis said that persons living on annuities
> Are longer lived than others ...
> Some ... *do* never die.
> Lord Byron, *Don Juan*, 1824

give a man enough rope and he will hang himself (*English*) Allow people with a wild or criminal character enough opportunity (or freedom) and they will infallibly bring about their own downfall. Thomas Fuller, *Holy War*, 1639 (attributed by some to the French satirical writer Rabelais, in *Pantagruel*, 1532). Variants include 'give a thief enough rope and he'll hang himself', which was first recorded in 1678.

> Give you women but rope enough, you'll do your own business.
> Samuel Richardson, *Sir Charles Grandison*, 1754

give and be blessed (*English*) Those who give generously to others will receive divine favour. Edward Hall, *Chronicle*, 1548.

give and spend and God will send (*English*) Those who pass their wealth on to others will find fate looks kindly on them. H.G. Bohn, *A Handbook of Proverbs*, 1855.

give and take is fair play (*English*) In dealings with others a person cannot complain if they lose some things while gaining others. Fanny Burney, *Evelina*, 1778.

> Give and take is fair play. All I say is, let it be a fair stand-up fight.
> Frederick Marryat, *Newton Forster*, 1832

give a slave a rod and he'll beat his master (*English*) Given the chance, an employee or servant will gladly thrash his employer or master. J. Clarke, *Paroemiographia Anglo-Latina*, 1639.

give credit where credit is due (*Hebrew*) Those who deserve recognition for their efforts should be honoured accordingly. Bible, Romans 13:7. Formerly found with 'honour' in the place of 'credit'.

Render therefore to al men their dew: ... to whom honour, honour.

Romans 13:7

give losers leave to speak (*English*) It is good manners to allow people on the losing side a chance to speak. Sir Thomas More, *Works*, 1533.

And well such losers may have leave to speak.

William Shakespeare, *Henry VI Part 2*, 1590–91

give me a child for the first seven years, and you may do what you like with him afterwards (*Spanish/French*) What a child learns before the age of seven determines his or her future character, regardless of what is subsequently learnt. V.S. Lean, *Collecteana*, 1902–04. Lean associated it particularly with the Jesuits, who were founded by Saint Ignatius Loyola in 1534. Centuries later the Russian revolutionary leader Lenin coined his own version of it: 'give us a child for eight years and it will be a Bolshevik for ever'. Also found in the form 'give me a child for the first seven years, and he is mine for life'. *See also* the CHILD is the father of the man.

give neither counsel nor salt till you are asked for it (*English*) It is unlucky to offer advice or salt to anyone else unless it is specifically requested. H.G. Bohn, *A Handbook of Proverbs*, 1855. Superstition insists that it is unwise to allow salt to be taken out of the house, either as a gift or as a loan, because the luck of the household goes with it. This is especially true if the loan takes place at New Year. If salt is actually borrowed, it is unwise for the borrower to repay the loan, as this is also unlucky. As regards the giving of counsel (sometimes rendered as 'advice'), other proverbs counter with the view 'good counsel never comes amiss' and 'good counsel never comes too late'.

give the devil his due (*English*) Even the most wicked people usually have a few redeeming features, which must (albeit reluctantly) be acknowledged. John Lyly, *Pappe with Hatchet*, 1589.

The Cavaliers (to give the Divell his due) fought very valiantly.

Prince Rupert's Declaration, 1642

giving is dead and restoring very sick (*English*) People are not as generous today as they used to be. J. Sandford, *The Garden of Pleasure*, 1573.

he gives twice who gives quickly (*Roman*) Those who honour their obligations promptly will be doubly appreciated by their creditors. Geoffrey Chaucer, *The Legend of Good Women*, *c.*1385 (also recorded in the writings of Publilius Syrus).

I did really ask the favour twice; but you have been even with me by granting it so speedily. *Bis dat qui cito dat.*

James Boswell, *Life of Johnson*, 1791

he that gives to be seen will relieve none in the dark (*English*) Those who like their generosity to be publicly known are unlikely to be so generous in making private gifts. Thomas Fuller, *Gnomologia*, 1732.

if you give a jest, you must take a jest (*English*) Those who play practical jokes on others must be prepared to be the victim of practical jokes in return. Jonathan Swift, *A Complete Collection of Polite and Ingenious Conversation*, 1738. Other proverbs along similar lines include 'the biter is sometimes bit', 'such answer as man gives, such will he get' and 'one ill word asks another.'

it is not given to every man to go to Corinth (*Roman*) Some rare pleasures or privileges are to be enjoyed only by the rich or the very lucky. Horace, *Epistles*, *c.*19BC. Horace was referring to Lais, the famous courtesan of Corinth, who charged the highest prices for her favours.

Lais an harlot of *Corinthe* ... was for none but lordes and gentlemen that might well paie for it. Whereof came up a proverbe, that it was not every man to go unto *Corinthe*.

Nicholas Udall, 1542

to give a thing and take a thing, is to wear the devil's gold ring (*Greek*) It is ignoble to give something and then to ask for it back again. J. Bridges, *Sermon at Paul's Cross*, 1571 (also found in essence in the writings of Plato). Often heard as a schoolchildren's playground rhyme. Related proverbs include 'give a thing and take again and you shall ride in hell's wain'.

Give a Thing, and take a Thing, Is the ill Man's Goud Ring. A Cant among Children, when they demand a Thing again, which they had bestowed.

James Kelly, *A Complete Collection of Scotish Proverbs*, 1721

who gives to all denies all (*English*) Those who offer everything intend to give nothing at all. Randle Cotgrave, *A Dictionary of the French and English Tongues*, 1611.

~ *See also* AGE does not give sense – it only makes

one go slowly; BETTER give a penny than lend twenty; the COW gives good milk but kicks over the pail; do not BLAME God for having created the tiger, but thank him for not having given it wings; ELBOW-GREASE gives the best polish; EXPERIENCE is a comb which nature gives us when we are bald; a FOOL may give a wise man counsel; a GIFT long waited for is sold not given; GOD gives the milk but not the pail; the HAND that gives, gathers; he that hath a WIFE and children hath given hostages to fortune; he that would HANG his dog gives out first that he is mad; if the COUNSEL be good, no matter who gave it; if the OLD dog bark, he gives counsel; it is BETTER to give than to receive; a MAN cannot give what he hasn't got; MONDAY's child is fair of face, Tuesday's child is full of grace; Wednesday's child is full of woe, Thursday's child has far to go; Friday's child is loving and giving, Saturday's child works hard for its living; and the child that's born on the Sabbath day, is fair and wise and good and gay; NEVER give a sucker an even break; NOTHING costs so much as what is given us; what ONE day gives us, another takes away from us.

gladness. *See* a MAN of gladness seldom falls into madness; SADNESS and gladness succeed each other.

glass. glasses and lasses are brittle ware (*English*) Young girls, like glass, are fragile and easily endangered. G. Torriano, *Italian Proverbs,* 1666.

> After all his strife he wan but a Strumpet, that for all his travails he reduced (I cannot say reclaymed) but a straggeler: which was as much in my judgement, as to strive for a broken glasse which is good for nothing.
>
> John Lyly, *Euphues: The Anatomy of Wit*, 1578

~*See also* the DEVIL's behind the glass; FAME is a magnifying glass; the FIRST glass for thirst, the second for nourishment, the third for pleasure, and the fourth for madness; PEOPLE who live in glass houses shouldn't throw stones.

glitter. *See* ALL that glitters is not gold.

glory. *See* NEVER rely on the glory of the morning or on the smile of your mother-in-law.

glove. *See* a CAT in gloves catches no mice.

glowing coals sparkle oft (*English*) A passionate, lively mind will express itself in frequent outbursts of ideas. T. Draxe, *Bibliotheca Scholastica*, 1616.

gluttony. gluttony kills more than the sword (*Roman*) Over-indulgence in the good things in life is responsible for more deaths than the more obvious threats of violence and the like. Alexander Barclay, *The Ship of Fools*, 1509. According to another proverb, gluttony is a particular danger to the English: 'gluttony is the sin of England.' The Greeks insist that 'surfeit has killed more than famine', while a French proverb observes 'gourmands make their grave with their teeth'.

> More perish by a surfet then the sword.
>
> John Lyly, *Euphues and His England*, 1580

~ *See also* a BELLY full of gluttony will never study willingly.

gnaw the bone which is fallen to thy lot (*English*) A sensible person reconciles himself to his lot in life (often quoted with reference to a man's wife). John Ray, *A Collection of English Proverbs*, 1678.

goat. the goat must browse where she is tied (*English*) Individuals must do the best they can within the bounds set by poverty or other limitations. Randle Cotgrave, *A Dictionary of the French and English Tongues*, 1611. Also found in the form 'the goat must bleat where she is tied'.

~ *See also* if the BEARD were all, the goat might preach.

God. God comes at last when we think he is furthest off (*English*) Just when it seems God will not intervene in human affairs, His influence is felt. J. Howell, *Paroemiographia*, 1659. Related proverbs include 'God comes with leaden feet but strikes with iron hands' and 'God is at the end, when we think he is furthest off it'.

God defend me from my friends; from my enemies I can defend myself (*English/French*) It is easier to protect yourself from your enemies than from your friends, from which quarter it is harder to anticipate an attack. Anthony Rivers, *Dictes or Sayings of the Philosophers*, 1477. In keeping with the theme of traitorous friends, the saying was adopted in 1956 by Gavin Maxwell for the title of his book about Sicilian bandit Salvatore Giuliano, *God Protect Me From My Friends*. Sometimes encountered in the shortened form 'save us from our friends'.

God gives the milk but not the pail (*English*) God provides man with the things he needs, but it is up to man to do the work necessary to obtain them. *The Spectator*, 18 May 1912. Related proverbs include 'God is a good worker but He loves to be helped'.

God heals and the physician hath the thanks (*English*) When an illness is successfully treated it is the doctor who gets the patient's gratitude, rather than God, who has ordained their recovery. George Herbert, *Outlandish Proverbs*, 1640. An Italian equivalent runs 'if the patient dies, the doctor has killed him, but if he gets well, the saints have saved him'.

> God heals and the doctor takes the fee.
>
> Benjamin Franklin, *Poor Richard's Almanack*, 1736

God helps those who help themselves (*Greek*) Providence is on the side of the person who works hard in pursuit of his own interests. R. Taverner, *Proverbs or Adages with New Additions, gathered out of the Chiliades of Erasmus*, 1546 (also found in the writings of Aeschylus, Euripides and Aesop). In Aesop's fable, a cart-driver calls on the help of the god Hercules when his cart gets stuck in the mud, only to be berated by Hercules for not first attempting to free it himself. A French version, found in La Fontaine's *Fables*, runs *aide-toi, le ciel t'aidera* (help yourself, heaven will help you). This slogan was adopted by a French radical political society in 1824. Another French equivalent includes 'God never builds us bridges, but he gives us hands', while the Spanish have 'while waiting for water from heaven, don't stop irrigating'. The Chinese have 'the gods cannot help those who do not seize opportunities'. A waggish rejoinder of unknown origins runs 'God helps those who helps themselves, but God help those who are caught helping themselves'. *See also* FORTUNE helps those who help themselves.

> God likes to assist the man who toils.
>
> Aeschylus, *Fragments*, fifth century BC

God help the poor, for the rich can help themselves (*English*) The poor must rely on divine aid because they are unable to defend themselves as the wealthy can. Thomas Dekker, *Work for Armourers*, 1609. Related proverbs include 'God help the rich, the poor can beg'.

God is always on the side of the big battalions (*French*) Good fortune inevitably seems to favour the stronger side in any contest. A. Graydon, *Memoirs*, 1822 (earlier recorded in a letter by Madame de Sévigné, 22 December 1673). Also found in the forms 'Providence is always on the side of the big battalions' and 'God sides with the strongest'. The saying is particularly associated with Napoleon, although it goes back much further and may be found, as 'the gods are on the side of the strongest', in Tacitus. Others to quote it have included the Comte de Bussy and Voltaire, who wrote: *On dit que Dieu est toujours pour les gros bataillons*.

> Someone has observed that Providence is always on the side of the big dividends.
>
> Saki, *Reginald*, 1904

God is better pleased with adverbs than with nouns (*English*) It is not what a person achieves that is important in the eyes of heaven so much as how they achieve it. *Complete History of England*, 1570.

> This man not only lives, but lives well, remembring alwayes the old adage, that God is the rewarder of adverbes, not of nownes.
>
> John Ford, *The Line of Life*, 1620

God is where He was (*English*) God is ever-present and constant in providing comfort to man. J. Palsgrave, *L'Éclaircissement de la langue française*, 1530. Another proverb emphasizing the constancy of God runs 'there is God when all is done'.

God keep me from the man that has but one thing to mind (*English*) Those who are obsessed with a particular cause or interest often make poor company. James Kelly, *A Complete Collection of Scotish Proverbs*, 1721. Related proverbs include 'God deliver me from a man of one book'.

God made man, man made money (*English*) God created mankind, but mankind itself invented most of the ills that beset it. The proverb is attributed to John Oldland, who coined it in the early eighteenth century in response to a lawyer with whom he was involved in a legal suit for debt.

> God mead man,
> And man mead money,
> God mead bees,
> And bees mead honey,
> But the Devil mead lawyers an' 'tornies,
> And pleac'd 'em at U'ston and Doten i' Forness.
>
> John Oldland, quoted in the *Lonsdale Magazine*, 1820

God made the country, and man made the town (*Roman*) God is the source of nature and goodness in the world, but the towns and their accompanying evils were invented by man. Abraham Cowley, quoted in J. Wells, *Poems*, 1667 (also found in Varro's *De Re Rustica*, *c.*35BC). The saying became better known in its modern form after it was quoted by Cowper in *The Task*, 1785. Variants include 'God the first garden made, and the first city Cain'.

> There is a saying that if God made the country, and man the town, the Devil made the little country town.
>
> H. Tennyson, *Memoir*, 25 January 1870

God makes the back to the burden (*English*) Heaven suits the person for the task in hand, so that they will be able to perform what is asked of them. William Cobbett, *Weekly Register*, 12 January 1822.

> Heaven suits the back to the burden.
>
> Charles Dickens, *Nicholas Nickleby*, 1839

God never sends mouths but He sends meat (*English*) Heaven will always answer the needs of the righteous and deserving and will ensure that no child is born without also providing the means for its sustenance. William Langland, *Piers Plowman*, 1377.

> For lente nevere was lyf but lyflode were shapen.
>
> William Langland, *Piers Plowman*, 1377

God send you joy, for sorrow will come fast enough (*English*) May you enjoy the blessings of heaven, to counter the sorrows that are sure to come. *London Prodigal*, 1605.

God sends meat, but the devil sends cooks (*English*) Good can easily be perverted by evil (just as a bad cook can readily ruin good ingredients). A. Borde, *Dietary of Health*, 1542. Related proverbs include 'God sends corn and the devil mars the sack'.

> This Goose is quite raw: Well, God sends Meat, but the Devil sends Cooks.
>
> Jonathan Swift, *Polite Conversation*, 1738

God's in his heaven, all's right with the world (*English*) Everything is fine. J. Palsgrave, *L'Éclaircissement de la langue française*, 1530. An older version of the proverb, intended to console others in times of trouble, ran 'God is where he was'.

> The snail's on the thorn: God's in his heaven –
> All's right with the world.
>
> Robert Browning, *Works*, 1841

the gods send nuts to those who have no teeth (*French/Spanish/English*) All too often, favours and benefits seem to be bestowed on those who are too old or are otherwise debarred from enjoying them. *American Speech*, 1929. In the French version it is 'bread' rather than 'nuts', while the Spanish complain 'God gives almonds to those who have no teeth'.

God tempers the wind to the shorn lamb (*French*) Heaven protects the weak and the defenceless. Laurence Sterne, *A Sentimental Journey through France and Italy: Maria*, 1768. The proverb as used by Sterne was a reworking of the older French saying, *Dieu mesure le froid à la brebis tondue* (God measures the cold to the shorn sheep, recorded in 1594). In the earlier versions, before Sterne, it was always a 'sheep' rather than a 'lamb' that was shorn (lambs, in fact, are never shorn). Related proverbs include 'God sends cold after clothes'.

> Although we cannot turn away the wind, we can soften it; we can temper it, if I may say so, to the shorn lambs.
>
> Charles Dickens, *The Old Curiosity Shop*, 1841

there are God's poor and the devil's poor (*English*) The poor may be divided into those who are fated to be so and those who have made themselves so. T. Adams, *Sermons*, 1629.

where God builds a church, the devil will build a chapel (*English*) Wickedness will often be found flourishing in close proximity to what is good. T. Becon, *Works*, 1560.

> Wherever God erects a House of Prayer,
> The Devil always builds a Chapel there:
> And 'twill be found upon Examination,
> The latter has the largest congregation.
>
> Daniel Defoe, *The True-born Englishman*, 1701

where God will help, nothing does harm (*English*) Those who enjoy the protection of heaven will be safe from all danger. *Havelock*, *c.*1300. Variants include 'where God will help, none can hinder', 'where God helps, nought harms' and 'what God will, no frost can kill'.

whom God loves, his bitch brings forth pigs (*Spanish*) Those who enjoy divine favour may expect all manner of miraculous strokes of good fortune. John Ray, *A Collection of English Proverbs*, 1813.

whom the gods love die young (*Greek*) The good and the godly are selected by heaven to die first. W. Hughe, *Troubled Man's Medicine*, 1546 (also quoted by Plautus). The proverb is supposed to have had its origins in a story told by the Greek historian Herodotus in his *History*, *c.*445BC. In this tale, the dutiful Cleobis and Biton help a woman to pull her cart to the temple to celebrate the festival of Here. In her gratitude, the woman begs Here to bestow upon the two lads the greatest blessing in her power – and the two boys die in their sleep. It was left to the poet Menander to coin the proverb itself when he retold the same story over a century later. The proverb has often been inscribed on the gravestones of those who have died young. Philosophers have pondered the accuracy of the saying and have justified it by explaining that it is the 'young at heart' (whatever their age) who find favour with heaven. Variant forms include 'God takes soonest those whom he loves best'. *See also* only the GOOD die young.

> I was meant to die young and the gods do not love me.
>
> Robert Louis Stevenson, letter, 1894

whom the gods would destroy, they first make mad (*Greek*) When heaven marks someone down for death, it first deprives him of his reason. Ben Jonson, *Catiline*, 1611. Euripides and Publius Syrus also recorded versions of the proverb, the latter as 'he whom Fortune would ruin she robs of his wits'. A modern reworking, introduced by Cyril Connolly in *The Unquiet Grave* (1944), runs 'whom the gods would destroy, they first call promising'.

> When God will punish, hee will first take away the understanding.
>
> George Herbert, *Outlandish Proverbs*, 1640

~ *See also* ALL things are possible with God; come DAY, go day, God send Sunday; the DANGER past and God forgotten; do not BLAME God for having created the tiger, but thank him for not having given it wings; GIVE and spend and God will send; he that SERVES God for money will serve the devil for better wages; MAN proposes, but God disposes; MAN's extremity is God's opportunity; the MILLS of God grind slowly, yet they grind exceeding small; the NEARER the church, the further from God; put your TRUST in God and keep your powder dry; the RIVER passed and God forgotten; the ROBIN and the wren are God's cock and hen; SOON todd, soon with God; SPEND and God will send; take the GOODS the gods provide; the VOICE of the people is the voice of God; we must not LIE down and cry God help us; a WHISTLING woman and a crowing hen are neither fit for God nor men; who ERRS and mends to God himself commends; you cannot SERVE God and Mammon.

godliness. *See* CLEANLINESS is next to godliness.

going. when the going gets tough, the tough get going (*US*) When the chips are down, people of truly strong character are spurred into action. This slogan is popularly attributed to Joseph P. Kennedy, father of US President J.F. Kennedy. In the 1980s the inspirational intent of the late President's father was lampooned in a slogan for T-shirts: 'when the going gets tough, the tough go shopping.'

gold. gold goes in at any gate except heaven's (*English*) Wealth will buy a person access to any place, except heaven. T. Adams, *Sermons*, 1629.

gold is an orator (*English*) Wealth can be as persuasive as any amount of argument. William Shakespeare, *Richard III*, 1592.

gold may be bought too dear (*English*) Even something very desirable is not worth having at too high a price. John Heywood, *A Dialogue containing … the Proverbs in the English Tongue*, 1546.

> The fact is, in my opinion, that we often buy money very much too dear.
>
> William Thackeray, *Barry Lyndon*, 1844

when we have gold we are in fear, when we have none we are in danger (*English*) Wealth breeds fear because those who have it are afraid of losing it, while those who do not have it fear the vulnerable position they are in. T. Draxe, *Bibliotheca Scholastica*, 1616.

~ *See also* ALL that glitters is not gold; an ASS loaded with gold still eats thistles; BEAUTY provoketh thieves sooner than gold; EVERY honest miller has a thumb of gold; an INCH of gold will not buy an inch of time; it is GOOD to make a bridge of gold to a flying enemy; LOOK to a gown of gold and you will at least get a sleeve of it; a MAN of straw is worth a woman of gold; no LOCK will hold against the power of gold; ONE for sorrow, two for joy; three for a girl, four for a boy; five for silver, six for gold; seven for a secret, never to be told; eight for heaven, nine for hell; and ten for the devil's own self; the STREETS of London are paved with gold; to GIVE a thing, and take a thing, is to wear the devil's gold ring; TRY your skill in gilt first and then in gold.

golden. the golden age never was the present age (*English*) People always believe that things were better in the past. Thomas Fuller, *Gnomologia*, 1732.

a golden key can open any door (*English*) Money will gain a person access to any place. John Lyly, *Euphues and His England*, 1580. Another proverb warns that there is in fact one door that will not open to a golden key, however, 'the gates of heaven are not unlocked with a golden key'.

> Who is so ignorant that knoweth not, gold be a
> key for every locke, chieflye with his Ladye.
> John Lyly, *Euphues and His England*, 1580

~ *See also* KILL not the goose that lays the golden egg; POISON is poison though it comes in a golden cup; SILENCE is golden; SPEECH is silver, silence is golden; we must not LOOK for a golden life in an iron cage.

good. as good play for nought as work for nought (*English*) If you are not going to be paid you might as well take things easy doing what you want as engage in harder toil. Nicholas Udall, *Flowers out of Terence*, 1533.

> The fee is ten guineas ... as good play for nothing,
> you know, as work for nothing.
> Walter Scott, letter, 1808

at a good bargain, make a pause (*English*) It is sensible to think twice when offered what appears to be a bargain, in case it is not all it seems to be. George Herbert, *Outlandish Proverbs*, 1640. Also encountered in the form 'at a good pennyworth, think twice'.

> 'Think twice of a good bargain', says the proverb.
> Maria Edgeworth, *The Parent's Assistant*, 1796

good ale is meat, drink and cloth (*English*) A good beer provides all a person really needs to survive. Beaumont and Fletcher, *The Scornful Lady*, *c.*1612.

> O my lord, my ale is meat, drink, and cloth.
> Jonathan Swift, *Dialogues*, 1738

good and quickly seldom meet (*English*) It is rare for a thing to be done both quickly and well. George Herbert, *Outlandish Proverbs*, 1640.

a good beginning makes a good ending (*Roman*) Care taken at the start of a task is likely to be rewarded by things turning out well at the end. *Proverbs of Hending*, *c.*1300 (also quoted by Quintilian). *See also* WELL begun is half done.

> But in proverbe I have herd seye
> That who that wel his werk begynneth
> The rather a good ende he wynneth.
> John Gower, *Confessio Amantis*, *c.*1390

the good Bernard does not see everything (*English*) Even the wise and good cannot know everything. Geoffrey Chaucer, *The Legend of Good Women*, *c.*1385. Saint Bernard of Clairvaux (1091–1153) was a French theologian and reformer, who was dubbed the Mellifluous Doctor and was the last of the fathers of the Catholic Church. He founded more than 70 monasteries and was canonized in 1174. *See also* even HOMER sometimes nods.

> Bernard the monk ne say nat al pardee!
> Geoffrey Chaucer, *The Legend of Good Women*, *c.*1385

good broth may be made in an old pot (*English*) It is not necessary to have new or perfect utensils to produce a good result. G. Torriano, *Italian Proverbs*, 1666.

good cheap is dear (*English*) Something that appears to be a bargain because it is sold cheap may prove expensive in that you would never have bought it in the first place if it had not appeared to be such a good buy. George Herbert, *Outlandish Proverbs*, 1640.

good clothes open all doors (*English*) Those who wear decent clothes will find others more ready to offer them opportunities. Thomas Fuller, *Gnomologia*, 1732.

good company is the shortest cut (*English*) Those who travel with good companions find the journey passes quickly. J. Clarke, *Paroemiographia Anglo-Latina*, 1639.

a good conscience is a continual feast (*English*) A clear conscience will prove a lasting source of consolation. Francis Bacon, *The Advancement of Learning*, 1605. *See also* a CONTENTED mind is a continual feast.

> A good conscience is a continual Christmas.
> Benjamin Franklin, *Works*, *c.*1736

good counsel never comes amiss (*English*) Good advice is always worth listening to. T. Draxe, *Bibliotheca Scholastica*, 1616. Related proverbs include 'good counsel has no price'.

a good dog deserves a good bone (*English*) Good conduct deserves a reward. Randle Cotgrave, *A Dictionary of the French and English Tongues*, 1611.

A good dog deserves, sir, a good bone.

Ben Jonson, *A Tale of a Tub*, 1633

a good example is the best sermon (*English*) Setting a good example by one's own conduct is more effective than simply telling others how to behave. Thomas Fuller, *Gnomologia*, 1732. *See also* PRACTISE what you preach.

a good face is a letter of recommendation (*Roman*) An honest face says as much about a person's character as any praise from a third party. T. Shelton, translation of *Don Quixote*, 1620 (also found in the writings of Publius Syrus). On much the same lines is 'a good face needs no paint' ('paint' being make-up). Another proverb, however, warns that 'good fame is better than a good face'.

There was a passport in his very looks.

Laurence Sterne, *A Sentimental Journey*, 1768

good fences make good neighbours (*English*) Clear and strong boundaries help maintain cordial relations between states, neighbours, friends and the like (in the most practical sense by preventing animals straying from one property to another and doing damage). E. Rogers, letter, 1640. *See also* a GOOD lawyer makes a bad neighbour; a HEDGE between keeps friendship green.

My apple trees will never get across
And eat the cones under his pines, I tell him.
He only says, 'Good fences make good neighbours'.

Robert Frost, 'North of Boston', 1914

good finds good (*English*) Good attracts good. George Herbert, *Outlandish Proverbs*, 1640.

a good hay year a bad fog year (*English*) A good hay harvest will be followed by bad weather. R. Inwards, *Weather Lore*, 1893.

a good heart cannot lie (*English*) Those who are truly virtuous will not stoop to telling lies. George Herbert, *Outlandish Proverbs*, 1640.

a good horse cannot be of a bad colour (*English/Scottish*) The quality of a horse (or anything else) is more important than its appearance. J. Carmichaell, *Proverbs in Scots*, 1628. Superstition harbours particular doubts about horses that are white in colour, although piebald horses are lucky and a wish may be made on meeting one. Another proverb has it that 'a dapple-grey horse will sooner die than tire'. *See also* APPEARANCES are deceptive.

It is observed by some, that there is no good horse of a bad colour.

Izaak Walton, *The Compleat Angler*, 1653

a good husband makes a good wife (*English*) Men who treat their wives well will find their wives behave well too. T. Draxe, *Bibliotheca Scholastica*, 1616.

the good is the enemy of the best (*English*) The temptation to settle for what is good detracts from the willingness to strive for what is even better. J. Kelman, *Thoughts on Things Eternal*, 1912. *See also* the BEST is the enemy of the good.

a good Jack makes a good Jill (*English*) A good example will inspire others (usually, a good husband will have a beneficial influence on his wife). W. Painter, *Palace of Pleasure*, 1623. Alternative views include 'a good Jill may mend the bad Jack' and 'a bad Jack may have as bad a Jill'. *See also* EVERY Jack has his Jill; a GOOD husband makes a good wife.

A good Jack makes a good Gill ... Inferiours imitate the manners of superiours ... wives of their husbands.

John Ray, *A Collection of English Proverbs*, 1670

a good judge conceives quickly, judges slowly (*English*) A wise judge takes his time before reaching a conclusion. George Herbert, *Outlandish Proverbs*, 1640. Related proverbs include 'from a foolish judge, a quick sentence' and 'he that passes judgment as he runs, overtakes repentance'. *See also* a JUDGE knows nothing unless it has been explained to him three times.

a good lawyer makes a bad neighbour (*English*) Lawyers make bad neighbours, because they are in a position to use their knowledge of the law to their own advantage. Randle Cotgrave, *A Dictionary of the French and English Tongues*, 1611. Also found as 'a good lawyer, an evil neighbour'. *See also* GOOD fences make good neighbours.

a good lawyer must be a great liar (*English/French*) To succeed in the law a man must be an accomplished liar. J. Smith, *Grammatica Quadrilinguis*, 1674.

good luck never comes too late (*English*) Good fortune is always welcome, no matter how late it comes. Michael Drayton, *Mooncalf*, *c.*1610.

good men are scarce (*English*) Men of real worth and character are only rarely encountered. D. Tuvill, *Essays Moral and Theological*, 1609. Also encountered in the form 'a good man is hard to find'. US filmstar Mae West is said to have contributed her own typically suggestive version of this latter variant, 'a hard man is good to find'.

> Maids, make much of one; good men are scarce.
> Thomas Fuller, *Gnomologia*, 1732

a good name is better than a good girdle (*English*) It is better to have a good reputation than wealth alone (an allusion to the belt or girdle from which people once suspended their purses). Equivalent proverbs include 'good fame is better than a good face', 'a good name is better than riches' and 'a good name is worth gold'. Another proverb adds 'a good name keeps its lustre in the dark'.

good riding at two anchors (*Greek*) There is safety in having two skills, jobs or other sources of security. John Heywood, *A Dialogue containing ... the Proverbs in the English Tongue*, 1546 (also quoted by Pindar). A longer version of the proverb runs 'good riding at two anchors, men have told, for if one break the other may hold'.

> Have more strings to thy bow then one, it is safe riding at two ankers.
> John Lyly, *Euphues: The Anatomy of Wit*, 1578

a good salad may be the prologue to a bad supper (*English*) An excellent salad is no guarantee that the meal to follow will be equally good. G. Torriano, *Select Italian Proverbs*, 1642.

good seed makes a good crop (*English*) The quality of what you produce depends on the quality of what you start out with. *Dialogue of Salomon and Marcolphus*, 1492. *See also* as you SOW, so shall you reap.

a good surgeon must have an eagle's eye, a lion's heart and a lady's hand (*English*) It takes keen eyesight, courage and delicacy of touch to make a man a good surgeon. L. Wright, *Display of Dutie*, 1589.

a good tale is none the worse for being twice told (*English*) A good story will bear repeating. Walter Scott, *Old Mortality*, 1816. Related proverbs include 'a good tale ill told is marred in the telling'.

good things are hard (*Greek*) The good things in life are obtained only with effort. R.C. Trench, *On the Lessons in Proverbs*, 1853 (quoting Solon and Pittacus).

a good tongue is a good weapon (*English*) The ability to speak well is a valuable gift. James Kelly, *A Complete Collection of Scottish Proverbs*, 1721. Related proverbs include 'who has not a good tongue ought to have good hands' and 'it is a good tongue that says no ill and a better heart that thinks none'.

a good tree brings forth good fruit (*English*) Good breeds good. Berners, *Huon*, *c.*1534.

good ware makes quick markets (*Roman*) Good quality merchandise will quickly find a buyer. Randle Cotgrave, *A Dictionary of the French and English Tongues*, 1611 (quoting Plautus).

a good wife and health is a man's best wealth (*English*) The best things a man can have are a good wife and good health. James Kelly, *A Complete Collection of Scottish Proverbs*, 1721. Another proverb observes 'a good wife's a goodly prize saith Solomon the wise'.

good wine engendreth good blood (*English*) The drinking of wine promotes healthy blood and emotional strength. G.B. Gelli, *Fearful Fancies of the Florentine Cooper*, 1568.

> This same young sober-blooded boy doth not love me; ... but that's no marvel, he drinks no wine.
> William Shakespeare, *Henry IV, Part 2*, *c.*1598

good wine needs no bush (*English*) If something is of high enough quality, it needs no recommendation but may stand by its own merits. John Lydgate, *Pilgrimage of Man*, 1430. Bacchus, the Roman god of wine, was often depicted with garlands of vine and ivy leaves and ever since Roman times taverns and vintners' shops have been distinguished by bushy displays (or pictures) of vines and ivy. The significance of ivy in vintners' signs was that ivy was reputed to counter the effects of over-indulgence in alcohol (thus implying that the wine being offered was good). Equivalent sentiments may be found in a number of European languages, including French, German and Italian.

> If it be true that good wine needs no bush, 'tis true that a good play needs no epilogue.
> William Shakespeare, *As You Like It*, *c.*1599

a good winter brings a good summer (*English*) Mild winters are followed by warm summers. T. Draxe, *Bibliotheca Scholastica*, 1616.

he hath a good judgement that relieth not wholly on his own (*Italian*) A wise person listens to the advice of others and does not rely solely on his own opinion. G. Torriano, *Select Italian Proverbs*, 1642.

he is a good dog who goes to church (*English*) A person might make the effort to appear good and to behave as expected, even if he is not really as worthy as he might seem (just as a dog attending church yet remains a dog). Walter Scott, *Woodstock*, 1826.

> Bevis ... fell under the proverb which avers, 'He is a good dog which goes to church'; for ... he behaved himself ... decorously.
>
> Walter Scott, *Woodstock*, 1826

he is a good physician who cures himself (*English*) Doctors are quick to offer cures to others but should be judged by how they treat themselves. John Lydgate, *Daunce of Machabree*, c.1430.

he that hath a good harvest may be content with some thistles (*English*) Those who are doing well overall should not mind the odd minor setback or inconvenience. J. Clarke, *Paroemiologia Anglo-Latina*, 1639.

if you can't be good, be careful (*US/English*) If you cannot resist misbehaving, make sure you don't land yourself in trouble (typically, of a sexual nature). A.M. Binstead, *Pitcher in Paradise*, 1903. The saying was popularized in the United States as early as 1907 through the song 'Be Good! If You Can't Be Good, be Careful!' Wags have added their own versions, including 'if you can't be careful, have fun', 'if you can't be careful, name it after me' and 'if you can't be careful, buy a pram'.

it is a good horse that never stumbles (*English*) Even the best horses (and, by extension, people) make mistakes sometimes. J. Palsgrave, *L'Éclaircissement de la langue française*, 1530. A fuller variant of the proverb runs 'it is a good horse that never stumbles, and a good wife that never grumbles'. *See also* even HOMER sometimes nods.

> He's a good horse that never stumbled, and a better wife that never grumbled. Both so rare, that I never met with either.
>
> James Kelly, *A Complete Collection of Scotish Proverbs*, 1721

it is a good thing to eat your brown bread first (*English*) If a person has to suffer misfortune in life (represented by brown bread, formerly thought inferior to white) it is best for them if they suffer it at a relatively young age for then life can only get better. R. Forby, *The Vocabulary of East Anglia*, 1830.

it is good fishing in troubled waters (*English*) There are plentiful opportunities for advantage when confusion and conflict abound. Richard Grafton, *Chronicles*, 1568.

> Thinking it (as the proverb saith) best fishing in troubled waters.
>
> Sir John Harington, *Orlando Furioso*, 1591

it is good to be merry and wise (*English*) It is good policy to remain sensible even when greatly enjoying yourself. Nicholas Udall, *Ralph Roister Doister*, c.1530.

> Come, come, George, let's be merry and wise.
>
> Beaumont and Fletcher, *The Knight of the Burning Pestle*, 1611

it is good to be merry at meat (*English*) Good spirits at mealtimes are to be welcomed. T. Draxe, *Bibliotheca Scholastica*, 1616.

it is good to have a cloak for the rain (*English*) It is good to have an expedient for every difficulty. John Skelton, *Magnyfycence*, c.1520. Another proverb along the same lines runs 'don't have thy cloak to make when it begins to rain'.

it is good to have company in misery (*English*) Those who face hardship of some kind will find solace in the companionship of others. Geoffrey Chaucer, *Troilus and Criseyde*, c.1385–90. Variants include 'company's good if you are going to be hanged'.

> 'Tis some comfort to have a companion in our sufferings.
>
> Susannah Centlivre, *The Busy Body*, 1709

it is good to learn at other men's cost (*English*) It is better to learn from others' bad experiences rather than from one's own. T. Tusser, *Five Hundred Points of Good Husbandry*, 1573. Related proverbs include 'learn wisdom by the follies of others'.

it is good to make a bridge of gold to a flying enemy (*Greek*) When an enemy is defeated, it is wise to let him make good his escape, lest he turn to fight again because his route has been cut off. Plutarch, *Themistocles*, first century AD. The proverb is attributed originally to Aristides, who advised the victorious Themistocles to allow the vanquished Xerxes to escape via a bridge of boats across the Hellespont. In some instances it is a bridge of silver, rather than one of gold.

> You may have heard a military proverb: that it

> is a good thing to make a bridge of gold to a flying enemy.
>
> Robert Louis Stevenson, *The Master of Ballantrae*, 1889

it takes a good many shovelfuls of earth to bury the truth (*Swiss*) The truth will always reveal itself in the end. R.C. Trench, *On the Lessons in Proverbs*, 1853.

no good apple on a sour stock (*English*) Those who are born into bad families are unlikely to turn out well themselves. William Langland, *Piers Plowman*, 1393.

no good building without a good foundation (*English*) No project will prosper if the initial work on which it is based is not sound. R. Percyvall, *A Spanish Grammar*, 1599.

on a good bargain, think twice (*English*) If something is offered at what appears to be a very reasonable price, caution should be exercised as it may have some hidden flaw. George Herbert, *Outlandish Proverbs*, 1640.

the only good Indian is a dead one (*US*) Red Indians are so dangerous and so evil that only when they are dead can they be trusted. J.M. Cavanaugh, *Congressional Globe*, 1868. This saying dates from the days of the Indian Wars in the United States, but it has since been adapted to attack many other nationalities (for instance, the Germans and the Japanese during the Second World War).

> She did not know why the government made treaties with Indians. The only good Indian was a dead Indian.
>
> Laura Ingalls Wilder, *Little House on the Prairie*, 1935

only the good die young (*Greek*) The virtuous and the innocent always seem to die before their time. Daniel Defoe, *Character of Dr S. Annesley*, 1697. *See also* whom the GODS love die young.

> Heaven gives its favourites early death.
>
> Lord Byron, *Childe Harolde's Pilgrimage*, 1812

that is not good language which all understand not (*English*) The worst language is that which cannot be readily understood. George Herbert, *Outlandish Proverbs*, 1640.

that which is good for the head is evil for the neck and the shoulders (*English*) Anything that is deemed good for one part of the body is almost certain to be bad for another part of it. James I, *A Counterblaste to Tobacco*, 1604. Related proverbs include 'that which is good for the back is bad for the head' and 'good for the liver may be bad for the spleen'.

there is a good time coming (*Scottish*) Better times are on their way (usually spoken by way of consolation when times are bad). Walter Scott, *Rob Roy*, 1818.

there is no good accord where every man would be a lord (*English*) It is impossible to reach agreement when those involved are all determined to have their way. John Heywood, *A Dialogue containing … the Proverbs in the English Tongue*, 1546.

when good cheer is lacking, our friends will be packing (*English*) People who are always in a bad mood will find their friends desert them. J. Clarke, *Paroemiologia Anglo-Latina*, 1639.

~ *See also* ALL good things must come to an end; ALL publicity is good publicity; a BAD custom is like a good cake, better broken than kept; BAD money drives out good; BARE words are no good bargain; BEAR with evil and expect good; the BEST is the enemy of the good; the BETROTHED of good is evil, the betrothed of life is death, the betrothed of love is divorce; BETTER a good cow than a cow of a good kind; BOOKS and friends should be few and good; BRAG is a good dog, but Holdfast is better; a CHANGE is as good as a rest; the COW gives good milk but kicks over the pail; CRACK was a good dog but he got hung for barking; ENOUGH is as good as a feast; EVERYTHING is good in its season; EVIL communications corrupt good manners; FAR-FETCHED and dear bought is good for ladies; FIRE and water are good servants but bad masters; from HELL, Hull and Halifax, Good Lord deliver us; he goes not out of his WAY that goes to a good inn; he is an ILL companion that has a good memory; he KNOWS best what good is that has endured evil; he that BRINGS good news knocks hard; HOPE is a good breakfast but a bad supper; 'IF' and 'an' spoils many a good charter; if in FEBRUARY there be no rain, 'tis neither good for hay nor grain; if the COUNSEL be good, no matter who gave it; an ILL agreement is better than a good judgement; an INCH is as good as a mile; into the MOUTH of a bad dog often falls a good bone; it is never a BAD day that hath a good night; it's an ILL wind that blows nobody any good; JACK is as good as his master; a JADE eats as much as a good horse; JOAN is as good as my lady in the dark; a LEAP YEAR is never a good sheep year; LEARNING makes a good man better and an ill man worse; LEAVE off while the play is good; a LIAR ought to have a good memory; a LISPING lass is good to kiss; LISTENERS never hear any good of themselves; LITERATURE is a good staff but a bad crutch; LITTLE and good fills the trencher; a LITTLE of what you fancy does you good; MANY a good cow hath an evil calf; a MISS is as good as a mile; the MONTH that comes in good will go out bad; NEXT to no wife, a good wife is best; a NOD is as good as a wink to a blind horse; no MAN can be a good ruler unless he hath first been ruled; no NEWS is good news; not a LONG day but a good heart rids work; an OLD man in a house is a good sign; ONE bad general is better than two good ones; ONE good turn deserves another; one NEVER loses by doing a good turn; ONE reason is as good as fifty; OPEN confession is good for the soul; PRAISE makes good men better and bad men worse; a RAGGED colt may make a good horse; RIGHT mixture makes good mortar; the ROAD to hell is paved with good intentions; SEE a pin and pick it up, all the day you'll have good luck; SHORT counsel is good counsel; SHORT rede, good rede; a SMILING boy seldom proves a good servant; SORROW is good for nothing but sin; that is not ALWAYS good in the maw that is sweet in the mouth; there is but an HOUR in a day between a good housewife and a bad; there is but ONE good mother-in-law, and she is dead; there is no such THING as good small beer, good brown bread, or a good old woman; there is NOTHING so good for the inside of a man as the outside of a horse; there's MANY a good cock come out of a tattered bag; there's MANY a good tune played on an old fiddle; there's ONE good wife in the country, and every man thinks he hath her; there was NEVER a good town but had a mire at one end of it; TOUCH wood, it's sure to come good; an UNTOWARD boy may make a good man; when the WIND is in the east, 'tis neither good for man nor beast; where OLD age is evil, youth can learn no good; you can have too MUCH of a good thing.

goodness is not tied to greatness (*Greek*) Goodness and greatness do not necessarily go together. J. Clarke, *Paroemiologia Anglo-Latina*, 1639.

goods. take the goods the gods provide (*Roman*) Accept without demurring what comes to you for free. John Dryden, *Alexander's Feast* (also quoted by Plautus).

> 'It is only because I am the governor's son,' Silverbridge pleaded ... 'What of that? Take the goods the gods provide you.'
>
> Anthony Trollope, *The Duke's Children*, 1880

~ *See also* HAP and halfpenny goods enough; a MAN may lose his goods for want of demanding them.

goose. a goose quill is more dangerous than a lion's claw (*English*) More harm may be done with a pen than with a more obvious weapon. Thomas Fuller, *Gnomologia*, 1732. *See also* the PEN is mightier than the sword.

~ *See also* ALL geese are swans; the CALF, the goose, the bee: the world is ruled by these three; FEATHER by feather the goose is plucked; he that EATS the king's goose shall be choked with his feathers; KILL not the goose that lays the golden egg; on SAINT Thomas the Divine kill all turkeys, geese and swine; what's SAUCE for the goose is sauce for the gander; a WILD goose never lays a tame egg.

gorse. when the gorse is out of bloom, kissing's out of fashion (*English*) When the gorse flowers, it is the season for romance (gorse remains in bloom for much of the year). M.A. Denham, *Proverbs relating to Seasons, etc.*, 1846. *See also* when the FURZE is in bloom, my love's in tune.

got. if you've got it, flaunt it (*US*) Do not be shy about your good points (typically sexually attractive physical features). Among other instances, the slogan was heard in the 1967 Mel Brooks's film comedy *The Producers*.

what is got over the devil's back is spent under his belly (*English*) Money acquired dishonestly is fated to be squandered on the pursuit of debauched pleasure. Gosson, *Plays Confuted*, 1582.

> What's got over the devil's back (that's by knavery), must be spent under his belly (that's by lechery).
>
> Thomas Middleton, *Michaelmas Term*, 1607

~*See also* a MAN cannot give what he hasn't got.

gotten. *See* a FRIEND is not so soon gotten as lost; SOON gotten, soon spent.

gout. *See* DRINK wine and have the gout, drink no wine and have the gout too.

govern. *See* LAW governs man, and reason the law; REASON governs the wise man and cudgels the fool.

government. *See* only FOOLS exult when governments change.

gown. *See* LOOK to a gown of gold and you will at least get a sleeve of it; the TAILOR must cut three sleeves to every woman's gown.

grace. grace will last, beauty will blast (*English*) Good character will long outlast physical attractiveness. *Proverbis of Wysdom*, *c.*1450. Also encountered as 'grace will last, favour will blast'. A French proverb on similar lines runs 'without grace beauty is an unbaited hook'.

~ *See also* BLUSHING is a sign of grace; MONDAY's child is fair of face, Tuesday's child is full of grace; Wednesday's child is full of woe, Thursday's child has far to go; Friday's child is loving and giving, Saturday's child works hard for its living; and the child that's born on the Sabbath day, is fair and wise and good and gay; PRIDE and grace dwell never in one place.

grain. grain by grain the hen fills her belly (*English*) Little by little the desired result is achieved. Middleton and Rowley, *The Spanish Gipsy*, 1623.

~ *See also* if in FEBRUARY there be no rain, 'tis neither good for hay nor grain.

grandmother. *See* don't TEACH your grandmother to suck eggs.

grape. *See* there is a DEVIL in every berry of the grape.

grasp all, lose all (*English*) Those who try to grab too much for themselves risk holding on to nothing at all. Layamon, *Brut*, *c.*1205. Variants include 'he that grasps at too much holds nothing fast'.

> Who imbraceth much, litle closeth.
> John Florio, *Firste Fruites*, 1578

grass. the grass is always greener on the other side of the fence (*English*) What others have always seems more attractive than what you have yourself. H. and M. Williams, *Plays of the Year*, 1959. Although known in this form only from the twentieth century, earlier versions of the proverb may be found as far back as the sixteenth century – for instance, as 'the corne in an other mans ground semeth ever more fertyll and plentifull then doth oure owne'. Variants include 'the grass is always greener on the other side of the hill', 'the other side of the road always looks cleanest' and, in the United States, 'the grass is always greener in the next man's yard'. *See also* FORBIDDEN fruit tastes sweetest.

> The apples on the other side of the wall are the sweetest.
> George Herbert, *Outlandish Proverbs*, 1640

while the grass grows, the steed starves (*English*) Some things come too late to do any good (just as a horse might starve while the grass to feed him is still growing). *Douce MS*, *c.*1350.

> *Rosencrantz* How can that be when you have the voice of the king himself for your succession in Denmark?
> *Hamlet* Ay, sir, but 'While the grass grows,' – the proverb is something musty.
> William Shakespeare, *Hamlet*, *c.*1600

~ *See also* RAIN on the green grass, and rain on the tree, and rain on the house-top, but not upon me.

grave. *See* if you DRINK in your pottage, you'll cough in your grave; if you would have FRUIT, you must bring the leaf to the grave; the MORE thy years, the nearer thy grave; there will be SLEEPING enough in the grave; we shall LIE all alike in our graves.

grease. *See* the SQUEAKING wheel gets the grease.

great. great bodies move slowly (*English*) Large organizations operate very slowly. James Kelly, *A Complete Collection of Scottish Proverbs*, 1721.

a great book is a great evil (*Greek*) Large books may impress because of their great size, although they may lack any greatness in content and thus exert an undesirable influence. Callimachus, *Fragments*, third century BC. An English variant runs 'a wicked book is the wickeder because it cannot repent'.

> Oftentimes it falls out … a great Booke is a great mischiefe.
> Robert Burton, *Anatomy of Melancholy*, 1628

a great dowry is a bed full of brambles (*Scottish*) Men who marry wealthy women may find they have to accept many undesirable things along with their bride's dowry. George Herbert, *Outlandish Proverbs*, 1640. An Irish proverb cautions 'where there is a dowry there is danger'.

the greater the right, the greater the wrong (*English*) Justice taken to the extreme can become an extreme wrong. Richard Grafton, *Chronicle*, 1569. Sometimes encountered, particularly in the legal context, as the Latin tag *summus jus, summa injuria*.

the greater the sinner, the greater the saint (*English*) The more wicked a person's past, the more remarkable is their subsequent reformation. Richard Graves, *The Spiritual Quixote*, 1772.

the greater the truth, the greater the libel (*English*) If something is undeniably true then any attempt to refute it is doubly damnable. Robert Burns, *The Reproof*, 1787. The maxim is often quoted in discussion of libel actions and is particularly associated with William Murray, 1st Earl of Mansfield, who was a leading judge of the King's Bench in the eighteenth century.

> 'The greater the truth, the greater the libel,' said Warburton, with a sneer.
>
> Edward Bulwer-Lytton, *Pelham*, 1828

the greatest calf is not the sweetest veal (*English*) The best meat or other produce does not necessarily come from the biggest animal, plant and so on. William Camden, *Remains concerning Britain*, 1636.

the greatest clerks be not the wisest men (*English/French*) Education does not necessarily imply wisdom. Geoffrey Chaucer, 'The Reeve's Tale', *The Canterbury Tales*, *c.*1387 (also found, as 'the greatest scholars are not the wisest men', in Rabelais).

> It is true that I long syth haue redde and herde that the best clerkes ben not the wysest men.
>
> William Caxton, *Reynard the Fox*, 1481

the greatest crabs be not all the best meat (*English*) The best meat does not necessarily come from the biggest animals. John Heywood, *A Dialogue containing ... the Proverbs in the English Tongue*, 1546.

the greatest talkers are the least doers (*English*) Talkative people are the least likely to be high achievers. William Shakespeare, *Richard III*, *c.*1592.

> Talkers are no good doers: be assur'd
> We go to use our hands and not our tongues.
>
> William Shakespeare, *Richard III*, *c.*1592

a great fortune is a great slavery (*English*) Great wealth brings with it great responsibilities. Thomas Fuller, *Gnomologia*, 1732. Related proverbs include 'great honours are great burdens'.

great men have great faults (*English*) Remarkable men often have serious flaws in their character. T. Draxe, *Bibliotheca Scholastica*, 1616.

great minds think alike (*English*) People of distinction share a similar viewpoint (often said when two people congratulate themselves on separately thinking of something or doing something at the same moment). D. Belchier, *Hans Beer-Pot*, 1618. *See also* GREAT wits jump.

great oaks from little acorns grow (*English*) Big things can develop from small beginnings. Geoffrey Chaucer, *Troilus and Criseyde*, *c.*1385–90. Much the same sentiment was voiced in various forms as far back as classical times, the most famous versions including *magnum in parvo* (a lot in a little).

> The greatest Oaks have been little Acorns.
>
> Thomas Fuller, *Gnomologia*, 1732

great trees keep down little ones (*English*) It is difficult for underlings to advance when they are perpetually in the shade of their masters. Thomas Fuller, *The Holy State and the Profane State*, 1642. An Italian proverb observes that 'great trees give more shade than fruit'.

great wits have short memories (*English*) The brightest minds often prove forgetful. John Dryden, *Sir Martin Mar-all*, 1668.

great wits jump (*English*) People of strong intellect will reach the same conclusion at much the same time. *Wit for Money*, 1691. *See also* GREAT minds think alike.

> Great wits jump: – for the moment Dr Slop cast his eyes upon his bag ... the very same thought occurred.
>
> Laurence Sterne, *Tristram Shandy*, 1767

he that has a great nose thinks everybody is speaking of it (*English*) It is easy for someone who fancies they have some defect or weakness to imagine everyone else is talking about it. Thomas Fuller, *Gnomologia*, 1732. Related sayings include 'his nose will abide no jests'.

I went to the Court for the first time to-day, and, like the man with the large nose, thought everybody was thinking of me and my mishaps.

Walter Scott, *Journal*, 24 January 1826

there's no great loss without some gain (*English*) Disappointments or other losses often bring with them some compensatory benefit. David Fergusson, *Scottish Proverbs*, 1641. *See also* EVERY cloud has a silver lining; what you LOSE on the swings you gain on the roundabouts.

~ *See also* BETTER a little fire to warm us than a great one to burn us; BUILDING and marrying of children are great wasters; the COMMAND of custom is great; DEATH is the great leveller; a GOOD lawyer must be a great liar; GOODNESS is not tied to greatness; he that is DRUNK is as great as a king; KEEP yourself from the anger of a great man, from the tumult of a mob, from a man of ill fame, from a widow that has been thrice married, from a wind that comes in at a hole, and from a reconciled enemy; the LEAST boy always carries the greatest fiddle; LIGHT cares speak, great ones are dumb; a LITTLE body often harbours a great soul; a LITTLE fire burns up a great deal of corn; LITTLE fishes slip through nets but great fishes are taken; a LITTLE leak will sink a great ship; LITTLE strokes fell great oaks; LITTLE thieves are hanged, but great ones escape; NATURE, time and patience are the three great physicians; POVERTY is no disgrace, but it is a great inconvenience; SEEM not greater than thou art; SMALL sorrows speak; great ones are silent; a SMALL spark makes a great fire; THRIFT is a great revenue; a TRULY great man never puts away the simplicity of a child.

greed. *See* NEED makes greed.

greedy folks have long arms (*Scottish*) Those who desire something strongly enough will go to great lengths to get it. James Kelly, *A Complete Collection of Scotish Proverbs*, 1721.

Greek. when Greek meets Greek, then comes the tug of war (*English/Dutch*) When two people of the same calibre or courage engage, the contest that ensues will be fierce. Nathaniel Lee, *The Rival Queens*, 1677. The proverb has its origins in the spirited resistance that was put up by Greek cities to attacks by Philip of Macedon and Alexander the Great. Nathaniel Lee's original line actually ran 'when Greeks join'd Greeks then was the tug of war'. Another proverb that casts a more dubious light upon the Greek national character runs 'after shaking hands with a Greek, count your fingers'.

Meantime ... Greek was meeting Greek only a few yards off. Mr Hardie was being undermined by a man of his own calibre.

Charles Reade, *Hard Cash*, 1863

~ *See also* BEWARE of Greeks bearing gifts.

green. a green winter makes a fat churchyard (*English*) A mild winter promises many deaths to come. J. Swan, *Speculum Mundi*, 1635. Scientists have been known to accept the truth of this proverb, explaining that a mild winter fosters epidemics that might not flourish in colder weather. Variants include 'a green Yule makes a fat churchyard' and 'green Christmas, full churchyard'.

A green yule makes a fat Church-yard. This, and a great many proverbial Observations, upon the Seasons of the Year, are groundless.

James Kelly, *A Complete Collection of Scotish Proverbs*, 1721

a green wound is soon healed (*English*) Injuries and insults are best healed while still fresh. John Lyly, *Euphues*, 1579.

~ *See* the GRASS is always greener on the other side of the fence; a HEDGE between keeps friendship green; NEW beer, new bread and green wood will make a man's hair grow through his hood; RAIN on the green grass, and rain on the tree, and rain on the house-top, but not upon me.

grey. grey hairs are death's blossoms (*English*) The appearance of grey hairs are a warning of life passing. R.C. Trench, *On the Lessons in Proverbs*, 1853. Sometimes heard with reference to white rather than grey hairs.

This whyte top wryteth myne olde yeres.

Geoffrey Chaucer, *The Canterbury Tales*, *c.*1387

the grey mare is the better horse (*English*) The wife is superior (either in character or in terms of running the marriage) to the husband. John Heywood, *A Dialogue containing ... the Proverbs in the English Tongue*, 1546.

The vulgar proverb, that the grey mare is the better horse, originated, I suspect, in the preference generally given to the grey mares of Flanders over the finest coach horses of England.

Thomas Macaulay, *The History of England from the Accession of James II*, 1849

~ *See also* ALL cats are grey in the dark; EVENING red and morning grey help the traveller on his way; HORNS and grey hairs do not come by years.

grief. *See* ALL things grow with time, except grief; he that TALKS much of his happiness, summons grief; MARRIAGE halves our griefs, doubles our joys, and quadruples our expenses; no DAY passeth without some grief; ONE grief drives out another.

grieve. *See* what the EYE does not see, the heart does not grieve over.

grind. *See* the MILL cannot grind with the water that is past; the MILLS of God grind slowly, yet they grind exceeding small; the MILL that is always going grinds coarse and fine.

grip. *See* NOTHING should be done in haste but gripping a flea.

grist. *See* ALL is grist that comes to the mill.

groat. *See* he KENS his groats among other folk's kail; a PIN a day is a groat a year.

grope. he that gropes in the dark finds that he would not (*English*) Those who venture into territory with which they are unfamiliar are likely to stumble across things they would rather not find. J. Howell, *Paroemiographia*, 1659.

ground. *See* the BEST remedy against an ill man is much ground between; BETWEEN two stools you fall to the ground; he that LIES upon the ground can fall no lower.

groundly. *See* WALK groundly, talk profoundly, drink roundly, sleep soundly.

grow. a growing youth has a wolf in his belly (*English*) The young have a voracious appetite. Benjamin Jowett, *Life*, 1886.

~ *See also* ABSENCE makes the heart grow fonder; ALL things grow with time, except grief; FOLLY grows without watering; GREAT oaks from little acorns grow; he who NEVER fails will never grow rich; ILL weeds grow apace; LAUGH and grow fat; the MORE camomile is trodden on, the faster it grows; the MORE you tramp on a turd the broader it grows; NEW beer, new bread and green wood will make a man's hair grow through his hood; ONE for the mouse, one for the crow, one to rot, one to grow; when the MISTRESS is the master, parsley grows the faster; while the GRASS grows, the steed starves.

growth. *See* CONFIDENCE is a plant of slow growth.

grunt. *See* what can you EXPECT from a pig but a grunt?

guess. *See* NONE can guess the jewel by the casket.

guest. *See* a CONSTANT guest is never welcome; an UNBIDDEN guest knoweth not where to sit.

guide. *See* GEAR is easier gained than guided.

guilty. a guilty conscience needs no accuser (*English*) Those who are conscious that they have committed an offence need not be reminded of it. Geoffrey Chaucer, *The Canterbury Tales*, *c.*1387. Variants include 'a guilty conscience is a thousand witnesses', 'suspicion always haunts the guilty mind' and 'he declares himself guilty who justifies himself before accusation'.

A guilty Conscience self accuses. A Man that has done ill ... shews his Guilt.

James Kelly, *A Complete Collection of Scotish Proverbs*, 1721

~ *See also* EVERYONE is innocent until proved guilty.

gut no fish till you get them (*English*) Do not count on something until you have it securely in your possession. James Kelly, *A Complete Collection of Scotish Proverbs*, 1721. *See also* don't COUNT your chickens before they are hatched.

gutter. *See* he who REPAIRS not his gutter repairs his whole house.

guy. See NICE guys finish last.

habit. *See also* OLD habits die hard; VICE is often clothed in virtue's habit.

hail brings frost in the tail (*English*) Hail is usually followed by a period of very cold weather, with frost. J. Clarke, *Paroemiologia Anglo-Latina*, 1639. Another proverb claims 'a hailstorm by day denotes a frost at night'.

hair. hair and hair makes the carle's head bare (*Roman*) Through regular, small reductions everything may eventually be lost. J. Clarke, *Paroemiologia Anglo-Latina*, 1639. Also encountered in the form 'pull hair and hair and you'll make the carle bald'.
no hair so small but hath his shadow (*Roman*) Even the most apparently insignificant person has his or her hopes, influence, desires and so forth. John Lyly, *Sapho and Phao*, 1584.

> Affirming, that as ... the smallest haires have their shadowes: so the meanest swaines had their fancies.
> Thomas Lodge, *Rosalynde*, 1590

take the hair of the dog that bit you (*English*) To counter the adverse effects of something the best policy is to take a little more of it (usually quoted in reference to overindulgence in alcohol and treatment of consequent hangovers). The proverb has its roots in the traditional notion that consuming the burnt hair of a dog would prove an antidote to its bite. *See also* LIKE cures like.

~ *See also* FRIDAY's hair and Sunday's horn go to the devil on Monday morn; GREY hairs are death's blossoms; HORNS and grey hairs do not come by years; NEW beer, new bread and green wood will make a man's hair grow through his hood; ONE hair of a woman draws more than a team of oxen.

half. half a loaf is better than no bread (*English*) A meagre amount of something is better than nothing at all. John Heywood, *A Dialogue containing ... the Proverbs in the English Tongue*, 1546. Variants include 'half an egg is better than an empty shell'.

> You know the Proverb of the half Loaf, Ariadne,
> a Husband that will deal thee some Love is better
> than one who can give thee none.
> Aphra Behn, *The Rover*, 1681

half an hour is soon lost at dinner (*English*) Time passes quickly when a person is busy eating. Jonathan Swift, *Polite Conversation*, 1738.
the half is better than the whole (*Greek*) In some circumstances, it is best to settle for something less, because ultimately this means one will be better off. Hugh Latimer, *Sermon before King's Majesty*, 1550. The proverb is also to be found in the Greek poet Hesiod's *Works and Days*, eighth century BC. Hesiod quoted the saying to his brother Perseus in order to settle a legal dispute between them without having to go to court, implying that it was better to accept half of an estate than press on in the hope of getting the whole estate, only to find it much reduced after court proceedings due to legal costs. Related proverbs include 'the half sheweth what the whole meaneth'.

> Unhappy they to whom God has not revealed,
> By a strong light which must their sense control,
> That half a great estate's more than the whole.
> Abraham Cowley, *Essays in Verse and Prose*, 1668

half the truth is often a whole lie (*English/US*) A person may be more seriously misled by a partial truth than by an outright lie. Benjamin Franklin, *Poor Richard's Almanack*, 1758.

That a lie which is half a truth is ever the blackest of lies,
That a lie which is all a lie may be met and fought with outright,
But a lie which is part a truth is a harder matter to fight.

Alfred, Lord Tennyson, 'The Grandmother', *Poems*, 1859

half the world doesn't know how the other half lives (*French*) Much of humanity lives in ignorance of the radically different existences led by their fellows. J. Hall, *Holy Observations*, 1607 (also quoted by Philippe de Commines in his *Memoires*, 1509, and by Rabelais in *Pantagruel*, 1532).

It is a common saying, that One Half of the
World does not know how the other Half lives.

Benjamin Franklin, *Poor Richard's Almanack*, 1755

half warned, half armed (*English*) To have knowledge of an approaching threat makes it much easier to fend it off. John Heywood, *A Dialogue containing ... the Proverbs in the English Tongue*, 1546.

~ *See also* BELIEVE nothing of what you hear, and only half of what you see; CALF love, half love, old love, cold love; a DANGER foreseen is half avoided; a DISEASE known is half cured; a FAULT confessed is half redressed; the FIRST blow is half the battle; he that has an ILL name is half hanged; a MAN surprised is half beaten; NEVER do things by halves; PLEASING ware is half sold; they SAY so is half a lie; TWO boys are half a boy, and three boys are no boy at all; WELL begun is half done; WOOD half burnt is easily kindled.

half-done. *See* FOOLS and bairns should never see half-done work.

halfpenny. *See* HAP and halfpenny goods enough.

halfway. *See* do not MEET troubles halfway.

Halifax. *See* from HELL, Hull and Halifax, good Lord deliver us.

hall. hall benches are slippery (*English*) Those who seek a place in the halls of the rich and powerful are warned that such favours are easily lost. Robert Henryson, *Morall Fabillis of Esope*, *c.*1450. Also encountered in the form 'hall binks are sliddery'.

~ *See also* AFTER a famine in the stall comes a famine in the hall; BRING a cow to the hall and she'll run to the byre; do on the HILL as you would do in the hall; 'tis MERRY in hall when beards wag all.

halloo. don't halloo till you are out of the wood (*English/US*) Don't expose yourself until all threat of danger is removed. Benjamin Franklin, *Papers*, 1770 (variants may be found in the writings of Sophocles and Cicero). To 'halloo' (to shout aloud or whistle) while in a wood and thus attract attention to oneself was formerly considered unwise, as woods could harbour all manner of hidden danger. Also encountered in the form 'don't shout till you are out of the wood'. *See also* CALL the bear 'uncle' till you are safe across the bridge; don't COUNT your chickens before they are hatched.

Don't holla till you are out of the wood. This
is a night for praying rather than boasting.

Charles Kingsley, *Hereward the Wake*, 1866

halt. *See* it is HARD halting before a cripple.

halter. *See* it is ILL talking of a halter in the house of a man that was hanged.

halve. *See* MARRIAGE halves our griefs, doubles our joys, and quadruples our expenses; a TROUBLE shared is a trouble halved.

halves. *See* HALF.

hammer. *See* the CHURCH is an anvil which has worn out many hammers.

hand. the hand that gives, gathers (*English*) Those who behave generously towards others will enjoy rewards for their generosity in the future. J. Howell, *Paroemiographia*, 1659.

the hand that rocks the cradle rules the world (*US*) Those who have influence over children (or at an early stage in the development of something) ultimately have the greatest influence of all. William Ross Wallace, 'The Hand that Rules the World', 1865. *See also* GIVE me a child for the first seven years, and you may do what you like with him afterwards.

They say that man is mighty,
He governs land and sea,
He wields a mighty sceptre
O'er lesser powers that be;

But a mightier power and stronger
Man from his throne has hurled,
And the hand that rocks the cradle
Is the hand that rules the world.

William Ross Wallace, 'The Hand that Rules the World', 1865

he that hath his hand in the lion's mouth must take it out as well as he can (*English*) Those who find themselves in severe trouble must do what they can to get themselves out of it. Walter Scott, *Ivanhoe*, 1819.

put not thy hand between the bark and the tree (*English*) Do not interfere in an argument between close relatives. John Heywood, *A Dialogue containing ... the Proverbs in the English Tongue*, 1546. The danger is that the person interfering will find himself 'pinched' between the two parties.

It were a foly for mee, to put hande betweene
the barke and the tree.

John Heywood, *A Dialogue containing ... the Proverbs in the English Tongue*, 1546

~ *See also* a BIRD in the hand is worth two in the bush; COLD hands, warm heart; the DEVIL finds work for idle hands; DIRTY hands make clean money; don't BITE the hand that feeds you; EMPTY hands no hawks allure; the EYE of the master does more work than both his hands; FINGERS were made before forks and hands before knives; FULL cup, steady hand; GIVE a clown a finger and he will take your hand; a GOOD surgeon must have an eagle's eye, a lion's heart and a lady's hand; he CARRIES fire in one hand and water in the other; if IFS and ands were pots and pans, there'd be no work for tinkers' hands; INDUSTRY is fortune's right hand, and frugality her left; it's ILL putting a naked sword in a madman's hand; a LONG tongue is a sign of a short hand; MANY hands make light work; ONE hand for oneself and one for the ship; ONE hand washes the other; ONE pair of heels is often worth two pairs of hands; SOW with the hand and not with the sack; when you go to DANCE take heed who you take by the hand.

handle. he that handles thorns shall prick his fingers (*English*) Those who deal with problematic matters must expect to experience difficulties. Nicholas Breton, *Works*, 1616.

~ *See also* PUDDINGS and paramours should be hotly handled.

handsome. handsome is as handsome does (*English*) Good character is proved more through deeds than through mere good looks, promises and the like. Geoffrey Chaucer, *The Canterbury Tales*, *c.*1387. Originally 'handsome' referred to refined or gentlemanly behaviour rather than physical appearance alone. A variant form more usually directed at women runs 'pretty is as pretty does'. A Yiddish equivalent cautions that 'handsome is not what is handsome, but what pleases'. *See also* BEAUTY is only skin deep; GRACE will last, beauty will blast.

By my troth, he is a proper man; but he is proper
that proper doth.

Thomas Dekker, *The Shoemaker's Holiday*, 1600

he that is not handsome at twenty, wise at forty and rich at fifty, will never be rich, wise or handsome (*English*) There comes a time in life when it becomes clear that if not already attained, good looks, wisdom and wealth are unlikely ever to be enjoyed. George Herbert, *Outlandish Proverbs*, 1640.

hang. do not hang all your bells upon one horse (*English*) Do not leave all your wealth to one child alone. J. Howell, *Paroemiographia*, 1659.

hang a dog on a crab-tree and he'll never love verjuice (*English*) People and animals learn to hate those things that have caused them hurt in the past. John Ray, *A Collection of English Proverbs*, 1670.

hang a thief when he's young and he'll no' steal when he's old (*Scottish*) Take drastic action at an early stage and any threat of trouble will be nipped in the bud. A. Henderson, *Scottish Proverbs*, 1832.

Hang a thief when he's young, and he'll no' steal
when he's auld.

A. Henderson, *Scottish Proverbs*, 1832

hanging and wiving go by destiny (*English*) A person's choice of marriage partner is decided by fate (as is their own ultimate end). John Heywood, *A Dialogue containing ... the Proverbs in the English Tongue*, 1546. Also encountered in the form 'hanging and wedding go by destiny'.

The ancient saying is no heresy,
Hanging and wiving goes by destiny.

William Shakespeare, *The Merchant of Venice*, *c.*1596

he that would hang his dog gives out first that he is mad (*English*) Those about to commit some wicked or disgraceful deed will often protect themselves in advance by some pretence designed to justify it. J. Palsgrave, *L'Éclaircissement de la langue française*, 1530.

he was hanged that left his drink behind (*English*) Ill luck will attend any person who leaves without first finishing his drink. *Roxborough Ballads*, *c.*1640. One north of England variant runs 'he will be hanged for leaving his liquor, like the saddler of Bawtry'. The aforesaid saddler of Bawtry was sentenced to be hanged in York and, as was customary, was offered the chance to take a last drink at a local tavern before being taken to the gallows and executed. The saddler, however, turned down the drink and was accordingly dispatched by the hangman without further delay – only for a reprieve to arrive moments later. If the saddler had agreed to slake his thirst, he would have been saved – hence the proverb.

you might as well be hanged for a sheep as for a lamb (*English*) If you are going to transgress the rules you might as well aim for the highest possible prize, as the penalty if you are caught will be the same (as was true of sheep-stealing in former times). John Ray, *A Collection of English Proverbs*, 1678. *See also* IN for a penny, in for a pound.

> So in for the lamb, as the saying is, in for the sheep.
> Samuel Richardson, *Clarissa*, 1748

~ *See also* ALL the keys hang not at one man's girdle; ALMOST was never hanged; BETTER to hang than to hold; the BOUGHS that bear most hang lowest; CONFESS and be hanged; CRACK was a good dog but he got hung for barking; CREAKING doors hang the longest; EVERY herring must hang by its own gill; GIVE a dog a bad name and hang him; GIVE a man enough rope and he will hang himself; he that has an ILL name is half hanged; he that KILLETH a man when he is drunk shall be hanged when he is sober; he that will be RICH before night may be hanged before noon; if at CHRISTMAS ice hangs on the willow, clover may be cut at Easter; if you're BORN to be hanged then you'll never be drowned; it is ILL talking of a halter in the house of a man that was hanged; LITTLE thieves are hanged, but great ones escape; PAY well, command well, hang well; a RICH man's money hangs him oftentimes; there are MORE ways of killing a dog than hanging it; WAR makes thieves, and peace hangs them.

hap. hap and halfpenny goods enough (*English*) If luck is on a person's side then it matters little that they start with no more than half a penny to their name. J. Clarke, *Paroemiologia Anglo-Latina*, 1639.

~ *See also* SET hard heart against hard hap.

ha'porth. *See* don't SPOIL the ship for a ha'porth of tar.

happen. *See* ACCIDENTS will happen in the best regulated families; the BRIDE goes to her marriage-bed but knows not what shall happen to her; it CHANCETH in an hour that happeneth not in seven years; the UNEXPECTED always happens; WORSE things happen at sea.

happiness. happiness takes no account of time (*English*) Those who are enjoying themselves have little sense of time passing. Matthew Prior, *Alma*, 1718. A German variant runs 'to the happy man no hour strikes'.

~ *See also* he that TALKS much of his happiness, summons grief; MEMORY of happiness makes misery woeful.

happy. happy is he that is happy in his children (*English*) Contented and well-behaved children bring their parents much pleasure. Thomas Fuller, *Gnomologia*, 1732. Representing the child's view, another proverb runs 'happy is the child whose father goes to the devil'.

happy is the bride the sun shines on (*English*) It is a good omen for the future of a marriage if the sun shines on a bride on her wedding day. Robert Herrick, *Hesperides*, 1648. *See also* BLESSED are the dead the rain rains on.

> The four old bells rang out merrily, and 'Blessed is the bride whom the sun shines on.' 'I have had a great deal of sunshine today,' she said. 'I hope it is a good omen,' I said. 'I hope so,' she said, sweetly and seriously.
> Francis Kilvert, Diary, 1 January 1873

happy is the country which has no history (*English*) The history of a nation may prove as much a hindrance as a help, and thus young countries, which lack a long history, may be considered freer agents. Thomas Carlyle, *Frederick the Great*, 1858–65.

> History, which is, indeed, little more than the register of the crimes, follies and misfortunes of mankind.
>
> Edward Gibbon, *The History of the Decline and Fall of the Roman Empire*, 1766–88

happy is the wooing that is not long a-doing (*English*) Short engagements are much more likely to result in a happy outcome than longer periods of wooing. Robert Burton, *Anatomy of Melancholy*, 1621.

> What signifies shilly-shally? What says the old proverb? – 'Happy is the wooing, that is not long a–doing'.
>
> Samuel Richardson, *Sir Charles Grandison*, 1753

if you would be happy for a week take a wife; if you would be happy for a month kill a pig; but if you would be happy all your life plant a garden (*English*) No pleasure is as lasting as a garden. Thomas Fuller, *The History of the Worthies of England*, 1661. Variants suggest the recipe for a happy life lies in honesty, rather than gardening , as for instance in 'let him that would be happy for a day, go to the barber; for a week, marry a wife; for a month, buy him a new horse; for a year, build him a new house; for all his life time, be an honest man'. A related proverb advises 'he that marries a wife is happy a month, but he that gets a fat benefice lives merrily all his life'.

> I say the Italian-humor, who have a merry Proverb, Let him that would be happy for a Day, go to the Barber; for a Week, marry a Wife; for a Month, buy him a New-horse; for a Year, build him a New-house; for all his Life-time, be an Honest man.
>
> Thomas Fuller, *The History of the Worthies of England*, 1661

~ *See also* BETTER be happy than wise; CALL no man happy till he dies; a DEAF husband and a blind wife are always a happy couple; if SAINT Paul's Day be fair and clear, it will betide a happy year; it is MISERY enough to have been once happy.

harbour. *See* a LITTLE body often harbours a great soul.

hard. hard cases make bad law (*Roman*) Complicated or exceptional legal cases tend to confuse understanding of the law. G. Hayes, 1854, quoted in W.S. Holdsworth, *The History of English Law*, 1926 (the proverb may also be found in essence as far back as the writings of Sallust in the first century BC).

hard words break no bones (*English*) Verbal criticism may be resented but cannot cause a person actual physical harm. *Towneley Play of Noah*, *c.*1450. *See also* STICKS and stones may break my bones, but names will never hurt me.

> I often tell 'em how wrong folks are to say that soft words butter no parsnips, and hard words break no bones.
>
> Anthony Trollope, *The Last Chronicle of Barsetshire*, 1867

it is hard halting before a cripple (*English*) It is difficult to deceive a person in something they have personal experience of (just as a crippled person will not be deceived by somebody pretending to be lame). Geoffrey Chaucer, *Troilus and Criseyde*, *c.*1385–90.

it is hard to be wretched but worse to be known so (*English*) Having to put up with the sympathy of others when one experiences misfortune is harder than putting up with the misfortune itself. George Herbert, *Outlandish Proverbs*, 1640.

it is hard to pay for bread that has been eaten (*Danish*) A person will rue having to pay retrospectively for something that they have already consumed or enjoyed. *See also* EATEN bread is soon forgotten.

it is hard to turn tack upon a narrow bridge (*English*) It is difficult to change course when there is little room to manoeuvre. Thomas Fuller, *Gnomologia*, 1732.

it's hard to wive and thrive both in a year (*English*) A man cannot expect to get married and at the same time expect his business not to be disrupted. *Towneley Plays*, *c.*1410. Another proverb, however, recognizes the futility in warning others not to marry in the form 'wives must be had, be they good or bad'. The man who feels he has to marry should at least go about his choice with care, another proverb cautioning that 'in wiving and thriving a man should take counsel of all the world'.

> You can't expect to wive and thrive in the same year.
>
> Jonathan Swift, *Polite Conversation*, 1738

~ *See also* the BIGGER they are, the harder they fall; he that BRINGS good news knocks hard; the FIRST seven years are the hardest; FORECAST is better than work hard; GOOD things are hard; if the COCK moult before the hen we shall have weather thick and thin, but if the hen moult before the cock we shall have weather hard as a block; it is EASY to fall into a trap but hard to get out again; KEEPING is harder than winning; MONDAY's child is fair of face, Tuesday's child is full of grace; Wednesday's child is full of woe, Thursday's child has far to go; Friday's child is loving and giving, Saturday's child works hard for its living; and the child that's born on the Sabbath day, is fair and wise and good and gay; OLD habits die hard; SET hard heart against hard hap; THINGS that are hard to come by are much set by.

harden. *See* the SAME heat that melts the wax will harden the clay.

harder. *See* HARD.

hardly. *See* a FALSE tongue hardly speaks truth.

hare. hare is melancholy meat (*English*) Those who eat hare will suffer a depression of their spirits. T. Kendall, *Flowers of Epigrams*, 1577. Also found in the form 'he hath devoured a hare'.

> Hare, a black meat, melancholy, and hard of digestion.
>
> Robert Burton, *Anatomy of Melancholy*, 1621

hares may pull dead lions by the beard (*English*) The most humble and timid may taunt the powerful with impunity after the latter have been brought down. G. Pettie, *Guazzo's Civil Conversation*, 1581.

> You are the hare of whom the proverb goes,
> whose valour plucks dead lions by the beard.
>
> William Shakespeare, *King John*, *c.*1595

~ *See also* as the BLIND man catches the hare; FIRST catch your hare; if you RUN after two hares you will catch neither; the TORTOISE wins the race while the hare is sleeping; you cannot RUN with the hare and hunt with the hounds.

harm. harm watch, harm catch (*English*) A person who is always anxious about coming to harm will attract harm. William Caxton, *Reynard the Fox*, 1481.

> Harm watch, harm catch, he says.
>
> Ben Jonson, *Bartholomew Fair*, 1614

~ *See also* be WARNED by others' harm; he that DRINKETH well sleepeth well, and he that sleepeth well thinketh no harm; where GOD will help, nothing does harm; a WOMAN and a cherry are painted for their own harm.

harpoon. *See* however BIG the whale may be, the tiny harpoon can rob him of life.

harvest. *See* he that hath a GOOD harvest may be content with some thistles.

haste. haste is from the devil (*Arabic*) Those who fail to take enough time over something invite ill results. J. Howell, *Familiar Letters*, 1633. Also found as 'haste is from hell'. A related proverb warns 'a hasty man never wants woe', while another warns that 'haste comes not alone' (meaning haste always brings trouble with it). *See also* HASTY climbers have sudden falls.

haste makes waste (*English*) Doing things too quickly may result in wasted effort and materials. Geoffrey Chaucer, *The Canterbury Tales*, *c.*1387. A fuller version, recorded in 1678, runs 'haste makes waste, and waste makes want, and want makes strife between the good man and his wife'. Equivalents elsewhere include the Dutch 'haste is prodigal'.

> The proverbe seith … in wikked haste is no profit.
>
> Geoffrey Chaucer, *The Canterbury Tales*, *c.*1387

make haste slowly (*Greek/Roman*) Going slowly but steadily is often the quickest way to get something done. Geoffrey Chaucer, *Troilus and Criseyde*, *c.*1385–90 (also quoted by Suetonius). The proverb was a favourite saying of Emperor Caesar Augustus, who popularized it in its Latin version *festina lente*, which is still heard. Plutarch expressed the same sentiment as 'hair by hair you will pull out the horse's tail', and quoted a story about the general Sertorius to illustrate it. According to him, Sertorius felt the need to impress upon his troops the effectiveness of slow, patient effort over thoughtless haste. He commanded two of his men, one strong and one weak, to pluck all the hairs from the tails of two horses. The strong man tried to pull out all the hairs at once and could make little impression, but the weak man pulled out hair after single hair until at length the job was successfully done. Proverbs to a similar effect from elsewhere in the world include the Chinese saying 'it is better to get one's clothes wet than to hurry'. The Italians, meanwhile, observe that 'three things only are done well in haste: flying from the plague, escaping quarrels, and catching fleas'. *See also* MORE haste, less speed.

He hasteth wel that wisly kan abyde.

Geoffrey Chaucer, *Troilus and Criseyde*, *c.*1385–90

~ *See also* MARRY in haste and repent at leisure; MORE haste, less speed; NOTHING should be done in haste but gripping a flea.

hasty. the hasty bitch bringeth forth blind whelps (*Roman*) Things done in haste are liable to turn out badly. R. Robinson, translation of Thomas More's *Utopia*, 1556 (also quoted by Livy).

But as the latin proverbe sayeth: the hastye bitche bringeth furth blind whelpes. For when this my worke was finished, the rudeness therof shewed it to be done in poste haste.

R. Robinson, translation of Thomas More's *Utopia*, 1556

hasty climbers have sudden falls (*English*) Those who ascend rapidly in the world are just as likely to fall to earth without warning. *Digby Plays*, *c.*1480. By much the same token another proverb advises the climbers to 'make no more haste when you come down than when you went up'.

Great clymbers fall unsoft.

Edmund Spenser, *The Shepheardes Calendar*, 1579

hasty love is soon hot and soon cold (*English*) Love or friendship that is quickly kindled can just as quickly be extinguished. John Heywood, *A Dialogue containing … the Proverbs in the English Tongue*, 1546. Related proverbs include 'a hasty meeting, a hasty parting'.

the hasty man never wants woe (*English*) Those who act in haste are likely to regret their actions. Geoffrey Chaucer, *Troilus and Criseyde*, *c.*1385–90.

'The hastie person never wants woe,' they say.

George Chapman, Ben Jonson and John Marston, *Eastward Ho*, 1605

hat. *See* GIVE a cob a hat and a pair of shoes and he'll last for ever.

hatch. *See* don't COUNT your chickens before they are hatched; he that MISCHIEF hatcheth, mischief catcheth.

hatchet. *See* do not REMOVE a fly from your friend's forehead with a hatchet; when the TREE is fallen, all go with their hatchet.

hate (noun). *See* BETTER a dinner of herbs than a stalled ox where hate is.

hate (verb). LOVE as in time to come thou shouldest hate and hate as thou shouldest in time to come, love; ONE beggar does not hate another as much as one doctor hates another; the TREASON is loved but the traitor is hated.

haw. *See* MANY haws, many snows; MANY hips and haws, many frosts and snaws; when ALL fruit falls, welcome haws.

hawk. hawks will not pick out hawks' eyes (*English*) Those engaged in the same profession (typically, criminal or dependent upon profiting by the loss of others) will not prey on one another. J. Sanforde, *The Garden of Pleasure*, 1573. The proverb is sometimes encountered with reference to crows rather than hawks.

I wadna … rest my main dependence on the Hielandmen – hawks winna pike out hawks' een. – They quarrel amang themsells … but they are sure to join … against a' civilized folk.

Walter Scott, *Rob Roy*, 1817

~ *See also* EMPTY hands no hawks allure.

hay. make hay while the sun shines (*German*) Make the most of any opportunity when it is presented. John Heywood, *A Dialogue containing … the Proverbs in the English Tongue*, 1546 (though also recorded in German satirist Sebastian Brant's *Das Narrenschiff* as early as 1494). In farming, ripe hay should be harvested at the first opportunity, in case it is lost through bad weather (a particular threat given the changeable nature of English weather patterns). *See also* GATHER ye rosebuds while ye may; NEVER put off till tomorrow what you can do today; PROCRASTINATION is the thief of time; STRIKE while the iron is hot; take TIME by the forelock.

We must lose no time; we must make our hay while shines the sun.

Charles Reade, *The Cloister and the Hearth*, 1861

~*See also* a GOOD hay year a bad fog year; if in FEBRUARY there be no rain, 'tis neither good for hay nor grain; a SWARM of bees in May is worth a load of hay; a THOUSAND pounds and a bottle of hay is all one thing at doomsday; a WET May brings plenty of hay.

hazelnut. *See* the MORE hazelnuts, the more bastard children.

head. he that hath a head of wax must not walk in the sun (*Roman*) Those in potentially vulnerable positions should not take unnecessary risks. George Herbert, *Outlandish Proverbs*, 1640. *See also* PEOPLE who live in glass houses shouldn't throw stones.

> If your head is wax, don't walk in the Sun.
>
> Benjamin Franklin, *Poor Richard's Almanack*, 1749

when the head acheth all the body is the worse (*English*) A person with a sore head feels infirm in all his or her limbs. Wright, *Political Songs from John to Edward II*, *c.*1230.

~ *See also* a BALD head is soon shaven; be not a BAKER if your head be of butter; the COMFORTER's head never aches; DRY feet, warm head, bring safe to bed; the FISH always stinks from the head downwards; HAIR and hair makes the carle's head bare; if the COCK crows on going to bed, he's sure to rise with a watery head; LAWYERS' houses are built on the heads of fools; the MOB has many heads but no brains; a QUIET tongue makes a wise head; a SPUR in the head is worth two in the heel; a STILL tongue makes a wise head; that which is GOOD for the head is evil for the neck and the shoulders; there are MANY ways of dressing a calf's head; TURNIPS like a dry bed but a wet head; TWO heads are better than one; where MACGREGOR sits is the head of the table; a WISE head makes a still tongue; YORKSHIRE born and Yorkshire bred, strong in the arm and weak in the head; you cannot put an OLD head on young shoulders.

headache. *See* a CROWN is no cure for the headache.

heal. *See* a BROKEN leg is not healed by a silk stocking; GOD heals and the physician hath the thanks; a GREEN wound is soon healed; it's ILL healing of an old sore; PHYSICIAN, heal thyself; though the WOUND be healed, a scar remains; TIME heals all wounds.

health. health is better than wealth (*Hebrew*) Good health is more valuable than mere riches. Apocrypha, Ecclesiasticus 30. Variants include 'health is great riches', 'the first wealth is health', 'good health is above wealth' and 'a healthy man is a successful man'. Another proverb counters this view, alleging that 'health without money is half an ague'. A Yiddish saying runs 'your health comes first; you can always hang yourself later'. Ideally, of course, a person will possess both health and wealth together, in which case they will allegedly enjoy a third benefit, according to another old proverb: 'health and wealth create beauty.'

> Health and strength is above all gold.
>
> Ecclesiasticus 30

health is not valued till sickness comes (*English*) It is only when a person is ill that they consider their health important. G. Torriano, *Select Italian Proverbs*, 1642. Related proverbs include 'a healthy body is the guest-chamber of the soul; a sick, its prison' and the Welsh 'next to sickness, health is sweet'.

~ *See also* a GOOD wife and health is a man's best wealth; POVERTY is the mother of health; WEALTH is enemy to health.

healthy. *See* EARLY to bed and early to rise, makes a man healthy, wealthy and wise; he that goes to BED thirsty riseth healthy.

heap. *See* RICHES are like muck, which stink in a heap, but spread abroad make the earth fruitful.

hear. hear all, see all, say nowt (*English*) It is good policy to be vigilant, but also to keep your observations to yourself. *Proverbs of Wisdom*, 1400. A proverb of Yorkshire origins. The fullest version runs 'hear all, see all, say nowt, tak' all, keep all, gie nowt, and if tha ever does owt for nowt do it for thysen'. *See also* SEE no evil, hear no evil, speak no evil.

> It seems queer, that you do it and get no profit.
> I should think you've forgotten the Yorkshire
> proverb, 'An' if tha does owt for nowt, do it
> for thysen.'
>
> D.H. Lawrence, letter, 1 February 1913

hear much, speak little (*English*) It is good policy to listen to others, but keep one's own counsel. *Peter Idel's Instructions*, *c.*1420. Other proverbs delivering a similar message include 'hear twice before you speak once', 'from hearing comes wisdom; from speaking, repentance', and 'he that hears much and speaks not at all shall be welcome both in bower and hall'.

> Give every man thine ear, but few thy voice.
>
> William Shakespeare, *Hamlet*, 1600–1

~ *See also* ASK no questions and hear no lies; BELIEVE nothing of what you hear, and only half of what you see; CHILDREN should be seen and not heard; do not ALL you can, spend not all you have, believe not all you hear, and tell not all you know; DREAM of a funeral and you hear of a marriage; EACH bird loves to hear himself sing; EVERY ass loves to hear himself bray; go ABROAD and you'll hear news of home; he who SAYS what he likes shall hear what he does not like; if the ADDER could hear and the blindworm could see, neither man nor beast would ever go free; LISTENERS never hear any good of themselves; SEE no evil, hear no evil, speak no evil; there are NONE so deaf as those who will not hear; what CHILDREN hear at home soon flies abroad; the YOUNG cock crows as he heard the old one.

heart. what comes from the heart goes to the heart (*English*) Anything that is born of real emotion will stir emotion in others when they hear of it. J. Platt, *Morality*, 1878.

when the heart is a fire some sparks will fly out of the mouth (*English*) When a person's heart is swollen with pride they will be tempted to boast. Thomas Fuller, *Gnomologia*, 1732. Variants include 'when the heart is full the tongue will speak' and 'what the heart thinketh the tongue speaketh'. A German proverb warns that 'fire in the heart sends smoke into the head', while the French observe that 'the mouth obeys poorly when the heart murmurs'.

~ *See also* ABSENCE makes the heart grow fonder; COLD hands, warm heart; EVERY heart hath its own ache; FAINT heart ne'er won fair lady; FAIR face and a foul heart; a GENTLE heart is tied with an easy thread; a GOOD heart cannot lie; a GOOD surgeon must have an eagle's eye, a lion's heart and a lady's hand; a HEAVY purse makes a light heart; HOME is where the heart is; HOPE deferred makes the heart sick; HUMBLE hearts have humble desires; if it were not for HOPE, the heart would break; it is a POOR heart that never rejoices; the JOY of the heart makes the face merry; a KIND heart loseth nought at last; KIND hearts are soonest wronged; a LIGHT purse makes a heavy heart; NEAREST the heart, nearest the mouth; not a LONG day but a good heart rids work; NOTHING agreeth worse than a lady's heart and a beggar's purse; PLEASE your eye and plague your heart; a PROUD heart and a beggar's purse agree not well together; put a STOUT heart to a stey brae; SET hard heart against hard hap; the WAY to a man's heart is through his stomach; what the EYE does not see, the heart does not grieve over.

hearty. a hearty welcome is the best cheer (*English*) Hospitality can lift a person's spirits more than anything else. Randle Cotgrave, *A Dictionary of the French and English Tongues*, 1611.

> Welcome is the best dish upon the table.
> Nathan Bailey, *Dictionary*, 1736

heat. *See* if you can't STAND the heat, get out of the kitchen; OLD pottage is sooner heated than new made; the SAME heat that melts the wax will harden the clay; they must HUNGER in frost that will not work in heat.

heaven. no coming to heaven with dry eyes (*English*) Those aspiring to sainthood, or simply a place in heaven, must expect to suffer while on earth. T. Adams, *Sermons*, 1629. Related proverbs include 'there is no going to heaven in a sedan'.

heaven protects children, sailors and drunken men (*English*) The young, seafarers and drunkards, being variously exposed to danger through innocence, occupation or incapacity, often seem to survive the worst perils unscathed, as though blessed with divine protection. T. Hughes, *Tom Brown at Oxford*, 1861. Another proverb (quoted by William Shakespeare) suggests that widows should be added to the list of those who enjoy divine protection: 'heaven is the widow's champion and defence.' The Greeks, meanwhile, believe simply that 'heaven protects the just'.

> Heaven, they say, protects children, sailors, and drunken men; and whatever answers to Heaven in the academical system protects freshmen.
> T. Hughes, *Tom Brown at Oxford*, 1861

~ *See also* CROSSES are ladders that lead to heaven; GENTLEMEN and rich men are venison in heaven; GOD's in his heaven, all's right with the world; GOLD goes in at any gate except heaven's; HUSBANDS are in heaven whose wives scold not; in RAIN and sunshine cuckolds go to heaven; it is EASIER for a camel to go through the eye of a needle than it is for a rich man to enter into the kingdom of heaven; MARRIAGES are made in heaven; MEET on the stairs and you won't meet in heaven; no COMING to heaven with dry eyes; ONE for sorrow, two for joy; three for a girl, four for a boy; five for silver, six for gold; seven for a secret, never to be told; eight for heaven, nine for hell; and ten for the devil's own self; ORDER is heaven's first law; a SHORT prayer reaches heaven; they that be in HELL ween there is no other heaven; the WAY to heaven is alike in every place; who SPITS against heaven it falls in his face.

heavy. a heavy purse makes a light heart (*English*) A rich man is a happy man. Alexander Barclay, *Eclogues*, *c.*1510. *See also* a LIGHT purse makes a heavy heart.

> A heavy purse makes a light heart. There
> 'tis exprest.
>
> Ben Jonson, *The New Inn*, 1631

~ *See also* LIGHT burdens far heavy; LIGHT gains make heavy purses; a LIGHT heeled mother makes a heavy heeled daughter; a LIGHT purse makes a heavy heart.

hedge. a hedge between keeps friendship green (*English*) Maintaining some privacy even from one's closest friends helps to keep relationships on a healthy footing. J. Mapletoft, *Select Proverbs*, 1707. *See also* GOOD fences make good neighbours; LOVE your neighbour, yet pull not down your hedge.

~ *See also* a LEAN dog to get through the hedge; LOVE your neighbour, yet pull not down your hedge; a LOW hedge is easily leaped over; MEN leap over where the hedge is lowest; ONE man may steal a horse, while another may not look over a hedge.

heed. take heed is a fair thing (*English*) It is always sensible to take care in going about something. Geoffrey Chaucer, *Troilus and Criseyde*, *c.*1385–90. Also encountered in the form 'take heed is good rede'.

> Take heede is a faire thing. Beware this blindnesse.
>
> John Heywood, *A Dialogue containing … the Proverbs in the English Tongue*, 1546

take heed of an ox before, of a horse behind, of a monk on all sides (*English*) There is danger in standing in front of an ox, behind a horse (or ass), and anywhere in the vicinity of a clergyman. George Herbert, *Outlandish Proverbs*, 1640.

take heed of reconciled enemies and of meat twice boiled (*English*) Do not trust former enemies when they claim to be friends once more. Geoffrey Chaucer, *c.*1386. Related proverbs include 'a reconciled friend is a double enemy'.

> Beware of meat twice boiled and an old foe
> reconcil'd.
>
> Benjamin Franklin, *Poor Richard's Almanack*, 1733

~ *See also* the MOON does not heed the barking of dogs; when you go to DANCE take heed who you take by the hand.

heel. *See* CLEAN heels, light meals; FOLLOW not truth too near the heels, lest it dash out thy teeth; ONE pair of heels is often worth two pairs of hands; a SPUR in the head is worth two in the heel.

heeled. *See* a LIGHT heeled mother makes a heavy heeled daughter.

heir. *See* LAND was never lost for want of an heir; WALNUTS and pears you plant for your heirs.

hell. from hell, Hull and Halifax, Good Lord deliver us (*English*) May we never find ourselves in hell, Hull or Halifax. A. Copley, *Wits, Fits, etc.*, 1594. Hull formerly had a reputation for strict government and harsh treatment of vagrants and beggars, while Halifax reputedly had its own notorious 'Gibbet Law', which made possible the summary execution of anyone found guilty of stealing cloth. It has been suggested that 'hell' was originally intended to signify Elland, another cloth-making town in the same area.

hell and Chancery are always open (*English*) Lawyers, like demons, are always ready to do mischief. Thomas Fuller, *Gnomologia*, 1732.

hell hath no fury like a woman scorned (*English*) A woman's anger is more to be feared than anything else on Earth. Beaumont and Fletcher, *The Knight of Malta*, 1625.

> Heav'n has no Rage, like Love to Hatred turn'd,
> Nor hell a Fury, like a Woman scorn'd.
>
> William Congreve, *The Mourning Bride*, 1697

they that be in hell ween there is no other heaven (*English*) People who have always lived in desperate conditions are unable to imagine a better life. John

Heywood, *A Dialogue containing ... the Proverbs in the English Tongue*, 1546. Equivalents in other languages include the Italian 'he who is in hell knows not what heaven is'.

~ *See also* ENGLAND is the paradise of women, the hell of horses and the purgatory of servants; he that would go to SEA for pleasure, would go to hell for a pastime; OLD maids lead apes in hell; ONE for sorrow, two for joy; three for a girl, four for a boy; five for silver, six for gold; seven for a secret, never to be told; eight for heaven, nine for hell; and ten for the devil's own self; the ROAD to hell is paved with good intentions; there are no FANS in hell; there is no REDEMPTION from hell; when WAR begins hell opens.

help. he helps little that helps not himself (*English*) Those who wish to help others should first help themselves. J. Sandford, *The Garden of Pleasure*, 1573.
help you to salt, help you to sorrow (*English*) At table, it is unlucky to pass the salt to another person. G. Torriano, *Italian Proverbs*, 1666.

> No one would at table spoon salt on to another person's plate, for 'Help you to salt, help you to sorrow'.
>
> Flora Thompson, *Lark Rise to Candleford*, 1945

~ *See also* ART helps nature, and experience art; EVENING red and morning grey help the traveller on his way; EVERY little helps; FORTUNE helps those who help themselves; GOD helps those who help themselves; GOD help the poor, for the rich can help themselves; he that is FALLEN cannot help him that is down; he that will not be COUNSELLED cannot be helped; a MOUSE may help a lion; MUSIC helps not the toothache; SLOW help is no help; THREE helping one another bear the burthen of six; TWO things a man should never be angry at: what he can help and what he cannot help; we must not LIE down and cry God help us; where GOD will help, nothing does harm.

hempe. when hempe is spun, England is done (*English*) When the reigns of Henry, Edward, Mary, Philip and Elizabeth (whose initials make up the word 'hempe') come to an end England will fall. Francis Bacon, *Essays*, 1625.

hen. if the hen does not prate, she will not lay (*Italian*) Scolding women make the best housewives. G. Torriano, *Select Italian Proverbs*, 1642. Proverbs on a similar theme include 'it is not the hen that cackles most which lays most eggs' and 'it is no good hen that cackles in your house and lays in another's'.

> If you would have a Hen lay, you must bear with her cackling.
>
> Thomas Fuller, *Gnomologia*, 1732

~ *See also* GRAIN by grain the hen fills her belly; he that would have EGGS must endure the cackling of hens; if the COCK moult before the hen we shall have weather thick and thin, but if the hen moult before the cock we shall have weather hard as a block; it is a SAD house where the hen crows louder than the cock; NEVER offer your hen for sale on a rainy day; the ROBIN and the wren are God's cock and hen; a WHISTLING woman and a crowing hen are neither fit for God nor men.

herb. no herb will cure love (*Roman*) There is no medicine that will relieve the symptoms of love. Geoffrey Chaucer, *The Legend of Good Women*, *c.*1385.

~ *See also* BETTER a dinner of herbs than a stalled ox where hate is.

Hercules. not even Hercules could contend against two (*Greek*) Even the strongest must yield to superior odds. R. Taverner, *Proverbs or Adages with New Additions, gathered out of the Chiliades of Erasmus*, 1539. Sometimes encountered in the abbreviated form 'not Hercules against two'.

> But Hercules himself must yield to odds.
>
> William Shakespeare, *Henry VI, Part 3*, 1590–1

heresy. *See* TURKEY, heresy, hops and beer came into England all in one year.

hero. *See* no MAN is a hero to his valet.

herring. *See* EVERY herring must hang by its own gill.

hesitate. he who hesitates is lost (*English*) In certain circumstances the taking of an immediate decision is of paramount importance. Joseph Addison, *Cato*, 1713. Equivalents in other languages include the Greek proverb 'the gods hate those who hesitate'.

> It has often been said of woman that she who

doubts is lost ... never thinking whether or no there be any truth in the proverb.

Anthony Trollope, *Can You Forgive Her?*, 1865

hew. he that hews too high may get a chip in his eye (*English*) Those who are over-ambitious risk harming their own interests (sometimes quoted in reference to those who marry above their social rank). John Gower, *Confessio Amantis*, *c.*1390. Also found in the forms 'he that climbs too high may get a chip in his eye' and 'he that looks too high may get a chip in his eye'.

hide. don't hide your light under a bushel (*Hebrew*) Don't conceal your talents or good qualities from others. Edward Lytton, *Kenelm*, 1873 (based on a passage in the Bible, Matthew 5:15). 'Bushel' in this case signifies the wooden or earthenware vessel that was formerly used for the purposes of measurement.

Neither do men lyght a candell, and put it under a busshell, but on a candlestick, and it lighteth all them which are in the house.

William Tyndale, Bible, Matthew 5:15, 1526–34

hide nothing from thy minister, physician and lawyer (*English*) It is foolish to keep anything secret from those who may influence your spiritual, corporeal or legal state. John Florio, *First Fruites*, 1578.

To friend, lawyer, doctor, tell plain your whole case;
Nor think on bad matters to put a good face.

Benjamin Franklin, *Poor Richard's Almanack*, 1748

those who hide can find (*English*) Those who hide things are the most likely to be able to find them again. *Seven Sages of Rome*, *c.*1400. Also found in the form 'hiders are good finders'.

~ *See also* the BAIT hides the hook; CATS hide their claws; if the DOCTOR cures, the sun sees it, but if he kills, the earth hides it; LOVE and a cough cannot be hid.

high. a high building, a low foundation (*English*) Tall buildings (and other ambitious enterprises) require deep foundations (or good preparation). W. Camden, *Remains concerning Britain*, 1623.

the higher the monkey climbs the more he shows his tail (*Hebrew*) The more a person enjoys advancement the more his weaknesses reveal themselves. John Wycliffe, Bible, Proverbs 3:35, *c.*1395.

The higher you climb, the more you shew your A—. Verified in no instance more than in Dulness aspiring. Emblematized also by an Ape climbing and exposing his posteriors.

Alexander Pope, *Dunciad*, 1743

the higher the tree, the sweeter the plum (*English*) The best fruit comes from the top of the tree. J. Howell, *Paroemiographia*, 1659. A fuller version of the proverb runs 'the higher the tree, the sweeter the plum, the better the shoe, the blacker the thumb'. Variants include 'the higher the plum tree, the riper the plum, the richer the cobbler, the blacker his thumb'.

the highest flood has the lowest ebb (*English*) Extreme events are accompanied by equally extreme lulls or reversals. Wright, *Songs*, *c.*1555.

high places have their precipices (*English*) Those who occupy the most senior positions have the furthest to fall when things go wrong. Thomas Fuller, *Gnomologia*, 1732. Variants on the theme include 'the higher standing, the lower fall'. Another proverb observes 'high regions are never without storms'. *See also* HIGH winds blow on high hills.

high winds blow on high hills (*Roman*) Those who occupy the highest positions must expect to be exposed to the greatest pressures. *Ancrene Riwle*, *c.*1225 (quoting Horace). *See also* HIGH places have their precipices.

~ *See also* he that HEWS too high may get a chip in his eye; he will SHOOT higher who shoots at the moon than he who aims at a tree; LOOK high and fall low; when BALE is highest, boot is nighest.

highway. the highway is never about (*English*) The main road is often a more direct route than any other. J. Chamberlain, *Letters*, 1623. Variants include 'he that leaves the highway to cut short commonly goes about'.

~ *See also* TRASH and trumpery is the highway to beggary.

hill. do on the hill as you would do in the hall (*English*) Always behave well, regardless of your surroundings. Alexander Barclay, *The Ship of Fools*, 1509.

Accustom yourself to act with discretion and good manners at all times.

James Kelly, *A Complete Collection of Scotish Proverbs*, 1721

~ *See* BLUE are the hills that are far away; FOG on the

hill, water to the mill; fog in the hollow, fine day to follow; he that comes FIRST to the hill may sit where he will; he that STAYS in the valley shall never get over the hill; HIGH winds blow on high hills; MIST from the hill brings water to the mill; when the CLOUDS go up the hills, they'll come down by the mills.

hind. *See* BEWARE of the forepart of a woman, the hind part of a mule and all sides of a priest.

hinder. *See* MEAT and mass never hindered man; WORK today for you know not how much you may be hindered tomorrow.

hindmost. *See* EVERY man for himself and the devil take the hindmost.

hip. *See* MANY hips and haws, many frosts and snaws.

hire. he who hires the horse must ride before (*English*) A person who pays for something is entitled to enjoy it to the full, before all others. J. Clarke, *Paroemiographia Anglo-Latina*, 1639.

~ *See also* the LABOURER is worthy of his hire.

history. history repeats itself (*English*) History goes in cycles. George Eliot, *Scenes of Clerical Life*, 1858.

> History, we know, is apt to repeat itself.
> George Eliot, *Scenes of Clerical Life*, 1858

~ *See also* HAPPY is the country which has no history.

hit. *See* a BLOT is not blot unless it be hit; he that ONCE hits will be ever shooting; he that SHOOTS oft shall at last hit the mark.

hither. *See* when a COUPLE are newly married the first month is honeymoon, or smick smack; the second is hither and thither; the third is thwick thwack; the fourth the devil take them that brought thee and I together.

hobby-horse. *See* EVERY man has his hobby-horse.

hog. a hog that's bemired endeavours to bemire others (*English*) Those whose reputations are besmirched get their revenge by besmirching others. Thomas Fuller, *Gnomologia*, 1732.

~ *See also* the CAT, the Rat and Lovell our Dog rule all England under an Hog; it is ILL to drive black hogs in the dark.

hoist. hoist your sail when the wind is fair (*English*) Embark on new enterprises when conditions are ideal. B. Melbancke, *Philotimus*, 1583. *See also* make HAY while the sun shines; STRIKE while the iron is hot.

> A man should strike while the iron is hot, and hoist sail while the wind is fair.
> Walter Scott, *The Fortunes of Nigel*, 1822

~ *See also* if the RAIN comes before the wind, lower your topsails and take them in; if the wind comes before the rain, lower your topsails and hoist them again.

hold. what you have, hold (*English*) Defend what is yours, rather than yearn for what belongs to others. *Towneley Play of the Killing of Abel*, *c.*1450. Variants include 'hold fast when you have it'. Another proverb warns 'he that will have all, loseth all'.

> It is better hold that I have then go from doore to doore and crave.
> *Towneley Play of the Killing of Abel*, *c.*1450

who holds his peace and gathers stones will find a time to throw them (*English*) Those who bide their time to take their revenge will eventually identify an ideal opportunity to get their own back. A.T. Quiller-Couch, *Hetty Wesley*, 1903.

~ *See also* BETTER to hang than to hold; he cannot SPEAK well that cannot hold his tongue; he that goes to LAW holds a wolf by the ears; he that KNOWS not how to hold his tongue, knows not how to talk; he that WORST may shall hold the candle; if on the TREES the leaves still hold, the coming winter will be cold; no LOCK will hold against the power of gold.

Holdfast. *See* BRAG is a good dog, but Holdfast is better.

hole. the hole calls the thief (*English*) Thieves and other ill-doers are drawn to the opportunity to enrich themselves. George Herbert, *Outlandish Proverbs*, 1640.

~ *See also* an ANT hole may collapse an embankment; BETTER a clout than a hole out; the FOX preys furthest from his hole; he who PEEPS through a hole may see what will vex him; KEEP yourself from the anger of a great man, from the tumult of a mob, from a man of ill fame, from a widow that has been thrice married, from a wind that comes in at a hole, and from a reconciled enemy; the MOUSE that has only one hole is easily taken.

hollow. *See* FOG on the hill, water to the mill; fog in the hollow, fine day to follow.

home. home is home, as the devil said when he found himself in the Court of Session (*Scottish*) The law is crooked and unjust, and thus a natural home for the devil. W. Motherwell, quoted in A. Henderson, *Scottish Proverbs*, 1832. The Scottish Court of Session, founded in 1532, is the senior civil tribunal in Scotland.
home is home, though it be never so homely (*English*) A person always feels most relaxed in his or her own home, no matter how humble it may be. John Heywood, *A Dialogue containing ... the Proverbs in the English Tongue*, 1546. According to a Spanish proverb, 'home, my own home, tiny though thou be, to me thou seemest an abbey'. Italian tradition provides 'to every bird its nest is fair'.

> The saying is, that home is home, be it never so homely.
> Charles Dickens, *Dombey and Son*, 1848

home is where the heart is (*Roman*) The emotions of most people are rooted in their homes, no matter how widely they might travel from it. J.J. McCloskey, 1870, quoted in Goldberg and Heffner, *Davy Crockett and Other Plays*, 1940 (also recorded in various forms as far back as Pliny, who may have coined it). Variants include the Greek 'home is dear, home is best' and 'home is where you hang your hat' (a proverb of more recent US origin).
home, sweet home (*English*) The greatest contentment and solace is to be found at home (often quoted on returning home after a hard day). John Howard Payne, 'Home, Sweet Home', 1823. The proverb was a favourite subject for needlework samplers in the nineteenth century, when the US-born lyricist John Howard Payne's rather sentimental song, set to the music of Sir Henry Bishop, was hugely popular on both sides of the Atlantic. Payne may well have derived his inspiration from a variety of earlier proverbial phrases along similar lines, including 'home is home, though it be never so homely' and 'for home though homely twere, yet it is sweet', a line from an English translation of Ariosto's *Orlando Furioso*, 1591.
~ *See also* ALTHOUGH the sun shine, leave not thy cloak at home; an ARGUS abroad but a mole at home; CHARITY begins at home; CURSES, like chickens, come home to roost; the DEVIL is at home; DRY bread at home is better than roast meat abroad; EAST, west, home's best; an ENGLISHMAN's home is his castle; the EVENING brings all home; EVERY dog is a lion at home; go ABROAD and you'll hear news of home; he who would BRING home the wealth of the Indies must carry the wealth of the Indies with him; it is a SHAME to steal but a worse to carry home; the LONGEST way round is the shortest way home; MANY go out for wool and come home shorn; SELDOM comes a loan laughing home; there's no PLACE like home; what CHILDREN hear at home soon flies abroad; a WOMAN's place is in the home.

homely. *See* HOME is home, though it be never so homely.

Homer. even Homer sometimes nods (*Greek*) Even the great have their lapses. Horace, *De Arte Poetica*, *c.*20BC. *See also* to ERR is human, to forgive divine; it is a GOOD horse that never stumbles.

> I think it shame when the worthy Homer nods; but in so long a work it is allowable if drowsiness comes on.
> Horace, *De Arte Poetica*, *c.*20BC

honest. an honest look covereth many faults (*Italian*) An honest appearance can conceal all manner of sins. G. Torriano, *Select Italian Proverbs*, 1642. Also found in the form 'an honest good look covereth many faults'. Another proverb warning against reliance upon honest appearances cautions that there is 'nobody so like an honest man as an arrant knave'.
honest men marry quickly, wise men not at all (*English*) Good men see no threat in marriage and enter into it willingly, but wise men know better and remain single. James Howell, *Epistolae Ho-Elianae; or Familiar Letters*, 1645–55.
you cannot make people honest by Act of Parliament (*English*) It is impossible to persuade a person to be honest unless they choose to be so themselves. Ben Jonson, *The Devil is an Ass*, 1631. Also encountered with the word 'sober' replacing 'honest'.

> If he were to be made honest by an act of parliament, I should not alter in my faith of him.
> Ben Jonson, *The Devil is an Ass*, 1631

~ *See also* EVERY honest miller has a thumb of gold; when THIEVES fall out honest men come by their own.

honesty. honesty is the best policy (*Greek*) The wise man chooses to be honest in all his dealings. Edwin Sandys, *Europae Speculum*, 1599. The proverb is common to several European languages and was quoted by Cervantes in *Don Quixote* in 1615. Another English proverb supports the main contention, with a minor proviso: 'knavery may serve for a turn, but honesty is best at long run.' An Italian proverb, meanwhile, concludes that although honesty may be the best policy 'there is always less money, less wisdom, and less honesty than people imagine'.

> My policy was chosen from the proverb, Random;
> I thought honesty the best.
> George Colman the Younger, *Ways and Means*, 1788

~ *See also* BEAUTY and honesty seldom agree.

honey. honey catches more flies than vinegar (*English*) A kindly, soft-voiced approach is likely to get better results than aggression. G. Torriano, *Italian Proverbs*, 1666. Along similar lines is the proverb 'cover yourself with honey and the flies will eat you'.

> Tart Words make no Friends: spoonful of honey
> will catch more flies than Gallon of Vinegar.
> Benjamin Franklin, *Poor Richard's Almanack*, 1744

honey is dear bought if licked off thorns (*English*) Something desirable may come at such a cost as to make it not worth having. *Old English Homilies*, *c.*1175. Equivalent proverbs include 'honey is sweet, but the bee stings' and 'no honey without gall'.

> He that licks honey from a nettle pays too dear for it.
> Thomas Fuller, *Gnomologia*, 1732

~ *See also* BEES that have honey in their mouths have stings in their tails; a DEAD bee will make no honey; it is not with SAYING honey, honey, that sweetness will come into the mouth; OLD bees yield no honey; where the BEE sucks honey the spider sucks poison.

honeymoon. *See* when a COUPLE are newly married the first month is honeymoon, or smick smack; the second is hither and thither; the third is thwick thwack; the fourth the devil take them that brought thee and I together.

honour (noun). **honour and ease are seldom bedfellows** (*English*) Those who seek to live honourably will often encounter moral dilemmas along the way. J. Clarke, *Paroemiologia Anglo-Latina*, 1639. Variants include 'honour and profit lie not in one sack'.

honour buys no beef (*English*) A good reputation does not in itself bring any tangible benefit. Thomas Shadwell, *The Sullen Lover*, 1668. Also encountered in the form 'honour buys no beef in the market'. Other equivalents include 'honour without profit is a ring on the finger'. *See also* VIRTUE is its own reward.

> I am not ambitious of that. As the excellent
> proverb says, 'Honour will buy no beef'.
> Thomas Shadwell, *The Sullen Lover*, 1668

honours change manners (*Roman*) Those who receive honours and accolades are all too prone to adopt a superior, arrogant attitude to others around them. John Lydgate, *Chaucer*, *c.*1430. Variants include the Scottish 'lordships change manners'.

> How I have offended the Lord of Lindesay I know
> not, unless honours have changed manners.
> Walter Scott, *The Abbot*, 1820

there is honour among thieves (*English*) Criminals observe their own code of honour between themselves. P.A. Motteux, *Don Quixote*, 1703 (much the same sentiment was expressed in classical times by Cicero and Publilius Syrus among others). *See also* DOG does not eat dog; HAWKS will not pick out hawks' eyes.

> A plague on it when thieves cannot be true one
> to another.
> William Shakespeare, *Henry IV, Part 1*, *c.*1597

~ *See also* he that DESIRES honour is not worthy; the MORE cost, the more honour; the MORE danger, the more honour; the POST of honour is the post of danger; a PROPHET is not without honour save in his own country.

honour (verb). *See* a FAIR death honours the whole life.

hood. *See* NEW beer, new bread and green wood will make a man's hair grow through his hood.

hoof. *See* EVERY devil has not a cloven hoof; THREE things are not to be trusted: a cow's horn, a dog's tooth and a horse's hoof.

hook. a hook is well lost to catch a salmon (*English*) Sometimes it is desirable to accept a small sacrifice in order to gain a much greater prize. T. Draxe, *Bibliotheca Scholastica*, 1633.

~ *See also* the BAIT hides the hook.

hope. hope and have (*English*) If a person hopes for something strongly enough the chances are they will eventually achieve it. *The Bugbears*, c.1566. Also encountered in the form 'hope well and have well'. Contrasting proverbs, however, warn that 'too much hope deceiveth' and 'hope often deludes the foolish man'.

> Spee well, and have well … That is, hope and expect good things, and it will fall out accordingly.
> James Kelly, *A Complete Collection of Scotish Proverbs*, 1721

hope deferred makes the heart sick (*Hebrew*) The postponement of expected benefit is singularly galling. John Wycliffe, Bible, Proverbs 13:13.

> And felt what kind of sickness of the heart it was which arises from hope deferred.
> Laurence Sterne, *A Sentimental Journey*, 1768

hope for the best and prepare for the worst (*English*) It is good policy to strive for the best possible outcome, but at the same time to guard against things going awry. Norton and Sackville, *Gorboduc*, 1565.

> It's best to hope the best, though of the worst affrayd.
> Edmund Spenser, *The Faerie Queene*, 1590

hope is a good breakfast but a bad supper (*English*) Hope at the beginning of an enterprise is fine, but it is less healthy if only hope is left at the end. W. Rawley, *Resuscitatio*, 1661. Related proverbs include 'he that lives on hope will die fasting' and 'hope is the poor man's bread'.

hope springs eternal in the human breast (*English*) Mankind is incurably optimistic, however bad things might get. Alexander Pope, *Essay on Man*, 1732. *See also* EVERY cloud has a silver lining; the DARKEST hour is just before the dawn; never SAY die; TOMORROW is another day.

> Hope springs eternal in the human breast:
> Man never is, but always to be, blest.
> The soul, uneasy and confin'd from home,
> Rests and expatiates in a life to come.
> Alexander Pope, *Essay on Man*, 1732

if it were not for hope, the heart would break (*English*) When everything else goes wrong, hope alone staves off despair. *Ancrene Wisse*, 1250. Related proverbs include 'he that wants hope is the poorest man alive' and 'he that hopes not for good, fears not evil'.

> No harm in hoping, Jack! My uncle says, Were it not for hope, the heart would break.
> Samuel Richardson, *Clarissa*, 1748

~ *See also* he that LIVES in hope dances to an ill tune; the HORSES of hope gallop, but the asses of experience go slowly; NEVER quit certainty for hope; where there's LIFE there's hope.

hopefully. *See* it is BETTER to travel hopefully than to arrive.

hops. *See* PLENTY of ladybirds, plenty of hops; TURKEY, heresy, hops and beer came into England all in one year.

horn. horns and grey hairs do not come by years (*English*) It is not time alone that makes men cuckolds or gives them grey hair. John Ray, *A Collection of English Proverbs*, 1678.

~ *See also* BUTTER is once a year in the cow's horn; a CURST cow has short horns; FRIDAY's hair and Sunday's horn go to the devil on Monday morn; he that BLOWS best bears away the horn; THREE things are not to be trusted: a cow's horn, a dog's tooth and a horse's hoof; TRAMP on a snail and she'll shoot out her horns; up CORN, down horn.

horse. have a horse of your own and then you may borrow another's (*Welsh*) If you have a horse of your own, there is more chance that you will be able to persuade another person to lend you theirs. J. Howell, *Paroemiographia*, 1659. Related proverbs include 'a horse, a wife, and a sword may be shewed but not lent'.

horses for courses (*English*) Some personalities are better suited to particular enterprises, situations, interests and so on, than others. A.E.T. Watson, *Turf*, 1891. The saying is derived from the world of horse-racing, and it refers to the fact that different courses suit particular mounts. *See also* there is no ACCOUNTING for tastes.

the horses of hope gallop, but the asses of experience go slowly (*Russian*) One's hopes may run on unchecked, but the person who knows better from past experience will exercise caution.

~ *See also* ALL lay loads on a willing horse; a BOISTEROUS horse must have a rough bridle; a BONNY bride is soon buskit and a short horse is soon wispit; CHOOSE a horse made and a wife to make; a COLT you may break, but an old horse you never can; do not HANG all your bells upon one horse; don't CHANGE horses in midstream; don't put the CART before the horse; ENGLAND is the paradise of women, the hell of horses and the purgatory of servants; a GOOD horse cannot be of a bad colour; the GREY mare is the better horse; he that hath a WHITE horse and a fair wife is never without trouble; he who HIRES the horse must ride before; if TWO ride on a horse, one must ride behind; if WISHES were horses, beggars would ride; if you can't RIDE two horses at once, you shouldn't be in the circus; it is a GOOD horse that never stumbles; it is a PROUD horse that will not bear his own provender; it is too LATE to shut the stable door after the horse has bolted; a JADE eats as much as a good horse; LEND not horse, nor wife, nor sword; the MAN who is born in a stable is a horse; a MAN without religion is like a horse without a bridle; the MASTER's eye maketh the horse fat; METTLE is dangerous in a blind horse; NEVER look a gift horse in the mouth; a NOD is as good as a wink to a blind horse; ONE man may steal a horse, while another may not look over a hedge; ONE thing thinketh the horse, and another he that saddles him; a RAGGED colt may make a good horse; SET the saddle on the right horse; a SHORT horse is soon curried; take HEED of an ox before, of a horse behind, of a monk on all sides; there is NOTHING so good for the inside of a man as the outside of a horse; THREE things are not to be trusted: a cow's horn, a dog's tooth and a horse's hoof; a WILLOW will buy a horse before an oak will pay for a saddle; you can LEAD a horse to water, but you can't make him drink; you may BREAK a horse' back, be he never so strong.

horseback. *See* AGUES come on horseback but go away on foot; SET a beggar on horseback, and he'll ride to the devil; SICKNESS comes on horseback, but goeth away on foot.

horseman. *See* BEHIND the horseman sits black care.

hostage. *See* he that hath a WIFE and children hath given hostages to fortune.

hostess. *See* the FAIRER the hostess, the fouler the reckoning.

hot. hot love is soon cold (*English*) Over-passionate love soon dies. R. Whitford, *Werke for Householders*, 1537. Related proverbs include 'hot love, hasty vengeance'.

> I hope that such hot love cannot be so soone colde.
> John Lyly, *Euphues: The Anatomy of Wit*, 1578

hot sup, hot swallow (*English*) It is best to have a hot drink with hot food (rather than a cold drink with hot food). J. Clarke, *Paroemiologia Anglo-Latina*, 1639.

~ *See also* the DEVIL to pay and no pitch hot; an ENGLISH summer, three hot days and a thunderstorm; HASTY love is soon hot and soon cold; in the COLDEST flint there is hot fire; LAD's love's a busk of broom, hot awhile and soon done; a LITTLE pot is soon hot; SOON hot, soon cold; STRIKE while the iron is hot.

hotly. *See* PUDDINGS and paramours should be hotly handled.

hound. *See* you cannot RUN with the hare and hunt with the hounds.

hour. an hour in the morning is worth two in the evening (*English*) Work is best done in the morning, when a person is fresh and willing. William Hone, *Every-day Book*, 1827. A variant of the proverb recommends an hour's work before breakfast, as this is worth two hours at any later time.

an hour may destroy what an age was a building (*English*) Something that takes a great deal of time to build up may be undone in just a moment. Thomas Fuller, *Gnomologia*, 1732. Variants include 'one hour's cold will spoil seven years' warming'.

an hour of pain is as long as a day of pleasure (*English*) Time seems to pass much slower for those who are suffering than it does for those who are enjoying themselves. Thomas Fuller, *Gnomologia*, 1732.

there is but an hour in a day between a good housewife and a bad (*English*) It only takes an hour a day for a conscientious housekeeper to keep things in good order. William Hone, *Every-day Book*, 1827.

~ *See also* the DARKEST hour is just before the dawn; HALF an hour is soon lost at dinner; it CHANCETH in an hour that happeneth not in seven years; LOSE an hour in the morning, chase it all day; ONE hour's sleep before midnight is worth two after; PUT off the evil hour as long as you can; SIX hours' sleep for a man, seven for a woman and eight for a fool; there are only TWENTY-FOUR hours in the day.

house. a house divided against itself cannot stand (*Hebrew*) Internal dissension will quickly result in the disintegration of any organization or enterprise. Bible, Mark 3:23–26 (also found in the fables of Aesop). *See also* DIVIDE and rule; UNITED we stand, divided we fall.

> How can Satan cast out Satan? And if a kingdom be divided against itself, that kingdom cannot stand. And if a house be divided against itself, that house cannot stand. And if Satan rise up against himself, and be divided, he cannot stand, but hath an end.
> Mark 3:23–26.

the house shows the owner (*English*) The character of a householder is reflected in the kind of house he or she lives in. Randle Cotgrave, *A Dictionary of the French and English Tongues*, 1611.

~ *See also* the BACK door robs the house; BETTER one house spoiled than two; BURN not your house to fright away the mice; by the STREET of by and by one arrives at the house of never; CHOOSE not a house near an inn or in a corner; COMMEND not your wife, wine, nor house; FOOLS build houses, and wise men live in them; he who REPAIRS not his gutter repairs his whole house; in the ANTS' house the dew is a flood; it is a SAD house where the hen crows louder than the cock; it is ILL talking of a halter in the house of a man that was hanged; a LAMB in the house, a lion in the field; LAWYERS' houses are built on the heads of fools; LEARNING is better than house and land; a LITTLE house well filled, a little land well tilled, and a little wife well willed; LOOK to thyself when thy neighbour's house is on fire; an OLD man in a house is a good sign; PEOPLE who live in glass houses shouldn't throw stones; THREE things drive a man out of his house: smoke, rain and a scolding wife; TWO fools in a house are too many.

house-going. a house-going parson makes a church-going people (*English*) A priest who visits his parishioners will be rewarded by more of his parishioners visiting his church. *British Weekly*, 2 January 1913.

household. *See* a GENTLE housewife mars the household; WOEFUL is the household that wants a woman.

housekeeper. *See* FAT housekeepers make lean executors.

house-top. *See* RAIN on the green grass, and rain on the tree, and rain on the house-top, but not upon me.

housewife. *See* a GENTLE housewife mars the household; there is but an HOUR in a day between a good housewife and a bad.

however. *See* however BIG the whale may be, the tiny harpoon can rob him of life.

howl. one must howl with the wolves (*English*) It is good policy to go along with the prevailing opinion of the majority. Arthur Conan Doyle, *Uncle Bernac*, 1897.

> Napoleon's power is far too great to be shaken. This being so, I have tried to serve him, for it is well to howl when you are among wolves.
> Arthur Conan Doyle, *Uncle Bernac*, 1897

~ *See also* who KEEPS company with the wolf will learn how to howl.

hue. *See* BLACK will take no other hue.

Hull. *See* from HELL, Hull and Halifax, good Lord deliver us; OXFORD for learning, London for wit, Hull for women, and York for a tit.

human. *See* HOPE springs eternal in the human breast; to ERR is human, to forgive divine.

humble hearts have humble desires (*English*) Timid, retiring people tend to have relatively modest ambitions. George Herbert, *Outlandish Proverbs*, 1640.

humble-bee. a humble-bee in a cow-turd thinks himself a king (*English*) A person may feel proud of themselves even in the most humble of circumstances. J. Howell, *Paroemiographia*, 1659.

hump. *See* the HUNCHBACK does not see his own hump, but sees his companion's.

hunchback. the hunchback does not see his own hump, but sees his companion's (*English*) People are much better at seeing faults in others than they are at seeing failings in themselves. Robert Herrick, *Hesperides*. 1648.

hundred. a hundred pounds of sorrow pays not one ounce of debt (*English*) Remorse does nothing to repay one's financial obligations to others. George Herbert, *Outlandish Proverbs*, 1640. The version that Herbert quotes runs 'a hundred loade of thought will not pay one ounce of debts'. *See also* a POUND of care will not pay an ounce of debt.

~ *See also* the BUYER has need of a hundred eyes, the seller of but one; it will ALL be one in a hundred years' time; ONE father is more than a hundred schoolmasters.

hung. *See* HANG.

hunger. hunger and cold deliver a man up to his enemy (*Spanish*) Cold and lack of food undermine any man's ability to resist his enemies. John Ray, *A Collection of English Proverbs*, 1813.

hunger breaks through stone walls (*English*) Hunger will drive men to desperate measures, overwhelming any obstacles in the way. John Heywood, *A Dialogue containing ... the Proverbs in the English Tongue*, 1546.

> They said they were an-hungry; sigh'd forth
> proverbs: That hunger broke stone walls.
> William Shakespeare, *Coriolanus*, *c.*1608

hunger drives the wolf out of the wood (*Italian*) Necessity will force individuals out of their familiar home territory in search of new opportunities. William Caxton, *Cato*, 1483.

> This one ... I own is the child of necessity. Hunger,
> thou knowest, brings the wolf out of the wood.
> Tobias Smollett, *Gil Blas*, 1748

hunger is the best sauce (*Roman*) All food tastes good to a person who is very hungry. Cicero, *De Finibus*, first century BC. Related proverbs include 'hunger finds no fault with the cookery', 'hunger makes hard beans sweet', 'hunger is good kitchen meat' and 'hungry dogs will eat dirty puddings', which was quoted by Horace. A US equivalent runs 'hunger finds no fault with mouldy corn'.

> Nor do you Find fault with the sauce, keen hunger
> being the best.
> Philip Massinger, *Unnatural Combat*, 1639

they must hunger in frost that will not work in heat (*English*) Those who neglect their work in the summer will starve in winter because they have not laid up the reserves that they will need. John Heywood, *A Dialogue containing ... the Proverbs in the English Tongue*, 1550.

hungry. hungry bellies have no ears (*Roman*) Those who are obsessed by hunger will be deaf to reason. R. Taverner, *Proverbs or Adages with New Additions, gathered out of the Chiliades of Erasmus*, 1539 (quoting Cato the Elder). A Spanish version runs 'an empty stomach will not listen to anything'. Hunger does, however, aid a person's other senses according to the Scottish proverbs 'a hungry man smells meat afar off' and 'a hungry man sees far'. A Russian proverb remarks upon the insatiable character of the belly: 'the belly is ungrateful – it always forgets we already gave it something'.

> It is a hard thing to perswade the belly, because
> it has no ears.
> Izaak Walton, *The Compleat Angler*, 1653

hungry flies bite sore (*English*) Flies that are hungry have a fiercer bite than those that are full. John Heywood, *A Dialogue containing ... the Proverbs in the English Tongue*, 1546.

a hungry man is an angry man (*English*) Hunger makes men irascible and liable to fight. D. Fergusson, *Scottish Proverbs*, *c.*1641. A French variant on the same theme insists that 'a hungry wretch is half mad'.

hunt. *See* the DOG that is idle barks at his fleas, but he that is hunting feels them not; you cannot RUN with the hare and hunt with the hounds.

hurt. he that hurts another hurts himself (*English*) A person who harms another harms himself, as his conscience will give him no peace and his own reputation will be indelibly stained. John Florio, *First Fruites*, 1578.

~ *See also* he THREATENS many that hurts any; MALICE hurts itself most; no man is ANGRY that feels not himself hurt; STICKS and stones may break my bones, but names will never hurt me; what you don't KNOW can't hurt you.

husband. the husband is always the last to know (*English*) In cases of marital or other domestic discord it is always the husband (or alternatively the wife) who is the last to hear about it. John Marston, *What you Will*, 1604.

> 'It is with love as with cuckoldom' – the suffering party is at least the third, but generally the last who knows anything about the matter.
>
> Laurence Sterne, *Tristram Shandy*, 1756

husbands are in heaven whose wives scold not (*English*) Men whose wives do not scold them are much to be envied by those with nagging wives. John Heywood, *A Dialogue containing ... the Proverbs in the English Tongue*, 1546. Related proverbs include the Greek 'man's best possession is a sympathetic wife' (quoted by Euripides) and two sayings of US origin, 'a smoky chimney and a scolding wife are two bad companions' and 'a quiet wife is mighty pretty'. Another saying of US origin observes drily 'it's a sweet sorrow to bury a nagging wife'.

~ *See also* the CALMEST husbands make the stormiest wives; a DEAF husband and a blind wife are always a happy couple; a GOOD husband makes a good wife; a LEWD bachelor makes a jealous husband.

hussy. *See* a CARELESS hussy makes many thieves; CATS eat what hussies spare.

hypocrisy can find out a cloak for every rain (*English*) Hypocrites change their views according to the circumstances they find themselves in. *New Custom*, 1573.

I

I today, you tomorrow (*Roman*) You will soon suffer the fate I suffer now. Variants include 'Today it is my turn, tomorrow yours' and the Latin *Hodie mihi, cras tibi* or *Sors hodierna mihi cras erit illa tibi*, in which form it was scratched on a wall by Lady Jane Grey while she was imprisoned in the Tower of London shortly before her execution. Christopher Marlowe, *The Jew of Malta*, *c.*1592.

ice. if the ice will bear a man before Christmas, it will not bear a duck after (*English*) If the ice is thick on the water at Christmas, it is unlikely to be strong enough to stand on in the weeks to follow. M.A. Denham, *A Collection of Proverbs ... relating to the Weather*, 1846. Also encountered in the form 'if the ice will bear a goose before Christmas, it will not bear a duck after' (and sometimes heard with a mouse replacing the duck). Variants include 'when November's ice will bear a duck winter will be all slush and muck'.

like ice, anger passes away (*Roman*) No one stays angry for long. Quoted in Ovid.

~ *See also* if at CHRISTMAS ice hangs on the willow, clover may be cut at Easter; INJURIES don't use to be written on ice; let EVERY man sweep the ice with his own broom; no one LIKES to be the first to step on the ice; the RICH man has his ice in the summer and the poor man gets his in the winter; TRUST not one night's ice.

idle. idle bairns are the devil's workhouses (*Scottish*) Children who have nothing better to do are bound to get up to mischief. Other Scottish proverbs along similar lines include 'idle dogs worry sheep'.

an idle brain is the devil's workshop (*English*) Those who have little to think about easily fall into bad ways. W. Perkins, *Works*, 1602. Variants on the same theme include 'an idle head is a box for the wind', 'an idle person is the devil's cushion' and 'the devil tempts all, but the idle man tempts the devil'. *See also* the DEVIL finds work for idle hands; IDLENESS is the root of all evil.

idle people have the least leisure (*English*) It is those with the most time on their hands who always seem to complain the most about not having enough time to do what they want to do. John Ray, *A Collection of English Proverbs*, 1678. Another proverb observes, 'idle people take the most pains'. *See also* the BUSIEST men have the most leisure.

> 'Got a great deal to do,' retorted Jog, who, like all thoroughly idle men, was always dreadfully busy.
> Robert Smith Surtees, *Sponge's Sporting Tour*, 1853

idle people lack no excuses (*English*) Lazy people always have excuses for not doing something. J. Withals, *A Short Dictionary in Latin and English*, 1616.

an idle youth, a needy age (*English*) Those who do not work hard in their youth will find they have nothing laid by to help them in old age. Randle Cotgrave, *A Dictionary of the French and English Tongues*, 1611. Other versions include 'be not idle and you shall not be longing'.

it is idle to swallow the cow and choke on the tail (*English*) Only a fool gives up on a job when most of the work has already been done. J. Howell, *Paroemiographia*, 1659.

~ *See also* the BUSY man has few idle visitors; the

DEVIL finds work for idle hands; the DOG that is idle barks at his fleas, but he that is hunting feels them not; he that is BUSY is tempted but by one devil, he that is idle by a legion.

idleness. idleness is the root of all evil (*English*) Those who have nothing to do are vulnerable to temptation. Geoffrey Chaucer, *The Canterbury Tales*, *c.*1387. Variants include 'idleness is the parent of all vice', 'of idleness comes no goodness', 'idleness is the key of beggary', 'idleness is the mother of poverty' and 'idleness must thank itself if it go barefoot'. *See also* the DEVIL finds work for idle hands; an IDLE brain is the devil's workshop; the LOVE of money is the root of all evil.

Idleness is the Root of all Evil; the World's wide enough, let 'em bustle.

George Farquhar, *The Beaux' Stratagem*, 1707

idleness turns the edge of wit (*English*) Sloth makes the mind dull and blunts a person's wits. Bodenham, *Belvedere*, 1600. Also encountered as 'idleness makes the wit rust' and 'idleness is the canker of the mind'.

Sloth tourneth the edge of wit, study sharpeneth the mind.

John Lyly, *Euphues: The Anatomy of Wit*, 1578

if. 'if' and 'an' spoils many a good charter (*English*) Many a good intention or plan comes to nothing because of the conditions that come with it. Sir Thomas More quoted much the same proverb *c.*1535: 'what quod the protectour thou servest me I wene with iffes and with andes'.

Then he came with his If's and And's.

Samuel Richardson, *Clarissa*, 1748

if ifs and ands were pots and pans, there'd be no work for tinkers' hands (*English*) Optimistic views of future possibilities must be tempered by a salutary reminder that these are dependent on other (probably unlikely) things happening first. Charles Kingsley, *Alton Locke*, 1850.

ignorance. ignorance is a voluntary misfortune (*English*) The ignorant have only themselves to blame for not paying more attention to getting a good education. *Politeuphuia*, 1597, attributed to J.Bodenham.

ignorance is bliss (*Roman*) Sometimes it is better not to know. Thomas Gray, 'Ode on a Distant Prospect of Eton College', 1742 (also found in various forms in the writings of Sophocles and Erasmus). Also encountered in its fuller form 'where ignorance is bliss, 'tis folly to be wise', a direct quotation from Gray's poem. Other proverbs on similar themes include 'ignorance is the peace of life' and the French 'ignorance and incuriosity are two very soft pillows'. An old Roman proverb runs 'what one knows it is sometimes useful to forget'. Among other diverse comments on the nature of ignorance are 'ignorance is the mother of devotion' and 'ignorance is the mother of impudence'. *See also* what the EYE does not see, the heart does not grieve over; KNOWLEDGE is power; he that KNOWS nothing, doubts nothing.

Thought would destroy their paradise.
No more; where ignorance is bliss,
'Tis folly to be wise.

Thomas Gray, 'Ode on a Distant Prospect of Eton College', 1742

ignorance is the mother of devotion (*English*) Devotion to someone or something is typically found in those who are ignorant of the real truth about their idol or other object of their admiration. Bishop Jewell, *Works*, 1202.

Your ignorance is the mother of your devotion to me.

John Dryden, *Secret Love*, 1668

ignorance is the mother of impudence (*Greek*) Ignorance often leads to arrogance and errors. Attributed to Socrates. Also found in the form 'ignorance breeds impudence'. Other proverbs expressing similar sentiments include the Hebrew 'ignorance and conceit go hand in hand' and the US 'ignorance is the womb of monsters'.

His ignorance is the mother of his impudence,
and the nurse of his obstinacy.

Charles Spurgeon, *John Ploughman's Talk*, 1869

ignorance of the law is no excuse (*English*) It is no defence to claim that one did not know that what one has done was illegal. Thomas Hoccleve, *The Regiment of Princes*, *c.*1412. This principle has been enshrined in a legal maxim, rendered in Latin as *ignorantia iuris neminem excusat*.

Ignorance of the Law excuses no man; not that all Men know the Law, but because 'tis an excuse every man will plead, and no man can tell how to confute him.

John Selden, *Table-Talk*, 1654

~ *See also* ADMIRATION is the daughter of ignorance; ART has no enemy but ignorance; it is BETTER to conceal one's knowledge than to reveal one's ignorance; WONDER is the daughter of ignorance.

ill. he can ill pipe that lacketh his upper lip (*English*) It is impossible to do something if you lack the necessary equipment, knowledge, funds and so forth. John Heywood, *A Dialogue containing ... the Proverbs in the English Tongue*, 1546.

he is an ill companion that has a good memory (*English*) No one likes a companion who remembers everything that is said or done when others are intoxicated or otherwise inclined to let slip things they would rather were forgotten. White Kennett, *Erasmus' Praise of Folly*, 1683.

he may ill run that cannot go (*English*) A person who cannot do an easy thing well is unlikely to succeed when he or she is faced with something much more difficult. John Heywood, *A Dialogue containing ... the Proverbs in the English Tongue*, 1546. Also found as 'ill run that cannot go'.

> In vain he attempts an uneasy task, who is not equal to an easy one.
>
> James Kelly, *A Complete Collection of Scotish Proverbs*, 1721

he that does you an ill turn will never forgive you (*English*) A person who causes harm to another will continue to harbour a grudge against their victim (inspired by a troubled conscience). James Kelly, *A Complete Collection of Scotish Proverbs*, 1721.

he that has an ill name is half hanged (*English*) Those with bad reputations are much more likely to be condemned when suspected of some crime. 1400, quoted in C. Brown, *Religious Lyrics of the XIVth Century*, 1957. *See also* GIVE a dog a bad name and hang him.

> Your hero makes laws to get rid of your thief, and gives him an ill name that he may hang him.
>
> Thomas Love Peacock, *Maid Marian*, 1822

he that hath done ill once will do it again (*English*) Those who have acted badly once are likely to do so again in the future. J. Mapletoft, *Select Proverbs*, 1707.

an ill agreement is better than a good judgement (*English*) There is more to be gained by reaching an out-of-court settlement with a rival, no matter how unsatisfactory, than there is by pursuing what may be a good case in law. George Herbert, *Outlandish Proverbs*, 1640.

an ill bird lays an ill egg (*English*) Bad things must be expected of bad people or organizations. G. Pettie, *Guazzo's Civil Conversation*, 1581. Equivalent proverbs include 'ill seed, ill weed'.

ill comes in by ells and goes out by inches (*English*) Misfortunes accumulate faster than they go. George Herbert, *Outlandish Proverbs*, 1640.

ill doers are ill dreaders (*Roman*) Those who do evil are often those who fear evil the most. Alexander Barclay, *The Ship of Fools*, 1509 (also quoted by Plautus). Also encountered in the form 'ill doers are ill deemers'. *See also* EVIL doers are evil dreaders.

> Put me not to quote the old saw, that evil doers are evil dreaders.
>
> Walter Scott, *The Fair Maid of Perth*, 1828

ill egging makes ill begging (*English*) Through enticement and flattery a person may be persuaded to act in an evil manner. William Camden, *Remains concerning Britain*, 1605.

ill luck is worse than found money (*English*) It is unlucky to keep money found by chance. Robert Greene, *The Art of Coney-Catching*, 1591.

an ill master makes an ill servant (*English*) Those who behave badly must expect their servants or employees to do likewise, following their example. G. Torriano, *Italian Proverbs*, 1666. Among related proverbs is 'an ill servant will never be a good master'.

an ill turn is soon done (*English*) It often takes little effort to cause harm. James Kelly, *A Complete Collection of Scottish Proverbs*, 1721.

ill weeds grow apace (*English/French*) Evil accumulates much faster than good (just as rank weeds grow faster than flowers and herbs). *c.*1470, quoted in *Anglia*, 1918.

> 'Ay,' quoth my uncle Gloucester, 'Small herbs have grace: great weeds do grow apace' ... I would not grow so fast, Because sweet flow'rs are slow and weeds make haste.
>
> William Shakespeare, *Richard III*, *c.*1592

ill will never said well (*English*) If a person feels resentment or other bad feeling towards another this is likely to colour any comments they make about them. *Roman de la Rose*, *c.*1400. Also found in the form 'evil will never said well.'

it is ill fishing before the net (*English*) It is foolish for a person to rely on something before they have got possession of it (just as it is unwise of a fisherman to count on catching anything before his nets have even been pulled in). Sir Philip Sidney, *First Arcadia*, 1590.

He that fishes afore the net, lang or he fish get.

David Fergusson, *Scottish Proverbs*, 1641

it is ill jesting with edged tools (*English*) It is unwise to fool with things that have the potential to cause great harm. Wager, *The Longer Thou Livest*, *c.*1568.

Sir Apish, jesting with matrimony is playing
with edged tools.

Henry Fielding, *Love in Several Masques*, 1728

it is ill sitting at Rome and striving with the Pope (*Scottish*) It is bad policy to pick arguments with someone or cause them some offence when you are at their mercy. J. Carmichaell, *Proverbs in Scots*, 1628.

it is ill talking of a halter in the house of a man that was hanged (*English*) It is tactless to discuss topics that are likely to cause offence in particular company. S. Palmer, *Moral Essays on Proverbs*, 1710.

Don't talk of a halter in the company of him
whose father was hanged.

S. Palmer, *Moral Essays on Proverbs*, 1710

it is ill to drive black hogs in the dark (*English*) It is bad policy to offer advice when you have an incomplete grasp of the facts. John Ray, *A Collection of English Proverbs*, 1678.

How can they advise, if they see but a part?
'Tis very ill driving black hogs in the dark.

Benjamin Franklin, *Poor Richard's Almanack*, July 1748

it's an ill bird that fouls its own nest (*English*) Those who commit some crime or act against their own fellows are particularly deserving of condemnation. *The Owl and the Nightingale*, 1250. Variants include 'it's a foul bird that defiles its own nest' and, on a slightly different tack, 'it's an ill bird that pecks out the dam's eyes'. *See also* there is HONOUR among thieves; the JAY bird don't rob his own nest.

An olde proverbe seyde ys in englyssh: men
seyn 'that brid or foule ys dyshonest, what that
he be and holden ful chirlyssh, that useth to
defoule his oone nest.

Thomas Hoccleve, *Minor Poems*, 1402

it's an ill dog that deserves not a crust (*Greek*) There is a spark of goodness in even the most evil persons, making them deserving of modest acts of kindness. John Ray, *A Collection of English Proverbs*, 1670.

it's an ill wind that blows nobody any good (*English*) It is rare indeed that someone somewhere does not enjoy benefit from even the worst of situations. John Heywood, *A Dialogue containing ... the Proverbs in the English Tongue*, 1546. The proverb is of nautical origins, referring to the fact that the wind that is blowing in the wrong direction for one ship is probably blowing another ship where it wants to go. *See also* every CLOUD has a silver lining.

Ill blows the wind that profits nobody.

William Shakespeare, *Henry VI, Part 3*, *c.*1591

it's ill healing of an old sore (*English*) Long-standing grievances are not easily reconciled. John Heywood, *A Dialogue containing ... the Proverbs in the English Tongue*, 1659.

it's ill putting a naked sword in a madman's hand (*English*) It is reckless to give a weapon of any kind to a person who is in a mood to use it. John Heywood, *A Dialogue containing ... the Proverbs in the English Tongue*, 1546.

it's ill speaking between a full man and a fasting (*Scottish*) There is little chance of two parties agreeing when one has what the other has not (specifically, when one has eaten and the other is hungry). D. Fergusson, *Scottish Proverbs*, 1641.

Ye maun eat and drink, Steenie ... for we do
little else here, and it's ill speaking between a
fou man a fasting.

Walter Scott, *Redgauntlet*, 1824

it's ill waiting for dead men's shoes (*English*) Those who hope to benefit through promotion and the like on the death of others may have a very long (and bitter) time to wait. J. Palsgrave, *L'Éclaircissement de la langue française*, 1530.

That's but sma' gear, puir thing; she had a sair
time o't with the auld leddy. But it's ill waiting
for dead folk's shoon.

Walter Scott, *Guy Mannering*, 1815

there were no ill language if it were not ill taken (*English*) Insults and bad language are significant only if they have an impact on those who hear them. George Herbert, *Outlandish Proverbs*, 1640.

~ *See also* the BARGAIN is ill made where neither party gains; the BEST remedy against an ill man is much ground between; BETTER untaught than ill taught; by doing NOTHING we learn to do ill; DISEASES are the price for ill pleasures; he that LIVES in hope dances to an ill tune; he that makes himself an ASS must not take it ill if men ride him; he that MARRIES late marries ill; he who DEPENDS on another dines ill and sups worse; KEEP yourself from the anger of a great man, from the tumult of a mob, from a man of ill fame, from a widow that has been thrice married, from a wind that comes in at a hole, and from a reconciled enemy; LEARNING makes a good man better and an ill man worse; MANY a one says well that thinks ill; NEVER speak ill of the dead; no FENCE against ill fortune; ONE ill word asketh another; out of the NORTH all ill comes forth; SAY no ill of the year till it be past; a SOW may whistle, though it has an ill mouth for it; they that THINK none ill are soonest beguiled; THREE ills come from the north: a cold wind, a shrinking cloth and a dissembling man; when CHILDREN stand still they have done some ill; who cometh LATE lodgeth ill; who UNDERSTANDS ill answers ill.

ill-gotten gains seldom prosper (*Greek*) Dishonestly acquired goods rarely bring any real benefit with them. Edmund Spenser, *Mother Hubbard's Tale*, 1591 (also quoted by Hesiod in *Opera et Dies* in the eighth century BC). Also found as 'ill-gotten goods thrive not' and 'ill-gotten goods thrive not to the third heir'. Equivalent proverbs include 'ill gotten, ill spent', which was quoted by Plautus and Cicero.

> Ill-gotten goods ne'er thrive; I played the thief,
> and now am robbed myself.
> Ben Jonson, *The Case is Altered*, 1609

imitation is the sincerest form of flattery (*English*) Attempts made to imitate someone or something should be accepted as a compliment. Charles Caleb Colton, *Lacon*, 1820. The proverb was usually originally encountered without the words 'form of'.

impossible. *See* the DIFFICULT we do at once, the impossible takes a little longer; NOTHING is impossible.

impression. *See* FIRST impressions are the most lasting.

impudence. *See* IGNORANCE is the mother of impudence.

inch. an inch is as good as a mile (*English*) It makes little difference in the long run whether a man is defeated by a narrow margin or a large one. John Heywood, *A Dialogue containing ... the Proverbs in the English Tongue*, 1546. The proverb was originally often rendered with 'yard' or 'ell' (about 45 inches, based on the length of a person's forearm) in the place of 'mile'. *See also* a MISS is as good as a mile.

> His great surprise was, that so small a pistol could
> kill so big a man ... an inch was as good as an ell.
> Walter Scott, *The Heart of Midlothian*, 1818

an inch of gold will not buy an inch of time (*Chinese*) Long life cannot be bought with money.

~ *See also* ILL comes in by ells and goes out by inches; MEN are not to be measured by inches.

incline. *See* as the TWIG is bent, so is the tree inclined.

inconvenience. *See* BETTER a mischief than an inconvenience; POVERTY is no disgrace, but it is a great inconvenience.

increase. *See* WINE and youth increase love.

index. *See* the FACE is the index of the mind; SPEECH is the index of the mind.

Indian. *See* the only GOOD Indian is a dead one.

Indies. *See* he who would BRING home the wealth of the Indies must carry the wealth of the Indies with him.

indispensable. *See* no MAN is indispensable.

industry is fortune's right hand, and frugality her left (*English*) Hard work and thrift will be rewarded. *Havelok the Dane*, *c.*1300.

> ... a proverb which has been worth ten times
> more to me than all my little purse contained.
> Maria Edgeworth, *Popular Tales*, 1799

infallible. *See* no MAN is infallible.

infect. *See* ONE scabbed sheep infects the whole flock.

infinite. *See* GENIUS is an infinite capacity for taking pains.

ingratiating. *See* ARTFUL speech and an ingratiating demeanour rarely accompany virtue.

inheritance. *See* BEAUTY is no inheritance; SERVICE is no inheritance.

injure. *See* the ROTTEN apple injures its neighbours.

injury. injuries don't use to be written on ice (*English*) Bad deeds done by others are not quickly forgotten. Thomas Fuller, *Gnomologia*, 1732. Variations on the theme include 'injuries are written in brass', the Greek 'injuries may be forgiven, but not forgotten' and the Zulu 'the injured never forgets; it is the offender who forgets'.

~ *See also* CONTEMPT will sooner kill an injury than revenge; NEGLECT will kill an injury sooner than revenge.

inn. *See* CHOOSE not a house near an inn or in a corner; he goes not out of his WAY that goes to a good inn; a MAN knows his companion in a long journey and a little inn.

innocent. *See* EVERYONE is innocent until proved guilty.

insatiable. *See* THREE things are insatiable: priests, monks and the sea.

inscription. *See* EACH cross hath its inscription.

inside. *See* there is NOTHING so good for the inside of a man as the outside of a horse.

inspiration. *See* NINETY per cent of inspiration is perspiration.

intention. *See* the ROAD to hell is paved with good intentions.

interest will not lie (*English*) Interest in something will persuade a person to do what he or she would not otherwise venture to do. John Bunyan, *Work of Jesus Christ*, 1688.

> Our English proverb is, Interest will not lie; interest will make a man do that which otherwise he would not do.
>
> John Bunyan, *Work of Jesus Christ*, 1688

invention. *See* NECESSITY is the mother of invention.

invite. *See* a BAD padlock invites a picklock.

Ireland. *See* ENGLAND's difficulty is Ireland's opportunity.

Irishman. put an Irishman on the spit and you can always get another Irishman to baste him (*English/Irish*) The Irish population has always been riven by political and other differences and an Irishman will jump at the opportunity to harm an opponent, regardless of their shared nationality. George Bernard Shaw, *John Bull's Other Island*, 1907.

iron. he must have iron nails that scratches a bear (*English*) Those who challenge those who wield great power must have the means to protect themselves from retaliation. John Ray, *A Collection of English Proverbs*, 1678.

iron not used soon rusts (*English*) A tool, or a person's brain, that is not used regularly will soon decay. Variants include 'iron with use grows bright' and 'drawn wells are seldom dry'. *See also* a USED key is always bright.

~ *See also* MANY irons in the fire, some must cool; STRIKE while the iron is hot; we must not LOOK for a golden life in an iron cage.

island. *See* in SETTLING an island, the first building erected by a Spaniard will be a church; by a Frenchman, a fort; by a Dutchman, a warehouse; and by an Englishman, an alehouse.

Italians are wise before the deed, the Germans in the deed, the French after the deed (*English*) Italians think before acting, while Germans think as they act and the French act before they think. George Herbert, *Outlandish Proverbs*, 1640.

itch and ease can no man please (*English*) A person who attempts to ease an itch by scratching it only ends up with a worse hurt. John Heywood, *A Dialogue containing … the Proverbs in the English Tongue*, 1546. A similar opinion is expressed in the proverb 'he that will not bear the itch must endure the smart', but rather the opposite is suggested in 'an itch is worse than a smart'.

J

Jack. Jack is as good as his master (*English*) All men are equal, although some be servants and others masters. J. Stevens, *Spanish and English Dictionary*, 1706.

> Is it the general opinion of seamen before the mast? Come, tell us. Jack's as good as his master in these matters.
>
> Charles Reade and Dion Boucicault, *Foul Play*, 1868

Jack of all trades is master of none (*English*) Those who claim mastery of a wide range of skills are unlikely in reality to be really adept at anything. Maria Edgeworth, *Popular Tales*, 1800. Also encountered in the form 'Jack of all trades is of no trade'. Equivalents in other languages include the French saying 'when one is good at everything, one is good at nothing' and the German proverb 'the master of one trade will support a wife and seven children: the master of seven trades will not support himself'.

> Old Lewis Baboon was a sort of Jack of all trades, which made the rest of the tradesmen jealous.
>
> John Arbuthnot, *John Bull*, 1712

Jack would be a gentleman if he could speak French (*English*) Mocking the pretensions of a person who aspires to being a member of the gentry (who in former times spoke French as the language of the English court). Similarly jocular variants include 'Jack would be a gentleman if he had money'.

~ *See also* ALL work and no play makes Jack a dull boy; EVERY Jack has his Jill; a GOOD Jack makes a good Jill.

jade. a jade eats as much as a good horse (*English*) It costs just as much to keep a poor quality horse (or by extension, a wife or similar) as it does to keep a good one. George Herbert, *Outlandish Proverbs*, 1640.

jam tomorrow and jam yesterday, but never jam today (*English*) Promises may be made of good times to come, or references made to good times past, but only rarely are these promises realized in the present. Lewis Carroll, *Through the Looking-Glass*, 1871.

> 'The rule is, jam to-morrow and jam yesterday – but never jam to-day.' 'It *must* come sometimes to "jam to-day",' Alice objected. 'No, it can't,' said the Queen.
>
> Lewis Carroll, *Through the Looking-Glass*, 1871

January. a January spring is worth nothing (*English*) Mild weather in January is no guarantee that there will be mild weather in the months to follow. M.A. Denham, *Proverbs relating to the Weather*, 1846. Another proverb is more explicit, 'a summerish January, a winterish spring', while another exclaims 'January warm, the Lord have mercy!' Other ominous signs for the months to come that may be detected in January include the first signs of growing grass.

jaundice. to the jaundiced eye all things look yellow (*English*) Those with a cynical view of life will see the bad in everything. Geoffrey Chaucer, *The Canterbury Tales*, *c.*1387. It was formerly widely believed that all people with jaundice saw the world with a yellow tint.

> All looks yellow to the jaundic'd eye.
>
> Alexander Pope, *Essay on Criticism*, 1709

jaw. don't let your jaws outrun your claws (*English*) Don't live beyond your means. W. Harrison, *Description of England*, 1577.

~ *See also* JOUK and let the jaw go by.

jay. the jay bird don't rob his own nest (*West Indian*) Thieves do not steal from their fellows. *See also* there is HONOUR among thieves; it's an ILL bird that fouls its own nest.

jealous. *See* a LEWD bachelor makes a jealous husband.

jealousy. jealousy shuts one door and opens two (*English*) Jealousy breeds suspicion. S. Palmer, *Moral Essay on Proverbs*, 1710.

~ *See also* LOVE is never without jealousy.

jest. *See* DOGS begin in jest and end in earnest; if you GIVE a jest, you must take a jest; it is ILL jesting with edged tools; LEAVE a jest when it pleases you best; there's MANY a true word spoken in jest.

jewel. *See* FAIR play is a jewel; NONE can guess the jewel by the casket; PLAIN dealing is a jewel.

Jew. the Jews spend at Easter, the Moors at marriages, the Christians in suits (*English*) While others variously devote their wealth to their religion or their marriages, Christians spend their money on lawsuits. George Herbert, *Outlandish Proverbs*, 1640.

> Is it not a sad thing that … it should become a proverb that 'the Jew spends all in his passover, the Moor in his marriage, and the Christian in his lawsuits?'
>
> J. Taylor, *Sunday Sermon*, 1651–3

Jill. *See* EVERY Jack has his Jill; a GOOD Jack makes a good Jill.

Joan is as good as my lady in the dark (*English*) Matters of rank are unimportant in certain circumstances (just as all women, ugly or beautiful, are the same in the dark). Anthony Munday, *The Downfall of the Earl of Huntingdon*, 1601.

> Much also we shall omit about confusion of Ranks, and Joan and My Lady.
>
> Thomas Carlyle, *Sartor Resartus*, 1838

job. if a job's worth doing, it's worth doing well (*English*) Having decided to do something, it is worth making the extra effort to do the job well, rather than leaving things slipshod. Lord Chesterfield, letter, 10 March 1746. Often encountered with the word 'thing' replacing 'job'. Charles Dickens often quoted the proverb, while G.K. Chesterton offered comfort to those who make the extra effort but find the results do not match their expectations: 'if a thing is worth doing, it is worth doing badly'. *See also* don't SPOIL the ship for a ha'porth of tar.

> 'If a thing's worth doing at all,' said the Professor … 'it's worth doing well.'
>
> H.G. Wells, *Bealby*, 1915

join. *See* if you can't BEAT 'em, join 'em.

joke. a joke breaks no bones (*English*) Jokes do no real physical harm. James Boswell, quoting Samuel Johnson in his *Life of Johnson*, 1781. Also found as 'a jest breaks no bones.'

> A joke, the proverb says, breaks no bones; but it may break a bookseller.
>
> Lord Byron, *Works*, 1819

a joke never gains over an enemy, but often loseth a friend (*English*) A joke will never defeat one's enemies, but may cause offence to one's friends. Thomas Fuller, *Gnomologia*, 1732.

jollity. there is no jollity but hath a smack of folly (*English*) Merriment and foolishness are closely allied. George Herbert, *Outlandish Proverbs*, 1640.

jouk and let the jaw go by (*Scottish*) When faced with strong opposition it may be best not to resist in order to avoid trouble. James Kelly, *A Complete Collection of Scotish Proverbs*, 1721. 'Jouk' is a Scottish dialect word for 'stoop', while 'jaw' signifies a torrent of water.

> Gang your ways hame, like a gude bairn – jouk and let the jaw gae by.
>
> Walter Scott, *Rob Roy*, 1817

journey. *See* a MAN knows his companion in a long journey and a little inn; in SPORTS and journeys men are known.

Jove but laughs at lovers' perjury (*Roman*) The gods will forgive lies told in the pursuit of love. William Shakespeare, *Romeo and Juliet*, *c.*1593 (also quoted by Tibullus in *Elegies* in the first century BC). Also encountered in the form 'Jove laughs at lovers' lies'.

Love endures no Tie,
And Jove but laughs at Lovers Perjury!
John Dryden, *Poems*, 1700

joy. joy and sorrow are next door neighbours (*English*) Happiness and unhappiness can follow each other in quick succession. Related proverbs include 'God send you joy, for sorrow will come fast enough', 'laugh before breakfast, you'll cry before supper' and 'if you sing before breakfast, you'll cry before night'. The close relationship between joy and sorrow is further stressed in the proverb 'no joy without annoy', which was quoted by Geoffrey Chaucer in 'The Nun Priest's Tale', *The Canterbury Tales*, *c.*1387.

the joy of the heart makes the face merry (*English*) A happy disposition shows itself in a person's face. T. Wright, *The Passions of the Mind*, 1601. Variant forms include 'the joy of the heart fairly colours the face' and 'the heart's mirth doth make the face fayre'.

~ *See also* GOD send you joy, for sorrow will come fast enough; MARRIAGE halves our griefs, doubles our joys, and quadruples our expenses; ONE for sorrow, two for joy; three for a girl, four for a boy; five for silver, six for gold; seven for a secret, never to be told; eight for heaven, nine for hell; and ten for the devil's own self.

joyful. *See* REMEMBRANCE of past sorrow is joyful.

judge (noun). **a judge knows nothing unless it has been explained to him three times** (*English*) Only after constant repetition will a judge understand anything. *See also* a GOOD judge conceives quickly, judges slowly.

no one should be judge in his own cause (*English*) All judges should be impartial and have no personal interest in the cases they hear. R. Pecock, *Repressor of Blaming of Clergy*, *c.*1449. The principle is enshrined in a legal maxim, rendered in Latin as *nemo debet esse iudex in propria causa*. A related proverb warns 'he who will have no judge but himself, condemns himself'.

No man is a good judge in his own cause. I
believe I am tolerably impartial.
John Wesley, letter, 3 November 1775

~ *See also* a GOOD judge conceives quickly, judges slowly; he whose FATHER is judge goes safe to his trial.

judge (verb). **don't judge a man by the words of his mother, listen to the comments of his neighbours** (*Yiddish*) To find out what a man is really like do not rely on what his mother says, as her views will be biased, but talk to his neighbours.

judge not, that ye be not judged (*Hebrew*) Do not condemn others for their failings, in case you find yourself similarly condemned. Bible, Matthew 7:1. Related proverbs include 'who judges others, condemns himself'.

Deme ye noman, and ye shal not be demed.
William Caxton, *Reynard the Fox*, 1481

you can't judge a book by its cover (*US*) One cannot judge inner character by outward appearances. *American Speech*, 1929. *See also* APPEARANCES are deceptive.

~ *See also* a BLIND man cannot judge colours; a GOOD judge conceives quickly, judges slowly; NEVER judge by appearances; THINGS present are judged by things past.

judgement. *See* he hath a GOOD judgement that relieth not wholly on his own; an ILL agreement is better than a good judgement.

July. *See* he who BATHES in May will soon be laid in clay, he who bathes in June will sing a merry tune, he who bathes in July will dance like a fly.

jump. *See* GREAT wits jump.

June. *See* CALM weather in June sets corn in tune; a DRIPPING June sets all in tune; he who BATHES in May will soon be laid in clay, he who bathes in June will sing a merry tune, he who bathes in July will dance like a fly.

just. a just war is better than an unjust peace (*Roman*) A war fought for good reasons is preferable to a peace founded on injustice. Samuel Daniel, *A History of the Civil Wars between York and Lancaster*, 1595 (also found in the writings of Tacitus).

For oft we see a wicked peace
To be well chang'd for war.
Samuel Daniel, *Ulysses and Siren*, 1605

be just before you're generous (*English*) Bear in mind your existing obligations before acting generously to third parties. E. Haywood, *Female Spectator*, 1745.

> I owe every farthing of my money … There's an old proverb – be just before you're generous.
> Frederick Marryat, *Peter Simple*, 1834

justice. *See* the CLERK makes the justice; MERCY surpasses justice.

justify. *See* the END justifies the means.

justly. *See* WEIGH justly and sell dearly.

kail. *See* he KENS his groats among other folk's kail.

ka me, ka thee (*English*) You do me a favour and I will do you a favour in return. John Heywood, *A Dialogue containing … the Proverbs in the English Tongue*, 1546. *See also* you SCRATCH my back and I'll scratch yours.

> Ka me, ka thee – it is a proverb all over the world.
> Walter Scott, *Kenilworth*, 1821

keep. keep a thing seven years and you'll always find a use for it (*English*) Never assume a thing is useless, because time will reveal how it may be usefully employed. W. Painter, *Palace of Pleasure*, 1623.

> According to the Proverb; Keep a thing seven years, and then if thou hast no use on't throw't away.
> Thomas Killigrew, *Parson's Wedding*, 1663

keep bad men company and you'll soon be of their number (*English*) Those who mix with bad company will inevitably be influenced by them. George Herbert, *Outlandish Proverbs*, 1640. The sentiment is reinforced in the related 'keep not ill men company, lest you increase the number' and 'he keeps his road well enough who gets rid of bad company', while a parallel moral is voiced in the variant 'keep good men company and you shall be of the number.' *See also* who KEEPS company with the wolf will learn how to howl.

keeping is harder than winning (*English*) It is often harder to hold on to good fortune (be it in the shape of a good woman, wealth, or something else) than it is to gain it in the first place. Geoffrey Chaucer, *Troilus and Criseyde*, *c.*1385–90.

keep no more cats than will catch mice (*English*) Keep only what is useful. J. Dare, *Counsellor Manners*, 1673. This is often quoted with reference to employees or family members who fail to earn their keep.

> Keep no more Cats than will Catch Mice. Ecquipage and Attendance … must be agreeable to Character, Dignity and Fortune.
> S. Palmer, *Moral Essays on Proverbs*, 1710

keep something for the sore foot (*English*) Save something for when one is old, ill or otherwise hard-pressed. James Kelly, *A Complete Collection of Scotish Proverbs*, 1721. Much the same advice is offered in the related 'keep something for him that rides on the white horse.' *See also* SAVE something for a rainy day.

> Preserve something for age, distress, and necessity.
> James Kelly, *A Complete Collection of Scotish Proverbs*, 1721

keep your mouth shut and your eyes open (*English*) It is good policy to say little but remain vigilant to what goes on around you. S. Palmer, *Moral Essays on Proverbs*, 1710. Variants include the US proverb 'keep your eyes wide open before marriage, and half shut afterwards'.

> Keep your mouth close an' your een open.
> Allan Ramsay, *A Collection of Scots Proverbs*, 1737

keep yourself from the anger of a great man, from the tumult of a mob, from a man of ill fame, from a widow that has been thrice married, from a wind that comes in at a hole, and from a reconciled enemy (*English*) Advice for a safe, contented life. J. Mapletoft, *Select Proverbs*, 1707.

keep your shop and your shop will keep you (*English*) Look after your business and you will prosper by it. George Chapman and others, *Eastward Ho*, 1605.

Variants include 'keep your house and your house will keep you'.

> I would earnestly recommend this adage to every mechanic in London, 'Keep your shop, and your shop will keep you.'
>
> Oliver Goldsmith, in *The Bee*, 17 November 1759

keep your weather-eye open (*English*) Keep a good lookout for changes in the weather (or for trouble of any kind). Admiral Smyth, *Sailor's Word-Book*, 1867. Originally a nautical proverb: lookouts on ships were supposed to keep their 'weather-eye' towards the wind, watching for sudden squalls.

who keeps company with the wolf will learn how to howl (*Spanish*) Those who mix with bad company will learn their evil ways. John Florio, *Second Fruites*, 1591. The traditional identification of the wolf with wickedness is reinforced in several other proverbs, among them 'the wolf doth something every week that keeps him from going to church on Sunday' and 'the wolf knows what the ill beast thinks'. The fact that there is no reforming such a creature is underlined by such proverbs as 'the wolf may lose his teeth, but never his nature' and 'the wolf must die in his own skin'. *See also* KEEP bad men company and you'll soon be of their number.

> Tho' you have kept company with a wolf you have not learnt how to howl of him.
>
> Samuel Richardson, *Clarissa*, 1748

why keep a dog and bark yourself? (*English*) It is senseless to do something yourself when you are paying someone else to do it. B. Melbancke, *Philotimus*, 1583.

> What? keep a dog and bark my self. That is, must I keep servants, and do my work my self.
>
> John Ray, *A Collection of English Proverbs*, 1670

~ *See also* an APPLE a day keeps the doctor away; a BAD custom is like a good cake, better broken than kept; DAUGHTERS and dead fish are no keeping wares; DEATH keeps no calendar; DESERT and reward seldom keep company; the EARTHEN pot must keep clear of the brass kettle; EXPERIENCE keeps a dear school; GOD keep me from the man that has but one thing to mind; GREAT trees keep down little ones; a HEDGE between keeps friendship green; he who GETS doth much, but he who keeps doth more; it is EASY to keep a castle that was never assaulted; it is EASY to rob an orchard when none keeps it; a MAN is known by the company he keeps; MEN count up the faults of those who keep them waiting; ONE sword keeps another in the scabbard; PAINS to get, care to keep, fear to lose; PRAISE the sea but keep on land; put your TRUST in God, and keep your powder dry; a SERVANT and a cock should be kept but a year; THREE may keep a secret, if two of them are dead; an UNLAWFUL oath is better broken than kept; who hath no MORE bread than need must not keep a dog.

keeper. *See* FINDERS keepers, losers weepers.

ken. he kens his groats among other folk's kail (*Scottish*) The wise man can always recognize what is rightfully his, even when it has been mixed up with someone else's belongings or outpourings. David Fergusson, *Scottish Proverbs*, 1641.

> 'D'ye think, sir, I dinna ken my ain groats in ither folk's kail?'
>
> Dean Ramsay, *Reminiscences*, 1857

kept. *See* KEEP.

kettle. *See* the EARTHEN pot must keep clear of the brass kettle; the POT calls the kettle black.

key. *See* ALL the keys hang not at one man's girdle; a GOLDEN key can open any door; KISSES are keys; SLOTH is the key to poverty; a USED key is always bright.

kick. *See* the COW gives good milk but kicks over the pail.

kid. *See* where the DAM leaps over, the kid follows.

kill. he that killeth a man when he is drunk shall be hanged when he is sober (*English*) Acts done in the heat of the moment or when under the influence of alcohol may still have to be answered for subsequently. John Heywood, *A Dialogue containing … the Proverbs in the English Tongue*, 1546.

killing no murder (*English*) In certain circumstances killing someone should be regarded as no crime. Sexby and Titus, *Killing Noe Murder*, 1657 (a notorious Royalist-backed pamphlet, published in Holland, that called for the assassination of the Lord Protector, Oliver Cromwell). Colonel Edward Sexby, one of the authors of the celebrated pamphlet, was a Leveller who in 1657 narrowly failed to kill Cromwell himself. Sometimes attributed to Irish origins.

> In Ireland, not only cowards, but the brave 'die many times before their death'. There killing is no murder.
>
> Maria Edgeworth, *Castle Rackrent*, 1800

kill not the goose that lays the golden egg (*Greek*) Do not make changes that will result in the loss of some benefit to yourself. William Caxton, *Aesop's Fables*, 1484. *See also* don't THROW the baby out with the bathwater.

> A man … had a goose, which everie daie laid him a golden egge, hee … kild his goose, thinking to have a mine of golde in her bellie, and finding nothing but dung, … wisht his goose alive.
>
> John Lyly, *Pappe with Hatchet*, *c.*1589

~ *See also* ANYONE can kill a trussed foe; CARE killed the cat; CONTEMPT will sooner kill an injury than revenge; CURIOSITY killed the cat; FAR shooting never killed bird; GLUTTONY kills more than the sword; he was CURSED in his mother's belly that was killed by a cannon; if the DOCTOR cures, the sun sees it, but if he kills, the earth hides it; if you would be HAPPY for a week take a wife; if you would be happy for a month kill a pig; but if you would be happy all your life plant a garden; it is not the BURDEN but the overburden that kills the beast; it is not WORK that kills, but worry; it is the PACE that kills; NEGLECT will kill an injury sooner than revenge; on SAINT Thomas the Divine kill all turkeys, geese and swine; PERSEVERANCE kills the game; there are MORE ways of killing a cat than choking it with cream; there are MORE ways of killing a dog than choking it with butter; there are MORE ways of killing a dog than hanging it.

kind (noun). *See* BETTER a good cow than a cow of a good kind; CAT will to kind.

kind (adj.). **a kind heart loseth nought at last** (*English*) Kindness is its own reward. J. Clarke, *Paroemiologia Anglo-Latina*, 1639. Related proverbs include 'kindnesses, like grain, increase by sowing.'

kind hearts are soonest wronged (*English*) It is often those who act with kindness towards others who are most easily hurt. Nicholas Breton, *Proverbs*, 1616.

~ *See also* you've got to CRUEL to be kind.

kindle. kindle not a fire that you cannot extinguish (*English*) Do not start trouble that might overwhelm you. B.R., *Euterpe*, 1584.

~ *See also* WOOD half burnt is easily kindled.

kindness. kindness is lost that is bestowed on children and old folks (*Greek*) The young and the very old will soon forget any kindness showed them. Alexander Barclay, *The Ship of Fools*, 1509 (originally attributed to Aristotle).

~ *See also* a FORCED kindness deserves no thanks.

king. the king can do no wrong (*English*) An absolute monarch is the source of ultimate legal authority, and is thus technically above the law, being immune to the actions of the courts. John Selden, *Table-Talk*, 1689. The principle is enshrined in the legal maxim *rex non potest peccare*. The proverb may be applied to anybody who occupies a position of supreme influence. In 1977 disgraced US president Richard Nixon quoted it in an attempt to justify his actions during the Watergate scandal prior to his resignation: 'When the President does it, that means it is not illegal.'

> The King can do no wrong … The prerogative of the crown extends not to do any injury: it is created for the benefit of the people, and therefore cannot be exerted to their prejudice.
>
> William Blackstone, *Commentaries on the Laws of England*, 1765

the king can make a knight, but not a gentleman (*English*) Aristocratic fine manners are inbred and cannot be acquired by virtue of rank or bestowed by others, even by monarchs. John Selden, *Table-Talk*, 1689.

kings have long arms (*Greek*) The influence of the powerful may extend a considerable distance. R. Taverner, *Proverbs or Adages with New Additions, gathered out of the Chiliades of Erasmus*, 1539 (also quoted by Ovid in *Heroides*, AD166). Related proverbs include 'kings have many ears and many eyes', which may be found in the writings of Lucian. The notion of long-armed influence is most familiar in Britain in the phrase 'the long arm of the law'.

> Kings have long Arms, but misfortune longer.
>
> Benjamin Franklin, *Poor Richard's Almanack*, 1752

a king without learning is but a crowned ass (*English*) A monarch who lacks education is a fool, despite the fact that he is of high status in society. John Berners, *Huon of Bordeaux*, *c.*1534.

~ *See also* a CAT may look at a king; EAT peas with the king and cherries with the beggar; he that EATS the king's goose shall be choked with his feathers; he that is DRUNK is as great as a king; a HUMBLE-BEE in a cow-turd thinks himself a king; in the COUNTRY of the blind, the one-eyed man is king; I wouldn't CALL the king my cousin; LAWS go as kings like; MUST is for the king; a PECK of March dust is worth a king's ransom; the PEOPLE's love is the king's lifeguard.

kingdom. *See* CONTENT is more than a kingdom; it is EASIER for a camel to go through the eye of a needle than it is for a rich man to enter into the kingdom of heaven; my MIND to me a kingdom is.

kinsman. *See* a NEAR friend is better than a far-dwelling kinsman.

kirk. *See* if PHYSIC do not work, prepare for the kirk.

kiss (noun). **kisses are keys** (*English*) Kisses are likely to lead to more intimate relations. J. Clarke, *Paroemiologia Anglo-Latina*, 1639. A fuller version of the proverb runs 'wanton kisses are keyes of sin.' A similar sentiment is expressed in 'do not make me kiss, and you will not make me sin.'

~ *See also* where COBWEBS are plenty, kisses are scarce

kiss (verb). **he that kisseth his wife in the market-place shall have many teachers** (*English*) People are always ready to give their advice when they see an opportunity to do so, especially in public, even where it has not been requested. W. Camden, *Remains concerning Britain*, 1605. Variants include 'he that sits to work in the market-place shall have many teachers'. **kissing goes by favour** (*English*) People are free to bestow their favours (as they do their kisses) on whoever they choose. William Camden, *Remainings concerning Britain*, 1605.

> Kissing goes by Favour. Men shew Regard, or do Service, to People as they affect.
>
> James Kelly, *A Complete Collection of Scotish Proverbs*, 1721

to kiss a man's wife or wipe his knife is a thankless office (*English*) Said when a person is ultimately denied the pleasure that another enjoys. J. Clarke, *Paroemiologia Anglo-Latina*, 1639.

~ *See also* the CAT and dog may kiss, yet are none the better friends; he that WIPES the child's nose kisseth the mother's cheek; a LISPING lass is good to kiss; MANY kiss the child for the nurse's sake; 'tis TIME to fear when tyrants seem to kiss; when the GORSE is out of bloom, kissing's out of fashion.

kitchen. kitchen physic is the best physic (*English*) The best remedies are to be found in the kitchen (in other words, a good diet may do more to improve the health than medicine can). W. Bullein, *Bulwarke of Defence*, 1562.

~ *See also* if the LAIRD slight the lady, so will all the kitchen boys; if you can't STAND the heat, get out of the kitchen.

kite. *See* a LEG of a lark is better than the body of a kite.

kitten. *See* WANTON kittens make sober cats.

knapsack. *See* EVERY soldier has the baton of a field-marshal in his knapsack.

knave. knaves and fools divide the world (*English*) The entire population of the world is either wicked or stupid. John Ray, *A Collection of English Proverbs*, 1670. **knaves and whores go by the clock** (*English*) Only the wicked charge by the hour. J. Howell, *Paroemiographia*, 1659. By much the same token, another proverb has it that 'one of the four and twenty politics of a knave is to stay long at his errand'.

~ *See also* BETTER be a fool than a knave; a CRAFTY knave needs no broker; EARLY master, long knave; GIVE a child all he shall crave and a dog while his tail doth wave and you'll have a fair dog and a foul knave; the MORE knave, the better luck; there is no PACK of cards without a knave.

knavery. there is knavery in all trades (*English*) Every trade and occupation has its rogues and ways of cheating customers. Martin Parker, *Knavery in all Trades*, 1632. A fuller version of the proverb runs 'there's knavery in all trades, but most in tailors.'

knee. *See* a DOG's nose and a maid's knees are always cold.

knife. *See* FINGERS were made before forks and hands before knives; NEVER catch at a falling knife or friend; to KISS a man's wife or wipe his knife is a thankless office; the SAME knife cuts bread and fingers; STIR with a knife, stir up strife.

knight. *See* the KING can make a knight, but not a gentleman.

knives. *See* KNIFE.

knock. *See* a BRIBE will enter without knocking; FORTUNE knocks once at least at every man's gate; GIFTS enter without knocking; he that BRINGS good news knocks hard; OPPORTUNITY seldom knocks twice at any man's door.

know. he knows best what good is that has endured evil (*English*) Only a person who has personal experience of evil can really distinguish what is genuinely good. H.G. Bohn, *A Handbook of Proverbs*, 1855.

he knows how many beans make five (*English*) He is no fool and is not easily deceived. John Galt, *Laurie Todd*, 1830. This proverb refers to an ancient trick question, in which a person is first asked how many beans make five (five) and is then asked how many blue beans make five white ones. The answer is five, peeled.

he that knows little, often repeats it (*English*) Those who possess only a few facts or stories take every opportunity to repeat them. J. Mapletoft, *Select Proverbs*, 1707. Another proverb along similar lines claims 'who knows most, speaks least'.

he that knows nothing, doubts nothing (*French*) Those who know no better have no reason to question anything. Randle Cotgrave, *A Dictionary of the French and English Tongues*, 1611.

he that knows not how to hold his tongue, knows not how to talk (*English*) Those who do not know when it is the right time to remain silent do not know when it is the right time to say something. *Politeuphuia*, 1597, attributed to J. Bodenham.

know thyself (*Greek*) Self-knowledge should be the goal of everyone. J. Trevisa, *Higden's Polychronicon*, 1387 (also attributed to Solon and found in the writings of Pausanias and Juvenal, among other classical writers). The proverb was originally inscribed at the temple of Apollo at Delphi.

> Know then thyself, presume not God to scan;
> The proper study of Mankind is Man.
> Alexander Pope, *Essay on Man*, 1732

what you don't know can't hurt you (*English*) Some secrets are best left undisclosed, as knowledge of them would only cause trouble. G. Pettie, *Petite Pallace*, 1576. *See also* IGNORANCE is bliss.

> So long as I know it not, it hurteth mee not.
> George Pettie, *Petite Pallace*, 1576

when you don't know what to do – wait (*English*) It is better to do nothing when in doubt what to do. G.J. Whyte-Melville, *Uncle John*, 1874.

you cannot know wine by the barrel (*English*) Outward appearances are no indication of inner quality. Randle Cotgrave, *A Dictionary of the French and English Tongues*, 1611. *See also* APPEARANCES are deceptive.

you should know a man seven years before you stir his fire (*English*) You should wait until you know someone very thoroughly before you assume you are entitled to interfere in their private life. Charles Dibdin, *Professional Life*, 1803.

~ *See also* BETTER the devil you know than the devil you don't know; the BRIDE goes to her marriage-bed but knows not what shall happen to her; a CARPENTER is known by his chips; the CAT knows whose lips she licks; come LIVE with me and you'll know me; the COW knows not the worth of her tail till she loses it; a DISEASE known is half cured; do not ALL you can, spend not all you have, believe not all you hear, and tell not all you know; the ENGLISH never know when they are beaten; HALF the world doesn't know how the other half lives; he that has no CHILDREN knows not what is love; the HUSBAND is always the last to know; in SPORTS and journeys men are known; it is a WISE child that knows its own father; it is BETTER to be a cuckold and not know it, than be none and everybody say so; it is HARD to be wretched but worse to be known so; a JUDGE knows nothing unless it has been explained to him three times; LITTLE knoweth the fat man what the lean man thinketh; a MAN is known by the company he keeps; a MAN knows his companion in a long journey and a little inn; MORE people know Tom Fool than Tom Fool knows; MUCH water goes by the mill that the miller knows not of; NECESSITY knows no law; the SACK is known by the sample; TELL not all you know, nor do all you can; THINKING is very far from knowing; the TREE is known by its fruit; an UNBIDDEN guest knoweth not where to sit; WARS are sweet to those that know them not; WEALTH is best known by want; we NEVER know the worth of the water till the well is dry; WORK today for you know not how much you may be hindered tomorrow; YEARS know more than books; you NEVER know what you can do till you try.

knowledge. knowledge is power (*English*) Those who have knowledge of something are automatically put at an advantage. Francis Bacon, *Meditationes Sacrae: De Haeresibus*, *c.*1626. Another proverb supports this view, stating that at the very least 'knowledge is no burden'. Knowledge has its limitations, however, as evidenced by the proverbs 'knowledge makes one laugh, but wealth makes one dance' and 'knowledge without practice makes but half an artist.' Other proverbs go further still, warning that 'knowledge is folly, except grace guide it' and that 'a little knowledge can be dangerous.' *See also* FOREWARNED is forearmed; IGNORANCE is bliss; MONEY is power.

A man of knowledge encreaseth strength.
Proverbs 24:5

~ *See also* it is BETTER to conceal one's knowledge than to reveal one's ignorance; WANT of care does us more damage than want of knowledge; ZEAL without knowledge is the sister of folly.

known. *See* KNOW.

L

labour is light where love doth pay (*English*) Work goes easily when it is done for reasons of love. Thomas Drayton, *Ideas*, 1594.

labourer. the labourer is worthy of his hire (*Hebrew*) A good workman is entitled to payment for his service. Bible, Luke 10:7.

> Your service will not be altogether gratuitous, my old friend – the labourer is worthy of his hire.
> Walter Scott, *St Ronan's Well*, 1824

lack (noun). *See* in LOVE is no lack.

lack (verb). *See* he can ILL pipe that lacketh his upper lip; IDLE people lack no excuses; when GOOD cheer is lacking, our friends will be packing; when the DEVIL is dead, he never lacks a chief mourner.

ladder. go down the ladder when thou marriest a wife, go up when thou choosest a friend (*English*) When it comes to choosing a wife, the sensible man does not marry above his rank (even though he may choose friends of superior social status). John Ray, *A Collection of English Proverbs*, 1678.

~ *See also* CROSSES are ladders that lead to heaven; STEP after step the ladder is ascended; when an ASS climbs a ladder we may find wisdom in women.

ladies. *See* LADY.

lad. if the lad go to the well against his will, either the can will break or the water will spill (*English*) Those who are forced to do something against their will are likely to make a bad job of it. James Kelly, *A Complete Collection of Scotish Proverbs*, 1721.

lad's love's a busk of broom, hot awhile and soon done (*English*) The love of young men, like the flowers of the broom, does not last long. John Ray, *A Collection of English Proverbs*, 1670.

lady. when our Lady falls in our Lord's lap, then let England beware a sad clap (*English*) When the feast of the Virgin Mary (25 March) coincides with Easter then England will suffer a severe blow. E. Gayton, *Pleasant Notes upon Don Quixote*, 1654. Also encountered in the form 'when our Lady falls in our Lord's lap, then let England beware a sad mishap' and 'when our Lady falls in our Lord's lap, then let the clergyman look to his cap' (a variant indicating the proverb's origins in the English Reformation). *See also* when EASTER falls in our Lady's lap, then let England beware of a rap.

~ *See also* FAINT heart ne'er won fair lady; FAR-FETCHED and dear-bought is good for ladies; the GIST of a lady's letter is in the postscript; a GOOD surgeon must have an eagle's eye, a lion's heart and a lady's hand; if the LAIRD slight the lady, so will all the kitchen boys; JOAN is as good as my lady in the dark; NOTHING agreeth worse than a lady's heart and a beggar's purse; the OPERA isn't over till the fat lady sings; when EASTER falls in our Lady's lap, then let England beware of a rap; where ROSEMARY flourishes the lady rules.

ladybird. *See* PLENTY of ladybirds, plenty of hops.

laid. *See* LAY.

laird. if the laird slight the lady, so will all the kitchen boys (*Scottish*) If a person speaks badly of his own wife, or of his possessions, he must expect others to speak badly of her, or them, as well. James Kelly, *A Complete Collection of Scotish Proverbs*, 1721.

lamb. a lamb in the house, a lion in the field (*English*) The ideal man is gentle at home but brave and fierce when he goes out into the world. Thomas Usk, *The Testament of Love*, c.1387.

~ *See also* DEATH devours lambs as well as sheep; GOD tempers the wind to the shorn lamb; go to BED with the lamb and rise with the lark; if the OLD year goes out like a lion, the new year will come in like a lamb; MARCH comes in like a lion and goes out like a lamb; you might as well be HANGED for a sheep as for a lamb.

lame. the lame foot overtakes the swift one in the end (*English*) The person who works doggedly at a task will eventually overtake the person who rushes at it. J.A. Froude, *Short Studies*, 1867–77. Related proverbs include 'the lame goes as far as your staggerer' and 'a lame traveller should get out betimes'.
the lame tongue gets nothing (*English*) Those who are incapable or unwilling to put their case verbally are unlikely to gain any reward. William Camden, *Remains concerning Britain*, 1605.

~ *See also* PUNISHMENT is lame but it comes.

lament. *See* SHORT pleasure, long lament.

land. he that hath land hath quarrels (*English*) Anyone who owns land has to accept that it is likely to lead to contention of some kind in the future. George Herbert, *Outlandish Proverbs*, 1640. Also found as 'he that hath land hath war'. Another proverb warns 'he that hath some land, must have some labour'.
land was never lost for want of an heir (*Italian*) There is never any shortage of heirs when it comes to the estates of the rich. John Ray, *A Collection of English Proverbs*, 1678.

~ *See also* the DUMB man gets no land; EVERY land has its own law; LEARNING is better than house and land; a LITTLE house well filled, a little land well tilled, and a little wife well willed; ONE acre of performance is worth twenty of the Land of Promise; PRAISE the sea but keep on land; you BUY land you buy stones, you buy meat you buy bones.

lane. *See* it is a LONG lane that has no turning.

language. *See* that is not GOOD language which all understand not; there were no ILL language if it were not ill taken.

lap. *See* there's no LEAPING from Delilah's lap into Abraham's bosom; when EASTER falls in our Lady's lap, then let England beware of a rap; when our LADY falls in our Lord's lap, then let England beware a sad clap.

lapwing. the lapwing cries farthest from her nest (*English*) To deceive predators, lapwings attempt to draw attention away from their nest by making as much noise as they can from a distance. John Lyly, *Euphues and His England*, 1580.

> Far from her nest the lapwing cries away: My heart prays for him, though my tongue do curse.
> William Shakespeare, *The Comedy of Errors*, c.1593

larder. no larder but hath its mice (*English*) Wherever good things are stored up there will be thieves and others hoping to help themselves. Thomas Fuller, *Gnomologia*, 1732.

large. *See* MEN cut large thongs of other men's leather; a SHOE too large trips you up.

lark. *See* go to BED with the lamb and rise with the lark; if the SKY falls we shall catch larks; a LEG of a lark is better than the body of a kite.

lass. the lass in the red petticoat shall pay for all (*English*) Debts incurred by young men shall, they hope, be paid off through marriage to a wealthy woman. J. Wilson, *The Cheats*, 1662.

~ *See also* GLASSES and lasses are brittle ware; a LISPING lass is good to kiss.

last (noun). *See* let the COBBLER stick to his last.

last (verb). *See* COURTESY on one side never lasts long; FIRST impressions are the most lasting; GIVE a cob a hat and a pair of shoes and he'll last for ever; GRACE will last, beauty will blast; LONG foretold long last, short notice soon past; the OFFSPRING of those that are very young or very old lasts not; an

OLD cart, well used, may last out a new one abused; while the THUNDER lasted two bad men were friends.

last (adj.). **it is the last straw that breaks the camel's back** (*Roman*) When things are at breaking point it takes very little to swing the balance. J. Bramhall, *The Defence of True Liberty of Human Actions*, 1655 (also quoted by Seneca). Variants over the years have included 'it is the last feather that breaks the horse's back'.

As the last straw breaks the laden camel's back, this piece of underground information crushed the sinking spirits of Mr Dombey.
Charles Dickens, *Dombey and Son*, 1848

the last benefit is most remembered (*English*) The most recent favour or profit is the one that comes first to mind. Thomas Fuller, *Gnomologia*, 1732. By the same token, another proverb has it that 'the last evil smarts most'.

last but not least (*English*) The last person, thing, notion and so on is not necessarily the least important. John Lyly, *Euphues and his England*, 1580.

Though last, not least in love.
William Shakespeare, *Julius Caesar*, 1599–1600

the last drop makes the cup run over (*English*) When things are on the brink it requires only the smallest additional thing or event to tip the scales. Thomas Fuller, *The Church History of Britain*, 1655. *See also* it is the LAST straw that breaks the camel's back.

last make fast (*English*) The last person to come through a door or gate should close it behind him. *Douce MS*, *c.*1350.

our last garment is made without pockets (*Italian*) All men are fated to die and thus to be deprived of all their earthly possessions. R.C. Trench, *On the Lessons in Proverbs*, 1853. The last garment in question is a shroud. *See also* SHROUDS have no pockets.

~ *See also* a BOW long bent at last waxeth weak; the CORD breaketh at the last by the weakest pull; the FAIREST rose at last is withered; GOD comes at last when we think he is furthest off; he who LAUGHS last laughs longest; the HUSBAND is always the last to know; it is not LOST that comes at last; a KIND heart loseth nought at last; LONG looked for comes at last; NICE guys finish last; PATRIOTISM is the last refuge of a scoundrel; the PITCHER goes so often to the well that it is broken at last; there are no BIRDS in last year's nest; they that WALK much in the sun will be tanned at last; WOMEN must have the last word.

latch. *See* a CROW on the thatch, soon death lifts the latch.

late. it is too late to shut the stable door after the horse has bolted (*Roman*) It is useless taking precautions to prevent something that has already happened. *Douce MS*, *c.*1350 (also quoted by Plautus). Alternative versions of the proverb include 'when your daughter is stolen, close Pepper Gate', Pepper Gate being a gate on the road leading out of Chester that on one occasion was belatedly ordered to be closed on the mayor's orders after the mayor's own daughter eloped with her lover.

It was only shutting the Stable Door after the Stead was stoln.
Daniel Defoe, *Robinson Crusoe*, 1719

it is too late to spare when the bottom is bare (*Greek*) It is too late to rein in your spending when there is nothing left. R. Taverner, *Proverbs or Adages with New Additions, gathered out of the Chiliades of Erasmus*, 1539 (quoting Hesiod and Seneca).

late children, early orphans (*English*) Children who are born to elderly parents are likely to be orphaned at a relatively early age. Benjamin Franklin, *Poor Richard's Almanack*, 1742.

late repentance is seldom true (*English*) Those who repent their misdeeds tardily are probably not sincere. Hugh Latimer, *Works*, 1552.

who cometh late lodgeth ill (*English*) Those who arrive last will have the least choice of accommodation. R. Sandford, *The Garden of Pleasure*, 1573. By the same token, another proverb runs 'he that cometh last to the pot is soonest wroth'.

He who cometh in late, has an ill lodging.
Thomas Fuller, *Gnomologia*, 1732

~ *See also* AFTER wit comes too late; BETTER late than never; the EARLY man never borrows from the late man; GOOD luck never comes too late; he that MARRIES late marries ill; he that RISETH late must trot all day; it is NEVER too late to learn; it is NEVER too late to mend; REPENTANCE comes too late; when a THING is done, advice comes too late.

Latin. *See* TACE is Latin for candle.

laugh. he is not laughed at that laughs at himself first (*English*) Making fun at your own expense is a way of forestalling the gibes of others. Thomas Fuller, *Gnomologia*, 1732.

he who laughs last laughs longest (*English*) He who finishes up on top at the end of something enjoys the most lasting victory. John Masefield, *The Widow in the Bye-Street*, 1912. The proverb in its modern form is closely related to the more old-fashioned 'he laughs best who laughs last', which was first recorded in both French and Italian and was being heard in English as early as 1706, when Sir John Vanbrugh quoted it in his play *The Country House*. Archaic equivalents include 'better the last smile than the first laughter'.

In this life he laughs longest who laughs last.
John Masefield, *The Widow in the Bye-Street*, 1912

laugh and grow fat (*English*) A person with a jovial, jolly nature grows fat on the comforts of a carefree life. John Harington, *The Metamorphosis of Ajax*, 1596.

He seems to have reversed the old proverb of
'laugh and be fat'.
Walter Scott, *Peveril of the Peak*, 1823

laugh and the world laughs with you, weep and you weep alone (*Greek*) Others are always ready to keep company with those who approach the world in a confident frame of mind, but those who are gloomy and troubled will find themselves shunned. Ella Wheeler Wilcox, 'Solitude', 1883 (the same sentiments were expressed by Horace many centuries before).

Rejoyce with them that doe rejoice, and weepe
with them that weepe.
Romans 12:15

laugh before breakfast, you'll cry before supper (*English*) Those who rejoice too early (perhaps literally before breakfast) may find their premature joy reversed later on. James Kelly, *A Complete Collection of Scotish Proverbs*, 1721. Sometimes encountered with 'sing' in the place of 'laugh'. Equivalent proverbs include 'laugh at leisure, you may weep before night'.

let them laugh that win (*English*) Those who come out on top are entitled to congratulate themselves. John Heywood, *A Dialogue containing … the Proverbs in the English Tongue*, 1546.

So, so, so, so. They laugh that win.
William Shakespeare, *Othello*, *c.*1602

~ *See also* a FOOL will laugh when he is drowning; he CARES not whose child cry so his laugh; JOVE but laughs at lovers' perjury; LOVE laughs at locksmiths; SELDOM comes a loan laughing home.

laughter is the best medicine (*English*) A good laugh is the best remedy for most ills. Opinions about the efficacious effects of laughter are not unanimous: another proverb warns 'laugh till you cry, sorrow till you die'.

law. he that goes to law holds a wolf by the ears (*English*) Any person who takes a complaint to the courts risks bringing down the wrath of the law upon himself. Robert Burton, *Anatomy of Melancholy*, 1621.

law governs man, and reason the law (*English*) Man is bound by the law, which in turn (at least in theory) is governed by logic and reason. Thomas Fuller, *Gnomologia*, 1732.

law makers should not be law breakers (*Greek*) Those who make the laws should observe them. Geoffrey Chaucer, *The Canterbury Tales*, *c.*1387.

the law is a bottomless pit (*English*) Pursuing a case through the courts will exhaust the richest purse. John Arbuthnot, *John Bull*, 1712. Archaic equivalents include 'law is a lickpenny' and 'law is a pick-purse'. Another proverb warns 'lawsuits consume time, and money, and rest, and friends'.

Law is a bottomless pit; it is a cormorant, a
harpy, that devours everything.
John Arbuthnot, *John Bull*, 1712

the law is an ass (*English*) Laws are not always wise, just or sensible. George Chapman, *Revenge for Honour*, 1634.

'If the law supposes that,' said Mr Bumble …
'the law is a ass – a idiot.'
Charles Dickens, *Oliver Twist*, 1838

laws go as kings like (*Spanish*) Laws are dictated by those in power. J. Ormsby, *Quixote*, 1885. *See also* NEW lords, new laws.

~ *See also* AGREE, for the law is costly; EVERY land has its own law; HARD cases make bad law; IGNORANCE of the law is no excuse; in a THOUSAND pounds of law there's not an ounce of love; the MORE laws, the more offenders; NECESSITY knows no law; NEW lords, new laws; ORDER is heaven's first law; a

PENNYWEIGHT of love is worth a pound of law; POSSESSION is nine points of the law; SELF-PRESERVATION is the first law of nature; SHOW me the man and I'll show you the law; there's ONE law for the rich and another for the poor; where DRUMS beat, laws are silent; a WISE lawyer never goes to law himself.

lawfully. that may be lawfully done which cannot be forborne (*English*) Necessity can constitute a legal defence. Samuel Johnson, *Lives of the Poets*, 1779–81.

lawyer. lawyers' houses are built on the heads of fools (*English*) Lawyers earn their salaries through the foolishness of their clients, who in the course of pursuing frequently hopeless cases run up huge legal bills. George Herbert, *Outlandish Proverbs*, 1640. Related proverbs to much the same effect include 'lawyers' gowns are lined with the wilfulness of their clients'.
a lawyer's opinion is worth nothing unless paid for (*English*) A lawyer gives good advice only when he has been paid. William Shakespeare, *King Lear*, 1605.

> Then 'tis like the breath of an unfee'd lawyer, you gave me nothing for't.
>
> William Shakespeare, *King Lear*, 1605

~ *See also* the DEVIL makes his Christmas pies of lawyers' tongues and clerks' fingers; a GOOD lawyer makes a bad neighbour; a GOOD lawyer must be a great liar; HIDE nothing from thy minister, physician and lawyer; a MAN who is his own lawyer has a fool for a client; an OLD physician and a young lawyer; a WISE lawyer never goes to law himself.

lay. *See* ALL lay loads on a willing horse; the BEST laid schemes of mice and men gang oft agley; he that DINES and leaves lays the cloth twice; he who BATHES in May will soon be laid in clay, he who bathes in June will sing a merry tune, he who bathes in July will dance like a fly; if the HEN does not prate, she will not lay; an ILL bird lays an ill egg; it is EASIER to raise the devil than to lay him; KILL not the goose that lays the golden egg; a WILD goose never lays a tame egg; WINTER finds out what summer lays up.

lay-overs for meddlers (*English/US*) Those who meddle in matters that do not concern them will be punished ('lay-overs' – or 'layers' – being smacks). F. Grose, *Classical Dictionary of the Vulgar Tongue*, 1785. Quoted as a threat to over-inquisitive or impertinent children.

lazy. lazy folk take the most pains (*English*) Lazy people end up having to do more work in the long run. John Ray, *A Collection of English Proverbs*, 1678. Also found as 'idle people have the most labour'.

> It is not much ease that lazy people get by all their scheming, for they always take the most pains in the end.
>
> Charles Spurgeon, *John Ploughman*, 1869

~ *See also* a LEAN fee is a fit reward for a lazy clerk; LONG and lazy, little and loud.

lead. you can lead a horse to water, but you can't make him drink (*English*) A person may be engineered into a position to do something, but it may prove more difficult to persuade them actually to do it. *Old English Homilies*, *c.*1175. Related proverbs include 'let a horse drink when he will, not what he will'.

> 'Well,' said she ... 'one man can take a horse to water but a thousand can't make him drink.'
>
> Anthony Trollope, *Barchester Towers*, 1857

~ *See also* ALL roads lead to Rome; CROSSES are ladders that lead to heaven; FATE leads the willing but drives the stubborn; if the BLIND lead the blind, both shall fall into the ditch; OLD maids lead apes in hell.

leaf. *See* DEEDS are fruits, words are but leaves; if on the TREES the leaves still hold, the coming winter will be cold; if you would have FRUIT, you must bring the leaf to the grave.

leak. *See* a LITTLE leak will sink a great ship; OLD vessels must leak.

lean (verb)**. lean not on a reed** (*English*) It is foolish to rely on something or someone weak or uncertain. Thomas Fuller, *Gnomologia*, 1732.

lean (adj.)**. a lean dog to get through the hedge** (*English*) Lean people seem to recover from illness more easily than those who carry more weight. V.S. Lean, *Collecteana*, 1902–04.
a lean fee is a fit reward for a lazy clerk (*English*) Those who do not work hard do not deserve much in return. *Politeuphuia*, 1597, attributed to J. Bodenham.

lean liberty is better than fat slavery (*English*) Freedom of any kind is better than slavery, however comfortable one's circumstances may be. Thomas Fuller, *Gnomologia*, 1732.

~ *See also* FAT housekeepers make lean executors; FAT paunches make lean pates; LITTLE knoweth the fat man what the lean man thinketh.

leap. if you leap into a well providence is not bound to fetch you out (*English*) Those who find themselves in difficult circumstances as a result of their own actions should not rely upon fate to rescue them. Thomas Fuller, *Gnomologia*, 1732.

there's no leaping from Delilah's lap into Abraham's bosom (*English*) Those who live lives of sin and debauchery on Earth cannot expect to enter Heaven, the abode of Abraham, when they die.

~ *See also* if ONE sheep leap o'er the dyke, all the rest will follow; LOOK before you leap; a LOW hedge is easily leaped over; MEN leap over where the hedge is lowest; where the DAM leaps over, the kid follows.

leap year. a leap year is never a good sheep year (*English*) Livestock never prosper in leap years. J. Chamber, *Treatise against Judicial Astrology*, 1601.

learn. he that would learn to pray, let him go to sea (*English*) Only those who have been exposed to the perils of the sea know what it is to pray with sincerity. Randle Cotgrave, *A Dictionary of the French and English Tongues*, 1611.

learn young, learn fair (*English*) What is learned at a young age remains with a person. David Fergusson, *Scottish Proverbs*, 1641. Related proverbs include 'what is learned young is hard to lose' and 'whoso learneth young forgets not when he is old'.

we must learn to walk before we can run (*English*) A person must learn basic skills before going on to more complex challenges. *Douce MS*, *c.*1350.

> Ffyrst must us crepe and sythen go.
>
> *Towneley Play of the First Shepherds*, *c.*1450

~ *See also* the ACOLYTE at the gate reads scriptures he has never learned; a BARBER learns to shave by shaving fools; by doing NOTHING we learn to do ill; by WRITING you learn to write; don't go NEAR the water until you learn how to swim; an EVIL lesson is soon learned; he that QUESTIONETH nothing, nothing learneth; it is GOOD to learn at other men's cost; it is NEVER too late to learn; LIVE and learn; SOON learnt, soon forgotten; where OLD age is evil, youth can learn no good; who KEEPS company with the wolf will learn how to howl; WISE men learn by others' faults, fools by their own; you're NEVER too old to learn.

learning. learning is better than house and land (*English*) A good education is more valuable than the possession of property. Samuel Foote, *Taste*, 1752. Variants include 'when house and land are gone and spent, then learning is most excellent'.

> When ign'rance enters, folly is at hand;
> Learning is better far than house and land.
>
> David Garrick, prologue to Oliver Goldsmith, *She Stoops to Conquer*, 1773

learning makes a good man better and an ill man worse (*English*) Knowledge can be used for both good and bad ends. William Camden, *Remains concerning Britain*, 1614. Another proverb making much the same point runs 'learning in a prince is like a knife in the hand of a madman'.

~ *See also* a KING without learning is but a crowned ass; a LITTLE learning is a dangerous thing; OXFORD for learning, London for wit, Hull for women, and York for a tit; there is no ROYAL road to learning.

least. the least boy always carries the greatest fiddle (*English*) The weakest always have to bear the greatest burden, because they cannot refuse the demands others make of them. John Ray, *A Collection of English Proverbs*, 1670.

least said, soonest mended (*English*) The less one says after committing some lapse of good behaviour the less time it will take to repair relationships with those thus offended. *The Parlement of Byrdes*, *c.*1460. Formerly usually encountered in the form 'little said soon amended'.

> I should be angry if I proceed in my guesses
> – and little said is soon amended.
>
> Samuel Richardson, *Clarissa*, 1748

~ *See also* the GREATEST talkers are the least doers; IDLE people have the least leisure; LAST but not least; they BRAG most that can do the least; whom we LOVE best, to them we can say least.

leather. *See* MEN cut large thongs of other men's leather; there is NOTHING like leather.

leave (noun). **leave is light** (*English*) It is no great task to request permission to do something (usually spoken to those who have failed to request leave to do something). John Heywood, *A Dialogue containing … the Proverbs in the English Tongue*, 1546.

> I am sorry, however, that he took it without leave … Leave, they say, is light.
>
> Benjamin Franklin, *Works*, 1757

~ *See also* GIVE losers leave to speak; PAINTERS and poets have leave to lie.

leave (verb). **leave a jest when it pleases you best** (*English*) Jokes at the expense of others are best abandoned before they cause resentment. George Herbert, *Outlandish Proverbs*, 1640.

leave no stone unturned (*Greek*) Spare no effort or neglect no possibility when looking for something or undertaking some task. *Dice-Play*, *c.*1550 (also quoted by Euripides and Pliny).

leave off while the play is good (*English*) Quit while you are ahead. *Douce MS*, *c.*1350.

> When I saw our host break ranks … I e'en pricked off with myself while the play was good.
>
> Walter Scott, *The Monastery*, 1820

leave well alone (*Roman*) If something is more or less satisfactory as it stands it is best not to interfere with it. Geoffrey Chaucer, *Envoy to Bukton*, *c.*1386 (also quoted by Terence in the second century BC). Often encountered as 'let well alone'. The saying was adopted as a maxim by the British prime minister Lord Melbourne in the mid-nineteenth century. *See also* if it ain't BROKE, don't fix it; let WELL alone; let SLEEPING dogs lie.

> He knew when to let well alone, a knowledge which is more precious than a knowledge of geography.
>
> Arnold Bennett, *The Card*, 1911

~ *See also* ALTHOUGH the sun shine, leave not thy cloak at home; the DEVIL always leaves a stink behind him; he has not LOST all who has one cast left; he that DINES and leaves lays the cloth twice; he was HANGED that left his drink behind; SLANDER leaves a scar behind it.

leaves. *See* LEAF.

left. *See* INDUSTRY is fortune's right hand, and frugality her left.

leg. a leg of a lark is better than the body of a kite (*English*) A little of something good is better than a lot of something inferior. John Heywood, *A Dialogue containing … the Proverbs in the English Tongue*, 1546.

> Yea, with delight, Say my lark's leg is better than a kite.
>
> John Bunyan, *Pilgrim's Progress*, 1684

~ *See also* the BELLY carries the legs and not the legs the belly; a BROKEN leg is not healed by a silk stocking; EVERYONE stretches his legs according to the length of his coverlet; he is like a CAT: fling him which way you will, he'll light on his legs; LIES have short legs; LOSE a leg rather than a life; there goes MORE to marriage than four bare legs in a bed; USE legs and have legs.

legion. *See* he that is BUSY is tempted but by one devil, he that is idle by a legion.

leisure. *See* the BUSIEST men have the most leisure; IDLE people have the least leisure; MARRY in haste and repent at leisure; there is LUCK in leisure.

lend. he that doth lend doth lose his money and friend (*English*) The person who agrees to lend money to a friend risks losing both his money and the friendship. William Shakespeare, *Hamlet*, *c.*1600. Related proverbs include 'lend and lose, so play fools' and 'he that lends, gives'. *See also* LEND your money and lose your friend.

> Neither a borrower or lender be;
> For loan oft loses both itself and friend.
>
> William Shakespeare, *Hamlet*, *c.*1600

lend not horse, nor wife, nor sword (*English*) Never lend out your horse, your wife or your sword (formerly many people's most valuable possessions). E. Hellowes, *Guevara's Epistles*, 1574. The order in which the three are listed varies: sometimes the horse and the sword are ranked before the wife.

lend only that which you can afford to lose (*English*) When you lend money, lend it on the assumption that it will never be returned and make sure that you will be able to bear the loss. Rowland Hill, *Commonplace Book*, *c.*1500. Variants include 'lend never that thing thou needest most'.

lend your money and lose your friend (*English*) If you lend money to your friend, your friendship is sure to suffer. William Shakespeare, *Hamlet*, *c.*1600. *See also* he that doth LEND doth lose his money and friend; neither a BORROWER nor a lender be.

> It is not the lending of our money that loses our friend; but the demanding it again.
> James Kelly, *A Complete Collection of Scottish Proverbs*, 1721

~ *See also* BETTER give a penny than lend twenty; DISTANCE lends enchantment to the view; FEAR lends wings; he who has but ONE coat cannot lend it.

lender. *See* NEITHER a borrower nor a lender be.

length. length begets loathing (*English*) Anything that goes on too long will be resented by those upon whom it is inflicted. C. Jarvis, *Don Quixote*, 1742.

~ *See also* be the DAY never so long, at length cometh evensong; EVERYONE stretches his legs according to the length of his coverlet; with the ANCIENT is wisdom, and in the length of days understanding.

lengthen. *See* as the DAY lengthens, so the cold strengthens.

Lent. *See* MARRY in Lent, and you'll live to repent; SALMON and sermon have both their season in Lent.

leopard. a leopard can't change its spots (*Hebrew*) It is impossible for a person (or animal) to transform their inherited nature. Bible, Jeremiah 13:23. An Ashanti variant runs 'the rain beats a leopard's skin, but it does not wash off the spots'.

> Can the Ethiopian change his skin, or the leopard his spots?
> Jeremiah 13:23

less. less of your courtesy and more of your purse (*English*) Rather than give your advice, give your money. T. Adams, *Sermons*, 1629. Also encountered in the form 'less of your counsel and more of your cost'.

> Less of your courtship, I pray, and more of your coin.
> Thomas Fuller, *Gnomologia*, 1732

~ *See also* LITTLE gear, less care; MORE haste, less speed; the MORE said, the less done; THINK much, speak little and write less; TWO in distress makes sorrow less.

lesser. *See* BIG fleas have little fleas upon their backs to bite them, and little fleas have lesser fleas, and so *ad infinitum*; of TWO evils choose the lesser.

lesson. *See* an EVIL lesson is soon learned.

letter. *See* the GIST of a lady's letter is in the postscript; a GOOD face is a letter of recommendation.

leveller. *See* DEATH is the great leveller.

lewd. a lewd bachelor makes a jealous husband (*English*) Men who are licentious when single often turn into the most jealous husbands. J. Mapletoft, *Select Proverbs*, 1707.

liar. a liar is not believed when he speaks the truth (*Roman*) Those who have a reputation for telling lies will be ignored when they attempt to tell the truth. Anthony Rivers, *Dictes or Sayings of the Philosophers*, 1477 (also quoted by Cicero).

a liar is worse than a thief (*English*) It is morally less defensible to be a liar than it is to be a thief. W. Painter, *Chaucer New Painted*, 1623. *See also* SHOW me a liar and I will show you a thief.

> But sure the proverbe is as true as briefe,
> A lyer's ever worse then a thiefe.
> John Taylor, *All the Workes of John Taylor, the Water Poet*, 1630

a liar ought to have a good memory (*Roman*) Those who tell lies must make sure they remember what they have said, as they may easily be caught out in their lies. Thomas Wyatt, *Poetical Works*, 1542 (also quoted by Quintilian and Saint Jerome). Related proverbs include 'liars begin by imposing upon others, but end by deceiving themselves'.

> A Lyar should have a good Memory. Lest he tell the same Lye different ways.
> James Kelly, *A Complete Collection of Scottish Proverbs*, 1721

~ *See also* a BOASTER and a liar are all one; COMMON fame is a common liar; DEBTORS are liars; a GOOD lawyer must be a great liar; SHOW me a liar and I will show you a thief.

libel. *See* the GREATER the truth, the greater the libel.

liberty. liberty is not licence (*English*) Freedom is not the same as licence to do whatever you want. John Milton, sonnet, 1645. Often quoted in discussions of the nature of democracy.

> Licence they mean when they cry liberty.
>
> John Milton, sonnet, 1645

~ *See also* he that MARRIES for wealth sells his liberty; LEAN liberty is better than fat slavery; the PRICE of liberty is eternal vigilance.

licence. *See* LIBERTY is not licence.

lick. *See* the CAT knows whose lips she licks; he is a POOR cook that cannot lick his own fingers; HONEY is dear bought if licked off thorns.

lie (noun). **a lie travels around the world while truth is putting on her boots** (*English*) Lies, being frequently more salacious and interesting, spread much faster than truths. Charles Haddon Spurgeon, *John Ploughman's Talk*, 1869 (also attributed tentatively to Mark Twain). The saying enjoyed new currency after it was quoted by British prime minister James Callaghan in the House of Commons in 1976.

lies have short legs (*English*) Lies are easily unmasked and are rarely believed for long. J. Sandford, *The Garden of Pleasure*, 1573. Also encountered in the form 'lies have short wings'.

> A lie has no leg, but a scandal has wings.
>
> Thomas Fuller, *Gnomologia*, 1732

~ *See also* ASK no questions and hear no lies; a BLISTER will rise upon one's tongue that tells a lie; HALF the truth is often a whole lie; MISUNDERSTANDING brings lies to town; ONE lie makes many; they SAY so is half a lie.

lie (verb). **he that lies upon the ground can fall no lower** (*Roman*) Those who are at rock bottom can fall no further. Alexander Barclay, *Mirrour of Good Manners*, 1570.

> I am not now in Fortune's power, he that is down can fall no lower.
>
> Samuel Butler, *Hudibras*, 1663

if you lie down with dogs, you will get up with fleas (*Roman*) Those who mix with undesirable company will pick up undesirable habits. J. Sandford, *The Garden of Pleasure*, 1573 (also quoted by Seneca).

> They have a certain spice of the disease; For they that sleep with dogs shall rise with fleas.
>
> John Webster, *The White Devil*, 1612

we must not lie down and cry God help us (*English*) Those in trouble should not rely solely on God to help them but should make an effort to help themselves. George Chapman, *The May Day*, 1611. Also encountered in the form 'lie not in the mire and say God help me'.

> There's no good in lying down and crying God help us!
>
> Charles Spurgeon, *John Ploughman*, 1869

we shall lie all alike in our graves (*English*) Death makes all men equal. J. Clarke, *Paroemiologia Anglo-Latina*, 1639.

~ *See also* as a TREE falls, so shall it lie; as you make your BED, so you must lie in it; COMPLIMENTING is lying; get a NAME to rise early, and you may lie all day; a GOOD heart cannot lie; he that will SWEAR will lie; INTEREST will not lie; it is a SIN to lie against the devil; let SLEEPING dogs lie; PAINTERS and poets have leave to lie; SEE a pin and let it lie, you'll want a pin before you die; SOLDIERS and travellers may lie by authority; there is no WHISPERING but there is lying; a TRAVELLER may lie with authority; TRUTH lies at the bottom of a well; where the DEER is slain, some of her blood will lie.

life. life begins at forty (*English*) People enjoy new zest for life when they reach the age of forty. William B. Pitkin, *Life Begins at Forty*, 1932. Professor Pitkin's book tackled the challenge offered by the increasing amount of leisure time that was becoming available to the middle-aged. The phrase subsequently became the title of a popular hit song by Jack Yellen and Ted Shapiro, memorably recorded by Sophie Tucker in 1937. Another proverb warns that 'life is half spent before we know what it is'.

life is just a bowl of cherries (*US*) Life is full of delights and pleasures (intended sarcastically). Ray Henderson, 'Life is just a bowl of cherries', 1931. Henderson's song, with lyrics by Lew Brown, was written for the Broadway musical show *George White's Scandals of 1931*. Related proverbs include 'life would be too smooth if it had no rubs in it' ('rubs' being 'obstacles') and 'life wasn't meant to be easy', a line from George Bernard Shaw's *Back to Methuselah*, which was also a favourite catchphrase of Australian prime minister Malcolm Fraser in the late 1970s.

life isn't all beer and skittles (*English*) No one can expect to lead a completely carefree existence. Charles Dickens, *The Pickwick Papers*, 1836.

The men … fell in for their first march, when they began to realize that a soldier's life was not all beer and skittles.

Rudyard Kipling, *Drums Fore and Aft*, 1888

life is sweet (*English*) It is good to be alive. *Patience*, *c.*1350.

All this is very true; but life is sweet for all that.

Henry Fielding, *Jonathan Wild*, 1743

where there's life there's hope (*Greek*) Hope cannot be extinguished as long as a person clings to life. R. Taverner, *Proverbs or Adages with New Additions, gathered out of the Chiliades of Erasmus*, 1539 (also quoted by Cicero and Terence). Also encountered as 'while there's life there's hope'.

While there's life, there's hope, he cry'd;
Then why such haste? so groan'd and dy'd.

John Ray, *A Collection of English Proverbs*, 1670

~ *See also* ART is long, life is short; the BEST things in life are free; the BETROTHED of good is evil, the betrothed of life is death, the betrothed of love is divorce; BREAD is the staff of life; a CAT has nine lives; CHILDREN and fools have merry lives; he that DESPISES his own life is soon master of another's; a FAIR death honours the whole life; he that hath TIME hath life; however BIG the whale may be, the tiny harpoon can rob him of life; if you would be HAPPY for a week take a wife; if you would be happy for a month kill a pig; but if you would be happy all your life plant a garden; LOSE a leg rather than a life; my SON is my son till he gets him a wife, but my daughter's my daughter all the days of her life; VARIETY is the spice of life; we must not LOOK for a golden life in an iron cage.

lifeguard. *See* the PEOPLE's love is the king's lifeguard.

lifeless. he is lifeless that is faultless (*English*) Perfect people make dull company. John Heywood, *A Dialogue containing … the Proverbs in the English Tongue*, 1546.

lift. *See* a CROW on the thatch, soon death lifts the latch.

light (noun). *See* don't HIDE your light under a bushel; MANY hands make light work; the WAY to see divine light is to put out thine own candle.

light (verb). *See* a CANDLE lights others and consumes itself; he is like a CAT: fling him which way you will, he'll light on his legs.

light (adj.). **light burdens far heavy** (*English*) Even the lightest of burdens becomes heavy if carried a considerable distance. John Heywood, *A Dialogue containing … the Proverbs in the English Tongue*, 1546.

We use to day, light burdens far carried are heavy.

John Bunyan, *Greatness of the Soul*, 1682

light cares speak, great ones are dumb (*Roman*) People tend to complain of minor problems but to remain silent about things that concern them more greatly. Joshua Sylvester, *The Divine Weeks and Works*, 1621 (quoting Seneca).

light come, light go (*English*) What comes easily, goes just as easily. Geoffrey Chaucer, *The Canterbury Tales*, *c.*1387. Also found as 'lightly gained, quickly lost'. *See also* EASY come, easy go.

Our honestest customers are the thieves … with them and with their purses 'tis lightly come, and lightly go.

Charles Reade, *The Cloister and the Hearth*, 1861

light gains make heavy purses (*English*) Small but swift financial gains can quickly multiply. John Heywood, *A Dialogue containing … the Proverbs in the English Tongue*, 1546. Not unrelated is the proverb 'a light purse makes a heavy heart'. *See also* look after the PENNIES and the pounds will look after themselves.

a light heeled mother makes a heavy heeled daughter (*English*) Hard-working mothers make their children lazy by doing everything for them. John Ray, *A Collection of English Proverbs*, 1670.

a light purse makes a heavy heart (*English*) Lack of money will depress the spirits. H. Chettle, *Piers Plainnes*, 1595. Variants include 'a light purse is a heavy curse'. *See also* a HEAVY purse makes a light heart.

~ *See also* CLEAN heels, light meals; a HEAVY purse makes a light heart; LABOUR is light where love doth pay; LEAVE is light; a WILLING mind makes a light foot.

lightning never strikes the same place twice (*US*) If a particular spot has been struck by lightning it is highly unlikely to be struck by a second bolt at a later date. P.H. Myers, *Prisoner of the Border*, 1857. In fact there is no factual justification for the notion of lightning never striking the same plot twice: certain high buildings, including the Empire State Building in New York, have been hit hundreds of times over the years. There are also several unlucky individuals who claim to have been struck by lightning on more than one occasion.

like (verb). **like it or lump it** (*English*) Accept what is offered with good grace, no matter how unsatisfactory it is, because it is all that is on offer. John Neal, *The Down-Easters*, 1833.

> Well, what I always say is, people must take me as they find me, and if they don't like it they can lump it.
>
> W. Somerset Maugham, *Of Human Bondage*, 1915

no one likes to be the first to step on the ice (*Yugoslavian*) No one likes to be the first to expose themselves to risk.

who likes not his business, his business likes not him (*English*) No man will prosper in a business for which he has no liking. T. Wright, *Essays on the Middle Ages*, 1846. Related proverbs include 'he that thinks his business below him will always be above his business' and 'business neglected is business lost'.

~ *See also* GIVE me a child for the first seven years, and you may do what you like with him afterwards; he who SAYS what he likes shall hear what he does not like; LAWS go as kings like; TURNIPS like a dry bed but a wet head.

like (adj.). **like breeds like** (*English*) Offspring take after their parents. R Edgeworth, *Sermons*, 1557. *See also* like FATHER like son.

> Like men, like manners:
> Like breeds like, they say.
>
> Alfred, Lord Tennyson, *Poems*, 1842

like cures like (*Roman*) Treat a problem by employing its characteristics against itself. C. Bede, *Verdant Green*, 1853. The approach has become one of the guiding principles of homoeopathic medicine, although it might also be quoted in many other contexts. *See* take the HAIR of the dog that bit you.

like will to like (*Greek*) Those with similar backgrounds or characters will tend to flock together. *Scottish Legendary*, *c.*1375 (also quoted by Homer and Cicero). Also found in the fuller form 'like will to like, quoth the devil to the collier'. Equivalent sayings include 'like loves like' and 'likeness causeth liking'. *See also* BIRDS of a feather flock together.

> Like will to like, each Creature loves his kind.
>
> Robert Herrick, *Hesperides*, 1648

likely. *See* UNLIKELIEST places are often likelier than those that are likeliest.

line. *See* no DAY without a line.

linen. *See* don't WASH your dirty linen in public; NEVER choose your women or your linen by candlelight.

lining. *See* EVERY cloud has a silver lining.

link. *See* a CHAIN is no stronger than its weakest link.

lion. if the lion's skin cannot, the fox's shall (*Roman*) What cannot be achieved through force must be achieved through cunning. J. Sandford, *The Garden of Pleasure*, 1573.

> And where the lion's hide is thin and scant, I'll firmly patch it with the fox's fell.
>
> George Chapman, *Alphonsus*, *c.*1634

the lion is not so fierce as he is painted (*English*) The reputations of famous people are often much exaggerated. Thomas Fuller, *The Historie of the Holy Warre*, 1639.

> The lion is not so fierce as they paint him.
>
> George Herbert, *Outlandish Proverbs*, 1640

~ *See also* as a BEAR has no tail, for a lion he'll fail; BEAT the dog before the lion; DESTROY the lion while he is yet but a whelp; EVERY dog is a lion at home; a GOOD surgeon must have an eagle's eye, a lion's heart and a lady's hand; a GOOSE quill is more dangerous than a lion's claw; HARES may pull dead lions by the beard; he that hath his HAND in the lion's mouth must take it out as well as he can; if the OLD year goes out like a lion, the new year will come in like a lamb; a LAMB in the house, a lion in the field; a LIVE dog is better than a dead lion; a MAN is a lion in his own cause; MARCH comes in like a lion and goes out like a lamb; a MOUSE may help a lion.

lip. *See* the CAT knows whose lips she licks; he can ILL pipe that lacketh his upper lip; SCALD not your lips in another man's pottage; there's MANY a slip 'twixt cup and lip.

lisp. a lisping lass is good to kiss (*English*) Girls with lisps make the best kissers. John Ford, *The Lady's Trial*, 1639.

listen. *See* don't JUDGE a man by the words of his mother, listen to the comments of his neighbours.

listeners never hear any good of themselves (*English*) Those who listen in to other people's conversations will only hear things about themselves they would rather not hear. *Mercurius Elencticus*, 1647. A related saying runs 'men love to hear well of themselves'.

> 'If it is fated that listeners are never to hear any good of themselves,' said Mrs Browdie, 'I can't help it, and I am very sorry for it.'
>
> Charles Dickens, *Nicholas Nickleby*, 1839

literature is a good staff but a bad crutch (*English*) Those who rely upon literature to make their living will find it inadequate as a source of revenue. Samuel Smiles, *Self-Help*, 1859.

little. by little and little the bird makes his nest (*English*) Through small repeated efforts the final aim is achieved. T. Wright, *Essays on the Middle Ages*, 1846. The same sentiment is voiced in such parallel sayings as 'little and often fills the purse' and 'little and good fills the trencher'.

little and good fills the trencher (*English*) Good quality food satisfies the appetite, even if modest in quantity. George Herbert, *Outlandish Proverbs*, 1640.

little birds that can sing and won't sing must be made to sing (*English*) Those who unreasonably refuse to cooperate must expect to be pressured to do as required. John Ray, *A Collection of English Proverbs*, 1678.

> *The bird that can sing, and will not sing, should be gar'd sing.* Spoken when we use rough means to perverse people.
>
> James Kelly, *A Complete Collection of Scotish Proverbs*, 1721

a little body often harbours a great soul (*English*) Small people often have generous, noble natures. Randle Cotgrave, *A Dictionary of the French and English Tongues*, 1611. A rather contrary proverb insists that 'the little cannot be great unless he devour many'.

a little fire burns up a great deal of corn (*English*) A rumour or other small act of mischief can cause a great deal of damage. William Shakespeare, *Henry VI Part 3*, *c.*1592.

little fish are sweet (*English*) Small treats or gifts may be enjoyed just as much as larger ones. R. Forby, *Vocabulary of East Anglia*, 1830.

little fishes slip through nets but great fishes are taken (*English*) Insignificant people may escape attention whereas more prominent people are more likely to be spotted. Alexander Barclay, *The Ship of Fools*, 1509.

little gear, less care (*Scottish*) The less wealth a person has, the less they have to worry about. James Kelly, *A Complete Collection of Scotish Proverbs*, 1721. Also encountered in the form 'little goods, little care'.

a little house well filled, a little land well tilled, and a little wife well willed (*English*) The ideal condition for a man is to have a well-stocked house, a well-managed plot of land, and a willing wife. R. Taverner, *Proverbs or Adages with New Additions, gathered out of the Chiliades of Erasmus*, 1539. Also encountered in the rather fuller version 'a little gound well tilled, a little house well filled, a little wife well willed, would make him live that were half killed'.

little knoweth the fat man what the lean man thinketh (*English*) It is difficult for a person to know what another person in an entirely different situation might be thinking. George Herbert, *Outlandish Proverbs*, 1640.

a little leak will sink a great ship (*English*) It can take only a minor problem to bring about the demise of a major enterprise. Thomas Fuller, *The Holy State*, 1642.

> Beware of little expenses, a small leak will sink a great ship.
>
> Benjamin Franklin, *Poor Richard's Almanack*, 1745

a little learning is a dangerous thing (*English*) Incomplete knowledge of something can be more dangerous than no knowledge of it at all. Alexander Pope, *Essay on Criticism*, 1711. Also encountered as 'a little knowledge is a dangerous thing'. Other proverbs warning of the potential dangers of education include 'learning in a prince is like a knife in the hand of a madman'. Ambrose Bierce, meanwhile, dismissed learning as 'the kind of ignorance distinguishing the studious'. *See also* IGNORANCE is bliss.

> A little learning is a dang'rous thing;

Drink deep, or taste not the Pierian spring:
There shallow draughts intoxicate the brain,
And drinking largely sobers us again.
Alexander Pope, *Essay on Criticism*, 1711

a little of what you fancy does you good (*English*) A little self-indulgence now and then can only be good for you. Fred W. Leigh and George Arthurs, 'A little of what you fancy does you good', *c.*1890. This song title acquired proverbial status after it was taken up by music hall singer Marie Lloyd and became one of her most celebrated hits. When Lloyd sang it the inference was that the self-indulgence in question was sexual in nature, but the line has since been quoted in reference to a much wider range of pleasures, including the consumption of chocolates and alcohol.

little pitchers have big ears (*English*) Children overhear many things that they are not intended to hear (usually quoted as a warning not to discuss adult matters in front of the young). John Heywood, *A Dialogue containing ... the Proverbs in the English Tongue*, 1546. The 'ears' of a pitcher are its handles.

Archbishop Good madam, be not angry with the child.
Queen Elizabeth Pitchers have ears.
William Shakespeare, *Richard III*, *c.*1592

a little poison embitters much sweetness (*English*) It takes only a little ill feeling to disrupt a previously harmonious relationship. *Old English Homilies*, *c.*1175.

One droppe of poyson infecteth the whole tunne of wine.
John Lyly, *Euphues and his England*, 1581

a little pot is soon hot (*English*) People small of stature are often more irascible than those who are somewhat larger. John Heywood, *A Dialogue containing ... the Proverbs in the English Tongue*, 1546.

Now were I not a little pot and soon hot, my very lips might freeze to my teeth.
William Shakespeare, *The Taming of the Shrew*, *c.*1592

little strokes fell great oaks (*Roman*) Repeated small efforts will finally overcome great obstacles. Geoffrey Chaucer, *The Romaunt of the Rose*, *c.*1400 (also quoted by Diogenianus in the second century AD). Variants include 'an oak is not felled at a single stroke'.

And many strokes, though with a little axe,
Hews down and fells the hardest-timber'd oak.
By many hands your father was subdued.
William Shakespeare, *Henry VI, Part 3*, *c.*1591

little things please little minds (*Roman*) Trivial people are satisfied with trivial things. G. Pettie, *Petite Pallace*, 1576 (also quoted by Ovid). Variants include 'little things are great to little men'. Another proverb bluntly states 'little things are pretty'.

Little things affect little minds.
Benjamin Disraeli, *Sybil*, 1845

little thieves are hanged, but great ones escape (*English*) Those who are guilty of petty offences tend to be hounded by the authorities, while those guilty of much more serious crimes often seem to escape notice. J. Clarke, *Paroemiologia Anglo-Latina*, 1639.

there is no little enemy (*English*) All enemies are dangerous, however tempting it may be to dismiss them as harmless. J. Howell, *Paroemiographia*, 1659.

~ *See also* ASK much to have a little; BETTER a little fire to warm us than a great one to burn us; BIG fish eat little fish; BIG fleas have little fleas upon their backs to bite them; BIRDS in their little nests agree; from a CHOLERIC man withdraw a little, from him that says nothing for ever; the DIFFICULT we do at once, the impossible takes a little longer; EVERY little helps; GREAT oaks from little acorns grow; GREAT trees keep down little ones; HEAR much, speak little; he HELPS little that helps not himself; he is not POOR that hath little, but he that desireth much; he that KNOWS little, often repeats it; he who BEGINS too much accomplishes little; LONG and lazy, little and loud; LOVE me little, love me long; a MAN knows his companion in a long journey and a little inn; MUCH cry and little wool; MUCH smoke, little fire; THINK much, speak little and write less; WIT without wisdom is but little worth.

live (verb). **come live with me and you'll know me** (*English*) In order to know someone really well you must live with them. Sean O'Casey, *Juno and the Paycock*, 1925.

I only seen him twice; if you want to know me, come an' live with me.
Sean O'Casey, *Juno and the Paycock*, 1925

he lives long who lives well (*English*) Those who

pursue full, worthwhile lives may be thought of as long-lived, whatever age they are when they die. T. Wilson, *The Art of Rhetoric*, 1553. Variants include 'he lives long that lives till all are weary of him', 'better to live well than long', and 'it is not how long but how well we live'.

he that lives in hope dances to an ill tune (*English*) Those who have only hope to rely on for the future find themselves in a far from satisfactory position. John Florio, *Second Fruites*, 1591. Other proverbs warn, 'he that lives in hope danceth without music', 'he that lives on hope hath a slender diet' and 'who lives by hope will die by hunger'.

> He that liveth in Hope, danceth without a Fiddle.
> Thomas Fuller, *Gnomologia*, 1732

he that lives long suffers much (*English*) A long life brings with it a proportionate amount of suffering. T. Shelton, *Cervantes' Don Quixote*, 1620. Related proverbs include 'he that lives most dies most' and 'he that lives longest must fetch his wood farthest'.

he that would live for aye must eat sage in May (*Roman*) Those who eat sage in May will enjoy good health into old age. John Ray, *A Collection of English Proverbs*, 1678. Other pieces of proverbial advice for a long life include 'if you would live ever you must wash milk from your liver'.

> He that would live for aye, must eat butter and sage in May.
> Thomas Fuller, *Gnomologia*, 1732

he who lives by the sword dies by the sword (*Hebrew*) Those who adopt violent methods shall meet a violent end themselves. Bible, Matthew 26:52.

> All they that take the sword shall perish with the sword.
> Matthew 26:52

I have lived too near a wood to be frightened by owls (*English*) Those who have long familiarity of something are unlikely to be frightened by it. Jonathan Swift, *Dialogues*, 1738.

live and learn (*English*) Learn the lessons offered by experience (often said of bitter or disappointing experiences). G. Gascoigne, *Glass of Government*, 1575. A Yiddish variant runs 'as we live, so we learn'.

> I was innocent myself once, but *live and learn* is an old saying, and a true one.
> David Garrick, *Miss in her Teens*, 1747

live and let live (*Dutch*) Act with tolerance to others, as you would wish them to do to you. Gerard de Malynes, *Ancient Law-Merchant*, 1622. The proverb is found in several European languages. *See also* DO as you would be done by; it takes ALL sorts to make a world.

> You knows, master, one must live and let live, as the saying is.
> Tobias Smollett, *Sir Launcelot Greaves*, 1762

live in the shade (*Greek*) It is best to live a quiet, sober life rather than one devoted to the pursuit of pleasure. Dean Plumptre, *Ecclesiastes*, 1896.

no living man all things can (*Roman*) No one can be good at everything. J. Clarke, *Paroemiologia Anglo-Latina*, 1639 (quoting Virgil).

they that live longest, see most (*English*) Those who live to an advanced age have the benefit of the greatest experience. T. Shelton, *Cervantes' Don Quixote*, 1620.

who lives well dies well (*English*) Those who have lived full, worthwhile lives can die in peace. Richard Pynson, *Kalendar of Shepherds*, 1506. Related proverbs include 'he that liveth wickedly can hardly die honestly'. *See also* they DIE well that live well.

~ *See also* an ARTIST lives everywhere; as a MAN lives so shall he die; as LONG as I live I'll spit in my parlour; BRAVE men lived before Agamemnon; FOOLS build houses, and wise men live in them; GIVE a man an annuity and he'll live for ever; HALF the world doesn't know how the other half lives; he PREACHES well that lives well; he who FIGHTS and runs away, lives to fight another day; if you WISH to live and thrive, let a spider run alive; LOVE lives in cottages as well as in courts; MAN cannot live by bread alone; MARRY in Lent, and you'll live to repent; PEOPLE who live in glass houses shouldn't throw stones; a REED before the wind lives on, while mighty oaks do fall; they DIE well that live well; THREATENED men live long; we are BORN crying, live complaining and die disappointed; we must EAT to live and not live to eat; you must ASK your neighbour if you shall live in peace.

live (adj.). **a live dog is better than a dead lion** (*Hebrew*) Something alive or active, however imperfect, is preferable to something that has more qualities, but is dead or otherwise useless. Bible, Ecclesiastes 9:4. Variants include 'better be a live ass than a dead lion'.

When the lion is shot, the dog gets the spoil. So he had come in for Katherine, Alan's lioness. A live dog is better than a dead lion.
D.H. Lawrence, *The Woman Who Rode Away*, 1928

lives. *See* LIFE.

lizard. *See* whom a SERPENT has bitten, a lizard alarms.

load (noun). *See* ALL lay loads on a willing horse; only an ELEPHANT can bear an elephant's load; a SWARM of bees in May is worth a load of hay.

load (verb). *See* an ASS loaded with gold still eats thistles.

loaf. *See* GIVE a loaf and beg a slice; HALF a loaf is better than no bread; a SLICE off a cut loaf isn't missed.

loan. *See* SELDOM comes a loan laughing home.

loathing. *See* LENGTH begets loathing.

lock. no lock will hold against the power of gold (*English*) Money will open all doors. John Lyly, *Euphues and His England*, 1580. *See also* a GOLDEN key can open any door.

And who is so ignorant that knoweth not, gold be a Key for every locke?
John Lyly, *Euphues and His England*, 1580

locksmith. *See* LOVE laughs at locksmiths.

lodge. *See* who cometh LATE lodgeth ill.

loft. *See* SEPTEMBER blow soft, till the fruit's in the loft.

lofty. *See* MACKEREL sky and mares' tails make lofty ships carry low sails.

log. *See* CROOKED logs make straight fires.

London. *See* OXFORD for learning, London for wit, Hull for women, and York for a tit; the STREETS of London are paved with gold.

long (verb). EASTER so longed for is gone in a day.

long (adj., adv.). **as long as I live I'll spit in my parlour** (*Scottish*) A man is entitled to behave as he wishes in his own house. James Kelly, *A Collection of Scotish Proverbs*, 1721. Also encountered in the form 'as long as I live I'll fart at my own fireside'.

it is a long lane that has no turning (*English*) Runs of bad fortune do not last forever. *Stationers' Register*, 1633.

It is a long lane that has no turning – Do not despise me for my proverbs.
Samuel Richardson, *Clarissa*, 1748

long absent, soon forgotten (*English*) People or things not constantly present are soon forgotten about. Randle Cotgrave, *A Dictionary of the French and English Tongues*, 1611. *See also* out of SIGHT, out of mind.

long and lazy, little and loud (*English*) Those who are tall tend to be idle, while those who are short make up for their lack of stature by making as much noise as possible. T. Whytehorne, *Autobiography*, *c.*1576. The fullest form of the proverb runs 'long and lazy, little and loud; fat and fulsome, pretty and proud'. Variants include 'long and lazy, little and loud, fair and sluttish, foul and proud' and 'fair and foolish, black and proud, long and lazy, little and loud'.

Long and lazie. That was the Proverb. Let my mistress be Lasie to others, but be long to me.
Robert Herrick, *Hesperides*, 1648

longest at the fire soonest finds cold (*Scottish*) Those who are used to a life of ease and pleasure are the least able to cope with harsher conditions. James Kelly, *A Complete Collection of Scotish Proverbs*, 1721.

the longest day must have an end (*English*) Even the worst and most disappointing days will come to an end after twenty-four hours. John Lyly, *Euphues and His England*, 1580. Variants include 'the longest night will have an end'.

But it sufficeth that the day will end.
William Shakespeare, *Julius Caesar*, 1599

the longest way round is the shortest way home (*English*) Sometimes it is quicker to avoid short cuts and take the longer route. John Lyly, *Euphues and His England*, 1580. Another English proverb supports this contention: 'he that leaves the highway, to cut short, commonly goes about.'

long foretold long last, short notice soon past (*English*) If a barometer gives long advance warning of weather to come, that weather will remain for a long time, but if there is little warning then it will come and go very quickly. A. Steinmetz, *Manual of Weathercasts*, 1866.

The barometer is … misleading … Boots … read a poem which was printed over the top of the oracle, about 'Long foretold, long last; Short notice, soon past'.

Jerome K. Jerome, *Three Men in a Boat*, 1889

long looked for comes at last (*English*) Those who wait patiently will eventually get what they have waited for. William Shakespeare, *The Taming of the Shrew*, 1593–4.

a long tongue is a sign of a short hand (*English*) Those who make many promises often fail to keep them. George Herbert, *Outlandish Proverbs*, 1640.

not a long day but a good heart rids work (*English*) Work is accomplished faster through determination than through long hours. Randle Cotgrave, *A Dictionary of the French and English Tongues*, 1611.

one can go a long way after one is weary (*English*) A person may still keep going even when they are tired. R.C. Trench, *On the Lessons in Proverbs*, 1853.

~ *See also* ART is long, life is short; BARNABY bright, Barnaby bright, the longest day and the shortest night; be the DAY never so long, at length cometh evensong; a BOW long bent at last waxeth weak; CHILDREN have wide ears and long tongues; CLEAR autumn, windy winter; warm autumn, long winter; COURTESY on one side never lasts long; the DAY is short and the work is long; the DIFFICULT we do at once, the impossible takes a little longer; EARLY master, long knave; EVEN reckoning makes long friends; a FOOL's tongue is long enough to cut his own throat; a GIFT long waited for is sold not given; GREEDY folks have long arms; had I REVENGED every wrong, I had not worn my skirts so long; HAPPY is the wooing that is not long a-doing; he LIVES long who lives well; he PULLS with a long rope that waits for another's death; he that FALLS in the dirt, the longer he stays there the fouler he is; he that LIVES long suffers much; he who LAUGHS last laughs longest; he who SUPS with the devil should have a long spoon; an HOUR of pain is as long as a day of pleasure; KINGS have long arms; LOVE me little, love me long; a MAN knows his companion in a long journey and a little inn; NEVER is a long time; OLD sins cast long shadows; PUT off the evil hour as long as you can; the SHORT cut is often the longest way round; SHORT pleasure, long lament; SHORT reckonings make long friends; SHORT visits make long friends; a STERN chase is a long chase; they that LIVE longest see most; THREATENED men live long.

look (noun). **looks breed love** (*English*) It is through visual impressions that love is inspired. R. Taverner, *Proverbs or Adages with New Additions, gathered out of the Chiliades of Erasmus*, 1539. Variants include 'loving comes by looks'.

Tell me where is fancy bred? … It is engender'd
in the eyes,
With gazing fed.

William Shakespeare, *The Merchant of Venice*, c.1596

~ *See also* a CHEERFUL look makes a dish a feast; an HONEST look covereth many faults; a PROUD look makes foul work in a fine face.

look (verb). **he that looks not before finds himself behind** (*English*) Those who do not think ahead will find themselves falling behind those who do. George Herbert, *Outlandish Proverbs*, 1640.

if it looks like a duck, walks like a duck and quacks like a duck, it's a duck (*US*) If something acts in a certain, unmistakable way there is no denying its true identity. Walter Reuther, 1950s. This relatively modern addition to the proverbial stock was introduced by Reuther, a union leader who was suggesting how a communist might be identified.

look after the pennies and the pounds will look after themselves (*English*) Take care about gathering in the smallest amounts of money and soon you will find you have a considerable amount. Lord Chesterfield, letter, 5 February 1750. Chesterfield attributed the proverb to William Lowndes, Secretary to the Treasury under William and Mary, Queen Anne and George I. Related proverbs include 'penny and penny laid up will be many'. *See also* EVERY little helps.

Take care of the pence and the pounds will take care of themselves is as true of personal habits as of money.

George Bernard Shaw, *Pygmalion*, 1912

look before you leap (*Greek*) Carefully assess the risks before committing yourself to some course of action. *Douce MS*, c.1350. Also encountered in the form 'look ere you leap'. *See also* RECULER pour mieux sauter.

When you feel tempted to marry, think of our

four sons and two daughters, and look twice
before you leap.
Charlotte Brontë, *Shirley*, 1849

look high and fall low (*English*) Those who aim high are at the greatest risk of disaster. John Ray, *A Collection of English Proverbs*, 1670. Ray's fuller version of the proverb renders it in the form 'look high and fall into a cowturd'. Related proverbs warning against over-ambition include 'look not too high lest a chip fall in your eye'.

look for your money where you lost it (*English*) If you lose money in business or at gambling the best policy is to try to reclaim it by the same means. V.S. Lean, *Collectanea*, 1902–4.

look to a gown of gold and you will at least get a sleeve of it (*English*) Those who set their standards high will achieve greater things than those who are less ambitious. Walter Scott, *Redgauntlet*, 1824.

look to the end (*Roman*) When contemplating doing something always consider what the end result will be. William Shakespeare, *The Comedy of Errors*, 1592–3. Also known in its Latin form, *Respice finem*.

look to the main chance (*English*) Seize the opportunity to improve your own interests. John Lyly, *Euphues and his England*, 1580. Also encountered in the form 'have an eye to the main chance'.

The education of Mr Jonas had been conducted …
on the strictest principles of the main chance.
The very first word he learnt to spell was 'gain'.
Charles Dickens, *Martin Chuzzlewit*, 1843–4

look to thyself when thy neighbour's house is on fire (*Roman*) When disaster strikes those close to you it is wise to take steps to safeguard your own interests. Horman, *Vulgaria*, 1519 (also found in Virgil and Horace).

we must not look for a golden life in an iron cage (*English*) It is unrealistic to expect things to go perfectly in an imperfect world. T. Draxe, *Bibliotheca Scholastica*, 1616.

~ *See also* ALWAYS look on the bright side; a CAT may look at a king; the DEVIL looks after his own; LONG looked for comes at last; a MAN is as old as he feels, and a woman as old as she looks; NEVER look a gift horse in the mouth; ONE man may steal a horse, while another may not look over a hedge; on PAINTING and fighting look aloof; those who PLAY at bowls must look out for rubbers; to the JAUNDICED eye all things look yellow.

lookers-on see most of the game (*Roman*) Those who watch while others act see more of the action than they do and so their advice should be taken seriously. J. Palsgrave, in *Acolastus*, 1529 (also quoted by Seneca). Also found as 'lookers-on see more of the game'.

A stander-by, sir, sees more than a gamester.
John Vanbrugh, *The Mistake*, 1706

lord. *See* EVERYBODY loves a lord; from HELL, Hull and Halifax, Good Lord deliver us; NEW lords, new laws; a NOD from a lord is a breakfast for a fool; there is no GOOD accord where every man would be a lord; when our LADY falls in our Lord's lap, then let England beware a sad clap.

lose. he has not lost all who has one cast left (*English*) All is not lost while there is still a chance to succeed. R. Codrington, *The Second Part of Youth's Behaviour*, 1664. Related proverbs include 'all is not lost that is in danger'.

if you lose your time you cannot get money or gain (*English*) Those who waste time cannot hope to profit by it. T. Draxe, *Bibliotheca Scholastica*, 1616.

lose a leg rather than a life (*English*) Sometimes it is necessary to sacrifice something in order to save what is more valuable. Thomas Fuller, *Gnomologia*, 1732.

lose an hour in the morning, chase it all day (*English*) An hour's work lost in the morning will never be made up. Samuel Smiles, *Self-Help*, 1859. Variants include 'lost time is never found again'. *See also* he that RISETH late must trot all day.

lose nothing for asking (*English*) Nothing is lost by asking for something. George Herbert, *Outlandish Proverbs*, 1640.

what you lose on the swings you gain on the roundabouts (*English*) What you lose in the course of one enterprise you will make up for in what you gain in the course of another. P.R. Chalmers, *Green Days and Blue Days*, 1912. Variant forms include 'what we lose in hake, but gain in herring', a saying once common among fishermen, who knew that if they caught no hake they stood a better chance of catching herring, which hake tended to drive away. *See also* EVERY cloud has a silver lining.

you cannot lose what you never had (*English*) You should not lament what is lost if it was never yours to call your own in the first place. Christopher Marlowe, *Hero and Leander*, 1593.

> 'He has broke all; there's half a line and a good hook lost.' 'I and a good Trout too.' 'Nay, the Trout is not lost, for ... no man can lose what he never had.'
>
> Izaak Walton, *The Compleat Angler*, 1676

~ *See also* a BLEATING sheep loses a bite; CATCH not at the shadow and lose the substance; the COW knows not the worth of her tail till she loses it; GRASP all, lose all; he that doth LEND doth lose his money and friend; it SIGNIFIES nothing to play well if you lose; a JOKE never gains over an enemy, but often loseth a friend; a KIND heart loseth nought at last; LEND only that which you can afford to lose; LEND your money and lose your friend; LOOK for your money where you lost it; a MAN may lose his goods for want of demanding them; a MERCHANT that gains not, loseth; one NEVER loses by doing a good turn; PAINS to get, care to keep, fear to lose; the SUN loses nothing by shining into a puddle; a TALE never loses in the telling; you WIN a few, you lose a few.

loser. losers are always in the wrong (*Spanish*) Those who are on the losing side are always assumed to have been in the wrong. H.G. Bohn, *A Handbook of Proverbs*, 1855.

~ *See also* FINDERS keepers, losers weepers; GIVE losers leave to speak.

loss. *See* he that BORROWS must pay again with shame or loss; ONE man's loss is another man's gain; there's no GREAT loss without some gain.

lost. it is lost that is unsought (*English*) Things that lie neglected and forgotten are effectively lost. John Heywood, *A Dictionary containing ... the Proverbs in the English Tongue*, 1546.

it is not lost that comes at last (*English*) Nothing is lost while there is still time to regain it. Robert Herrick, *Hesperides*, 1648.

lost time is never found again (*English*) Time once lost cannot be reclaimed. Benjamin Franklin, *The Way to Wealth*, 1736.

~ *See also* ALL is lost that is put into a riven dish; BETTER lost than found; for WANT of a nail the shoe was lost; a FRIEND is not so soon gotten as lost; HALF an hour is soon lost at dinner; he who HESITATES is lost; a HOOK is well lost to catch a salmon; in too MUCH dispute truth is lost; KINDNESS is lost that is bestowed on children and old folks; LAND was never lost for want of an heir; an OCCASION lost cannot be redeemed; there is NOTHING lost by civility; TIME lost cannot be recalled; 'tis BETTER to have loved and lost than never to have loved at all; what a NEIGHBOUR gets is not lost.

lot. *See* GNAW the bone which is fallen to thy lot.

lottery. *See* MARRIAGE is a lottery.

loud. *See* ACTIONS speak louder than words; it is a SAD house where the hen crows louder than the cock; LONG and lazy, little and loud.

louse. *See also* BETTER a louse in the pot than no flesh at all; SUE a beggar and get a louse.

love (noun). **in love is no lack** (*English*) Those who are in love need nothing else. John Heywood, *A Dialogue containing ... the Proverbs in the English Tongue*, 1546.

love and a cough cannot be hid (*English*) There is no keeping love secret, just as a cough cannot be suppressed. *Cursor Mundi*, 1325.

> If there are two things not to be hidden – love and a cough – I say there is a third, and that is ignorance.
>
> George Eliot, *Romola*, 1863

love begets love (*English*) Love promotes love in others. Robert Herrick, *Hesperides*, 1648. Sometimes encountered in the Latin version *amor gignit amorem* (love produces love). Related proverbs include 'likeness begets love'.

> Love love begets, then never be
> Unsoft to him who's smooth to thee.
>
> Robert Herrick, *Hesperides*, 1648

love cannot be compelled (*English*) It is impossible to command love against its inclination. Geoffrey Chaucer, *The Canterbury Tales*, *c.*1387.

> Ne may love be compeld by maisterie.
>
> Edmund Spenser, *The Faerie Queene*, 1590

love conquers all (*Roman*) Love will triumph over all obstacles. Also encountered in the Latin form *amor vincit omnia*.

love does much, money does everything (*French*) Money succeeds where all else, including love, cannot. Jan Gruter, *Florilegium Ethicopoliticum*, 1611. Another proverb, furthermore, advises that 'love lasts as long as money endures'.

love is blind (*Greek*) Those who are in love are blinded to things that they would otherwise notice (typically faults in the object of their desire). Geoffrey Chaucer, *The Canterbury Tales*, *c.*1387 (also quoted by Theocritus and Plautus). Perhaps significantly, in classical Rome it was customary for sculptors to depict the god of love Cupid blindfolded. A rather cynical proverb adds 'love is blind – and when you get married you get your eyesight back'.

> If love is blind, love cannot hit the mark.
>
> William Shakespeare, *Romeo and Juliet*, *c.*1593

love is free (*English*) People are free to choose whom they love. Geoffrey Chaucer, 'The Knight's Tale', *The Canterbury Tales*, *c.*1387. Variants on the same theme include 'love is lawless'.

love is full of fear (*Greek*) Love can give rise to all manner of fears. Geoffrey Chaucer, *Troilus and Criseyde*, *c.*1385–90 (quoted by Ovid). Also found in the form 'love is full of trouble'.

> Fie, fie, fond love! thou art so full of fear.
>
> William Shakespeare, *Venus and Adonis*, 1593

love is love's reward (*English*) The reward that all lovers seek is love in return. John Dryden, *Palamon and Arcite*, 1700. Another proverb has it that 'love is the true price of love'.

love is never without jealousy (*English*) Lovers are always jealous. William Shakespeare, *Venus and Adonis*, 1593. Variants include 'love being jealous makes a good eye look asquint'.

> The reward of love is jealousy.
>
> Thomas Fuller, *Gnomologia*, 1732

love laughs at locksmiths (*English*) Love will triumph, despite all attempts to hinder it. George Colman the Younger, *Love Laughs at Locksmiths*, 1803. *See also* LOVE will find a way.

> Were beauty under twenty locks kept fast,
> Yet love breaks through and picks them all at last.
>
> William Shakespeare, *Venus and Adonis*, *c.*1592

love lives in cottages as well as in courts (*English*) Love can flourish regardless of class or social status. John Ray, *A Collection of English Proverbs*, 1670.

> Conjugal love much more, for they who live in cottages ... seldom marry for interest, wealth, or court favour.
>
> James Kelly, *A Complete Collection of Scotish Proverbs*, 1721

love makes the world go round (*Italian*) Human affairs are motivated by love. Lewis Carroll, *Alice's Adventures in Wonderland*, 1865 (also quoted by Jacopone da Todi and Dante). *See also* MONEY makes the world go round.

> In for a penny, in for a pound,
> 'Tis love that makes the world go round.
>
> W.S. Gilbert, *Iolanthe*, 1882

the love of money is the root of all evil (*Hebrew*) The desire for money leads men into all manner of selfishness and wickedness. Bible, 1 Timothy 6:7–10. Sometimes encountered in the truncated form 'money is the root of all evil', which has a somewhat altered meaning. Twentieth-century reworkings of the ancient proverb have included 'the lack of money is the root of all evil'. *See also* you cannot SERVE God and Mammon.

> For the love of money is the root of all evil,
> leading men to flounder in their Christian faith
> and fall into deep unhappiness.
>
> 1 Timothy 6:7–10

love will creep where it cannot go (*English*) Where love may not proceed openly it is pursued with stealth and caution. *Towneley Plays*, *c.*1400.

love will find a way (*English*) Love cannot be denied and will find a way through all obstacles in the end. T. Deloney, *The Gentle Craft*, 1607. Also encountered in the form 'love will find out the way'.

when love puts in, friendship is gone (*English*) It is impossible for friendship to survive when love takes its place. John Lyly, *Euphues*, 1579.

~ *See also* ALL's fair in love and war; be off with the OLD love before you are on with the new; the BEST smell is bread, the best savour salt, the best love that of children; the BETROTHED of good is evil, the betrothed of life is death, the betrothed of love is divorce; CALF love, half love, old love, cold love; COLD pudding will settle your love; the COURSE of true love never did run smooth; the FALLING out of friends is the renewal of love; FANNED fires and forced love never did well yet; FAULTS are thick where love is thin; FOLLOW love and it will flee thee;

flee love and it will follow thee; HASTY love is soon hot and soon cold; he that has no CHILDREN knows not what is love; HOT love is soon cold; in a THOUSAND pounds of law there's not an ounce of love; LABOUR is light where love doth pay; LAD's love's a busk of broom, hot awhile and soon done; LOOKS breed love; LUCKY at cards, unlucky in love; a MAN has choice to begin love but not to end it; no HERB will cure love; of SOUP and love the first is the best; OLD love will not be forgotten; ONE love expels another; a PENNYWEIGHT of love is worth a pound of law; the PEOPLE's love is the king's lifeguard; PITY is akin to love; PRAISE the child and you make love to the mother; the QUARREL of lovers is the renewal of love; SALT water and absence wash away love; SOUND love is not soon forgotten; when POVERTY comes in at the door, love flies out of the window; when DISTRUST enters in at the foregate, love goes out at the postern; when the FURZE is in bloom, my love's in tune; WINE and youth increase love.

love (verb). **love as in time to come thou shouldest hate and hate as thou shouldest in time to come, love** (*Greek*) Treat those you love as though one day they will become your enemy, and your enemy as though one day he or she will become your friend. R. Taverner, *Proverbs or Adages with New Additions, gathered out of the Chiliades of Erasmus*, 1539 (also quoted by Aristotle).

love me little, love me long (*English*) The best love is bestowed in a spirit of moderation and constancy, rather than precipitately and passionately. *Archiv*, 1500.

> Love me little, love me long. A Dissuasive from shewing too much, and too sudden Kindness.
>
> James Kelly, *A Complete Collection of Scotish Proverbs*, 1721

love me, love my dog (*English*) If you love me, you must also undertake to love everything about me. *Early Miscellany*, *c.*1480. The saying is associated with Saint Bernard of Clairvaux (1090–1153), who should not be confused with Saint Bernard of Menthon or Montjoux (*c.*996–*c.*1081), the French Benedictine monk who founded two hospices in the Alps and after whom Saint Bernard dogs were named.

> That you must love me, and love my dog … we could never yet form a friendship … without the intervention of some third anomaly … the understood dog in the proverb.
>
> Charles Lamb, *Popular Fallacies*, 1826

love your friend with his fault (*Italian*) A person must accept the shortcomings of their friends. Jeremy Taylor, *The Rule and Exercises of Holy Living*, 1650.

> A modern proverb says 'Love your friend with his foible'.
>
> Edward Fitzgerald, *Polonius*, 1852

love your neighbour, yet pull not down your hedge (*English*) By all means maintain close relations with your neighbours, but for your friendship to prosper make sure that there remains some guarantee to protect your privacy. George Herbert, *Outlandish Proverbs*, 1640. *See also* GOOD fences make good neighbours; a HEDGE between keeps friendship green.

one cannot love and be wise (*Roman*) Any person who falls in love will find their good sense deserting them. T. Berthelet, *Erasmus' Sayings of Wise Men*, *c.*1527 (also quoted by Publilius Syrus). Other proverbs along the same lines run 'love and knowledge live not together' and 'love is without reason'. On the other hand, another proverb advises 'love makes a wit of a fool'.

> If a man could not love and be wise, surely he could flirt and be wise at the same time.
>
> George Eliot, *Middlemarch*, 1872

whom we love best, to them we can say least (*English*) Those who are in love often find it hard to communicate their feelings to those who are the object of their affection. William Shakespeare, *The Two Gentlemen of Verona*, 1594–5.

~ *See also* ALL cats love fish but fear to wet their paws; EACH bird loves to hear himself sing; CRAFT must have clothes but truth loves to go naked; EVERY ass loves to hear himself bray; EVERYBODY loves a lord; HANG a dog on a crab-tree and he'll never love verjuice; MISERY loves company; MONDAY's child is fair of face, Tuesday's child is full of grace; Wednesday's child is full of woe, Thursday's child has far to go; Friday's child is loving and giving, Saturday's child works hard for its living; and the child that's born on the Sabbath day, is fair and wise and good and gay; 'tis BETTER to have loved and lost than never to have loved at all; the TREASON is loved but the traitor is hated; who DAINTIES love, shall beggars prove; whom GOD loves, his bitch brings forth pigs; whom the GODS love die young.

Lovell. *See* the CAT, the Rat and Lovell our Dog rule all England under an Hog.

lover. *See* JOVE but laughs at lovers' perjury; the QUARREL of lovers is the renewal of love.

low. a low hedge is easily leaped over (*English*) Small obstacles are easily negotiated. Jan Gruter, *Florilegium Ethicopoliticum*, 1611. *See also* MEN leap over where the hedge is lowest.

~ *See also* the BOUGHS that bear most hang lowest; he that LIES upon the ground can fall no lower; a HIGH building, a low foundation; the HIGHEST flood has the lowest ebb; LOOK high and fall low; MACKEREL sky and mares' tails make lofty ships carry low sails; MEN leap over where the hedge is lowest.

lower. *See* if the RAIN comes before the wind, lower your topsails and take them in; if the wind comes before the rain, lower your topsails and hoist them again.

lowly sit, richly warm (*English*) People who occupy humble positions are more comfortable than those in more precarious senior posts. John Ray, *A Collection of English Proverbs*, 1670.

luck. there is luck in leisure (*English*) It is sometimes sensible not to consider carefully before taking action. G. Meriton, *Yorkshire Dialogue*, 1683. *See also* LOOK before you leap; MORE haste, less speed.

there is luck in odd numbers (*Roman*) Odd numbers are luckier than even numbers. William Shakespeare, *The Merry Wives of Windsor*, c.1598 (also quoted by Virgil). In the ancient world odd numbers were considered the fundamental numbers of nature, with nine, for instance, representing the Deity (according to Pythagoras), and it was probably thus that they acquired a reputation for being lucky. *See also* THIRD time lucky.

> Good luck lies in odd numbers ... They say there is divinity in odd numbers, either in nativity, chance or death.
>
> William Shakespeare, *The Merry Wives of Windsor*, c.1598

~ *See also* BAD luck is fertile; CARE and diligence bring luck; the DEVIL's children have the devil's luck; FOOLS for luck; GOOD luck never comes too late; ILL luck is worse than found money; the MORE knave, the better luck; the PROPERER the man, the worse luck; SEE a pin and pick it up, all the day you'll have good luck; that VOYAGE never has luck where each one has a vote.

lucky. lucky at cards, unlucky in love (*English*) Those who are lucky in gambling will enjoy less luck in love affairs (usually quoted as compensation to someone who has just lost a gambling stake of some kind). T.W. Robertson, *Society*, 1866. Variants include 'lucky in life, unlucky in love'.

> Well, Miss, you'll have a sad Husband, you have such good Luck at Cards.
>
> Jonathan Swift, *Polite Conversation*, 1738

~ *See also* it is BETTER to be born lucky than rich; THIRD time lucky.

lump. *See* LIKE it or lump it.

lunch. *See* there is no such THING as a free lunch.

lurk. *See* the DEVIL lurks behind the cross; PRIDE may lurk under a threadbare cloak.

luxury. *See* ANGER can be an expensive luxury.

MacGregor. where MacGregor sits is the head of the table (*English*) Wherever an influential person settles, there power settles also. R.W. Emerson, *American Scholar*, 1837. The name concerned varies; the MacGregor sometimes quoted is thought by some to be the Scottish outlaw hero Rob Roy MacGregor.

mackerel. mackerel sky and mares' tails make lofty ships carry low sails (*English*) Dappled white clouds high in the sky are a sign of troubled, rainy weather in the offing. R. Inwards, *Weather Lore*, 1869. Variants include 'mackerel scales, furl your sails'.

~ *See also* THROW out a sprat to catch a mackerel.

mad. *See also* BUTTER is mad twice a year; he that would HANG his dog gives out first that he is mad; ONE mad action is not enough to prove a man mad; whom the GODS would destroy, they first make mad.

made. *See* MAKE.

madman. *See* FOOLS and madmen speak the truth; it's ILL putting a naked sword in a madman's hand.

madness. *See* the FIRST glass for thirst, the second for nourishment, the third for pleasure, and the fourth for madness; a MAN of gladness seldom falls into madness.

magnifying glass. *See* FAME is a magnifying glass.

Mahomet. *See* if the MOUNTAIN will not go to Mahomet, Mahomet must go to the mountain.

maid. maids say nay and take (*English*) Demure young women often say no when they really mean yes. John Heywood, *Two Hundred Epigrams*, 1562. The impossibility of understanding the way young women think is recognized by a Russian proverb that runs 'a maiden's heart is a dark forest'.

> Play the maid's part, still answer nay, and take it.
> William Shakespeare, *Richard III*, 1594

~ *See also* BACHELORS' wives and maids' children be well taught; a DOG's nose and a maid's knees are always cold; OLD maids lead apes in hell; when the BELLY is full the mind is among the maids.

main. *See* LOOK to the main chance.

maintain. what maintains one vice would bring up two children (*English*) The pursuit of vice is costly. Benjamin Franklin, in Arber's *English Garner*, 1758.

~ *See also* it is EASIER to build two chimneys than to maintain one.

maker. *See* LAW makers should not be law breakers.

malady. *See* MUCH meat, much malady.

male. *See* the FEMALE of the species is more deadly than the male.

malice hurts itself most (*English*) Ill feeling towards others eats away at the person who harbours it. John Clarke, *Paroemiologia Anglo-Latina*, *c.*1639. Variants include 'malice drinks its own poison', 'malice feeds on the living', and 'he that keeps malice harbours a viper in his heart'. Other proverbs add 'malice hath a sharp sight and strong memory', 'malice is mindful', and 'malice seldom wants a mark to shoot at'.

> Malice drinketh up the greatest part of its own poison.
> Thomas Fuller, *Gnomologia*, 1732

malt. *See* a SOFT fire makes a sweet malt.

Mammon. *See* you cannot SERVE God and Mammon.

man. as a man lives so shall he die (*Hebrew*) The character of a man's life will be reflected in the manner in which he meets his death, when it is too late for him to change the pattern of his existence. Bible, Ecclesiastes 11:3. In its fullest form the proverb is sometimes given as 'as a man lives so shall he die, as a tree falls, so shall it lie'.

if a man deceive me once, shame on him, but if he deceive me twice, shame on me (*English*) Those who allow themselves to be duped twice by the same party have only themselves to blame. Nathan Bailey, *An Universal Etymological English Dictionary*, 1736.

if a man once fall, all will tread on him (*English*) Any man brought low by scandal or some other setback will find everyone bands together to join in criticism of him. J. Palsgrave, *L'Éclaircissement de la langue française*, 1530.

it is the men who make a city (*Greek*) The character of a city depends more upon its inhabitants than upon the physical realities of bricks and mortar. Thomas Fuller, *Gnomologia*, 1732 (also quoted by Thucydides).

> It is men who make a city, not walls, or ships without crews.
>
> Thucydides, *History of the Peloponnesian War*, fifth century BC

a man apt to promise is apt to forget (*English*) Those who make promises frequently are unlikely to take them seriously. Thomas Fuller, *Gnomologia*, 1732.

a man at thirty must be either a fool or a physician (*Roman*) Any man who has not learned to look after his health by the age of thirty is a fool. Tacitus, *Annals*, first century AD. Tacitus attributed the saying to the Emperor Tiberius, who lived to the ripe old age of seventy-eight. When Plutarch cited the proverb he altered the relevant age to sixty.

a man can die but once (*English*) Mortals need suffer death only once. William Shakespeare, *Henry IV, Part 2*, *c.*1598.

> Death of one person can be paid but once.
>
> William Shakespeare, *Antony and Cleopatra*, *c.*1606

a man can do no more than he can (*English*) It is futile asking someone to do more than they are capable of. J. Palsgrave, *L'Éclaircissement de la langue française*, 1530. Related proverbs include 'man doth what he can, and God what He will'.

a man cannot give what he hasn't got (*English*) It is impossible to give something not actually in one's possession. Samuel Johnson, quoted by James Boswell, 1775.

man cannot live by bread alone (*Hebrew*) There is more to life than the maintenance of mere bodily existence. Bible, Deuteronomy 8:3 and Matthew 4:4.

> Man canna live by bread alone, but he assuredly canna live without it.
>
> John Buchan, *Witch Wood*, 1927

a man cannot spin and reel at the same time (*English*) A person cannot do two things at the same time. John Ray, *A Collection of English Proverbs*, 1678. Also encountered with 'weave' in the place of 'reel'.

a man cannot whistle and drink at the same time (*English*) It is impossible to do two things at the same time. J. Howell, *Paroemiographia*, 1659.

a man has choice to begin love but not to end it (*English*) People are free to fall in love as they choose, but cannot similarly decide when their love will end. H.G. Bohn, *A Handbook of Proverbs*, 1855.

man is a bubble (*Greek*) The life of a man does not last long and leaves as little impression. R. Taverner, *Proverbs or Adages with New Additions, gathered out of the Chiliades of Erasmus*, 1539.

> Man is but a bubble, or bladder of the water.
>
> R. Taverner, *Proverbs or Adages with New Additions, gathered out of the Chiliades of Erasmus*, 1539

a man is a lion in his own cause (*English*) When a person has a vested interest in something he or she will work at it more assiduously than would be the case otherwise. David Fergusson, *Scottish Proverbs*, 1641.

a man is as old as he feels, and a woman as old as she looks (*English*) The age of a woman may be judged from her appearance, while a man may decide it from his inner condition. Mortimer Collins, 'How Old Are You?', 1855. Wags have since varied the proverb as follows, 'a man is as old as the woman he feels'. Also encountered in Italian.

> O wherefore our age be revealing?
> Leave that to the registry books!
> A man is as old as he's feeling,
> A woman as old as she looks.
>
> Mortimer Collins, 'How Old Are You?', 1855

a man is known by the company he keeps (*English*) A person's character may be judged by the quality of his friends and associates. M. Coverdale, *H. Bullinger's Christian State of Matrimony*, 1541 (it may also be found in various forms in the writings of Euripides and Aesop). Formerly usually quoted in discussing a woman's choice of marriage partners. Less often heard English equivalents include 'bad company is the ruin of a good character' and 'as a man is, so is his'. The proverb is also found in other European languages. An Italian variant, recorded in 1574, goes 'Tel me with whom thou doest goe, and I shall know what thou doest', while a Spanish version, quoted by Cervantes in *Don Quixote* in 1615, runs 'Tell me what company you keep, and I'll tell you what you are'. *See also* BIRDS of a feather flock together.

> There is a proverb, Mrs Joyner, 'You may know him by his company'.
>
> William Wycherley, *Love in a Wood*, 1672

man is the measure of all things (*Greek*) Man is capable of subjugating all things to his will. George Chapman, *Caesar and Pompey*, 1631 (also quoted by Plato).

> As of all things man is said the measure,
> So your full merits measure forth a man.
>
> George Chapman, *Caesar and Pompey*, 1631

man is to man a wolf (*Roman*) Men can behave with animal viciousness to those perceived to be their rivals. Cornelius Agrippa, *The Vanity of Arts and Sciences*, 1569 (also quoted by Plautus). A contrasting view is offered by the proverb 'man is to man a god' and the more equivocal 'man is to man either a god or a wolf'.

> I mourn the pride and avarice that make man a wolf to man.
>
> William Cowper, *The Task*, 1785

a man knows his companion in a long journey and a little inn (*English*) Those who travel together and share the same accommodation will know each other very well by journey's end. Thomas Fuller, *Gnomologia*, 1732.

a man may lose his goods for want of demanding them (*English*) Those who fail to assert their ownership of their own property risk losing it altogether. T. Draxe, *Bibliotheca Scholastica*, 1616.

a man must take such as he finds, or such as he brings (*English*) A person must accept things as they are, unless he or she has better to offer. Geoffrey Chaucer, *The Canterbury Tales*, *c.*1387. *See also* take what you FIND or what you bring.

> I have herd seyd, man sal taa of twa thinges,
> Slyk as he fyndes, or taa slyk as he bringes.
>
> Geoffrey Chaucer, *The Canterbury Tales*, *c.*1387

a man of gladness seldom falls into madness (*English*) People who adopt a generally optimistic attitude to life are unlikely to be driven mad by their experiences. J. Howell, *Paroemiographia*, 1659.

a man of many trades begs his bread on Sunday (*English*) People who pursue many different lines of business are unlikely to do as well as people who concentrate on one particular trade. James Kelly, *A Complete Collection of Scotish Proverbs*, 1721. Contrasting proverbs include 'many ventures make a full freight'.

a man of straw is worth a woman of gold (*English/French*) A feeble and relatively ineffective man is, by virtue of his sex, still the equal of the most accomplished woman. John Florio, *Second Fruites*, 1591.

a man of words and not of deeds is like a garden full of weeds (*English*) A man who is unwilling to back his promises with action is of little worth. J. Howell, *Paroemiographia*, 1659.

man proposes, but God disposes (*Hebrew*) Men may initiate enterprises, but it is God who decides how they turn out. Bible, Proverbs 16:9 (also quoted by William Langland, *Piers Plowman*, in 1377, by Thomas à Kempis in 1420 and before him in variant forms by Plato). It is also found in most other European languages and has equivalents elsewhere in the world, the Chinese for instance having 'man may plan, but Heaven executes', while a Yiddish saying runs 'man rides but God holds the reins' and the Polish have 'man shoots but God carries the bullet'. Related proverbs in English include 'man doth what he can and God what He will'.

> A man's heart deviseth the way: but the Lord directeth his steps.
>
> Proverbs 16:9

a man's best friend is his dog (*English*) The one companion a man can rely on to be faithful is his dog. Alexander Pope, *Letters*, 1737. Another proverb advises 'a man, a horse and a dog are never weary of each other's company'.

Histories are more full of examples of the fidelity of dogs than of men.

Alexander Pope, *Letters*, 1737

a man's destiny is always dark (*English*) It is impossible to know what the future has in store. George Herbert, *Outlandish Proverbs*, 1651.

man's extremity is God's opportunity (*English*) It is when life is at its least bearable that people are most likely to turn to religious faith to keep them going. T. Adams, *Works*, 1629.

a man's studies pass into his character (*Roman*) A man will be influenced by what he learns. Francis Bacon, *Essays*, 1612 (also quoted by Ovid in his *Heroides*). Sometimes encountered in the form 'a man's character passes into his studies'.

a man surprised is half beaten (*English*) A person caught unawares is automatically at a disadvantage. Thomas Fuller, *Gnomologia*, 1732.

a man that breaks his word bids others be false to him (*English*) A person who does not behave honestly towards others cannot expect them to behave honestly in return. Edward Hall, *Hall's Chronicle*, 1548.

the man who is born in a stable is a horse (*English*) A person will acquire the manners and characteristics of his upbringing. M. Scott, *Tom Cringle's Log*, 1833. Also encountered in the contrasting form 'a man is not a horse because he was born in a stable'.

a man who is his own lawyer has a fool for a client (*English*) Anyone who relies on his own judgement in the courts rather than employ someone with relevant specialist knowledge is a fool. Philadelphia *Port Folio*, 1809.

a man will never change his mind if he has no mind to change (*English*) Those who have no opinion about something have no views that may be changed. R.C. Trench, *On the Lessons in Proverbs*, 1853.

a man without religion is like a horse without a bridle (*Roman*) A person who has no religious faith lacks a direction in life. Robert Burton, *Anatomy of Melancholy*, 1621. Another proverb suggests that lack of material possessions is more important: 'a man without money is no man at all'.

Justice and religion are the two chief props ... of a ... commonwealth: ... as Sabellicus delivers, a man without religion is like an horse without a bridle.

Robert Burton, *Anatomy of Melancholy*, 1621

men are blind in their own cause (*English*) If a person has a vested interest in something they are likely to dismiss arguments that appear to run contrary to that interest, no matter how well founded the criticisms might be. John Heywood, *A Dialogue containing ... the Proverbs in the English Tongue*, 1546.

men are not to be measured by inches (*English*) Great men are not necessarily great in physical stature. John Florio, *Montaigne*, 1603.

God doth not measure men by inches. People of small stature may have stout hearts.

James Kelly, *A Complete Collection of Scotish Proverbs*, 1721

men count up the faults of those who keep them waiting (*French*) It is bad policy to keep others waiting, as they will while away the time considering your faults.

men cut large thongs of other men's leather (*English*) People are more inclined to waste raw materials when others have paid for them. *Proverbs of Hending*, 1300.

The comparative wastefulness wherewith that which is another's is too often used: Men cut broad thongs from other men's leather.

R.C. Trench, *On the Lessons in Proverbs*, 1853

men leap over where the hedge is lowest (*English*) Those in the weakest position make the easiest targets for others. John Heywood, *A Dialogue containing ... the Proverbs in the English Tongue*, 1546. Variants include 'everyone leaps over the dyke where it is lowest'. *See also* a LOW hedge is easily leaped over.

Men loup the dike where it is leaghest. That is, oppress and over-run those who are least able to resist them.

James Kelly, *A Complete Collection of Scotish Proverbs*, 1721

men's years and their faults are always more than they are willing to own (*English*) Men are always unwilling to the full extent of either their age or their sins. H.G. Bohn, *A Handbook of Proverbs*, 1855.

no man can be a good ruler unless he hath first been ruled (*English*) Only those who have experienced the rule of another will rule wisely when they assume power. R. Taverner, *Proverbs or Adages with New Additions, gathered out of the Chiliades of Erasmus*, 1539.

no man can serve two masters (*Hebrew*) It is impossible to be faithful to more than one master or ideal simultaneously. Bible, Matthew 6:24. The proverb made its first appearance in English literature in a collection of political songs around 1330. Related proverbs include 'no man can do two things at once'. *See also* you cannot SERVE God and Mammon.

> Men cannot serve two masters.
>
> George Bernard Shaw, *Saint Joan*, 1924

no man cries stinking fish (*English*) No one speaks ill of their own wares or attributes (including fish-mongers advertising their fish); generally quoted as a warning against anything that is being advertised, on the grounds that goods of reasonable quality sell themselves and thus require no advertising. L. Price, *A Map of Merry Conceits*, 1656.

> I replied that I was a young gentleman of large fortune (this was not true; but what is the use of crying bad fish?).
>
> William Thackeray, *Barry Lyndon*, 1844

no man is a hero to his valet (*French*) The aura of mystique is much reduced with intimate knowledge of a person's personal character. John Florio, *Montaigne's Essays*, 1603. The saying is most commonly attributed to the seventeenth-century Frenchwoman Madame Cornuel, though much the same may be found in the writings of Plutarch and Montaigne. *See also* FAMILIARITY breeds contempt.

> And to his very valet seemed a hero.
>
> Lord Byron, *Beppo*, 1818

no man is angry that feels not himself hurt (*English*) For a man to be truly angry he must have suffered some personal affront. Coined or repeated by Francis Bacon. A US proverb offers a different insight into the workings of anger: 'to be angry is to punish yourself for another's faults.'

no man is indispensable (*English*) No individual is irreplaceable (usually referring to an employee in a company, team or other organization and recommending humility to those inclined to believe in their own self-importance).

no man is infallible (*English*) Nobody is perfect or immune from making mistakes.

no man is wise at all times (*Roman*) Even those who are very wise make mistakes. J. Clarke, *Paroemiologia Anglo-Latina*, 1639 (also quoted by Pliny). *See also* even HOMER sometimes nods.

> I was tired of being always wise, and could not help gratifying their request, because I loved to see them happy.
>
> Oliver Goldsmith, *The Vicar of Wakefield*, 1766

that which a man causes to be done, he does himself (*English*) Responsibility for an action rests with the person who ordered it done, as well as with his agent. Roger L'Estrange, *Aesop's Fables*, 1692. Sometimes encountered in the Latin version: *Qui facit per alium facit per se*. *See also* if you WANT a thing done well, do it yourself.

> That which a man causes to be done, he does himself, and 'tis all a case whether he does it by practice, precept, or example.
>
> Roger L'Estrange, *Aesop's Fables*, 1692

whatever man has done, man may do (*English*) It stands to reason that anything one man can do can be done by others. Charles Reade, *Hard Cash*, 1863. Another proverb on contrasting lines runs 'a man that does what no other man does is wondered at by all'.

~ *See also* AGE and wedlock bring a man to his night-cap; ALL men are mortal; APPAREL makes the man; as SOON as man is born he begins to die; BACCHUS hath drowned more men than Neptune; a BAD woman is worse than a bad man; the BEST laid schemes of mice and men gang oft agley; the BEST of men are but men at best; BETTER be an old man's darling than a young man's slave; the BETTER gamester the worser man; BUSINESS makes a man as well as tries him; the CHILD is the father of the man; CHILDREN are to be deceived with comfits and men with oaths; COMMAND your man and do it yourself; do as MOST men do and men will speak well of you; don't JUDGE a man by the words of his mother, listen to the comments of his neighbours; EARLY to bed and early to rise, makes a man healthy, wealthy and wise; EVERY elm has its man; EVERY man can rule a shrew but he who has her; GOD made man, man made money; GOD made the country, and man made the town; a GOOD wife and health is a man's best wealth; GREAT men have great faults; if my AUNT had been a man, she'd have been my uncle; if the ADDER could hear and the blindworm could see, neither man nor beast would ever go free; in SPORTS and journeys men are known; like MASTER, like man; MANNERS maketh man; MANY men have many minds; MARRIAGE makes or mars a man; MEAT and mass never hindered man; the MIND is the man; MONEY makes a man; NEEDLES and pins, needles and pins, when a man marries his trouble begins; NINE tailors make a man; no MOON, no man; SHOW me the man and I'll show you the law; SIX hours' sleep for a man, seven for a woman and eight for a fool; so MANY men, so many opinions; the STYLE is the man; the TAILOR makes the man; there is NOTHING so good for the inside of a man as the outside of a horse; THREE things drive a man out of his house: smoke, rain and a scolding wife; TODAY a man, tomorrow none; TRIM TRAM, like master like man; an UNTOWARD boy may make a good man; the WAY to a man's heart is through his stomach; when the WIND is in the east, 'tis neither good for man nor beast; a WHISTLING woman and a crowing hen is neither fit for God nor men; WINE and wenches empty men's purses; WINE hath drowned more men than the sea.

Manchester. what Manchester says today, the rest of England says tomorrow (*English*) Radical thinking may originate not in capitals or at the heads of organizations but in more remote areas. Rudyard Kipling, *A Day's Work*, 1898. The proverb is often encountered with other cities (both British and US) usurping the place of Manchester, which owed its claim to original thought to its reputation as a champion of free trade in the 1840s.

manners. manners maketh man (*English*) It is by a person's standards of civilized behaviour that he may be judged. *Douce MS*, *c.*1350. Also found as 'manners make the man'. According to another proverb 'manners and money make a gentleman'.

> The difference is, that in days of old Men made
> the manners; manners now make men.
> Lord Byron, *Don Juan*, 1824

~ *See also* EVIL communications corrupt good manners; HONOURS change manners; MEAT is much, but manners is more; OTHER times, other manners.

manure. *See* the BEST manure is under the farmer's foot.

many. many a good cow hath an evil calf (*English*) Good character in parents is no guarantee of good character in their offspring. John Heywood, *A Dialogue containing ... the Proverbs in the English Tongue*, 1546. *See also* like FATHER, like son.

many a mickle makes a muckle (*English*) A lot of small amounts amassed together will amount to a considerable total. *Ancrene Wisse*, 1250. The original form of the proverb ran 'many a little makes a mickle' ('mickle' signifying a considerable amount), or alternatively 'many a pickle makes a mickle'. 'Muckle', a mock-dialect nonsense word suggesting a large quantity of something, first appeared in the late eighteenth century.

> A Scotch adage, than which nothing in nature is
> more true ... 'many mickles make a muckle'.
> George Washington, *Writings*, 1793

many a one says well that thinks ill (*English*) Many people say kind things that they do not mean. Jonathan Swift, *Polite Conversation*, 1738.

many dishes make many diseases (*English*) People who eat too much risk damaging their health. Robert Burton, *Anatomy of Melancholy*, 1624.

many drops make a shower (*English*) Tiny things may combine to make something much more significant. George Pettie, *A Petite Pallace of Pettie His Pleasure*, 1576. Related proverbs include 'many drops of water will sink a ship'. *See also* look after the PENNIES and the pounds will look after themselves.

many go out for wool and come home shorn (*Spanish*) Those who set out to acquire some benefit for themselves may only end up worse off. J. Minsheu, *Dialogues in Spanish*, 1599.

> To wander through the world ... without once
> considering how many there goe to seeke for
> wooll, that returne againe shorne themselves.
> Thomas Shelton, *Cervantes' Don Quixote*, 1612

many hands make light work (*Greek*) The more people help the less work each will have to do. *Sir Beves*, *c.*1330 (also quoted in variant forms by Hesiod and other writers in classical times). One variant in which the Romans knew the proverb ran 'by the hands of many a great load is lightened'.

> Most Hands dispatch apace,
> And make light work, (the proverb says).
> Samuel Butler, *Hudibras*, 1678

many haws, many snows (*Scottish*) If plants produce many haws then the winter that follows will be severe. Robinson, *Whitby Glossary*, 1855. Variants include 'many haws, cold toes'. *See also* MANY hips and haws, many frosts and snaws.

many hips and haws, many frosts and snaws (*English*) The more hips and haws in the autumn, the more severe the winter will be. M.A. Denham, *A Collection of Proverbs ... relating to the Weather*, 1846. *See also* many HAWS, many snows.

many irons in the fire, some must cool (*English*) A person who tries to pursue several projects at once will find that some at least fail to prosper or hold their interest. W. Paget, *Letter to Somerset*, *c.*1549.

Make haste, then; for I have more irons in the fire.
John Dryden, *An Evening's Love*, 1671

many kiss the child for the nurse's sake (*English*) In certain circumstances kindness or favours may be shown to someone in order to impress a third party. John Heywood, *A Dialogue containing ... the Proverbs in the English Tongue*, 1546 (also recorded in thirteenth-century manuscripts). Another proverb on the subject of kissing hands warns 'many kiss the hand they wish cut off.' *See also* PRAISE the child and you make love to the mother.

Many one kisses the bairn for love of the nurrish.
That is, shows their kindness to the companions, friends, or relations, of those upon whom they have a design, which they hope by their influence to effect.
James Kelly, *A Complete Collection of Scottish Proverbs*, 1721

many men have many minds (*Roman*) The more people are involved, the more opinions will be voiced. Geoffrey Chaucer, 'The Squire's Tale', *The Canterbury Tales*, *c.*1387 (also quoted by Terence).

Diverse wits affected divers beene.
Edmund Spenser, *The Faerie Queene*, 1596

many sands will sink a ship (*English*) Small things can multiply to produce a great effect. Robert Burton, *Anatomy of Melancholy*, 1621.

many talk of Robin Hood who never shot with his bow (*English*) Some people boast of deeds in which they had no role. Geoffrey Chaucer, *Troilus and Criseyde*, *c.*1385–90.

many women, many words (*English*) Where women congregate there will always be plenty of chatter. *The Castle of Perseverance*, *c.*1425.

so many countries, so many customs (*Greek*) Every country boasts its own distinctive cultural identity. *Anglo-Saxon Gnomic Verses*, *c.*1100 (also recorded in a hymn by the Greek poet Pindar in the fifth century BC). Equivalent proverbs are found in several other European languages. *See also* OTHER times, other manners; so MANY men, so many opinions.

In sondry londes, sondry ben usages.
Geoffrey Chaucer, *Troilus and Criseyde*, *c.*1385–90

so many men, so many opinions (*Roman*) Every man has his own unique set of opinions and individual outlook on the world. Geoffrey Chaucer, *The Canterbury Tales*, *c.*1387 (also quoted by Terence). Also found as 'so many men, so many minds' and as 'so many heads, so many wits'. *See also* so many COUNTRIES, so many customs; MANY men have many minds.

Doctors differ. So many persons, so many minds.
Samuel Richardson, *Sir Charles Grandison*, 1754

so many mists in March, so many frosts in May (*English*) The prevalence of mist in March is an indication of how much frost will lie on the ground in May. A. Hopton, *Concordancy of Years*, 1612.

there are many ways of dressing a calf's head (*English*) There are many ways of saying or doing a foolish thing (or, if one way of doing something does not work, there is always another way that may be tried next). Seventeenth century. The proverb is an allusion to the banquets held by members of the Calves' Head Club, which was dedicated to ridiculing the memory of Charles I, deemed by his enemies to have been a 'foolish' king whose folly expressed itself in many and varied forms. The club first met in 1693; at its annual banquet on the anniversary of the king's execution, 30 January, those present enjoyed a large dish of calves' heads dressed in different ways to represent Charles and his closest supporters. The last banquet was held in 1735.

Their bill of fare was a large dish of calves' heads, dressed several ways, by which they represented the king and his friends who had suffered in his cause; a large pike with a small one in its mouth, as an emblem of tyranny; a large cod's head by which they intended to represent the person of the king singly; a boar's head with an apple in its mouth, to represent the king as bestial ...
Ned Ward (attributed), *Secret History of the Calves' Head Club, or the Republicans Unmasked*, *c.*1700

there's many a good cock come out of a tattered bag (*English*) Many good things emerge from unpromising situations. C.S. Burne, *Shropshire Folklore*, 1883. The proverb had its origins in cockfighting.

there's many a good tune played on an old fiddle (*English*) Old age is not necessarily a bar to worthwhile achievement. Samuel Butler, *The Way of All Flesh*, 1902. Equivalent proverbs include 'good broth may be made in an old pot'.

> Beyond a haricot vein in one of my legs I'm as young as ever I was. Old indeed! There's many a good tune played on an old fiddle.
>
> Samuel Butler, *The Way of All Flesh*, 1902

there's many a slip 'twixt cup and lip (*English*) Things can go amiss even at the very last moment before they are finally made secure (just as a drink may be dropped or slopped before the cup reaches the mouth). R. Taverner, *Proverbs or Adages with New Additions, gathered out of the Chiliades of Erasmus,* 1539 (also quoted by Erasmus).

there's many a true word spoken in jest (*English*) Very often a comment intended humorously turns out to be (or may turn out to be) more accurate than anyone expected. Geoffrey Chaucer, *The Canterbury Tales*, *c.*1387. In some circumstances the proverb may be quoted when a seriously intended comment that has been delivered in a lighthearted fashion seems likely to be dismissed as a joke. Related proverbs include 'the truest jests sound worst in guilty ears' and 'a true jest is no jest'.

> There actually are Johannis churches here … as well as Apollinaris ones … There is many a true word spoken in jest.
>
> George Bernard Shaw, *Widowers' Houses*, 1898

too many boatmen will run the boat up to the top of the mountain (*Japanese*) An overmanned ship (or organization) will surely come to grief. *See also* too many COOKS spoil the broth.

too many cooks spoil the broth (*English*) If too many people interfere in a job only chaos and confusion will result (as will happen in any kitchen when more than one person attempts to supervise the cooking). *The Life of Carew*, 1575. The proverb is known in other European languages, including Dutch ('too many cooks make the porridge too salt'). A Turkish equivalent runs 'two captains will sink the ship', while the Polish have 'where there are six cooks, there is nothing to eat'.

> She professes to keep her own counsel … 'Too many Cooks spoil the Broth'.
>
> Jane Austen, *The Watsons*, *c.*1805

~ *See also* ABUNDANCE, like want, ruins many; although there EXIST many thousand subjects for elegant conversation, there are persons who cannot meet a cripple without talking about feet; a CARELESS hussy makes many thieves; COWARDS die many times before their death; he KNOWS how many beans make five; he that KISSETH his wife in the marketplace shall have many teachers; he THREATENS many that hurts any; he who COMMENCES many things finishes but a few; an HONEST look covereth many faults; 'IF' and 'an' spoils many a good charter; it takes a GOOD many shovelfuls of earth to bury the truth; a MAN of many trades begs his bread on Sunday; the MOB has many heads but no brains; ONE butcher does not fear many sheep; ONE funeral makes many; ONE lie makes many; RICH folk have many friends; TWO fools in a house are too many.

mar. *See* a GENTLE housewife mars the household; go FORWARD and fall, go backward and mar all; MARRIAGE makes or mars a man.

March. March comes in like a lion and goes out like a lamb (*English*) The month of March usually begins with severe weather, which calms and becomes mild by the end. J. Fletcher, *Wife for a Month*, 1625. Occasionally heard with the lion and the lamb reversed. Variants include 'March comes in with an adder's head and goes out with a peacock's tail'. Among other proverbs reflecting upon the variability of the weather in March is 'March many weathers'.

> Charming and fascinating he resolved to be. Like March, having come in like a lion, he purposed to go out like a lamb.
>
> Charlotte Brontë, *Shirley*, 1849

~ *See also* as NOVEMBER so the following March; if APPLES bloom in March, in vain for them you'll search; if apples bloom in April, then they'll be plentiful; if apples bloom in May, you may eat them night and day; on the FIRST of March, the crows begin to search; a PECK of March dust is worth a king's ransom; so MANY mists in March, so many frosts in May.

march. *See* an ARMY marches on its stomach.

mare. *See* the GREY mare is the better horse; MACKEREL sky and mares' tails make lofty ships carry low sails; MONEY makes the mare to go; NOTHING so bold as a blind mare.

mark. *See* he that SHOOTS oft shall at last hit the mark.

market. *See* BUY in the cheapest market and sell in the dearest; GENTRY sent to market will not buy one bushel of corn; GOOD ware makes quick markets; a MONEYLESS man goes fast through the market; SEND a fool to market and a fool he'll return; THREE women make a market.

market-place. *See* he that KISSETH his wife in the market-place shall have many teachers.

marriage. marriage halves our griefs, doubles our joys, and quadruples our expenses (*English*) Marriage has its benefits but always proves expensive. V.S. Lean, *Collecteana*, 1902–04.

marriage is a lottery (*English*) The achievement of a successful marriage with an ideal partner is more a matter of chance than of choice and all who enter into it are taking a risk. Ben Jonson, *The Tale of a Tub*, 1633. A fuller French version of the proverb runs 'marriage is a lottery in which men stake their liberty and women their happiness'. *See also* MARRIAGES are made in heaven.

> I smile to think how like a lottery
> These weddings are.
> Ben Jonson, *The Tale of a Tub*, 1633

marriage makes or mars a man (*Italian*) Marriage to the right partner will seal a man's happiness, while marriage to the wrong partner will break him. J. Howell, letter, 1625. A somewhat extreme Spanish version of the proverb runs 'the day you marry you either kill yourself or save yourself'.

marriages are made in heaven (*Hebrew*) The choice of marital partners is directed by God. W. Painter, *The Palace of Pleasure*, 1567 (also quoted in the *Midrash* in AD550). The sentiment may also be found in French. Variants include 'wedding is destiny, and hanging likewise'. A less well-known English proverb runs 'if marriages are made in heaven, some had few friends there'. *See also* HANGING and wiving go by destiny; MARRIAGE is a lottery.

> House and riches are the inheritance of fathers:
> and a prudent wife is from the Lord.
> Proverbs 19:14

~ *See also* DREAM of a funeral and you hear of a marriage; the JEWS spend at Easter, the Moors at marriages, the Christians in suits; there goes MORE to marriage than four bare legs in a bed.

marriage-bed. *See* the BRIDE goes to her marriage-bed but knows not what shall happen to her.

marry. he that marries a widow and three children marries four thieves (*English*) The man who marries a widow with children will find they rob him of all his wealth. John Ray, *A Collection of English Proverbs*, 1670. On not dissimilar lines is 'he that marries a widow and two daughters has three back doors to his house'. Husbands of widows are further warned that 'he who marries a widow will often have a dead man's head thrown in his dish' (meaning that the second husband will have to withstand constant comparison with the first), 'never marry a widow unless her first husband was hanged' and also that 'it's dangerous marrying a widow, because she hath cast her rider'. On a more positive, if cynical, note another proverb observes that 'it is as easy to marry a widow as to put a halter on a dead horse'. Another encourages the man thinking of marrying a widow not to delay: 'marry a widow before she leaves mourning'.

he that marries for wealth sells his liberty (*English*) Those who marry rich women for their money will have to live under the domination of their wives. George Herbert, *Outlandish Proverbs*, 1640. Related proverbs include the Italian 'he who marries for love without money hath merry nights and sorry days'.

he that marries late marries ill (*English*) People who marry late are unlikely to enjoy a happy married life. Thomas Nashe, *Works*, 1589. Equivalent proverbs include 'he that marries ere he be wise will die ere he thrive' and 'he who marries early will leave a widow'. The Germans, meanwhile, have the succinct saying 'early marriage, long love'.

marry in haste and repent at leisure (*French/Italian*) Those who get married without taking time to question the wisdom of it will live to regret it in the years to come. W. Painter, *The Palace of Pleasure*, 1566 (also quoted in variant forms centuries earlier by Socrates and Philemon among others).

> He who would marry is on the road to repentance.
> Philemon, *Fragments*, *c.*300BC

marry in Lent, and you'll live to repent (*English*) It is unlucky to marry during the season of Lent, as marriages contracted then offend heaven and will not prosper. Mrs G.L. Banks, *Manchester Man*, 1876.

marry in May and rue the day (*Roman*) May is the unluckiest month of the year and thus the one month to avoid when choosing a wedding date. *Poor Robin's Almanack*, 1675 (also quoted by Ovid). Also encountered in the forms 'marry in May, rue for aye' and 'marry in May, repent alway'. Less well known equivalents include 'married in May will soon decay' and 'to wed in May is to wed poverty'.

marry with your match (*Roman*) When seeking a partner in marriage, it is best to choose someone from the same rank and station as yourself. John Clarke, *Paroemiologia Anglo-Latina*, 1639 (also quoted by Ovid). Variants include 'marry a wife of thine own degree', 'marry thy like' and the Spanish 'let everyone marry an equal'. *See also* MEDDLE with your match.

~ *See also* BUILDING and marrying of children are great wasters; go down the LADDER when thou marriest a wife, go up when thou choosest a friend; he that TELLS his wife news is but newly married; HONEST men marry quickly, wise men not at all; it is BETTER to marry a shrew than a sheep; KEEP yourself from the anger of a great man, from the tumult of a mob, from a man of ill fame, from a widow that has been thrice married, from a wind that comes in at a hole, and from a reconciled enemy; NEEDLES and pins, needles and pins, when a man marries his trouble begins; when a COUPLE are newly married the first month is honeymoon, or smick smack; the second is hither and thither; the third is thwick thwack; the fourth the devil take them that brought thee and I together; a YOUNG man should not marry yet, an old man not at all.

martyr. *See* the BLOOD of the martyrs is the seed of the Church; he that BRINGETH himself into needless dangers dieth the devil's martyr; it is not the SUFFERING but the cause which makes a martyr.

mass. *See* MEAT and mass never hindered man.

master. like master, like man (*Roman*) The character of a man is reflected in that of his servants or employees. J. Palsgrave, *L'Éclaircissement de la langue française*, 1530 (also quoted by Cicero).

> The Proverbe be true that sayes, 'like master, like man', and I may add, 'like lady, like maid'. Lady Hercules was fine, but her maid was still finer.
>
> Thomas Shelton, *Cervantes' Don Quixote*, 1620

the master's eye maketh the horse fat (*Greek*) A person takes special care to nurture what belongs to him (and is also prone to see what belongs to him as being perhaps better than it really is). Hugh Latimer, *Sermons*, 1552 (also quoted by Aristotle).

> It is the eye of the master that fatteth the horse, and the love of the woeman, that maketh the man.
>
> John Lyly, *Euphues: The Anatomy of Wit*, 1578

masters should be sometimes blind, and sometimes deaf (*English*) There are occasions when a master is best advised to turn a blind eye to the misdemeanours of his underlings. Thomas Fuller, *Gnomologia*, 1732.

~ *See also* the EYE of a master does more work than both his hands; EARLY master, long knave; a FALLING master makes a standing servant; FIRE and water are good servants but bad masters; GIVE a slave a rod and he'll beat his master; he that DESPISES his own life is soon master of another's; he that has a WIFE has a master; he that TEACHES himself has a fool for his master; if MONEY be not thy servant, it will be thy master; an ILL master makes an ill servant; JACK is as good as his master; JACK of all trades is master of none; let your PURSE be your master; no MAN can serve two masters; the SCHOLAR teacheth the master; TRIM TRAM, like master like man; when the MISTRESS is the master, parsley grows the faster.

master-blow. *See* RESERVE the master-blow.

mastiff. *See* YELPING curs will raise mastiffs.

match. *See* MARRY with your match; MEDDLE with your match.

matter. *See* if the COUNSEL be good, no matter who gave it.

maun. *See* he that will to CUPAR maun to Cupar.

maw. *See* that is not ALWAYS good in the maw that is sweet in the mouth.

May. May chickens come cheeping (*English*) As May

is the unluckiest month of the year, when evil spirits roam abroad, any young born in that month are unlikely to be worth keeping. A. Hislop, *Proverbs of Scotland*, 1868. In times gone by this superstition was so firmly believed that litters of kittens and other young animals were routinely destroyed. It was also supposed that human children born in May were unlikely to prosper and would probably die before reaching maturity – thus the Cornish proverb 'May chets bad luck begets' ('chets' being 'children'). Variants include 'May birds are aye cheeping'. *See also* MARRY in May and rue the day.

~ *See also* APRIL showers bring forth May flowers; BUTTON up to the chin till May comes in; the CUCKOO comes in April, and stays the month of May, sings a song at midsummer, and then goes away; he that would LIVE for aye must eat sage in May; he who BATHES in May will soon be laid in clay, he who bathes in June will sing a merry tune, he who bathes in July will dance like a fly; if APPLES bloom in March, in vain for them you'll search; if apples bloom in April, then they'll be plentiful; if apples bloom in May, you may eat them night and day; MARRY in May and rue the day; ne'er CAST a clout till May be out; so MANY mists in March, so many frosts in May; a SWARM of bees in May is worth a load of hay; a WET May brings plenty of hay.

meadow. *See* a THIN meadow is soon mowed.

meal. *See* CLEAN heels, light meals.

mean. *See* ONE year's seeding means seven years' weeding; SILENCE means consent; SPEAK not of my debts unless you mean to pay them.

means. *See* the END justifies the means; he who WILLS the end wills the means.

measure (noun). **there is a measure in all things** (*Greek*) Moderation should be exercised in all circumstances. Geoffrey Chaucer, *Troilus and Criseyde*, *c.*1385–90 (also quoted by Horace). *See also* MODERATION in all things.

> If the prince be too important, tell him there is measure in every thing.
>
> William Shakespeare, *Much Ado About Nothing*, *c.*1598

~ *See also* EAT at pleasure, drink by measure; FEED by measure and defy the physician; MAN is the measure of all things; WEIGHT and measure take away strife.

measure (verb). **don't measure other people's corn by one's own bushel** (*English*) Refrain from judging other's behaviour or efforts and so forth by one's own standards. W. Saltonstall, *Picturae Loquentes*, 1631.

> Pray do not measure my corn with your bushel, old Drybones!
>
> John Gay, *The Wife of Bath*, 1713

measure thrice and cut once (*English*) It is good policy to measure something carefully before buying it. John Florio, *Second Frutes*, 1591. Variants include 'measure thrice what thou buyest and cut it but once'.

> Measure twice, cut but once. Take good deliberation before you fall to actual execution.
>
> James Kelly, *A Complete Collection of Scotish Proverbs*, 1721

~ *See also* MEN are not to be measured by inches.

meat. meat and mass never hindered man (*Scottish*) A man should give time to the eating of meat and the taking of mass, as these can only give him new strength to tackle his work. J. Carmichaell, *Proverbs in Scots*, 1628. Variants include 'meat and matins hinder no man's journey' and 'prayers and provender hinder no man's journey'.

> I beg to remind you of an old musty saw, that meat and mass never hindered man.
>
> Robert Louis Stevenson, *Catriona*, 1893

meat is much, but manners is more (*English*) A person should never forget their table manners, however hungry he or she is. J. Clarke, *Paroemiologia Anglo-Latina*, 1639. Also encountered in the form 'meat is much, but mense is better'.

when meat is in anger is out (*English*) People who are well fed are less likely to be angry. J. Clarke, *Paroemiologia Anglo-Latina*, 1639.

~ *See also* BONES bring meat to town; DRY bread at home is better than roast meat abroad; GOD never sends mouths but He sends meat; GOD sends meat, but the devil sends cooks; GOOD ale is meat, drink and cloth; the GREATEST crabs be not all the best meat; HARE is melancholy meat; it is GOOD to be merry at meat; MUCH meat, much malady; NEW meat begets a new appetite; ONE man's meat is another man's poison; POOR men seek meat for their stomach; rich men stomach for their meat; QUICK at meat, quick at work; SMALL birds must have meat; take HEED of reconciled enemies and of meat twice boiled; you BUY land you buy stones, you buy meat you buy bones.

medal. *See* EVERY medal hath its reverse.

meddle. meddle with your match (*English*) Contend with your equal (often addressed to those who pick on their inferiors). Ben Jonson, *Every Man in his Humour*, 1598. *See also* MARRY with your match.

> Meddle with your match. Spoken by people of age, when young people jest upon them too wantonly: or by weak people, when insulted by the more strong and robust.
>
> James Kelly, *A Complete Collection of Scottish Proverbs*, 1721

~ *See also* BUSY folks are always meddling.

meddler. *See* LAY-OVERS for meddlers.

medicine. there is no medicine against death (*English*) The one incurable disease is death. William Cowper, *Yearly Bill of Mortality*, 1787. Variants include 'there is no medicine for fear'. *See also* there is a REMEDY for everything except death.

> No medicine, though it oft can cure,
> Can always balk the tomb.
>
> William Cowper, *Yearly Bill of Mortality*, 1787

~ *See also* LAUGHTER is the best medicine; READY money is a ready medicine.

meet. do not meet troubles halfway (*Roman*) There is no point exposing yourself to trouble before you need to. J.C. Hutcheson, *Crown and Anchor*, 1896 (also quoted by Seneca). *See also* never TROUBLE trouble till trouble troubles you.

> Are you come to meet your trouble? The fashion of the world is to avoid cost, and you encounter it.
>
> William Shakespeare, *Much Ado About Nothing*, c.1598

meet on the stairs and you won't meet in heaven (*English*) Bad luck will befall those who pass each other on the same set of stairs. R. Hunt, *West of England*, 1865. The superstition that it is unlucky to pass on the stairs is thought to date from rougher times: people were deemed particularly vulnerable to attack from assassins when climbing or descending stairs because it was more difficult to draw their swords to defend themselves from any sudden attack. To avoid the bad luck that might be provoked by crossing on the stairs, tradition suggests either waiting until the other person has passed on their way or undertaking such precautions as crossing the fingers.

~ *See also* although there EXIST many thousand subjects for elegant conversation, there are persons who cannot meet a cripple without talking about feet; EXTREMES meet; GOOD and quickly seldom meet; it is MERRY when friends meet; I was ANGERED, for I had no shoes – than I met a man who had no feet; when GREEK meets Greek then comes the tug of war.

melancholy. *See* HARE is a melancholy meat; he is a FOOL that is not melancholy once a day.

melt. *See* the SAME heat that melts the wax will harden the clay.

même. *See* PLUS ça change, plus, c'est la même chose.

memory. memory is the treasure of the mind (*English*) A person's memory is full of treasures. T. Wilson, *Rhetorique*, 1560. Also encountered in the forms 'memory is the treasury and guardian of all things' and 'memory is the treasurer of the mind'. A Chinese proverb, however, insists that 'a good memory is not equal to pale ink' and the Spanish suggest that 'memory, like women, is usually unfaithful'.

> Memory ... is the treasure-house of the mind.
>
> Thomas Fuller, *The Holy State and the Profane State*, 1642

memory of happiness makes misery woeful (*English*) Memories of happy times make bad times even harder to bear. John Lydgate, *The Fall of Princes*, 1431–8. Variants include the Roman 'the remembrance of past pleasures adds to present sorrows' and the Italian 'no greater grief than to remember days of joy when misery is at hand' (as coined by Dante).

> The consideration of pleasures past greatly augments the pain present.
>
> *Politeuphuia*, 1597, attributed to J. Bodenham

~ *See also* CREDITORS have better memories than debtors; GREAT wits have short memories; he is an ILL companion that has a good memory; a LIAR ought to have a good memory.

men. *See* MAN.

mend. either mend or end (*English*) If something is imperfect and cannot be improved, it is best to dispense with it altogether. John Florio, *Montaigne*, dedication, 1603.

I would set my life on any chance,
To mend it or be rid on't.
William Shakespeare, *Macbeth*, *c.*1604

~ *See also* the BEST go first, the bad remain to mend; it is NEVER too late to mend; LEAST said, soonest mended; when THINGS are at the worst they soon begin to mend; who ERRS and mends to God himself commends; a WOMAN and a ship ever want mending.

merchant. a merchant that gains not, loseth (*English*) A businessman who fails to make a profit must be judged as failing. H. Estienne, *World of Wonders*, 1607. On the other hand, another proverb asserts that 'he that loseth is a merchant as well as he that gains'.

~ *See also* QUICK returns make rich merchants.

mercy. mercy surpasses justice (*English*) The demands of justice can be swayed by the impulse to show mercy. Geoffrey Chaucer, *Troilus and Criseyde*, *c.*1385–90. Variants include the Russian 'clemency is the support of justice'.

Here may men see that mercy passeth right.
Geoffrey Chaucer, *Troilus and Criseyde*, *c.*1385–90

mercy to the criminal may be cruelty to the people (*English*) In showing leniency to a criminal it is possible that a court is exposing the general populace to future harm. Joseph Addison, *Spectator*, 1711. Related proverbs include 'nothing emboldens sin as much as mercy'.

In the public administration of justice, mercy to one may be cruelty to others.
Joseph Addison, *Spectator*, 1711

merry. it is merry when friends meet (*English*) Friends meet in a friendly atmosphere. T. Draxe, *Bibliotheca Scholastica*, 1616. Variants include 'it is merry when gossips meet', 'it is merry when maltmen meet', and 'it is merry when knaves meet'. Related proverbs include 'merry meet merry part'.

merry is the company till the reckoning comes (*English*) Merrymaking tends to come to an end when the time to settle up the bill arrives. John Ray, *A Collection of English Proverbs*, 1678. Also encountered in the form 'merry is the feast-making till we come to the reckoning'.

merry nights make sorry days (*English*) Those who over-indulge themselves in the evening will regret it the following day. *Folk-Lore*, 1896.

'tis merry in hall when beards wag all (*English*) It is a sure sign, during a feast, that everyone is enjoying themselves when their beards are seen to wag (with laughter). *King Alisaunder*, *c.*1310.

Be merry, be merry, my wife has all ... 'Tis merry in hall when beards wag all.
William Shakespeare, *Henry IV, Part 2*, *c.*1598

~ *See also* ALL are not merry that dance; a CHERRY year, a merry year; a plum year, a dumb year; CHILDREN and fools have merry lives; he who BATHES in May will soon be laid in clay, he who bathes in June will sing a merry tune, he who bathes in July will dance like a fly; it is GOOD to be merry and wise; it is GOOD to be merry at meat; the JOY of the heart makes the face merry; the MORE the merrier.

Merryman. *See* the BEST doctors are Dr Diet, Dr Quiet and Dr Merryman.

messmate before a shipmate, shipmate before a stranger, stranger before a dog (*English*) The recommended order in which sailors choose their comrades. Admiral W.H. Smyth, *Sailor's Word-Book*, 1867. Also encountered in the variant form 'a messmate before a shipmate, a shipmate before a stranger, a stranger before a dog, but a dog before a soldier'.

met. *See* MEET.

mettle. mettle is dangerous in a blind horse (*English*) Spirit or zeal may not be welcome in individuals who do not know how to harness it. S. Ward, *Sermons*, 1636.

Metal is dangerous in a blind mare. And so is bigotry, and blind zeal, in an ignorant fellow.
James Kelly, *A Complete Collection of Scotish Proverbs*, 1721

~ *See also* put a COWARD to his mettle and he'll fight the devil.

mice. *See* MOUSE.

mickle. *See* MANY a mickle makes a muckle.

midge. *See* the MOTHER of mischief is no bigger than a midge's wing.

midnight. *See* ONE hour's sleep before midnight is worth two after.

midstream. *See* don't CHANGE horses in midstream.

midsummer. *See* the CUCKOO comes in April, and stays the month of May, sings a song at midsummer, and then goes away.

mieux. *See* RECULER pour mieux sauter.

might is right (*Greek*) Usual standards of justice can be overwhelmed by the influence of the powerful. 1327, quoted in T. Wright, *Political Songs*, 1839 (also quoted in Plato's *Republic*, by Plautus and by Lucan in *Pharsalia*). Also found as 'might makes right' and 'might overcomes right'. Other variants include the German 'a handful of might is better than a sackful of right' and the Spanish 'there is no argument like that of the stick'.

> O, that right should thus overcome might!
> William Shakespeare, *Henry IV, Part 2*, *c.*1598

mighty. *See* the PEN is mightier than the sword; a REED before the wind lives on, while mighty oaks do fall.

mile. *See* AFTER dinner rest a while, after supper walk a mile; EVERY mile is two in winter; an INCH is as good as a mile; a MISS is as good as a mile; SIT awhile and go a mile.

milk. *See* the COW gives good milk but kicks over the pail; GOD gives the milk but not the pail; it's no USE crying over spilt milk; why BUY a cow when milk is so cheap?; you cannot SELL the cow and sup the milk.

mill. the mill cannot grind with the water that is past (*English*) It is impossible to make anything of times or opportunities that have already passed. T. Draxe, *Adages*, 1616. Related proverbs include 'mills will not grind if you give them not water'.
mills and wives are ever wanting (*English*) Mills, like women, are a constant source of expense. George Herbert, *Outlandish Proverbs*, 1640.
the mills of God grind slowly, yet they grind exceeding small (*English*) It may take a long time to get your revenge on someone, but when you do it is sure to be doubly crushing. George Herbert, *Outlandish Proverbs*, 1640.

> Though the mills of God grind slowly, yet they
> grind exceeding small;
> Though with patience He stands waiting, with
> exactness grinds He all.
> Henry Wadsworth Longfellow, 'Retribution', 1870

the mill that is always going grinds coarse and fine (*English*) People who are always talking are bound to say stupid things as well as intelligent things. P.W. Joyce, *English as We Speak*, 1910.

~ *See also* ALL is grist that comes to the mill; FOG on the hill, water to the mill; fog in the hollow, fine day to follow; MIST from the hill brings water to the mill; MUCH water goes by the mill that the miller knows not of; when the CLOUDS go up the hills, they'll come down by the mills.

miller. *See* EVERY honest miller has a thumb of gold; MUCH water goes by the mill that the miller knows not of.

mind (noun). **the mind is the man** (*Roman*) A person should be judged by his or her intellectual abilities. D. Rogers, *Naaman*, 1642 (quoting Cicero). Given by Cicero as 'each man's mind is himself'.
my mind to me a kingdom is (*Greek*) Whatever their status, a person is the ruler in their own mind. Sir E. Dyer, 'My Mind to Me a Kingdom is', 1588 (quoting Seneca).

> I am no gentleman born, I must confess; but my
> mind to me a kingdom is.
> Ben Jonson, *The Case is Altered*, 1609

~ *See also* a CONTENTED mind is a continual feast; the FACE is the index of the mind; GOD keep me from the man that has but one thing to mind; GREAT minds think alike; LITTLE things please little minds; a MAN will never change his mind who has no mind to change; MANY men have many minds; MEMORY is the treasure of the mind; out of SIGHT, out of mind; SPEECH is the index of the mind; TRAVEL broadens the mind; when the BELLY is full the mind is among the maids; a WILLING mind makes a light foot; a WISE man changes his mind, a fool never will.

mind (verb). **mind your own business** (*English*) Do not pay unwarranted interest in the affairs of others, but concentrate instead on your own. J. Clarke, *Paroemiologia Anglo-Latina*, 1639. Related proverbs include 'mind what you must live by'.

~ *See also* TAILORS and writers must mind the fashion.

minister. *See* HIDE nothing from thy minister, physician and lawyer.

miracle. *See* the AGE of miracles is past.

mire. *See* there was NEVER a good town but had a mire at one end of it.

mirror. *See* the BEST mirror is an old friend.

mirth. the mirth of the world dureth but a while (*English*) Joy is always temporary. R. Sandford, *The Garden of Pleasure*, 1573.

~ *See also* an OUNCE of mirth is worth a pound of sorrow.

mischief. he that mischief hatcheth, mischief catcheth (*English*) Those who create mischief must expect to be the victim of mischief themselves. W. Camden, *Remains concerning Britain*, 1605. A Roman equivalent runs 'he prepares evil for himself who plots mischief for others'.

mischief comes by the pound and goes away by the ounce (*English*) Troubles tend to arrive suddenly in a heap and to go away only gradually. R. Sandford, *The Garden of Pleasure*, 1573. Related proverbs include 'misfortunes come on wings and depart on foot'.

> The yll commeth by poundes and goeth away by ounces.
>
> John Florio, *First Frutes*, 1578

mischief has swift wings (*English*) Mischief spreads very quickly. *Sir T. Smith's Voyage into Russia*, 1605.

no mischief but a woman or a priest is at the bottom of it (*Roman*) Women and the clergy are at the root of most disputes to beset mankind. Hugh Latimer, *Second Sermon before Edward VI*, 1549 (also quoted by Juvenal).

> Such a plot must have a woman in it.
>
> Samuel Richardson, *Sir Charles Grandison*, 1754

~ *See also* BETTER a mischief than an inconvenience; the MOTHER of mischief is no bigger than a midge's wing.

miser. *See* the DEVIL's mouth is a miser's purse.

misery. it is misery enough to have been once happy (*English*) For those who have fallen on bad times it is particularly painful to be reminded of how happy they once were. Bullein, *Bulwark of Defence*, 1562.

> *Miserum est fuisse felicem* ... it is a great miserie to have beene happy.
>
> Robert Burton, *Anatomy of Melancholy*, 1624

misery loves company (*English*) Those who feel depressed find consolation in the company of others, particularly if they are similarly afflicted. John Lyly, *Euphues: The Anatomy of Wit*, 1578. *See also* ADVERSITY makes strange bedfellows.

> If misery loves company, misery has company enough.
>
> Henry David Thoreau, *Journal*, 1 September 1851

~ *See also* it is GOOD to have company in misery; MEMORY of happiness makes misery woeful.

misfortune. misfortunes never come singly (*English*) If something goes wrong the chances are something else will too. *King Alisaunder*, *c.*1300. Also found in the form 'misfortunes never come alone'. A fuller version of this proverb is 'blessings do not come in pairs, misfortunes never come singly', while other variants include the Welsh 'misfortunes come by forties' and 'a misfortune and a friar are seldom alone'. *See also* BLESSINGS do not come in pairs, misfortunes never come singly; it never RAINS but it pours.

> When sorrows come, they come not single spies, but in battalions.
>
> William Shakespeare, *Hamlet*, *c.*1600

~ *See also* IGNORANCE is a voluntary misfortune; one has ALWAYS strength enough to bear the misfortunes of one's friends; our WORST misfortunes are those which never befall us.

misreckoning is no payment (*English*) Paying someone less than is due to them is little better than paying them nothing at all. John Heywood, *A Dialogue containing ... the Proverbs in the English Tongue*, 1546. Also encountered in the form 'wrong reckoning is no payment'.

miss (noun). **a miss is as good as a mile** (*English*) Failing by a narrow margin is in the final analysis no better than failing by a wider margin. William Camden, *Remains concerning Britain*, 1614. The proverb was originally given as 'an inch in a miss is as good as an ell' (an ell being an archaic measurement equivalent to forty-five inches). *See also* an INCH is as good as a mile.

> A narrow shave; but a miss is as good as a mile.
> George Bernard Shaw, *Arms and the Man*, 1894

miss (verb). *See* a SLICE off a cut loaf isn't missed; you NEVER miss the water till the well runs dry.

mist. mist from the hill brings water to the mill (*English*) Mist on high ground warns of wet weather to come. R.P. Chope, *Hartland Dialect*, 1891. Variants include 'when the mist comes from the hill, then good weather it doth spill; when the mist comes from the sea, then good weather it will be'. Another version is specific to anglers: 'when the mist creeps up the hill, fisherman out and try your skill; when the mist begins to nod, fisherman then put up your rod'.

~ *See also* so MANY mists in March, so many frosts in May.

mistake. if you don't make mistakes you don't make anything (*English*) Those who are not prepared to risk making mistakes will never achieve anything. Joseph Conrad, *An Outcast of the Islands*, 1896. *See also* NOTHING ventured, nothing gained.

> It's only those who do nothing that make no mistakes, I suppose.
> Joseph Conrad, *An Outcast of the Islands*, 1896

~*See also* he is the BEST general who makes the fewest mistakes.

mistress. when the mistress is the master, parsley grows the faster (*English*) Parsley grows best in a garden where the woman rules the household. Charlotte Burne, *Shropshire Folk-Lore*, 1883.

misty. a misty morning may have a fine day (*English*) Mist in the morning is often a sign of fine weather to come. James Kelly, *A Complete Collection of Scotish Proverbs*, 1721.

misunderstanding brings lies to town (*English*) Lies and rumours often arise out of mistakes and misunderstandings. J. Clarke, *Paroemiologia Anglo-Latina*, 1639. Related proverbs include the Scottish 'ill hearing maks wrang rehearsing'.

mixen. *See* BETTER wed over the mixen than over the moor.

mixture. *See* RIGHT mixture makes good mortar.

mob. the mob has many heads but no brains (*English*) Mobs can include many intelligent individuals but rarely act intelligently. Thomas Fuller, *Gnomologia*, 1732. Variants include 'a mob is a monster with many hands but no brains'.

> A mob's a monster; heads enough but no brains.
> Benjamin Franklin, *Poor Richard's Almanack*, November 1747

~ *See also* KEEP yourself from the anger of a great man, from the tumult of a mob, from a man of ill fame, from a widow that has been thrice married, from a wind that comes in at a hole, and from a reconciled enemy.

mocking is catching (*English*) Those who scorn others for their faults may well find they have fallen prey to the same faults themselves. John Heywood, *Play of Love*, 1533. Also encountered in the forms 'hanging's stretching, mocking's catching' and 'scorning is catching'.

> Mocking is catching. Spoken to discourage people from mimicking any man's imperfections, lest you contract a habit of them.
> James Kelly, *A Complete Collection of Scotish Proverbs*, 1721

moderation in all things (*Greek*) It is sensible to be moderate in everything you do. Herman Melville, *Mardi*, 1849 (also quoted by Hesiod in *Works and Days*). Variants include 'drink moderately, love moderately, live moderately; everything in moderation'. *See also* there is a MEASURE in all things.

mole. *See* an ARGUS abroad but a mole at home.

molehill. *See* don't make a MOUNTAIN out of a molehill.

Monday. Monday's child is fair of face, Tuesday's child is full of grace; Wednesday's child is full of woe, Thursday's child has far to go; Friday's child is loving and giving, Saturday's child works hard for its living; and the child that's born on the Sabbath day, is fair

and wise and good and gay (*English*) The day upon which a person is born gives an indication of their underlying character. A.E. Bray, *Traditions of Devon*, 1838. A related proverbial rhyme suggests which are the best days of the week for getting married: 'Monday for wealth, Tuesday for health, Wednesday the best day of all; Thursday for crosses, Friday for losses, Saturday no luck at all.'

~ *See also* FRIDAY's hair and Sunday's horn go to the devil on Monday morn; SNEEZE on a Monday, you sneeze for danger.

money. if money be not thy servant, it will be thy master (*Italian*) Those who fail to achieve mastery over money will find it gains mastery over them. G. Torriano, *Select Italian Proverbs*, 1666. Also found in the form 'money is a good servant but a bad master'.

money begets money (*English*) Money, once obtained, attracts more money to it. T. Wilson, *Discourse upon Usury*, 1572. Also found as 'money draws money'. Related proverbs include 'money is often lost for want of money'. *See also* MONEY makes money.

> We have got to recollect that money makes money, as well as makes everything else.
> Charles Dickens, *Our Mutual Friend*, 1865

money has no smell (*Roman*) Money carries with it no taint of wherever it might have come from. Arnold Bennett, *Mr Prohack*, 1922. The proverb arose from a comment by the Roman emperor Vespasian, responding to his son Titus's reservations about raising money via a tax imposed on public lavatories: 'and yet it comes from urine'. Another proverb with the same meaning is the English 'money is welcome though it come in a dirty clout', first recorded in the mid-sixteenth century.

> He understood in a flash the deep wisdom of that old proverb ... that money has no smell.
> Arnold Bennett, *Mr Prohack*, 1922

money isn't everything (*English/US*) The getting of money is not the only consideration in life. Eugene O'Neill, *Marco Millions*, 1927. Another proverb, though, warns 'he that wants money wants all things'.

money is power (*English*) Wealth brings with it influence. N. Ames, *Almanack*, 1741. Much the same sentiment is expressed in the proverb 'all things are obedient to money' (which was quoted in classical times by Horace among others). Related proverbs upon the potency of money include 'money is the sinews of war' and 'money is the sinews of love'.

money makes a man (*English*) A man with money is taken more seriously by the world at large, regardless of his other qualities or flaws. R.L. Greene, *Early English Carols*, 1500. A fuller version of the proverb runs 'money makes a man free everywhere'. Also found in the form 'money is the man'.

> Money most truly and fearfully 'makes the man'. A difference in income, as you go lower, makes more and more difference ... in all which polishes the man.
> Charles Kingsley, *Alton Locke*, 1850

money makes friends enemies (*English*) Money can easily come between friends. Thomas Fuller, *Gnomologia*, 1732. Variants include the French 'money makes strangers'.

money makes money (*English*) Money can be used to make more money. T. Wilson, *Discourse upon Usury*, 1572. Variants include 'money would be gotten if there were money to get it with'. A less well-known proverb advises 'if thou wouldst keep money, save money; if thou wouldst reap money, sow money'. *See also* MONEY begets money.

> Money, says the proverb, makes money. When you have got a little, it is often easy to get more.
> Adam Smith, *The Wealth of Nations*, 1776

money makes the mare to go (*English*) Anything can be accomplished with money. 1500, quoted in R.L. Greene, *Early English Carols*, 1935. Equivalent proverbs include 'money makes the old wife trot', 'money will make the pot boil' and the French 'money makes dogs dance'.

money makes the world go round (*US*) It is money that motivates all the world's important activities. Fred Ebb and John Kander, song title, *Cabaret*, 1966. A related proverb runs 'money governs the world'. Centuries before the phrase was made famous as the song from *Cabaret* it had been voiced elsewhere in various disguised forms, including a seventeenth-century Dutch version. *See also* LOVE makes the world go round.

money never comes out of season (*English*) Money is always welcome. T. Draxe, *Bibliotheca Scholastica*, 1616.

money talks (*English*) The promise of money buys any favour or influence that a person may desire. G. Torriano, *Italian Proverbs*, 1666. Although it is only in the twentieth century that the proverb has appeared in its modern form, the same sentiment has been voiced in various forms many centuries previously and equivalents may be found in many European languages. Examples from elsewhere include 'money answers all things', 'if money go before, all ways lie open' and the Italian 'the tongue hath no force when golde speaketh'.

> Money will say more in one moment than the most eloquent lover can in years.
>
> Henry Fielding, *The Miser*, 1733

~ *See also* ALL things are obedient to money; BAD money drives out good; BEAUTY is potent, but money is omnipotent; DALLY not with women or money; DIRTY hands make clean money; a FOOL and his money are soon parted; GOD made man, man made money; he that doth LEND doth lose his money and friend; he that SERVES God for money will serve the devil for better wages; if you LOSE your time you cannot get money or gain; ILL luck is worse than found money; LEND your money and lose your friend; LOOK for your money where you lost it; LOVE does much, money does everything; the LOVE of money is the root of all evil; READY money is a ready medicine; READY money will away; a RICH man's money hangs him oftentimes; SAMSON was a strong man yet he could not pay money before he had it; TELL money after your own father; TIME is money; TRADE is the mother of money; where there's MUCK, there's money; you PAYS your money and you takes your choice.

moneyless. a moneyless man goes fast through the market (*English*) A person with no money to spend has no reason to linger where things might be purchased. James Kelly, *A Complete Collection of Scottish Proverbs*, 1721. The proverb is sometimes quoted to convey the idea that those who are in need of something will hurry to where it might be obtained. Also found in the form 'a silverless man goes fast through the market'.

monk. a monk out of his cloister is like a fish out of water (*Roman*) Monks are only at home in a monastery. Geoffrey Chaucer, *The Canterbury Tales* (prologue), *c.*1387.

~ *See also* the COWL does not make the monk; the DEVIL sick would be a monk; a RUNAWAY monk never praises his convent; take HEED of an ox before, of a horse behind, of a monk on all sides; THREE things are insatiable: priests, monks and the sea.

monkey. *See* the HIGHER the monkey climbs the more he shows his tail; if you PAY peanuts, you get monkeys; SOFTLY, softly, catchee monkey.

month. the month that comes in good will go out bad (*English*) A month that begins with fine weather will end with bad weather. R. Inwards, *Weather Lore*, 1893.

~ *See also* the CUCKOO comes in April, and stays the month of May sings a song at midsummer, and then goes away; if you would be HAPPY for a week take a wife; if you would be happy for a month kill a pig; but if you would be happy all your life plant a garden; NEVER eat an oyster unless there is an R in the month; the NIGHTINGALE and cuckoo sing both in one month; when a COUPLE are newly married the first month is honeymoon, or smick smack; the second is hither and thither; the third is thwick thwack; the fourth the devil take them that brought thee and I together.

moon. the moon does not heed the barking of dogs (*Roman*) It is futile to rant against nature or against other things or persons that are incapable of change. John Lyly, *Euphues and His England*, 1580.

> Doth the moon care for the barking of a dog? They detract, scoffe, and raile (saith one), and bark at me on every side; but I … vindicate myself by contempt alone.
>
> Robert Burton, *Anatomy of Melancholy*, 1621

no moon, no man (*English*) Babies born at the time when there is no moon (in other words, when it is between cycles) are unlikely to prosper. Thomas Hardy, *The Return of the Native*, 1878. Superstition claims that babies born at this time are unlikely to live beyond puberty. The ideal time for childbirth is during the waxing of a new moon.

> 'No moon, no man.' 'Tis one of the truest sayings ever spit out. The boy never comes to anything that's born at new moon.
>
> Thomas Hardy, *The Return of the Native*, 1878

~ *See also* the FULL moon brings fair weather; he

will SHOOT higher who shoots at the moon than he who aims at a tree; a PALE moon doth rain, a red moon doth blow; a white moon doth neither rain nor snow.

Moor. *See* the JEWS spend at Easter, the Moors at marriages, the Christians in suits.

moor. *See* BETTER wed over the mixen than over the moor.

more. the more camomile is trodden on, the faster it grows (*English*) Some things, such as love and virtue, grow stronger the harsher they are treated (just as camomile lawns are supposed to grow better when walked upon). William Shakespeare, *Henry IV, Part 1*, *c.*1597.

> For ne'er was simple camomile so trod on, yet still I grow in love.
>
> James Shirley, *Hyde Park*, 1637

the more cost, the more honour (*Scottish*) The more expensive a thing is, the more desirable it is to some. David Fergusson, *Scottish Proverbs*, 1641. Expressing much the same sentiment is the English proverb 'what costs little, is less esteemed'.

> Spoken to them that propose an expensive thing, when a cheaper would do.
>
> James Kelly, *A Complete Collection of Scottish Proverbs*, 1721

the more danger, the more honour (*English*) There are more opportunities to win respect when the peril is greatest. Francis Beaumont and John Fletcher, *Women Pleased*, *c.*1625.

more haste, less speed (*English*) Doing something too quickly may ultimately mean it takes longer to accomplish than if it is done at a steadier pace. *Douce MS*, *c.*1350. A longer version, recorded in 1721, runs 'the more haste, the worse speed, quoth the tailor to his long thread'. Equivalents include 'haste trips up its own heels', the Scottish 'fools' haste is nae speed' and the Tunisian 'in haste is regret, in slowness peace'. *See also* make HASTE slowly; SLOW but sure wins the race.

> A mod'rate pace is best indeed.
> The greater hurry, the worse speed.
>
> Edward Ward, *Hudibras Redivivus*, 1705

more have repented speech than silence (*English*) Those who speak their mind are more likely to regret it later than those who say nothing at all. George Herbert, *Outlandish Proverbs*, 1640. Related proverbs include 'no reply is best.'

the more hazelnuts, the more bastard children (*English*) More children are born out of wedlock in the wake of a good crop of hazelnuts. Northall, *Folk-phrases*, 1844. Hazelnuts are traditionally associated with fertility, perhaps originally because going out to collect hazelnuts in former times provided lovers with an excuse to meet away from the watchful eyes of their mentors (in Germany to 'go a-nutting' was actually a synonym for making love). Hazel twigs used to be carried at weddings, and hazelnuts feature in numerous charms and spells connected with love. As well as being good years for babies, bountiful hazelnut years are also reputed to coincide with a burgeoning in the number of prostitutes.

the more knave, the better luck (*English*) The more unprincipled a person is, the more they seem to benefit by strokes of good fortune. Hugh Latimer, *Sermons*, 1550. Related proverbs include 'the more knaves, the worse company'.

the more laws, the more offenders (*English*) The more rules there are to break, the more offences will be committed. J. Palsgrave, *L'Éclaircissement de la langue française*, 1530.

the more one drinks the more one may (*English*) The more a person gets used to drinking alcohol the more they find they can consume. T. Draxe, *Bibliotheca Scholastica*, 1616.

more people know Tom Fool than Tom Fool knows (*English*) People in the public eye are known by more people than they know themselves. S. Holland, *Wit and Fancy in a Maze*, 1656. The name Tom Fool was traditionally applied both to simpletons and to the Fools of historical drama. Also encountered with 'Jack' in the place of 'Tom Fool'.

> It was no satisfaction to me that I knew not their faces, for they might know mine ... according to the old English proverb, 'that more knows Tom Fool, than Tom Fool knows'.
>
> Daniel Defoe, *Colonel Jack*, 1723

the more said, the less done (*English*) The more time people spend discussing something the less likely it is to get done. George Colman, *Polly Honeycombe*, 1760.

more than enough is too much (*English*) A superfluity of anything is too much. John Heywood, *Two Hundred Epigrams*, 1562.

the more the fox is cursed, the better he fares (*English*) The greater the volume of complaint against someone or something, the greater it must be assumed has been that person or thing's success. Spelman, *Dialogue*, c.1580. Also encountered in the form 'the fox fares best when he is banned'.

> The Foxe fares ever best, when he is cursed.
>
> Ben Jonson, *Volpone*, 1605

the more the merrier (*English*) The greater the number the better the end result. *The Pearl*, c.1380. A fuller version of the proverb points out the contrasting advantages of a smaller number of people at a party or meal: 'the more the merrier; the fewer the better fare'. *See also* too MANY cooks spoil the broth.

> The old proverb comes true – 'the more the merrier: but the fewer the better fare'.
>
> Charles Kingsley, *Westward Ho!*, 1855

the more thy years, the nearer thy grave (*English*) The older a person is, the less time they have left to them. W. Camden, *Remains concerning Britain*, 1605.

the more wicked, the more fortunate (*English*) The wicked often seem to have the best luck. George Herbert, *Outlandish Proverbs*, 1640. This is somewhat countered by another proverb that warns 'a wicked man is his own hell'.

the more you get, the more you want (*Greek*) A little of something good only feeds the appetite for more. R. Rolle, *Psalter*, c.1340 (also quoted by Horace in his *Epistles*). Variants in other languages include the French *plus il en a, plus il en veut*.

> My more having would be a source
> To make me hunger more.
>
> William Shakespeare, *Macbeth*, c.1604

the more you stir, the worse it will stink (*English*) The more you probe into others' secrets the greater trouble you will provoke. John Heywood, *A Dialogue containing … the Proverbs in the English Tongue*, 1546.

> I have spoken … but let it alone; the more it is stirred, the more it will stink.
>
> Thomas Shelton, *Don Quixote*, 1620

the more you tramp on a turd the broader it grows (*Scottish*) The more a person tries to stamp out vicious rumours about themselves the wider the rumours are dispersed. David Fergusson, *Scottish Proverbs*, 1641.

there are more old drunkards than old doctors (*French*) Medical men may criticize the habits of habitual drunkards, but there is no guarantee that they will live as long.

there are more ways of killing a cat than choking it with cream (*English*) There is more than one way of doing something. Sydney Smith, *John Smith's Letters*, 1839. Also encountered in the variant form 'there's more than one way to skin a cat'. 'Butter' sometimes replaces 'cream'.

> Hold on yet awhile. More ways of killing a cat than choking her with cream.
>
> Charles Kingsley, *Westward Ho!*, 1855

there are more ways of killing a dog than choking it with butter (*English*) There are many alternatives when it comes to doing something. W.T. Thompson, *Chronicles of Pineville*, 1845.

> A proverb always had to be capped. No one could say, 'There's more ways of killing a dog than hanging it' without being reminded, 'nor of choking it with a pound of fresh butter.'
>
> Flora Thompson, *Lark Rise to Candleford*, 1945

there are more ways of killing a dog than hanging it (*English*) There is more than one way to do something. John Ray, *A Collection of English Proverbs*, 1670.

there goes more to marriage than four bare legs in a bed (*English*) There is more to achieving happiness in marriage than compatibility in sexual matters (the challenges of parenthood being one of the consequences thus implied). John Heywood, *A Dialogue containing … the Proverbs in the English Tongue*, c.1549.

> A sort of penny-wedding it will prove, where all men contribute to the young folks' maintenance, that they may not have just four bare legs in a bed together.
>
> Walter Scott, *The Fortunes of Nigel*, 1822

who hath no more bread than need must not keep a dog (*English*) Those who have only enough food to feed themselves will have nothing left over to feed a dog. George Herbert, *Outlandish Proverbs*, 1640.

you can have no more of a cat than her skin (*English*) Apart from its skin, a cat produces nothing of commercial value. H.G. Wright, *Arthur Hall of Grantham*, 1570.

you can have no more of a fox than the skin (*English*) You cannot get more from someone or something than there is to be had. Alexander Barclay, *Eclogues*, c.1514. *See also* you can have no MORE of a cat than her skin, you cannot get BLOOD from a stone.

~ *See also* an ANGLER eats more than he gets; BACCHUS hath drowned more men than Neptune; BIRTH is much but breeding more; CONTENT is more than a kingdom; DIET cures more than doctors; the EYE of the master does more work than both his hands; FOUR eyes see more than two; GLUTTONY kills more than the sword; he who GETS doth much, but he who keeps doth more; the HIGHER the monkey climbs the more he shows his tail; HONEY catches more flies than vinegar; KEEP no more cats than will catch mice; LESS of your courtesy and more of your purse; a MAN can do no more than he can; MEAT is much, but manners is more; MEN's years and their faults are always more than they are willing to own; MUCH would have more; the OLDER the crab-tree the more crabs it bears; ONE father is more than a hundred schoolmasters; ONE hair of a woman draws more than a team of oxen; RESPECT a man, he will do the more; SCORN at first makes after-love the more; SHIPS fear fire more than water; there are PLENTY more fish in the sea; who hath a FAIR wife needs more than two eyes.

morn. *See* FRIDAY's hair and Sunday's horn go to the devil on Monday morn.

morning. morning dreams come true (*Greek*) Things dreamt after midnight are sure to come true. J. Palsgrave, *Acolastus*, 1540 (also quoted by Horace in *Satires*).

> And all the morning dreams are true.
> Ben Jonson, *Love Restored*, 1616

~ *See also* CLOUDY mornings turn to clear afternoons; EVENING red and morning grey help the traveller on his way; a FOUL morning may turn to a fair day; a GAUDY morning bodes a wet afternoon; LOSE an hour in the morning, chase it all day; a MISTY morning may have a fine day; NEVER rely on the glory of the morning or on the smile of your mother-in-law; a RAINBOW in the morning is the shepherd's warning; a rainbow at night is the shepherd's delight; RED sky at night, shepherd's delight; red sky in the morning, shepherd's warning.

mortal. *See* ALL men are mortal.

mortar. *See* RIGHT mixture makes good mortar.

moss. *See* a ROLLING stone gathers no moss.

most. do as most men do and men will speak well of you (*English*) Those who fall in with the opinions and behaviour of their fellows are most likely to win their approval. John Heywood, *A Dialogue containing ... the Proverbs in the English Tongue*, 1546.

that which one most anticipates soonest comes to pass (*Roman*) It is often the thing that is most expected that happens first. Quoted by Horace.

~ *See also* the BUSIEST men have the most leisure; EMPTY vessels make the most sound; FIRST impressions are the most lasting; the LAST benefit is most remembered; LAZY folk take the most pains; LOOKERS-ON see most of the game; MALICE hurts itself most; SHALLOW streams make most din; they BRAG most that can do least; they that LIVE longest, see most.

mother. it is not as thy mother says but as thy neighbours say (*English*) Close relations are less likely to tell the truth about one than a person with whom one is less intimately connected. Thomas Fuller, *Gnomologia*, 1732. Related proverbs include 'the mother's breath is aye sweet'.

like mother, like daughter (*Hebrew*) Daughters take after their mothers both in character and mannerisms. Bible, Ezekiel 16:44. Variants include 'like mistress, like maid'. *See also* like FATHER, like son.

> Every one that useth proverbs shall use this
> proverb against thee, saying, As is the mother,
> so is her daughter.
> Ezekiel 16:44

the mother of mischief is no bigger than a midge's wing (*English/Scottish*) Grave consequences can result from the smallest item of gossip or unsubstantiated rumour. J. Carmichaell, *Proverbs in Scots*, 1628.

~ *See also* a CHILD may have too much of his mother's blessing; CHILDREN suck the mother when they are young and the father when they are old; don't JUDGE a man by the words of his mother, listen to the comments of his neighbours; EXPERIENCE is the mother of wisdom; a FAIR day in winter is the mother of a storm; he that WIPES the child's nose kisseth the mother's cheek; he that would the DAUGHTER win, must with the mother first begin; he was CURSED in his mother's belly that was killed by a cannon; IGNORANCE is the mother of devotion; IGNORANCE is the mother of impudence; a LIGHT heeled mother makes a heavy heeled daughter; NECESSITY is the mother of invention; NIGHT is the mother of counsel; POVERTY is the mother of health; PRAISE the child, and you make love to the mother; TRADE is the mother of money; TRUST is the mother of deceit.

mother-in-law. *See* NEVER rely on the glory of the morning or on the smile of your mother-in-law; there is but ONE good mother-in-law, and she is dead.

moult. *See* if the COCK moult before the hen we shall have weather thick and thin, but if the hen moult before the cock we shall have weather hard as a block.

mountain. don't make a mountain out of a molehill (*Greek*) Don't exaggerate minor problems so that they become major ones. William Roper, *Life of More*, 1557. Equivalents in other European languages, all descended from an ancient Greek saying, include the French 'to make an elephant out of a fly'.

> Those people are ever swelling mole hills to
> mountains.
>
> Samuel Foote, *The Lame Lover*, c.1760

if the mountain will not go to Mahomet, Mahomet must go to the mountain (*Arabic*) If it is impossible to do something the easy way then it must be done the hard way. Francis Bacon, *Essays*, 1597. According to Bacon, in his essay 'Of Boldness', Mahomet promised the faithful that he would call a mountain to him and preach from the top of it – but when he called the mountain did not come. Mahomet calmly explained that this was a sign of God's mercy, for had the mountain moved to where they stood they would all have been crushed. He then announced that as the mountain would not come to him, he would have to go to the mountain. The mountain has since been identified as Mount Safa near Mecca. Bacon may have produced his English version of the proverb after reading the Arabic *Anecdotes of Chodja Nas'reddin Dschocha er Rumi*: 'if the palm tree does not come to Dschocha, Dschocha will go to the palm tree.'

> Neither Kitty nor I can change our habits, even
> for friendship ... Mountains cannot stir ... but
> Mahomet can come to the mountain as often
> as he likes.
>
> Edward Bulwer-Lytton, *The Caxtons*, 1849

~ *See also* FAITH will move mountains; too MANY boatmen will run the boat up to the top of the mountain.

mourner. *See* when the DEVIL is dead, he never lacks a chief mourner.

mouse. a mouse in time may bite in two a cable (*English*) Given enough time, a relatively insignificant effort may result in great achievements. John Heywood, *A Dialogue containing ... the Proverbs in the English Tongue*, 1546.

> Rogues ... like rats, ofte bite the holy cords a-twain
> Which are too intrinse t'unloose.
>
> William Shakespeare, *King Lear*, 1605–06

a mouse may help a lion (*English*) The small and insignificant may still provide invaluable service to the great and powerful. *Mirror for Magistrates*, 1563. The proverb has its origins in Aesop's fable about the lion and the rat, which was first printed in English by William Caxton in 1484. Another proverb, however, warns the humble not to be overcome with a sense of their own importance: 'a mouse must not think to cast a shadow like an elephant.''

the mouse that has only one hole is easily taken (*Roman*) The fugitive who has only one place of safety to shelter in will soon be located. Geoffrey Chaucer, *The Canterbury Tales*, c.1387 (also quoted by Plautus). Also found in several other European languages.

> The mouse that always trusts to one poor hole,
> Can never be a mouse of any soul.
>
> Alexander Pope, *The Wife of Bath*, 1717

~ *See also* the BEST laid schemes of mice and men gang oft agley; BURN not your house to fright away the mice; a CAT in gloves catches no mice; it is a BOLD mouse that breeds in the cat's ear; KEEP no more cats than will catch mice; let the CAT wink and let the mouse run; NEVER let the plough stand to catch a mouse; no LARDER but hath its mice; ONE for the mouse, one for the crow, one to rot, one to grow; POUR not water on a drowned mouse; SILENCE catches a mouse; TWO cats and a mouse, two wives in one house, two dogs and a bone, never agree in one; when the CAT's away, the mice will play.

mouth. into the mouth of a bad dog often falls a good bone (*French*) Bad people get their share of good luck. J. Clarke, *Paroemiologia Anglo-Latina*, 1639.

out of the mouths of babes and sucklings (*Hebrew*) The young may, however unwittingly, voice great truths or perceptive insights. Bible, Psalms 8:2 and Matthew 21:16.

> Jesus saith unto them, Yea, have yee never read,
> Out of the mouth of babes and sucklings thou
> hast perfected praise.
> Matthew 21:16

~ *See also* BEES that have honey in their mouths have stings in their tails; a CLOSE mouth catches no flies; the DEVIL's mouth is a miser's purse; GOD never sends mouths but He sends meat; he that hath his HAND in the lion's mouth must take it out as well as he can; he who has ONCE burnt his mouth always blows his soup; it is not with SAYING honey, honey, that sweetness will come into the mouth; KEEP your mouth shut and your eyes open; NEAREST the heart, nearest the mouth; NEVER look a gift horse in the mouth; a SHUT mouth never fills a black coffin; a SOW may whistle, though it has an ill mouth for it; a THISTLE is a fat salad for an ass's mouth; that is not ALWAYS good in the maw that is sweet in the mouth; when the HEART is a fire some sparks will fly out of the mouth; when the WIND is in the south it blows the bait into the fish's mouth.

move. *See* FAITH will move mountains; GREAT bodies move slowly.

mow. *See* EARLY sow, early mow; a THIN meadow is soon mowed.

much. much coin, much care (*Greek*) Great riches bring with them the cares of responsibility and the anxiety that they will be lost. J. Clarke, *Paroemiologia Anglo-Latina*, 1639 (also quoted by Horace).

> Care follows increasing wealth.
> Horace, *Odes*, first century BC

much cry and little wool (*English*) Those who boast much of what they have to offer often turn out to have the least to offer in reality. J. Fortescue, *On the Governance of England*, 1475. *See also* EMPTY vessels make the most sound.

> Thou wilt at best but suck a bull,
> Or shear swine, all cry and no wool.
> Samuel Butler, *Hudibras*, 1663

much meat, much malady (*English*) Those who overeat lay themselves open to all manner of disease and physical ailment. *Politeuphuia*, 1597, attributed to J. Bodenham. Also found as 'much meat, many maladies'.

much smoke, little fire (*English*) When much fuss is made about something, the chances are there is very little substance to it. *Brewer's Phrase and Fable*, 1959.

much water goes by the mill that the miller knows not of (*English*) Many more things go astray or are stolen than the owner is aware of. John Heywood, *A Dialogue containing ... the Proverbs in the English Tongue*, 1546. A Scottish equivalent runs, 'mickle water goes by the miller when he sleeps'.

> What, man! more water glideth by the mill
> than wots the miller of.
> William Shakespeare, *Titus Andronicus*, c.1593

much would have more (*Greek*) Those who have a little of something good greatly desire more of it. *Douce MS*, c.1350 (also quoted by Horace). Also encountered in the form 'he that much hath much behoveth'. *See also* the MORE you get, the more you want.

> Much would have more; but often meets with less.
> Thomas Fuller, *Gnomologia*, 1732

in too much dispute truth is lost (*English*) Sight of the truth tends to be obscured when it is much argued over. A. Wilson, *History of Great Britain*, 1653.

you can have too much of a good thing (*English*) It is possible to have too much of anything, however desirable it may originally be. B. Burgh, *Cato*, 1483. Also found in the forms 'too much of a thing is good for nothing', 'too much of ought is good for nought', and 'too much breaks the bag'. *See also* ENOUGH is as good as a feast.

> Why then, can one desire too much of a
> good thing?
> William Shakespeare, *As You Like It*, c.1599

~ *See also* ASK much to have a little; BIRTH is much but breeding more; HEAR much, speak little; he is not POOR that hath little, but he that desireth much; he that LIVES long suffers much; he that TALKS much of his happiness, summons grief; he who GETS doth much, but he who keeps doth more; a LITTLE poison embitters much sweetness; LOVE does much, money does everything; MEAT is much, but manners is more; MORE than enough is too much; NOTHING costs so much as what is given us; an OLD sack asketh much patching; ONE beggar does not hate another as much as one doctor hates another; ONE enemy is too much; they that WALK much in the sun will be tanned at last; THINGS that are hard to come by are much set by; THINK much, speak little and write less.

muck. where's there's muck, there's money (*English*) Where there is muck – be it in the form of soil, dirt, dung or industrial grime – there is money to be made. John Ray, *A Collection of English Proverbs*, 1678. The saying was coined in the late sixteenth century when farmers first learned that spreading dung and other 'muck' on their land would promote their crops and enjoyed new currency after the Industrial Revolution when factories, a source of new wealth, belched out soot and smoke. Also found, in northern England as 'where there's muck, there's brass'. Other variants include 'muck and money go together'.

~ *See* RICHES are like muck, which stink in a heap, but spread abroad make the earth fruitful.

muckle. *See* MANY a mickle makes a muckle.

mud. *See* ALL that breed in the mud are not eels; EASTER in snow, Christmas in mud; Christmas in snow, Easter in mud.

mule. *See* BEWARE of the forepart of a woman, the hind part of a mule and all sides of a priest; ONE mule doth scrub another.

multitude. *See* CHARITY covers a multitude of sins.

murder. murder will out (*English*) It is impossible to keep terrible crimes such as murder secret. *Cursor Mundi*, *c.*1325. Variants include 'murder cannot be hid'. *See also* TRUTH will out.

O blisful god, that art so just and trewe!
Lo, how that thou biwreyest mordre alway,
Mordre wol out, that see we day by day.
Geoffrey Chaucer, *The Canterbury Tales*, *c.*1387

~ *See also* KILLING no murder.

music. music hath charms (*English*) One of the properties of music is the soothing of a troubled mind. William Congreve, *The Mourning Bride*, 1697. The fuller version, 'music hath charms to soothe the savage breast' is equally well known. The Spanish, meanwhile, have 'where there is music there can be nothing bad'. A contrasting proverb, however, runs 'all music jars when the soul's out of tune'.

Music hath charms to soothe the savage breast,
To soften rocks or bend a knotted oak.
William Congreve, *The Mourning Bride*, 1697

music helps not the toothache (*English*) Music may have many qualities, but has its limitations and cannot ease physical pain. George Herbert, *Outlandish Proverbs*, 1640.

must. must is for the king (*English*) Only monarchs are entitled to insist upon others doing as they say. George Chapman, *An Humorous Day's Mirth*, 1599. Also encountered in the form 'must is a king's word'.

mustard. *See* SYMPATHY without relief is like mustard without beef.

mutton. *See* ONE shoulder of mutton draws down another.

N

nail. nail drives out nail (*Greek*) The old is inevitably replaced by the new. *Ancrene Wisse*, 1250 (also found in the writings of Aristotle). Also found as 'one nail drives out another'. The origins of the proverb lie in the practice of using a new nail as a punch to dislodge an old one.

> As one nail by strength drives out another,
> So the remembrance of my former love
> Is by a newer object quite forgotten.
>
> William Shakespeare, *The Two Gentlemen of Verona*, c.1594

~ *See also* for WANT of a nail the shoe was lost; he must have IRON nails that scratches a bear.

naked. *See* ANYTHING will fit a naked man; CRAFT must have clothes but truth loves to go naked; it's ILL putting a naked sword in a madman's hand.

nakedness. *See* TRUTH's best ornament is nakedness.

name. get a name to rise early, and you may lie all day (*English*) Those who enjoy a good reputation may trade on it to enjoy easy benefits. Swetnam, *School of Defence*, 1617.

> I would not have a man depend too much upon this proverb; for a good name is soon lost, and hardly to be retrieved.
>
> James Kelly, *A Complete Collection of Scotish Proverbs*, 1721

names and natures do often agree (*English*) A person's character is often reflected by their name. J. Clarke, *Paroemiologia Anglo-Latina*, 1639. Related proverbs include 'names are debts'.

no names, no pack drill (*English*) By keeping the names of guilty parties secret no one can be punished (pack drill, drilling at length while carrying a heavy backpack, being a standard punishment for minor transgressions in the armed forces). O. Onions, *Peace in our Time*, 1923.

> I know some as are as sweet as the blossoms that bloom in the May – oh, no names, no pack drill.
>
> Sean O'Casey, *Juno and the Paycock*, 1925

~ *See* GIVE a dog a bad name and hang him; a GOOD name is better than a good girdle; he that has an ILL name is half hanged; a ROSE by any other name would smell as sweet; STICKS and stones may break my bones, but names will never hurt me.

Naples. *See* SEE Naples and die.

narrow. *See* it is HARD to turn tack upon a narrow bridge; WIDE will wear but narrow will tear.

nation. *See* the ENGLISH are a nation of shopkeepers.

natural. it is as natural to die as to be born (*English*) Death is a natural part of the business of living. Thomas Fuller, *Gnomologia*, 1732. Also encountered in the form 'dying is as natural as living'. Other expressions of the naturalness of death from around the world include the Greek 'all things are born of earth, all things earth takes again', the Italian 'what belongs to nature lasts to the grave' and the Malay 'flowers and buds fall and the old and ripe fall'.

nature. nature abhors a vacuum (*Roman*) An empty space of any kind runs contrary to the natural order of things. Thomas Cranmer, *Answer to Gardiner*, 1551 (derived ultimately from Plutarch).

> Whatever philosophy may determine of material

nature, it is certainly true of intellectual nature, that it abhors a vacuum: our minds cannot be empty.

Samuel Johnson, letter, 20 June 1771

nature does nothing in vain (*Greek*) There is a purpose behind all the workings of nature. G. Harvey, *Marginalia*, *c.*1580 (also found in the writings of Aristotle).

Nature which doth nothing in vain.

Francis Bacon, *The Advancement of Learning*, 1605

nature passes nurture (*English*) A person's inbred character will always have more influence than what they are taught. Stapylton, *Juvenal*, 1647. Sometimes quoted in reference to art, supporting the view that art can be but a pale imitation of nature. The same point is made by numerous other proverbs from around the world, among them the French 'nature is stronger than education', the Greek 'you will never make a crab walk straight forward' and the Tunisian 'a dog's tail, even after forty years of stretching, will come out crooked'. *See also* NURTURE passes nature.

nature, time and patience are the three great physicians (*English*) The passage of time and natural healing processes are the best treatments known to man. J. Mapletoft, *Select Proverbs*, 1707. Related proverbs include the Roman 'the physician cures, nature makes well'.

nature will have its course (*English*) Natural processes cannot be denied. *Beryn*, *c.*1400. Another proverb advises that 'nature is conquered by obeying her', although the French observe that 'drive away nature and back it comes at a gallop' and the Americans have 'drive nature out the door and it will return by the window'. The Russians similarly acknowledge the unswervable character of nature in the saying 'no matter how much you feed a wolf he will always return to the forest'. The Portuguese have 'whatever the bee sucks turns to honey and whatever the wasp sucks turns to venom'.

~ *See also* ART helps nature, and experience art; CUSTOM is a second nature; EXPERIENCE is a comb which nature gives us when we are bald; NAMES and natures do often agree; NURTURE passes nature; SELF-PRESERVATION is the first law of nature; though you CAST out nature with a fork, it will still return.

nay. *See* he that WILL not when he may, when he will he shall have nay; MAIDS say nay and take.

near. don't go near the water until you learn how to swim (*English*) Do not undertake any risky enterprise until you have acquired the skills necessary to accomplish it. H.G. Bohn, *Hand-Book of Proverbs*, 1855. *See also* it is the BEST swimmers who drown.

a near friend is better than a far-dwelling kinsman (*English*) Sometimes a friend whose ready help can be relied on is better than that of a relative whose assistance may be more difficult to obtain. R. Taverner, *Proverbs or Adages with New Additions, gathered out of the Chiliades of Erasmus*, 1545. Other proverbs along similar lines include the Welsh 'a Christian neighbour is better than a brother five miles away', the Chinese 'better good neighbours near than relatives at a distance', and the Italian 'far water does not put out near fire'.

the nearer the bone, the sweeter the flesh (*English*) The choicest portions of something are often to be found in close proximity to the poorest. Bartholomew, *On the Properties of Things*, 1398. Another proverb with a rather different viewpoint has it that 'flesh is aye fairest that is farthest from the bone', a saying formerly often applied to those who are plump but healthy looking. Variants include the Scottish 'the nearer the rock, the sweeter the grass'.

The nearer the bane the sweeter, as your honours weel ken.

Walter Scott, *The Bride of Lammermoor*, 1819

the nearer the church, the further from God (*English/French/German*) Those who live nearest the church and make a show of following its tenets in public often turn out to be the least sincere in their faith. Robert Manning of Brunne, *Handlyng Synne*, *c.*1303. Variants include the Scottish 'near the kirk but far frae grace' and 'the nearer Rome, the worse Christian' and 'the nearer the Pope, the worse Christian', which both date from the Reformation. The French have 'near the monastery, last at mass'.

For the nearer the church – the proverb is somewhat musty.

Walter Scott, *Redgauntlet*, 1824

nearest the heart, nearest the mouth (*Scottish*) Said to those who inadvertently speak the name of a person close to them rather than another name they intended to say. David Fergusson, *Scottish Proverbs*, 1641.

Spoken to them who, designing to name one person, by mistake names another, perhaps a mistress or sweetheart.

James Kelly, *A Complete Collection of Scottish Proverbs*, 1721

near is my coat but nearer my skin (*English*) In the last resort a person will, however reluctantly, put his own interests (represented by his own skin) above all other concerns. *Ballads*, *c.*1579 (also found in the writings of Plautus). Variant forms include 'near is my kirtle, but nearer is my smock', 'the smock is nearer than the petticoat' and 'near is my shirt but nearer my skin'.

And though to fortune near be her petticoat,
Yet nearer is her smock, the queen doth note.

Ben Jonson, *The Alchemist*, 1612

~ *See also* the BEST fish swim near the bottom; FOLLOW not truth too near the heels, lest it dash out thy teeth; the MORE thy years, the nearer thy grave.

necessary. *See* a BRIDLE for the tongue is a necessary piece of furniture.

necessity. necessity and opportunity may make a coward valiant (*English*) Even the cowardly will respond with courage when they have no other option, or if given reason enough. Randle Cotgrave, *A Dictionary of the French and English Tongues*, 1611. Also encountered in the form 'necessity makes even the timid brave', in which form it may be found in the writings of the Roman historian Sallust, and among the Scottish as 'put a coward to his mettle and he'll fight the devil'.

necessity is the mother of invention (*Roman*) Need prompts all manner of ingenuity. Roger Ascham, *Toxophilus*, 1545. Similar proverbs include the Roman 'necessity is the mistress of art' and the US 'want is the mother of industry' and 'necessity is a good teacher'. The Persians, meanwhile, had 'necessity turns a lion into a fox'. *See also* NEEDS must when the devil drives.

I soaled my Shoes with wood, which I cut from a
Tree ... No man could more verify the Truth ...
That, Necessity is the Mother of Invention.

Jonathan Swift, *Gulliver's Travels*, 1726

necessity knows no law (*Roman*) All rules are cast aside when circumstances dictate action. William Langland, *Piers Plowman*, 1377 (also quoted by Publilius Syrus and other classical authors). German Chancellor Bethmann-Hollweg quoted the proverb in the Reichstag on 4 August 1914 in justification of his country's invasion of Belgian territory. Seneca recognized that 'necessity is a tremendous weapon' and a proverb of US origin runs 'necessity is the argument of tyrants'. Other variants include the Egyptian 'necessity has its own rules' and the Greek 'necessity has no law'. *See also* NEEDS must when the devil drives.

So spake the Fiend, and with necessitie,
The Tyrant's plea, excus'd his devilish deeds.

John Milton, *Paradise Lost*, 1667

neck. *See* that which is GOOD for the head is evil for the neck and the shoulders.

need (noun). **need makes greed** (*English*) Those in want are often tempted to be greedy when the opportunity arises. James Kelly, *A Complete Collection of Scotish Proverbs*, 1721.

needs must when the devil drives (*English*) One must do whatever is necessary when circumstances leave no other choice. John Lydgate, *Assembly of the Gods*, *c.*1450. Sometimes shortened to 'needs must'. Related proverbs include 'need makes the old wife trot', 'need and night make the lame to trot' and 'need will have its course'.

He must needs go that the devil drives.

William Shakespeare, *All's Well that Ends Well*, *c.*1602

~ *See also* ALL countries stand in need of Britain; the BUYER has need of a hundred eyes, the seller of but one; a FRIEND in need is a friend indeed; PROVE thy friend ere thou have need; WEAK men had need be witty; who hath no MORE bread than need must not keep a dog.

need (verb). See a BLIND man's wife needs no paint; a CRAFTY knave needs no broker; the EFFECT speaks, the tongue needs not; GOOD wine needs no bush; a GUILTY conscience needs no accuser; he that will not be SAVED needs no preacher; who hath a FAIR wife needs more than two eyes; who hath SKIRTS of straw needs fear the fire.

needle. needles and pins, needles and pins, when a man marries his trouble begins (*English*) Marriage brings with it many troubles. James Halliwell-Phillipps, *Nursery Rhymes and Tales of England*, 1843. Also found with 'girl' rather than 'man'.

~ *See also* it is EASIER for a camel to go through the eye of a needle than it is for a rich man to enter into the kingdom of heaven.

needless. *See* he that BRINGETH himself into needless dangers dieth the devil's martyr.

needy. *See* an IDLE youth, a needy age.

negative. *See* TWO negatives make an affirmative.

neglect will kill an injury sooner than revenge (*English*) An insult or other offence loses its impact sooner when the victim chooses to forget it rather than exact vengeance for it. Owen Felltham, *Resolves, Divine, Morall, Politicall*, 1620–28. Variants on much the same theme include the Spanish 'no revenge is more honourable than the one not taken' and the Italian 'to forget a wrong is the best revenge', although the Sudanese take the opposite view, insisting that 'the man who does not take revenge is the nephew of an ass'.

> Neglect kills injuries; revenge increases them.
> Benjamin Franklin, *Poor Richard's Almanack*, 1733–58

neighbour. what a neighbour gets is not lost (*English*) Favours won by friends or neighbours may also indirectly bring benefit to you. L. Wager, *Mary Magdalene*, 1567. An opposite view is expressed in the Spanish saying 'what my neighbour eats does my stomach no good'.

your neighbour's apples are the sweetest (*Yiddish*) What belongs to another always seems more desirable than what one has oneself. *See also* FORBIDDEN fruit tastes sweetest.

~ *See also* DANGER is next neighbour to security; don't JUDGE a man by the words of his mother, listen to the comments of his neighbours; GOOD fences make good neighbours; a GOOD lawyer makes a bad neighbour; it is not as thy MOTHER says but as thy neighbours say; JOY and sorrow are next door neighbours; LOOK to thyself when thy neighbour's house is on fire; LOVE your neighbour, yet pull not down your hedge; the ROTTEN apple injures its neighbours; you must ASK your neighbour if you shall live in peace.

neither. neither a borrower nor a lender be (*English*) Borrowing or lending money, especially from or to one's friends, is but an invitation to trouble. William Shakespeare, *Hamlet*, *c.*1600. The proverb doubtless descends from such biblical injunctions as 'the borrower is servant to the lender' (Proverbs, 22:7). Equivalents in other languages include the Lebanese 'whether you lend or borrow, you will sink without trace'. *See also* LEND your money and lose your friend.

> Neither a borrower nor a lender be;
> For loan oft loses both itself and friend,
> And borrowing dulls the edge of husbandry.
> William Shakespeare, *Hamlet*, *c.*1600

~ *See also* the BARGAIN is ill made where neither party gains; CORPORATIONS have neither bodies to be punished nor souls to be damned; GIVE neither counsel nor salt till you are asked for it; if in FEBRUARY there be no rain, 'tis neither good for hay nor grain; if the ADDER could hear and the blindworm could see, neither man nor beast would ever go free; if you RUN after two hares you will catch neither.

Neptune. *See* BACCHUS hath drowned more men than Neptune.

nest. *See* BIRDS in their little nests agree; by LITTLE and little the bird makes his nest; DESTROY the nests and the birds will fly away; it's an ILL bird that fouls its own nest; the JAY bird don't rob his own nest; the LAPWING cries farthest from her nest; there are no BIRDS in last year's nest.

net. the net fills though the fisherman sleeps (*Greek*) Good things may still come to those who do nothing to help themselves. White-Kennett, *Erasmus' In Praise of Folly*, 1683. The Greeks derived the proverb from the Athenian general Timotheus, who enjoyed great good fortune in his campaigns despite not being an outstanding thinker. Another Greek proverb employing similar imagery runs 'the net of the sleeper catches fish'.

~ *See also* ALL is fish that comes to the net; in VAIN the net is spread in sight of the bird; it is ILL fishing before the net; it is in VAIN to cast your net where there is no fish; LITTLE fishes slip through nets but great fishes are taken; the ROUGH net is not the best catcher of birds.

nettle. *See* ANGRY men make themselves beds of nettles; if you GENTLY touch a nettle it'll sting you for your pains; in DOCK, out nettle.

never. he that never climbed never fell (*English*) Those who never risk themselves will never come to grief as a result. John Heywood, *A Dialogue containing ... the Proverbs in the English Tongue*, 1546. A related proverb adds 'who climbs high his fall is great'. *See also* NOTHING ventured, nothing gained.

> Crabshaw replied ' ... who never climbed,
> never fell.'
>
> Tobias Smollett, *Sir Launcelot Greaves*, 1762

he who never fails will never grow rich (*English*) Those who are not prepared when necessary to risk failure and learn from it are unlikely to achieve success. Charles Spurgeon, *John Ploughman's Talk*, 1869. The sentiment is supported by another proverb, which runs 'failure teaches success'. The French, meanwhile, have the proverb 'one learns by failing'.

it is never too late to learn (*English*) Age is no bar to learning. Roger L'Estrange, *Seneca's Morals*, 1678. *See also* you can't TEACH an old dog new tricks; you're never too OLD to learn.

it is never too late to mend (*English*) Things can still be put right, however much time has passed. Robert Greene, *Never Too Late*, 1590. *See also* a STITCH in time saves nine.

it never rains but it pours (*English*) Minor misfortunes pile up on one another, as if deliberately to increase the victim's misery. John Arbuthnot, *It Cannot Rain but it Pours*, 1726.

> A wife with a large fortune too. It never rains
> but it pours, does it, Mr Thorne?
>
> Anthony Trollope, *Barchester Towers*, 1857

never catch at a falling knife or friend (*Scottish*) Take care in offering assistance to friends in trouble because their troubles might pull you down also. J.H. Friswell, *Gentle Life*, 1864.

never choose your women or your linen by candlelight (*English*) Do not select something without being able to see it clearly (for example, not by flattering candlelight). J. Sandforde, *Garden of Pleasure*, 1573. Equivalent proverbs are found in other European languages, including Swedish ('one should choose one's bedfellow whilst it is daylight').

> Fine linnen, girls and gold so bright. Chuse not
> to take by candlelight.
>
> Benjamin Franklin, *Poor Richard's Almanack*, 1737

never do things by halves (*English*) If you are going to do something, do it properly. Hanway, *Travels*, 1753. Related proverbs include 'do it well that thou may'st not do it twice' and 'do well and have well'.

never eat an oyster unless there is an R in the month (*English*) Oysters should only be eaten in months that are spelt with an R in them, as they are unpalatable at other times. W. Harrison, *Description of England*, 1577. In fact, this proverb is based on good sense, as the months between May and August are the breeding season for English oysters (although in practice imported oysters are now available at any time of the year). The legal close season for oysters in England, however, runs from 15 June to 4 August. In connection with the scarcity of native English oysters on menus during the close season comes another proverb, 'who eats oysters on Saint James's Day will never want'. Saint James's Day falls on 25 July, well into the close season, and thus anyone who could arrange for such a luxury as oysters on such a date could be presumed to be immensely rich. Another, largely archaic, saying runs: 'oysters are ungodly, because they are eaten without grace; uncharitable because we leave nought but shells; and unprofitable because they must swim in wine.' Not dissimilar is the proverb 'oysters are a cruel meat, because we eat them alive; an uncharitable meat, for we leave nothing to the poor; and an ungodly meat, because we never say grace'.

> Oisters ... must not bee eaten in those monethes,
> which in pronouncing wante the letter R.
>
> W. Vaughan, *Directions for Health*, 1600

never give a sucker an even break (*US*) Never be tempted to offer a fair chance to anyone, no matter how gullible or stupid they are. *Collier's*, 28 November 1925. This piece of advice has been attributed to, among others, US film and stage comedian W.C. Fields, who is thought to have included it as an ad lib in the musical *Poppy* in 1923, and to playwright Edward Albee.

never is a long time (*English*) Given enough time, most things are possible (usually quoted in response to someone who claims something will never happen). Geoffrey Chaucer, *The Canterbury Tales*, *c.*1387. Variants include 'never is a long day'.

> Nevere to thryve were to long a date.
>
> Geoffrey Chaucer, *The Canterbury Tales*, *c.*1387

never judge by appearances (*Hebrew*) Do not rely on physical appearance as a guide to character. Bible, John 7:24. One of many proverbs with biblical origins – although many centuries later, in 1891, the wit Oscar Wilde, in *The Picture of Dorian Gray*, observed 'it is only the shallow people who do not judge by appearances'. Variants include 'you cannot judge a tree by its bark'. *See also* APPEARANCES are deceptive; the COWL does not make the monk; FINE feathers make fine birds.

> Judge not according to the appearance, but judge righteous judgement.
>
> John 7:24

never let the plough stand to catch a mouse (*English*) Never let yourself be distracted by trifles from the business in hand. John Ray, *A Collection of English Proverbs*, 1678. Another proverb advises that 'the plough goes not well if the ploughman hold it not', while yet another warns that it is unsafe to entrust the ploughing to anyone else: 'he that by the plough would thrive himself must either hold or drive'.

never look a gift horse in the mouth (*English/European*) Those who receive presents or favours should not examine them too carefully for faults in case they should appear ungrateful. Saint Jerome, fifth century AD. Looking a horse in the mouth is a recognized procedure in buying and selling horses, because checking its teeth gives a reliable indication of the animal's age (in times gone by some unscrupulous dealers filed down the teeth of their horses in order to make them seem younger). National variants include the Italian 'don't worry about the colour of a gift horse'. *See also* BEGGARS can't be choosers.

never offer your hen for sale on a rainy day (*Scottish*) It is bad policy to attempt to sell anything when the market is quiet. James Kelly, *A Complete Collection of Scotish Proverbs*, 1721.

never praise a ford till you get over (*English*) It is foolhardy to express thanks for a successful outcome until that outcome is actually realized. T. Draxe, *Bibliotheca Scholastica*, 1633.

never put off till tomorrow what you can do today (*English*) It is good policy to do things right away, instead of putting them off to a later date. Geoffrey Chaucer, *The Canterbury Tales*, *c.*1387. *See also* make HAY while the sun shines; PROCRASTINATION is the thief of time; there is no TIME like the present; TOMORROW never comes.

> No procrastination; never put off till to-morrow what you can do to-day.
>
> Lord Chesterfield, letter, 26 December 1749

never quit certainty for hope (*Greek*) Never exchange a certain advantage for another that depends on chance. Quoted by the Greek poet Hesiod in the 8th century BC.

never rely on the glory of the morning or on the smile of your mother-in-law (*English*) Good weather in the morning and the goodwill of your mother-in-law are not to be trusted. J.W.R. Scott, *The Foundations of Japan*, 1922.

never say die (*English*) Never give up hope. Charles Dickens, *The Pickwick Papers*, 1837.

never sigh but send (*English*) Those who sigh for their lovers would do much better to send for them. John Ray, *A Collection of English Proverbs*, 1678. The fuller version of the proverb runs 'never sigh but send, he'll come if he be unhanged'.

> Come, miss, never sigh, but send for him.
>
> Jonathan Swift, *Dialogues*, 1738

never speak ill of the dead (*Greek*) Never criticize those who are no longer living and are thus unable to defend themselves. R. Taverner, *'Flores aliquot sententiarum*, 1540. The saying is sometimes attributed to the Spartan lawgiver Chilon in the sixth century BC. Also encountered in the form 'speak well of the dead'. Related proverbs include 'speak not of a dead man at the table'.

> He that has too much feeling to speak ill of the dead ... will not hesitate ... to destroy ... the reputation ... of the living.
>
> Samuel Johnson, *Lives of the Poets*, 1781

never tell tales out of school (*English*) Refrain from spreading abroad what has been told to you in confidence. William Tyndale, *The Practice of Prelates*, 1530.

> Write us, my good girl, a long, gossiping letter ... tell me any silly thing you can recollect ... we will never tell tales out of school.
>
> Mary Lamb, letter, 1805

never tread on a sore toe (*English*) Avoid antagonizing someone by touching on sensitive issues. H.G. Bohn, *A Handbook of Proverbs*, 1855.

never trouble trouble till trouble troubles you (*English*) Never provoke trouble unnecessarily. *Folk-Lore Journal*, 1884. *See also* do not MEET troubles half-way.

never trust a tailor that does not sing at his work (*English*) A tailor who does not sing as he works is thinking how to cheat his customer. Beaumont and Fletcher, *Knight of the Burning Pestle*, 1611.

never work with children or animals (*US*) Those who enter business partnerships (especially in the sphere of showbusiness) with children or animals are sure to experience difficult times. Often attributed to US comedian W.C. Fields.

one never loses by doing a good turn (*English*) Those who do good turns for others will never suffer by their actions. R. Codrington, *The Second Part of Youth's Behaviour*, 1664. Related proverbs include 'one never loses anything by politeness'.

there is never a Saturday without some sunshine (*English*) The sun always shines on Saturdays, if only for a brief moment. Robert Southey, *The Doctor*, 1835.

there was never a good town but had a mire at one end of it (*English*) Every town (and person) has its imperfections. James Kelly, *A Complete Collection of Scotish Proverbs*, 1721.

we never know the worth of water till the well is dry (*English*) It is often only when it is too late and the supply of water or something else has run out that a person begins to appreciate it. Thomas Fuller, *Gnomologia*, 1732. *See also* you NEVER miss the water till the well runs dry.

you never know what you can do till you try (*English*) Lack of confidence that you can do something should not hold you back from at least attempting to do it. William Cobbett, *A Year's Residence in the USA*, 1818.

> I have often heard my poor old uncle say that no man knows what he can do till he tries.
>
> Captain Frederick Marryat, *Frank Mildmay*, 1829

you never miss the water till the well runs dry (*English/Scottish*) It is only when something is no longer available that you start to miss it and value it. J. Carmichaell, *Proverbs in Scots*, 1628. *See also* we NEVER know the worth of water till the well is dry.

you're never too old to learn (*Roman*) Age is no bar to learning. Alexander Barclay, *Eclogues*, 1530 (also found in the writings of Seneca). *See also* it is never too LATE to learn.

you should never touch your eye but with your elbow (*English*) The eyes are delicate and should never be touched. George Herbert, *Outlandish Proverbs*, 1640. The same advice was sometimes extended to the ears and the teeth. There is some evident good sense behind the proverb, as eye diseases are often highly contagious and easily exacerbated by rubbing and so forth. Also found in many other European languages.

~ *See also* BETTER late than never.

new. new beer, new bread and green wood will make a man's hair grow through his hood (*English*) Those who spend money with abandon will soon find themselves reduced to poverty. W. Ellis, *The Modern Husbandman*, 1750. Also found in the form 'new bread, new beer, and green wood will bring ruin to any man's house'.

a new broom sweeps clean (*English*) A person newly promoted to a post will show greater zeal than his or her predecessor. John Heywood, *A Dialogue containing ... the Proverbs in the English Tongue*, 1546. Although the proverb was recorded in the sixteenth century, popular tradition derives it from an incident that occurred during the first Dutch War of 1652. The story goes that the Dutch admiral Van Tromp lashed a broom to the mast of his flagship as a warning that he would 'sweep' the English navy from the seas; in reply, the English admiral Robert Blake had a horsewhip bound to the mast of his own flagship – and subsequently drove the Dutch ships off (sailors also tied brooms to the mast to indicate that their ship was for sale). In reality, the proverb almost certainly arose from the fact that old-fashioned brooms, comprising a bundle of green stems tied to a long handle, rapidly lost their effectiveness as the sticks dried out and became far less efficient than when new. New appointees are often succinctly described as 'new brooms'. An Irish proverb, however, adds the rider: 'a new broom sweeps clean, but the old brush knows all the corners.'

new church, old steeple, poor town and proud people (*English*) Describing the character of a town where there is enough money to rebuild the church but not enough to put up a new steeple. Harland and Wilkinson, *Lancashire Legends*, 1873.

new lords, new laws (*English*) When new people take control changes in the law are inevitable. E. Hall, *Chronicle*, 1547. *See also* LAWS go as kings like.

> 'I was lately married to a woman, and she's my vocation now.' ... 'New lords new laws, as the saying is.'
>
> Thomas Hardy, *Far From the Madding Crowd*, 1874

new meat begets a new appetite (*English*) The appearance of fresh dishes of food (or other enticing things) does much to renew the appetite of the diner. T. Draxe, *Bibliotheca Scholastica*, 1616. Also encountered in the form 'new dishes beget new appetites'.

new things are fair (*English*) Anything new is thereby attractive. Geoffrey Chaucer, *The Legend of Good Women*, *c.*1385. Also encountered as 'everything new is fine'. The Germans, however, have the proverb 'ever something new, seldom something good'. *See also* what is NEW cannot be true.

> Men loven of propre kynde newefangelnesse.
>
> Geoffrey Chaucer, *The Canterbury Tales*, *c.*1387

what is new cannot be true (*English*) Never trust a novelty. J. Clarke, *Paroemiologia Anglo-Latina*, 1639. The fuller form of the proverb is 'what is new cannot be true, and what is true cannot be new'. The proverb is countered by another ancient saying, 'newer is truer'. *See also* NEW things are fair.

> I found that generally what was new was false.
>
> James Boswell, *Life of Johnson*, 1791

when a new book appears, read an old one (*English*) Stick to what you know you will enjoy, or have already found yourself to be content with. A.C. Benson, *From a College Window*, 1907. Benson attributed this quip, often sarcastically directed at anyone rooted in their own prejudices, to Charles Lamb.

you can't put new wine in old bottles (*Hebrew*) You can't always marry new ideas or innovations with old contexts. Bible, Matthew, 9:17. Because new wine expands as it matures, it is inadvisable to put it in old bottles (formerly made of skin) as the old skin will not stretch as new skin does, and therefore bursts and the wine is lost. *See also* you can't TEACH an old dog new tricks.

~ *See also* ALWAYS something new out of Africa; at EASTER let your clothes be new, or else be sure you will it rue; be off with the OLD love before you are on with the new; EVERYONE has a penny to spend at a new alehouse; if the OLD year goes out like a lion, the new year will come in like a lamb; an OLD cart, well used, may last out a new one abused; OLD pottage is sooner heated than new made; OLD reckonings make new quarrels; there is NOTHING new under the sun; TRUST not a new friend nor an old enemy; you can't TEACH an old dog new tricks.

newly. *See* he that TELLS his wife news is but newly married; when a COUPLE are newly married the first month is honeymoon, or smick smack; the second is hither and thither; the third is thwick thwack; the fourth the devil take them that brought thee and I together.

news. no news is good news (*English/Italian*) When no news about something is to be had this may be accepted as a good sign, as bad news would be communicated soon enough. James I, letter, 1616 (although also attributed to Italian sources of an earlier date).

~ *See* BAD news travels fast; go ABROAD and you'll hear news of home; he that BRINGS good news knocks hard; he that TELLS his wife news is but newly married.

next. next to no wife, a good wife is best (*English*) A man should aim to remain a bachelor all his life if he wishes to enjoy himself, but if he must marry a good wife is preferable to a bad one. Thomas Fuller, *The Holy State and The Profane State*, 1642. Another proverb has it that 'a man's best fortune or his worst is a wife'. David Garrick, in *The Irish Widow* (1772), quoted a traditional saying that ran 'wife a mouse, quiet house; wife a cat, dreadful that'.

~ *See* as AUGUST so the next February; CLEANLINESS is next to godliness; DANGER is next neighbour to security; JOY and sorrow are next door neighbours.

nibble. *See* the FISH will soon be caught that nibbles at every bait.

nice. a nice wife and a back door will soon make a rich man poor (*English*) A wealthy man will soon find his riches gone if he has an extravagant wife and dishonest servants (who come and go by the back door). *Proverbs of Good Counsel*, *c.*1450. *See also* the BACK door robs the house.

nice guys finish last (*US*) It takes a certain degree of ruthlessness to succeed in life. *c.*1946 (commonly attributed to Leo Durocher, manager of the Brooklyn Dodgers baseball team, 1951–4). Usually quoted in justification for some unscrupulous act.

~ *See also* when the BALE is highest, boot is nighest.

night. night is the mother of counsel (*Greek*) Night-time is the best time for thinking and making plans. J. Sandford, *The Garden of Pleasure*, 1573 (also found in the writings of Menander). Also found in English as 'darkness and night are mothers of thought', in Arabic as 'night bears dark children', in Turkish as 'night is a pregnancy', in Italian as 'night is the mother of thoughts', in Danish as 'the best advice is found on the pillow', and in the Russian 'take thy thoughts to bed with thee, for the morning is wiser than the evening'.

> Untroubled night, they say, gives counsell best.
>
> Edmund Spenser, *The Faerie Queene*, 1590.

the night is no man's friend (*German*) No man is safe during the hours of darkness, when evil spirits roam. R.C. Trench, *On the Lessons in Proverbs*, 1853.

what's done by night appears by day (*English*) Deeds committed in secrecy will inevitably come to light eventually. John Gower, *Confessio Amantis*, *c.*1390.

> Day … night's scapes doth open lay.
>
> William Shakespeare, *Lucrece*, *c.*1594

~ *See also* if APPLES bloom in March, in vain for them you'll search; if apples bloom in April, then they'll be plentiful; if apples bloom in May, you may eat them night and day; BARNABY bright, Barnaby bright, the longest day and the shortest night; a BLUSTERING night, a fair day follows; FRIDAY night's dream on the Saturday told, is sure to come true be it never so old; he that RUNS in the night stumbles; he that will be RICH before night may be hanged before noon; it is never a BAD day that hath a good night; MERRY nights make sorry days; a RAINBOW in the morning is the shepherd's warning; a rainbow at night is the shepherd's delight; RED sky at night, shepherd's delight; red sky in the morning, shepherd's warning; TRUST not one night's ice.

nightcap. *See* AGE and wedlock bring a man to his nightcap.

nightingale. a nightingale cannot sing in a cage (*English*) The artist needs to work in freedom in order to be able to express his or her art properly. Thomas Fuller, *Gnomologia*, 1732. Variants on the same theme include the US proverb 'a bird in a cage is less than half a bird' and 'a bird in a cage puts all heaven in a rage'.

the nightingale and cuckoo sing both in one month (*English*) A person who celebrates a stroke of good fortune or success should remember that misfortune or humiliation may follow on its heels. Thomas D'Urfey, *Quixote*, 1696.

nimble. a nimble ninepence is better than a slow shilling (*English*) A small sum of money put to work wisely may yield better results than a large amount of money left unused. *Notes and Queries*, 1851. Also found as 'a nimble ninepence is better than a dead shilling' or as 'a nimble penny is worth a slow sixpence'.

nine. nine tailors make a man (*French*) It takes the work of nine tailors – or nine tailors themselves – to make a man. Thomas Dekker and John Webster, *Northward Ho*, 1605. The origins of the proverb are disputed, with some authorities suggesting a real man may be distinguished by his possession of sets of clothes from nine different tailors, while others claim that tailors are physically feeble as a consequence of their work and thus it takes nine (or, sometimes, two or three) of them to amount to a man. Yet others claim a link with the 'nine tailors' rung by bell-ringers – an allusion to the tradition of ringing a funeral bell nine times for a man, six for a woman and three for a child. Another proverb casting tailors in a dubious light runs 'a hundred tailors, a hundred weavers and a hundred millers make three hundred thieves'.

> Does it not stand on record that the English Queen Elizabeth, receiving a deputation of Eighteen Tailors, addressed them with 'Good morning, gentlemen both!'
>
> Thomas Carlyle, *Sartor Resartus*, 1838

~ *See also* a CAT has nine lives; ONE for sorrow, two for joy; three for a girl, four for a boy; five for silver, six for gold; seven for a secret, never to be told; eight for heaven, nine for hell; and ten for the devil's own self; PARSLEY seed goes nine times to the devil;

POSSESSION is nine points of the law; SEVEN may be company but nine are confusion; a STITCH in time saves nine.

ninepence. *See* a NIMBLE ninepence is better than a slow shilling.

ninety per cent of inspiration is perspiration (*US*) Great things are achieved not so much by inspiration but by diligence and hard work. Thomas Edison.

noble. the noblest vengeance is to forgive (*English*) There is more satisfaction in forgiving an enemy than there is in exacting revenge. W. Baldwin, *Treatise of Moral Philosophie*, 1550.

noblesse oblige (*French*) The aristocracy, or those who occupy positions of high standing, have responsibilities as well as rights. Duc de Levis, *Maximes et Preceptes*, 1808 (though similar sentiments were expressed centuries before by Aeschylus and Euripides).

nobody. nobody calls himself rogue (*English*) Nobody speaks ill of themselves. H.G. Bohn, *A Handbook of Proverbs*, 1855. Also encountered in the form 'nobody hath too much prudence or virtue'.

~ *See also* EVERYBODY's business is nobody's business; it's an ILL wind that blows nobody any good; what BELONGS to everybody belongs to nobody.

nod (noun)**. a nod from a lord is a breakfast for a fool** (*English*) The foolish derive great satisfaction from the acknowledgment of their betters. Thomas Fuller, *Gnomologia*, 1732. Also found as 'a nod from a lord is a dinner for a fool'.

a nod is as good as a wink to a blind horse (*English*) The smallest hint may convey a wealth of meaning (usually quoted when a person wants to hint at something he or she does not feel able to divulge in more explicit terms). William Godwin, *Caleb Williams*, 1794. The phrase enjoyed a revival in the early 1970s when it was repeated, as 'nudge, nudge, say no more, a nod is as good as a wink to a blind horse' in a famous *Monty Python* television comedy sketch, in which it was used to suggest all manner of sexual innuendo.

> A wink's as good as a nod with some folks.
>
> Dorothy Wordsworth, *Journal*, 1802

nod (verb)**.** *See* even HOMER sometimes nods.

none. none but the brave deserve the fair (*English*) Only those of heroic character should aspire to win the most beautiful women. John Dryden, *Poems*, 1697.

> All the proverbs were on his side. 'None but the brave deserve the fair,' said his cousin.
>
> Anthony Trollope, *Phineas Redux*, 1873

none can guess the jewel by the casket (*English*) It is impossible to judge by appearances.

there are none so blind as those who will not see (*English*) Some people fail to see the truth of a matter simply because they refuse to contemplate the possibility that they may be wrong. John Heywood, *A Dialogue containing ... the Proverbs in the English Tongue*, 1546. *See also* there are NONE so deaf as those who will not hear.

> 'None so blind as those that won't see.'
> Baxter was credulous and incredulous for
> precisely the same reason ... A single effort
> of the will was sufficient to exclude from his
> view whatever he judged hostile to his
> immediate purpose.
>
> Edward Fitzgerald, *Polonius*, 1852

there are none so deaf as those who will not hear (*English*) Those who are determined not to listen are the hardest to persuade. John Heywood, *A Dialogue containing ... the Proverbs in the English Tongue*, 1546. The proverb is rendered in French as *il n'y a de pire sourd que celui qui ne veut pas entendre*. Related proverbs include 'deaf people always hear better than they say they do', a saying of US origin. *See also* there are NONE so blind as those who will not see.

~ *See also* a BAD excuse is better than none; a FRIEND to all is a friend to none; a GOOD tale is none the worse for being twice told; he that GIVES to be seen will relieve none in the dark; it is a BAD cause that none dare speak in; it is BETTER to be a cuckold and not know it, than be none and everybody say so; it is EASY to rob an orchard when none keeps it; ONE of these days is none of these days; the SEA and the gallows refuse none; they that THINK none ill are soonest beguiled; TODAY a man, tomorrow none; when we have GOLD we are in fear, when we have none we are in danger.

noon. *See* he that will be RICH before night may be hanged before noon.

north. out of the north all ill comes forth (*English*) The north of the British Isles is the source of great trouble. Michael Drayton, *England's Heroical Epistles*, 1597. A less well-known proverb goes into more detail, 'the north for greatness, the east for health, the south for neatness, the west for wealth', while another runs 'the north of England for an ox, the south for a sheep and the middle part for a man'.

the north wind doth blow and we shall have snow (*English*) When the wind blows from the north it brings cold weather with it. Ralph Inwards, *Weather Lore*, 1893. Related proverbs advise 'when the wind is in the north, the skilful fisher goes not forth' and 'when the wind's in the north you mustn't go forth'. By way of contrast, though, another proverb runs 'a northern air brings weather fair'.

~ *See also* THREE ills come from the north: a cold wind, a shrinking cloth and a dissembling man.

nose. *See* a DOG's nose and a maid's knees are always cold; don't CUT off your nose to spite your face; he that has a GREAT nose thinks everybody is speaking of it; he that WIPES the child's nose kisseth the mother's cheek.

nothing. by doing nothing we learn to do ill (*Roman*) Those who are idle are easily tempted. George Herbert, *Outlandish Proverbs*, 1640.

he that has nothing is frightened of nothing (*English*) He who has nothing to lose cannot be frightened. William Roper, *Life of More*, *c.*1557. Another proverb, though, observes that 'he that hath nothing is not contented'.

nothing agreeth worse than a lady's heart and a beggar's purse (*English*) A man without money cannot hope to support a woman with expensive tastes. John Heywood, *A Dialogue containing ... the Proverbs in the English Tongue*, 1546. Also found as 'nothing agreeth worse than a lord's heart and a beggar's purse'.

nothing comes of nothing (*Greek*) Nothing can happen if one has nothing to start with. Geoffrey Chaucer, *Boethius*, *c.*1374. Related proverbs include 'where nothing is, nothing can be had' and 'if you put nothing into your purse you can take nothing out'. The philosopher Xenophanes quoted the proverb as the founding principle upon which his theory of the eternity of matter was based. According to Persius, in *Satires*, 'from nothing nothing, and into nothing can nothing return'.

> Nothing will come of nothing. Speak again.
>
> William Shakespeare, *King Lear*, 1605

nothing costs so much as what is given us (*English*) The receipt of a gift or favour from someone puts the receiver under a debt to that person. Thomas Fuller, *Gnomologia*, 1732.

nothing dries sooner than a tear (*Roman*) Public demonstrations of sorrow or grief are often short-lived, suggesting insincerity. T. Wilson, *The Arte of Rhetorique*, 1560 (also found in the writings of Cicero). Sometimes found in the form 'nothing dries sooner than a woman's tears'.

> These are but moonish shades of griefs or fears;
> There's nothing sooner dries than women's tears.
>
> John Webster, *The White Devil*, 1612

nothing for nothing (*English*) Everything must be paid for. T. Brown, *Works*, 1704. A fuller version sometimes quoted among Americans goes 'nothing don't get nothing for nothing, nowhere, no time, nohow'. Another proverb runs, 'nothing for nothing, and very little for a halfpenny'. *See also* you don't get SOMETHING for nothing.

> Nothing for nothing, young man.
>
> George Eliot, *Romola*, 1863

nothing is burdensome as a secret (*French*) Keeping a secret is the most difficult thing in the world.

nothing is certain but death and taxes (*English*) The only things that can be relied on to happen are the coming of death and the arrival of tax demands. Daniel Defoe, *History of the Devil*, 1726. Formerly also encountered as 'nothing is certain but death and quarter day' (quarter days being the days upon which taxes were due).

> In this world nothing can be said to be certain,
> except death and taxes.
>
> Benjamin Franklin, letter, 13 November 1789

nothing is certain but the unforeseen (*English*) What has not been envisaged is always the one thing that actually happens. J.A. Froude, *Oceana*, 1886. *See also* the UNEXPECTED always happens.

nothing is impossible (*English*) All things can be achieved. J.C. Bridge, *Cheshire Proverbs*, 1917. One variant form runs 'naught's impossible, as the old woman said when they told her her cauf [calf] had swallowed the grindstone'. Related proverbs include 'nothing is impossible to a willing heart'. *See also* never SAY die.

nothing should be done in haste but gripping a flea (*English*) Nothing should be done without careful thought beforehand, with the exception of killing a flea (which must be done immediately before it can escape). N. L'Estrange, *Anecdotes and Traditions*, 1655.

> Nothing to be done in haste, but gripping of Fleas ... Spoken when we are unreasonably urged to make haste.
>
> James Kelly, *A Complete Collection of Scotish Proverbs*, 1721

nothing so bad but it might have been worse (*English*) However bad things might appear, there is consolation in the fact that they are still not as bad as they might be. Walter Scott, *Rob Roy*, 1817. *See also* always LOOK on the bright side.

nothing so bold as a blind mare (*Scottish*) A person unaware of the true state of things will venture where others will not. J. Carmichaell, *Proverbs in Scots*, 1628.

nothing succeeds like success (*French*) Success breeds success. A.D. Richardson, *Beyond Mississippi*, 1867.

nothing ventured, nothing gained (*English*) Only by making an attempt to do something is there any chance of achieving it. John Heywood, *A Dialogue containing ... the Proverbs in the English Tongue*, 1546. Also found in French, Spanish and other European languages. Variants in English include 'nothing venture, nothing have', the form in which it was quoted by Geoffrey Chaucer in *Troilus and Criseyde*, *c.*1385–90, 'nothing venture, nothing win', 'nothing seek, nothing find' and 'nought lay down nought take up'. The French and Spanish have 'he who will not risk himself will never go to the Indies' – a reference to the trading links those countries had with the West Indies in former times. *See also* FAINT heart ne'er won fair lady.

> I'm sorry the gentleman's daunted – nothing venture, nothing have – but the gentleman knows best.
>
> Charles Dickens, *The Old Curiosity Shop*, 1841

there is nothing like leather (*English*) Those with vested interests in or specialist knowledge of something are first to recommend their own wares, services, and so on. Roger L'Estrange, *Aesop*, 1692. The proverb is also heard in a literal context, usually applauding the hardwearing qualities of leather. The story goes that when a certain town was threatened by a siege the town council called a meeting to discuss how best to fortify their defences. A shipbuilder immediately recommended wooden walls and the stonemason spoke up in favour of stone, but the local currier had no doubts: 'there is nothing like leather'.

> 'I dare say, my remark came from the professional feeling of there being nothing like leather,' replied Mr Hale.
>
> Elizabeth Gaskell, *North and South*, 1855

there is nothing lost by civility (*English*) Good manners cost nothing. G. and W. Grossmith, *Diary of a Nobody*, 1892. *See also* CIVILITY costs nothing.

there is nothing new under the sun (*Hebrew*) Every supposedly new idea or feat has in reality been conceived or performed somewhere, sometime before. Bible, Ecclesiastes 1:9. Sometimes found in the abbreviated form 'nothing new'. Proverbs expressing similar sentiments include 'there's never a new fashion but it's old' and the German 'there is nothing new but what has grown old' or 'there is nothing new but what has been forgotten'.

> My dear fellow! There is nothing new under the sun.
>
> George Orwell, *Coming Up for Air*, 1939

there is nothing so good for the inside of a man as the outside of a horse (*English*) Horse-riding is superlative for promoting a man's well-being. G.W.E. Russell, *Social Silhouettes*, 1906. The saying enjoyed revived attention in 1987 when it was quoted by President Ronald Reagan and described as one of his favourite proverbs. Before him it had also been heard on the lips of Rear Admiral Grayson, personal physician to President Woodrow Wilson, and allegedly on those of British prime minister Lord Palmerston.

~ *See also* BELIEVE nothing of what you hear, and only half of what you see; BETTER say nothing than nothing to the purpose; BETTER sit idly than work for nothing; BLESSED is he who expects nothing, for he shall never be disappointed; from a CHOLERIC man withdraw a little, from him that says nothing for ever; he is RICH enough that wants nothing; he that hath no PATIENCE hath nothing; he that KNOWS nothing, doubts nothing; he that QUESTIONETH nothing, nothing learneth; HIDE nothing from thy minister, physician and lawyer; if you would be POPE you must think of nothing else; it SIGNIFIES nothing to play well if you lose; a JANUARY spring is worth nothing; a JUDGE knows nothing unless it has been explained to him three times; the LAME tongue gets nothing; a LAWYER's opinion is worth nothing unless paid for; LOSE nothing for asking; NATURE does nothing in vain; she SMELLS best that smells of nothing; SOMETHING is better than nothing; SORROW is good for nothing but sin; the SUN loses nothing by shining into a puddle; THINGS that are above us are nothing to us; where GOD will help, nothing does harm; you don't get SOMETHING for nothing.

notice. *See* LONG foretold long last, short notice soon past.

nought. he that hath nought shall have nought (*English*) Those who start with nothing are unlikely to acquire anything. Alexander Barclay, *Ship of Fools*, 1509. The French, however, offer the indigent the consoling observation 'he goes safely who has nothing', while US tradition observes that 'the man who is everything is nothing' and the English note that 'where nothing is to be had even the king must lose his right'.

nought is never in danger (*English*) A worthless thing or person is never to be considered in danger because no one would have any regrets if something did happen to it or them (usually quoted after the person or object in question has narrowly escaped disaster). J. Clarke, *Paroemiologia Anglo-Latina*, 1639.

> 'He was nearly killed last time' ... 'Oh, nought's never in danger!' observed Bob Spangles.
>
> Robert Smith Surtees, *Sponge's Sport*, 1853

there comes nought out of the sack but what was there (*English*) It is impossible to get more out of something than was put in in the first place. L. Evans, *Withals Dictionary Revised*, 1586.

~ *See also* as GOOD play for nought as work for nought; a KIND heart loseth nought at last; ONCE nought, twice somewhat.

noun. *See* GOD is better pleased with adverbs than with nouns.

nourish. *See* DESIRES are nourished by delays.

nourishment. See the FIRST glass for thirst, the second for nourishment, the third for pleasure, and the fourth for madness.

November. as November so the following March (*English*) The weather in November will repeat itself the following spring. R. Inwards, *Weather Lore*, 1893. Other proverbs on the subject of the weather in November include 'if there's ice in November that will bear a duck, there'll be nothing after but sludge and muck', 'November take flail, let ship no more sail' and 'thunder in November a fertile year to come'.

nowadays. *See* there are no CHILDREN nowadays.

nowt. there's nowt so queer as folk (*English*) People are infinitely unpredictable. *English Dialect Dictionary*, 1905.

~ *See also* HEAR all, see all, say nowt; when in DOUBT, do nowt.

number. *See* KEEP bad men company and you'll soon be of their number; there is LUCK in odd numbers; there is SAFETY in numbers.

nurse. *See* MANY kiss the child for the nurse's sake.

nurture passes nature (*French*) Education and upbringing outweigh a person's inbred character. Randle Cotgrave, *A Dictionary of the French and English Tongues*, 1611. *See also* NATURE passes nurture.

> But you see how Education altereth Nature.
>
> John Lyly, *Euphues: The Anatomy of Wit*, 1578

nut. *See* APPLES, pears and nuts spoil the voice; the GODS send nuts to those who have no teeth.

oak. an oak is not felled at one stroke (*English*) It takes persistence and hard work to accomplish great things. *Romaunce of the Rose*, *c.*1400.

> An old oak is not felled at a blow.
>
> Robert Burton, *Anatomy of Melancholy*, 1621

when the oak is before the ash, then you will get only a splash (*English*) If the oak trees produce leaves before the ash, then the coming months will see little rain and the summer (and consequently the harvest) will be a fine one. *Notes & Queries*, 1852. The proverb further advises, 'when the ash is before the oak, then you may expect a soak'. Curiously, in Cornwall and other parts of Europe if the oak comes into leaf before the ash this is treated as a sign of a poor summer in store.

~ *See also* BEWARE of the oak, it draws the stroke; avoid the ash, it courts the flash; GREAT oaks from little acorns grow; LITTLE strokes fell great oaks; a REED before the wind lives on, while mighty oaks do fall; a WILLOW will buy a horse before an oak will pay for a saddle.

oath. *See* CHILDREN are to be deceived with comfits and men with oaths; an UNLAWFUL oath is better broken than kept.

obedience. *See* the FIRST duty of a soldier is obedience.

obedient. *See* ALL things are obedient to money.

obey. *See* the BOUND must obey.

oblige. *See* NOBLESSE oblige.

obtain. *See* he that can STAY obtains.

occasion. an occasion lost cannot be redeemed (*Roman*) Lost opportunities rarely come again. T. Draxe, *Bibliotheca Scholastica*, 1616. Also encountered in the form 'occasion is bald behind'.

~ *See also* he is not a WISE man who cannot play the fool on occasion.

odd. *See* there is LUCK in odd numbers.

odious. *See* COMPARISONS are odious.

offender. offenders never pardon (*Roman*) It is not for those who have committed some offence to pardon themselves. George Herbert, *Outlandish Proverbs*, 1640 (also found in Tacitus).

> Forgiveness to the Injur'd does belong;
> But they ne'r pardon who have done the wrong.
>
> John Dryden, *The Conquest of Granada*, 1672

~ *See also* the MORE laws, the more offenders.

offer. *See* NEVER offer your hen for sale on a rainy day.

office. out of office, out of danger (*English*) Losing a particular post or job might at the same time deliver a person from threats that came with it. Philip Massinger, *A New Way to Pay Old Debts*, 1633.

~ *See also* to KISS a man's wife or wipe his knife is a thankless office.

officer. *See* the THIEF doth fear each bush an officer.

offspring. the offspring of those that are very young or very old lasts not (*English*) Children born to the very young or very old cannot be expected to live long. George Herbert, *Outlandish Proverbs*, 1640.

oft. *See* the BEST laid schemes of mice and men gang oft agley.

often. *See* the DOCTOR is often more to be feared than the disease; HALF the truth is often a whole lie; he that KNOWS little, often repeats it; into the MOUTH of a bad dog often falls a good bone; ONE pair of heels is often worth two pairs of hands; the PITCHER goes so often to the well that it is broken at last; PROSPECT is often better than possession; the SHORT cut is often the longest way round; UNLIKELIEST places are often likelier than those that are likeliest; VICE is often clothed in virtue's habit.

oftentimes. *See* a RICH man's money hangs him oftentimes.

oil. *See* TRUTH and sweet oil always come to the top.

old. be off with the old love before you are on with the new (*English*) It is advisable to end old relationships before embarking on new ones. R. Edwards, *Damon and Pithias*, 1571.

> It is best to be off wi' the old love
> Before you be on wi' the new.
> Walter Scott, *The Bride of Lammermoor*, 1819

if the old dog bark, he gives counsel (*Roman*) If an old or experienced person gives warning others should pay heed to what they say. George Herbert, *Outlandish Proverbs*, 1640. Variants include 'an old dog barks not in vain'.

if the old year goes out like a lion, the new year will come in like a lamb (*English*) If the year ends with bad weather, the new year will see an improvement in prevailing weather conditions. R. Inwards, *Weather Lore*, 1893.

old and tough, young and tender (*English*) Toughness comes with age and experience. John Ray, *A Collection of English Proverbs*, 1678.

old bees yield no honey (*English*) The elderly are poor workers and bring in little of worth. John Ray, *A Collection of English Proverbs*, 1670. Not unrelated is 'old cattle breed not'.

an old cart, well used, may last out a new one abused (*English*) Something used but well-maintained can outlast something much newer. Thomas Fuller, *Gnomologia*, 1732.

an old cat sports not with her prey (*English*) Those with experience do not waste unnecessary time and energy as they go about their business. George Herbert, *Outlandish Proverbs*, 1640. Similar sentiments are expressed in 'an old dog barks not in vain' and the wisdom of experience is further evidenced in another proverb that runs 'put an old cat to an old rat'.

the older the crab-tree the more crabs it bears (*English*) The older cantankerous people get the more foolish and vicious they become. Richard Whately, *Annotations on Bacon's Essays*, 1856.

the older the wiser (*English*) Wisdom comes with age. J. Clarke, *Paroemiologia Anglo-Latina*, 1639. Contrasting proverbs include 'the older the worse' and 'the older the more covetous'. *See also* there's no FOOL like an old fool.

old fish and young flesh feed men best (*English*) The meat of mature fish and the company of young women are the best possible fare for a man. John Heywood, *A Dialogue containing … the Proverbs in the English Tongue*, 1546.

> There goes a saying, and 'twas shrewdly said,
> Old fish at table, but young flesh in bed.
> Alexander Pope, 'January and May', 1717

an old fox is not easily snared (*English*) A person experienced in the ways of the world is not easily duped. R. Taverner, *Proverbs or Adages with New Editions, gathered out of the Chiliades of Erasmus*, 1539. Related proverbs include 'old foxes want no tutors'.

> A little experience and practice will inure us to it: *vetula vulpes*, as the proverb saith, *laques haud capitur*, an old fox is not so easily taken in a snare.
> Robert Burton, *Anatomy of Melancholy*, 1621

old friends and old wine are best (*English*) Friendships that have been tried and tested over the years should be cherished most, as should vintage wines. T. Draxe, *Bibliotheca Scholastica*, 1633. Variants include 'old friends and old wine and old gold are best' and 'old fish, old oil and an old friend are the best'. Another proverb along similar lines runs 'old wood is best to burn, old horse to ride, old books to read, and old wine to drink'.

I love everything that's old! old friends, old times, old manners, old books, old wine.

Oliver Goldsmith, *She Stoops to Conquer*, 1773

old habits die hard (*English/US*) It is difficult to break old habits, no matter how undesirable they may be. Benjamin Franklin, quoted in the *London Chronicle*, 1758. *See also* you can't TEACH an old dog new tricks.

old love will not be forgotten (*English*) Lovers always remember their early love affairs. T. Heywood and R. Brome, *Late Lancashire Witches*, 1634.

old maids lead apes in hell (*English*) Old women who die unmarried are fated in punishment to keep the company of apes in the underworld. George Gascoigne, *Posies*, 1575.

Therefore I will ... lead his apes into hell ... and there will the devil meet me ... and say, Get you to heaven, Beatrice, get you to heaven; here's no place for you maids: so deliver I up my apes.

William Shakespeare, *Much Ado About Nothing*, *c.*1598

an old man in a house is a good sign (*English*) Advice is more likely to be reliable if received from someone with the experience of age. John Ray, *A Collection of English Proverbs*, 1678.

an old man never wants a tale to tell (*English*) The elderly always have a story to relate, regardless of the subject or whether the audience is willing. Thomas Fuller, *Gnomologia*, 1732. Other proverbs along similar lines include 'old wives were aye good maidens', a wry observation that some elderly people are rarely short of stories that prove how wonderful they were in their youth.

old men are twice children (*Greek*) In old age men and women return to the simple innocence of their infancy, as though children once more. R. Taverner, *Proverbs or Adages with New Additions, gathered out of the Chiliades of Erasmus*, 1539 (also found in the writings of Aristophanes).

They say an old man is twice a child.

William Shakespeare, *Hamlet*, *c.*1600

old men go to death, death comes to young men (*English*) The aged seek death as a release, but the young have to be actively sought out by death. Francis Bacon, *Apophthegms*, 1625. Related proverbs include 'the old man has his death before his eyes; the young man behind his back'. *See also* YOUNG men may die, but old men must die.

old men will die and children soon forget (*English*) It is in the nature of things that the old die and are forgotten by those they leave behind. *Black Letter Ballads*, *c.*1567.

an old ox makes a straight furrow (*English*) Those with age and experience on their side do the best job. J. Howell, *Paroemiographia*, 1659. Other ox-themed proverbs similarly emphasize the ability of the experienced to look after themselves and their own affairs, among them 'an old ox will find a shelter for himself' and 'old oxen have stiff horns.'

an old physician and a young lawyer (*English*) Old doctors, who have a wealth of experience to draw on, and young lawyers, who have more time and energy to devote to their clients, are the best. George Herbert, *Outlandish Proverbs*, 1640.

Commonly, physicians, like beer, are best when they are old; and lawyers, like bread, when they are young and new.

Thomas Fuller, *The Holy State and the Profane State*, 1642

an old poacher makes the best gamekeeper (*English*) It is good policy to employ a former practitioner of some craft (usually criminal) to combat others engaged in the same activities. Geoffrey Chaucer, *The Canterbury Tales*, *c.*1387. *See also* set a THIEF to catch a thief.

old pottage is sooner heated than new made (*English*) Quarrels between old lovers are sooner reconciled than disputes between those more recently united. John Ray, *A Collection of English Proverbs*, 1670. Also found as 'old porridge is sooner warmed than new made'.

old praise dies unless you feed it (*English*) Most people need constant reassurance and praise, as past compliments are soon forgotten. George Herbert, *Outlandish Proverbs*, 1640.

old reckonings make new quarrels (*English*) Long-standing differences of opinion often give rise to new conflicts. Randle Cotgrave, *A Dictionary of the French and English Tongues*, 1611. By the same token, another proverb has it that 'old sores are hardly cured'.

an old sack asketh much patching (*English*) Things that are old and well used tend to need more attention and restoration if they are to continue to be serviceable. John Heywood, *A Dialogue containing ... the Proverbs in the English Tongue*, 1546. A somewhat contrasting view is expressed in the proverb 'an old cart well used may outlast a new one abused.'

old sins cast long shadows (*English*) Offences committed in one's youth come back to provoke guilt in one's old age. Agatha Christie, *Sad Cypress*, 1940. Related proverbs include 'old sin makes new shame'.

old soldiers never die, they simply fade away (*English*) Veteran soldiers, having proved that they have discovered how to survive all the risks and hardships of life in the armed forces, seem as a rule to live to an advanced age, as though they do not recognize death's dominion over them. J. Foley, 'Old Soldiers Never Die', 1920. Foley's song, which originated the proverb, was written in the wake of the First World War and remained lastingly popular. It began as a parody of the gospel hymn 'Kind Words Never Die'.

old vessels must leak (*English*) Elderly items of equipment (and people) tend to be unreliable. G. Torriano, *Select Italian Proverbs*, 1642.

an old wise man's shadow is better than a young buzzard's sword (*English*) The wisdom of experience outweighs the reckless courage of youth. George Herbert, *Outlandish Proverbs*, 1640. The link between age and wisdom is perhaps most concisely expressed in the form of the proverb 'older wiser'.

there's one good wife in the country, and every man thinks he hath her (*English*) Good wives are scarce, but their cunning is such that every married man is fooled into thinking his own spouse is perfect. T. Shelton, *Cervantes' Don Quixote*, 1620.

> They say, that every married man should believe there's but one good wife in the world, and that's his own.
>
> Jonathan Swift, *Dialogues*, 1738

'tis an old rat that won't eat cheese (*English*) Men or women who are immune to the lure of flattery or luxury are rare indeed. *Brewer's Phrase and Fable*, 1958. The notion is that an old rat has learned from experience not to be tempted by the cheese that is placed in a trap.

where old age is evil, youth can learn no good (*English*) If adults set a bad example, it must be expected that youth will follow it. T. Draxe, *Bibliotheca Scholastica*, 1633.

you cannot put an old head on young shoulders (*English*) It is useless to expect the young to behave with the wisdom of their elders. H. Smith, *Preparative to Marriage*, 1591.

> We should not expect to find old heads upon young shoulders.
>
> Charles Dickens, *Martin Chuzzlewit*, 1850

~ *See also* the BEST mirror is an old friend; the BEST wine comes out of an old vessel; BETTER be an old man's darling than a young man's slave; CALF love, half love, old love, cold love; CHILDREN suck the mother when they are young and the father when they are old; a COLT you may break, but an old horse you never can; FRIDAY night's dream on the Saturday told, is sure to come true be it never so old; GOOD broth may be made in an old pot; HANG a thief when he's young and he'll no' steal when he's old; he that would be WELL old must be old betimes; he WRONGS not an old man that steals his supper from him; it's ILL healing of an old sore; KINDNESS is lost that is bestowed on children and old folks; a MAN is as old as he feels, and a woman as old as she looks; NEW church, old steeple, poor town and proud people; the OFFSPRING of those that are very young or very old lasts not; REMOVE an old tree and it will die; there are MORE old drunkards than old doctors; there is no such THING as good small beer, good brown bread, or a good old woman; there's MANY a good tune played on an old fiddle; there's no FOOL like an old fool; TRUST not a new friend nor an old enemy; when a NEW book appears, read an old one; you cannot CATCH old birds with chaff; you cannot SHIFT an old tree without it dying; you can't put NEW wine in old bottles; you can't TEACH an old dog new tricks; the YOUNG cock crows as he heard the old one; YOUNG folks think old folks to be fools, but old folks know young folks to be fools; a YOUNG man should not marry yet, an old man not at all; YOUNG men may die, but old men must die; YOUNG saint old devil; YOUTH and old age will never agree.

omelette. you cannot make an omelette without breaking eggs (*French*) Sometimes it is necessary to accept some minor loss in order to achieve one's aim (usually directed at someone who hopes to get something for nothing). T.P. Thompson, *Audi Alteram Partem*, 1859 (also cited in the *Dictionnaire de l' Académie*, 1878). This saying has been variously attributed to Robespierre and Napoleon.

> 'My dear Flora, you cannot make an omelette without breaking eggs,' said I.
>
> Robert Louis Stevenson, *Saint Ives*, 1897

omnipotent. *See* BEAUTY is potent, but money is omnipotent.

once. he that once hits will be ever shooting (*English*) A person who once tastes success at something will be tempted to try to repeat this success over and over again. T. Wilson, *Rhetorique*, 1560.

> He that once hits, is ever bending.
>
> George Herbert, *Outlandish Proverbs*, 1640

he who has once burnt his mouth always blows his soup (*German*) We learn from bad experiences to be cautious the next time. *See also* once BITTEN, twice shy.

once a priest, always a priest (*English*) Once a person takes holy orders they will always be at heart a priest, even if subsequently defrocked. G.A. Sala, *Twice Round the Clock*, 1859. The proverb had particular reference in Tudor times, when many converts to the newly established Church of England were presumed by their enemies to retain Roman Catholic leanings, despite their disavowals of the Church of Rome. Variants include 'once a bishop, always a bishop'.

> You must be quite sure, Stephen, that you have a vocation because it would be terrible if you found afterwards that you had none. Once a priest always a priest, remember.
>
> James Joyce, *A Portrait of the Artist as a Young Man*, 1916

once a thief, always a thief (*English*) A person once guilty of theft will always be dishonest. J. Stevens, *Spanish and English Dictionary*, 1706. Historical variants include 'once a knave, always a knave' and 'once a devil, always a devil'. Another colourful saying alleges 'the thief is sorry he is to be hanged, but not that he is a thief'.

once a whore, always a whore (*English*) Prostitutes (and by extension, politicians and others who 'sell' themselves to others) can never be redeemed, as they are inclined to such immorality by nature. H. Parrot, *Laquei Ridiculosi*, 1613.

once bitten, twice shy (*English*) Bad experiences teach a person to be more cautious another time. Robert Smith Surtees, *Sponge's Sporting Tour*, 1853. *See also* a BURNT child dreads the fire.

> Once bit twice shy. He had no mind to be kidnapped.
>
> Joseph Conrad, *Rescue*, 1920

once nought, twice somewhat (*English*) What may be forgivable if done only once may be unforgivable if repeated and thus deserving of punishment. *Folk-Lore Journal*, 1889. Also found as 'once nowt, twice summat'.

~ *See also* BUTTER is once a year in the cow's horn; CHRISTMAS comes but once a year; the DIFFICULT we do at once, the impossible takes a little longer; FORTUNE knocks once at least at every man's gate; he is a FOOL that is not melancholy once a day; he that hath done ILL once will do it again; if a MAN deceive me once, shame on him, but if he deceive me twice, shame on me; if a MAN once fall, all will tread on him; it is MISERY enough to have been once happy; a MAN can die but once; MEASURE thrice and cut once; SCORE twice before you cut once.

one. but one egg and that addled too (*Spanish*) Said when a person comes up with only one idea or suggestion, and that a poor one. Thomas Fuller, *Gnomologia*, 1732.

> Praise thyself chick, thou hast laid an egg, and that a bad one.
>
> J. Collins, *A Dictionary of Spanish Proverbs*, 1823

he who has but one coat cannot lend it (*Spanish*) A person cannot lend what he needs himself. H.G. Bohn, *A Handbook of Proverbs*, 1855.

if one sheep leap o'er the dyke, all the rest will follow (*English*) If one person does something many others are likely to follow suit. James Kelly, *A Complete Collection of Scotish Proverbs*, 1721. Often encountered in the shorter form 'one sheep follows another'.

> Call in the other fellow, who has some common sense. One sheep will leap the ditch when another goes first.
>
> Walter Scott, *Old Mortality*, 1816

if one will not another will (*English*) If one person refuses to do something the chances are that someone else will. John Heywood, *A Dialogue containing … the Proverbs in the English Tongue*, 1546. Also encountered in the fuller forms 'if one will not another will; so are all maidens married' and 'if one will not another will; the morn's that market day'.

one acre of performance is worth twenty of the Land of Promise (*English*) A deed performed is of far more practicable value than a mere promise. Thomas Nashe, *Have with you to Saffron Walden*, 1596.

one bad general is better than two good ones (*English*) The guidance of a single person, however dubious, is still preferable to that of divided counsels. V.S. Lean, *Collecteana*, 1902–4.

one beggar does not hate another as much as one doctor hates another (*Polish*) In terms of professional rivalry, there is nothing to match that between doctors.

one business begets another (*English*) If one business prospers it promotes the establishment of further related enterprises. Thomas More, *Works*, 1528.

one butcher does not fear many sheep (*Greek*) The brave do not fear the hostile intentions of those who are far weaker than they are, however many they be in number. R.C. Trench, *On the Lessons in Proverbs*, 1853 (attributed to the Macedonian leader Alexander the Great).

one cloud is enough to eclipse all the sun (*English*) A single misfortune may be enough to make a person forget all their other advantages. Thomas Fuller, *Gnomologia*, 1732.

one enemy is too much (*English*) A person is not safe while he has an enemy. George Herbert, *Outlandish Proverbs*, 1640. Much the same sentiment may be found in proverbs elsewhere in the world, among them the Spanish 'of enemies the fewer the better'. Another proverb advises that 'one enemy can do more hurt than ten friends can do good', while the French warn that 'an enemy never sleeps' and an Arabic proverb advises 'better a thousand enemies outside the house than one inside'. Another saying recommends that the best policy is to 'make your enemy your friend', but another of US origin advises 'love your enemy, but don't put a gun in his hand'. Those who are unwilling or unable to reconcile themselves with their enemies may find consolation in the proverbs 'if you have no enemies it is a sign fortune has forgot you' and 'he that has no enemies has no friends'.

one Englishman can beat three Frenchmen (*English*) A single Englishman is the equal of three foreigners. William Shakespeare, *Henry V*, *c.*1598.

> My men ... there are three privateers ... It's just a fair match for you – one Englishman can always beat three Frenchmen.
>
> Captain Frederick Marryat, *Peter Simple*, 1834

one father can support ten children; ten children cannot support one father (*German*) Parents feel more obligation to support their children than children feel towards supporting their parents. R.C. Trench, *On the Lessons in Proverbs*, 1853. Related proverbs include 'one father is enough to govern one hundred sons, but not a hundred sons one father'. The French, meanwhile, summarize a father as 'a banker provided by nature'.

one father is more than a hundred schoolmasters (*English*) Children are more profoundly influenced by their fathers than by their school teachers. George Herbert, *Outlandish Proverbs*, 1640.

one for sorrow, two for joy; three for a girl, four for a boy; five for silver, six for gold; seven for a secret, never to be told; eight for heaven, nine for hell; and ten for the devil's own self (*English*) Seeing one magpie is unlucky, according to superstition, although various interpretations may be attached to the sightings of two or more. T. Park, note in Brand's *Antiquities*, *c.*1780. The reputation of the magpie as an ill-starred bird is derived from Christian mythology, the magpie allegedly refusing to enter Noah's Ark and subsequently declining to wear full mourning black at the Crucifixion. The popular rhyme is known in a number of variations. One recorded in Lancashire in the middle of the nineteenth century runs: 'one for anger, two for mirth, three for a wedding, four for a birth, five for rich, six for poor, seven for a bitch, eight for a whore, nine for a burying, ten for a dance, eleven for England, twelve for France.'

one for the mouse, one for the crow, one to rot, one to grow (*English*) When sowing it is advisable to give up three seeds for lost for every one that will take root. *Notes & Queries*, 1850.

one funeral makes many (*English*) The death of one person is likely to be followed by the deaths of others (specifically, among the mourners who brave the elements at the funeral). R.D. Blackmore, *Perlycross*,

1894. Superstition insists, incidentally, that deaths (like accidents) tend to happen in threes. In parts of eastern England, the death of a woman was considered particularly ominous, a notion expressed in the saying 'if churchyard opens for a she, it will open for three'. Variants include 'one funeral makes another'.

one good turn deserves another (*English*) Favours should always be repaid. *Bulletin of John Rylands Library*, *c.*1400. Parallel, now archaic, sayings with the same meaning included 'giffe gaffe is one good turn for another'. *See also* KA me, ka thee; you SCRATCH my back and I'll scratch yours.

> If you'll be so kind to ka me one good turn,
> I'll be so courteous to kob you another.
>
> Thomas Dekker and John Ford, *The Witch of Edmonton*, *c.*1623

one grief drives out another (*English*) New sorrows expel old ones. James Mabbe, *Celestina*, 1631.

one hair of a woman draws more than a team of oxen (*English*) A woman may use her influence on others to achieve far more than may otherwise be achieved by brute strength. John Florio, *Second Fruites*, 1591.

> And beauty draws us with a single hair.
>
> Alexander Pope, *The Rape of the Lock*, 1712

one hand for oneself and one for the ship (*English*) Divide your attentions between serving others and looking after your own interests. *Port Folio*, 1799. The proverb has nautical origins, coming from the English shipyards where workers on new vessels were taught to secure themselves with one hand and keep the other free to do their work.

> The maxim, which says, 'one hand for the owner, and t'other for yourself,' … has saved many a hearty fellow from a fall that would have balanced the purser's books.
>
> James Fenimore Cooper, *The Pilot*, 1822

one hand washes the other (*Greek*) Favours are bestowed in the expectation of being rewarded. J. Sanforde, *Garden of Pleasure*, 1573 (also quoted by Epicharmus and Seneca). Also encountered in the fuller version, 'one hand washes the other, and both the face'. Variant forms include 'one hand claweth another' and 'one hand will not wash the other for nothing'. *See also* ONE good turn deserves another; you SCRATCH my back and I'll scratch yours.

> Hand washes hand.
>
> Seneca, *Apocolocyntosis divi Claudii*, first century AD

one hour's sleep before midnight is worth two after (*English*) Sleep taken before midnight will bring much more benefit than sleep taken after that hour. George Herbert, *Outlandish Proverbs*, 1640. Herbert, in fact, claims that an hour's sleep before midnight is worth no less than three hours' sleep later. *See also* EARLY to bed and early to rise, makes a man healthy, wealthy and wise.

one ill word asketh another (*English*) An unfriendly comment or insult is likely to inspire a similarly hostile retort. John Heywood, *Proverbs in the English Tongue*, 1550. A fuller variant runs 'one ill word meets another, an it were at the bridge of London'.

one lie makes many (*English*) A person who lies once will be obliged to back up his story with many more lies. Nicholas Udall, *Flowers out of Terence*, 1533. Variants include 'a lie begets a lie' and 'one trick needs another trick to back it up'.

one love expels another (*English*) Love tends to displace love. John Lyly, *Euphues*, 1579.

one mad action is not enough to prove a man mad (*English*) It takes more than an isolated instance of aberrant behaviour for a person to be declared mad. Thomas Fuller, *Gnomologia*, 1732.

one man may steal a horse, while another may not look over a hedge (*English*) Some people are in a position to take full advantage of the opportunities life offers (both legal and illegal) with impunity, while other less privileged people find they are scarcely in a position to do anything at all without being called to account. John Heywood, *A Dialogue containing … the Proverbs in the English Tongue*, 1546. In *The Irish Widow*, in 1772, David Garrick adapted the proverb to lampoon the Irish: 'but an Englishman may look over the hedge, while an Irishman must not stale a horse.'

> Strange how one artist may steal a horse while another may not look over a hedge.
>
> Arnold Bennett, *Things That Have Interested Me*, 1921

one man's loss is another man's gain (*English*) What is a loss to one man may result in profit to another. T. Berthelet, *Erasmus' Sayings of Wise Men*, *c.*1527.

> Doubtless one man's loss is another man's gain.
>
> Walter Scott, *The Pirate*, 1821

one man's meat is another man's poison (*Roman*) What one person values and enjoys another man will detest or complain of. John Heywood, *A Dia-*

logue containing ... the Proverbs in the English Tongue, 1546 (also quoted by Lucretius in *De Rerum Natura* in 45BC). *See also* BEAUTY is in the eye of the beholder.

> It is more true of novels than perhaps of anything else, that one man's food is another man's poison.
>
> Anthony Trollope, *Autobiography*, 1883

one mule doth scrub another (*Roman*) Fools and rogues flatter or otherwise help one another. J. Palsgrave, *Acolastus*, 1540. Also encountered with 'ass' or 'horse' in the place of 'mule'.

> In Latine, *Mulus mulum scabit*, one Mule scratcheth another; by which the Ancients signified, that courtesies done unto friends, ought to be requited with reciprocall offices of friendship.
>
> Thomas Coryat, *Thomas Coriate Traveller for the English Wits: Greeting*, 1616

one of these days is none of these days (*English*) Things that are put off to another day never get done. *Comes Facundus*, 1658. Related proverbs include 'one today is worth two tomorrows'.

one pair of heels is often worth two pairs of hands (*English*) Sometimes it is preferable to be able to run away from a situation than to attempt to grapple with it. *Gammer Gurton's Needle*, 1575. *See also* DISCRETION is the better part of valour.

> I ... made two pair of legs (and these were not mine, but my mare's) worth one pair of hands ... I e'en pricked off with myself.
>
> Walter Scott, *The Monastery*, 1820

one picture is worth ten thousand words (*US*) More may be said in a picture than in any amount of words. Frederick R. Barnard, in *Printers' Ink*, 8 December 1921. Barnard claimed a Chinese origin for the proverb, but it seems more likely that he actually coined it himself.

one potter envies another (*Greek*) It is natural for artists or craftsmen to resent their rivals. D. Dyke, *Works of Philemon*, 1633.

one reason is as good as fifty (*English*) Further reasons and proofs are superfluous if one has already been accepted. M. Prior, *Alma*, 1718.

one scabbed sheep infects the whole flock (*Roman*) It takes only one tainted or infected individual to contaminate everyone or everything in the vicinity. *Douce MS*, *c*.1350 (also quoted by Juvenal). Also encountered in the form 'one scabbed sheep mars a whole flock'.

> From one rude Boy that's us'd to mock,
> Ten learn the wicked Jest;
> One sickly Sheep infects the Flock,
> And poysons all the rest.
>
> Isaac Watts, *Divine Songs*, 1728

one shoulder of mutton draws down another (*English*) The more mutton a person eats the more they want to eat. John Ray, *A Collection of English Proverbs*, 1670. Also encountered in the form 'one shoulder of mutton drives down another'.

one step at a time (*English*) It is best to take things steadily, tackling each problem as it arises. Rudyard Kipling, *Kim*, 1901.

> It's beyond me. We can only walk one step at a time in this world.
>
> Rudyard Kipling, *Kim*, 1901

one swallow does not make a summer (*Greek*) It should not be assumed that because one good thing has happened that everything will go well from now on (just as the arrival of the first swallow does not necessarily mean summer is now properly under way). R. Taverner, *Proverbs or Adages with New Additions, gathered out of the Chiliades of Erasmus*, 1539 (also quoted in Aristotle's *Nicomachean Ethics*, as 'one swallow does not make a spring'). Related proverbs include 'one fair day in winter makes not birds merry' and 'one fair day assureth not a good summer'.

> One foul wind no more makes a winter, than one swallow makes a summer.
>
> Charles Dickens, *Martin Chuzzlewit*, 1844

one sword keeps another in the scabbard (*English*) If one party makes a display of strength, another party is likely to be dissuaded from making a similar display. Samuel Purchas, *Hakluytas Posthumus, or Purchas his Pilgrimes*, 1625. Also found in the form 'one sword keeps another in the sheath'.

one thief robs another (*English*) Thieves are not above stealing from one another. *Sir John Oldcastle*, 1600. *See also* there is HONOUR among thieves.

one thing thinketh the horse, and another he that saddles him (*English*) Differences in opinion can often be accounted for by the contrast between the situations of the parties concerned. César Oudin, *A Grammar Spanish and English*, 1622. Also found as 'one thing thinketh the horse, and another he that rides him'. Variants include 'one thing thinketh the bear and another he that leadeth him.'

one today is worth two tomorrows (*English*) A single good deed done today is better than the promise that you will do two good deeds tomorrow. W. Secker, *Nonsuch*, 1660.

one volunteer is worth two pressed men (*English*) A person who gives his services voluntarily is much more valuable than a person who is forced to work against his will. T. Hearne, *Journal*, 1705. The saying dates from the days of the press gangs, when unwilling men were kidnapped ('pressed') and obliged to do service in the Royal Navy.

one wedding brings another (*English*) When one wedding takes place it is almost inevitable that another will quickly follow. M. Parker, *Wooing Maid*, 1634. *See also* ONE funeral makes many.

> The cook says at breakfast-time that one wedding makes many.
>
> Charles Dickens, *Dombey and Son*, 1848

one woodcock does not make a winter (*English*) The sight of a single woodcock (which may be first spotted as early as October) does not necessarily mean winter has arrived. J. Swetnam, *School of Defence*, 1617.

> One swallow makes not a spring, nor one woodcock a winter.
>
> John Ray, *A Collection of English Proverbs*, 1670

one year's seeding means seven years' weeding (*English*) Allow weeds or other undesirable things to go unchecked just once and you will find it takes much more time to retrieve the situation later. Harland and Wilkinson, *Lancashire Legends*, 1873.

there is but one good mother-in-law, and she is dead (*English*) There is no such thing as a good mother-in-law. Wise, *New Forest*, 1863. Equivalents include 'the best mother-in-law wears a green overcoat' (in other words, is dead and buried). Other proverbs concerning mothers-in-law include 'the mother-in-law remembers not that she was a daughter-in-law', the Arabic 'a mother-in-law is cold iron fallen to earth', and the Lebanese 'a mother-in-law is a fever, a sister-in-law is a poisonous serpent'. See also NEVER rely on the glory of the morning or on the smile of your mother-in-law.

there's one law for the rich and another for the poor (*English*) The rich get more lenient treatment from the legal establishment than the poor do. Captain Frederick Marryat, *The King's Own*, 1830. Related proverbs include 'laws catch flies, but let the hornets go free', recorded in the early fifteenth century, and 'laws are like cobwebs: while the small flies are caught the great break through'. Another takes a broader approach: 'rich men have no faults'. Much the same sentiment is expressed in the traditional rhyme: 'the law doth punish man or woman that steals the goose from off the common, but lets the greater felon loose that steals the common from the goose.'

> Is there nothing smuggled besides gin? Now, if the husbands and fathers of these ladies – those who have themselves enacted the laws – wink at their infringement, why should not others do so? … There cannot be one law for the rich and another for the poor.
>
> Captain Frederick Marryat, *King's Own*, 1830

what one day gives us, another takes away from us (*English*) A stroke of good fortune one day may easily be cancelled out by misfortune the next. George Herbert, *Outlandish Proverbs*, 1651.

when one door shuts, another opens (*English/Irish*) When one opportunity disappears another is sure to present itself. D. Rowland, *Lazarillo*, 1586. A rather cynical modern reworking of the proverb runs, 'one door closes and another door closes'. *See also* EVERY cloud has a silver lining.

~ *See also* ALL the keys hang not at one man's girdle; an ATHEIST is one point beyond the Devil; BETTER one house spoiled than two; a BIRD never flew on one wing; a BOASTER and a liar are all one; the BUYER has need of a hundred eyes, the seller of but one; COURTESY on one side never lasts long; do not HANG all your bells upon one horse; do not make FISH of one and flesh of another; don't put ALL your eggs in one basket; EVERY dog is allowed one bite; FRIENDSHIP cannot stand always on one side; GENTRY sent to market will not buy one bushel of corn; GOD keep me from the man that has but one thing to mind; he has not LOST all who has one cast left; he that CHASTENS one chastens twenty; he that is BUSY is tempted but by one devil, he that is idle by a legion; a HUNDRED pounds of sorrow pays not one ounce of debt; if TWO ride on a horse, one must ride behind; it is EASIER to build two chimneys than to maintain one; it will ALL be one in a hundred years' time; JEALOUSY shuts one door and opens two; the MOUSE that has only one hole is easily taken; an OAK is not felled at one stroke; PRIDE and grace dwell never in one place; the RISING of one man is the falling of another; SAYING is one thing, and doing another; a THOUSAND pounds and a bottle of hay is all one thing at doomsday; a THOUSAND probabilities do not make one truth; TRUST not one night's ice; TWO cats and a mouse, two wives in one house, two dogs and a bone, never agree in one; TWO heads are better than one; VENTURE not all in one bottom; what MAINTAINS one vice would bring up two children.

one-eyed. *See* in the COUNTRY of the blind, the one-eyed man in king.

open. open confession is good for the soul (*Scottish*) Making a clean breast of things promotes spiritual health. *c.*1641, quoted in E. Beveridge, *D. Fergusson's Scottish Proverbs*, 1924. Sometimes spoken sarcastically when someone boasts of wrongs they have committed.

an open door may tempt a saint (*English*) Even the best of people may be tempted to go astray if the opportunity to steal or otherwise enrich themselves is made too easy. J. Howell, *Paroemiographia*, 1659. Variants include 'at open doors dogs come in', in which form the proverb was first recorded around 1200.

~ *See also* a BAD bush is better than an open field; a DOOR must either be shut or open; a GOLDEN key can open any door; GOOD clothes open all doors; HELL and Chancery are always open; JEALOUSY shuts one door and opens two; KEEP your mouth shut and your eyes open; KEEP your weather-eye open; when ONE door shuts, another opens; when WAR begins hell opens.

opera. the opera isn't over till the fat lady sings (*US*) A situation is not resolved until the last chance of a further change has passed. *Washington Post*, 13 June 1978. The phrase is thought to have arisen through the clichéd notion that all grand operas culminate in an oversized prima donna delivering an aria, typically clad in Nordic horned helmet and costume. In fact, few operas end like this (with the notable exception of *Tristan and Isolde*). Alternatively, in the 1970s US opera singer Kate Smith was often called upon to sing 'God Bless America' before home games of the Philadelphia Flyers ice hockey team: every time she sang, the team won and consequently games were deemed a foregone conclusion before play had even started. A third suggested origin relates to steam engines. In former times ships' boilers were commonly dubbed 'fat ladies' and it was only when a sufficient head of steam had been raised, signalled by a safety whistle sounding, that an engine could be operated. In recent years the phrase has been enthusiastically taken up by football commentators to communicate the fact that changes in a final scoreline are possible right up to the last whistle.

~ *See also* BED is the poor man's opera.

opinion. opinion rules the world (*English*) The world is much influenced by opinions and reputations. Markham, *The English House-wife*, 1615.

~ *See also* he that COMPLIES against his will is of his own opinion still; a LAWYER's opinion is worth nothing unless paid for; so MANY men, so many opinions.

opportunity. opportunity makes a thief (*English*) The realization that it is possible to make easy gains through an act of dishonesty will tempt many an otherwise honest person. *Hali Meidenhad*, *c.*1220. One variant applies the same idea to love, 'opportunity makes a lover' and yet another insists 'opportunity is whoredom's bawd'.

> Opportunity makes the thief … Therefore, masters … ought to secure their moneys and goods under lock and key, that they do not give … a temptation to steal.
>
> John Ray, *A Collection of English Proverbs*, 1670

opportunity seldom knocks twice at any man's door (*English*) Opportunities should be grasped whenever they present themselves, as it is unlikely they will come again. G. Fenton, *Bandello*, 1567. Another proverb with much the same message runs, 'occasion is bald behind'. Also related is 'an occasion lost cannot be redeemed'. In the form 'opportunity knocks (but once)' the proverb provided the title for a celebrated British television talent show that ran from the mid-1950s to 1977.

~ *See also* ENGLAND's difficulty is Ireland's opportunity; MAN's extremity is God's opportunity; NECESSITY and opportunity may make a coward valiant.

orator. *See* GOLD is an orator.

orchard. *See* it is EASY to rob an orchard when none keeps it.

order is heaven's first law (*English*) Self-discipline is the first requisite for the person who hopes to win divine approval (or harmony of any kind). Alexander Pope, *Essay on Man*, 1734.

> 'Order is Heaven's first law,' and a mind without order can by no possibility be either a healthy or a happy mind.
>
> Mrs Craik, *Woman's Thoughts*, 1858

ornament. *See* TRUTH's best ornament is nakedness.

orphan. *See* LATE children, early orphans.

other. other times, other manners (*Greek*) Different standards of behaviour are appropriate in different eras. G. Pettie, *Petite Pallace*, 1576 (also found in the writings of Pindar). *See also* when in ROME, do as the Romans do.

~ *See also* be WARNED by others' harm; BLACK will take no other hue; a CANDLE lights others and consumes itself; don't MEASURE other people's corn by one's own bushel; the GRASS is always greener on the other side of the fence; HALF the world doesn't know how the other half lives; he CARRIES fire in one hand and water in the other; he is not FIT to command others that cannot command himself; he KENS his groats among other folk's kail; a HOG that's bemired endeavours to bemire others; it is GOOD to learn at other men's cost; a MAN that breaks his word bids others be false to him; MEN cut large thongs of other men's leather; ONE hand washes the other; a ROSE by any other name would smell as sweet; SADNESS and gladness succeed each other; they that be in HELL ween there is no other heaven; when TWO friends have a common purse one sings and the other weeps; WISE men learn by others' faults, fools by their own.

ounce. an ounce of mirth is worth a pound of sorrow (*English*) A little wit or humour balances out a great deal of sadness. G. Pettie, *Petite Pallace*, 1576.

an ounce of practice is worth a pound of precept (*English*) A little practical experience is better than any amount of theoretical study. T. Whythorne, *Autobiography*, *c.*1576. Variants include 'an ounce of good fortune is worth a pound of forecast' and 'an ounce of discretion is worth a pound of learning', 'discretion' here signifying ingrained wit.

> We are convinced of the justice of the old saying, that an ounce of mother wit is worth a pound of clergy.
>
> Sydney Smith, 'Persecuting Bishops', *Edinburgh Review*, 1850

~ *See also* a HUNDRED pounds of sorrow pays not one ounce of debt; in a THOUSAND pounds of law there's not an ounce of love; MISCHIEF comes by the pound and goes away by the ounce; a POUND of care will not pay an ounce of debt.

outrun. *See* don't let your JAWS outrun your claws.

overcome. *See* DANGERS are overcome by dangers; he that ENDURES is not overcome.

overgrow. *See* the WEEDS overgrow the corn.

overtake. *See* the LAME foot overtakes the swift one in the end.

overthrow. *See* the BEST cart may overthrow.

owl. the owl was a baker's daughter (*English*) There is no predicting how a person's character may be changed by circumstances. William Shakespeare, *Hamlet*, *c.*1600. The proverb alludes to a Gloucestershire legend that a baker's daughter was turned into an owl in punishment after she objected to the generous size of a loaf that her mother was preparing for Christ when he begged for something to eat.

> Well, God 'ield you! They say the owl was a baker's daughter.
>
> William Shakespeare, *Hamlet*, *c.*1600

~ *See also* I have LIVED too near a wood to be frightened by owls.

own. *See* MEN's years and their faults are always more than they are willing to own.

owner. *See* the HOUSE shows the owner.

ox. *See* BEAUTY draws more than oxen; BETTER a dinner of herbs than a stalled ox where hate is; the BLACK ox treads on one's foot; an OLD ox makes a straight furrow; ONE hair of a woman draws more than a team of oxen; take HEED of an ox before, of a horse behind, of a monk on all sides; you must PLOUGH with such oxen as you have.

Oxford for learning, London for wit, Hull for women, and York for a tit (*English*) Traditional saying listing the best qualities of various English cities ('tit' being a dialect term for a horse). W. C. Hazlitt, *English Proverbs*, 1869.

oyster. *See* he was a BOLD man that first ate an oyster; NEVER eat an oyster unless there is an R in the month.

P

pace. it is the pace that kills (*English*) Going about something too energetically for too long can have fatal consequences. William Thackeray, *Pendennis*, 1850. The ideal pace to tackle something was formerly alleged to be that of the average alderman, and those who approached things in a sensible, leisurely manner were said to be 'paced like an alderman'. *See also* it is not WORK that kills, but worry.

> You're going too fast, and can't keep up the
> pace ... it will kill you.
> William Thackeray, *Pendennis*, 1850

~ *See also* SOFT pace goes far.

pack (noun). **there is no pack of cards without a knave** (*English*) It is inevitable that in any group of people, animals and the like there will be at least one villain or rogue. Nicholas Breton, *Pasquils Fooles-Cappe*, 1600.

~ *See also* no NAMES, no pack drill.

pack (verb). when GOOD cheer is lacking, our friends will be packing.

package. *See* the BEST things come in small packages.

paddle your own canoe (*US*) Rely upon yourself. Captain Frederick Marryat, *Settlers in Canada*, 1844. It was popularized by a poem by Sarah Bolton in 1854 and was also quoted by President Abraham Lincoln.

> Voyage upon life's sea,
> To yourself be true,
> And, whatever your lot may be,
> Paddle your own canoe.
> Sarah Bolton, in *Harper's Magazine*, May 1854

padlock. *See* a BAD padlock invites a picklock; WEDLOCK is a padlock.

page. make a page of your own age (*English*) Do your own errands, rather than ask someone else to act as your servant or page. Robert Armin, *A Nest of Ninnies*, 1608.

> Folk may just mak a page o' their ain age, and ...
> gang their ain errands.
> Walter Scott, *Rob Roy*, 1818

paid. *See* PAY.

pail. *See* the COW gives good milk but kicks over the pail; GOD gives the milk but not the pail.

pain (noun). **pain is forgotten where gain follows** (*English*) Injuries or offences suffered hurt much less after the victim has got some reward through them. W. Camden, *Remains concerning Britain*, 1636.

pain is gain (*Greek*) A person tends to learn more from pain and suffering than from joy or ease. Quoted by Dean Plumptre in 1881.

pain past is pleasure (*English*) There is satisfaction to be gained from remembering past suffering, and a person may be judged to be richer for the experience. G. Fenton, *Bandello*, 1567. Another proverb along similar lines runs 'past labour is pleasant' (also found as 'labours once done be sweet').

~ *See also* an HOUR of pain is as long as a day of pleasure; no PLEASURE without pain; PRIDE feels no pain.

pain (verb). *See* FLY the pleasure which paineth afterward.

pains. pains to get, care to keep, fear to lose (*English*) Wealth is hard to acquire, and once attained creates in the possessor anxiety that it will be lost. T. Draxe, *Bibliotheca Scholastica*, 1633. Related proverbs include 'pains is the price that God putteth upon all things'.

~ *See also* GENIUS is an infinite capacity for taking pains; if you GENTLY touch a nettle it'll sting you for your pains; LAZY folk take the most pains; no GAINS without pains.

paint (noun). *See* a BLIND man's wife needs no paint.

paint (verb). *See* the DEVIL is not as black as he is painted; the LION is not so fierce as he is painted; a WOMAN and a cherry are painted for their own harm.

painters and poets have leave to lie (*Roman*) Artists have licence to depart from the truth in their work. J. Harington, *Apologie of Poetrie*, 1591 (quoting Horace). Also found as 'painters and poets may lie by authority' and sometimes extended to include astronomers and travellers.

painting. on painting and fighting look aloof (*English*) It is best to view works of art from a distance to get the best effect, just as it is good policy not to get too close to a brawl for fear of getting hurt. George Herbert, *Outlandish Proverbs*, 1640.

pair. *See* GIVE a cob a hat and a pair of shoes and he'll last for ever; ONE pair of heels is often worth two pairs of hands.

pale. a pale moon doth rain, a red moon doth blow; a white moon doth neither rain nor snow (*English*) Traditional weather prediction based on the colour of the moon. J. Clarke, *Paroemiologia Anglo-Latina*, 1639.

paleness. the paleness of the pilot is a sign of a storm (*English*) The true nature of a situation may be gauged from inspection of the person who knows most about it. Robert Greene, *The Looking-Glass*, 1594.

pan. *See* if IFS and ands were pots and pans, there'd be no work for tinkers' hands.

paper. *See* the FAIRER the paper, the fouler the blot; a WHITE wall is a fool's paper.

paradise. *See* ENGLAND is the paradise of women, the hell of horses and the purgatory of servants.

paramour. *See* PUDDINGS and paramours should be hotly handled.

pardon. pardon all but thyself (*English*) Forgive others who do wrong, but be highly critical of your own misdeeds. Randle Cotgrave, *A Dictionary of the French and English Tongues*, 1611.

~ *See also* OFFENDERS never pardon.

parliament. *See* you cannot make people HONEST by Act of Parliament.

parlour. *See* as LONG as I live I'll spit in my parlour.

parsley. parsley seed goes nine times to the devil (*English*) Parsley must go nine times to hell before it will start to grow. R. Barnsley, in *Wit Restored*, 1658. Tradition insists that the devil will claim the first eight sowings (presumably an attempt to explain why parsley takes so long to germinate) and that only really wicked people can grow it in abundance. Also found as 'parsley must be sown nine times'.

> People say parsley seed goes seven times (some are moderate, discarding the holy number as unfit, and say five) to the Old Lad, it is so long a-germinating.
>
> D.H. Lawrence, letter, 4 May 1908

~ *See also* the BABY comes out of the parsley bed; when the MISTRESS is the master, parsley grows the faster.

parsnip. *See* FINE words butter no parsnips.

parson. *See* a HOUSE-GOING parson makes a church-going people; PINCH on the parson's side.

part (noun). **if you're not part of the solution, you're part of the problem** (*English*) If you are not in tune with what is perceived to be the solution to some problem then by implication you only contribute to the problem itself. Malcolm Bradbury, *The History Man*, 1975.

~ *See also* BEWARE of the forepart of a woman, the hind part of a mule and all sides of a priest; DISCRETION is the better part of valour.

part (verb). *See* the BEST of friends must part; a FOOL and his money are soon parted.

party. *See* the BARGAIN is ill made where neither party gains.

pas. *See* CE n'est que le premier pas qui coûte.

pass. *See* FANCY passes beauty; like ICE, anger passes away; a MAN's studies pass into his character; NATURE passes nurture; no DAY passeth without some grief; NURTURE passes nature; the RIVER passed and God forgotten; that which one MOST anticipates soonest comes to pass.

passion. when passion entereth at the foregate, wisdom goeth out of the postern (*English*) Passion overrules good sense. Thomas Fuller, *Gnomologia*, 1732. Another proverb warns 'passion will master you, if you do not master your passion'. *See also* when DISTRUST enters in at the foregate, love goes out at the postern.

past. past cure, past care (*English*) When something has gone beyond the point where anything can be done there is no point worrying about it. William Shakespeare, *Love's Labour's Lost*, *c.*1594.

Things past redress are now with me past care.
William Shakespeare, *Richard II*, *c.*1595

~ *See also* the AGE of miracles is past; the DANGER past and God forgotten; DEAD folks are past fooling; LONG foretold long last, short notice soon past; the MILL cannot grind with the water that is past; PAIN past is pleasure; REMEMBRANCE of past sorrow is joyful; SAY no ill of the year till it be past; THINGS past cannot be recalled; THINGS present are judged by things past; TIMES past cannot be recalled; a WORD spoken is past recalling.

pastime. *See* he that would go to SEA for pleasure, would go to hell for a pastime.

pasture. *See* CHANGE of pasture makes fat calves.

patch. *See* an OLD sack asketh much patching.

pate. *See* FAT paunches make lean pates.

paternoster. *See* no PENNY, no paternoster.

path. *See* EVERY path hath a puddle.

patience. he that hath no patience hath nothing (*English*) Patience is the one essential quality, without which a person has nothing. Randle Cotgrave, *A Dictionary of the French and English Tongues*, 1611. Another proverb adds 'he that hath patience, hath fat thrushes for a farthing'. Not everyone is capable of exercising patience, however, as evidenced by 'patience is a flower that grows not in every one's garden' (also found as 'let patience grow in your garden alway').

patience is a virtue (*English*) Those who await things with patience are to be admired. William Langland, *Piers Plowman*, 1377. Other proverbs celebrating patience include 'patience is the best remedy', 'patient men win the day' and 'patience is a plaster for all sores'. Those who find it easy to be patient will be pleased to learn that their offspring will profit by their example, according to the saying 'be patient and you shall have patient children'. Another proverb, however, laments that 'patience with poverty is a poor man's remedy' and another warns that 'patience under old injuries invites new ones'.

Pacience is an heigh vertue, certeyn.
Geoffrey Chaucer, *The Canterbury Tales*, *c.*1387

patience perforce (*English*) Sometimes there is no option but to be patient. George Gascoigne, *Patience Perforce*, 1575. A fuller version of the saying, found in William Shakespeare's *Antony and Cleopatra* (1606–07), runs 'patience perforce is medicine for a mad dog'.

But patience perforce; he must abie
What future and his fate on him will lay
Edmund Spenser, *The Faerie Queene*, 1590

~ *See also* NATURE, time and patience are the three great physicians; no REMEDY but patience.

patriotism is the last refuge of a scoundrel (*English*) Calling on patriotic feeling is the last resort of the man who has no better argument to offer. Samuel Johnson, quoted in James Boswell, *Life of Johnson*, 1791.

Paul. Paul's will not always stand (*English*) Nothing, not even St Paul's cathedral, lasts for ever. G. Harvey, *Works*, 1593.

~ *See also* if SAINT Paul's Day be fair and clear, it will betide a happy year.

paunch. *See* FAT paunches make lean pates.

pause. *See* at a GOOD bargain, make a pause.

paved. *See* the ROAD to hell is paved with good intentions; the STREETS of London are paved with gold.

paw. *See* ALL cats love fish but fear to wet their paws; take the CHESTNUTS out of the fire with the cat's paw.

pay. he who pays the piper calls the tune (*English*) The person who provides the money for something is entitled to dictate how things should proceed. James Kelly, *A Complete Collection of Scotish Proverbs*, 1721. The saying derives from the hiring of musicians for public and private celebrations. Also related is the saying 'as you pipe, I must dance', which signifies the need to do what another person pays you to do. *See also* they that DANCE must pay the fiddler.

if you pay not a servant his wages, he will pay himself (*English*) Servants or employees who are not paid as promised will help themselves to what they think they are entitled. Thomas Fuller, *Gnomologia*, 1732. Related proverbs include 'he that cannot pay, let him pray'.

if you pay peanuts, you get monkeys (*English*) Those who pay low wages cannot expect good work from their staff. L. Coulthard, in *Director*, August 1966.

it pays to advertise (*US*) Advertising one's wares in some way will assuredly improve sales. The premise on which the whole advertising industry is based, this sloganistic advice probably entered common currency around the 1870s, when the power of advertising was first acknowledged on a big scale. One form in which it was recorded around 1870 was: 'the man who on his trade relies must either bust or advertise.' An earlier saying supporting the practice of advertising was the French 'the sign brings customers', but others questioned its usefulness: the Scottish doubted the wisdom of such activity in the pithy 'gude ale needs nae wisp', while the Romans regarded it as highly suspicious, as evidenced by their saying 'puffed goods are putrid'. Cole Porter wrote a song titled 'It Pays to Advertise' while he was still at Yale University, around 1912.

> The codfish lays ten thousand eggs,
> The homely hen lays one.
> The codfish never cackles
> To tell you what she's done.
> And so we scorn the codfish,
> While the humble hen we prize,
> Which only goes to show you
> That it pays to advertise.
>
> Anonymous, quoted in *Bartlett's Familiar Quotations*, 1980

pay beforehand was never well served (*English*) The person who pays for work in advance will find that the work proceeds slowly and not to their satisfaction. John Florio, *Second Fruites*, 1591. Also found as 'he that payeth beforehand shall have his work ill done'.

> It is common to see tradesmen, and labourers,
> to go about a piece of work with great uneasiness,
> which is to pay a just debt.
>
> James Kelly, *A Complete Collection of Scotish Proverbs*, 1721

pay well, command well, hang well (*English*) Advice to military commanders attributed to Ralph Hopton, a general in the Cavalier army during the English Civil War. Quoted in David Lloyd, *Memoires*, 1668.

you pays your money and you takes your choice (*English*) Once you have paid over your money you are free to choose (though usually with the implication that you are faced with two equally uninspiring alternatives). *Punch*, 1846.

~ *See also* DEATH pays all debts; the DEVIL to pay and no pitch hot; he that BORROWS must pay again with shame or loss; a HUNDRED pounds of sorrow pays not one ounce of debt; it is HARD to pay for bread that has been eaten; LABOUR is light where love doth pay; the LASS in the red petticoat shall pay for all; a LAWYER's opinion is worth nothing unless paid for; a PHYSICIAN is an angel when employed but a devil when one must pay him; PITCH and pay; a POUND of care will not pay an ounce of debt; SAMSON was a strong man yet he could not pay money before he had it; SPEAK not of my debts unless you mean to pay them; TALKING pays no toll; they that DANCE must pay the fiddler; the THIRD time pays for all; a WILLOW will buy a horse before an oak will pay for a saddle.

payment. *See* MISRECKONING is no payment.

pea. *See* EAT peas with the king and cherries with the beggar.

peace. peace makes plenty (*English/French*) Prosperity comes with peace. *Reliquae Antiquae*, fifteenth century. The fuller version of the proverb, known in several variant forms, runs 'peace maketh plenty, plenty maketh pride, pride maketh war, war maketh poverty, poverty maketh peace'.

Peace, dear nurse of arts, plenties, and joyful births.
William Shakespeare, *Henry V*, *c.*1598

~ *See also* a CRAFTY fellow never has any peace; if you WANT peace, prepare for war; a JUST war is better than an unjust peace; SOLDIERS in peace are like chimneys in summer; WAR makes thieves, and peace hangs them; who HOLDS his peace and gathers stones will find a time to throw them; you must ASK your neighbour if you shall live in peace.

peacemaker. *See* the STICK is the surest peacemaker.

peacock. the peacock hath fair feathers, but foul feet (*English*) Even the most magnificent and beautiful people or animals have some flaw, of which they are very conscious. T. Draxe, *Bibliotheca Scholastica*, 1616. Other proverbs relating to peacocks include 'when the peacock loudly calls, look out for storms and squalls', 'no peacock envies another peacock his tail' and the Burmese 'the sparrow is sorry for the peacock at the burden of its tail'.

peanut. *See* if you PAY peanuts, you get monkeys.

pearl. *See* don't CAST your pearls before swine.

pear. *See* APPLES, pears and nuts spoil the voice; WALNUTS and pears you plant for your heirs.

peck. a peck of March dust is worth a king's ransom (*English*) A dry March is unusual and therefore much to be valued. John Heywood, *Play of Weather*, 1533.

~ *See also* you've got to EAT a peck of dirt before you die.

peep. he who peeps through a hole may see what will vex him (*English*) Those who spy on others may see things that will upset them. J. Mapletoft, *Select Proverbs*, 1707.

pen. the pen is mightier than the sword (*Roman*) The writer wields more power than the soldier. Claus Petri, 1520 (also quoted by Cicero). According to William Shakespeare, in *Hamlet*, 'many wearing rapiers are afraid of goose-quills'. Other proverbs relating to pens include 'pen and ink is wit's plough'. See also a GOOSE quill is more dangerous than a lion's claw.

Beneath the rule of men entirely great,
The pen is mightier than the sword.
Edward Bulwer-Lytton, *Richelieu*, 1839

pens may blot but they cannot blush (*English*) Shameful or wicked things are easier written than spoken. T. Draxe, *Bibliotheca Scholastica*, 1616.

penny. in for a penny, in for a pound (*English*) If you are going to do something, you might as well commit yourself to it fully. E. Ravenscroft, *Canterbury Guests*, 1695. *See also* you might as well be HANGED for a sheep as for a lamb.

Now, gentlemen, I am not a man who does
things by halves. Being in for a penny, I am ready
as the saying is to be in for a pound.
Charles Dickens, *The Old Curiosity Shop*, 1841

no penny, no paternoster (*English*) If no fee is forthcoming, no service will be performed. William Tyndale, *The Obedience of a Christian Man*, 1528. The proverb derives from the practice of priests demanding payment before carrying out religious services. Related proverbs include 'no penny, no pardon'.

Who at a dead lift,
Can't send for a gift
A pig to the priest for a roster,
Shall heare his clarke say ...
No pennie, no Pater Noster.
Robert Herrick, *Hesperides*, 1648

a penny at a pinch is worth a pound (*English*) A small amount of money available when it is needed is worth more than a greater amount when it is not needed. J. Withals, *A Short Dictionary in Latin and English*, 1616. Related proverbs include 'a penny in the purse is better than a friend at Court' and 'a penny in pocket is a good companion'.

a penny in purse will bid me drink when all the friends I have will not (*English*) There is no greater temptation to go out for a drink than money in one's pocket. John Ray, *A Collection of English Proverbs*, 1678.

a penny saved is a penny earned (*English*) By saving a penny you end up a penny better off, just as if you had actually earned it. George Herbert, *Outlandish Proverbs*, 1640. Also found as 'a penny saved is a penny got'. The opposite opinion is expressed by the proverb 'every penny that's saved is not gotten' and others advise that 'sometimes a penny well spent is better than a penny ill spared' and 'the penny is ill saved that shames the master'.

> I saved five pounds out of the brick-maker's affair ... It's a very good thing to save one, let me tell you: a penny saved, is a penny got!
> Charles Dickens, *Bleak House*, 1853

a penny soul never came to twopence (*English*) Mean or narrow-minded people are doomed to failure. Samuel Smiles, *Self-Help*, 1859.

penny wise, pound foolish (*English*) A person who is niggardly in parting with small amounts of money but careless when it comes to larger sums is a fool. E. Topsell, *Four-footed Beasts*, 1607.

> He never would insure his ricks ... Miss Diana has often told him he deserved to have his ricks take fire for being penny wise and pound foolish.
> Mrs Henry Wood, *Trevlyn Hold*, 1864

~ *See also* a BAD penny always turns up; BETTER give a penny than lend twenty; EVERYONE has a penny to spend at a new alehouse; a FRIEND in court is better than a penny in purse; LOOK after the pennies and the pounds will look after themselves.

pennyweight. a pennyweight of love is worth a pound of law (*English*) It is cheaper to reconcile oneself with one's enemies than to engage in lawsuits with them. James Kelly, *A Complete Collection of Scotish Proverbs*, 1721.

pennyworth. *See* they that DEAL with the devil get a dear pennyworth.

people. like people, like priest (*Hebrew*) The common masses ape the views of their priest (or other leader), whether they be right or wrong. Bible, Hosea 4:9. *See also* like PRINCE, like people.

> Like priest, like people ... Always taken in the worse sense.
> John Ray, *A Collection of English Proverbs*, 1670

the people's love is the king's lifeguard (*English*) A monarch's best protection is the love of his people. *Gentleman's Magazine*, 1738.

people who live in glass houses shouldn't throw stones (*English*) Those who are themselves in a vulnerable position, open to criticism, should refrain from finding fault with others. Geoffrey Chaucer, *Troilus and Criseyde*, *c.*1385–90. One tradition attributed the saying in its modern form to James I, who allegedly quoted it to his favourite, the Duke of Buckingham, who had encouraged mobs to break the windows of his opponents and then complained when his own windows were broken in retaliation. *See also* the POT calls the kettle black.

> People who live in glass houses have no right to throw stones.
> George Bernard Shaw, *Widowers' Houses*, 1892

~ *See also* don't MEASURE other people's corn by one's own bushel; FAME is but the breath of the people; a HOUSE-GOING parson makes a church-going people; IDLE people have the least leisure; IDLE people lack no excuses; like PRINCE, like people; MERCY to the criminal may be cruelty to the people; MORE people know Tom Fool than Tom Fool knows; NEW church, old steeple, poor town and proud people; PIE-LID makes people wise; the VOICE of the people is the voice of God; you cannot make people HONEST by Act of Parliament; you may FOOL all of the people some of the time, some of the people all of the time, but not all of the people all of the time.

perfect. *See* PRACTICE makes perfect.

perforce. *See* PATIENCE perforce.

performance. *See* ONE acre of performance is worth twenty of the Land of Promise.

perfume. *See* BEAUTY without virtue is a flower without perfume.

perish. we perish by permitted things (*Roman*) It is not always indulgence in forbidden things that destroys a person, but over-indulgence in what is allowed. R.C. Trench, *On the Lessons in Proverbs*, 1853.

perjury. *See* JOVE but laughs at lovers' perjury.

permit. *See* the FIRST faults are theirs that commit them, the second theirs that permit them; we PERISH by permitted things.

perseverance kills the game (*English*) It is through persistence that a person gets what they want. John Ray, *A Collection of English Proverbs*, 1813.

person. *See* although there EXIST many thousand subjects for elegant conversation, there are persons who cannot meet a cripple without talking about feet.

perspiration. *See* NINETY per cent of inspiration is perspiration.

persuasion. the persuasion of the fortunate sways the doubtful (*English*) The arguments of those who seem more fortunate than their fellows are always persuasive. George Herbert, *Outlandish Proverbs*, 1640.

petticoat. *See* the LASS in the red petticoat shall pay for all.

philosopher. *See* it is not the BEARD that makes the philosopher.

physic. if physic do not work, prepare for the kirk (*English*) If the medicine or other remedy does not work then it is likely the patient will die. Geoffrey Chaucer, 'The Knight's Tale', *The Canterbury Tales*, *c.*1387.

~ *See also* KITCHEN physic is the best physic; TEMPERANCE is the best physic.

physician. physician, heal thyself (*Hebrew*) Sort out your own problems before venturing to advise others who suffer from the same failings. Bible, Luke 4:23.

> Ye will surely say to me this proverb, Physician, heal thyself; whatever we have heard done in Capernaum, do also here in thy country.
> Luke 4:23

a physician is an angel when employed but a devil when one must pay him (*English*) It is the lot of a doctor to be welcome when working to cure a patient but unwelcome when he demands his fee. Walter Scott, *The Abbot*, 1820. Related proverbs include 'the physician owes all to the patient but the patient owes nothing to him but a little money'.

~ *See also* FEED by measure and defy the physician; GOD heals and the physician hath the thanks; he is a GOOD physician who cures himself; HIDE nothing from thy minister, physician and lawyer; a MAN at thirty must be either a fool or a physician; NATURE, time and patience are the three great physicians; an OLD physician and a young lawyer; a YOUNG physician fattens the churchyard.

pick. *See* CHILDREN and chicken must always be pickin'; HAWKS will not pick out hawks' eyes; he that would make a PUN would pick a pocket; SEE a pin and pick it up, all the day you'll have good luck.

picklock. *See* a BAD padlock invites a picklock.

pickpocket. *See* a BEGGAR may sing before a pickpocket.

picture. pictures are the books of the unlearned (*English*) Pictures may convey depths of meaning to those who cannot read and are thus unable to glean the same information from books. Thomas Fuller, *The History of the Worthies of England*, 1660.

~ *See also* EVERY picture tells a story; ONE picture is worth ten thousand words.

pie. *See* the DEVIL makes his Christmas pies of lawyers' tongues and clerks' fingers.

piece. a piece of a churchyard fits everybody (*English*) All mortals must die. George Herbert, *Outlandish Proverbs*, 1640. Another proverb observes that 'no churchyard is so handsome that a man would desire straight to be buried there'.

~ *See also* a BRIDLE for the tongue is a necessary piece of furniture; he who has been BITTEN by a snake fears a piece of string.

pie-crust. *See* PROMISES, like pie-crust, are made to be broken.

pie-lid makes people wise (*English*) Those who eat lots of pie crust will become wise (an allusion to the fact that by only by eating the pie lid can a person ascertain what is inside). John Lyly, *Midas*, 1592.

pig. pigs might fly, if they had wings (*English*) Something is as unlikely to come to pass as pigs are to fly. Thomas Fuller, *Gnomologia*, 1732. Often heard in the shortened form 'pigs might fly'. An alternative runs 'pigs may fly, but they are very unlikely birds'. According to a lesser known saying, 'pigs fly in the air with their tails forward'.

~ *See also* CHILD's pig but father's bacon; if you would be HAPPY for a week take a wife; if you would be happy for a month kill a pig; but if you would be happy all your life plant a garden; what can you

EXPECT from a pig but a grunt?; whom GOD loves, his bitch brings forth pigs.

pill. if the pills were pleasant they would not want gilding (*English*) If something has been disguised to look good it is probably not so good underneath. T. Draxe, *Bibliotheca Scholastica*, 1616.

> Apothecaries would not give pills in sugar unless they were bitter.
>
> J. Clarke, *Paroemiologia Anglo-Latina*, 1639

~ *See also* BITTER pills may have blessed effects.

pilot. *See* in a CALM sea every man is a pilot; the PALENESS of the pilot is a sign of a storm.

pin. a pin a day is a groat a year (*English*) By saving even the most inexpensive items over a long period a person may find themselves substantially better off. Joseph Addison, *The Spectator*, 295, 1712.

~ *See also* it is a SIN to steal a pin; NEEDLES and pins, needles and pins, when a man marries his trouble begins; SEE a pin and let it lie, you'll want a pin before you die; SEE a pin and pick it up, all the day you'll have good luck.

pinch. pinch on the parson's side (*English*) If a person is short of money he or she should reduce what they pay to the church (as tithes, alms, etc.). U. Fulwell, *Ars Adulandi*, 1576. Also found as 'pinch on the priest's side'.

> Pinch on the parsons side my Lorde, the whorsons have too much.
>
> U. Fulwell, *Ars Adulandi*, 1576

~ *See also* a PENNY at a pinch is worth a pound.

pine. the pine wishes herself a shrub when the axe is at her root (*English*) A prominent person may wish that he or she was less conspicuous when they find themselves picked out for hostile attention. Thomas Fuller, *Gnomologia*, 1732.

pint. *See* you can't FIT a quart into a pint pot.

pipe. *See* he can ILL pipe that lacketh his upper lip.

piper. *See* he who PAYS the piper calls the tune.

pippin. *See* PLANT the crab-tree where you will, it will never bear pippins.

piss not against the wind (*Italian*) Do not run contrary to the general flow. G. Torriano, *Select Italian Proverbs*, 1642.

> *Chi piscia contra il vento si bagna la commiscia.* He that pisseth against the wind, wets his shirt. It is to a man's own prejudice, to strive against the stream.
>
> John Ray, *A Collection of English Proverbs*, 1670

pit. *See* the LAW is a bottomless pit.

pitch. pitch and pay (*English*) Throw down your money without delay, pay ready money. *Piers of Fulham*, fifteenth century.

> But you your promise once did breake. Give me your hand, that you will pitch and pay.
>
> H. Clapham, *Errour on Left Hand*, 1608

~ *See also* the DEVIL to pay and no pitch hot; he that TOUCHES pitch shall be defiled.

pitcher. the pitcher goes so often to the well that it is broken at last (*English*) A particular trick or subterfuge, previously lucrative on many occasions, finally fails to achieve the desired result. *Ayenbite of Inwit*, 1340. The proverb is often quoted in reference to longstanding practices that have been revealed to be dishonest. Also encountered in several other European languages, including French, Dutch and Portuguese.

> A pot may goo so longe to water that at the laste it cometh to broken hoom.
>
> William Caxton, *Reynard the Fox*, 1481

~ *See also* LITTLE pitchers have big ears.

pity (noun)**. pity is akin to love** (*English*) To feel pity for someone requires emotions close to love. William Shakespeare, *Twelfth Night*, *c.*1601. Variants include 'pity is but one remove from love'.

> I pity you – that's a degree to love.
>
> William Shakespeare, *Twelfth Night*, *c.*1601

pity cureth envy (*English*) It is impossible to envy someone for whom one feels pity. Thomas Fuller, *Gnomologia*, 1732.

pity (verb). *See* BETTER be envied than pitied; that SICK man is not to be pitied who hath his cure in his sleeve.

place. a place for everything and everything in its place (*English*) The person who keeps everything neatly in order will enjoy a peaceful and trouble-free existence. George Herbert, *Outlandish Proverbs*, 1640. It is thought that the proverb resulted from an amalgamation of two earlier sayings, 'there is a place for everything' and 'everything in its place' – though one authority suggests it derives from the necessity recognized by early printers to keep their type in proper order. Related sayings include 'everything is good in its season'. *See also* CLEANLINESS is next to godliness.

there's no place like home (*English*) Being in one's own home brings a particular pleasure that can be enjoyed nowhere else. John Howard Payne, 'Home, Sweet Home', 1823. The US-born Payne wrote the song for the London musical stage as part of the musical play *Clari, the Maid of Milan*, and it became a great favourite on both sides of the Atlantic in the Victorian era. *See also* EAST, west, home's best; HOME is where the heart is; HOME, sweet home.

> Mid pleasures and palaces though we may roam,
> Be it ever so humble, there's no place like home!
> A charm from the skies seems to hallow us there,
> Which, seek through the world, ne'er is met with
> elsewhere.
>
> John Howard Payne, 'Home, Sweet Home', 1823

~ *See also* HIGH places have their precipices; LIGHTNING never strikes the same place twice; PRIDE and grace dwell never in one place; UNLIKELIEST places are often likelier than those that are likeliest; the WAY to heaven is alike in every place; a WOMAN's place is in the home.

plague. *See* PLEASE your eye and plague your heart.

plain dealing is a jewel (*English*) Honesty in all one's dealings with others is an ideal much to be valued. B. Melbancke, *Philotimus*, 1583. Equivalent sayings include 'the plain fashion is best'. The rarity of honesty in everyday dealings is lamented in the proverbial sayings 'plain dealing is dead, and died without issue' and 'plain dealing is praised more than practised'. Another warns 'plain dealing is a jewel, but he that useth it shall die a beggar'.

> Plain dealing is a jewel; but they that wear it, are out of fashion.
>
> Thomas Fuller, *Gnomologia*, 1732

planet. *See* it RAINS by planets.

plant (noun). *See* CONFIDENCE is a plant of slow growth.

plant (verb). **plant the crab-tree where you will, it will never bear pippins** (*English*) It is unrealistic to expect good things to come from a bad source. John Lyly, *Euphues*, 1579.

~ *See also* he that goes BAREFOOT must not plant thorns; if the BRAIN sows not corn, it plants thistles; if you would be HAPPY for a week take a wife; if you would be happy for a month kill a pig; but if you would be happy all your life plant a garden; it is not SPRING until you can plant your foot upon twelve daisies; WALNUTS and pears you plant for your heirs.

play (noun). *See* ALL work and no play makes Jack a dull boy; FAIR play is a jewel; GIVE and take is fair play; he that will CHEAT at play will cheat you anyway; if you PLAY with boys you must take the boys' play; LEAVE off while the play is good.

play (verb). **he that plays with cats must expect to be scratched** (*English*) Any person who engages in potentially risky enterprises must not be surprised if they suffer some harm as a result. S. Palmer, *Moral Essays on Proverbs*, 1710.

if you play with boys you must take boys' play (*English*) If a person joins in with rough play (or other business) they must be prepared to accept rough handling. Thomas Fuller, *Gnomologia*, 1732. Related proverbs include 'play with children and let the saints alone'.

if you play with fire you get burnt (*English*) Those who flirt with danger risk coming to harm. H. Vaughan, *Silex Scintillans*, 1655. *See also* FIRE and water are good servants, but bad masters.

play in summer starve in winter (*English*) Those who do not work diligently or store things up when times are good will find they have nothing when times are hard. *Poor Robin's Almanack*, July 1669.

play the game (*English*) Obey the rules, deal fairly with others. Geoffrey Chaucer, 'The Clerk's Tale', *The Canterbury Tales*, *c.*1387.

those who play at bowls must look out for rubbers (*English*) While setting about some difficult or perilous task beware of possible obstacles and impediments. William Shakespeare, *Richard II*, *c.*1595. The origins of the proverb lie in the game of bowls, in which the slightest irregularity in the ground might affect the way in which the bowls run. A 'rubber' denotes the collision of two bowls.

Lady Madam, we'll play at bowls.
Queen 'Twill make me think the world is full of rubs.
William Shakespeare, *Richard II*, *c.*1595

~ *See also* as GOOD play for nought as work for nought; CHILDREN and fools must not play with edged tools; it SIGNIFIES nothing to play well if you lose; the PORPOISE plays before a storm; there's MANY a good tune played on an old fiddle; TURN about is fair play; when the CAT's away, the mice will play.

pleasant. *See* if the PILLS were pleasant they would not want gilding.

please. please your eye and plague your heart (*English*) Those who choose partners (or other things) primarily for their appearances are likely to suffer in the long run. A. Brewer, *The Lovesick King*, *c.*1617. *See also* APPEARANCES are deceptive.

Many a substantial farmer ... would be glad to marry her; but she was resolved to please her eye, if she should plague her heart.
Tobias Smollett, *Roderick Random*, 1748

you can't please everyone (*English*) It is impossible to satisfy all sides all the time. E. Paston, letter, 16 May 1472. Other proverbs warn 'he had need rise betimes that would please everybody', 'he that all men will please shall never find ease' and 'he that would please all and himself too, undertakes what he cannot do'.

~ *See also* the CLOCK goes as it pleases the clerk; the FIRST dish pleaseth all; GOD is better pleased with adverbs than with nouns; ITCH and ease can no man please; LEAVE a jest when it pleases you best; LITTLE things please little minds; the TALE runs as it pleases the teller.

pleasing ware is half sold (*English*) A person who particularly likes something being offered for sale will probably pay more than the asking price. Randle Cotgrave, *A Dictionary of the French and English Tongues*, 1611. Variants include the Scottish 'liked gear is half bought'.

pleasure. no pleasure without pain (*English*) Some effort or sacrifice is required before anything can be enjoyed. G. Pettie, *Petite Pallace*, 1576. Also encountered in the form 'no pleasure without repentance'.

His store of pleasure must be sauced with pain.
Christopher Marlowe, *Dr Faustus*, *c.*1590

the pleasures of the rich are bought with the tears of the poor (*English*) The less privileged often suffer the consequences of the pleasure-seeking activities of the wealthier classes. T. Draxe, *Bibliotheca Scholastica*, 1633. According to the popular music-hall song 'She was Poor, but She was Honest': 'it's the rich what gets the pleasure, it's the poor what gets the blame.' Other variations include 'the pleasures of the mighty are the tears of the poor'.

~ *See also* BUSINESS before pleasure; DISEASES are the price for ill pleasures; EAT at pleasure, drink by measure; the FIRST glass for thirst, the second for nourishment, the third for pleasure, and the fourth for madness; FLY the pleasure which paineth afterward; he that would go to SEA for pleasure would go to hell for a pastime; an HOUR of pain is as long as a day of pleasure; PAIN past is pleasure; SHORT pleasure, long lament.

plentiful. *See* if APPLES bloom in March, in vain for them you'll search; if apples bloom in April, then they'll be plentiful; if apples bloom in May, you may eat them night and day.

plenty. plenty makes poor (*Roman*) Those who enjoy considerably increased wealth may still consider themselves poor, as their needs have also grown at a similar rate. Edmund Spenser, *The Faerie Queene*, 1590. On the other hand, another proverb has it that 'plenty breeds pride'.

Abundance makes me poor.
John Fletcher, *The Lover's Progress*, 1623

plenty of ladybirds, plenty of hops (*English*) A year when there are lots of ladybirds will be a good year for the hop harvest. W.C. Hazlitt, *English Proverbs*, 1869.

there are plenty more fish in the sea (*English*) If one opening fails to meet one's expectations, there are many more opportunities waiting to be seized instead (usually quoted with reference to potential partners as consolation for disappointed lovers). G. Harvey,

Letter-Book, *c.*1573. Originally encountered in the form 'there are as good fish in the sea as ever came out of it' and also found as 'the sea hath fish for every man'.

> There's fish in the sea, no doubt of it,
> As good as ever came out of it.
> W.S. Gilbert, *Patience*, 1881

~ *See also* PEACE makes plenty; a WET May brings plenty of hay; where COBWEBS are plenty, kisses are scarce.

plough (noun). *See* he that COUNTS all costs will never put plough in the earth; NEVER let the plough stand to catch a mouse.

plough (verb). **you must plough with such oxen as you have** (*English*) A person must do the best he or she can with the tools at his or her disposal. John Ray, *A Collection of English Proverbs*, 1678. A ploughman who has only one ox available for the work is warned by another saying that 'to plough with an ox and an ass together' is a recipe for disaster.

pluck. *See* FEATHER by feather the goose is plucked; if you would ENJOY the fruit, pluck not the flower.

plum. *See* a CHERRY year, a merry year; a plum year, a dumb year; the HIGHER the tree, the sweeter the plum.

plus ça change, plus c'est la même chose (*French*) The more things change, the more they stay the same. Alphonse Karr, *Les Guêpes*, 1849. Often encountered in the abbreviated form *plus ça change*.

poacher. *See* an OLD poacher makes the best gamekeeper.

pocket. *See* the DEVIL dances in any empty pocket; he that would make a PUN would pick a pocket; our LAST garment is made without pockets; SHROUDS have no pockets.

poet. a poet is born not made (*English*) The ability to write poetry (or to engage in other artistic activities) depends upon a person's natural talent rather than acquired skills. Philip Sidney, *An Apologie for Poetrie*, *c.*1581. A related proverb advises that 'poets are born but orators are made'.

~ *See also* PAINTERS and poets have leave to lie.

point. *See* an ATHEIST is one point beyond the devil; POSSESSION is nine points of the law.

poison. poison is poison though it comes in a golden cup (*English*) Poison is no less effective when served up in a fine vessel. G. Pettie, *Petite Pallace*, 1576.

> Doe we not commonly see that in paynted pottes is hidden the deadlyest poyson?
> John Lyly, *Euphues: The Anatomy of Wit*, 1578

~ *See also* a LITTLE poison embitters much sweetness; ONE man's meat is another man's poison; where the BEE sucks honey the spider sucks poison.

policy. policy goes beyond strength (*English*) Sometimes a little cunning achieves more than brute strength. G. Harvey, *Marginalia*, *c.*1590.

> Policy help'd above strength.
> George Chapman, *Alphonsus*, *c.*1634

~ *See also* HONESTY is the best policy.

polish. *See* ELBOW-GREASE gives the best polish.

politeness. *See* PUNCTUALITY is the politeness of princes.

politics makes strange bedfellows (*English*) Unlikely alliances are forged in the course of political compromise. P. Hone, *Diary*, 9 July 1839. *See also* ADVERSITY makes strange bedfellows.

pool. *See* STANDING pools gather filth.

poor. a poor man's table is soon spread (*English*) When a person has very little, it does not take long to set it out. T. Draxe, *Bibliotheca Scholastica*, 1616.

he is a poor cook that cannot lick his own fingers (*English*) Those who are unable (or otherwise unwilling) to enjoy the fruits of their labours in even the most modest fashion should be pitied. J. Stanbridge, *Vulgaria*, *c.*1510. The implication is that it is in human nature for someone acting to promote or safeguard the interests of another party to be tempted to glean some benefit for themselves.

> *He's a sarry cook that may not lick his own fingers.*
> Apply'd satirically to receivers, trustees, guardians, and other managers. Signifying that they will take a share of what is among their hands.
> James Kelly, *A Complete Collection of Scottish Proverbs*, 1721

he is not poor that hath little, but he that desireth much (*English*) A man will consider himself poor if he has not sufficient wealth to do as he wants. G. Colville, 1556. Related proverbs include 'a poor man wants some things, a covetous man all things'.

it is a poor dog that is not worth whistling for (*English*) Few people are completely useless. John Heywood, *A Dialogue containing ... the Proverbs in the English Tongue*, 1546.

it is a poor family that has neither a whore nor a thief in it (*Spanish*) Few families can boast of having no rogues or other badly behaved members among their number (usually quoted in response to criticism of a family member). J. Howell, *Paroemiographia*, 1659.

it is a poor heart that never rejoices (*English*) No one should feel guilty for engaging in celebration (often quoted in defence of drinking alcohol or some other indulgence). Captain Frederick Marryat, *Peter Simple*, 1834.

> What happened when I reached home you may guess ... Ah! Well, it's a poor heart that never rejoices.
>
> Charles Dickens, *Barnaby Rudge*, 1841

poor men seek meat for their stomach; rich men stomach for their meat (*English*) The poor have to work hard for their food, while the more wealthy engage in work or exercise simply to raise an appetite to eat. A. Copley, *Wits, Fits and Fancies*, 1595. Another proverb comparing the contrasting lots of the rich and the poor observes 'poor and liberal, rich and covetous', while another offers the poor the consolation that 'poor men go to heaven as soon as the rich'.

the poorer the church, the purer the church (*English*) Money corrupts, and thus the less a church possesses the closer its congregation is to heaven. W.C. Hazlitt, *English Proverbs*, 1869.

~ *See also* BED is the poor man's opera; CHARITY and pride do both feed the poor; CHILDREN are poor men's riches; GOD help the poor, for the rich can help themselves; make the VINE poor and it will make you rich; NEW church, old steeple, poor town and proud people; a NICE wife and a back door will soon make a rich man poor; the PLEASURES of the rich are bought with the tears of the poor; PLENTY makes poor; the RICH man has his ice in the summer and the poor man gets his in the winter; there are GOD's poor and the devil's poor; there's ONE law for the rich and another for the poor.

Pope. if you would be Pope you must think of nothing else (*English*) Those who seek the top job must be totally single-minded in their quest to win the post. J. Mapletoft, *Select Proverbs*, 1707.

~ *See also* it is ILL sitting at Rome and striving with the Pope.

porpoise. the porpoise plays before a storm (*English*) According to tradition, porpoises frolic in the water when they know a storm is on the way (often quoted when someone behaves in a frivolous manner even though disaster is in the offing). George Chapman and others, *Eastward Ho*, 1605.

> That cardinal ... lifts up's nose, like a foul porpoise before a storm.
>
> John Webster, *The Duchess of Malfi*, 1623

porridge. *See* EVERYTHING tastes of porridge; SAVE your breath to cool your porridge.

port. *See* ANY port in a storm.

possession. possession is nine points of the law (*English*) Possession of property or land is tantamount to legal ownership. *Edward III*, 1595. This time-honoured proverb is not in fact supported by any specific law, though in practice it has some claims to validity. The 'nine points' (sometimes eleven) have been listed as (1) a good deal of money, (2) a good deal of patience, (3) a good cause, (4) a good lawyer, (5) a good counsel, (6) good witnesses, (7) a good jury, (8) a good judge and (9) good luck.

> In those days possession was considerably more than eleven points of the Law. The baron was therefore convinced that the earl's outlawry was infallible.
>
> Thomas Love Peacock, *Maid Marian*, 1822

~ *See also* PROSPECT is often better than possession.

possible. *See* ALL's for the best in the best of all possible worlds; ALL things are possible with God.

post. the post of honour is the post of danger (*Roman*) The greatest honours come with the greatest risks. Lord Berners, *Huon*, 1533.

For I remembered your old Roman axiom, the more the danger, still the more the honour.
John Fletcher, *Rule a Wife and Have a Wife*, 1624

postscript. *See* the GIST of a lady's letter is in the postscript.

postern. a postern door makes a thief (*English*) Any house with a back door is vulnerable to thieves and other evil-doers. *Proverbs of Good Counsel*, *c.*1450.

The Postern Door Makes Thief and Whore.
Thomas Fuller, *Gnomologia*, 1732

~ *See also* when DISTRUST enters in at the foregate, love goes out at the postern; when PASSION entereth at the foregate, wisdom goeth out of the postern.

pot. the pot calls the kettle black (*Spanish/Arabic*) It is hypocritical for a person to accuse another of something of which they themselves are equally guilty. Miguel de Cervantes, *Don Quixote*, 1615. Similar proverbs may be found in several other European languages, including German and French – the latter in the form 'dirty-nosed folk always want to wipe other folks' noses'. Equivalents in English include 'the kiln calls the oven burnt house'.

As another old proverb says, do not let the kettle call the pot black-arse!
Aphra Behn, *The Feign'd Courtezans*, 1679

~ *See also* BETTER a louse in the pot than no flesh at all; the EARTHEN pot must keep clear of the brass kettle; GOOD broth may be made in an old pot; if IFS and ands were pots and pans, there'd be no work for tinkers' hands; a LITTLE pot is soon hot; a WATCHED pot never boils; you can't FIT a quart into a pint pot.

potent. *See* BEAUTY is potent, but money is omnipotent.

pottage. *See* if you DRINK in your pottage, you'll cough in your grave; OLD pottage is sooner heated than new made; SCALD not your lips in another man's pottage.

potter. *See* ONE potter envies another.

poultry. *See* the SLEEPING fox catches no poultry.

pound. a pound of care will not pay an ounce of debt (*English*) Worrying about one's debts does nothing to reduce them. L. Wright, *Display of Dutie*, 1589. *See also* a HUNDRED pounds of sorrow pays not one ounce of debt.

~ *See also* a HUNDRED pounds of sorrow pays not one ounce of debt; in a THOUSAND pounds of law there's not an ounce of love; in for a PENNY, in for a pound; LOOK after the pennies and the pounds will look after themselves; MISCHIEF comes by the pound and goes away by the ounce; an OUNCE of mirth is worth a pound of sorrow; an OUNCE of practice is worth a pound of precept; a PENNY at a pinch is worth a pound; a PENNYWEIGHT of love is worth a pound of law; PENNY wise, pound foolish; a THOUSAND pounds and a bottle of hay is all one thing at doomsday.

pour. pour not water on a drowned mouse (*English*) Do not insult those who are already down on their knees. J. Clarke, *Paroemiologia Anglo-Latina*, 1639.

Take pity on poor miss; don't throw water on a drowned rat.
Jonathan Swift, *Dialogues*, 1738

~ *See* it NEVER rains but it pours.

poverty. poverty breeds strife (*English*) Lack of money engenders quarrels, particularly between man and wife. John Ray, *A Collection of English Proverbs*, 1678. *See also* when POVERTY comes in at the door, love flies out of the window.

poverty is no disgrace, but it is a great inconvenience (*English*) It is possible to deny that poverty is the fault of the person concerned, but this does not lessen its unwelcome impact. John Florio, *Second Fruites*, 1591. Variants include the Yiddish 'poverty is no disgrace, but no honour either'. Another proverb enlarges on the feelings of shame associated with poverty: 'poverty is not a shame, but the being ashamed of it is.'

'Poverty's no disgrace, but 'tis a great inconvenience' was a common saying among the Lark Rise people …
Flora Thompson, *Lark Rise to Candleford*, 1945

poverty is not a crime (*English*) It is not generally the fault of the poor that they are destitute. John Florio, *Second Fruites*, 1591. Variants include 'poverty is no sin' and the Spanish 'poverty is not perversity'.

Mrs Nickleby ... said through her tears that poverty was not a crime.

Charles Dickens, *Nicholas Nickleby*, 1839

poverty is the mother of health (*English*) Those who have no money for more elaborate fare eat more sparingly and sensibly and thus enjoy improved health. William Langland, *Piers Plowman*, 1377. Another proverb, of Japanese origins, claims 'the poor sleep soundly'.

when poverty comes in at the door, love flies out of the window (*English*) The strains created by lack of money can break down loving relationships. William Caxton, *A Game of Chess*, 1474. Also related are 'poverty parteth fellowship' and 'love lasteth as long as the money endureth'. Another proverb warns that love is not the only victim of poverty, claiming that 'there is no virtue that poverty destroyeth not'.

~ *See also* BASHFULNESS is an enemy to poverty; BEAR wealth, poverty will bear itself; he who is CONTENT in his poverty is wonderfully rich; SLOTH is the key to poverty.

powder. *See* put your TRUST in God and keep your powder dry.

power. power corrupts (*English*) When a person gains power the temptation is to misuse it. Anthony Trollope, *The Prime Minister*, 1876. The proverb is often encountered in the fuller form 'power tends to corrupt, and absolute power corrupts absolutely'.

We know that power does corrupt, and that we cannot trust kings to have loving hearts.

Anthony Trollope, *The Prime Minister*, 1876

~ *See also* ANGER without power is folly; KNOWLEDGE is power; MONEY is power; no LOCK will hold against the power of gold.

practice makes perfect (*Greek*) To be really good at something you must repeat it over and over again. Thomas Norton, *Ordinall of Alchimy*, 1477 (also quoted in various forms by Publilius Syrus, Periander and Pliny the Younger). Formerly usually encountered in the form 'use maketh mastery'.

Use makes perfect.

Walter Scott, *The Antiquary*, 1816

~ *See also* an OUNCE of practice is worth a pound of precept.

practise what you preach (*English*) If you tell other people how to behave, you should behave the same way yourself. William Langland, *Piers Plowman*, 1377. Another proverb confirms the notion as follows: 'he preaches well that lives well'. *See also* a GOOD example is the best sermon.

Divines do not always practise what they preach.

Charles Dickens, *The Old Curiosity Shop*, 1840

praise (noun). **praise is not pudding** (*English*) Flattery and praise may be pleasing, but they bring no actual benefit in themselves. Alexander Pope, *The Dunciad*, 1728. A related proverb observes 'praise without profit puts little in the pot'.

Since t'is not improbable, that a Man may receive more solid Satisfaction from *Pudding*, while he is *living*, than from *Praise*, after he is *dead*.

Benjamin Franklin, *Poor Richard's Almanack*, 1750

praise makes good men better and bad men worse (*English*) Praise encourages the virtuous to greater good, but has the opposite effect upon the wicked. Thomas Fuller, *Gnomologia*, 1732. Another proverb along similar lines warns 'praise none too much, for all are fickle'.

~ *See also* OLD praise dies unless you feed it.

praise (verb). **praise no man till he is dead** (*English*) Reserve final judgement on a person until they are dead, for only then is it possible to make a definitive statement about their worth. R. Taverner, *Proverbs or Adages with New Additions, gathered out of the Chiliades of Erasmus*, 1540. Equivalents include 'praise day at night' (warning against praising the day until the day is actually over).

praise the child and you make love to the mother (*English*) Those who wish to win over a mother can do no better than compliment their offspring. William Cobbett, *Advice to Young Men*, 1829. Variants include 'he that wipes the child's nose kisses the mother's cheek'.

praise the sea but keep on land (*English*) By all means admire the sea, but do not venture upon it and thus expose yourself to risk. John Florio, *Second Fruites*, 1591. A less well-known proverb that similarly warns of the dangers of venturing on the sea ominously advises 'he that would learn to pray, let him go to sea'. Other equivalents include 'praise a hill but keep below' (also found in the form 'praise a hill but keep on the plain'). *See also* he that would go to SEA for pleasure, would go to hell for a pastime.

~ *See also* ADMONISH your friends in private, praise them in public; EVERY cook praises his own broth; let EVERY man praise the bridge he goes over; NEVER praise a ford till you get over; a RUNAWAY monk never praises his convent.

prate. *See* if the HEN does not prate, she will not lay.

pray. *See also* an ANGRY man is not fit to pray; the FAMILY that prays together stays together; he that would LEARN to pray, let him go to sea.

prayer. *See* a SHORT prayer reaches heaven.

preach. he preaches well that lives well (*English*) Those who preach by their own example are better than those who do not live by the standards that they preach. Thomas Fuller, *Gnomologia*, 1732.

he that preaches war is the devil's chaplain (*English*) Those who encourage others to go to war (or to engage in other hostilities) are in league with the devil. R. Codrington, *The Second Part of Youth's Behaviour*, 1664.

~ *See also* if the BEARD were all, the goat might preach; PRACTISE what you preach.

preacher. *See* he that will not be SAVED needs no preacher.

precept. *See* EXAMPLE is better than precept; an OUNCE of practice is worth a pound of precept.

precipice. *See* HIGH places have their precipices.

premier. *See* CE n'est que le premier pas qui coûte.

prepare. *See* HOPE for the best and prepare for the worst; if PHYSIC do not work, prepare for the kirk; if you WANT peace, prepare for war; in FAIR weather prepare for foul.

Presbyterianism is no religion for a gentleman (*English*) Presbyterianism, being essentially a 'low church' branch of Christianity, is not grand and noble enough for the high-born. This inflammatory remark is traditionally attributed to Charles II, who harboured secret Catholic sympathies, and was directed at the Presbyterian Duke of Lauderdale, who promptly switched faiths. In *The New Forcers of Conscience* John Milton voiced his own proverbial view of the matter, insisting that beyond their names there is little in reality to choose between such reformed faiths as Presbyterianism and the older versions: 'New Presbyter is but Old Priest writ large'.

present. *See* the GOLDEN age never was the present age; no TIME like the present; THINGS present are judged by things past.

preserve. *See* he who SERVES is preserved.

press. *See* ONE volunteer is worth two pressed men.

prettiness dies first (*English*) Good looks do not last long. George Herbert, *Outlandish Proverbs*, 1640. Another proverb questioning the advantages of prettiness warns 'prettiness makes no pottage' while another even more blunt saying has it that 'a pretty pig makes an ugly old sow'.

prevent. *See* a STUMBLE may prevent a fall.

prevention is better than cure (*English*) It is better to forestall a problem before it arises than treat it after it has already become established. Henry de Bracton, *De Legibus*, *c.*1240.

prey. *See* the FOX preys furthest from his hole; an OLD cat sports not with her prey.

price. the price of liberty is eternal vigilance (*Irish*) Liberty must be carefully guarded against all threats. John Philpot Curran, 1790. The saying was later adopted as a maxim by the US reformer Wendell Phillips in 1852.

~ *See also* DISEASES are the price for ill pleasures; EVERY man has his price.

prick. *See* he that HANDLES thorns shall prick his fingers; it EARLY pricks that will be a thorn.

pride. pride and grace dwell never in one place (*English*) It is impossible for a vain person to behave graciously. James Kelly, *A Complete Collection of Scottish Proverbs*, 1721.

pride feels no pain (*English*) Pride persuades people to accept and ignore pain and difficulty if giving in to it will lead to some loss of face. T. Adams, *The Devil's Banquet*, 1614. The proverb is usually quoted in reference to clothing, explaining why many people will endure some degree of bodily discomfort in order to look good. Related proverbs include 'pride feels no frost' and 'pride feels no cold'.

> Pride feels no cold. Spoken ... to Beaus with their open Breasts, and Ladies with their extravagant Hoops.
>
> James Kelly, *A Complete Collection of Scottish Proverbs*, 1721

pride goes before a fall (*Hebrew*) Displays of arrogance are all too often quickly followed by humiliation. Bible, Proverbs 16:18. Formerly also encountered in the forms 'pride will have a fall' and 'pride never left his master without a fall'. Other variants include 'pride goeth before destruction', in which form it is quoted in the Geneva Bible.

> 'Pride shall have a fall, and it always was and will be so!' observes the housemaid.
>
> Charles Dickens, *Dombey and Son*, 1816

pride may lurk under a threadbare cloak (*English*) Even the poor have their pride. Thomas Fuller, *Gnomologia*, 1732.

pride must abide (*English*) Those who are arrogant must put up with critical remarks from others. Elizabeth Gaskell, *North and South*, 1855. Other proverbs along similar lines include 'pride scorns the vulgar yet lies at its mercy' and 'pride will spit in pride's face'.

> I kept myself up with proverbs as long as I could;
> 'Pride must abide' – and such wholesome pieces of pith!
>
> Elizabeth Gaskell, *North and South*, 1855

~ *See also* CHARITY and pride do both feed the poor.

priest. the priest forgets that he was clerk (*English*) People who have been promoted tend to forget that they were once in posts as humble as their subordinates. John Heywood, *Johan Johan the husbande, Tyb his wife and syr Jhan the preest*, 1533.

~ *See also* BEWARE of the forepart of a woman, the hind part of a mule and all sides of a priest; like PEOPLE, like priest; no MISCHIEF but a woman or a priest is at the bottom of it; ONCE a priest, always a priest; THREE things are insatiable: priests, monks and the sea.

prince. like prince, like people (*English*) The character and behaviour of a monarch influences that of his people. T. Draxe, *Bibliotheca Scholastica*, 1616. Equivalents include 'like priest, like people'. By the same token, rulers are warned that 'the prince that is feared of many must of necessity fear many'. *See also* like PEOPLE, like priest.

~ *See* PUNCTUALITY is the politeness of princes; put not your TRUST in princes; SPIES are the ears and eyes of princes; whosoever DRAWS his sword against the prince must throw the scabbard away.

private. *See* ADMONISH your friends in private, praise them in public.

probability. *See* a THOUSAND probabilities do not make one truth.

problem. *See* if you're not PART of the solution you're part of the problem.

procrastination is the thief of time (*English*) Putting things off results only in time being wasted. Edward Young, 'Night Thoughts', 1742 (similar thoughts were voiced at an earlier date by Seneca and Erasmus, among others). Equivalents in other languages include the Dutch 'stay but a while, you lose a mile' and the Spanish 'when the fool has made up his mind the market has gone by'. In 1891 Oscar Wilde offered a contrasting view of time-wasting in *The Picture of Dorian Gray*: 'he was always late on principle, his principle being that punctuality is the thief of time'. *See also* NEVER put off till tomorrow what you can do today; there is no TIME like the present; TOMORROW never comes.

> Procrastination is the thief of time;
> Year after year it steals, till all are fled,
> And to the mercies of a moment leaves
> The vast concerns of an eternal scene.
>
> Edward Young, 'Night Thoughts', 1742

proffer. proffered service stinks (*English*) If a person extols the virtues of the goods or services they are offering then the chances are that they are exaggerating them. *Douce MS*, *c.*1350.

> When I go to market to sell, my commodity stinks; but when I want to buy ... it can't be had for love or money.
>
> Tobias Smollett, *Humphry Clinker*, 1771

profoundly. *See* WALK groundly, talk profoundly, drink roundly, sleep soundly.

prologue. *See* a GOOD salad may be the prologue to a bad supper.

promise (noun). **promise is debt** (*English*) As soon as you make a promise to someone you are under an obligation to them. Geoffrey Chaucer, *The Canterbury Tales*, *c.*1387.

promises, like pie-crust, are made to be broken (*English*) It is inevitable that all promises will be broken. *Heraclitus Ridens*, 1681. Another proverb runs 'promises are either broken or kept'.

> 'Promises like that are mere pie-crust,' said Ralph.
> Anthony Trollope, *Ralph the Heir*, 1871

~ *See also* ONE acre of performance is worth twenty of the Land of Promise.

promise (verb). *See* a MAN apt to promise is apt to forget.

proof. the proof of the pudding is in the eating (*English*) The true worth of something is revealed when it is put to the test in practice. *King Alisaunder*, *c.*1300. In the Middle Ages favourite delicacies of the populace included bulky meat puddings enclosed in a length of intestine or in dough – the only sure way to test (or 'prove') them to see if they were cooked all the way through was to taste them.

> The thin soft cakes ... were done liberal justice to in the mode which is best proof of cake as well as pudding.
> Walter Scott, *The Fair Maid of Perth*, 1828

proper. the properer the man, the worse luck (*English*) The more proper (and thus honest) a person is the worse they tend to fare in life. J. Day, *Isle of Gulls*, 1606.

property has its duties as well as its rights (*English*) Landowners have obligations as well as privileges. J.E.T. Rogers, *Industrial and Commercial History*, 1891.

prophet. a prophet is not without honour save in his own country (*Hebrew*) While a person may be acknowledged for his gifts and good points further abroad, his virtues often remain unrecognized closer to home. Bible, Matthew 13:58. *See also* FAMILIARITY breeds contempt.

> A prophet is not without honour, except in his own country, and in his own house.
> Matthew 13:58

propose. *See* MAN proposes, but God disposes.

prospect is often better than possession (*English*) It is sometimes better to anticipate possession of something than actually to have it. Thomas Fuller, *Gnomologia*, 1732.

prosper. *See* CHEATS never prosper; ILL-GOTTEN gains seldom prosper; WINE counsels seldom prosper.

prosperity lets go the bridle (*English*) When things are going well a person is tempted to pay less attention to keeping control and may thus come to grief. George Herbert, *Outlandish Proverbs*, 1640.

protect. *See* HEAVEN protects children, sailors and drunken men.

proud. a proud heart and a beggar's purse agree not well together (*English*) Those who have no money cannot afford to be arrogant. John Lydgate, *Minor Poems*, *c.*1430. Related proverbs include 'he is a proud beggar that makes his own alms'.

> A proud mind and a poor purse are ill met.
> Thomas Fuller, *Gnomologia*, 1732

a proud look makes foul work in a fine face (*English*) A haughty expression can make the prettiest or noblest face ugly. Thomas Fuller, *Gnomologia*, 1732. Related proverbs include 'proud looks lose hearts, but courteous words win them'.

it is a proud horse that will not bear his own provender (*English*) No one should be too proud to look after their own business themselves. John Heywood, *A Dialogue containing ... the Proverbs in the English Tongue*, 1546.

~ *See also* NEW church, old steeple, poor town and proud people.

prove. prove thy friend ere thou have need (*Greek*) A sensible person tests the strength of another's friendship before the day when he or she might have to rely upon it. John Heywood, *A Dialogue containing ... the Proverbs in the English Tongue*, 1546 (quoting Cato).

~ *See also* EVERYONE is innocent until proved guilty; the EXCEPTION proves the rule; ONE mad action is not enough to prove a man mad; a SMILING boy seldom proves a good servant; who DAINTIES love, shall beggars prove.

provender. *See* it is a PROUD horse that will not bear his own provender.

provide. provide for the worst, the best will save itself (*English*) Always prepare for the worst possible outcome rather than the best. John Heywood, *A Dialogue containing ... the Proverbs in the English Tongue*, 1546.

> 'Tis good however to prepare for the worst,
> and the best (as they say) will help itself.
> Roger L'Estrange, *Citt and Bumpkin*, 1680

~ *See also* take the GOODS the gods provide.

providence. *See* if you LEAP into a well providence is not bound to fetch you out.

provoke. *See* BEAUTY provoketh thieves sooner than gold.

public. *See* ADMONISH your friends in private, praise them in public; don't WASH your dirty linen in public.

publicity. *See* ALL publicity is good publicity.

pudding. puddings and paramours should be hotly handled (*Scottish*) Puddings, like love affairs, are best when heated. David Fergusson, *Scottish Proverbs*, 1641. A cautionary note is sounded, however, by another proverb that runs 'pudding is poison when it is too much boiled'.

~ *See also* COLD pudding will settle your love; a GENTLEMAN without an estate is a pudding without suet; PRAISE is not pudding; the PROOF of the pudding is in the eating; SCORNFUL dogs will eat dirty puddings; those that EAT black pudding will dream of the devil.

puddle. *See* EVERY path hath a puddle; the SUN loses nothing by shining into a puddle.

puff not against the wind (*English*) It is foolish to try to resist the general flow of things. W. Camden, *Remains concerning Britain*, 1614.

pull (noun). *See* the CORD breaketh at the last by the weakest pull.

pull (verb). **he pulls with a long rope that waits for another's death** (*English*) Those who wait on the death of others in the hope of advancement may have a very long time to wait. George Herbert, *Outlandish Proverbs*, 1640.

pull devil, pull baker (*English*) Said to encourage two parties competing over the same prize, and implying that unscrupulous tactics will be employed. George Colman the Elder, *Rolliad*, 1759. Also encountered with 'parson' instead of 'baker'.

> Then my mither and her quarrelled, and pu'ed
> me twa ways at anes, as if ilk had and end o'
> me, like Punch and the Deevil rugging about the
> Baker at the fair.
> Walter Scott, *Old Mortality*, 1816

~ *See also* HARES may pull dead lions by the beard; it is EASIER to pull down than to build up; LOVE your neighbour, yet pull not down your hedge.

pun. he that would make a pun would pick a pocket (*English*) Those who are given to making puns are of such low character that they would be quite capable of committing other nefarious acts. Alexander Pope, *The Dunciad*, 1729. Pope was actually quoting critic John Dennis, who had remarked to the composer Purcell, 'any man who would make such an execrable pun would not scruple to pick my pocket' (though the phrase is often attributed to Samuel Johnson). According to Pope, Dennis was inspired to make the remark after Purcell had complained about the lack of service by a waiter (or 'drawer') in a particular tavern and had then likened the tavern in question to a table – because neither had a drawer.

> A great Critick formerly ... declared He that
> would pun would pick a Pocket.
> Alexander Pope, *The Dunciad*, 1729 (note)

punctuality. punctuality is the politeness of princes (*French*) It is a sign of good breeding to turn up to meetings and so forth on time. Samuel Smiles, *Self-Help*, 1859 (generally attributed originally to Louis XVIII, who listed it among his favourite sayings). Also encountered in the form 'punctuality is the politeness of kings'.

punctuality is the soul of business (*English*) Promptness in all things to essential to good business. T.C. Haliburton, *Wise Saws*, 1853.

punish. *See* CORPORATIONS have neither bodies to be punished nor souls to be damned.

punishment. punishment is lame but it comes (*English*) Punishment for wickedness may come slowly, but it always comes eventually. George Herbert, *Outlandish Proverbs*, 1640. Sometimes found with 'overtakes' in the place of 'comes'.

~ *See also* EVERY sin brings its punishment with it; SERVICE without reward is punishment.

pupil. *See* TODAY is yesterday's pupil.

pure. to the pure all things are pure (*Hebrew*) Those who are pure in spirit see all that is good and holy in the world around them. Bible, Titus 1:15.

> Unto the pure all things are pure, but unto
> them that are defiled, and unbeleeving, is
> nothing pure.
> Titus 1:15

~ *See also* the POORER the church, the purer the church.

purgatory. *See* ENGLAND is the paradise of women, the hell of horses and the purgatory of servants.

purpose. *See* BETTER say nothing than nothing to the purpose; the DEVIL can quote scripture for his own purpose.

purse. let your purse be your master (*English*) It is good policy to be guided in your lifestyle by what you can afford. J. Clarke, *Paroemiologia Anglo-Latina*, 1639. Another proverb on similar lines runs 'ask thy purse what thou should'st buy'. Those who fail to pay heed to their purses are warned 'wrinkled purses make wrinkled faces' and also that 'an empty purse frightens away friends'.

~ *See also* a BEGGAR's purse is bottomless; be it for BETTER, be it for worse, do you after him that beareth the purse; the DEVIL's mouth is a miser's purse; an EMPTY purse fills the face with wrinkles; a FRIEND in court is better than a penny in purse; a HEAVY purse makes a light heart; he that has not SILVER in his purse should have silk on his tongue; he that SHOWS his purse bribes the thief; LESS of your courtesy and more of your purse; LIGHT gains make heavy purses; a LIGHT purse makes a heavy heart; NOTHING agreeth worse than a lady's heart and a beggar's purse; a PENNY in purse will bid me drink when all the friends I have will not; a PROUD heart and a beggar's purse agree not well together; when TWO friends have a common purse one sings and the other weeps; WINE and wenches empty men's purses; WRINKLED purses make wrinkled faces; you can't make a SILK purse out of a sow's ear.

put off the evil hour as long as you can (*English*) Try to delay the hour when you must tackle some distasteful task as long as possible. Jonathan Swift, *Dialogues*, 1738.

Q

quack. *See* if it LOOKS like a duck, walks like a duck and quacks like a duck, it's a duck.

quadruple. *See* MARRIAGE halves our griefs, doubles our joys, and quadruples our expenses.

quarrel (noun). **the quarrel of lovers is the renewal of love** (*Roman*) Lovers or friends who have quarrelled and then been reconciled will find their relationship thereby strengthened. R. Edwardes, *Paradise of Dainty Devises*, 1576 (also found in the writings of Terence). *See also* the FALLING out of friends is the renewal of love.

> She would ... picke quarrells upon no occasion, because she would be reconciled to him againe ... The falling out of lovers is the renuing of love.
> Robert Burton, *Anatomy of Melancholy*, 1624

~ *See also* it takes TWO to make a quarrel; OLD reckonings make new quarrels.

quarrel (verb). *See* he that hath LAND hath quarrels.

quarrelsome dogs get dirty coats (*English*) Those who engage habitually in argument and confrontation must expect rough handling from time to time. S. Lover, *Handy Andy*, 1842.

quart. *See* you can't FIT a quart into a pint pot.

quarter-master. he'll be quarter-master wherever he comes (*English*) Said of a person who likes to be in command wherever he is. T. Wilson, *Discorse upon Usury*, 1572.

Queen Anne is dead (*English*) What purports to be fresh news is in fact already known by everyone. Ballad, quoted in Lady Pennyman, *Miscellanies*, 1722. This rather sarcastic saying was born in the confusion that surrounded reports of the death of Queen Anne in 1714. The demise of the queen (from erysipelas) was of particular import as she was childless (despite having been pregnant seventeen times) and there was much controversy over the succession, with the rival factions being represented by the Protestant Hanoverians and the Catholic James Edward Stuart. On her deathbed the queen finally nominated the Hanoverian George I to succeed her, thus settling the question: her death some two days later was thus of comparatively little interest and effectively 'old news'. To compound the confusion, rumours of her death circulated from the moment that the announcement concerning the succession was made. A fuller version of the saying runs 'as dead as Queen Anne the day after she died'. Less often heard is another English proverb along similar lines, 'Queen Elizabeth is dead' (again signifying stale news). A French equivalent is *c'est vieux comme le Pont-Neuf* (that's as old as the Pont-Neuf), the Pont-Neuf being the oldest bridge spanning the Seine in Paris.

> Tell 'em Queen Anne's dead, my lady.
> George Colman the Younger, *The Heir-at-Law*, 1797

queer. *See* there's NOWT so queer as folk.

quench. *See* ALMS quencheth sin; DIRTY water will quench fire; WATER afar quencheth not fire.

question (noun). **question for question is all fair** (*English*) Having answered a question a person has a right to ask one in return. Oliver Goldsmith, *She Stoops to Conquer*, 1773.

~ *See also* ASK a silly question and you'll get a silly answer; ASK no questions and hear no lies; FOOLS ask questions that wise men cannot answer; there are TWO sides to every question.

question (verb). **he that questioneth nothing, nothing learneth** (*English*) Those who do not ask questions will find nothing out. Thomas Fuller, *Gnomologia*, 1732.

~ *See also* that which cometh from ABOVE let no man question.

quick. quick at meat, quick at work (*English*) Those who eat their meals fastest are likely also to be the fastest workers. Randle Cotgrave, *A Dictionary of the French and English Tongues*, 1611.

quick returns make rich merchants (*Scottish*) Fortunes are to be made from customers who come back quickly to spend more money. Usually applied to drunkards who once sober return to make themselves drunk again. James Kelly, *A Complete Collection of Scottish Proverbs*, 1721.

~ *See also* GOOD ware makes quick markets.

quickly. quickly come, quickly go (*English*) What is easily obtained may be equally easily lost (often quoted in reference to money). B. Melbancke, *Philotimus*, 1583. *See also* EASY come, easy go.

~ *See also* ACT quickly, think slowly; GOOD and quickly seldom meet; a GOOD judge conceives quickly, judges slowly; he GIVES twice who gives quickly; HONEST men marry quickly, wise men not at all; WATER, fire and soldiers quickly make room.

quiet. a quiet conscience sleeps in thunder (*English*) Those who are not troubled by guilty acts sleep soundly. James Kelly, *A Complete Collection of Scottish Proverbs*, 1721. Related proverbs include 'quiet sleep feels no foul weather'.

a quiet tongue makes a wise head (*English*) Those who know how to keep silent when necessary are the wisest. John Heywood, *Epigrams*, 1562. *See also* a STILL tongue makes a wise head.

~ *See also* the BEST doctors are Dr Diet, Dr Quiet and Dr Merryman.

quietness is best (*English*) Silence is much to be valued; silence is golden. *George a Green*, 1599. Fuller versions of the proverb run 'quietness is best, as the fox said when he bit the cock's head off' and 'quietness is the best noise, as Uncle Johnny said when he knocked down his wife.'

> Quietnesse is a great treasure.
>
> R. Codrington, *The Second Part of Youth's Behaviour*, 1664

quill. *See* a GOOSE quill is more dangerous than a lion's claw.

quinine is made of the sweat of ship carpenters (*English*) Medicines and other things that are difficult to make are accordingly expensive to buy. F. Cowan, *Sea Proverbs*, 1894.

quit. quit while you are ahead (*English*) Leave off doing something while you are in a good position, thus avoiding any loss to one's winnings and the like. *Douce MS*, *c.*1350. Historical variants include 'leave off while the play is good'.

~ *See also* he BEGINS to die that quits his desires; NEVER quit certainty for hope.

quote. *See* the DEVIL can quote scripture for his own purpose.

quoth. *See* BATE me an ace, quoth Bolton.

R

R. *See* NEVER eat an oyster unless there is an R in the month.

race. the race is not to the swift, nor the battle to the strong (*Hebrew*) It is not necessarily the fastest and the strongest who always win. Bible, Ecclesiastes 9:11. A potential winner must, however, at least be in the race, as another less well-known proverb points out: 'the race is got by running'. It was this proverb that prompted US author and journalist Damon Runyon to remark 'the race is not always to the swift nor the battle to the strong, but that's the way to bet'.

> It is not honesty, learning, worth, wisdome, that preferres men, The race is not to the swift, nor the battell to the stronger.
>
> Robert Burton, *Anatomy of Melancholy*, 1632

~ *See also* SLOW but sure wins the race; the TORTOISE wins the race while the hare is sleeping.

rag. *See* the SLUGGARD must be clad in rags.

ragged. a ragged colt may make a good horse (*English*) A wild youth may yet turn out to be a reliable and worthy adult. R. Hill, *Commonplace Book*, *c.*1500.

> Aft a ragged cowte's been known
> To mak a noble aiver.
>
> Robert Burns, *Dream*, 1786

rain (noun)**. if the rain comes before the wind, lower your topsails and take them in; if the wind comes before the rain, lower your topsails and hoist them again** (*English*) Advice to sailors on sailing ships depending on whether the wind rises before or after the onset of rain. *Notes and Queries*, 1853.

in rain and sunshine cuckolds go to heaven (*English*) When the rain falls and the sun shines at the same time this means that those whose wives have betrayed them are on their way to heaven. John Florio, *Second Frutes*, 1591. Another proverb gnomically observes that 'cuckolds are Christians'.

rain before seven, fine before eleven (*English*) Rain early in the morning presages fine weather from eleven o'clock. *Notes & Queries*, 1853. A variant on the notion has produced the related proverb, 'if it rains at eleven, 'twill last till seven'. Also encountered in the form 'if rain begins at early morning light, 'twill end ere day at noon is bright'.

the rain comes south when the wind's in the south (*Scottish*) Expect heavy rainfall if it starts to rain when a southerly wind is blowing. A. Hislop, *Scottish Proverbs*, 1862. Another proverb runs 'rain from the south prevents the drought; but rain from the west is always best'.

rain, rain, go away, come again on Saturday (*English*) Traditional charm recited to keep the rain off. John Aubrey, *Gentilisme*, 1687. Also found with 'washing day' or 'another day' replacing 'Saturday'. Related sayings include 'rain, rain, go to Spain; come again another day: when I brew and when I bake, I'll give you a figgy cake'.

~ *See also* AFTER drought cometh rain; AFTER rain comes sunshine; after WIND comes rain; BLESSED are the dead that the rain rains on; BRIGHT rain makes fools fain; HYPOCRISY can find out a cloak for every rain; if CANDLEMAS Day be sunny and bright winter will have another flight; if Candlemas

Day be cloudy with rain, winter is gone and won't come again; if in FEBRUARY there be no rain, 'tis neither good for hay nor grain; it is GOOD to have a cloak for the rain; THREE things drive a man out of his house: smoke, rain and a scolding wife; the WEST wind always brings wet weather, the east wind wet and cold together, the south wind surely brings us rain, the north wind blows it back again.

rain (verb). **if it rains when the wind is in the east, it will rain for twenty-four hours at least** (*English*) An easterly wind is a sure sign of prolonged rain to come. John Aubrey, *Natural History of Wiltshire*, *c.*1685.

it rains by planets (*English*) The places where showers of rain fall are determined by the movement of the planets, or by the mysterious workings of Providence. Thomas Fuller, *Gnomologia*, 1632.

> This the country people use when it rains in one place and not in another; meaning that the showers are governed by the planets, which ... cause such uncertain wandering of clouds and falls of rain. Or ... the falls of showers are as uncertain as the motions of the planets are imagined to be.
>
> John Ray, *A Collection of English Proverbs*, 1670

rain on the green grass, and rain on the tree, and rain on the house-top, but not upon me (*English*) Traditional charm recited to keep the rain off. M.A. Denham, *A Collection of Proverbs ... relating to the Weather*, 1846. Another proverb observes 'to see it rain is better than to be in it'.

when it rains and the sun shines at the same time the devil is beating his wife (*French*) Weather superstition, seeking to provide an explanation for contrary climatic conditions. G. Torriano, *Select Italian Proverbs*, 1642. In many versions the devil uses a leg of mutton to beat his wife with.

> The Devil was beating his wife behind the door with a shoulder of mutton.
>
> Jonathan Swift, *Polite Conversation*, 1738

~ *See also* it NEVER rains but it pours; a PALE moon doth rain, a red moon doth blow; a white moon doth neither rain nor snow; SAINT Swithin's Day, if thou dost rain, for forty days it will remain; Saint Swithin's Day, if thou be fair, for forty days 'twill rain no more.

rainbow. a rainbow in the morning is the shepherd's warning; a rainbow at night is the shepherd's delight (*English*) A rainbow early in the day threatens bad weather, while one late in the day promises fine weather to come. L. Digges, *Prognostication*, 1555. The notion may have some basis in fact as rainbows appear only when there is moisture (such as may suggest approaching rain) in the air. Variants include 'if there be a rainbow at morn, put your hook in the corn; a rainbow at eve, put your head in the sheave', 'if there be a rainbow in the eve, it will rain and leave; but if there be a rainbow in the morrow, it will neither lend nor borrow', 'rainbow at noon, rain comes soon' and 'if the rainbow comes at night, the rain is gone quite'. *See also* RED sky at night, shepherd's delight; red sky in the morning, sailor's warning.

> A rainbow in the Eastern sky,
> The morrow will be fine and dry.
> A rainbow in the West that gleams,
> Rain tomorrow falls in streams.
>
> Chinese proverb

rainy. *See* NEVER offer your hen for sale on a rainy day; SAVE something for a rainy day.

raise. *See* the FLY sat upon the axletree of the chariot-wheel and said, what a dust do I raise!; it is EASIER to raise the devil than to lay him; YELPING curs will raise mastiffs.

rake. what the rake gathers, the fork scatters (*English*) What one generation carefully saves up the next generation may quickly dissipate. J. Lyly, *Euphues*, 1580.

> The fork is commonly the rake's heir.
>
> W. C. Hazlitt, *English Proverbs*, 1869

ransom. *See* a PECK of March dust is worth a king's ransom.

rap. *See* when EASTER falls in our Lady's lap, then let England beware of a rap.

rarely. *See* ARTFUL speech and an ingratiating demeanour rarely accompany virtue.

rat. rats desert a sinking ship (*English*) If an enterprise is about to collapse the first to leave are those with the least interest in what happens to it. T. Lupton, *A Thousand Notable Things*, 1579. Sailors have believed for centuries that rats know long in advance that a particular ship is doomed and will desert it long before it actually founders. By extension it is thought to be a good omen if rats are seen boarding a vessel. A realistic explanation for the belief suggests that rats will desert a ship if a vessel ships water and the bilges where the rats live are flooded. A leaking ship is likely to founder, hence the link between the rats' departure and any catastrophe that then befalls the vessel in question. The proverb is also encountered in the form 'rats desert a falling house': scientists confirm that rats may indeed be more sensitive than humans to minor earth tremors that may be the precursor of major earthquakes (in former times rats were often taken into caves and mines to provide warnings of imminent collapses). Rats are also supposed to vacate premises if someone within is close to death.

> A rotten carcass of a boat, ... the very rats instinctively have quit it.
> William Shakespeare, *The Tempest*, *c.*1610

~ *See also* the CAT, the Rat and Lovell our Dog rule all England under an Hog; 'tis an OLD rat that won't eat cheese.

reach. *See* a SHORT prayer reaches heaven; STRETCH your arm no further than your sleeve will reach.

read. *See* the ACOLYTE at the gate reads scriptures he has never learned; when a NEW book appears, read an old one.

ready. ready money is a ready medicine (*English*) A supply of readily available cash does much to make a person feel better and to solve any problems they may face. J. Conybeare, *Adagia*, *c.*1580.
ready money will away (*English*) Money that is easily accessible is easily spent. J. Taylor, *Works*, 1630.

reap. *See* as you SOW, so shall you reap; they that SOW the wind shall reap the whirlwind.

reason. reason governs the wise man and cudgels the fool (*English*) A wise man profits by using reason, while a fool is punished or humiliated by it. J. Mapletoft, *Select Proverbs*, 1707.
there is reason in the roasting of eggs (*English*) There is purpose behind every course of action, however bizarre. J. Howell, *Paroemiographia*, 1659.

> But there's reason in the roasting of eggs, and ... money is not so plentiful ... that your uncle can afford to throw it into the Barchester gutters.
> Anthony Trollope, *The Last Chronicle of Barset*, 1867

~ *See also* BECAUSE is a woman's reason; CUSTOM without reason is but ancient error; FRUIT out of season, sorrow out of reason; LAW governs man, and reason the law; ONE reason is as good as fifty.

recall. *See* THINGS past cannot be recalled; TIME lost cannot be recalled; TIMES past cannot be recalled; a WORD spoken is past recalling.

receive. *See* it is BETTER to give than to receive.

receiver. if there were no receivers, there would be no thieves (*English*) There would be no point in dishonesty if there were not others ready to reward it and profit by it. Geoffrey Chaucer, *The Canterbury Tales*, *c.*1387. Also found as 'no receiver, no thief'. Another proverb insists 'the receiver is as bad as the thief'.

> This proverbe preeves, Where be no receyvers, there be no theeves.
> John Heywood, *A Dialogue containing ... the Proverbs in the English Tongue*, 1546

reckoning. *See* EVEN reckoning makes long friends; the FAIRER the hostess, the fouler the reckoning; MERRY is the company till the reckoning comes; OLD reckonings make new quarrels; SHORT reckonings make long friends.

recommendation. *See* a GOOD face is a letter of recommendation; SELF-PRAISE is no recommendation.

reconcile. *See* KEEP yourself from the anger of a great man, from the tumult of a mob, from a man of ill fame, from a widow that has been thrice married, from a wind that comes in at a hole, and from a reconciled enemy; take HEED of reconciled enemies and of meat twice boiled.

reculer pour mieux sauter (*French*) Draw back and consider the situation before committing yourself. Michel de Montaigne, *Essays*, 1580 (also found in essence in the writings of Ovid). Often quoted in the original French, but also encountered in English as 'we must recoil a little, to the end we may leap the better'. *See also* LOOK before you leap.

> We must recoil a little, to the end we may leap the better.
> George Herbert, *Outlandish Proverbs*, 1640

red. red sky at night, shepherd's delight; red sky in the morning, shepherd's warning (*English*) A red sunset is a prelude of fine weather to come, while a red dawn presages bad weather in store. John Wycliffe, Matthew 26:2, *c.*1395. The proverb is based on a vestige of good sense, for the weather systems governing the British climate are generally formed in the Atlantic, to the west, and thus when the sun sets in the west it will appear red if the air approaching the British Isles is dry and warm. A red sun in the morning is less significant, as it rises in the east. The state of the coming weather systems are obviously of particular importance to both shepherds and sailors (shepherds and sailors being more or less interchangeable in the proverb). Related proverbs include 'if red the sun begins his race, expect that rain will flow apace' and 'if the sun in red should set, the next day surely will be wet; if the sun should set in grey, the next will be a rainy day'.

> Like a red morn, that ever yet betoken'd
> Wreck to the seaman ... Sorrow to shepherds.
> William Shakespeare, *Venus and Adonis*, *c.*1592

~ *See also* EVENING red and morning grey help the traveller on his way; the LASS in the red petticoat shall pay for all; a PALE moon doth rain, a red moon doth blow; a white moon doth neither rain nor snow.

rede. *See* SHORT rede, good rede.

redeem. *See* an OCCASION lost cannot be redeemed.

redemption. there is no redemption from hell (*English*) Some deeds are so wicked there can be no escape from guilt. William Langland, *Piers Plowman*, 1377. The saying acquired particular significance among the English through the nickname given to Exchequer Court, called 'Hell', where the king's debtors were pursued; money paid to the Exchequer was deemed irrecoverable thereafter.

redressed. *See* a FAULT confessed is half redressed.

reed. a reed before the wind lives on, while mighty oaks do fall (*English*) In difficult times the humble and insignificant may survive while those who would normally be considered their superiors perish. Geoffrey Chaucer, *Troilus and Criseyde*, *c.*1385–90. Variant forms include 'oaks may fall when reeds stand the storm'.

> Though I live obscure, yet I live cleane and honest, and when as the lofty oake is blowne downe, the silly reed may stand.
> Richard Burton, *Anatomy of Melancholy*, 1621

~ *See also* LEAN not on a reed.

reel. *See* a MAN cannot spin and reel at the same time.

refuge. *See* PATRIOTISM is the last refuge of a scoundrel.

refuse. *See* the SEA and the gallows refuse none.

regulate. *See* ACCIDENTS will happen in the best regulated families.

rejoice. *See* it is a POOR heart that never rejoices.

relief. *See* SYMPATHY without relief is like mustard without beef.

relieve. *See* he that GIVES to be seen will relieve none in the dark.

religion. *See* a MAN without religion is like a horse without a bridle; PRESBYTERIANISM is no religion for a gentleman.

rely. *See* he hath a GOOD judgement that relieth not wholly on his own; NEVER rely on the glory of the morning or on the smile of your mother-in-law.

remain. *See* the BEST go first, the bad remain to mend; SAINT Swithin's Day, if thou dost rain, for forty days it will remain; Saint Swithin's Day, if thou be fair, for forty days 'twill rain no more; though the WOUND be healed, a scar remains.

remedy. no remedy but patience (*Roman*) For some complaints or problems there is no solution except to wait for things to come right. *Letter of Muscovy Company*, 1557 (also found in the writings of Horace). *See also* TIME heals all wounds.

the remedy may be worse than the disease (*Roman*) Countermeasures may be so radical that some may consider them to be worse than the problems they are designed to solve. Francis Bacon, 'Of Sedition and Troubles', 1597 (also found in the writings of Publilius Syrus in the first century BC and in Seneca). This proverb was originally quoted in medical contexts but is now applied in many other situations.

> Things will therefore stand as they are; the remedy would be worse than the disease.
>
> Lord Byron, letter, 1807

there is a remedy for everything except death (*English*) Death is a malady for which there is no cure. John Lydgate, *The Dance of Machabree*, *c.*1430. Another proverb ignores the limitation imposed by death, claiming 'there is a remedy for everything, could men but find it'. *See also* there is no MEDICINE against death.

> There is a remedy for everything but death, said Don Quixote; for 'tis but having a Barke ready at the Sea side, and in spite of all the world we may embarke our selves.
>
> Thomas Shelton, *Cervantes' Don Quixote*, 1620

~ *See also* AVOIDANCE is the only remedy; the BEST remedy against an ill man is much ground between; DESPERATE diseases call for desperate remedies; no WRONG without a remedy.

remember. *See* the LAST benefit is most remembered.

remembrance of past sorrow is joyful (*English*) There is pleasure to be derived from recalling past sorrows and perils. William Shakespeare, *Romeo and Juliet*, 1594–5.

removal. *See* THREE removals are as bad as a fire.

remove. do not remove a fly from your friend's forehead with a hatchet (*Chinese*) Taking extreme measures to counter a minor problem may lead to considerably greater harm resulting.

remove an old tree and it will die (*English*) Interfere with something long-established and you risk destroying it altogether. Alexander Barclay, *Mirrour of Good Manners*, 1570. Also found as 'remove an old tree and it will wither to death'.

render unto Caesar that which is Caesar's (*Hebrew*) Hand over what you have to those who claim a stronger title to them. Bible, Matthew 22:21. The proverb is usually quoted in discussion of business affairs, particularly tax revenues demanded by government (echoing the original context – the taxes imposed on all Romans under the rule of Julius Caesar).

> Render therefore unto Caesar the things which are Caesar's; and unto God the things that are God's.
>
> Matthew 22:21

renewal. *See* the FALLING out of friends is the renewal of love; the QUARREL of lovers is the renewal of love.

repair. he who repairs not his gutter repairs his whole house (*English*) A person who fails to make timely repairs will find that eventually he or she will have to institute much more extensive repairs to counter damage done. John Ruskin, *The Seven Lamps of Architecture*, 1849. Variants include 'he who repairs not a part builds all'. *See also* a STITCH in time saves nine.

repeat. *See* he that KNOWS little, often repeats it; HISTORY repeats itself.

repent. *See* if you TRUST before you try, you may repent before you die; MARRY in haste and repent at leisure; MARRY in Lent, and you'll live to repent; MORE have repented speech than silence.

repentance comes too late (*English*) Repenting after the harm is done does nothing to reduce the effects. John Lydgate, *The Fall of Princes*, *c.*1440. A contrasting viewpoint is offered by the saying 'it is never too late to repent'. Other related proverbs include 'too late repents the rat when caught by the cat'.

~ *See also* LATE repentance is seldom true; SUDDEN friendship, sure repentance.

reproach. *See* the STING of a reproach is the truth of it.

reprove. *See* SATAN reproves sin.

reserve the master-blow (*Italian*) The wise master keeps back some of the secrets of his skill so that he is never overtaken by his pupil. G. Torriano, *Select Italian Proverbs*, 1659.

respect a man, he will do the more (*English*) Those who receive respect and praise are more likely to do more in return. J. Howell, *Paroemiologia*, 1659. Another proverb warns 'he that respects not is not respected.'

rest. *See* AFTER dinner rest a while, after supper walk a mile; a CHANGE is as good as a rest; DESIRE hath no rest; if ONE sheep leap o'er the dyke, all the rest will follow.

restore. *See* GIVING is dead and restoring very sick.

return. *See* the DOG returns to its vomit; he goes FAR that never returns; QUICK returns make rich merchants; SEND a fool to market and a fool he'll return; though you CAST out nature with a fork, it will still return.

reveal. *See* it is BETTER to conceal one's knowledge than to reveal one's ignorance; DRUNKENNESS reveals what soberness conceals; TRUTH should not always be revealed.

revenge. had I revenged every wrong, I had not worn my skirts so long (*English*) Those who become absorbed in exacting vengeance for every wrong done to them will have no time left to make money for themselves, and will thus find themselves reduced to wearing rags and tatters. R. Hill, *Commonplace Book*, 1500. Also found as 'had I revenged been of every harm, my coat had never kept me half so warm'.

revenge is a dish that is best eaten cold (*English*) Those who take their time over exacting their revenge on their enemies will find it has added savour. C. Lowe, *Prince Bismarck*, 1885. Also found in the form 'revenge is a dish that should be served cold'.

revenge is sweet (*Greek*) There is satisfaction to be had in exacting one's revenge on an enemy. William Painter, *The Palace of Pleasure*, 1566 (also found in essence in Homer's *Iliad* in the ninth century BC). An Italian proverb warns, however, that 'revenge is a morsel for God', being far too sweet for men.

> Revenge, at first, though sweet,
> Bitter 'ere long, back on itself recoils.
> John Milton, *Paradise Lost*, 1667

~ *See also* CONTEMPT will sooner kill an injury than revenge; NEGLECT will kill an injury sooner than revenge.

revenue. *See* THRIFT is a great revenue.

reverse. *See* EVERY medal hath its reverse.

revolutions are not made with rose-water (*French*) Major changes cannot be made without a certain degree of violence and disruption. 1789, Nicolas Chamfort, quoted in Marmontel, *Oeuvres*, 1818.

> On either side harm must be done before good
> can accrue – revolutions are not to be made
> with rose water.
> Lord Byron, letter, 3 October 1819

reward. *See* DESERT and reward seldom keep company; a LEAN fee is a fit reward for a lazy clerk; LOVE is love's reward; SERVICE without reward is punishment; VIRTUE is its own reward.

rich. he is rich enough that wants nothing (*Roman*) A person should be satisfied if they have enough for their needs. George Herbert, *Outlandish Proverbs*, 1640. Related proverbs include 'he is rich enough who lacks not bread', 'he is rich enough that needeth neither to flatter nor borrow' and 'why should a rich man steal?'

> He is rich that is satisfied.
> Thomas Fuller, *Gnomologia*, 1732

he that will be rich before night may be hanged before noon (*French*) Those who hope for rapid wealth must not be too fastidious about the methods they adopt to achieve their aim, even to the extent of committing crime. H. Estienne, *World of Wonders*, 1607.

rich folk have many friends (*English*) The rich are never short of flatterers who seek to become their friends. James Kelly, *A Complete Collection of Scotish Proverbs*, 1721. Also found as 'rich folk have routh of friends' ('routh' meaning 'plenty'). Much the same point is made by the proverb 'rich men have no faults', but another warns the wealthy that 'the rich knows not who is his friend.' The message is hammered home in 'they are rich who have true friends.'

the rich man has his ice in the summer and the poor man gets his in the winter (*English*) The difference between a rich man and a poor man lies not so much in what they can get but in the power the wealthy man has to get it when he wants it. W.B. Masterson, quoted in the *Morning Telegraph*, 27 October 1921. Another proverb suggests another way to judge real wealth, 'he is rich enough that wants nothing', while another runs, 'he is rich enough that needeth neither to flatter nor borrow'.

a rich man's money hangs him oftentimes (*English*) A person's wealth can easily prove their downfall. J. Withals, *A Short Dictionary in Latin and English*, 1616.

~ *See also* BEG from beggars and you'll never be rich; BEGGARS breed and rich men feed; GENTLEMEN and rich men are venison in heaven; GOD help the poor, for the rich can help themselves; he that is not HANDSOME at twenty, wise at forty and rich at fifty, will never be rich, wise or handsome; he who is CONTENT in his poverty is wonderfully rich; he who NEVER fails will never grow rich; it is BETTER to be born lucky than rich; it is EASIER for a camel to go through the eye of a needle than it is for a rich man to enter into the kingdom of heaven; make the VINE poor and it will make you rich; a NICE wife and a back door will soon make a rich man poor; the PLEASURES of the rich are bought with the tears of the poor; POOR men seek meat for their stomach; rich men stomach for their meat; QUICK returns make rich merchants; a SNOW year, a rich year; there's one LAW for the rich and another for the poor.

riches. riches are but the baggage of fortune (*English*) To become rich a person needs to have luck on their side. Francis Bacon, 'Riches', 1607–12. Also found as 'riches are but the baggage of virtue'.

> To bee rich is the gift of fortune.
>
> John Lyly, *Euphues*, 1580

riches are like muck, which stink in a heap, but spread abroad make the earth fruitful (*English*) Wealth hoarded up does nothing to improve the world, whereas money put to good use bestows benefit far and wide. Ben Jonson, *Every Man out of Humour*, 1599.

riches have wings (*Hebrew*) Wealth is easily lost. Bible, Proverbs 23:5.

> For riches taketh her to her wings, as an eagle, and flieth into the heaven.
>
> Proverbs 23:5

riches serve a wise man but command a fool (*English*) The wise make their money work for them, while the foolish let it rule their lives. Thomas Fuller, *Gnomologia*, 1732. Variants on similar lines include 'riches abuse them who know not how to use them'. A similar point is made by the proverb 'he is not fit for riches who is afraid to use them'.

~ *See also* CHILDREN are poor men's riches.

richly. *See* LOWLY sit, richly warm,

rid. *See* not a LONG day but a good heart rids work.

ride. he rides well that never falls (*English*) No one is immune from making mistakes. Thomas Malory, *Morte d'Arthur*, 1485. Also found as 'he rides sure that never fell'.

> He rode sure indeed, that never caught a fall in his life.
>
> Thomas Fuller, *Gnomologia*, 1732

he who rides a tiger is afraid to dismount (*Chinese*) Those who embark on perilous enterprises may find that it is unsafe to do anything but follow their course to the very end. W. Scarborough, *Collection of Chinese Proverbs*, 1875.

if you can't ride two horses at once, you shouldn't be in the circus (*English*) If you cannot meet the expected standard, you should not enter the fray. G. McAllister, *James Maxton*, 1935.

~ *See also* the DEVIL rides upon a fiddlestick; GOOD riding at two anchors; he that makes himself an ASS must not take it ill if men ride him; he who HIRES the horse must ride before; if TWO ride on a horse one must ride behind; if WISHES were horses, beggars would ride; SET a beggar on horseback, and he'll ride to the devil.

ridiculous. *See* from the SUBLIME to the ridiculous is but a step.

right (noun). *See* the GREATER the right, the greater the wrong; PROPERTY has its duties as well as its rights; TWO wrongs don't make a right.

right (adj./adv.). **do right and fear no man** (*English*) Do what is good and do not allow yourself to be cowed by any other person. *Book of Precedence*, *c.*1450. Related proverbs include 'do evil and look for the like'.

right mixture makes good mortar (*English*) If the ingredients are good then the final result is likely to be good. James Kelly, *A Complete Collection of Scotish Proverbs*, 1721.

∼ *See also* the CUSTOMER is always right; GOD's in his heaven, all's right with the world; INDUSTRY is fortune's right hand, and frugality her left; MIGHT is right; our COUNTRY, right or wrong; SET the saddle on the right horse.

ring. *See* as your WEDDING ring wears, your cares will wear away; BETTER no ring than a ring of rush; to GIVE a thing, and take a thing, is to wear the devil's gold ring.

ripe. *See* SOON ripe, soon rotten.

rise. he that riseth late must trot all day (*US*) A person who gets up late must spend the rest of the day working at top speed in order to catch up. Coined by Benjamin Franklin. *See also* an HOUR in the morning is worth two in the evening.

∼ *See* a BLISTER will rise upon one's tongue that tells a lie; EARLY to bed and early to rise, makes a man healthy, wealthy and wise; get a NAME to rise early, and you may lie all day; go to BED with the lamb and rise with the lark; he that FALLS today may rise tomorrow; he that goes to BED thirsty riseth healthy; he that will DECEIVE the fox must rise betimes; he that will THRIVE must rise at five; if the COCK crows on going to bed, he's sure to rise with a watery head; a STREAM cannot rise above its source.

rising. the rising of one man is the falling of another (*English*) For one person to progress or win promotion another person must suffer a demotion or disappointment of some kind. T. Draxe, *Bibliotheca Scholastica*, 1616.

∼ *See* a SUDDEN rising hath a sudden fall.

rive. *See* DOUBLE charge will rive a cannon.

riven. *See* ALL is lost that is put into a riven dish.

river. the river passed and God forgotten (*English*) Those who call on divine aid in time of trouble are all too apt to forget all about such assistance once the trouble is overcome. Randle Cotgrave, *A Dictionary of the French and English Tongues*, 1611.

∼ *See also* FOLLOW the river and you'll get to the sea.

road. the road to hell is paved with good intentions (*English*) Those who mean well often end up doing evil. E. Hellowes, *Guevara's Epistles*, 1574. Also (particularly in former times) encountered in the form 'hell is paved with good intentions'. Another proverb insists 'the road to hell is easy'.

> Hell is full of good meanings and wishings.
> George Herbert, *Outlandish Proverbs*, 1640

∼ *See also* ALL roads lead to Rome; there is no ROYAL road to learning; there will be RUBS in the smoothest road.

roast. *See* DRY bread at home is better than roast meat abroad.

roasting. *See* there is REASON in the roasting of eggs.

rob. *See* the BACK door robs the house; however BIG the whale may be, the tiny harpoon can rob him of life; it is EASY to rob an orchard when none keeps it; the JAY bird don't rob his own nest; ONE thief robs another.

robbery. *See* FAIR exchange is no robbery.

robin. if the robin sings in the bush then the weather will be coarse; but if the robin sings in the barn then the weather will be warm (*English*) Traditional rhyme to foretell the weather. R. Inwards, *Weather Lore*, 1893.
the robin and the wren are God's cock and hen (*English*) The humble robin and the wren are especially loved by Heaven. *Poetical Description of Song Birds*, 1787. The fuller version of the proverb runs, 'the robin and the wren are God's cock and hen; the martin and the swallow are God's mate and marrow'. Sometimes the sparrow takes the place of the robin. Legend has it that the robin acquired its red breast when it was singed while bringing water to souls tormented in the fires of hell, or alternatively that it was splashed with the blood of Christ as it tried to pull the thorns from his brow. The wren has traditionally been considered the wife of the robin and it is consequently risking the direst misfortune to kill either bird or destroy their eggs or nests. Another proverb warns 'he that hunts robin or wren will never prosper boy nor man'.

> In Hampshire we have this couplet, 'Little Cock Robin and Little Jenny Wren, Are God Almighty's little Cock and Hen.' And agreeably to this these birds are held sacred, no boys, however daring, venturing to take their nests or to kill them.
> W. Holloway, *Provincialisms*, 1838

Robin Hood. Robin Hood could brave all weathers but a thaw wind (*English*) The least bearable aspect of the weather is a 'thaw wind', a raw and penetrating wind that often blows from the south or south-east after a frost or snow. W. Neville, *The Life and Exploits of Robin Hood*, 1855. The proverb is especially well known in Yorkshire, the probable home territory of the semi-fictional outlaw hero. Inhabitants of the area around Rochdale might refer to a 'Robin Hood wind', a piercing cold wind from the north or east coming off Blackstone Edge.

~ *See also* MANY talk of Robin Hood who never shot with his bow.

rock (noun). *See* he who will not be RULED by the rudder must be ruled by the rock.

rock (verb). *See* the HAND that rocks the cradle rules the world.

rod. *See* GIVE a slave a rod and he'll beat his master; SPARE the rod and spoil the child.

rogue. *See* NOBODY calls himself rogue.

roll. a rolling stone gathers no moss (*English*) Those who are always busy consequently keep themselves clear of all unnecessary encumbrances. William Langland, *Piers Plowman*, 1362 (also found in the writings of Erasmus).

> Your popular rumour, unlike the rolling stone of the proverb, is one which gathers a deal of moss in its wanderings up and down.
> Charles Dickens, *The Old Curiosity Shop*, 1841

Roman. *See* when in ROME, do as the Romans do.

Rome. Rome was not built in a day (*French*) It takes time and effort to achieve the remarkable (just as it took centuries for Imperial Rome to be built). R. Taverner, *Proverbs or Adages with New Additions, gathered out of the Chiliades of Erasmus*, 1546. The proverb is occasionally heard in reference to other major cities, particularly Paris.

> As Rome ... had not been built in a day, so neither had Mademoiselle Gerard Moore's education been completed in a week.
> Charlotte Brontë, *Shirley*, 1849

when in Rome, do as the Romans do (*Roman*) When you find yourself in unfamiliar surroundings, it is good policy to compromise one's usual habits and customs and to imitate the manners and way of life of the inhabitants. Saint Ambrose, *Advice to Saint Augustine*, AD 387. The story goes that Saint Ambrose was approached by Saint Augustine for advice when the latter's mother – Saint Monica – arrived in Milan and expressed confusion about whether to fast on a Saturday (as they did in Rome) or to ignore the ruling (as they did in Milan). Saint Ambrose's considered opinion was that she should adapt her practice to whatever was the custom in the place in which she found herself: 'if you are at Rome, live after the Roman fashion; if you are elsewhere, live as they do there'. Much the same advice may be found in varying forms in numerous other cultures around the world. An equivalent, though now archaic, proverb from elsewhere in Europe ran 'never wear a brown hat in Friesland' – an allusion to the extraordinary headwear commonly adopted by inhabitants of that region (a knitted cap surmounted by a silk skull-cap, a metal turban and a high bonnet). Anyone who appeared on the streets wearing humbler head attire would be mocked and jeered.

~ *See also* ALL roads lead to Rome; BETTER to be first in a village than second at Rome; it is ILL sitting at Rome and striving with the Pope.

room. *See* there is ALWAYS room at the top; WATER, fire and soldiers quickly make room.

roost. *See* CURSES, like chickens, come home to roost.

root. *See* IDLENESS is the root of all evil; the LOVE of money is the root of all evil; the PINE wishes herself a shrub when the axe is at her root.

rope. *See* GIVE a man enough rope and he will hang himself; he PULLS with a long rope that waits for another's death.

rose. a rose by any other name would smell as sweet (*English*) It is not the name of something that distinguishes it, but its intrinsic character. William Shakespeare, *Romeo and Juliet*, c.1593.

> What's in a name? that which we call a rose
> By any other name would smell as sweet;
> So Romeo would, were he not Romeo called.
> William Shakespeare, *Romeo and Juliet*, c.1593

no rose without a thorn (*English*) Many desirable things, like roses, carry their own dangers with them. John Lydgate, *Bochas*, *c.*1435. Sometimes encountered in the fuller form 'no rose without a thorn, or a love without a rival'.

Hath not thy rose a thorn, Plantagenet?
William Shakespeare, *Henry VI, Part 1*, *c.*1590

~ *See also* ANYTHING may be spoken if it be under the rose; the FAIREST rose at last is withered.

rosebud. *See* GATHER ye rosebuds while ye may.

rosemary. where rosemary flourishes the lady rules (*English*) Rosemary will only flourish in the garden of a household where a woman dominates. H. Friend, *Flowers and Flower Lore*, 1884.

rose-water. *See* REVOLUTIONS are not made with rose-water.

rot. *See* ONE for the mouse, one for the crow, one to rot, one to grow.

rotten. the rotten apple injures its neighbours (*English*) Evil or corruption is contagious and will infect those close at hand unless quickly isolated. *Ayenbite of Inwit*, 1340.

The rotten apple spoils his companion.
Benjamin Franklin, *Poor Richard's Almanack*, 1736

~ *See also* SOON ripe, soon rotten; there is SMALL choice in rotten apples.

rough. take the rough with the smooth (*English*) Bad times and experiences must be accepted as a necessary accompaniment to the enjoyment of what is good. *Beryn*, *c.*1400.

One must take a little rough with one's smooth.
Jerome K. Jerome, *Three Men on a Bummel*, 1900

the rough net is not the best catcher of birds (*English*) Sometimes the use of rough language is not the best way to win an argument or win someone over. John Heywood, *A Dialogue containing … the Proverbs in the English Tongue*, 1550.

~ *See also* a BOISTEROUS horse must have a rough bridle.

roundabout. *See* what you LOSE on the swings you gain on the roundabouts.

roundly. *See* WALK groundly, talk profoundly, drink roundly, sleep soundly.

royal. there is no royal road to learning (*Greek*) The acquisition of knowledge can be achieved only through study. E. Stone, *Euclid's Elements*, 1745 (quoting Euclid).

There is no royal road to learning; no short cut to the acquirement of any valuable art.
Anthony Trollope, *Barchester Towers*, 1857

rub. there will be rubs in the smoothest road (*English*) One must expect to encounter setbacks whatever course of action one elects to follow. S. Palmer, *Moral Essays on Proverbs*, 1710.

rubber. *See* those who PLAY at bowls must look out for rubbers.

rudder. *See* he who will not be RULED by the rudder must be ruled by the rock; the TONGUE is the rudder of our ship.

rue. *See* at EASTER let your clothes be new, or else be sure you will it rue; MARRY in May and rue the day.

ruin. *See* ABUNDANCE, like want, ruins many.

rule (noun). *See* the EXCEPTION proves the rule; there is an EXCEPTION to every rule.

rule. he who will not be ruled by the rudder must be ruled by the rock (*English*) Those who will not listen to good advice or pay heed to changing circumstances must learn bitter lessons from experience (just as a ship that does not respond to the helm will be shipwrecked). G. Torriano, *Select Italian Proverbs*, 1642. Related proverbs include 'he that will not be ruled by his own dame shall be ruled by his step-dame'.

'He who will not be ruled by the rudder must be ruled by the rock', but ruled he must be.
B. Wilberforce, *Secret of Quiet Mind*, 1911

rule youth well, for age will rule itself (*English*) It is best to concentrate on keeping the young under control, for the older know better and will control themselves. David Fergusson, *Scottish Proverbs*, 1641.

Youth is rash and headstrong, but age sober and steadfast.
James Kelly, *A Complete Collection of Scotish Proverbs*, 1721

~ *See also* the CALF, the goose, the bee: the world is

ruled by these three; the CAT, the Rat and Lovell our Dog rule all England under an Hog; DIVIDE and rule; EVERY man can rule a shrew but he who has her; the HAND that rocks the cradle rules the world; no MAN can be a good ruler unless he hath first been ruled; OPINION rules the world; where ROSEMARY flourishes the lady rules.

ruler. *See* no MAN can be a good ruler unless he hath first been ruled.

run. he that runs in the night stumbles (*English*) Those who rush headlong into things of which they have no knowledge or experience are likely to come to grief. T. Draxe, *Bibliotheca Scholastica*, 1616. Also found as 'he that runs in the dark may well stumble.'

if you run after two hares you will catch neither (*English*) A person who divides his attention between trying to achieve two goals simultaneously is unlikely to attain either. Alexander Barclay, *The Ship of Fools*, 1509 (also found in the *Adages* of Erasmus).

> I am redie to take potions … yet one thing maketh to feare, that in running after two Hares, I catch neither.
>
> John Lyly, *Euphues and His England*, 1580

you cannot run with the hare and hunt with the hounds (*English*) It is impossible to align oneself with two clearly and actively opposed sides. John Lydgate, *Minor Poems*, 1449. A hunting proverb that was much quoted from Tudor times onwards.

> The whole thing … gave me a look of running with the hare and hunting with the hounds.
>
> Robert Louis Stevenson, *Catriona*, 1893

~ *See also* BRING a cow to the hall and she'll run to the byre; the COURSE of true love never did run smooth; he may ILL run that cannot go; he who FIGHTS and runs away, lives to fight another day; if you WISH to live and thrive, let a spider run alive; the LAST drop makes the cup run over; let the CAT wink and let the mouse run; STILL waters run deep; the TALE runs as it pleases the teller; too MANY boatmen will run the boat up to the top of the mountain; TWO dogs fight for a bone, and a third runs away with it; we must LEARN to walk before we can run; when the WELL is full it will run over; the WORLD runs on wheels; you NEVER miss the water till the well runs dry.

runaway. a runaway monk never praises his convent (*Italian*) People rarely speak well of those they have deserted. G. Torriano, *Select Italian Proverbs*, 1666.

rush (noun). *See* BETTER no ring than a ring of rush.

rush (verb). *See* FOOLS rush in where angels fear to tread.

Russian. *See* SCRATCH a Russian and you find a Tartar.

rust. *See* IRON not used soon rusts; it is BETTER to wear out than to rust out.

S

Sabbath. *See* MONDAY's child is fair of face, Tuesday's child is full of grace; Wednesday's child is full of woe, Thursday's child has far to go; Friday's child is loving and giving, Saturday's child works hard for its living; and the child that's born on the Sabbath day, is fair and wise and good and gay.

sack. the sack is known by the sample (*English*) The contents of a sack may be ascertained from a small sample. Thomas Fuller, *Gnomologia*, 1732.

~ *See also* BIND the sack before it be full; EMPTY sacks will never stand upright; an OLD sack asketh much patching; SOW with the hand and not with the sack; there comes NOUGHT out of the sack but what was there.

sad. it is a sad house where the hen crows louder than the cock (*English*) A house where a woman rules the roost is unlikely to be a happy house. J. Sandford, *The Garden of Pleasure*, 1573.

> They are sory houses, where the hennes crowe, and the cock holdes his peace.
>
> John Florio, *First Fruites*, 1578

~ *See* when our LADY falls in our Lord's lap, then let England beware a sad clap.

saddle. *See* ONE thing thinketh the horse, and another he that saddles him; SET the saddle on the right horse; a WILLOW will buy a horse before an oak will pay for a saddle.

sadness and gladness succeed each other (*English*) Happiness and unhappiness come to each person in turn. J. Clarke, *Paroemiologia Anglo-Latina*, 1639.

safe. no safe wading in an unknown water (*English*) There is risk involved in entering unknown territory of any kind. *Manifest Detection*, *c.*1552.

> No safe wading in uncouth waters. It is no wisdom to engage with dangers that we are not acquainted with.
>
> James Kelly, *A Complete Collection of Scotish Proverbs*, 1721

safe bind, safe find (*English*) Keep your valuables secure, so that you may find them again. John Bale, *King Johan*, *c.*1540. *See also* FAST bind, fast find.

> Safe bind, safe find – it may be once away and aye away.
>
> Walter Scott, *St Ronan's Well*, 1824

~ *See also* BETTER safe than sorry; CALL the bear 'uncle' till you are safe across the bridge; DRY feet, warm head, bring safe to bed; he that is too SECURE is not safe; he whose FATHER is judge goes safe to his trial; it is BEST to be on the safe side.

safety. safety first (*English*) Always make safety the first priority. W.R. Inge, *Assessment and Anticipation*, 1929.

there is safety in numbers (*Hebrew*) If you are one of large number of people, there is less chance that you will be singled out for attention. Bible, Proverbs 11:14.

> She determined to call upon them and seek safety in numbers.
>
> Jane Austen, *Emma*, 1815

sage. *See* he that would LIVE for aye must eat sage in May.

said. *See* SAY.

sail. *See* HOIST your sail when the wind is fair; MACKEREL sky and mares' tails make lofty ships carry low sails.

sailor. *See* HEAVEN protects children, sailors and drunken men.

Saint. if Saint Paul's Day be fair and clear, it will betide a happy year (*English*) If the weather on Saint Paul's Day (25 January) is fine a good year will follow. Robert of Avesbury, *History*, *c.*1340. Conversely, if it rains or snows on Saint Paul's Day a poor harvest later in the year is deemed inevitable. If the day turns out windy then warfare must shortly be expected; if it is cloudy then many people are fated to die soon.
on Saint Thomas the Divine kill all turkeys, geese and swine (*English*) The feast day of Saint Thomas the Apostle (21 December) is the last day on which animals should be slaughtered in preparation for Christmas. *An Agreeable Companion*, 1742. Variants include 'the day of Saint Thomas the Divine is good for brewing, baking and killing fat swine'.
Saint Swithin's Day, if thou dost rain, for forty days it will remain; Saint Swithin's Day, if thou be fair, for forty days 'twill rain no more (*English*) If it rains on Saint Swithin's Day (15 July) then it will rain consecutively for the next forty days. Ben Jonson, *Every Man Out of His Humour*, 1599. Saint Swithin (sometimes given as Saint Swithun) was bishop of Winchester until his death in 862. At his own request Swithin was buried humbly at a spot he chose himself in the grounds of Winchester cathedral – so that the 'sweet rain of heaven might fall upon his grave' – and there he remained until 15 July 871, when work was set in progress to move his body to a more prestigious location within the building itself. Heavy rain prevented the completion of this enterprise and after forty days' continual downpour the plan was given up altogether, the workers interpreting the deluge as a sign of the saint's disapproval. The tradition that rain that falls on Saint Swithin's Day will continue for another forty days has since become established as one of the best known of all British weather myths (despite the fact that in 963, regardless of the saint's wishes, his remains were sheltered from the elements through the building of a shrine over his grave). The notion has survived regardless of the fact that Saint Swithin's 15 July related to the Julian Calendar, not the Gregorian Calendar adopted several centuries later. Popular tradition has it that Saint Swithin brings rain on 15 July in order to christen the year's apples (an idea supported by the ancient rhyme 'till Saint Swithin's Day be past, the apples be not fit to taste'). Forecasters deny that the tradition can be relied upon, though they concede that mid-July often witnesses a fundamental change in weather patterns. In any case, another proverb insists that any bad weather ushered in by Saint Swithin will be mopped up by 24 August, Saint Bartholomew's Day: 'all the tears that Saint Swithin can cry, Saint Bartlemy's mantle wipes them dry'. Another less well-known proverb, meanwhile, suggests a similar interpretation for rain that falls a clear month earlier, on 15 June: 'if Saint Vitus' Day be rainy weather, it will rain for thirty days together'.

> O here, Saint Swithin's, the fifteen day, variable weather, for the most part rain ... why it should rain forty days after, now, more or less, it was rule held afore I was able to hold a plough.
> Ben Jonson, *Every Man Out of His Humour*, 1599

~ *See also* ALL are not saints that go to church; the GREATER the sinner, the greater the saint; an OPEN door may tempt a saint; a WOMAN is an angel at ten, a saint at fifteen, a devil at forty and a witch at fourscore; WOMEN are saints in church; YOUNG saint old devil.

sake. *See* MANY kiss the child for the nurse's sake.

salad. *See* a GOOD salad may be the prologue to a bad supper; a THISTLE is a fat salad for an ass's mouth.

sale. *See* NEVER offer your hen for sale on a rainy day.

salmon. salmon and sermon have both their season in Lent (*English*) Both salmon-fishing and sermons are at their best in the weeks leading up to Easter. J. Howell, *Paroemiographia*, 1659.

~ *See also* a HOOK is well lost to catch a salmon.

salt. salt water and absence wash away love (*English*) A sea voyage will always dampen one's ardour for lovers left behind. 1805, Horatio Nelson, quoted in Robert Southey's *Life of Nelson*, 1813.

> I'm very glad that we're off to-morrow – salt water cures love, they say, sooner than anything else.
> Captain Frederick Marryat, *Poor Jack*, 1840

~ *See also* the BEST smell is bread, the best savour salt, the best love that of children; GIVE neither counsel nor salt till you are asked for it; HELP you to salt, help you to sorrow.

salve. there's a salve for every sore (*English*) There is no ill that cannot be relieved one way or another. *The School House of Women*, 1542. Another proverb suggests 'seek your salve where you get your sore'.

> But let us hence, my sovereign, to provide a
> salve for any sore that may betide.
> William Shakespeare, *Henry VI, Part 3*, *c.*1591

same. the same heat that melts the wax will harden the clay (*English*) What has one effect on one person may have a completely opposite effect upon another. T. Adams, *Sermons*, 1629. Also encountered in the form 'the same sunshine that melts the wax will harden the clay'.

the same knife cuts bread and fingers (*English*) A knife carelessly used can cut fingers as well as the things it was intended to cut. John Lyly, *Euphues and his England*, 1580.

~ *See also* it is a SILLY fish that is caught twice with the same bait; LIGHTNING never strikes the same place twice; a MAN cannot spin and reel at the same time; a MAN cannot whistle and drink at the same time; you cannot have TWO forenoons in the same day.

sample. *See* the SACK is known by the sample.

Samson was a strong man yet he could not pay money before he had it (*English*) No one, no matter how strong, can pay money that they do not have. J. Howell, *Paroemiographia*, 1659. A fuller version of the proverb runs 'Salomon was a wise man, and Sampson was a strong man, yet neither of them could pay money till they had it'.

sand. *See* MANY sands will sink a ship.

Satan reproves sin (*English*) The devil will punish those who sin (usually quoted when one wrongdoer condemns another person for doing bad things). G. Torriano, *Select Italian Proverbs*, 1666.

satin. *See* SILKS and satins put out the fire in the chimney.

Saturday. Saturday's flit will never sit (*English*) Servants engaged on a Saturday will never stay for long. Sternberg, *The Dialect of Northamptonshire*, 1851. The proverb expressed an old superstition, and for centuries it was considered very unlucky for a person hopeful of a domestic post to turn up for their first day's work on a Saturday. A fuller version of the proverb runs 'Saturday servants never stay, Sunday servants run away'. Also encountered as 'Saturday's flittings, light sittings'.

~ *See also* FRIDAY night's dream on the Saturday told, is sure to come true be it never so old; MONDAY's child is fair of face, Tuesday's child is full of grace; Wednesday's child is full of woe, Thursday's child has far to go; Friday's child is loving and giving, Saturday's child works hard for its living; and the child that's born on the Sabbath day, is fair and wise and good and gay; RAIN, rain, go away, come again on Saturday; there is NEVER a Saturday without some sunshine.

sauce. what's sauce for the goose is sauce for the gander (*English*) What is good for one person can be presumed to be good for another (especially if discussing a husband and wife or other members of opposite sexes). John Ray, *A Collection of English Proverbs*, 1670. Some authorities suggest that the original sauce in question, the ideal accompaniment for both goose and gander at the table, was gooseberry sauce (thus, perhaps, the fruit's name). Others suggest that the proverb was derived from an older French saying.

> Teach them that 'sauce for goose is sauce
> for gander'.
> Lord Byron, *Don Juan*, 1823

~ *See also* HUNGER is the best sauce.

sauter. *See* RECULER pour mieux sauter.

save. he that will not be saved needs no preacher (*English*) There is no point trying to redeem those who are bent on a life of wickedness. John Ray, *A Collection of English Proverbs*, 1670.

save a thief from the gallows and he shall cut your throat (*English*) People with guilty consciences particularly resent those who offer them help. William Camden, *Remains Concerning Britain*, 1614. Variants include 'save a thief from the gallows and he shall hate you', 'save a thief from the gallows and he will be the first shall do thee a mischief', 'save a thief from the gallows and he will help to hang you' and 'save a stranger from the sea and he'll turn your enemy'.

> Whence else came the English proverb, that if you save a thief from the gallows, he shall be the first to cut your throat.
>
> Daniel Defoe, *Colonel Jack*, 1723

save something for a rainy day (*English*) It is good policy when times are good to save money or other benefits for future use when times are hard. J. Stubbes, *Anatomie of Abuses*, 1583. Related proverbs include 'save something for the man that rides on the white horse' (in other words, an old man – because of his white hair) and 'save while you may for age and want, no morning sun lasts a whole day'. *See also* KEEP something for the sore foot.

> I ... do provide for it by laying by something against a rainy day.
>
> Samuel Pepys, *Diary*, 31 October 1666

save your breath to cool your porridge (*English*) Do not expend your energy on things that are not important. Deloney, *The Gentle Craft*, *c.*1598.

> Instead of asking riddles ... ye would keep your breath to cool your porridge.
>
> Robert Louis Stevenson, *Kidnapped*, 1886

saving is getting (*English*) Money that is got by saving is just as valuable as money got by any other means. G. Torriano, *Select Italian Proverbs*, 1642. *See also* a PENNY saved is a penny earned.

~ *See also* a PENNY saved is a penny earned; PROVIDE for the worst, the best will save itself; a STITCH in time saves nine; SPEND not where you may save, spare not where you must spend.

savour. *See* the BEST smell is bread, the best savour salt, the best love that of children; the CASK savours of the first fill; WINE savours of the cask.

say. he who says what he likes shall hear what he does not like (*Roman*) Those who speak out loud everything they think, without regard for the feelings of others, are likely to attract hostile responses from others. R. Taverner, *Proverbs or Adages with New Additions, gathered out of the Chiliades of Erasmus*, 1539 (also quoted by Terence). Along the same lines is 'say little but think the more', first recorded in the fifteenth century.

> Peace husband ... speake no more than you should, least you heare what you would not.
>
> Robert Greene, *Pandosto*, 1588

it is not with saying honey, honey, that sweetness will come into the mouth (*Turkish*) Good things come only with hard work. R.C. Trench, *On the Lessons in Proverbs*, 1853.

say before they say (*English*) Always get your version of the story in first, before anyone else can give their version of events. H.G. Bohn, *A Handbook of Proverbs*, 1855.

saying is one thing, and doing another (*English*) It is one thing to say you will do something, but quite another actually to do it. John Heywood, *A Dialogue containing ... the Proverbs in the English Tongue*, 1546. *See also* ACTIONS speak louder than words.

> I see that *saying* and *doing* are two things, and hereafter I shall better observe this distinction.
>
> John Bunyan, *Pilgrim's Progress*, 1678

say no ill of the year till it be past (*English*) It is bad luck to condemn the way a year has gone until it is over. George Herbert, *Outlandish Proverbs*, 1640.

they say so is half a lie (*Italian*) Unauthenticated rumours are little better than lies. G. Torriano, *Select Italian Proverbs*, 1666. Also found in the form 'they say so is half a liar'.

~ *See also* BETTER say nothing than nothing to the purpose; DO as I say, not as I do; EASIER said than done; the FLY sat upon the axletree of the chariot-wheel and said, what a dust do I raise!; from a CHOLERIC man withdraw a little, from him that says nothing for ever; HEAR all, see all, say nowt; ILL will never said well; it is BETTER to be a cuckold and not know it, than be none and everybody say so; it is not as thy MOTHER says but as thy neighbours say; LEAST said, soonest mended; MANY a one says well that thinks ill; the MORE said, the less done; NEVER say die; what EVERYBODY says must be true; what MANCHESTER says today, the rest of England says tomorrow; whom we LOVE best, to them we can say least.

scabbard. *See* ONE sword keeps another in the scabbard; whosoever DRAWS his sword against the prince must throw the scabbard away.

scabbed. *See* ONE scabbed sheep infects the whole flock.

scald. a scalded cat fears cold water (*English*) Everyone learns to avoid what has caused them harm before, even to the extent of fearing what is actually quite harmless. Randle Cotgrave, *A Dictionary of the French and English Tongues*, 1611. Also encountered with 'dog' in the place of 'cat'. Equivalent sayings include 'whom a serpent has bitten, a lizard alarms' and 'he who is bitten by a serpent is afraid of a rope'. *See also* once BITTEN, twice shy; a BURNT child dreads the fire.

scald not your lips in another man's pottage (*English*) Do not get too involved in the affairs of others. T. Adams, *Sermons*, 1629.

scar. *See* SLANDER leaves a scar behind it; though the WOUND be healed, a scar remains.

scarce. *See* GOOD men are scarce; where COBWEBS are plenty, kisses are scarce.

scarlet. *See* an APE's an ape, a varlet's a varlet, though they be clad in silk or scarlet.

scatter. *See* what the RAKE gathers, the fork scatters.

scheme. *See* the BEST laid schemes of mice and men gang oft agley.

scholar. the scholar teacheth the master (*Roman*) Sometimes the pupil can become more learned than the teacher. J. Clarke, *Paroemiologia Anglo-Latina*, 1639 (quoting Juvenal). A Scottish variant runs 'the scholar may waur the master'.

school. *See* EXPERIENCE keeps a dear school; NEVER tell tales out of school.

schoolmaster. *See* ONE father is more than a hundred schoolmasters.

scold. *See* HUSBANDS are in heaven whose wives scold not; THREE things drive a man out of his house: smoke, rain and a scolding wife.

score twice before you cut once (*English*) Check twice before taking an irrevocable step. R. Holme, *Academy of Armory*, 1688. Originally a piece of advice commonly heard among leather workers. A fuller version of the proverb runs 'score twice before you cut once, else you cut yourself out of doors'.

scorn. scorn at first makes after-love the more (*English*) Love affairs that begin with mutual contempt are all the stronger when they blossom. William Shakespeare, *Two Gentlemen of Verona*, 1594–5.

~ *See also* HELL hath no fury like a woman scorned.

scornful dogs will eat dirty puddings (*Scottish*) Those who lack respect both for others and themselves will have no qualms in helping themselves to anything, no matter how poor or shameful. Bernard Mandeville, *The Virgin Unmasked*, 1709. Also encountered in the form 'hungry dogs will eat dirty puddings'.

scorpion. there is a scorpion under every stone (*Greek*) When things go against a person enemies will emerge from all sides. Erasmus, letter, *c.*1522 (quoting Sophocles).

scoundrel. *See* PATRIOTISM is the last refuge of a scoundrel.

scratch. scratch an Englishman and you'll find a seaman (*English*) All Englishmen are seafarers at heart.

scratch a Russian and you find a Tartar (*French*) Every Russian at heart has the aggressive and barbarous character of the Tartar. J. Gallatin, *Diary*, 2 January 1823 (often attributed originally to Napoleon). The proverb has since been adapted to refer to other nationalities – including, for instance, Puerto Rican: 'scratch a Puerto Rican and you find a Spaniard.'

you scratch my back and I'll scratch yours (*Greek*) You do me a favour, and I will do you a favour in return. Randle Cotgrave, *A Dictionary of the French and English Tongues*, 1611. Historical variants include 'scratch me and I'll scratch thee' and 'scratch my back and I'll claw your elbow'. Another interesting local variant is one recorded in Devon running 'scratch my back and I'll scratch your face' (supposedly a threat uttered by the 'demon of Dartmoor' against anyone who attempted to farm the moor). *See also* KA me, ka thee.

> We are all getting liberal now; and (provided you can scratch me if I scratch you) what do I care ... whether you are a Dustman or a Duke?
> Wilkie Collins, *The Moonstone*, 1868

~ *See also* EATING and scratching wants but a beginning; he must have IRON nails that scratches a bear; he that PLAYS with cats must expect to be scratched; TRUTH has a scratched face.

scripture. *See* the ACOLYTE at the gate reads scriptures he has never learned; the DEVIL can quote scripture for his own purpose.

scrub. *See* ONE mule doth scrub another.

sea. he that would go to sea for pleasure, would go to hell for a pastime (*English*) The man that would voluntarily go to sea is reckless of his own welfare. A.J. Boyd, *Shellback*, 1899. Heard chiefly among sailors. *See also* PRAISE the sea but keep on land.
the sea and the gallows refuse none (*English*) The sea and the gallows will claim anyone, regardless of rank. T. Gentleman, *England's Way to Win Wealth*, 1614. Other proverbs expressing similar sentiments include the French saying 'the sea has an enormous thirst and an insatiable appetite'.

~ *See also* FOLLOW the river and you'll get to the sea; he COMPLAINS wrongfully on the sea who twice suffers shipwreck; he that would LEARN to pray, let him go to sea; in a CALM sea every man is a pilot; PRAISE the sea but keep on land; there are PLENTY more fish in the sea; THREE things are insatiable: priests, monks and the sea; WINE hath drowned more men than the sea; WORSE things happen at sea.

seaman. *See* SCRATCH an Englishman and you'll find a seaman.

sea-mark. *See* let ANOTHER's shipwreck be your sea-mark.

search. *See* if APPLES bloom in March, in vain for them you'll search; if apples bloom in April, then they'll be plentiful; if apples bloom in May, you may eat them night and day; on the FIRST of March, the crows begin to search.

season. *See* EVERYTHING is good in its season; FRUIT out of season, sorrow out of reason; MONEY never comes out of season; SALMON and sermon have both their season in Lent.

second. second thoughts are best (*Greek*) Reappraisal brings better understanding. Ralph Holinshed, *Chronicles*, 1577 (also quoted by Euripides in *Hippolytus*).

> Second thoughts, they say, are best: I'll consider of it once again.
> John Dryden, *The Spanish Friar*, 1681

the second blow makes the fray (*English*) It takes two to make a fight, so it is only when the second person retaliates that conflict is properly joined. Francis Bacon, *The Colours of Good and Evil*, 1597. Also encountered in the fuller form 'the first blow makes the wrong, the second blow makes the fray'. *See also* it takes TWO to make a quarrel.

~ *See also* BETTER to be first in a village than second at Rome; BOLDNESS in business is the first, second and third thing; CUSTOM is a second nature; the FIRST faults are theirs that commit them, the second theirs that permit them; the FIRST glass for thirst, the second for nourishment, the third for pleasure, and the fourth for madness; when a COUPLE are newly married the first month is honeymoon, or smick smack; the second is hither and thither; the third is thwick thwack; the fourth the devil take them that brought thee and I together.

secret. wherever there is a secret there must be something wrong (*English*) Secrets are a sure sign that something is being kept hidden that ought to be revealed. Roger North, *Lives*, 1696.

~ *See also* he that TELLS a secret is another's servant; NOTHING is burdensome as a secret; ONE for sorrow, two for joy; three for a girl, four for a boy; five for silver, six for gold; seven for a secret, never to be told; eight for heaven, nine for hell; and ten for the devil's own self; THREE may keep a secret, if two of them are dead.

secure. he that is too secure is not safe (*English*) Those who think themselves safe may be lured into a false sense of security and thus be vulnerable to danger. Thomas Fuller, *Gnomologia*, 1732.

security. *See* DANGER is next neighbour to security.

see. see a pin and let it lie, you'll want a pin before you die (*English*) It is bad luck not to pick up a pin lying on the ground. James Halliwell-Phillipps, *Nursery Rhymes and Tales of England*, 1845. Variants on the usual proverb run 'see a pin and let it lie, all the day you'll have to cry', 'he that will not stoop for a pin, will never be worth a pound' and 'he that takes not up a pin, slights his wife'. *See also* SEE a pin and pick it up, all the day you'll have good luck.

see a pin and pick it up, all the day you'll have good luck (*English*) It is good luck to pick up a pin lying on the ground. Samuel Pepys, *Diary*, 2 January 1668. One superstition suggests that much depends upon which way the pin is pointing before is picked up: if it points away from the finder it brings good luck, but it threatens bad luck if it points towards the finder. An entirely different viewpoint, however, is expressed by the rival proverb 'pick up pins pick up sorrow'. James Joyce, in *Ulysses*, published in 1922, reports the belief among women that it is unlucky to pick up a pin, because it 'cuts' love. *See also* SEE a pin and let it lie, you'll want a pin before you die.

seeing is believing (*Roman*) Only when a person sees something with his or her own eyes are they certain to believe it. S. Harward, *MS*, 1609 (also quoted by Plautus). Another Roman proverb observed that 'men trust their ear less than their eyes'. Equivalents from other parts of the world include the Wolof saying 'deny, but what thou seest believe', the Scottish 'words are but wind but seeing's believing', the German 'what the eyes see the heart believes', the Italian 'who sees with the eye believes with the heart', the Japanese 'to hear a hundred times is not so good as to see once' and the Chinese 'what one hears is doubtful, what one sees is certain'.

> There's nothing like matter of fact; seeing is believing.
>
> John Arbuthnot, *The History of John Bull*, 1712

see Naples and die (*Italian*) Naples is the fairest city in the world, so having seen it the traveller might as well die, as he will never see anything better. G.A. Sala, *The American Revolution*, 1882. There is a darker side to this seemingly lighthearted boast, for Naples was once notorious for epidemics of typhoid and cholera, and as a result in former times many visitors did die after seeing the city. Occasionally applied to other cities (often sarcastically).

see no evil, hear no evil, speak no evil (*Japanese*) The proverb is supposed to have had its origins in the sixteenth-century carvings of Three Wise Monkeys over a doorway at the Sacred Stable at Nikko in Japan (each in turn with paws covering ears, eyes and mouth). *Army and Navy Stores Catalogue*, 1926. *See also* HEAR all, see all, say nowt.

~ *See also* BELIEVE nothing of what you hear, and only half of what you see; CHILDREN should be seen and not heard; a DWARF on a giant's shoulders sees further of the two; FOOLS and bairns should never see half-done work; FOUR eyes see more than two; the GOOD Bernard does not see everything; HEAR all, see all, say nowt; he that GIVES to be seen will relieve none in the dark; he who PEEPS through a hole may see what will vex him; the HUNCHBACK does not see his own hump, but sees his companion's; if the ADDER could hear and the blindworm could see, neither man nor beast would ever go free; if the DOCTOR cures, the sun sees it, but if he kills, the earth hides it; LOOKERS-ON see most of the game; SELDOM seen, soon forgotten; a STRANGER's eye sees clearest; they that LIVE longest, see most; there are NONE so blind as those who will not see; the WAY to see divine light is to put out thine own candle; what the EYE does not see, the heart does not grieve over.

seed. *See* the BLOOD of the martyrs is the seed of the Church; GOOD seed makes a good crop; PARSLEY seed goes nine times to the devil

seeding. *See* ONE year's seeding means seven years' weeding.

seek. seek and ye shall find (*Greek*) Those who actively pursue what they want are the most likely to be rewarded. Bible, Matthew 7:7 (also quoted by Sophocles in *Oedipus Tyrannus*). Related proverbs include 'as good seek nought as seek and find nought', 'who seeks what he should not, finds what he would not', 'seek that which may be found', 'he that seeketh findeth', and the worldly-wise 'he that seeks trouble never misses'.

Ask, and it shall be given you: seek, and ye shall find.
Matthew 7:7

~ *See also* POOR men seek meat for their stomach; rich men stomach for their meat.

seem. seem not greater than thou art (*Roman*) It is foolish to make out that you are something that you are not. Robert Burton, *Anatomy of Melancholy*, 1621.

~ *See also* BE what you would seem to be; SUCCESS makes a fool seem wise; 'tis TIME to fear when tyrants seem to kiss.

seen. *See* SEE.

seldom. seldom comes a loan laughing home (*English*) Loans are rarely settled in full and on time. *Proverbs of Hending*, *c.*1300.

A borrow'd loan should come laughing home.
What a man borrows he should return with thankfulness.
James Kelly, *A Complete Collection of Scottish Proverbs*, 1721

seldom seen, soon forgotten (*English*) When one is only rarely reminded of something it soon passes from one's memory altogether. *Douce MS*, *c.*1350. *See also* OUT of sight, out of mind.

~ *See also* BEAUTY and honesty seldom agree; DESERT and reward seldom keep company; GOOD and quickly seldom meet; HONOUR and ease are seldom bedfellows; ILL-GOTTEN gains seldom prosper; LATE repentance is seldom true; a MAN of gladness seldom falls into madness; OPPORTUNITY seldom knocks twice at any man's door; a SMILING boy seldom proves a good servant; WINE counsels seldom prosper.

self do, self have (*English*) Expect others to treat you as you treat them. John Heywood, *A Dialogue containing … the Proverbs in the English Tongue*, 1546.

Self deed, self fa. That is, as you do to others, so it will befall you.
James Kelly, *A Complete Collection of Scottish Proverbs*, 1721

self-praise is no recommendation (*English*) Those who speak well of themselves cannot be relied upon. T. Shelton, *Cervantes' Don Quixote*, 1612. Also encountered in the form 'self-praise comes aye stinking home'. Related proverbs include 'self-praise is odious', 'self-exaltation is the fool's paradise', 'let another man praise thee, not thine own mouth', 'he that praiseth himself spattereth himself', the Spanish 'self-praise disgraces', the Italian 'who praises himself fouls himself', and the French 'a man would scarcely have any pleasure if he never flattered himself'. Another proverb, of US origin, drily observes of those who flatter themselves that 'when you die your trumpeter will be buried'.

Self-praise is no recommendation, but I may say for myself that I am not so bad a man of business.
Charles Dickens, *Bleak House*, 1853

self-preservation is the first law of nature (*English*) The instinct to safeguard your own life and interests is paramount. R. Dallington, *Aphorisms*, 1613.

Self-preservation, Nature's first great Law.
Andrew Marvell, 'Hodge's Vision from the Monument', 1675

sell. you cannot sell the cow and sup the milk (*English*) When something is sold the former owner cannot expect to continue to enjoy any income or other benefit from it. James Kelly, *A Complete Collection of Scottish Proverbs*, 1721.

~ *See also* BUY in the cheapest market and sell in the dearest; a GIFT long waited for is sold not given; he that MARRIES for wealth sells his liberty; PLEASING ware is half sold; WEIGH justly and sell dearly; while the DUST is on your feet, sell what you have bought.

seller. *See* the BUYER has need of a hundred eyes, the seller of but one.

send a fool to market and a fool he'll return (*English*) A fool will never thrive in business, or any other dealings. G. Whitney, *Emblems*, 1586. Variants have a fool being sent 'far' or 'to France'.

You may go back again, like a fool as you came.
Jonathan Swift, *Polite Conversation*, 1738

~ *See* come DAY, go day, God send Sunday; GENTRY sent to market will not buy one bushel of corn; GIVE and spend and God will send; GOD never sends mouths but He sends meat; GOD sends meat, but the devil sends cooks; GOD send you joy, for sorrow will come fast enough; the GODS send nuts to those who have no teeth; NEVER sigh but send; SPEND and God will send; where the DEVIL cannot come, he will send.

sense. *See* AGE does not give sense – it only makes one go slowly.

sent. *See* SEND.

September blow soft, till the fruit's in the loft (*English*) A mild and gale-free September allows fruit to be gathered in undamaged, so is much to be hoped for. T. Tusser, *Five Hundred Points of Husbandry*, 1571.

sermon. *See* a GOOD example is the best sermon; SALMON and sermon have both their season in Lent.

serpent. whom a serpent has bitten, a lizard alarms (*Italian*) Those who have suffered harm from something learn to fear anything resembling the source of the original injury. G. Torriano, *Select Italian Proverbs*, 1666. *See also* he who has been BITTEN by a snake fears a piece of string.

servant. a servant and a cock should be kept but a year (*English*) Servants should be dismissed before they become too well rooted in their post and cease to give of their best (as is also true of cocks). Thomas Fuller, *Gnomologia*, 1732. A related proverb advises 'he that would be well served must know when to change his servants'. Other proverbs offering helpful advice on the management of servants (or employees) include 'don't take a servant off a midden', 'if you pay not a servant his wages, he will pay himself' and 'if you would have a good servant, take neither a kinsman nor a friend'. Another proverb advises that 'a servant is known by his master's absence' (in other words, by his or her behaviour when not under the direct control of the master). The ideal servant, another proverb states, has 'the back of an ass, the tongue of a sheep and the snout of a swine'. Servants, for their part, are advised 'a good servant should never be in the way and never out of the way', 'servants should put on patience when they put on a livery' and 'servants should see all and say nothing'. Those who dream of better things will be encouraged by the proverb 'he that hath not served knows not how to command', although another proverb conversely warns that 'servants make the worst masters'.

~ *See also* a COMMON servant is no man's servant; ENGLAND is the paradise of women, the hell of horses and the purgatory of servants; a FALLING master makes a standing servant; FIRE and water are good servants but bad masters; he that TELLS a secret is another's servant; if MONEY be not thy servant, it will be thy master; if you PAY not a servant his wages, he will pay himself; an ILL master makes an ill servant; no SILVER, no servant; a SMILING boy seldom proves a good servant.

serve. he that serves God for money will serve the devil for better wages (*English*) Those who do God's work for pay will presumably work for anyone else if the pay is greater. Sir Roger L'Estrange, *Aesop's Fables*, 1692.

he who serves is preserved (*Roman*) Those who prove their worth as servants or employees are likely to be retained and valued by their masters. *Record*, 7 June 1917. Related proverbs include 'he who serves well needs not ask his wages'.

you cannot serve God and Mammon (*Hebrew*) It is impossible to stay true to high moral principles and at the same time to pursue financial reward. Bible, Matthew 6:24. In the original biblical passage, concerning the Sermon on the Mount, the word 'mammon' is an approximation of the Aramaic word meaning wealth or gain. Later generations personalized Mammon as a demon associated with avarice and the acquisition of money.

> Lady Lufton ... would say of Miss Dunstable that it was impossible to serve both God and Mammon.
> Anthony Trollope, *Framley Parsonage*, 1860

~ *See also* FIRST come, first served; if you would be WELL served, serve yourself; no MAN can serve two masters; PAY beforehand was never well served; RICHES serve a wise man but command a fool; YOUTH must be served.

service. service is no inheritance (*English*) No servant or employee has the right to hand on his post to his children. Thomas Hoccleve, The *Regiment of Princes*, 1412.

> In Isbel's case and mine own. Service is no heritage.
> William Shakespeare, *All's Well That Ends Well*, *c.*1602

service without reward is punishment (*English*) Those who fail to pay for work done effectively punish the worker. T. Draxe, *Bibliotheca Scholastica*, 1616.

~ *See also* PROFFERED service stinks.

session. *See* HOME is home, as the devil said when he found himself in the Court of Session.

set. set a beggar on horseback, and he'll ride to the devil (*Roman*) Give power or opportunity to one not used to it and the person concerned will be overcome with pride and arrogance. G. Pettie, *Petite Pallace*, 1576. The proverb is known in various forms: according to these, a beggar on horseback will never alight, ride a gallop, ride to the gallows, run his horse out of breath or run his horse to death.

> It needs not … proud queen; unless the adage
> must be verified, that beggars mounted run their
> horse to death.
>
> William Shakespeare, *Henry VI, Part 3*, *c.*1591

set a thief to catch a thief (*Greek*) In order to detect those guilty of wrongdoing the best policy is to recruit someone experienced in such wrongdoing themselves. E. Gayton, *Pleasant Notes upon Don Quixote*, 1654 (similar thoughts were voiced centuries earlier by Callimachus, Cato the Younger and Geoffrey Chaucer among others). Related proverbs include 'a thief knows a thief, as a wolf knows a wolf'.

> A theef of venisoun, that hath forlaft
> His likerousnesse, and al his olde craft,
> Can kepe a forest best of any man.
>
> Geoffrey Chaucer, *The Canterbury Tales*, *c.*1387

set hard heart against hard hap (*Scottish*) Summon up your determination to overcome a strong challenge. J. Clarke, *Paroemiologia Anglo-Latina*, 1639. Also found in the form 'set stout heart to a stey brae'.

set the saddle on the right horse (*English*) The blame for something or the responsibility to do something must be consigned to the right party. Thomas Dekker and John Webster, *Westward Ho*, 1607.

> On all sides he laid about him like a man …
> putting consequence on premiss, and everywhere
> the saddle on the right horse.
>
> Thomas Carlyle, *Past and Present*, 1843

~ *See also* BROKEN bones well set become stronger; CALM weather in June sets corn in tune; a DRIPPING June sets all in tune; SOW dry and set wet; THINGS that are hard to come by are much set by.

settle. in settling an island, the first building erected by a Spaniard will be a church; by a Frenchman, a fort; by a Dutchman, a warehouse; and by an Englishman, an alehouse (*English*) The English consider a ready supply of ale to be more important than anything else. F. Grose, *A Provincial Glossary*, 1787.

~ *See also* COLD pudding will settle your love.

seven. seven may be company but nine are confusion (*English*) Seven is the perfect number for a social gathering, whereas nine guarantees uproar. Brathwaite, *The English Gentleman*, 1630. Also encountered in the form 'seven make a banquet, nine a riot'.

~ *See also* it CHANCETH in an hour that happeneth not in seven years; the FIRST seven years are the hardest; GIVE me a child for the first seven years, and you may do what you like with him afterwards; KEEP a thing seven years and you'll always find a use for it; ONE for sorrow, two for joy; three for a girl, four for a boy; five for silver, six for gold; seven for a secret, never to be told; eight for heaven, nine for hell; and ten for the devil's own self; ONE year's seeding means seven years' weeding; RAIN before seven, fine before eleven; SIX hours' sleep for a man, seven for a woman and eight for a fool; you should KNOW a man seven years before you stir his fire.

shade. *See* LIVE in the shade.

shadow. *See* CATCH not at the shadow and lose the substance; COMING events cast their shadows before; no HAIR so small but hath his shadow; OLD sins cast long shadows; an OLD wise man's shadow is better than a young buzzard's sword.

shallow streams make most din (*Scottish*) The least intelligent people tend to make the most noise. James Kelly, *A Complete Collection of Scotish Proverbs*, 1721.

shame. he that has no shame has no conscience (*English*) Those who have no shame cannot be expected to feel guilt for their actions. Thomas Fuller, *Gnomologia*, 1732. Related proverbs include 'shame is as it is taken'.

it is a shame to steal but a worse to carry home (*English*) Those who retain possession of stolen goods compound their guilt for the original theft. J. Clarke,

Paroemiologia Anglo-Latina, 1639. A somewhat contrary Arabic saying advises 'hide your shame in your house'.

~ *See also* he that BORROWS must pay again with shame or loss; if a MAN deceive me once, shame on him, but if he deceive me twice, shame on me; TELL the truth and shame the devil.

share. he who shares has the worst share (*Spanish*) Those who offer to share what they have often end up with the smaller portion. H.G. Bohn, *A Handbook of Proverbs*, 1855. Related proverbs include 'he who hath the least part of it shareth honey with the bear'.
share and share alike (*English*) Divide everything equally. Randle Cotgrave, *A Dictionary of the French and English Tongues*, 1611.

> They say, that a' man share and share equal-aquals in the creature's ulzie.
> Walter Scott, *The Pirate*, 1821

~ *See also* a TROUBLE shared is a trouble halved.

shares. *See* the DEVIL goes shares in gaming.

sharp. the sharper the storm, the sooner it's over (*Roman*) The more intense some experience or hardship is, the sooner it is likely to end. Francis Kilvert, *Diary*, 9 June 1872 (also quoted by Seneca in *Natural Questions*). Also encountered in the form 'the sharper the blast, the shorter 'twill last'.
a sharp stomach makes short devotion (*English*) People who are hungry do not linger long over saying grace. J. Clarke, *Paroemiographia Anglo-Latina*, 1639.

shave. *See* a BALD head is soon shaven; a BARBER learns to shave by shaving fools.

sheep. *See* a BLEATING sheep loses a bite; CARRION crows bewail the dead sheep and then eat them; DEATH devours lambs as well as sheep; if ONE sheep leap o'er the dyke, all the rest will follow; it is BETTER to marry a shrew than a sheep; a LEAP YEAR is never a good sheep year; ONE butcher does not fear many sheep; ONE scabbed sheep infects the whole flock; there's a BLACK sheep in every family; you might as well be HANGED for a sheep as for a lamb.

sheet. *See* the DIFFERENCE is wide that the sheets will not decide.

shepherd. *See* a RAINBOW in the morning is the shepherd's warning; a rainbow at night is the shepherd's delight; RED sky at night, shepherd's delight; red sky in the morning, shepherd's warning.

shift. you cannot shift an old tree without it dying (*English*) There comes a point where people or other things have become so firmly rooted over a long period of time that it becomes impossible to transplant them without destroying them completely. Alexander Barclay, *Mancinus' Mirror of Good Manners*, c.1518. *See also* you can't TEACH an old dog new tricks.

shilling. *See* a NIMBLE ninepence is better than a slow shilling.

shine. *See* ALTHOUGH the sun shine, leave not thy cloak at home; HAPPY is the bride the sun shines on; make HAY while the sun shines; the SUN loses nothing by shining into a puddle; when it RAINS and the sun shines at the same time the devil is beating his wife.

ship. ships fear fire more than water (*English*) The greatest dread of sailors is a fire breaking out on their ship. George Herbert, *Outlandish Proverbs*, 1640.

~ *See also* don't SPOIL the ship for a ha'porth of tar; a LITTLE leak will sink a great ship; MACKEREL sky and mares' tails make lofty ships carry low sails; MANY sands will sink a ship; ONE hand for oneself and one for the ship; QUININE is made of the sweat of ship carpenters; RATS desert a sinking ship; the TONGUE is the rudder of our ship; a WOMAN and a ship ever want mending.

shipmate. *See* MESSMATE before a shipmate, shipmate before a stranger, stranger before a dog.

shipwreck. *See* he COMPLAINS wrongfully on the sea who twice suffers shipwreck; let ANOTHER's shipwreck be you sea-mark.

shirtsleeves. from shirtsleeves to shirtsleeves in three generations (*English*) The fruits of the hard work of one generation will be frittered away by the second, so that the subsequent generation is obliged to work as hard as the first. N.M. Butler, *True and False Democracy*, 1907 (attributed to US businessman Andrew Carnegie). *See also* from CLOGS to clogs is three generations.

shoe. a shoe too large trips you up (*Roman*) Over-ambition can lead to disaster. Often quoted as a warning to those who aim to tackle more than they can manage.

~ *See also* EVERY shoe fits not every foot; for WANT of a nail the shoe was lost; GIVE a cob a hat and a pair of shoes and he'll last for ever; it's ILL waiting for dead men's shoes; I was ANGERED, for I had no shoes – then I met a man who had no feet.

shoemaker. the shoemaker's son always goes barefoot (*English*) Those who concentrate their efforts on meeting the demands of others may neglect to direct their skill towards the interests of their own family. John Heywood, *A Dialogue containing … the Proverbs in the English Tongue*, 1546. Related proverbs include 'who is worse shod than the shoemaker's wife?' Another proverb suggesting a rather contrary view claims that 'a shoemaker's son is a prince born'.

shoot. he that shoots oft shall at last hit the mark (*Roman*) Anyone who makes many attempts at something is likely in the end to achieve what he or she is aiming at. Thomas More, *Utopia*, 1551 (also quoted by Cicero).

> He that's always shooting, must sometimes hit.
>
> Thomas Fuller, *Gnomologia*, 1732

he will shoot higher who shoots at the moon than he who aims at a tree (*English*) The person who has great ambitions will achieve more impressive results than the person who aims much lower. Philip Sidney, *Arcadia*, 1590. Also encountered with 'sun' in the place of 'moon'.

> Who shootes at the mid-day Sunne, though he be sure he shall never hit the marke; yet as sure he is he shall shoote higher, than who ayms but at a bush.
>
> Philip Sidney, *Arcadia*, 1590

~ *See also* FAR shooting never killed bird; a FOOL's bolt is soon shot; he that ONCE hits will be ever shooting; MANY talk of Robin Hood who never shot with his bow; TRAMP on a snail and she'll shoot out her horns.

shop. *See* KEEP your shop and your shop will keep you; when the WARES be gone, shut up the shop windows.

shopkeeper. *See* the ENGLISH are a nation of shopkeepers.

shorn. *See* GOD tempers the wind to the shorn lamb; MANY go out for wool and come home shorn.

short. short counsel is good counsel (*English*) First thoughts are the most reliable. Roger of Wendover, *Chronicle*, 1235. The proverb is vividly illustrated in Roger of Wendover's *Chronicle* by the tale of Walcher, first Bishop of Durham, who fell into the hands of a mob in Gateshead in the year 1080: with the cry 'short rede, good rede, slay the bishop', his church was set ablaze and Walcher himself was put to death before anyone could voice any second thoughts.

the short cut is often the longest way round (*English*) What appears at first to offer a short cut in something may in the event turn out to require more time, effort or trouble. Francis Bacon, *The Advancement of Learning*, 1605. Variants include 'there is no short cut of a way without some ill way'.

> It is in life, as it is in ways, the shortest way is commonly the foulest, and surely the faire way is not much about.
>
> Francis Bacon, *The Advancement of Learning*, 1605

the shortest answer is doing (*English*) The quickest way to respond to a challenge is to act on it. George Herbert, *Outlandish Proverbs*, 1640.

short folk are soon angry (*Scottish*) People of small stature are the quickest to lose their temper. James Kelly, *A Complete Collection of Scotish Proverbs*, 1721. Related proverbs include 'short folk's heart is soon at their mouth' (implying that short people have the most passionate natures).

a short horse is soon curried (*English*) Minor tasks take little time. *Douce MS*, *c.*1350.

> A short tale is soon told – and a short horse soon curried.
>
> Walter Scott, *The Abbot*, 1820

short pleasure, long lament (*English*) Those who indulge in short-lived pleasures may repent them at length. *Coventry Plays*, 1468.

a short prayer reaches heaven (*English*) Concise requests are likely to be better received than long rambling ones. *Good Wyfe wold a Pylgremage*, *c.*1460.

short reckonings make long friends (*English*) Those who come to terms or settle their debts quickly are likely to enjoy lasting friendly relationships. R. Whitforde, *Work for Householders*, 1530. Also found with 'accounts' in the place of 'reckonings'. *See also* EVEN reckoning makes long friends.

short rede, good rede (*English*) The briefest advice is often the best. Roger of Wendover, *Chronicles*, 1235. The proverb is often associated with the death of the first Bishop of Durham who was killed in 1080 by a mob of local people chanting 'short rede, good rede, slay the bishop'.

short visits make long friends (*English*) Friends who do not overstay their welcome thus preserve their friendships. *Folk-Lore*, 1923.

~ *See also* ART is long, life is short; BARNABY bright, Barnaby bright, the longest day and the shortest night; a BONNY bride is soon buskit and a short horse is soon wispit; a CURST cow has short horns; the DAY is short and the work is long; GOOD company is the shortest cut; GREAT wits have short memories; LIES have short legs; the LONGEST way round is the shortest way home; LONG foretold long last, short notice soon past; a LONG tongue is a sign of a short hand; a SHARP stomach makes short devotion; WIDE ears and a short tongue.

shot. *See* SHOOT.

shoulder. *See* a DWARF on a giant's shoulders sees further of the two; ONE shoulder of mutton draws down another; that which is GOOD for the head is evil for the neck and the shoulders; you cannot put an OLD head on young shoulders.

shovelful. *See* it takes a GOOD many shovelfuls of earth to bury the truth.

show. he that shows his purse bribes the thief (*Scottish*) Those who display their wealth openly invite others to rob them. James Kelly, *A Complete Collection of Scottish Proverbs*, 1721. Variants include 'he that shows his purse longs to be rid of it'.

show me a liar and I will show you a thief (*English*) A person who is prepared to tell lies is also capable of stealing. R. West, *The Court of Conscience*, 1607. *See also* a LIAR is worse than a thief.

show me the man and I'll show you the law (*Scottish*) The impartiality of the law depends upon the impartiality of the judge. David Fergusson, *Scottish Proverbs*, 1641.

> A case of importance scarcely occurred, in which there was not some ground for bias or partiality on the part of the judges, who were so little able to withstand the temptation, that the adage 'Show me the man, and I will show you the law', became as prevalent as it was scandalous.
>
> Walter Scott, *The Bride of Lammermoor*, 1819

~ *See* the HIGHER the monkey climbs the more he shows his tail; the HOUSE shows the owner; if you cannot BITE, never show your teeth; SICKNESS shows us what we are.

shower. *See* APRIL showers bring forth May flowers; MANY drops make a shower.

shrew. *See* EVERY man can rule a shrew but he who has her; it is BETTER to marry a shrew than a sheep.

shrink. *See* THREE ills come from the north: a cold wind, a shrinking cloth and a dissembling man.

shrouds have no pockets (*Italian*) You cannot take your earthly wealth with you when you die. R.C. Trench, *On Lessons in Proverbs*, 1854. *See also* our LAST garment is made without pockets.

shrub. *See* the PINE wishes herself a shrub when the axe is at her root.

shut. a shut mouth never fills a black coffin (*US*) A person who keeps his silence is unlikely to be murdered for being an informant. This proverbial piece of advice was widely heard in US cities during the gangster era of the 1920s and 1930s.

~ *See also* AWAY goes the devil when he finds the door shut against him; a BOOK that is shut is but a block; the CAT shuts its eyes while it steals cream; a DOOR must either be shut or open; it is too LATE to shut the stable door after the horse has bolted; JEALOUSY shuts one door and opens two; KEEP your mouth shut and your eyes open; when ONE door shuts, another opens; when the WARES be gone, shut up the shop windows.

shy. *See* ONCE bitten, twice shy.

sib. *See* ALL Stuarts are not sib.

sick. that sick man is not to be pitied who hath his cure in his sleeve (*English*) Those who have the means to help themselves but fail to do anything in their interest do not deserve anybody else's pity. Thomas Fuller, *Gnomologia*, 1732.

~ *See also* the DEVIL sick would be a monk; GIVING is dead and restoring very sick; HOPE deferred makes the heart sick.

sickness. sickness comes on horseback, but goeth away on foot (*Dutch*) Illnesses come quickly, but are slow to recede. Randle Cotgrave, *A Dictionary of the French and English Tongues*, 1611. More prosaic versions of the same proverb include 'sickness comes in haste and goes at leisure'. *See also* AGUES come on horseback, but go away on foot.

sickness shows us what we are (*Roman*) Ill-health is a reminder of our own mortality. Thomas Fuller, *Gnomologia*, 1732 (also quoted by Lucretius).

~ *See also* the CHAMBER of sickness is the chapel of devotion; HEALTH is not valued till sickness comes.

side. *See* ALWAYS look on the bright side; BEWARE of the forepart of a woman, the hind part of a mule and all sides of a priest; the BREAD never falls but on the buttered side; COURTESY on one side never lasts long; EVERY man hath his weak side; FRIENDSHIP cannot stand always on one side; GOD is always on the side of the big battalions; the GRASS is always greener on the other side of the fence; it is BEST to be on the safe side; PINCH on the parson's side; take HEED of an ox before, of a horse behind, of a monk on all sides; there are TWO sides to every question.

sigh. *See* NEVER sigh but send.

sight. out of sight, out of mind (*English*) Anything (or anyone) that is not constantly in view is quickly forgotten. *Proverbs of Alfred*, *c.*1250. *See also* IGNORANCE is bliss.

> Sir John and the rest saw no more of her; and out of sight was out of mind.
>
> Charles Kingsley, *The Water Babies*, 1863

~ *See also* in VAIN the net is spread in the sight of the bird.

sign. *See* BLUSHING is a sign of grace; a LONG tongue is a sign of a short hand; an OLD man in a house is a good sign; the PALENESS of the pilot is a sign of a storm.

signify. it signifies nothing to play well if you lose (*English*) It is no consolation to say a person played or acted well if the final result goes against them. Thomas Fuller, *Gnomologia*, 1732. Related proverbs making much the same point include the blunt 'he plays well that wins'.

silence. silence catches a mouse (*English*) The silent, stealthy approach has the best results. J. Clarke, *Paroemiographia Anglo-Latina*, 1639. Related proverbs include 'silence doth seldom harm'. *See also* SOFTLY, softly catchee monkey.

> Saying nothing, till you be ready to put in execution, is the way to shun prevention, and effect your business.
>
> James Kelly, *A Complete Collection of Scotish Proverbs*, 1721

silence is a woman's best garment (*Greek*) It becomes a woman to keep her silence. R. Taverner, *Proverbs or Adages with New Additions, gathered out of the Chiliades of Erasmus*, 1539 (also quoted by Sophocles in *Ajax*). Also encountered in the form 'silence is the best ornament of a woman'. Another proverb archly observes 'silence is a fine jewel for a woman, but it's little worn'.

> Let your women keepe silence in the Churches, for it is not permitted unto them to speake.
>
> 1 Corinthians 14:34

silence is golden (*Swiss*) Silence is precious. W. White, *Eastern England*, 1865. *See also* SPEECH is silver, silence is golden

> Silence is golden, as her father used to say when she used to fly into tempers and wanted to say nasty things to everybody within range.
>
> Aldous Huxley, *Antic Hay*, 1923

silence is wisdom (*English*) The wise man keeps his peace. Geoffrey Chaucer, *Troilus and Criseyde*, *c.*1385–90. Also encountered in the form 'silence is counsel'.

silence means consent (*Roman*) If a person remains silent in a particular set of circumstances their silence may be taken to mean they have no objections to what is taking place or being proposed. William Wycliffe, *c.*1380, quoted in *Select English Works*, 1871. The principle has long been quoted in courts of law. Occasionally encountered in Latin, *qui tacet consentire videtur* and also as 'silence gives consent'. A French equivalent runs 'he consents enough who does not say a word'.

> But that you shall not say I yield, being silent,
> I would not speak.
> William Shakespeare, *Cymbeline*, *c.*1610

~ *See* MORE have repented speech than silence; SPEECH is silver, silence is golden.

silent. *See* BEWARE of a silent dog and still water; SMALL sorrows speak; great ones are silent; there is a TIME to speak, and a time to be silent; where DRUMS beat, laws are silent.

silk. silks and satins put out the fire in the chimney (*English*) Extravagant spending on clothes and other luxuries may mean that there is not enough money left for food and other necessaries. George Herbert, *Outlandish Proverbs*, 1640. Also encountered in the form 'silks and satins put out the kitchen fire'.

you can't make a silk purse out of a sow's ear (*English*) It is impossible to get perfect results when working with imperfect materials. Alexander Barclay, *Eclogues*, 1518. Sows' ears were once commonly used to make drawstring purses, but these were carried generally by the poor only, as the rich favoured purses made of silk and other much more delicate materials than sows' ears, which are coarse in texture and heavily bristled. Variants include 'you cannot make a horn of a pig's tail'.

> He remembered his uncle's saying that it took three generations to make a gentleman: it was a companion proverb to the silk purse and the sow's ear.
> W. Somerset Maugham, *Of Human Bondage*, 1915

~ *See also* an APE's an ape, a varlet's a varlet, though they be clad in silk or scarlet; a BROKEN leg is not healed by a silk stocking; the FAIREST silk is soonest stained; he that has not SILVER in his purse should have silk on his tongue.

silly. it is a silly fish that is caught twice with the same bait (*English*) Only a fool makes the same mistake twice. Thomas Fuller, *Gnomologia*, 1732.

~ *See also* ASK a silly question and you'll get a silly answer.

silver. he that has not silver in his purse should have silk on his tongue (*English*) Anyone who has no money needs all the advantages of a charming manner to improve their situation. J. Howell, *Paroemiographia*, 1659.

no silver, no servant (*English*) No one will work for someone who has no money. T. Draxe, *Bibliotheca Scholastica*, 1633.

~ *See also* EVERY cloud has a silver lining; he is WELL worth sorrow that buys it with silver; ONE for sorrow, two for joy; three for a girl, four for a boy; five for silver, six for gold; seven for a secret, never to be told; eight for heaven, nine for hell; and ten for the devil's own self; SPEECH is silver, silence is golden.

simple. *See* go to BATTERSEA to get your simples cut.

simplicity. *See* a TRULY great man never puts away the simplicity of a child.

sin. it is a sin to lie against the devil (*English*) It is a sin to lie to anyone, no matter how evil they may be themselves. Nicholas Ridley, *Works*, 1555.

it is a sin to steal a pin (*English*) Stealing something of small value is just as serious as stealing something worth a lot more. R. Whitford, *Werke for Householders*, 1537. Variants include 'he that will steal a pin will steal a better thing' and 'he that will steal an egg will steal an ox'.

> Children were taught to 'know it's a sin to steal a pin' ... when they brought home some doubtful finding.
> Flora Thompson, *Lark Rise to Candleford*, 1945

~ *See also* ALMS quencheth sin; CHARITY covers a multitude of sins; DISSEMBLED sin is double wickedness; EVERY sin brings its punishment with it; OLD sins cast long shadows; SATAN reproves sin; SORROW is good for nothing but sin.

sincerest. *See* IMITATION is the sincerest form of flattery.

sing. *See* a BEGGAR may sing before a pickpocket; the CUCKOO comes in April, and stays the month of May, sings a song at midsummer, and then goes away; EACH bird loves to hear himself sing; he who BATHES in May will soon be laid in clay, he who bathes in June will sing a merry tune, he who bathes in July will dance like a fly; if the ROBIN sings in the bush then the weather will be coarse; but if the robin sings in the barn then the weather will be warm; LITTLE birds that can sing and won't sing must be made to sing; NEVER trust a tailor that does not sing at his work; the NIGHTINGALE and cuckoo sing both in one month; a NIGHTINGALE cannot sing in a cage; the OPERA isn't over till the fat lady sings; when TWO friends have a common purse one sings and the other weeps.

singly. *See* MISFORTUNES never come singly.

sink. *See* a LITTLE leak will sink a great ship; MANY sands will sink a ship; RATS desert a sinking ship.

sinner. *See* the GREATER the sinner, the greater the saint.

sister. *See* ZEAL without knowledge is the sister of folly.

sit. sit a beggar at your table, and he will soon put his feet on it (*Russian*) Show kindness to the undeserving and they will only abuse it.

sit awhile and go a mile (*English*) Those who make sure they are well rested will perform best. J. Palsgrave, *L'Éclaircissement de la langue française*, 1530.

~ *See also* BEHIND the horseman sits black care; BETTER sit idly than work for nothing; he that comes FIRST to the hill may sit where he will; it is as CHEAP sitting as standing; it is ILL sitting at Rome and striving with the Pope; LOWLY sit, richly warm; SATURDAY's flit will never sit; an UNBIDDEN guest knoweth not where to sit; where MACGREGOR sits is the head of the table.

six. six feet of earth make all men equal (*English*) All men are equal in death (when buried six feet down). J. Howell, *Paroemiographia*, 1659.

six hours' sleep for a man, seven for a woman and eight for a fool (*Roman*) Anyone who takes more than the amount of sleep appropriate to their sex is either lazy or a fool. J. Wodroephe, *Spared Hours of a Soldier*, 1623. It was a favourite saying of George III. The proverb is known in several variants, which include 'five hours' sleep for a traveller, seven for a scholar, eight for a merchant and eleven for a knave'. Also related is 'the sluggard makes his night till noon' and 'nature requireth five, Custom taketh seven, Idleness takes nine and Wickedness eleven'.

~ *See also* ONE for sorrow, two for joy; three for a girl, four for a boy; five for silver, six for gold; seven for a secret, never to be told; eight for heaven, nine for hell; and ten for the devil's own self; THREE helping one another bear the burthen of six.

skeleton. *See* EVERY family has a skeleton in the cupboard.

skill. skill and confidence are an unconquered army (*English*) Those who have skill and confidence are ready to meet any challenge. George Herbert, *Outlandish Proverbs*, 1640. Variants include 'skill and assurance are an invincible couple'.

~ *See also* TRY your skill in gilt first and then in gold.

skin. *See* BEAUTY is only skin deep; if the LION's skin cannot, the fox's shall; NEAR is my coat, but nearer my skin; you can have no MORE of a cat than her skin; you can have no MORE of a fox than the skin.

skirt. who hath skirts of straw needs fear the fire (*English*) Those who are particularly vulnerable to particular dangers must be especially careful. R. Codrington, *The Second Part of Youth's Behaviour*, 1664.

~ *See also* the DEVIL gets up to the belfry by the vicar's skirts; had I REVENGED every wrong, I had not worn my skirts so long.

skittle. *See* LIFE isn't all beers and skittles.

skull. *See* FULL bellies make empty skulls.

sky. if the sky falls we shall catch larks (*Roman*) If something that is unlikely happens we shall be able to get a certain benefit by it (usually quoted sarcastically in response to those who speculate about the benefits they would get if something that is actually highly improbable were to take place). *Peter Idley's Instructions to his Son*, *c.*1445 (also quoted by Terence). *See also* PIGS might fly, if they had wings.

> I cannot be put off by the news that our system would be perfect if it were worked by angels ... just as I do not admit that if the sky fell we should all catch larks.
>
> George Bernard Shaw, *Misalliance*, 1914

~ *See also* MACKEREL sky and mares' tails make lofty ships carry low sails; RED sky at night, shepherd's delight; red sky in the morning, shepherd's warning.

slander leaves a scar behind it (*Roman*) Allegations always leave the taint of suspicion, even when the victim is officially cleared. T. Draxe, *Bibliotheca Scholastica*, 1616. Also encountered in the form 'slander leaves a score behind it'. *See also* FLING enough dirt and some will stick.

~ *See also* a GENEROUS confession disarms slander; TRUTH is no slander.

slave. *See* BETTER be an old man's darling than a young man's slave; GIVE a slave a rod and he'll beat his master.

slavery. *See* a GREAT fortune is a great slavery; LEAN liberty is better than fat slavery.

slay. *See* where the DEER is slain, some of her blood will lie.

sleep. he that sleeps bites no body (*English*) Those who sleep well do not vent their hostility upon others. *Merry Tales*, 1567.

let sleeping dogs lie (*English/French*) Avoid the provocation of potential trouble. Geoffrey Chaucer, *Troilus and Criseyde*, *c.*1385–90 (also recorded in French in the thirteenth century and found in other European languages). Variants include 'wake not a sleeping lion', in which form Sir Philip Sidney quoted it in *Arcadia* in 1580, and 'he that sleeps bites no body'. In *Henry IV, Part 2*, William Shakespeare quoted it in the form 'wake not a sleeping wolf'. Other less well-known proverbs warn of the dangers of disturbing hornets and stirring up stinking puddles. *See also* LEAVE well alone; let WELL alone.

> Take my advice, and speer as little about him as
> he does about you. Best to let sleeping dogs lie.
> Walter Scott, *Redgauntlet*, 1824

the sleeping fox catches no poultry (*English*) Those who spend all their time in bed will never get anything done. Benjamin Franklin, quoted in Arber's *E. Garner*, 1758. Related proverbs include 'let him that sleeps too sound borrow the debtor's pillow'.

sleep is the brother of death (*Greek*) Sleep is akin to death. *The Mirror of Magistrates*, 1563 (also quoted by Homer in the *Iliad*). Also encountered as 'sleep is the cousin of death'. Related sayings include 'sleep is the image of death'. Other proverbs take a more optimistic approach, among them the Italian 'bed is a medicine' and the German 'sleep to the sick is half health'.

> How wonderful is Death, Death and his brother
> Sleep!
> Percy Bysshe Shelley, *Queen Mab*, 1813

there will be sleeping enough in the grave (*English*) No one should over-indulge in sleep, as they will have sleep enough when they are dead. Benjamin Franklin, *The Way to Wealth*, 1736.

~ *See also* he that DRINKETH well sleepeth well, and he that sleepeth well thinketh no harm; let not a CHILD sleep upon bones; the NET fills though the fisherman sleeps; ONE hour's sleep before midnight is worth two after; a QUIET conscience sleeps in thunder; SIX hours' sleep for a man, seven for a woman and eight for a fool; the TORTOISE wins the race while the hare is sleeping; WALK groundly, talk profoundly, drink roundly, sleep soundly.

sleeve. *See* LOOK to a gown of gold and you will at least get a sleeve of it; STRETCH your arm no further than your sleeve will reach; that SICK man is not to be pitied who hath his cure in his sleeve; the TAILOR must cut three sleeves to every woman's gown.

slice. a slice off a cut loaf isn't missed (*English*) It is easy for something to be taken dishonestly, without being detected, from what is in the process of being properly dispersed. William Shakespeare, *Titus Andronicus*, *c.*1593. Also encountered in the form 'it is safe taking a shive of a cut loaf'. *See also* MUCH water goes by the mill that the miller knows not of.

> More water glideth by the mill
> Than wots the miller of; and easy it is
> Of a cut loaf to steal a shive.
> William Shakespeare, *Titus Andronicus*, *c.*1593

~ *See also* GIVE a loaf and beg a slice.

slight. *See* if the LAIRD slight the lady, so will all the kitchen boys.

slip. *See* he STANDS not surely that never slips; LITTLE fishes slip through nets but great fishes are taken; there's MANY a slip 'twixt cup and lip.

slippery. *See* HALL benches are slippery.

sloth is the key to poverty (*English*) Laziness inevitably leads to poverty. *Politeuphuia*, 1597, attributed to J. Bodenham. Other proverbs concerning sloth include 'sloth is the devil's cushion', 'sloth, like rust, consumes faster than labour wears', 'the slothful man is the beggar's brother' and 'sloth turneth the edge of wit'.

slow. slow but sure wins the race (*English*) Those who make steady, measured progress will in the end finish ahead of those who rush ahead too quickly. T. Draxe, *Bibliotheca Scholastica*, 1633. The moral behind the proverb was illustrated by one of Aesop's most famous fables, written in the sixth century BC, that of the fleet-footed hare and the plodding tortoise: the hare, confident of victory in a race against the tortoise, takes a rest, but wakes too late to catch up with the steadily plodding tortoise as it reaches the finishing post. Sometimes quoted in the abbreviated form 'slow but sure'. Variants include 'slow and steady wins the race'. Among related proverbs with similar meanings is 'the snail slides up the tower at last though the swallow mounteth it sooner'. *See also* LITTLE strokes fell great oaks.

> What signifies minding her? … if she be slow
> she's sure.
>
> Oliver Goldsmith, *The Vicar of Wakefield*, 1768

slow help is no help (*English*) Help that is too slow in coming is much the same as no help at all. R.C. Trench, *On the Lessons in Proverbs*, 1853.

~ *See also* CONFIDENCE is a plant of slow growth; a NIMBLE ninepence is better than a slow shilling.

slowly. *See* ACT quickly, think slowly; AGE does not give sense – it only makes one go slowly; CHURCH work goes on slowly; a GOOD judge conceives quickly, judges slowly; GREAT bodies move slowly; the HORSES of hope gallop, but the asses of experience go slowly; make HASTE slowly; the MILLS of God grind slowly, yet they grind exceeding small.

sluggard. the sluggard must be clad in rags (*English*) Lazy people will never have money for fine clothes. William Camden, *Remains concerning Britain*, 1605.

smack. *See* there is no JOLLITY but hath a smack of folly; when a COUPLE are newly married the first month is honeymoon, or smick smack; the second is hither and thither; the third is thwick thwack; the fourth the devil take them that brought thee and I together.

small. it's a small world (*English*) The world is smaller than popularly supposed (usually quoted on meeting someone unexpectedly or on discovering friends in common etc. with someone previously considered a complete stranger). G.A. Sala, *America Revisited*, 1886. Also found as 'the world is but a little place, after all'. Other proverbs reflecting upon the relative smallness of the world include 'the world is but a day's walk, for the sun goes about it in twenty-four hours'.

small birds must have meat (*Hebrew*) Children, like young birds, must be fed. William Shakespeare, *The Merry Wives of Windsor*, 1600–1 (quoting the Book of Job).

small invitation will serve a beggar (*English*) Beggars need little encouragement to help themselves. N.R., *Proverbs English, French, Dutch, etc. All Englished*, 1659.

small is beautiful (*US*) Small-scale things are preferable to things on a larger scale. E.F. Schumacher, *Small Is Beautiful*, 1973 (Schumacher himself attributed it to his publishers Anthony Blond and Desmond Briggs). The saying was adopted as a slogan by those opposed to attempts to combine small businesses in huge public conglomerations during the 1970s. *See also* the BEST things come in small packages; BIG is beautiful.

small sorrows speak; great ones are silent (*Roman*) People will share their minor sorrows with everyone, but are more reluctant to discuss more serious grievances. T. Hughes, *The Misfortunes of Arthur*, 1587 (also quoted by Seneca).

> The grief that does not speak whispers the o'er-
> fraught heart and bids it break.
>
> William Shakespeare, *Macbeth*, c.1604

a small spark makes a great fire (*English*) Apparently insignificant events can lead to great disruption or upheavals. G. Ashby, *Poems*, c.1470.

> How soon a little spark kindles into a flame.
>
> Samuel Richardson, *Clarissa*, 1748

there is small choice in rotten apples (*English*) There is little scope for choice when all alternatives are equally unappealing. William Shakespeare, *The Taming of the Shrew*, 1592.

> Faith, as you say, there's small choice in rotten apples.
>
> William Shakespeare, *The Taming of the Shrew*, c.1592

~ *See also* the BEST things come in small packages; the MILLS of God grind slowly, yet they grind exceeding small; no HAIR so small but hath his shadow; there is no such THING as good small beer, good brown bread, or a good old woman; WINK at small faults.

smell (noun). *See* the BEST smell is bread, the best savour salt, the best love that of children; MONEY has no smell.

smell (verb). **one is not smelt where all stink** (*English*) A guilty man may conceal himself in a crowd of similarly guilty men. T. Adams, *Sermons*, 1629.

she smells best that smells of nothing (*Roman*) The woman (or man) who wears no perfume at all smells the best. Meres, *Palladis*, 1598 (also quoted by Plautus). The idea behind the proverb is that any person who wears perfume must be suspected of wearing it to mask some personal odour that may well be offensive.

> *Mulier recte olet, ubi nihil olet*; then a woman smells best, when she hath no perfume at all.
>
> Robert Burton, *Anatomy of Melancholy*, 1621

~ *See also* a ROSE by any other name would smell as sweet.

smick smack. *See* when a COUPLE are newly married the first month is honeymoon, or smick smack; the second is hither and thither; the third is thwick thwack; the fourth the devil take them that brought thee and I together.

smile. a smiling boy seldom proves a good servant (*English*) The best servants or employees are those with diligent, serious natures. J. Howell, *Paroemiographia*, 1659.

> A laughing faced lad makes a lither servant. It is supposed such are too full of roguery to be diligent.
>
> James Kelly, *A Complete Collection of Scottish Proverbs*, 1721

~ *See* CIDER is treacherous because it smiles in the face and then cuts the throat; NEVER rely on the glory of the morning or on the smile of your mother-in-law; when FORTUNE smiles, embrace her.

smoke. the smoke follows the fairest (*Greek*) Envy clusters around those who are the most beautiful, gifted, intelligent etc. *Berkeley MS*, 1639 (also quoted by Aristophanes).

> The reek follows the fairest … This is in Aristophanes, and signifies that envy is a concomitant of excellency.
>
> James Kelly, *A Complete Collection of Scottish Proverbs*, 1721

the smoke of a man's own country is better than the fire of another's (*English*) People always prefer their own home or country to that of their neighbours. R. Taverner, *Proverbs or Adages with New additions, gathered out of the Chiliades of Erasmus*, 1539.

> The reek of my own house is better than the fire of another's.
>
> James Kelly, *A Complete Collection of Scottish Proverbs*, 1721

there's no smoke without fire (*Roman*) When rumours about something spread there is sure to be some nugget of truth at the bottom of it. Thomas Hoccleve, *Works*, c.1422 (also quoted by Plautus).

> There can no great smoke arise, but there must be some fire, no great reporte without great suspition.
>
> John Lyly, *Euphues: The Anatomy of Wit*, 1578

~ *See also* MUCH smoke, little fire; THREE things drive a man out of his house: smoke, rain and a scolding wife.

smooth. *See* the COURSE of true love never did run smooth; take the ROUGH with the smooth; there will be RUBS in the smoothest road.

snail. *See* TRAMP on a snail and she'll shoot out her horns.

snake. *See* he who has been BITTEN by a snake fears a piece of string.

snare. *See* an OLD fox is not easily snared.

snaw. *See* MANY hips and haws, many frosts and snaws.

sneeze on a Monday, you sneeze for danger (*English*) There is something to be gleaned from a sneeze, according to the day of the week on which it happens. Harland, *Lancashire Folk-Lore*, 1867. In full, the proverb is usually given as 'sneeze on a Monday, you sneeze for danger; sneeze on a Tuesday, you kiss a stranger; sneeze on a Wednesday, you sneeze for a letter; sneeze on a Thursday, for something better; sneeze on a Friday, you sneeze for sorrow; sneeze on a Saturday, your sweetheart tomorrow; sneeze on a Sunday, your safety seek, the devil will have you the whole of the week'.

snow. a snow year, a rich year (*English*) A year in which much snow falls will, by way of compensation, see plentiful harvests a few months later. J. Frampton, *Monardes*, 1580. Another proverb insists 'if February give much snow, a fine summer it doth foreshow'.

~ *See also* EASTER in snow, Christmas in mud; Christmas in snow, Easter in mud; the FILTH under the white snow the sun discovers; MANY haws, many snows; the NORTH wind doth blow and we shall have snow; a PALE moon doth rain, a red moon doth blow; a white moon doth neither rain nor snow.

sober. *See* he that KILLETH a man when he is drunk shall be hanged when he is sober; WANTON kittens make sober cats.

soberness. *See* DRUNKENNESS reveals what soberness conceals.

soft. soft and fair goes far (*English*) A calm and gentle demeanour will achieve more than a more brusque approach. *Beryn*, *c.*1400.

> Soft and fair, young lady. You that are going to be married think things can never be done too fast.
> Oliver Goldsmith, *The Good-Natured Man*, 1768

a soft answer turneth away wrath (*Hebrew*) A calm, composed manner will blunt the anger of others. William Wycliffe, Bible, Proverbs 15:1, 1382. Variants include the Roman 'a soft speech has its poison' and the Scottish 'a kindly word cools anger'. Another proverb recommends the use of 'soft words and hard arguments'.

> A soft answer turneth away wrath. There is no shield against wrongs so effectual as an unresisting temper.
> Robert Southey, letter, 19 July 1826

a soft fire makes a sweet malt (*English*) Too much haste will spoil the final result (just as too hot a fire will ruin the refining of a good malt whisky). Rowland Hill, *Commonplace Book*, 1530.

> Hold, hold (quoth Hudibras), soft fire,
> They say, does make sweet malt.
> Samuel Butler, *Hudibras*, 1663

soft pace goes far (*English*) Those who adopt a gentle, steady pace keep going the longest. C. Desainliens, *The French Littelton*, 1576.

~ *See also* FAIR and soft goes far in a day; SEPTEMBER blow soft, till the fruit's in the loft.

softly, softly, catchee monkey (*African*) A quiet, stealthy approach will result in success. G. Benham, *Cassell Dictionary of Quotations*, 1907. In the 1970s the proverb was adopted as the title of a highly popular British television police series.

~ *See* SPEAK softly and carry a big stick.

solano. *See* ASK no favour during the solano.

sold. *See* SELL.

soldier. soldiers and travellers may lie by authority (*English*) Those who have undoubted experience of the world are unlikely to be challenged when they exaggerate or lie about their experiences. J. Howell, *Paroemiographia*, 1659. *See also* a TRAVELLER may lie with authority.

soldiers in peace are like chimneys in summer (*English*) A soldier in peacetime has no role to play. A. Copley, *Wits, Fits, etc.*, 1594.

~ *See also* EVERY soldier has the baton of a field-marshal in his knapsack; the FIRST duty of a soldier is obedience; OLD soldiers never die, they simply fade away; WATER, fire and soldiers quickly make room.

solution. *See* if you're not PART of the solution, you're part of the problem.

someone. *See* if your EAR burns someone is thinking about you.

something. something is better than nothing (*English*) It is better to have something, no matter how imperfect, than nothing at all. John Heywood, *A Dialogue containing ... the Proverbs in the English Tongue*, 1546. Also encountered as 'somewhat is better than nothing'.

> A string of coral beads ... I could wish they had been oriental pearls, but something is better than nothing.
> Thomas Shelton, *Don Quixote*, 1620

you don't get something for nothing (*English*) Nothing comes without a price of some kind. P.T. Barnum, *Struggles and Triumphs*, 1870. Also encountered in somewhat jocular northern English dialect form, 'you don't get owt for nowt'. *See also* there is no such thing as a FREE lunch; NOTHING comes of nothing.

~ *See also* ALWAYS something new out of Africa; KEEP something for the sore foot; SAVE something for a rainy day; wherever there is a SECRET there must be something wrong.

sometimes. *See* the BITER is sometimes bit; MASTERS should be sometimes blind, and sometimes deaf.

somewhat. *See* ONCE nought, twice somewhat.

son. my son is my son till he gets him a wife, but my daughter's my daughter all the days of her life (*English*) Mothers relinquish influence over their sons when they get married and another woman intervenes, but retain a permanent leading role in the lives of their daughters. John Ray, *A Collection of English Proverbs*, 1670.

~ *See also* CLERGYMEN's sons always turn out badly; EVERY man is the son of his own works; like FATHER, like son; the SHOEMAKER's son always goes barefoot.

song. no song, no supper (*English*) Only those who have done some work or performed some service can expect to be rewarded. Beaumont and Fletcher, *Knight of the Burning Pestle*, 1611.

~ *See also* the CUCKOO comes in April, and stays the month of May, sings a song at midsummer, and then goes away.

soon. soon enough, if well enough (*English*) A thing is done in plenty of time if it is done correctly. Roger Ascham, *Toxophilus*, 1545.

> We do it soon enough, if that we do be well.
> George Herbert, *Outlandish Proverbs*, 1651

as soon as man is born he begins to die (*Roman*) Every minute of life brings a person closer to death. *King Edward III*, 1596.

> While man is growing, life is in decrease,
> And cradles rock us nearer to our tomb.
> Our birth is nothing but our death begun.
> Edward Young, *Night Thoughts*, 1742

soon gotten, soon spent (*English*) Money that is quickly earned is just as quickly spent. John Heywood, *A Dialogue containing ... the Proverbs in the English Tongue*, 1546.

soon hot, soon cold (*English*) Emotions that arise quickly subside equally quickly. Burgh and Lydgate, *Secrees*, *c.*1450.

soon learnt, soon forgotten (*English*) What is quickly learned or acquired is equally quickly forgotten or dissipated. Geoffrey Chaucer, *Troilus and Criseyde*, *c.*1385–90. *See also* soon GOTTEN, soon spent.

> 'Unless I heard the whole repeated, I cannot continue it,' she said. 'Yet it was quickly learned.' 'Soon gained, soon gone,' moralized the tutor.
> Charlotte Brontë, *Shirley*, 1849

soon ripe, soon rotten (*Roman*) Anything that matures quickly will soon become over-ripe (often quoted in reference to the young). William Langland, *Piers Plowman*, 1393.

> And that that rathest rypeth, roteth most saunest.
> William Langland, *Piers Plowman*, 1393

soon todd, soon with God (*English*) Children whose milk teeth appear early are fated to die prematurely. J. Howell, *Paroemiographia*, 1659. Many people interpret an early toothed (or 'todd') baby differently, insisting that the infant somehow knows that the mother will quickly become pregnant again, so gets its teeth early so that it will be the better able to fend for itself when the new arrival diverts the mother's attention – a notion often expressed as 'soon teeth, soon toes'. Also encountered in the form 'soon todd, soon turfed'.

we soon believe what we desire (*Roman*) We are easily deceived by our desires. Geoffrey Chaucer, 'The Tale of Melibee', *The Canterbury Tales*, *c.*1387 (also quoted by Seneca and other classical writers).

> We soon believe that we would have.
> T. Draxe, *Bibliotheca Scholastica*, 1616

~ *See also* a BALD head is soon shaven; BEAUTY provoketh thieves sooner than gold; a BELLOWING cow soon forgets her calf; a BONNY bride is soon buskit and a short horse is soon wispit; CONTEMPT will sooner kill an injury than revenge; a CROW on the thatch, soon death lifts the latch; EATEN bread is soon forgotten; an EVIL lesson is soon learned; the FAIREST silk is soonest stained; the FISH will soon be caught that nibbles at every bait; a FOOL and his money are soon parted; a FOOL's bolt is soon shot; a FRIEND is not so soon gotten as lost; a GREEN wound is soon healed; HALF an hour is soon lost at dinner; HASTY love is soon hot and soon cold; he that DESPISES his own life is soon master of another's; he who BATHES in May will soon be laid in clay, he who bathes in June will sing a merry tune, he who bathes in July will dance like a fly; HOT love is soon cold; if EVERY man would sweep his own doorstep the city would soon be clean; an ILL turn is soon done; IRON not used soon rusts; KEEP bad men company and you'll soon be of their number; KIND hearts are soonest wronged; LAD's love's a busk of broom, hot awhile and soon done; LEAST said, soonest mended; a LITTLE pot is soon hot; LONG absent, soon forgotten; LONGEST at the fire soonest finds cold; LONG foretold long last, short notice soon past; NEGLECT will kill an injury sooner than revenge; a NICE wife and a back door will soon make a rich man poor; NOTHING dries sooner than a tear; OLD men will die and children soon forget; OLD pottage is sooner heated than new made; a POOR man's table is soon spread; SELDOM seen, soon forgotten; the SHARPER the storm, the sooner it's over; SHORT folk are soon angry; a SHORT horse is soon curried; SIT a beggar at your table, and he will soon put his feet on it; SOUND love is not soon forgotten; that which one MOST anticipates soonest comes to pass; they that THINK none ill are soonest beguiled; a THIN meadow is soon mowed; what CHILDREN hear at home soon flies abroad; what is WELL done is done soon enough; when THINGS are at the worst they soon begin to mend.

sore. as sore fight wrens as cranes (*Scottish*) Little people can fight as furiously as those who are stronger or greater. David Fergusson, *Scottish Proverbs*, 1641.

> Little people (if rightly match'd) will fight as
> bitterly … as those who are stronger or bigger.
> James Kelly, *A Complete Collection of Scottish Proverbs*, 1721

~ *See also* BRAWLING curs never want sore ears; HUNGRY flies bite sore; it's ILL healing of an old sore; KEEP something for the sore foot; NEVER tread on a sore toe; STORE is no sore; there's a SALVE for every sore.

sorrow. sorrow comes unsent for (*English*) Sorrows come, regardless of the fact that no one wants them. Edmund Spenser, *The Shepheardes Calendar*, 1579. Also found as 'sorrow and ill weather come unsent for'. Related proverbs include 'sorrows come uninvited' and as 'sorrow is soon enough when it comes'.

> Sorrow, ne neede be hastened on:
> For he will come without calling anon.
> Edmund Spenser, *The Shepheardes Calendar*, 1579

sorrow is always dry (*English*) Those who are weighed down with sorrow frequently find respite in drink. John Bale, *Kynge Johan*, *c.*1540.

> Deborah, my life, grief, you know, is dry.
> Oliver Goldsmith, *The Vicar of Wakefield*, 1768

sorrow is good for nothing but sin (*English*) Only bad things can result from sorrow. William Camden, *Remains concerning Britain*, 1605. Related proverbs include 'sorrow will pay no debt'.

when sorrow is asleep wake it not (*English*) Do not stir up old sorrows. J. Howell, *Paroemiographia*, 1659.

~ *See also* FRUIT out of season, sorrow out of reason; GOD send you joy, for sorrow will come fast enough; he is WELL worth sorrow that buys it with silver; HELP you to salt, help you to sorrow; he that goes A-BORROWING, goes a-sorrowing; a HUNDRED pounds of sorrow pays not one ounce of debt; JOY and sorrow are next door neighbours; ONE for sorrow, two for joy; three for a girl, four for a boy; five for silver, six for gold; seven for a secret, never to be told; eight for heaven, nine for hell; and ten for the devil's own self; an OUNCE of mirth is worth a pound of sorrow; REMEMBRANCE of past sorrow is joyful; SMALL sorrows speak; great ones are silent; TWO in distress makes sorrow less.

sorry. *See* BETTER safe than sorry; MERRY nights make sorry days.

sort. *See* it takes ALL sorts to make a world.

soul. *See* BREVITY is the soul of wit; CORPORATIONS have neither bodies to be punished nor souls to be damned; the EYES are the window of the soul; a LITTLE body often harbours a great soul; OPEN confession is good for the soul; a PENNY soul never came to twopence; PUNCTUALITY is the soul of business.

sound (noun). **sound travelling far and wide a stormy day will betide** (*English*) If sounds travel a long way through the air this is a sign that wet weather is on the way. W. Roper, *Weather Sayings*, 1883.

~ *See also* EMPTY vessels make the most sound.

sound (verb). *See* a CRACKED bell can never sound well.

sound (adj.). **sound love is not soon forgotten** (*English*) The memory of true love lingers long after the relationship has ended. N.R., *Proverbs English, French, Dutch, etc. All Englished*, 1659.

soundly. *See* WALK groundly, talk profoundly, drink roundly, sleep soundly.

soup. of soup and love the first is the best (*Spanish*) Soup is of more practical use than love. Thomas Fuller, *Gnomologia*, 1732.

~ *See also* he who has ONCE burnt his mouth always blows his soup.

sour. *See* EVERY white hath its black and every sweet its sour; he DESERVES not the sweet that will not taste the sour; no GOOD apple on a sour stock; take the SWEET with the sour.

source. *See* a STREAM cannot rise above its source.

south. *See* the RAIN comes south when the wind's in the south; the WEST wind always brings wet weather, the east wind wet and cold together, the south wind surely brings us rain, the north wind blows it back again; when the WIND is in the south it blows the bait into the fish's mouth.

sow (noun). **a sow may whistle, though it has an ill mouth for it** (*English*) Someone may possess a basic skill, but is quite incapable of practising it with any distinction. Maria Edgeworth, letter, 19 October 1802.

~ *See also* you can't make a SILK purse out of a sow's ear.

sow (verb). **as you sow, so shall you reap** (*Hebrew*) In due course you will have to accept the consequences of your actions, good and bad. Bible, Galatians 6:7. Related proverbs include 'he that sows thistles shall reap prickles', 'he that soweth good seed shall reap good corn' and 'who sows little mows the less'. *See also* as you BAKE, so shall you brew; as you BREW, so shall you bake; as you make your BED, so you must lie in it.

> According to the several seeds that we sow we shall reap several sorts of grain.
>
> Walter Raleigh, *History of the World*, 1614

sow dry and set wet (*English*) Sow when the weather is fine and remove your plants when the weather is cold and wet. T. Tusser, *Five Hundred Points of Good Husbandry*, 1573.

sow with the hand and not with the sack (*Greek*) Do not deal out your seeds or other good things all at once. Sir John Harington, *Orlando Furioso*, 1591 (quoting Plutarch).

they that sow the wind shall reap the whirlwind (*Hebrew*) Those who live their lives recklessly, seeking to gain profit and ignoring risk to themselves, must face the possible consequences of their actions. Bible, Hosea 8:7.

> Indiscriminate profusion ... is sowing the wind to reap the whirlwind.
>
> Walter Scott, *The Black Dwarf*, 1816

~ *See also* if the BRAIN sows not corn, it plants thistles; EARLY sow, early mow.

spade. *See* CALL a spade a spade.

span. *See* SPIN.

Spaniard. *See* in SETTLING an island, the first building erected by a Spaniard will be a church; by a Frenchman, a fort; by a Dutchman, a warehouse; and by an Englishman, an alehouse.

spare. spare at the spigot, and let out at the bung-hole (*English*) While taking care not to lose some minor benefit, take care not to lose much more inadvertently in some other way. G. Torriano, *Select Italian Proverbs*, 1642. The proverb derives from the business of brewing, referring to the danger of a brewer paying so much attention to checking that the spigot, which regulates the flow from a cask via the tap, is completely sealed that he fails to notice that much more is being lost from the bung-hole, by means of which the cask is emptied. Also encountered in the form 'save at the spigot, and let out at the bung-hole'.

spare the rod and spoil the child (*Greek*) Those who

fail to discipline their children will find their offspring become selfish and ungovernable. Bible, Proverbs 13:24 (also quoted by the Greek poet Menander).

> Salamon seide ... *Qui parcit virge, odit filium*. The Englich of this latyn is ... Who-so spareth the sprynge, spilleth his children.
>
> William Langland, *Piers Plowman*, 1377

spare to speak and spare to speed (*English*) Those who do not speak up in defence of their own interests will not advance them. *Douce MS*, *c.*1350. Related proverbs include 'speak and speed, ask and have'.

spare well and have to spend (*English*) Those who live economically and thriftily will find that in the long term they have more money to spend. Miles Coverdale, *H. Bullinger's Christian State of Matrimony*, 1541. Variants include 'spare well and spend well' and 'know when to spend and when to spare, and you need not be busy; you'll ne'er be bare'. Another proverb recommends 'spare when you are young and spend when you are old'.

~ *See also* CATS eat what hussies spare; it is too LATE to spare when the bottom is bare; SPEND not where you may save, spare not where you must spend.

spark. *See* a SMALL spark makes a great fire; when the HEART is a fire some sparks will fly out of the mouth.

sparkle. *See* GLOWING coals sparkle oft.

sparrow-hawk. you can't make a sparrow-hawk of a buzzard (*English*) It is impossible to change the essential character of something. *Romaunce of the Rose*, *c.*1400.

speak. he cannot speak well that cannot hold his tongue (*English*) Good speakers know when to be silent. G. Torriano, *Select Italian Proverbs*, 1666. Another proverb advises 'who speaks not, errs not'.

speak fair and think what you will (*English*) Maintain a civil and courteous manner in public, but think whatever you like in private. Sir R. Barckley, *Discourse of the Felicity of Man*, 1598. Related proverbs include 'speak fitly, or be silent wisely'.

speak not of my debts unless you mean to pay them (*English*) It is impolite to discuss another's debts unless you intend to do something about them. George Herbert, *Outlandish Proverbs*, 1640.

speak softly and carry a big stick (*West African*) Maintain a calm and moderate demeanour when tackling contentious issues with others, but also remind other parties of the influence you could wield. This proverb, closely associated with the business of international diplomacy, is commonly attributed to US President Theodore Roosevelt, who quoted it in a speech he gave at the Minnesota State Fair in 1901, when he was discussing Latin-American relations.

speak when you are spoken to (*English*) It is good manners (particularly in children) to speak only when invited to in reply to others. T. Bowes, *La Primaudaye's French Academy*, 1586. *See also* CHILDREN should be seen and not heard.

~ *See also* ACTIONS speak louder than words; ANYTHING may be spoken if it be under the rose; a CASTLE that speaketh is near a surrender; do as MOST men do and men will speak well of you; the EFFECT speaks, the tongue needs not; a FALSE tongue hardly speaks truth; FOOLS and madmen speak the truth; GIVE losers leave to speak; HEAR much, speak little; he that has a GREAT nose thinks everybody is speaking of it; it is a BAD cause that none dare speak in; it's ILL speaking between a full man and a fasting; JACK would be a gentleman if he could speak French; a LIAR is not believed when he speaks the truth; LIGHT cares speak, great ones are dumb; NEVER speak ill of the dead; one may THINK that dares not speak; SEE no evil, hear no evil, speak no evil; SMALL sorrows speak; great ones are silent; SPARE to speak and spare to speed; that is WELL spoken that is well taken; there is a TIME to speak, and a time to be silent; there's MANY a true word spoken in jest; THINK first and speak afterwards; THINK much, speak little and write less; a WORD spoken is past recalling.

species. *See* the FEMALE of the species is more deadly than the male.

speech. speech is silver, silence is golden (*Swiss*) Speech may have great value, but silence, which allows time to think and ensures that secrets remain private, is much more precious. George Herbert, *Outlandish Proverbs*, 1640 (some suggest an Oriental origin). A Hebrew equivalent runs 'if a word be worth one shekel, silence is worth two'. *See also* SILENCE is golden.

> *Sprechen ist silbern, Schweigen ist golden* – speech is silver, silence is golden.
> Thomas Carlyle, in *Fraser's Magazine*, June 1834

speech is the index of the mind (*Greek*) The way a person talks reveals their inner preoccupations. Brathwaite, *The English Gentleman*, 1630 (also quoted by Erasmus). Also encountered in the forms 'speech is the picture of the mind' and 'speech shows what a man is'.

~ *See also* ARTFUL speech and an ingratiating demeanour rarely accompany virtue; MORE have repented speech than silence.

speed. *See* MORE haste, less speed; SPARE to speak and spare to speed.

spend. spend and God will send (*English*) Spend your money as you will, for Providence will surely look after your interests. *Douce MS*, *c.*1350. The underlying message is not so much that a person should be profligate with their wealth, but that refusal to spend where modest spending is appropriate may only end up in reduction to poverty in the long run. Sometimes encountered in the fuller form 'spend and God will send; spare and ever bare'. *See also* 'SPEND not where you may save; spare not where you must spend'.

> Solomon says, There is that scattereth, and yet aboundeth: And there is some that withholdeth more than is meet, and it tendeth to poverty.
> James Kelly, *A Complete Collection of Scottish Proverbs*, 1721

spend not where you may save, spare not where you must spend (*English*) It is foolish to spend when it would be possible to save your money, and also to refuse to spend when it is necessary. John Ray, *A Collection of English Proverbs*, 1678. Another proverb advises 'know when to spend and when to spare and you need not be busy, you'll never be bare'. A further variant runs 'in hard times the wise man cuts his expenses, the foolish spendthrift cuts his throat'.

what you spend, you have (*English*) You cannot lose what you have already spent or enjoyed. *c.*1300, quoted in M.R. James, *Catalogue of the Library of Pembroke College*, 1905. Sometimes given in the longer form 'what you spend, you have; what you give, you have; what you leave, you lose'.

> Ho, ho, who lies here?
> I the good Earle of Devonshire,
> And Maulde my wife, that was ful deare …
> That we spent, we had:
> That we gave, we have:
> That we lefte we lost.
> Edmund Spenser, *The Shepheardes Calendar*, 1579

~ *See also* do not ALL you can, spend not all you have, believe not all you hear, and tell not all you know; EVERYONE has a penny to spend at a new alehouse; GIVE and spend and God will send; the JEWS spend at Easter, the Moors at marriages, the Christians in suits; SOON gotten, soon spent; SPARE well and have to spend; what is GOT over the devil's back is spent under his belly.

spice. *See* VARIETY is the spice of life.

spider. *See* if you WISH to live and thrive, let a spider run alive; where the BEE sucks honey the spider sucks poison.

spies. *See* SPY.

spigot. *See* SPARE at the spigot, and let out at the bung-hole.

spill. *See* if the LAD go to the well against his will, either the can will break or the water will spill.

spilt. spilt wine is worse than water (*English*) It is regrettable when something good is wasted. James Kelly, *A Complete Collection of Scottish Proverbs*, 1721.

~ *See also* it's no USE crying over spilt milk.

spin. *See* a MAN cannot spin and reel at the same time; when ADAM delved and Eve span, who was then the gentleman?; when HEMPE is spun, England is done.

spirit. the spirit is willing but the flesh is weak (*Hebrew*) Sometimes a person's physical attributes are not equal to their aspirations. Walter Scott, *Journal*, 23 July 1827.

spit (noun). *See* put an IRISHMAN on the spit and you can always get another Irishman to baste him.

spit (verb). **who spits against heaven it falls in his face** (*English*) Those who attack or insult God will find that their ill wishes rebound upon them. Thomas North, *The Diall of Princes*, 1557. Also encountered in the form 'who spits against the wind it falls in his face'.

For your names
Of whore and murderess, they proceed from you,
As if a man should spit against the wind;
The filth returns in's face.
John Webster, *The White Devil*, 1612

~ *See also* as LONG as I live I'll spit in my parlour.

spite. *See* don't CUT off your nose to spite your face.

splash. *See* when the OAK is before the ash, then you will get only a splash.

spoil. don't spoil the ship for a ha'porth of tar (*English*) If you neglect minor repairs then you risk losing everything. John Day, *The Blind Beggar*, 1600. Most people assume the proverb is of nautical origins, but it is in reality related to agriculture, with 'ship' being a dialectical version of 'sheep'. Tar was formerly pasted on any sores and wounds that sheep suffered in order to keep flies off; injuries left thus untreated could fester and become maggot-ridden, thus leading to the animal's death. *See also* a STITCH in time saves nine.

'Never tyne the ship for want of a bit of tar,
Gerard', said this changeable mother.
Charles Reade, *The Cloister and the Hearth*, 1861

~ *See also* APPLES, pears and nuts spoil the voice; BETTER one house spoiled than two; 'IF' and 'an' spoils many a good charter; SPARE the rod and spoil the child; too MANY cooks spoil the broth.

spoke (noun). *See* the WORST spoke in a cart breaks first.

spoken. *See* SPEAK.

spoon. *See* he who SUPS with the devil should have a long spoon.

sport (noun). **in sports and journeys men are known** (*English*) A person's real character is revealed by sport and by travel. George Herbert, *Outlandish Proverbs*, 1640.

sport (verb). *See* an OLD cat sports not with her prey.

spot. *See* a LEOPARD can't change its spots.

sprat. *See* THROW out a sprat to catch a mackerel.

spread. *See* in vain the NET is spread in the sight of the bird; a POOR man's table is soon spread; RICHES are like muck, which stink in a heap, but spread abroad make the earth fruitful.

spring (noun). **it is not spring until you can plant your foot upon twelve daisies** (*English*) Only when the daisies are flourishing in close abundance can spring be properly said to have arrived. R. Chambers, *Book of Days*, 1863.

~ *See also* EARLY thunder, early spring; a JANUARY spring is worth nothing.

spring (verb). *See* HOPE springs eternal in the human breast.

spun. *See* SPIN.

spur. a spur in the head is worth two in the heel (*English*) A person will perform all the better for a drink beforehand. John Ray, *A Collection of English Proverbs*, 1670. The proverb related originally to riding, acknowledging the truth that a rider emboldened by drink will ride harder and more recklessly than a sober man will.

That's four good miles; but 'a spur in the head is worth two in the heel'.
Maria Edgeworth, *The Absentee*, 1812

~ *See* GILT spurs do not make the knight.

spy. spies are the ears and eyes of princes (*English*) Those in power rely on spies to bring them the information they need. George Herbert, *Outlandish Proverbs*, 1651.

squeak. the squeaking wheel gets the grease (*English*) Those who complain the loudest are the first to get attention. J. Bartlett, *Familiar Quotations*, 1937.

stable. *See* it is too LATE to shut the stable door after the horse has bolted; the MAN who is born in a stable is a horse.

staff. *See* BREAD is the staff of life; LITERATURE is a good staff but a bad crutch.

stain. *See* the FAIREST silk is soonest stained; TRUE blue will never stain.

stair. *See* MEET on the stairs and you won't meet in heaven.

stall. *See* AFTER a famine in the stall comes a famine in the hall; BETTER a dinner of herbs than a stalled ox where hate is.

stand. he stands not surely that never slips (*English*) Only those who have suffered setbacks before make sure they are secure when they set about new tasks. Randle Cotgrave, *A Dictionary of the French and English Tongues*, 1611.

if you can't stand the heat, get out of the kitchen (*English*) If you cannot bear the pressure, do not put yourself in a position where you will exposed to it. The saying is commonly attributed to US President Harry S. Truman, who quoted it when turning down the presidential nomination in 1952, though Truman himself credited Major-General Harry Vaughan as the originator. Truman quoted the proverb in his book *Mr Citizen* in 1960.

> He got in the way of justice ... You know what they say, if you don't like the heat, get out of the kitchen.
>
> Malcolm Bradbury, *The History Man*, 1975

standing pools gather filth (*English*) Dirt gathers on something (or someone) that is little used or disturbed. J. Clarke, *Paroemiologia Anglo-Latina*, 1639.

> Standing pools gather mud.
>
> James Kelly, *A Complete Collection of Scotish Proverbs*, 1721

~ *See also* ALL countries stand in need of Britain; CUT not the bough that thou standest upon; EMPTY sacks will never stand upright; EVERY tub must stand on its own bottom; a FALLING master makes a standing servant; FRIENDSHIP cannot stand always on one side; a HOUSE divided against itself cannot stand; it is as CHEAP sitting as standing; let the CHURCH stand in the churchyard; NEVER let the plough stand to catch a mouse; PAUL's will not always stand; UNITED we stand, divided we fall; when CHILDREN stand still they have done some ill.

starve. *See* FEED a cold and starve a fever; PLAY in summer starve in winter; while the GRASS grows, the steed starves.

stay. he that can stay obtains (*English*) Those who are prepared to bide their time are more likely to get what they want in the end. Randle Cotgrave, *A Dictionary of the French and English Tongues*, 1611.

> He that waits patiently, may come to be well served at last.
>
> James Kelly, *A Complete Collection of Scotish Proverbs*, 1721

he that stays in the valley shall never get over the hill (*English*) Only those who act to realize their ambitions can hope to achieve success. T. Draxe, *Bibliotheca Scholastica*, 1633.

~ *See also* the CUCKOO comes in April, and stays the month of May, sings a song at midsummer, and then goes away; the FAMILY that prays together stays together; he that FALLS in the dirt, the longer he stays there the fouler he is.

steady. *See* FULL cup, steady hand.

steal. *See also* CALL a man a thief and he will steal; the CAT shuts its eyes while it steals cream; HANG a thief when he's young and he'll no' steal when he's old; he WRONGS not an old man that steals his supper from him; it is a SHAME to steal but a worse to carry home; it is a SIN to steal a pin; ONE man may steal a horse, while another may not look over a hedge.

steed. *See* while the GRASS grows, the steed starves.

steel. *See* the TONGUE is not steel yet it cuts.

steeple. *See* NEW church, old steeple, poor town and proud people.

step. step after step the ladder is ascended (*English*) A man goes up in the world stage by stage rather than all in one go. Randle Cotgrave, *A Dictionary of the French and English Tongues*, 1611.

~ *See also* from the SUBLIME to the ridiculous is but a step; it is the FIRST step that is difficult; no one LIKES to be the first to step on the ice; ONE step at a time.

stern. a stern chase is a long chase (*English*) When two parties join in a bitter struggle the contest between them is likely to last a long time. James Fenimore Cooper, *The Pilot*, 1823.

> The Aurora ... had neared the chase about two miles. 'This will be a long chase, a stern chase always is.'
>
> Captain Frederick Marryat, *Mr Midshipman Easy*, 1836

stey. *See* put a STOUT heart to a stey brae.

stick (noun). **the stick is the surest peacemaker** (*French*) Peace is best maintained through the use of force. V.S. Lean, *Collecteana*, 1902–04.

sticks and stones may break my bones, but names will never hurt me (*English*) The criticisms, insults and taunts of others will never cause me any real hurt, as a beating with a stick or stone might. G.F. Northall, *Folk-Phrases*, 1894. Frequently heard between children in the course of playground squabbles. *See also* HARD words break no bones.

~ *See also* it is EASY to find a stick to beat a dog; SPEAK softly and carry a big stick.

stick (verb). *See* FLING enough dirt and some will stick; let the COBBLER stick to his last; no BUTTER will stick to his bread.

still. a still tongue makes a wise head (*English*) Those who keep their thoughts to themselves are wiser than those who share them with all and sundry. John Heywood, *Works*, 1562. *See also* a QUIET tongue makes a wise head.

still waters run deep (*Roman*) A placid surface may conceal turbulent emotions and complexities lurking beneath. *Cursor Mundi*, *c.*1400 (also found in the *Disticha*, written *c.*175BC and attributed by some to Cato). The proverb is usually quoted in reference to people who appear remote and cool in demeanour, warning that they may easily turn out to be not at all what they appear. It is a fact that waters that appear calm and smooth flowing on the surface may well mask strong and even dangerous currents below. Also encountered in the form 'silent waters run deep'. Another proverb that hints at dangers lurking in still waters warns 'serpents engender in still waters'. Shallow waters, accordingly, are the noisiest. *See also* SHALLOW streams make most din.

> Our passions are most like to floods and streams,
> The shallow murmur but the deep are dumb.
> Walter Raleigh, lines written to Elizabeth I, *c.*1599

~ *See also* BEWARE of a silent dog and still water; when CHILDREN stand still they have done some ill; a WISE head makes a still tongue.

still (adv.). *See* he that COMPLIES against his will is of his own opinion still.

sting (noun). **the sting is in the tail** (*English*) Something that appears generally good may bring a nasty surprise that is revealed only at the end. William Shakespeare, *The Taming of the Shrew*, *c.*1592.

> Who knows not where a wasp does wear his
> sting? In his tail.
> William Shakespeare, *The Taming of the Shrew*, *c.*1592

the sting of a reproach is the truth of it (*English*) Criticism is particularly painful to a victim when it is accurate. Thomas Fuller, *Gnomologia*, 1732.

~ *See also* BEES that have honey in their mouths have stings in their tails.

sting (verb). *See* if you GENTLY touch a nettle it'll sting you for your pains.

stink (noun). *See* the DEVIL always leaves a stink behind him; so we get the CHINK, we'll bear with the stink.

stink (verb). *See* the FISH always stinks from the head downwards; FISH and guests stink after three days; GARLIC makes a man wink, drink and stink; the MORE you stir, the worse it will stink; no MAN cries stinking fish; one is not SMELT where all stink; PROFFERED service stinks; RICHES are like muck, which stink in a heap, but spread abroad make the earth fruitful.

stir. stir with a knife, stir up strife (*English*) It is risking dire bad luck to stir a drink or food in the pot with a knife rather than a spoon. *Transcripts of the Devonshire Association*, 1900.

~ *See also* the MORE you stir, the worse it will stink; you should KNOW a man seven years before you stir his fire.

stitch. a stitch in time saves nine (*Roman*) Making minor repairs promptly prevents having to make more major repairs later. Thomas Fuller, *Gnomologia*, 1732 (also quoted in a variant form by Ovid). *See also* don't SPOIL the ship for a ha'porth of tar.

> A word in time saved nine; and now she was
> going to live in the country there was a chance
> for her to turn over a new leaf!
> John Galsworthy, *The Man of Property*, 1906

stock. *See* no GOOD apple on a sour stock.

stocking. *See* a BROKEN leg is not healed by a silk stocking.

stomach. *See* an ARMY marches on its stomach; EATING and drinking takes away one's stomach; POOR men seek meat for their stomach; rich men stomach for their meat; a SHARP stomach makes short devotion; the WAY to a man's heart is through his stomach.

stone. *See* BOIL stones in butter and you may sup the broth; CONSTANT dropping wears away the stone; DRIVE gently over the stones; HUNGER breaks through stone walls; LEAVE no stone unturned; PEOPLE who live in glass houses shouldn't throw stones; a ROLLING stone gathers no moss; STICKS and stones may break my bones, but names will never hurt me; there is a SCORPION under every stone; who HOLDS his peace and gathers stones will find a time to throw them; you BUY land you buy stones, you buy meat you buy bones; you cannot get BLOOD from a stone.

stone-dead hath no fellow (*English*) Death is the perfect solution (frequently voiced by proponents of the death penalty). *The Soddered Citizen*, *c.*1663.

stool. *See* BETWEEN two stools you fall to the ground.

store is no sore (*English*) There is no harm in storing up things for future use. John Heywood, *A Dialogue containing ... the Proverbs in the English Tongue*, 1546.

> Let my dressers crack with the weight of curious viands.
>
> Philip Massinger, *A New Way to Pay Old Debts*, 1633

storm. *See* AFTER a storm comes a calm; ANY port in a storm; a FAIR day in winter is the mother of a storm; the PALENESS of the pilot is a sign of a storm; the PORPOISE plays before a storm; the SHARPER the storm, the sooner it's over; VOWS made in storms are forgotten in calms.

stormy. *See* the CALMEST husbands make the stormiest wives; SOUND travelling far and wide a stormy day will betide.

story. *See* EVERY picture tells a story.

stout. put a stout heart to a stey brae (*Scottish*) Pluck up your courage to tackle a challenging task. A. Montgomerie, *The Cherry and the Cloe*, 1585. A 'stey brae' is, in Scottish dialect, a 'steep hill'.

> He ... shouted to me ... to 'pit a stoot hert tae a stey brae'.
>
> John Buchan, *Greenmantle*, 1916

straight. *See* CROOKED logs make straight fires; an OLD ox makes a straight furrow.

strange. *See* ADVERSITY makes strange bedfellows; FACT is stranger than fiction; POLITICS makes strange bedfellows; TRUTH is stranger than fiction.

stranger (noun)**. a stranger's eye sees clearest** (*English*) It is often the case that it takes a stranger unfamiliar with the way things stand to see things as they really are. Charles Reade, *The Cloister and the Hearth*, 1860.

~ *See also* MESSMATE before a shipmate, shipmate before a stranger, stranger before a dog.

straw. straws tell which way the wind blows (*English*) It is possible to observe by minor or trifling changes the general direction in which events are going (just as one might tell the direction in which the wind is blowing by tossing loose straws into the air). John Selden, *Table-Talk*, 1654.

> Such straws of speech show how blows the wind.
>
> Charles Reade, *The Cloister and the Hearth*, 1860

~ *See also* a DROWNING man will clutch at a straw; it is a DANGEROUS fire begins in the bed straw; it is the LAST straw that breaks the camel's back; a MAN of straw is worth a woman of gold; who hath SKIRTS of straw needs fear the fire; you can't make BRICKS without straw.

stream. a stream cannot rise above its source (*English*) There are natural limitations to what can be achieved by anyone or anything. S. Tuke, *The Adventures of Five Hours*, 1663. Also encountered in the form 'the stream can never rise above the spring-head'.

> Then what can Birth, or mortal Men bestow,
> Since Floods no higher their Fountains flow?
>
> John Dryden, *The Wife of Bath*, 1700

~ *See also* CROSS the stream where it is ebbest; don't CHANGE horses in midstream; SHALLOW streams make most din.

street. by the street of by and by one arrives at the house of never (*Spanish*) If one is always procrastinating, things will never get done. R.C. Trench, *On the Lessons in Proverbs*, 1853. *See also* PROCRASTINATION is the thief of time.

the streets of London are paved with gold (*English*) London, with its wealth of easy opportunities, is the place to go to if you want to make your fortune. *A New Account of Compliments; or, The Complete English Secretary, with a Collection of Playhouse Songs*, 1789. The proverb is associated by many people with the legend of Dick Whittington, the penniless youth destined to become Lord Mayor, who was lured to London by the rumour of streets paved with gold.

strength. *See* one has ALWAYS strength enough to bear the misfortunes of one's friends; POLICY goes beyond strength; UNION is strength; WISDOM goes beyond strength; a WOMAN's strength is in her tongue.

strengthen. *See* as the DAY lengthens, so the cold strengthens.

stretch. stretch your arm no further than your sleeve will reach (*English*) Do not attempt to exceed your own capabilities or resources (especially financial). Miles Coverdale, *H. Bullinger's Christian State of Matrimony*, 1541.

> Put your Hand no farther than your Sleeve will reach. That is, spend no more than your Estate will bear.
>
> James Kelly, *A Complete Collection of Scotish Proverbs*, 1721

~ *See also* EVERYONE stretches his legs according to the length of his coverlet.

strife. *See* POVERTY breeds strife; STIR with a knife, stir up strife; WEIGHT and measure take away strife.

strike. strike while the iron is hot (*French/English*) Act before the opportunity to do something slips away. Geoffrey Chaucer, *Troilus and Criseyde*, *c.*1385–90. The proverb has its origins in the business of the blacksmith, who works metal while it is still red-hot and pliable. *See also* make HAY while the sun shines; take TIME by the forelock.

> Where's the good of putting things off? Strike while the iron's hot; that's what I say.
>
> Charles Dickens, *Barnaby Rudge*, 1841

~ *See also* LIGHTNING never strikes the same place twice.

string. *See* he who has been BITTEN by a snake fears a piece of string.

strive. *See* it is ILL sitting at Rome and striving with the Pope.

stroke. *See* BEWARE of the oak, it draws the stroke; avoid the ash, it courts the flash; LITTLE strokes fell great oaks; an OAK is not felled at one stroke.

strong. *See* BROKEN bones well set become stronger; a CHAIN is no stronger than its weakest link; the RACE is not to the swift, nor the battle to the strong; SAMSON was a strong man yet he could not pay money before he had it; YORKSHIRE born and Yorkshire bred, strong in the arm and weak in the head; you may BREAK a horse's back, be he never so strong.

Stuart. *See* ALL Stuarts are not sib.

stubborn. *See* FACTS are stubborn things; FATE leads the willing but drives the stubborn.

study. *See* a BELLY full of gluttony will never study willingly; a MAN's studies pass into his character.

stumble. a stumble may prevent a fall (*English*) A minor mishap may prevent a more serious misfortune. Thomas Fuller, *Gnomologia*, 1732. One variant runs 'he that stumbles and falls not mends his pace'. Another less consolatory proverb remarks 'he who stumbles twice over the same stone deserves to break his shins'.

~ *See also* he that RUNS in the night stumbles; it is a GOOD horse that never stumbles.

style. the style is the man (*Roman*) The quality of a man may be determined by the way in which he does things and in how he presents himself (often applied to literary style). Robert Burton, *Anatomy of Melancholy*, 1621.

> To the Reader *Stylus virum arguit*, our style bewrays us.
>
> Robert Burton, *Anatomy of Melancholy*, 1621

subject. *See* although there EXIST many thousand subjects for elegant conversation, there are persons who cannot meet a cripple without talking about feet.

sublime. from the sublime to the ridiculous is but a step (*French*) It is all too easy to move from what is admirable to what is laughable. Thomas Paine, *The Age of Reason*, 1793. The proverb is commonly, but inaccurately, attributed to Napoleon, who is supposed to have quoted Paine's words when discussing the retreat from Moscow in 1812.

> The sublime and the ridiculous are often so nearly related that it is difficult to class them separately. One step above the sublime makes the ridiculous, and one step above the ridiculous makes the sublime again.
> Thomas Paine, *The Age of Reason*, 1793

substance. *See* CATCH not at the shadow and lose the substance.

subtlety is better than force (*English*) Cunning is always preferable to brute force. T. Draxe, *Bibliotheca Scholastica*, 1616.

succeed. *See* if at FIRST you don't succeed, try, try, try again; NOTHING succeeds like success; SADNESS and gladness succeed each other.

success. success makes a fool seem wise (*English*) Even fools can seem wise when they are fortunate enough to enjoy success, even if through no effort of their own. J. Mapletoft, *Select Proverbs*, 1707. Related proverbs include 'success makes fools admired, makes villains honest' and 'success is never blamed'. An earlier Roman equivalent, quoted by Seneca, runs 'successful villainy is called virtue'.

~*See also* NOTHING succeeds like success.

suck. *See* CHILDREN suck the mother when they are young and the father when they are old; don't TEACH your grandmother to suck eggs; where the BEE sucks honey the spider sucks poison.

sucker. *See* NEVER give a sucker an even break.

suckling. *See* out of the MOUTHS of babes and sucklings.

sudden. sudden friendship, sure repentance (*English*) Friendships that spring up quickly should not be relied upon. James Kelly, *A Complete Collection of Scotish Proverbs*, 1721.

a sudden rising hath a sudden fall (*English*) Those who rise up in the world very rapidly are liable to fall again just as quickly. John Lydgate, *The Fall of Princes*, *c.*1440.

~ *See also* HASTY climbers have sudden falls.

sue a beggar and get a louse (*English*) There is no point in suing someone with no assets with which to compensate you. R. Wilson, *The Cobblers Prophecy*, 1594.

> I guess it is some law phrase – but sue a beggar, and – your honour knows what follows.
> Walter Scott, *The Bride of Lammermoor*, 1819

suet. *See* a GENTLEMAN without an estate is a pudding without suet.

suffer. *See* he COMPLAINS wrongfully on the sea who twice suffers shipwreck; he that LIVES long suffers much.

sufferance. of sufferance cometh ease (*English*) Through patience comes relief. Geoffrey Chaucer, 'The Merchant's Tale', *The Canterbury Tales*, *c.*1387. Related proverbs include 'suffer the ill and look for the good'.

suffering. it is not the suffering but the cause which makes a martyr (*English*) A martyr is created by his sacrifice for a particular cause, not by his sacrifice alone. S. Torshell, *The Hypocrite Discovered*, 1644.

sufficient unto the day is the evil thereof (*Hebrew*) Confine your worries to the present, rather than concern yourself with what might possibly go wrong tomorrow. Bible, Matthew 6:34. *See also* don't CROSS the bridge until you get to it; TOMORROW is another day; TOMORROW never comes.

> Take, therefore, no thought for the morrow; for the morrow shall take thought for the things of itself. Sufficient unto the day is the evil thereof.
> Matthew 6:34

suit. *See* the JEWS spend at Easter, the Moors at marriages, the Christians in suits.

summer. there is no summer but it has a winter (*English*) Good times cannot be expected to go on forever. M.A. Denham, *A Collection of Proverbs ... relating to the Weather*, 1846.

~ *See also* an ENGLISH summer, three hot days and

a thunderstorm; a GOOD winter brings a good summer; ONE swallow does not make a summer; PLAY in summer starve in winter; the RICH man has his ice in the summer and the poor man gets his in the winter; SOLDIERS in peace are like chimneys in summer; WINTER finds out what summer lays up.

summon. *See* he that TALKS much of his happiness, summons grief.

sun. let not the sun go down on your wrath (*Hebrew*) Always repair any rifts or quarrels with others before retiring for the night. Bible.

the sun loses nothing by shining into a puddle (*Greek*) The good might be brought into contact with what is evil or loathsome and yet not be contaminated by it. R. Brunne, *Handlyng Synne*, 1303 (also quoted by Diogenes Laertius, who may have originated it, and Tertullian). Variants include 'the sun is never the worse for shining on a dunghill'.

> Though that holy writ speke of horrible synne, certes holy writ may nat been defouled, na-moore than the sonne that shyneth on the mixne.
>
> Geoffrey Chaucer, *The Canterbury Tales*, *c.*1387

where the sun enters the doctor does not (*Italian*) Those who get plenty of exposure to the sun will enjoy good health. *Times*, 6 June 1928.

~ *See also* ALTHOUGH the sun shine, leave not thy cloak at home; the FILTH under the white snow the sun discovers; HAPPY is the bride the sun shines on; he that hath a HEAD of wax must not walk in the sun; if the DOCTOR cures, the sun sees it, but if he kills, the earth hides it; make HAY while the sun shines; ONE cloud is enough to eclipse all the sun; there is NOTHING new under the sun; they that WALK much in the sun will be tanned at last; when it RAINS and the sun shines at the same time the devil is beating his wife.

Sunday. *See* as the FRIDAY, so the Sunday; come DAY, go day, God send Sunday; FRIDAY's hair and Sunday's horn go to the devil on Monday morn; a MAN of many trades begs his bread on Sunday.

sunny. *See* if CANDLEMAS Day be sunny and bright winter will have another flight; if Candlemas Day be cloudy with rain, winter is gone and won't come again.

sunshine. *See* after RAIN comes sunshine; in RAIN and sunshine cuckolds go to heaven; there is NEVER a Saturday without some sunshine.

sup. he who sups with the devil should have a long spoon (*English*) Those who enter into dealings with people of dubious reputation should take care not to get drawn in too deeply and must keep their wits about them. Geoffrey Chaucer, *The Canterbury Tales*, *c.*1387.

> He must have a long spoon that must eat with the Devil. What tell'st thou me of supping?
>
> William Shakespeare, *The Comedy of Errors*, *c.*1593

~ *See also* BOIL stones in butter and you may sup the broth; he who DEPENDS on another dines ill and sups worse; HOT sup, hot swallow; you cannot SELL the cow and sup the milk.

supper. *See* AFTER dinner rest a while, after supper walk a mile; a GOOD salad may be the prologue to a bad supper; he WRONGS not an old man that steals his supper from him; HOPE is a good breakfast but a bad supper; LAUGH before breakfast, you'll cry before supper; no SONG, no supper.

support. *See* ONE father can support ten children; ten children cannot support one father.

sure. *See* at EASTER let your clothes be new, or else be sure you will it rue; FRIDAY night's dream on the Saturday told, is sure to come true be it never so old; he STANDS not surely that never slips; if the COCK crows on going to bed, he's sure to rise with a watery head; SLOW but sure wins the race; the STICK is the surest peacemaker; SUDDEN friendship, sure repentance; TOUCH wood, it's sure to come good.

surgeon. *See* a GOOD surgeon must have an eagle's eye, a lion's heart and a lady's hand.

surpass. *See* MERCY surpasses justice.

surprise. *See* a MAN surprised is half beaten.

surrender. *See* a CASTLE that speaketh is near a surrender.

suspicion. suspicion has double eyes (*English*) Those who are suspicious are twice as watchful as their neighbours. William Shakespeare, *Henry IV Part 1*,

1597–8. Related proverbs include the Roman 'a suspicious mind sees everything on the dark side' and 'suspicion begets suspicion' and the Japanese 'suspicion raises hobgoblins in the dark'.

~ *See also* CAESAR's wife must be above suspicion.

Sussex won't be druv (*English*) Residents of Sussex are notoriously stubborn and cannot be persuaded to do anything against their own inclination. T. Wales, *Sussex Garland*, 1910.

swallow. *See* HOT sup, hot swallow; it is IDLE to swallow the cow and choke on the tail; ONE swallow does not make a summer.

swan. *See* ALL geese are swans.

swarm. a swarm of bees in May is worth a load of hay (*English*) Some things are best done in their proper season and will not prosper if done at any other time. S. Hartlib, *Reformed Commonwealth of Bees*, 1655. As regards bees, swarms that take to the wing later than May are less likely to produce much honey because nectar-bearing flowers will shortly be past their best – as witnessed by the proverb in its fuller form: 'A swarm of bees in May is worth a load of hay; a swarm of bees in June is worth a silver spoon; a swarm of bees in July is not worth a fly.' It has been suggested that 'a swarm of bees in June is worth a silver spoon' was a later addition, probably from the nineteenth century.

> As she reminded the children: A swarm in May's worth a rick of hay; and a swarm in June's worth a silver spoon; while a swarm in July isn't worth a fly.
> Flora Thompson, *Lark Rise to Candleford*, 1945

sway. *See* the PERSUASION of the fortunate sways the doubtful.

swear. he that will swear will lie (*English*) A person who will readily swear to something is just as ready to tell a lie. A. Dent, *The Plain Man's Pathway*, 1601.

if you swear you will catch no fish (*English*) A foul-mouthed fisherman will never get a bite. Thomas Heywood, *Fair Maid of the Exchange*, 1607. In former times the skippers of trawlers often prohibited swearing on board their vessels in order to promote the chances of bringing home a good catch (though it is also on record that one skipper faced with empty nets actually ordered his crew to swear in the hope that this would change their luck for the better).

sweat. *See* EAT till you sweat and work till you freeze; no SWEET without sweat; QUININE is made of the sweat of ship carpenters.

sweep. *See* if EVERY man would sweep his own doorstep the city would soon be clean; let EVERY man sweep the ice with his own broom; a NEW broom sweeps clean.

sweet. from the sweetest wine, the tartest vinegar (*English*) The bitterest experiences or emotions may stem from the most harmonious and pleasant sources (often quoted in reference to love that has turned sour). W. Painter, *The Palace of Pleasure*, 1567.

> The sweetest wine tourneth to the sharpest vineger.
> John Lyly, *Euphues: The Anatomy of Wit*, 1578

no sweet without sweat (*English*) Good things only come through hard work. J. Clarke, *Paroemiologia Anglo-Latina*, 1639.

take the sweet with the sour (*English*) Every man must be prepared to accept bad times along with the good. Alexander Barclay, *The Ship of Fools*, 1509. Variants include 'he deserves not sweet that will not taste of sour' and 'sweet meat will have sour sauce'.

> Thy wit is a very bitter sweeting; it is a most sharp sauce.
> William Shakespeare, *Romeo and Juliet*, c.1593

~ *See also* APPLES taste sweetest when they are going; the DEEPER the sweeter; EVERY white hath its black and every sweet its sour; FORBIDDEN fruit tastes sweetest; the GREATEST calf is not the sweetest veal; he DESERVES not the sweet that will not taste the sour; the HIGHER the tree, the sweeter the plum; HOME, sweet home; LIFE is sweet; LITTLE fish are sweet; the NEARER the bone, the sweeter the flesh; REVENGE is sweet; a ROSE by any other name would smell as sweet; a SOFT fire makes a sweet malt; that is not ALWAYS good in the maw that is sweet in the mouth; TRUTH and sweet oil always come to the top; WARS are sweet to those that know them not; your NEIGHBOUR's apples are the sweetest.

sweetness. *See* it is not with SAYING honey, honey, that sweetness will come into the mouth; a LITTLE poison embitters much sweetness.

swift. *See* the LAME foot overtakes the swift one in the end; MISCHIEF has swift wings; the RACE is not to the swift, nor the battle to the strong.

swim. *See* the BEST fish swim near the bottom; don't go NEAR the water until you learn how to swim; FISH must swim thrice; how we APPLES swim.

swimmer. *See* it is the BEST swimmers who drown.

swine. *See* don't CAST your pearls before swine; on SAINT Thomas the Divine kill all turkeys, geese and swine.

swing. *See* what you LOSE on the swings you gain on the roundabouts.

Swithin. *See* SAINT Swithin's Day, if thou dost rain, for forty days it will remain; Saint Swithin's Day, if thou be fair, for forty days 'twill rain no more

sword. *See* GLUTTONY kills more than the sword; he who LIVES by the sword dies by the sword; it's ILL putting a naked sword in a madman's hand; LEND not horse, nor wife, nor sword; an OLD wise man's shadow is better than a young buzzard's sword; ONE sword keeps another in the scabbard; the PEN is mightier than the sword; whosoever DRAWS his sword against the prince must throw the scabbard away.

sympathy without relief is like mustard without beef (*English*) Expressions of sympathy are empty words if they are not accompanied by active assistance. R.L. Gales, *Vanished Country Folk*, 1914. A Yiddish proverb offering a different opinion runs 'if you can't help your friend with money, help him at least with a sigh'.

T

table. *See* a POOR man's table is soon spread; SIT a beggar at your table, and he will soon put his feet on it; where MACGREGOR sits is the head of the table.

tace is Latin for candle (*English*) Silence is advisable. *Tace* in Latin means 'be silent'. Thomas Shadwell, *The Virtuoso*, 1676. The proverb suggests that silence will actually promote understanding, thus 'lighting a candle' in the darkness. In former times, it was customary for audiences in English theatres to toss candles on to the stage when they did not like a play: the management were supposed to take the hint and to dowse the lights and close the curtains.

> '*Tace*, madam,' answered Murphy, 'is Latin for a candle; I commend your prudence.'
> Henry Fielding, *Amelia*, 1751

tack. *See* it is HARD to turn tack upon a narrow bridge.

tail. make not thy tail broader than thy wings (*English*) It is a mistake to keep more servants than your station in life warrants. Francis Bacon, *Essays*, 1597.

~*See also* as a BEAR has no tail, for a lion he'll fail; BEES that have honey in their mouths have stings in their tails; the COW knows not the worth of her tail till she loses it; GIVE a child all he shall crave and a dog while his tail doth wave and you'll have a fair dog and a foul knave; HAIL brings frost in the tail; the HIGHER the monkey climbs the more he shows his tail; if you BUY the cow, take the tail into the bargain; it is IDLE to swallow the cow and choke on the tail; MACKEREL sky and mares' tails make lofty ships carry low sails; the STING is in the tail.

tailor. the tailor makes the man (*English*) A man must be judged by the work of his tailor – in other words, by the quality of his suit of clothes. William Shakespeare, *King Lear*, 1605. *See also* APPEARANCES are deceptive.

> Believe it, sir, That clothes do much upon the wit … and thence comes your proverb, The tailor makes the man.
> Ben Jonson, *The Staple of News*, 1625

the tailor must cut three sleeves to every woman's gown (*English*) Tailors will take every opportunity to charge their customers for work they have not actually done. *The Mirror of Mirth*, 1583.

tailors and writers must mind the fashion (*English*) In order to prosper, tailors and writers must adapt to the latest fashions. John Lyly, *Euphues: The Anatomy of Wit*, 1578.

~ *See also* NEVER trust a tailor that does not sing at his work; NINE tailors make a man.

take. you can't take it with you (*English*) It is not possible to take your earthly riches with you when you die, so you might as well make the most of them while you are still living. Also encountered in the fuller form 'you can't take it with you when you go'.

> For we brought nothing into the world, and it is certain we can carry nothing out.
> Timothy 6:7

tale. a tale never loses in the telling (*English*) Constant repetition of a story tends to lead to the exaggeration of its content. *The Schoolhouse of Women*, 1541. The notion is supported by another, less well-known, saying: 'the tale runs as it pleases the teller'.

Similar sentiments are expressed by 'a good tale is none the worse for being twice told'. A proverb that finds fault with the frequent repetition of the same stories, however, runs 'a tale twice told is cabbage twice sold', while another warns 'it ought to be a good tale that is twice told'.

> A Tale never loses in the telling. Fame or Report ... commonly receives an Addition as it goes from Hand to Hand.
>
> James Kelly, *A Complete Collection of Scotish Proverbs*, 1721

the tale runs as it pleases the teller (*English*) It is up to the narrator how a tale is told. Thomas Fuller, *Gnomologia*, 1732. Related proverbs include 'each tale is ended as it hath favour'.

~ *See also* DEAD men tell no tales; a GOOD tale is none the worse for being twice told; NEVER tell tales out of school; an OLD man never wants a tale to tell.

tale-teller. a tale-teller is worse than a thief (*English*) Lying is a worse sin than stealing. James Kelly, *A Complete Collection of Scotish Proverbs*, 1721.

~ *See also* ALE-SELLERS should not be tale-tellers.

talk. he that talks much of his happiness, summons grief (*English*) Those who talk openly about their own happiness invite misfortune. George Herbert, *Outlandish Proverbs*, 1640.

he that talks to himself talks to a fool (*English*) Talking to yourself is the first sign of madness. Thomas Fuller, *Gnomologia*, 1732.

talking pays no toll (*English*) Talk is free. George Herbert, *Outlandish Proverbs*, 1640.

talk is but talk (*English*) Talk alone achieves nothing. *Two Merry Milkmaids*, 1620. The fuller form of the proverb runs 'talk is but talk; it's money buys land'.

> Prate is but prate, its money buyes land.
>
> J. Ray, *A Collection of English Proverbs*, 1678.

talk of the devil and he is bound to appear (*Roman*) If you discuss someone when they are not present the chances are that they will unexpectedly appear. G. Torriano, *Select Italian Proverbs*, 1642 (also quoted by Terence and Cicero). Variants include 'talk of the devil and he'll either come or send' and the contrasting 'talk of an angel and you'll hear his wings'.

> They were the very men we spoke of – talk of the devil, and – humph?
>
> Walter Scott, *The Fortunes of Nigel*, 1822

~ *See also* although there EXIST many thousand subjects for elegant conversation, there are persons who cannot meet a cripple without talking about feet; he is like a BAGPIPE: he never talks till his belly be full; he that KNOWS not how to hold his tongue, knows not how to talk; it is ILL talking of a halter in the house of a man that was hanged; MANY talk of Robin Hood who never shot with his bow; MONEY talks; THINK with the wise, but talk with the vulgar; WALK groundly, talk profoundly, drink roundly, sleep soundly.

talker. *See* the GREATEST talkers are the least doers.

tame (verb). *See* ARTHUR could not tame a woman's tongue.

tame (adj.). *See* a WILD goose never lays a tame egg.

tan. *See* they that WALK much in the sun will be tanned at last.

tango. *See* it takes TWO to tango.

tar. *See* don't SPOIL the ship for a ha'porth of tar.

target. *See* BREAD and cheese be two targets against death.

tart. *See* from the SWEETEST wine, the tartest vinegar.

Tartar. *See* SCRATCH a Russian and you find a Tartar.

taste (noun). **tastes differ** (*English*) Every man has his own individual tastes, which are often at variance to those of others. J. Davis, *Travels in the USA*, 1803. Related proverbs include the English 'all feet tread not in one shoe' and the Scottish 'every man to his taste, as the man said when he kissed his cow'. The Romans, meanwhile, sagely observed that 'there are as many tastes as there are men'.

> Tastes differ ... I never saw a marine landscape that I admired less.
>
> Wilkie Collins, *The Moonstone*, 1868

~ *See also* EVERYONE to his taste; there is no ACCOUNTING for tastes.

taste (verb). *See* APPLES taste sweetest when they are going; EVERYTHING tastes of porridge; FORBIDDEN fruit tastes sweetest; he DESERVES not the sweet that will not taste the sour.

tattered. *See* there's MANY a good cock come out of a tattered bag.

taught. *See* TEACH.

taxes. *See* NOTHING is certain but death and taxes.

teach. don't teach your grandmother to suck eggs (*English*) It is impertinent to attempt to correct your elders or betters concerning things of which they have long experience themselves. Randle Cotgrave, *A Dictionary of the French and English Tongues*, 1611. Alternatives include warnings against teaching your grandmother to spin, to handle ducks and to sup sour milk. One variant runs 'don't teach your father how to get children'.

> A child may sometimes teach his grandmother
> to suck eggs.
> Henry Fielding, *Tom Jones*, 1749

he that teaches himself has a fool for his master (*English*) Those who try to teach themselves rather than consult proven teachers are fools. Ben Jonson, *Timber, of Discoveries*, 1640.

> Learn of the skilful: He that teaches himself,
> hath a fool for his master.
> Benjamin Franklin, *Poor Richard's Almanack*, 1741

you can't teach an old dog new tricks (*English*) It is impossible to persuade the old, who are established in their ways of life, to adopt new habits. J. Fitzherbert, *Husbandry*, 1530.

> The same renitency against conviction which is
> observed in old dogs, 'of not learning new tricks'.
> Laurence Sterne, *Tristram Shandy*, 1767

~ *See also* BACHELORS' wives and maids' children be well taught; BETTER untaught than ill taught; he who CAN does, he who cannot teaches; the SCHOLAR teacheth the master.

teacher. *See* EXPERIENCE is the best teacher; EXPERIENCE is the teacher of fools; he that KISSETH his wife in the market-place shall have many teachers.

team. *See* ONE hair of a woman draws more than a team of oxen.

tear (noun). *See* NOTHING dries sooner than a tear; the PLEASURES of the rich are bought with the tears of the poor.

tear (verb). *See* WIDE will wear but narrow will tear.

teeth. *See* TOOTH.

tell. he that tells a secret is another's servant (*English*) A person who divulges his or her secrets to another is at that person's mercy. George Herbert, *Outlandish Proverbs*, 1640.

> To him thou tellest thy secret, thou givest also
> thy liberty.
> J. Wodroephe, *The Spared Houres of a Soldier in His Travels*, 1623

he that tells his wife news is but newly married (*English*) Experienced husbands keep their wives in ignorance of what they know. *Proverbs of Alfred*, *c.*1275.

tell a woman she's a beauty and the devil will tell her so fifty times (*English*) A single compliment paid to a woman will be remembered by her many times and thus feed her vanity. S. Palmer, *Moral Essays on Proverbs*, 1710. Other proverbs lamenting the vanity of women include 'tell a woman she is fair and she will soon turn fool' and 'the more women look in their glass, the less they look to their house'.

tell it not in Gath (*English*) Do not say anything to your enemies about it. John Wyclif, Bible, 1382.

> The fact is – but tell it not in Gath – I was happier
> without them!
> Marie Corelli, *God's Good Man*, 1904

tell me with whom thou goest, and I'll tell thee what thou doest (*English*) A man, and his actions, will be influenced by the company he keeps. George Pettie, *Guazzo's Civil Conversation*, 1581.

tell money after your own father (*English*) Check money received from your relatives to ensure you have not been cheated. S. Hieron, *The Preacher's Plea*, 1604.

> Reckon money after all your kin.
> James Kelly, *A Complete Collection of Scotish Proverbs*, 1721

tell not all you know, nor do all you can (*English*) Never divulge the full extent of your private self and capabilities or knowledge to others. Benjamin Franklin, *Poor Richard's Almanack*, 1739.

tell the truth and shame the devil (*English*) Those who admit their faults should be encouraged by the thought that in so doing they heap shame on the devil who tempted them in the first place. W. Patten, *Expedition into Scotland*, 1548.

> And I can teach thee, coz, to shame the Devil
> By telling truth: tell truth, and shame the Devil.
> William Shakespeare, *Henry IV, Part 1*, *c.*1597

~ *See also* a BLISTER will rise upon one's tongue that tells a lie; BLOOD will tell; CHILDREN and fools tell the truth; DEAD men tell no tales; do not ALL you can, spend not all you have, believe not all you hear, and tell not all you know; EVERY picture tells a story; FRIDAY night's dream on the Saturday told, is sure to come true be it never so old; a GOOD tale is none the worse for being twice told; NEVER tell tales out of school; NEVER tell thy foe that thy foot acheth; an OLD man never wants a tale to tell; STRAWS tell which way the wind blows; a TALE never loses in the telling; TIME will tell.

teller. *See* the TALE runs as it pleases the teller.

temper. *See* GOD tempers the wind to the shorn lamb.

temperance is the best physic (*Roman*) Abstinence from alcohol is the best way to promote good health. H.G. Bohn, *A Handbook of Proverbs*, 1855. A variant of this proverb advises 'be temperate in wine, in eating, girls, and cloth, or the gout will seize you and plague you both'.

tempt. *See* he that is BUSY is tempted but by one devil, he that is idle by a legion; an OPEN door may tempt a saint.

ten. *See* ONE father can support ten children; ten children cannot support one father; ONE for sorrow, two for joy; three for a girl, four for a boy; five for silver, six for gold; seven for a secret, never to be told; eight for heaven, nine for hell; and ten for the devil's own self; ONE picture is worth ten thousand words; a WOMAN is an angel at ten, a saint at fifteen, a devil at forty and a witch at fourscore.

tender. *See* OLD and tough, young and tender.

thank. *See* do not BLAME God for having created the tiger, but thank him for not having given it wings.

thankless. *See* to KISS a man's wife or wipe his knife is a thankless office.

thanks. *See* a FORCED kindness deserves no thanks; GOD heals and the physician hath the thanks.

thatch. *See* a CROW on the thatch, soon death lifts the latch.

thaw. *See* ROBIN HOOD could brave all weathers but a thaw wind.

thick. *See* BLOOD is thicker than water; FAULTS are thick where love is thin; if the COCK moult before the hen we shall have weather thick and thin, but if the hen moult before the cock we shall have weather hard as a block.

thief. the thief doth fear each bush an officer (*English*) People with a guilty conscience live in constant fear of being found out. William Shakespeare, *Henry VI Part 3*, 1590–1.

when thieves fall out honest men come by their own (*English*) When criminals fall out among themselves, good men come back to the fore. John Heywood, *A Dialogue containing ... the Proverbs in the English Tongue*, 1546.

> Thanks to this quarrel, which confirms the old saying that when rogues fall out, honest people get what they want.
> Charles Dickens, *Martin Chuzzlewit*, 1850

~ *See also* ALL are not thieves that dogs bark at; BEAUTY provoketh thieves sooner than gold; CALL a man a thief and he will steal; a CARELESS hussy makes many thieves; HANG a thief when he's young, and he'll no' steal when he's old; he that MARRIES a widow and three children marries four thieves; he that SHOWS his purse bribes the thief; the HOLE calls the thief; if there were no RECEIVERS, there would be no thieves; it is a POOR family that has neither a whore nor a thief in it; a LIAR is worse than a thief; LITTLE thieves are hanged, but great ones escape; ONCE a thief, always a thief; ONE thief robs another; OPPORTUNITY makes a thief; a POSTERN door makes a thief; PROCRASTINATION is the thief of time; SAVE a thief from the gallows and he shall cut your throat; SET a thief to catch a thief; SHOW me a liar and I will show you a thief; a TALE-TELLER is worse than a thief; there is HONOUR among thieves; TWO daughters and a back door are three arrant thieves; WAR makes thieves, and peace hangs them.

thin. the thin end of the wedge is to be feared (*English*) It is wise to be cautious about something minor that might very well lead on to something much more threatening or problematic. R.D. Blackmore, *Tommy Upmore*, 1884.

a thin meadow is soon mowed (*English*) It does not take long to gather in a poor harvest. John Ray, *A Collection of English Proverbs*, 1670.

~ *See also* FAULTS are thick where love is thin; if the COCK moult before the hen we shall have weather thick and thin, but if the hen moult before the cock we shall have weather hard as a block.

thing. if a thing is worth doing, it's worth doing well (*English*) It is always worth taking a little extra effort when doing something that is worth doing. Lord Chesterfield, letter, 9 October 1746.

take things as they come (*English*) Do not anticipate possible problems, but deal with them as they arise. J. Davies, *The Scourge of Folly*, 1611. Also encountered in the form 'take things as you find them'.

there is no such thing as a free lunch (*US*) No favour or benefit comes free of some obligation in return. Mid-nineteenth century. The saying was formerly widely heard in saloon bars in reference to the snacks that were served free of charge to anyone who bought a drink. From the 1970s the phrase has been voiced frequently in discussion of economic affairs and particularly associated with the economist Milton Friedman (who made it the title of his 1975 book).

there is no such thing as good small beer, good brown bread, or a good old woman (*English*) Good old women are as rare as good small beer and good brown bread. Jonathan Swift, *Dialogues*, 1738. Related proverbs include 'some things I do not love; a good long mile, good small beer, and a good old woman'.

things done cannot be undone (*English*) There is no altering what is already done. *Good Wyfe wold a Pylgremage*, *c.*1460. *See also* what's DONE cannot be undone.

things past cannot be recalled (*English*) It is too late to change what has already been done. H. Medwall, *Nature*, 1500. *See also* what's DONE cannot be undone.

> Since a thing past can't be recalled ... we may be content.
>
> Maria Edgeworth, *Popular Tales*, 1804

things present are judged by things past (*English*) Developments in the present are inevitably compared with how things went in the past. J. Sandford, *The Garden of Pleasure*, 1573.

things that are above us are nothing to us (*Roman*) People tend to ignore those things that they cannot understand or aspire to. John Stubbes, *Anatomie of Abuses*, 1583. A contrasting proverb, however, claims that 'things that are below us are nothing to us'.

things that are hard to come by are much set by (*English*) Things that have been acquired with difficulty will be carefully guarded by the person who has obtained them. *Romaunce of the Rose*, *c.*1400. Variants include 'things hardly attained are long retained'.

> Hardlie come by, warilie kept.
>
> Robert Greene, *Works*, 1587

when a thing is done, advice comes too late (*English*) Advice given when it is too late for it to be acted upon is useless. R. Codrington, *The Second Part of Youth's Behaviour*, 1664. Variants on this theme include the Chinese 'when error is committed, good advice comes too late', the Danish 'advice after mischief is like medicine after death', and the Spanish 'advice comes after the rabbit has escaped'. Geoffrey Chaucer's version of it ran: 'advisement is good before the need.' The Germans, however, counter such declarations with their own proverb, insisting that 'good counsel never comes too late'.

when things are at the worst they soon begin to mend (*English*) Just when it seems that things can get no worse they are likely to improve. G. Whetstone, *Heptameron of Civil Discourses*, 1582. *See also* the DARKEST hour is just before the dawn; THINGS at the worst will mend.

> Things being at the worst, begin to mend.
>
> John Webster, *The Duchess of Malfi*, 1623

~ *See also* ALL good things must come to an end; ALL things are obedient to money; ALL things are possible with God; ALL things come to those who wait; ALL things grow with time, except grief; the BEST things are worst to come by; the BEST things come in small packages; the BEST things in life are free; the BEST things may be abused; BOLDNESS in business is the first, second and third thing; FACTS are stubborn things; FIRST things first; GOD keep me from the man that has but one thing to mind; GOOD things are hard; he that GAINS time gains all things; he who COMMENCES many things finishes but a few; if you WANT a thing done well, do it yourself; it is a GOOD thing to eat your brown bread first; KEEP a thing seven years and you'll always find a use for it; LITTLE things please little minds; MAN is the measure of all things; MODERATION in all things; NEVER do things by halves; NEW things are fair; no LIVING man all things can; ONE thing thinketh the horse, and another he that saddles him; SAYING is one thing, and doing another; take HEED is a fair thing; there is MEASURE in all things; a THOUSAND pounds and a bottle of hay is all one thing at doomsday; to GIVE a thing, and take a thing, is to wear the devil's gold ring; to the JAUNDICED eye all things look yellow; to the PURE all things are pure; THREE things are insatiable: priests, monks and the sea; THREE things are not to be credited; THREE things are not to be trusted: a cow's horn, a dog's tooth and a horse's hoof; THREE things drive a man out of his house: smoke, rain and a scolding wife; TIME devours all things; TIME tries all things; TWO things a man should never be angry at: what he can help and what he cannot help; we PERISH by permitted things; WORSE things happen at sea; the WORTH of a thing is what it will bring; you can have too MUCH of a good thing.

think. he that thinks amiss concludes worse (*English*) Those who think mistakenly are bound to come to wrong conclusions. George Herbert, *Outlandish Proverbs*, 1651.

one may think that dares not speak (*English*) A person may have their own private thoughts about something even if they dare not voice them aloud. T. Deloney, *Thomas of Reading*, 1597.

> I think, but dare not speak.
>
> William Shakespeare, *Macbeth*, 1605–06

they that think none ill are soonest beguiled (*English*) Those who refuse to believe evil in others are soonest fooled by them. John Heywood, *A Dialogue containing ... the Proverbs in the English Tongue*, 1546.

think first and speak afterwards (*English*) Always think before you speak. H.G. Bohn, *A Handbook of Proverbs*, 1855. Variants include 'think today and speak tomorrow'.

thinking is very far from knowing (*English*) Speculation about something is not the same as knowledge of something. J. Mapletoft, *Select Proverbs*, 1707.

think much, speak little and write less (*English*) Think as much as you like but exercise great self-restraint when it comes to actual expression of those thoughts. John Lydgate, *Minor Poems*, *c.*1430.

think on the end before you begin (*English*) Never do anything without having a clear idea of what you want to achieve in the end. *Cursor Mundi*, *c.*1300.

> Thus human life is best understood, by the wise man's rule, of regarding the end.
>
> Jonathan Swift, *Tale of a Tub*, 1704

he thinks not well that thinks not again (*English*) The person who allows no opportunity for second thoughts is unlikely to come out with the best ideas. Randle Cotgrave, *A Dictionary of the French and English Tongues*, 1611.

> He thinks ill that thinks not twice.
>
> George Herbert, *Outlandish Proverbs*, 1640

think with the wise, but talk with the vulgar (*Greek*) Those who wish to write well should think with wisdom, but write in the language of the common people. Roger Ascham, *Toxophilus*, 1545 (quoting Aristotle).

> Speak with the speech of the world, think with the thoughts of the few.
>
> J. Hay, *Pike County Ballads*, 1871

~ *See also* ACT quickly, think slowly; the CROW thinks her own birds fairest; EVIL be to him who thinks it; a FOOL thinks himself wise; GOD comes at last when we think he is furthest off; GREAT minds think alike; he that DRINKETH well sleepeth well, and he that sleepeth well thinketh no harm; he that has a GREAT nose thinks everybody is speaking of it; he that is WARM thinks all so; a HUMBLE-BEE in a cow-turd thinks himself a king; if your EAR burns someone is thinking about you; if you would be POPE you must think of nothing else; LITTLE knoweth the fat man what the lean man thinketh; MANY a one says well that thinks ill; on a GOOD bargain, think twice; ONE thing thinketh the horse, and another he that saddles him; SPEAK fair and think what you will; there's ONE good wife in the country, and every man thinks he hath her.

third. third time lucky (*English*) Difficult challenges are often successfully met on the third attempt. Robert Browning, letter, *c.*1840. Three is the number of the Holy Trinity and has long been considered lucky.

the third time pays for all (*English*) A third attempt

at something, if successful, makes up for previous failures. J. Higgins, *Mirror for Magistrates*, 1574. Related proverbs include 'the third time is never like the rest'.

> *Primo, secundo, tertio*, is a good play; and the old saying is, 'the third pays for all'.
> William Shakespeare, *Twelfth Night*, *c.*1601

~ *See also* BOLDNESS in business is the first, second and third thing; the FIRST glass for thirst, the second for nourishment, the third for pleasure, and the fourth for madness; TWO dogs fight for a bone, and a third runs away with it; when a COUPLE are newly married the first month is honeymoon, or smick smack; the second is hither and thither; the third is thwick thwack; the fourth the devil take them that brought thee and I together.

thirst. *See* the FIRST glass for thirst, the second for nourishment, the third for pleasure, and the fourth for madness.

thirsty. *See* he that goes to BED thirsty riseth healthy.

thirty. *See* a MAN at thirty must be either a fool or a physician.

thistle. a thistle is a fat salad for an ass's mouth (*English*) What another person may consider poor fare may be considered a feast by someone who has very little else to choose from. James Kelly, *A Complete Collection of Scotish Proverbs*, 1721.

~ *See also* the ASS loaded with gold still eats thistles; he that hath a GOOD harvest may be content with some thistles; if the BRAIN sows not corn, it plants thistles.

Thomas. *See* on SAINT Thomas the Divine kill all turkeys, geese and swine.

thong. *See* MEN cut large thongs of other men's leather.

thorn. *See* he that goes BAREFOOT must not plant thorns; he that HANDLES thorns shall prick his fingers; HONEY is dear bought if licked off thorns; it EARLY pricks that will be a thorn; no ROSE without a thorn.

thought. thought is free (*English*) There are no limitations on what a man may think. John Gower, *Confessio Amantis*, *c.*1390. The saying was a particular favourite of William Shakespeare and it appears in various guises in *Twelfth Night*, *Hamlet*, *Measure for Measure*, *Othello* and *The Tempest*.

> Fair lady, do you think you have fools in hand? – Now, sir, thought is free.
> William Shakespeare, *Twelfth Night*, *c.*1601

~ *See also* SECOND thoughts are best; the WISH is father to the thought.

thousand. in a thousand pounds of law there's not an ounce of love (*English*) The law is a hard-hearted business in which love has no place. Randle Cotgrave, *A Dictionary of the French and English Tongues*, 1611. Also encountered in the form 'in a thousand pounds worth of law there's not a shilling's worth of pleasure'.

a thousand pounds and a bottle of hay is all one thing at doomsday (*English*) Wealth and possessions will all become equally meaningless at the Day of Judgement. J. Howell, *English Proverbs*, 1659.

a thousand probabilities do not make one truth (*English*) What is thought probable is not necessarily accurate. H.G. Bohn, *A Handbook of Proverbs*, 1855.

~ *See also* although there EXIST many thousand subjects for elegant conversation, there are persons who cannot meet a cripple without talking about feet; ONE picture is worth ten thousand words.

thread. the thread breaks where it is weakest (*English*) A single flaw will compromise the strength of a thread – or anything else. George Herbert, *Outlandish Proverbs*, 1640. Related proverbs include 'a thread too fine spun will easily break'. *See also* a CHAIN is no stronger than its weakest link.

~ *See also* a GENTLE heart is tied with an easy thread.

threadbare. *See* PRIDE may lurk under a threadbare cloak.

threaten. he threatens many that hurts any (*Roman*) A person who causes injury to another will cause many more to feel threatened. G. Harvey, *Marginalia*, *c.*1590 (quoting Cato). Variants include 'there are more men threatened than stricken'.

> He threatens many, that hath iniur'd one.
> Ben Jonson, *Sejanus*, 1604

threatened men live long (*English*) Those whose lives are in some way endangered often live longest, as though in defiance of the threat made against them. Lady E. Wheathell, quoted in M. Saint C. Byrne's *Lisle Letters*, 1534.

> 'The proverb says that threatened men live long,' he tells her lightly.
>
> Charles Dickens, *The Mystery of Edwin Drood*, 1870

three. it takes three generations to make a gentleman (*English*) A genteel nature cannot be acquired but comes by birth and takes at least three generations. James Fenimore Cooper, *The Pioneers*, 1823.

> He remembered his uncle's saying that it took three generations to make a gentleman: it was a companion proverb to the silk purse and the sow's ear.
>
> William Somerset Maugham, *Of Human Bondage*, 1915

three helping one another bear the burthen of six (*English*) Those who work together as a team can achieve as much as twice their number working alone. George Herbert, *Outlandish Proverbs*, 1640.

three ills come from the north: a cold wind, a shrinking cloth and a dissembling man (*English*) The exports of northern England include freezing weather, cloth that shrinks when wet, and bad-tempered, argumentative people. Ben Jonson, *Bartholomew Fair*, 1614.

three may keep a secret, if two of them are dead (*English*) It is part of human nature to find the keeping of secrets well nigh impossible. John Heywood, *A Dialogue containing ... the Proverbs in the English Tongue*, 1546. Also found as 'three may keep counsel if two be away' and as 'two may keep counsel, if one of them's dead'. Variants include 'three are too many to keep a secret, and too few to be merry' and 'the secret of two no further will go, the secret of three a hundred will know'.

> Is your man secret? Did you ne'er hear say
> Two may keep counsel, putting one away?
>
> William Shakespeare, *Romeo and Juliet*, c.1593

three removals are as bad as a fire (*English*) Moving house three times results in as much damage to one's belongings as a fire. Benjamin Franklin, *Poor Richard's Almanack*, 1758.

> I never saw an oft removed Tree, Nor yet an oft removed Family, That throve so well, as those that settled be. And again, Three Removes are as bad as a Fire.
>
> Benjamin Franklin, *Poor Richard's Almanack*, 1758

three things are insatiable: priests, monks and the sea (*English*) Only the sea has as voracious an appetite as members of the clergy. H. Estienne, *World of Wonders*, 1607. One variant of the proverb links the greediness of priests, women and the sea. Another runs 'three things are untameable, idiots, women and the salt sea'.

three things are not to be credited (*English*) There are three things that should never be trusted at face value, namely, a woman when she weeps, a merchant when he swears, and a drunkard when he prays. B. Rich, *Ladies Looking Glasse*, 1616.

three things are not to be trusted: a cow's horn, a dog's tooth and a horse's hoof (*French*) Never trust something or someone who could cause you potential harm. John of Fourdun, *Scotichronicon*, c.1383 (recorded in French in the thirteenth century). The proverb exists in several variant forms. As well as advising against trusting animals that might suddenly turn against a man, other versions warn against trusting the weeping of a woman, the oaths of a merchant, the prayers of a drunkard and the laugh of an Englishman.

three things drive a man out of his house: smoke, rain and a scolding wife (*Roman*) A nagging wife ranks alongside a smoky house and a leaky roof as one of the three things guaranteed to make a husband flee his own home. Geoffrey Chaucer, 'The Tale of Melibe', *The Canterbury Tales*, c.1387 (though derived ultimately from the biblical Book of Proverbs).

> Poverty is hard, but debt is horrible; a man might as well have a smoky house and a scolding wife, which are said to be the two worst evils of our life.
>
> Charles Spurgeon, *John Ploughman's Talk*, 1869

three women make a market (*Italian*) It takes just three women to create market conditions. G. Torriano, *Select Italian Proverbs*, 1666. Also encountered in the form 'three women and a goose make a market'. Another proverb observes, rather sourly, that 'where there are women and geese there wants no noise'.

~ *See also* BETTER no doctor at all than three; the CALF, the goose, the bee: the world is ruled by these three; an ENGLISH summer, three hot days and a thunderstorm; FISH and guests stink after three days; from CLOGS to clogs is only three generations; from SHIRTSLEEVES to shirtsleeves in three generations;

he that MARRIES a widow and three children marries four thieves; a JUDGE knows nothing unless it has been explained to him three times; NATURE, time and patience are the three great physicians; ONE Englishman can beat three Frenchmen; ONE for sorrow, two for joy; three for a girl, four for a boy; five for silver, six for gold; seven for a secret, never to be told; eight for heaven, nine for hell; and ten for the devil's own self; the TAILOR must cut three sleeves to every woman's gown; TWO boys are half a boy, and three boys are no boy at all; TWO daughters and a back door are three arrant thieves; TWO's company, but three's a crowd.

thrice. *See* FISH must swim thrice; KEEP yourself from the anger of a great man, from the tumult of a mob, from a man of ill fame, from a widow that has been thrice married, from a wind that comes in at a hole, and from a reconciled enemy; MEASURE thrice and cut once.

thrift is a great revenue (*Roman*) Careful control of expenditure may contribute substantially to a person's wealth. J. Howell, *Paroemiographia*, 1659 (also quoted by Cicero). Variants include the Polish 'by thrift and work people grow rich'.

thrive. he that will thrive must first ask his wife (*English*) Before a man can prosper he must win the approval of his wife. 1500, quoted in R.L. Greene, *Early English Carols*, 1935. Related proverbs include 'first thrive and then wive'.

> He that would thrive, must ask his wife. It was lucky for me that I had one as much dispos'd to industry and frugality as myself.
> Benjamin Franklin, *Autobiography*, 1790

he that will thrive must rise at five (*English*) Those who wish to get on in life must rise early. G. Harvey, *Marginalia*, *c.*1590. A fuller version of the proverb runs 'he that will thrive must rise at five; he that hath thriven may lie till seven'.

~ *See also* FIRST thrive and then wive; he that WEDS before he's wise shall die before he thrive; if you WISH to live and thrive, let a spider run alive; it's HARD to wive and thrive both in a year.

throat. *See* CIDER is treacherous because it smiles in the face and then cuts the throat; a FOOL's tongue is long enough to cut his own throat; let not your TONGUE cut your throat; SAVE a thief from the gallows and he shall cut your throat.

throw. don't throw out your dirty water until you get in fresh (*English*) Do not part with what you have before you have made certain of your possession of its better replacement. David Fergusson, *Scottish Proverbs*, 1641. Also encountered in the form 'cast not out your foul water until you get in clean'.

> Mrs Giddy has discarded Dick Shuttle ... she was a fool to throw out her dirty water before she got clean.
> Jonathan Swift, *A Complete Collection of Polite and Ingenious Conversation*, 1738

don't throw the baby out with the bathwater (*German*) Take care not to reject what is valuable or essential when instituting change or reform. Thomas Carlyle, *The Nigger Question*, 1853 (also quoted in German by J. Kepler in *Tertius Interveniens*, 1610). The proverb was first introduced into English by the historian Thomas Carlyle, who was an authority on the German language. In Germany it is given as *Das Kind mit dem Bade ausschütten.*

> When changing we must be careful not to empty the baby with the bath in mere reaction against the past.
> George Bernard Shaw, *Everybody's Political What's What*, 1944

throw out a sprat to catch a mackerel (*English*) Sacrifice something of minor value to obtain something of much greater worth. William Hone, *Every-day Book*, 1826. Variants include 'set a herring to catch a whale'.

> It was their custom, Mr Jonas said ... never to throw away sprats, but as bait for whales.
> Charles Dickens, *Martin Chuzzlewit*, 1850

~ *See also* the BEST throw of the dice is to throw them away; PEOPLE who live in glass houses shouldn't throw stones; who HOLDS his peace and gathers stones will find a time to throw them; whosoever DRAWS his sword against the prince must throw the scabbard away.

thumb. *See* EVERY honest miller has a thumb of gold.

thunder. while the thunder lasted two bad men were friends (*Indian*) Even bad people will come together in the face of a common danger. A.C. Benson, *At Large*, 1908. Another proverb advises that 'when it thunders the thief becomes honest'.

~ *See also* EARLY thunder, early spring; a QUIET conscience sleeps in thunder.

thunderstorm. *See* an ENGLISH summer, three hot days and a thunderstorm.

Thursday. *See* MONDAY's child is fair of face, Tuesday's child is full of grace; Wednesday's child is full of woe, Thursday's child has far to go; Friday's child is loving and giving, Saturday's child works hard for its living; and the child that's born on the Sabbath day, is fair and wise and good and gay.

thwick thwack. *See* when a COUPLE are newly married the first month is honeymoon, or smick smack; the second is hither and thither; the third is thwick thwack; the fourth the devil take them that brought thee and I together.

tide. the tide never goes out so far but it always comes in again (*English*) The tide always comes back in after it has gone out. *Notes & Queries*, 1864 (identifying it as an old Cornish proverb). Variants include 'the tide keeps its course'.

~ *See also* TIME and tide wait for no man.

tie. See a GENTLE heart is tied with an easy thread; the GOAT must browse where she is tied; GOODNESS is not tied to greatness.

tiger. *See* do not BLAME God for having created the tiger, but thank him for not having given it wings; he who RIDES a tiger is afraid to dismount.

till. *See* a LITTLE house well filled, a little land well tilled, and a little wife well willed.

time. he that hath time hath life (*English*) A man with expectations of much time ahead of him may rejoice in life. John Florio, *First Fruites*, 1578.

> Then do not squander time, for that is the stuff
> life is made of.
>
> Benjamin Franklin, *The Way to Wealth*, 1736

no time like the present (*English*) Do not delay doing things that can be done at once. G. Legh, *The Accidence of Armoury*, 1562. *See also* PROCRASTINATION is the thief of time.

> 'There is no time like the present', cried Mr
> Bramble.
>
> Tobias Smollett, *Humphry Clinker*, 1771

take time by the forelock (*Greek*) Seize the opportunity before it passes by. Richard Mulcaster, *Positions*, 1581. The proverb has its origins in the ancient legend of the statue of Time by Lysippus, which supposedly depicted him as 'Opportunity', complete with a drooping forelock which others might grasp (though it could only be reached by those in front of him). The saying – sometimes extended to 'take time by the forelock for she is bald behind' – has also been attributed to Pittacus of Mitylene, a wise man who lived in the sixth century BC. Variant forms include 'take occasion by the forelock' and 'seize time by the forelock'. *See also* make HAY while the sun shines; NEVER put off till tomorrow what you can do today; PROCRASTINATION is the thief of time; STRIKE while the iron's hot.

> Tell her the joyous time wil not be staid,
> Unlesse she doe him by the forelock take.
>
> Edmund Spenser, *Sonnets*, 1595

there is a time for everything (*Hebrew*) There is an appropriate time for all things. Bible, Ecclesiastes 3:1. Recorded in English literature since at least the fourteenth century (it was quoted by Geoffrey Chaucer in *The Canterbury Tales* and subsequently by William Shakespeare). Also found in the form 'there is a time and a place for everything'.

> To everything there is a season, and a time to
> every purpose under the heaven.
>
> Ecclesiastes 3:1

there is a time to speak, and a time to be silent (*Hebrew*) In some circumstances it is appropriate to speak out, in others it is best to keep your silence. Bible, Ecclesiastes 3:7. Related proverbs include 'there is a time to wink, as well as to see'.

time and tide wait for no man (*English*) Do not delay doing something, as the chance to do it will pass. Geoffrey Chaucer, *The Canterbury Tales*, *c.*1387. Also found in the form 'time and tide stay for no man' and, in Scotland, as 'time bides na man'.

> Time and tide will wait for no man, saith the

adage. But all men have to wait for time and tide.

Charles Dickens, *Martin Chuzzlewit*, 1844

time devours all things (*Roman*) All things perish in time. H.G. Bohn, *A Handbook of Proverbs*, 1855. Related proverbs include 'time is a file that wears and makes no noise', 'time and patience will wear out stone posts' and 'time is the rider that breaks youth'.

time flies (*Roman*) Time, and with it the life of man, passes very quickly. Geoffrey Chaucer, *The Canterbury Tales*, *c.*1387 (also quoted in variant forms by Horace and Ovid among others). Often encountered in its original Latin form, *tempus fugit*. Equivalents include 'time fleeth away without delay' and 'take time when time cometh, for time will away'.

In reality, killing time
Is only the name for another of the multifarious ways
By which Time kills us.

Osbert Sitwell, 'Milordo Inglese'

time heals all wounds (*Greek*) All injuries heal with the passing of time. Geoffrey Chaucer, *Troilus and Criseyde*, *c.*1385–90 (also quoted by Euripides in *Alcestis*, *c.*438BC, by Menander and by Seneca). Often quoted in reference to the recently bereaved. Also found as 'time cures all things' and as 'time is the great healer'. A jovial modern reworking of the proverb runs 'time wounds all heels'.

Time is the great physician.

Benjamin Disraeli, *Henrietta Temple*, 1837

time is money (*Greek*) Time is an asset with its own monetary value – so it should not be wasted. T. Wilson, *Discourse upon Usury*, 1572 (also quoted by Antiphon as far back as 430BC and subsequently by Theophrastus).

'You don't come often to the club, Stout?' … 'No, time is money'.

Edward Bulwer-Lytton, *Money*, 1840

time lost cannot be recalled (*English*) Time spent cannot be reclaimed. Geoffrey Chaucer, *Troilus and Criseyde*, *c.*1385–90. Also found in the forms 'time lost we cannot win' and 'time past cannot be won again'.

And time lost may well be repented, but never recalled.

John Lyly, *Euphues and his England*, 1580

times change and we with time (*Roman*) All things, including ourselves, are changed by the passage of time. John Lyly, *Euphues: The Anatomy of Wit*, 1578.

The tymes are chaunged as Ovid sayeth, and wee are chaunged in the times.

John Lyly, *Euphues: The Anatomy of Wit*, 1578

times past cannot be recalled (*English*) Once time has passed by it cannot be lived again. Geoffrey Chaucer, *Troilus and Criseyde*, *c.*1385–90.

Volat irrevocabile tempus, time past cannot be recal'd.

Robert Burton, *Anatomy of Melancholy*, 1621

time tries all things (*English*) Everything is subject to the processes of time. *Republica*, 1553. Variants include 'time trieth truth'.

Time, I, that please some, try all.

William Shakespeare, *The Winter's Tale*, *c.*1611

time will tell (*English*) All things will be revealed with the passage of time. R. Taverner, *Proverbs or Adages with New Additions, gathered out of the Chiliades of Erasmus*, 1539. Less concise versions include 'time revealeth all things' and 'time is the father of truth'.

The doctor had looked very grave … and had said that time alone could tell.

E.H. Porter, *Pollyanna*, 1913

time works wonders (*English*) The passage of time can achieve remarkable changes for the better. A. Marten, *Exhortation to Defend the Country*, 1588.

Time does wonders.

Lord Byron, letter, 7 January 1815

'tis time to fear when tyrants seem to kiss (*English*) It is always an ominous sign when tyrants agree. William Shakespeare, *Pericles*, *c.*1608.

~ *See also* ACCUSING the times is but excusing ourselves; ALL things grow with time, except grief; COWARDS die many times before their death; HAPPINESS takes no account of time; he that GAINS time gains all things; if you LOSE your time you cannot get money or gain; an INCH of gold will not buy an inch of time; it will ALL be one in a hundred years' time; a JUDGE knows nothing unless it has been explained to him three times; LOST time is never found again; LOVE as in time to come thou shouldest hate and hate as thou shouldest in time to come, love; a MAN cannot spin and reel at the same time; a MAN cannot whistle and drink at the same time; a MOUSE in time may bite in two a cable; NATURE, time and patience are the three great physicians; NEVER is a long time; no MAN is wise at all times; ONE step at a time; OTHER times, other manners; PARSLEY seed goes nine times to the devil; PROCRASTINATION is the thief of time; a STITCH in time saves nine; TELL a woman she's a beauty and the devil will tell her so fifty times; there is a GOOD time coming; THIRD time lucky; the THIRD time pays for all; what may be done at ANY time will be done at no time; when it RAINS and the sun shines at the same time the devil is beating his wife; who HOLDS his peace and gathers stones will find a time to throw them; WORK expands so as to fill the time available; you may FOOL all of the people some of the time, some of the people all of the time, but not all of the people all of the time.

tinker. *See* if IFS and ands were pots and pans, there'd be no work for tinkers' hands.

tiny. *See* however BIG the whale may be, the tiny harpoon can rob him of life.

tit. *See* OXFORD for learning, London for wit, Hull for women, and York for a tit.

today. here today, gone tomorrow (*English*) Some things disappear almost as quickly as they come (often heard in reference to money). T. Draxe, *Bibliotheca Scholastica*, 1616. *See also* EASY come, easy go.
today a man, tomorrow none (*English*) The life of man is short. R. Taverner, *Proverbs or Adages with New Additions, gathered out of the Chiliades of Erasmus*, 1539. Related proverbs include 'today at cheer, tomorrow in bier', 'today gold, tomorrow dust', 'today a man, tomorrow a mouse' and 'today a man, tomorrow a cuckold'.
today is yesterday's pupil (*English*) What happens today depends very much upon what happened yesterday. Thomas Fuller, *Gnomologia*, 1732. Also encountered in the form 'today is the scholar of yesterday'.
today you, tomorrow me (*Roman*) It is your turn to do something today, but it will be my turn tomorrow. *Ancrene Wisse*, 1250. Also encountered in the reverse form, as 'today me, tomorrow you'. *See also* I today, you tomorrow.

> What haps to-day to me to-morrow may to you.
> Edmund Spenser, *The Faerie Queene*, 1596

~ *See also* BETTER an egg today than a chicken tomorrow; HERE today, gone tomorrow; he that FALLS today may rise tomorrow; I today, you tomorrow; JAM tomorrow and jam yesterday, but never jam today; NEVER put off till tomorrow what you can do today; ONE today is worth two tomorrows; what MANCHESTER says today, the rest of England says tomorrow; WORK today for you know not how much you may be hindered tomorrow.

todd. *See* SOON todd, soon with God.

toe. *See* NEVER tread on a sore toe.

together. *See* BIRDS of a feather flock together.

told. *See* TELL.

toll. *See* TALKING pays no toll.

Tom. *See* MORE people know Tom Fool than Tom Fool knows.

tomorrow. tomorrow is another day (*Spanish*) Things may improve on the morrow. J. Rastell, *Calisto and Meliboea*, *c.*1527 (also quoted by Fernando de Rojas in *La Celestina* in 1499 and subsequently by Cervantes). In the twentieth century the proverb provided the last line of the celebrated Hollywood movie *Gone with the Wind*, 1936. *See also* don't CROSS the bridge until you get to it; SUFFICIENT unto the day is the evil thereof.

> We will say no more of it at present ... To-morrow is a new day.
> Walter Scott, *St Ronan's Well*, 1824

tomorrow never comes (*English*) Things delayed until another day are unlikely ever to get done. Lord Berners, *Froissart*, 1523. Equivalents in other languages include the Spanish 'tomorrow is often the busiest day of the year'.

> To-morrow every fault is to be amended; but that To-morrow never comes.
> Benjamin Franklin, *Poor Richard's Almanack*, 1756

~ *See also* BETTER an egg today than a chicken tomorrow; DRUNKEN days have all their tomorrows; here TODAY, gone tomorrow; he that FALLS today may rise tomorrow; I today, you tomorrow; JAM tomorrow and jam yesterday, but never jam today; NEVER put off till tomorrow what you can do today; ONE today is worth two tomorrows; TODAY a man, tomorrow none; TODAY you, tomorrow me; what MANCHESTER says today, the rest of England says tomorrow; WORK today for you know not how much you may be hindered tomorrow.

tongue. let not your tongue cut your throat (*English*) Refrain from saying something that might harm your own interests. H.G. Bohn, *A Handbook of Proverbs*, 1855. Variants include 'let not thy tongue run away with thy brains' and 'the tongue talks at the head's cost'. Another proverb emphasizes the virtues of silence in the form 'keep your tongue between your teeth'.

the tongue ever turns to the aching tooth (*English*) A person's attention will always be diverted to whatever irritates them the most. George Pettie, *Guazzo's Civil Conversation*, 1581.

the tongue is not steel yet it cuts (*English*) A person may make a sharp impression with the words he or she speaks. Geoffrey Chaucer, *The Canterbury Tales*, *c.*1387. Variants include 'the tongue breaketh bone and herself hath none' and 'a tart temper never mellows with age; and a sharp tongue is the only edged tool that grows keener with constant use'.

the tongue is the rudder of our ship (*Italian*) The course that a person's life takes depends very much upon what they say. G. Torriano, *Select Italian Proverbs*, 1664.

~ *See also* ARTHUR could not tame a woman's tongue; a BLISTER will rise upon one's tongue that tells a lie; a BRIDLE for the tongue is a necessary piece of furniture; CHILDREN have wide ears and long tongues; the DEVIL makes his Christmas pies of lawyers' tongues and clerks' fingers; the EFFECT speaks, the tongue needs not; a FALSE tongue hardly speaks truth; a FOOL's tongue is long enough to cut his own throat; a GOOD tongue is a good weapon; he cannot SPEAK well that cannot hold his tongue; he that has not SILVER in his purse should have silk on his tongue; he that KNOWS not how to hold his tongue, knows not how to talk; the LAME tongue gets nothing; a LONG tongue is a sign of a short hand; a QUIET tongue makes a wise head; a STILL tongue makes a wise head; WIDE ears and a short tongue; a WISE head makes a still tongue; a WOMAN's strength is in her tongue.

tool. *See* a BAD workman blames his tools; CHILDREN and fools must not play with edged tools; it is ILL jesting with edged tools; what is a WORKMAN without his tools?

tooth. *See* CAST a bone in the devil's teeth; an EYE for an eye, and a tooth for a tooth; FOLLOW not truth too near the heels, lest it dash out thy teeth; the GODS send nuts to those who have no teeth; if you cannot BITE, never show your teeth; THREE things are not to be trusted: a cow's horn, a dog's tooth and a horse's hoof; the TONGUE ever turns to the aching tooth.

toothache. *See* MUSIC helps not the toothache.

top. *See* there is ALWAYS room at the top; too MANY boatmen will run the boat up to the top of the mountain; TRUTH and sweet oil always come to the top.

topsail. *See* if the RAIN comes before the wind, lower your topsails and take them in; if the wind comes before the rain, lower your topsails and hoist them again.

tortoise. the tortoise wins the race while the hare is sleeping (*English*) Those who set about a task slowly but surely may overtake those who take a rest before rushing at it. William Thackeray, *Pendennis*, 1850 (referring to Aesop's fable about the race between a tortoise and a hare in which the tortoise overtakes the hare while the latter is asleep).

touch. he that touches pitch shall be defiled (*Hebrew*) Those who mix with bad company are bound to be tainted themselves. Apocrypha, Ecclesiasticus 13:1. *See also* if you PLAY with fire you get burnt.

> 'There,' John would add, 'you can't touch pitch and not be mucked.'
>
> Robert Louis Stevenson, *Treasure Island*, 1883

touch wood, it's sure to come good (*English*) Potential misfortune may be avoided by touching wood without delay. R. Anderson, *Ballads in Cumberland Dialect*, 1805. This ancient superstition may go back to pagan tree worship, reinforced by reverence for the wooden Cross on which Christ was crucified. Tradition has it that it is not enough just to say the words, but that wood (preferably that of the sacred oak or ash) should actually be touched – though this stipulation is often ignored nowadays.

~ *See also* if you GENTLY touch a nettle it'll sting you for your pains; you should NEVER touch your eye but with your elbow.

tough. *See* OLD and tough, young and tender; when the GOING gets tough, the tough get going.

town. *See* BONES bring meat to town; GOD made the country, and man made the town; MISUNDERSTANDING brings lies to town; NEW church, old steeple, poor town and proud people; there was NEVER a good town but had a mire at one end of it.

trade. trade follows the flag (*English*) The expansion of national influence around the world will be rewarded by increased opportunities for trade. J.A. Froude, *Fraser's Magazine*, 1870. Many observers have refuted the accuracy of the proverb, alleging that the reverse is more usually true, with national influence being achieved through increased trade. Related proverbs include 'the flag protects the cargo'.

trade is the mother of money (*English*) There are always fortunes to be made through trade. T. Draxe, *Bibliotheca Scholastica*, 1633. Related proverbs include 'a handful of trade is worth a handful of gold' and the Yiddish 'a trade is a shield against poverty'.

~ *See also* EVERY man to his trade; JACK of all trades is master of none; a MAN of many trades begs his bread on Sunday; there are TRICKS in every trade; there is KNAVERY in all trades; TWO of a trade never agree.

traitor. *See* the TREASON is loved but the traitor is hated.

tramp. tramp on a snail and she'll shoot out her horns (*English*) Even the most humble and ineffectual will show their resentment of ill treatment. James Kelly, *A Complete Collection of Scotish Proverbs*, 1721.

~ *See also* the MORE you tramp on a turd the broader it grows.

trap. *See* it is EASY to fall into a trap but hard to get out again.

trash and trumpery is the highway to beggary (*English*) Those who spend lavishly on fine clothing and other luxuries will beggar themselves. John Ray, *A Collection of English Proverbs*, 1678.

travel (noun). **travel broadens the mind** (*English*) Exposure to different cultures, peoples and landscapes is always educational. Anthony Powell, *Venusberg*, 1933. Another proverb supports this view 'he that travels knows much', but another questions the worth of travel, thus: 'travel makes a wise man better, but a fool worse'. An old Roman proverb, meanwhile, observes that 'a man need not go away from home for instruction', while the Greeks advise 'see one mountain, one sea, one river, and see all'.

travel (verb). **he travels fastest who travels alone** (*English*) A traveller who goes without companions will experience fewer delays. Henry David Thoreau, *Walden, or Life in the Woods*, 1854.

> Down to Gehenna, or up to the Throne,
> He travels fastest who travels alone.
> Rudyard Kipling, *The Story of Gadsby*, 1888

~ *See also* BAD news travels fast; it is BETTER to travel hopefully than to arrive; a LIE travels around the world while truth is putting on her boots; SOUND travelling far and wide a stormy day will betide.

traveller. a traveller may lie with authority (*English*) Those who have travelled extensively may boast of their exploits without fear of contradiction. William Langland, *Piers Plowman*, *c.*1362. *See also* SOLDIERS and travellers may lie by authority.

> A good traveller is something at the latter end
> of a dinner; but one that lies three thirds ... should
> be once heard and thrice beaten.
> William Shakespeare, *All's Well That Ends Well*, *c.*1602

travellers change climates not conditions (*Roman*) Those who travel abroad may change their surroundings, but not their character. Thomas Fuller, *Church History of Britain*, 1655 (quoting Horace). Another Roman equivalent was 'they change their sky, not their soul, who run beyond the sea'. Much the same point is made by two English proverbs that run 'if an ass goes travelling he'll not come home a horse' and 'the crow went travelling abroad and came home just as black'.

~ *See also* EVENING red and morning grey help the traveller on his way; SOLDIERS and travellers may lie by authority.

travelling. *See* AGE can be a bad travelling companion.

treacherous. *See* CIDER is treacherous because it smiles in the face and then cuts the throat.

tread. *See* the BLACK ox treads on one's foot; FOOLS rush in where angels fear to tread; if a MAN once fall, all will tread on him; the more CAMOMILE is trodden on, the faster it grows; NEVER tread on a sore toe.

treason. the treason is loved but the traitor is hated (*Roman*) Traitors have no friends, even among those who stand to profit by their treason. C. Brooke, *Richard III*, 1614 (quoting Tacitus). On the other hand, another proverb of US origin observes that 'the successful traitor becomes a hero'.

> Hate then the traitor, but yet love the treason.
> John Dryden and Nathaniel Lee, *The Duke of Guise*, 1683

treasure. *See* MEMORY is the treasure of the mind.

tree. as a tree falls, so shall it lie (*Hebrew*) A person's ultimate end depends on the kind of life they have lead. Bible, Ecclesiastes 11:3.

> Where the tree falleth there it lyeth ... and every ones deathes daye is his domes day.
> John Lyly, *Euphues: The Anatomy of Wit*, 1578

if on the trees the leaves still hold, the coming winter will be cold (*English*) If leaves remain on the trees late into the autumn this is a sure sign of a severe winter to come. M. Stevenson, *Twelve Moneths*, 1661. Another proverb insists that if leaves show their undersides rain should be expected shortly.

like tree, like fruit (*English*) The quality of the fruit that a tree produces depends upon the quality of the tree itself. Geoffrey Chaucer, *The Canterbury Tales*, *c.*1387.

> Such as the tree is, such is the fruit.
> John Ray, *A Collection of English Proverbs*, 1670

the tree falls not at the first blow (*Italian*) Great feats are not accomplished at a single stroke. G. Torriano, *Piazza universale di proverbi italiani*, 1666.

the tree is known by its fruit (*Hebrew*) A person, organization, idea or other entity may be judged by the results that flow as a consequence. Bible, Matthew 12:33. Related proverbs include 'there is no tree but bears fruit'.

> If then the tree may be known by the fruit ... there is virtue in that Falstaff.
> William Shakespeare, *Henry IV, Part 1*, *c.*1597

when the tree is fallen, all go with their hatchet (*Greek*) Many people will gather round where there is hope of possible gain for little effort. George Pettie, *Guazzo's Civil Conversation*, 1581 (also quoted by Menander).

~ *See also* the APPLE never falls far from the tree; as the TWIG is bent, so is the tree inclined; a GOOD tree brings forth good fruit; GREAT trees keep down little ones; he that would EAT the fruit must climb the tree; he will SHOOT higher who shoots at the moon than he who aims at a tree; the HIGHER the tree, the sweeter the plum; put not thy HAND between the bark and the tree; RAIN on the green grass, and rain on the tree, and rain on the house-top, but not upon me; REMOVE an old tree and it will die; a WOMAN, a dog and a walnut tree, the more you beat them the better they be; you cannot SHIFT an old tree without it dying.

trencher. *See* LITTLE and good fills the trencher.

trial. *See* he whose FATHER is judge goes safe to his trial; TRUTH fears no trial.

trick. there are tricks in every trade (*English*) There are ways to cheat in every trade and occupation. M. Parker, *Knavery in all Trades*, 1632. Related proverbs include 'every monkey has his tricks'.

~ *See also* you can't TEACH an old dog new tricks.

tries, tried. *See* TRY.

trim tram, like master like man (*English*) Employees and servants tend to behave as their masters do. Thomas Middleton and William Rowley, *A Fair Quarrel*, 1617.

trip. *See* a SHOE too large trips you up.

trodden. *See* TREAD.

trot. *See* the DOG that trots about finds a bone; he that RISETH late must trot all day.

trouble (noun)**. a trouble shared is a trouble halved** (*English*) Talking through your troubles with others makes them seem less daunting. Dorothy L. Sayers, *Five Red Herrings*, 1931.

~ *See also* a CLEAR conscience can bear any trouble; he that hath a WHITE horse and a fair wife is never without trouble; NEEDLES and pins, needles and pins, when a man marries his trouble begins; NEVER trouble trouble till trouble troubles you.

trouble (verb). *See* it is GOOD fishing in troubled waters; NEVER trouble trouble till trouble troubles you.

true. true blue will never stain (*English*) True honesty and integrity will never be corrupted. *Roxburghe Ballads*, *c.*1630. The colour blue is traditionally associated with the Virgin Mary, herself deemed incorruptible. More likely, however, is the suggestion that the proverb is derived from the blue aprons worn by butchers, which, being dark in colour, tend not to show bloodstains. Variants include 'true blood may not lie'.

~ *See also* the COURSE of true love never did run smooth; FRIDAY night's dream on the Saturday told, is sure to come true be it never so old; LATE repentance is seldom true; MORNING dreams come true; there's MANY a true word spoken in jest; what EVERYBODY says must be true; what is NEW cannot be true.

truly. a truly great man never puts away the simplicity of a child (*Chinese*) The wise man preserves the inquiring innocence of the young.

trump. *See* CLUBS are trumps.

trumpery. *See* TRASH and trumpery is the highway to beggary.

trumpeter. *See* a DRY cough is the trumpeter of death.

truss. *See* ANYONE can kill a trussed foe.

trust (noun). **put not your trust in princes** (*Hebrew*) Rulers are but men beneath all their pomp, and no more to be trusted than any other men. Bible, Psalms 46:3.

put your trust in God and keep your powder dry (*English*) Put your faith in God to help you out of difficulty, but to be on the safe side also make preparations to intervene more actively to defend your interests. Colonel Blacker, *Oliver's Advice*, 1834. Commonly attributed to the English Parliamentarian leader Oliver Cromwell, addressing troops under his command during a river crossing at the time of the English Civil War. A more recent, equally down-to-earth, version of the old proverb was voiced during the Japanese attack on Pearl Harbor in the Second World War, when an unidentified chaplain in the US navy is alleged to have exhorted fellow-sailors with the words 'praise the Lord and pass the ammunition'. Another variation was repeated during the same conflict between Londoners who, realizing that German buzz bombs fell shortly after their engines cut out, would pray 'praise the Lord and keep the engine running'.

trust is the mother of deceit (*English*) When a person puts their trust in someone else the other person may be tempted to betray that trust. *Romaunce of the Rose*, *c.*1400. Similar thoughts are expressed in the proverbs 'he who trusteth not is not deceived' and 'in trust is treason'.

> My trust, like a good parent, did beget of him a
> falsehood in its contrary as great as my trust was.
> William Shakespeare, *The Tempest*, *c.*1610

trust (verb). **if you trust before you try, you may repent before you die** (*English*) Never trust those of whom you are not certain. *c.*1560, quoted in Huth, *Ancient Ballads*, 1867. Also heard in the more succinct form 'try before you trust'.

trust not a new friend nor an old enemy (*English*) Never place your trust in those you hardly know or in those with whom you were once on bad terms. *Ballad*, 1450. Variants include 'trust not the praise of a friend nor the contempt of an enemy'.

trust not one night's ice (*English*) It is unwise to put much faith in something that is only of very recent origin and has yet to be proved reliable. George Herbert, *Outlandish Proverbs*, 1651.

~ *See also* FIRST try and then trust; NEVER trust a tailor that does not sing at his work; THREE things are not to be trusted: a cow's horn, a dog's tooth and a horse's hoof.

truth. there is truth in wine (*Greek*) Wine encourages those who drink it to reveal truths they might otherwise keep hidden. R. Taverner, *Proverbs or Adages with New Additions, gathered out of the Chiliades of Erasmus*, 1545. Often attributed to Alcaeus.

> There is no saying truer than that ... there is
> truth in wine. Wine ... has the merit of forcing
> a man to show his true colours.
> Anthony Trollope, *He Knew He Was Right*, 1869

truth and sweet oil always come to the top (*Spanish*) The truth, like oil on water, always rises to the surface. George Herbert, *Outlandish Proverbs*, 1640. Also encountered as 'truth and oil are ever above'.

truth fears no trial (*English*) What is true will withstand all tests. William Shakespeare, *Love's Labour's Lost*, *c.*1594. Variants include 'truth fears no colours'. Among related proverbs is 'truth is truth to the end of the reckoning'.

> Sir, I will be as good as my word ... Fear no colours.
>
> William Shakespeare, *Henry IV, Part 2*, *c.*1598

truth has a scratched face (*English*) The truth attracts many critics. John Lyly, *Campaspe*, 1584. Related proverbs include 'truth finds foes where it should find none'. Those who tell the truth are warned by an Italian proverb 'he who would speak the truth must keep a sharp lookout, while a Turkish saying has it that 'he that speaks the truth must have one foot in the stirrup'.

truth is no slander (*English*) Criticism of another must be allowed if it is true. B. Melbancke, *Philotimus*, 1583.

> But that slander, sir, is found a truth now.
>
> William Shakespeare, *Henry VIII*, *c.*1612

truth is stranger than fiction (*Roman*) What happens in real life can be much more extraordinary than anything that would be countenanced by writers of fiction. Lord Byron, *Don Juan*, 1823. *See also* FACT is stranger than fiction.

> 'Tis strange – but true; for truth is always strange, –
> Stranger than fiction.
>
> Lord Byron, *Don Juan*, 1823

truth lies at the bottom of a well (*Greek*) The truth is often to be found deep down, well hidden. J. Wigand, *De Neutralibus*, 1562 (also quoted by Diogenes Laertius and Cicero). The proverb is often attributed to Democritus. Variants include the Greek 'nature has buried truth at the bottom of the sea'. A contrary view is expressed by the proverb 'truth lies on the surface of things'.

> Whilst the unlearned ... were all busied in getting down to the bottom of the well, where Truth keeps her little court ...
>
> Laurence Sterne, *Tristram Shandy*, 1758

truth's best ornament is nakedness (*English*) The truth is best delivered without any ornamentation. Thomas Fuller, *Gnomologia*, 1732. Also encountered in the form 'the truth shows best being naked'.

truth should not always be revealed (*English*) Sometimes it is for the best to keep the truth hidden. Thomas Usk, *The Testament of Love*, *c.*1387. Variants include 'all truth is not to be told at all times' and the French 'some truths are not for all men at all times'.

truth will out (*English*) The truth will always come out in the end. John Lydgate, *The Life of St Alban*, 1439. Variants include 'truth will prevail', 'truth and sweet oil always come to the top' and 'truth will sometimes break out, unlooked for'. *See also* MURDER will out.

> Truth will come to light; murder cannot be hid long; a man's son may, but in the end truth will out.
>
> William Shakespeare, *The Merchant of Venice*, *c.*1596

~ *See also* CHILDREN and fools tell the truth; CRAFT must have clothes but truth loves to go naked; DEEM the best till the truth be tried; FACE to face the truth comes out; a FALSE tongue hardly speaks truth; FOLLOW not truth too near the heels, lest it dash out thy teeth; FOOLS and madmen speak the truth; the GREATER the truth, the greater the libel; HALF the truth is often a whole lie; in too MUCH dispute truth is lost; it takes a GOOD many shovelfuls of earth to bury the truth; a LIAR is not believed when he speaks the truth; a LIE travels around the world while truth is putting on her boots; the STING of a reproach is the truth of it; TELL the truth and shame the devil; a THOUSAND probabilities do not make one truth.

try. try your skill in gilt first and then in gold (*English*) When learning a new trade or other profession it is best to start modestly before taking bigger risks. J. Clarke, *Paroemiographia Anglo-Latina*, 1639.

> Practise new and doubtful experiments in cheap commodities, or upon things of small value.
>
> John Ray, *A Collection of English Proverbs*, 1670

~ *See also* BUSINESS makes a man as well as tries him; DEEM the best till the truth be tried; FIRST try and then trust; if at FIRST you don't succeed, try, try, try again; if you TRUST before you try, you may repent before you die; TIME tries all things; you NEVER know what you can do till you try.

tub. *See* EVERY tub must stand on its own bottom.

Tuesday. *See* MONDAY's child is fair of face, Tuesday's child is full of grace; Wednesday's child is full of woe, Thursday's child has far to go; Friday's child is loving and giving, Saturday's child works hard for its living; and the child that's born on the Sabbath day, is fair and wise and good and gay.

tug. *See* when GREEK meets Greek, then comes the tug of war.

tumble. *See* an UNHAPPY man's cart is eith to tumble.

tumult. *See* KEEP yourself from the anger of a great man, from the tumult of a mob, from a man of ill fame, from a widow that has been thrice married, from a wind that comes in at a hole, and from a reconciled enemy.

tune. *See* CALM weather in June sets corn in tune; a DRIPPING June sets all in tune; he that LIVES in hope dances to an ill tune; he who BATHES in May will soon be laid in clay, he who bathes in June will sing a merry tune, he who bathes in July will dance like a fly; he who PAYS the piper calls the tune; there's MANY a good tune played on an old fiddle; when the FURZE is in bloom, my love's in tune; why should the DEVIL have all the best tunes?

turf. on the turf all men are equal, and under it (*English*) All men are equal on the racecourse, and in the grave. Robert Smith Surtees, *Handley Cross*, 1854.

turd. *See* the MORE you tramp on a turd the broader it grows.

turkey. turkey, heresy, hops and beer came into England all in one year (*English*) Legend has it that turkeys, hops and beer, and with them heresy, were all imported to England in the same year – according to some, in 1524. H. Buttes, *Diet's Dry Dinner*, 1599. Variants add carp and pike to the list. In fact there seems to be little historical basis for the tradition, hops for instance having come centuries earlier with the Romans.

~ *See also* on SAINT Thomas the Divine kill all turkeys, geese and swine.

turn (noun). **turn about is fair play** (*English*) As long as each party gets their turn, then the rules of fair play are deemed to be satisfied. *The Life of Captain Dudley Bradstreet*, 1755.

> You had your chance then; seems to me it's mine now. Turn about's fair play.
> Robert Louis Stevenson, *The Wrecker*, 1892

~ *See also* he that does you an ILL turn will never forgive you; an ILL turn is soon done; one GOOD turn deserves another; one NEVER loses by doing a good turn.

turn (verb). *See* a BAD penny always turns up; CLERGYMEN's sons always turn out badly; CLOUDY mornings turn to clear afternoons; even a WORM will turn; a FOUL morning may turn to a fair day; IDLENESS turns the edge of wit; it is a LONG lane that has no turning; it is HARD to turn tack upon a narrow bridge; a SOFT answer turneth away wrath; the TONGUE ever turns to the aching tooth.

turncoat. *See* WINE is a turncoat.

turnips like a dry bed but a wet head (*English*) Turnips thrive in well-drained ground. J.C. Bridge, *Cheshire Proverbs*, 1917.

twelve. *See* it is not SPRING until you can plant your foot upon twelve daisies.

twenty. *See* BETTER give a penny than lend twenty; he that CHASTENS one chastens twenty; he that is not HANDSOME at twenty, wise at forty and rich at fifty, will never be rich, wise or handsome; ONE acre of performance is worth twenty of the Land of Promise.

twenty-four. there are only twenty-four hours in the day (*English*) There is a limit to how much can be achieved in the course of a day's work. V.S. Lean, *Collecteana*, 1902–04.

~ *See also* if it RAINS when the wind is in the east, it will rain for twenty-four hours at least.

twice. *See* BUTTER is mad twice a year; CABBAGE twice cooked is death; a GOOD tale is none the worse for being twice told; he COMPLAINS wrongfully on the sea who twice suffers shipwreck; he GIVES twice who gives quickly; he that DINES and leaves lays the cloth twice; if a MAN deceive me once, shame on him, but if he deceive me twice, shame on me; it is a

SILLY fish that is caught twice with the same bait; LIGHTNING never strikes the same place twice; OLD men are twice children; on a GOOD bargain, think twice; ONCE bitten, twice shy; ONCE nought, twice somewhat; OPPORTUNITY seldom knocks twice at any man's door; SCORE twice before you cut once; take HEED of reconciled enemies and of meat twice boiled; WELL done is twice done; a WISE woman is twice a fool.

twig. as the twig is bent, so is the tree inclined (*English*) By influencing someone or something at an early age it is possible to influence how they develop later on (just as a tree will grow in the direction in which it is trained as a sapling). Alexander Pope, *Epistles to Several Persons*, 1732. A Scottish version runs 'thraw the wand while it is green'. Related proverbs concerning trees include 'a tree falls the way it leans'. *See also* GIVE me a child for the first seven years, and you may do what you like with him afterwards.

> 'Tis Education forms the common mind,
> Just as the Twig is bent, the Tree's inclined.
> Alexander Pope, *Epistles to Several Persons*, 1732

two. if two ride on a horse, one must ride behind (*English*) If two people participate in an enterprise together one inevitably must take the lead. William Shakespeare, *Much Ado About Nothing*, *c.*1598.

> An two men ride of a horse, one must ride behind.
> William Shakespeare, *Much Ado About Nothing*, *c.*1598

it takes two to make a bargain (*English*) The agreement of both sides must be obtained before any bargain can be sealed. John Lyly, *Euphues and His England*, 1580.

> 'Hold, hold, Sir,' cried Jenkinson, 'there are two words to that bargain.'
> Oliver Goldsmith, *The Vicar of Wakefield*, 1766

it takes two to make a quarrel (*English*) There can be no argument unless at least two parties disagree. J. Stevens, *Spanish and English Dictionary*, 1706.

> There must always be two parties to a quarrel, says the old adage.
> Charles Dickens, *Oliver Twist*, 1838

it takes two to tango (*US*) Many activities, including dancing the tango, necessarily require the participation of two people. Hofmann and Manning, 'Takes Two to Tango', 1952.

> There are lots of things you can do alone,
> But it takes two to tango.
> Hofmann and Manning, 'Takes Two to Tango', 1952

of two disputants the warmer is generally in the wrong (*English*) When two people argue it is likely to be the person who argues loudest who is mistaken. Charles Lamb, *Elia*, 1826.

of two evils choose the lesser (*Greek*) When faced with a choice of two unattractive alternatives, select the less risky course. Aristotle, *Nicomachean Ethics*, *c.*335BC. Plutarch turned the proverb to comic use in telling the story of a Spartan who, obliged to marry, chose a small wife, explaining he was thereby choosing the lesser of two evils. The proverb is found in several European languages. One Hebrew variant runs 'he is not called wise who knows good and ill, but he who can recognize of two evils the lesser'. Film star Mae West famously added her own version of the proverb when she quipped 'whenever I'm caught between two evils, I take the one I've never tried'.

> Since it is the lesser evil of the two, it is to be preferred.
> Henry Fielding, *The Temple Beau*, 1730

there are two sides to every question (*Greek*) There are always two ways of looking at things in any debate. Joseph Addison, *The Spectator*, 1711 (also quoted by Diogenes Laertius in the third century BC and attributed by him to Protagoras two centuries before that).

> Let them recollect this, that there are two sides to every question, and a downhill as well as an uphill road.
> Charles Kingsley, *The Water Babies*, 1863

two and two make four (*English*) Logic dictates that something must be so, despite all attempts to prove otherwise. Jeremy Collier, *Essays on Moral Subjects*, 1697.

> Even in the valley of the shadow of death two and two do not make six.
> Leo Tolstoy, attributed on his death when reconciliation with the Church was suggested, 1910

two blacks don't make a white (*English*) A wrong deed cannot be justified on the grounds that this is not the first time such a crime has been committed. James Kelly, *A Complete Collection of Scotish Proverbs*, 1721.

See also TWO wrongs don't make a right.

> But whatever satisfaction the pot may have in calling the kettle blacker than itself the two blacks do not make a white.
>
> George Bernard Shaw, *The Intelligent Woman's Guide to Socialism and Capitalism*, 1928

two boys are half a boy, and three boys are no boy at all (*English*) The greater the number of boys that help in doing something, the less effective their assistance becomes. Flora Thompson, *Country Calendar*, *c.*1930. *See also* too many COOKS spoil the broth.

> Their parents do not encourage the joining of forces ... we have a proverb here: 'Two boys are half a boy, and three boys are no boy at all.'
>
> Flora Thompson, *Country Calendar*, *c.*1930

two cats and a mouse, two wives in one house, two dogs and a bone, never agree in one (*English*) There can be no agreement between two cats, two wives, or two dogs when they have something to fight over. John Ray, *A Collection of English Proverbs*, 1670. Related proverbs include 'two kings in one kingdom do not agree well together' and 'two sparrows on one ear of corn make an ill agreement'.

two daughters and a back door are three arrant thieves (*English*) The wealth of a household can quickly disappear via spendthrift daughters and dishonest servants. David Fergusson, *Scottish Proverbs*, 1641.

two dogs fight for a bone, and a third runs away with it (*English*) While two parties quarrel over something, a third party may find the opportunity to snatch what is argued over for themselves. Geoffrey Chaucer, *The Canterbury Tales*, *c.*1387.

> I pray you, sirs, list to Esop's talk: Whilest two stout dogs were striving for a bone, There comes a cur and stole it from them both.
>
> *Arden of Feversham*, 1592

two fools in a house are too many (*English*) No household will prosper where both husband and wife are fools. John Lyly, *Euphues and His England*, 1580. Also encountered in the form 'two fools in a bed are too many'.

> Two Fools in a House are too many by a Couple.
>
> Thomas Fuller, *Gnomologia*, 1732

two heads are better than one (*Greek*) When two people apply themselves to a problem they are more likely to come up with a solution than one person tackling it alone. John Gower, *Confessio Amantis*, *c.*1390 (also quoted by Homer). Fuller versions of the proverb run 'two heads are better than one – or why do folks marry?', 'two heads are better than one, even if the one's a sheep's' and 'two heads are better than one quoth the woman when she had her dog with her to the market'. Formerly also found in the form 'two have more wit than one' and occasionally encountered as 'two eyes can see more than one'. *See also* FOUR eyes see more than two; too MANY cooks spoil the broth.

> Here comes brother Thomas; two heads are better than one; let us take his opinion.
>
> Samuel Foote, *The Nabob*, 1778

two in distress makes sorrow less (*English*) It is easier to cope with distress when there is someone else to share it with. H.G. Bohn, *A Handbook of Proverbs*, 1855.

two negatives make an affirmative (*English*) Two negatives cancel each other out. G. Harvey, *Works*, 1593.

two of a trade never agree (*Greek*) Different practitioners in the same trade will always be at odds with each other. Thomas Dekker, *The Honest Whore, Part 2*, *c.*1605 (also quoted by Hesiod in *Works and Days*).

> It is a common rule, and 'tis most true,
> Two of one trade never love: no more do you.
>
> Thomas Dekker, *The Honest Whore, Part 2*, 1630

two things a man should never be angry at: what he can help and what he cannot help (*English*) Anger is futile both when something can be done and when nothing can be done. Thomas Fuller, *Gnomologia*, 1732.

two wrongs don't make a right (*English*) Committing an offence on the grounds that this is not the first time the offence has been committed or that it is retaliation for some other wrong is not a legitimate defence. B. Rush, letter, 2 August 1783. Representing another view of affairs is the contrasting 'two negatives make an affirmative', which was quoted by William Shakespeare in *Twelfth Night* in 1601. *See also* TWO blacks don't make a white.

two's company, three's a crowd (*English*) Two people may enjoy a flourishing, intimate relationship, but the presence of a third party might hinder such enjoyment. John Heywood, *A Dialogue containing ... the*

Proverbs in the English Tongue, 1546. Usually quoted by lovers whose privacy is threatened by the unwanted presence of a third person. A less well-known proverb relates to somewhat larger numbers, observing 'seven make a banquet, nine a riot'. Also found in the form 'two is company, but three is none'. *See also* SEVEN may be company but nine are confusion.

when two friends have a common purse one sings and the other weeps (*English*) When two people share their money one of them is bound to do better out of it than the other. J. Mapletoft, *Select Proverbs*, 1707.

you cannot have two forenoons in the same day (*English*) It is impossible for the old to live their youth over again (commonly quoted when an elderly person regrets the physical infirmities that accompany old age). *Notes & Queries*, 1854.

~ *See also* BETTER one house spoiled than two; BETWEEN two stools you fall to the ground; a BIRD in the hand is worth two in the bush; BREAD and cheese be two targets against death; a DWARF on a giant's shoulders sees further of the two; EVERY mile is two in winter; FOUR eyes see more than two; GOOD riding at two anchors; if you can't RIDE two horses at once, you shouldn't be in the circus; if you RUN after two hares you will catch neither; it is EASIER to build two chimneys than to maintain one; JEALOUSY shuts one door and opens two; a MOUSE in time may bite in two a cable; no MAN can serve two masters; not even HERCULES could contend against two; ONE bad general is better than two good ones; ONE for sorrow, two for joy; three for a girl, four for a boy; five for silver, six for gold; seven for a secret, never to be told; eight for heaven, nine for hell; and ten for the devil's own self; ONE hour's sleep before midnight is worth two after; ONE pair of heels is often worth two pairs of hands; ONE today is worth two tomorrows; ONE volunteer is worth two pressed men; a SPUR in the head is worth two in the heel; THREE may keep a secret, if two of them are dead; what MAINTAINS one vice would bring up two children; while the THUNDER lasted two bad men were friends; who hath a FAIR wife needs more than two eyes.

twopence. *See* a PENNY soul never came to twopence.

tyrant. *See* 'tis TIME to fear when tyrants seem to kiss.

U

unasked. *See* FLIES come to feasts unasked.

unbidden. an unbidden guest knoweth not where to sit (*English*) A person who arrives uninvited should not expect necessarily to be welcomed as a guest. John Heywood, *A Dialogue containing ... the Proverbs in the English Tongue*, 1546. Variants include 'an unbidden guest must bring his stool with him' and 'who comes uncalled, sits unserved.'

> An unbidden guest
> Should travel as Dutchwomen go to church,
> Bear their stools with them.
> John Webster, *The White Devil*, 1612

uncalled. *See* come not to COUNSEL uncalled.

uncertain. *See* CHILDREN are certain cares but uncertain comforts.

uncle. *See* CALL the bear 'uncle' till you are safe across the bridge; if my AUNT had been a man, she'd have been my uncle.

unconquered. *See* SKILL and confidence are an unconquered army.

under. *See* ANYTHING may be spoken if it be under the rose; the BEST manure is under the farmer's foot.

understand. who understands ill answers ill (*English*) Those who misunderstand what is being said cannot be expected to reply wisely. Nathan Bailey, *An Universal Etymological English Dictionary*, 1736. Related proverbs include 'who wrong hears, wrong answer gives', 'ill hearing makes ill rehearsing' and 'misunderstanding brings lies to town'.

~ *See* that is not GOOD language which all understand not.

understanding. *See* with the ANCIENT is wisdom, and in the length of days understanding.

undone. *See* THINGS done cannot be undone; what's DONE cannot be undone.

unexpected. the unexpected always happens (*Roman*) The unforeseen is bound to come to pass. E.J. Hardy, *How to be Happy though Married*, 1885 (also found in the writings of Plautus). Variants include 'the unlooked for often comes'. *See also* NOTHING is certain but the unforeseen.

unforeseen. *See* NOTHING is certain but the unforeseen.

unhappy. an unhappy man's cart is eith to tumble (*Scottish*) An unfortunate person is more vulnerable to things going wrong. David Fergusson, *Scottish Proverbs*, 1641.

union is strength (*Greek*) Those who work together will find they have more influence than if they work separately. R. Williams, *Complete Writings*, 1654 (also found in Homer's *Iliad* and attributed to Periander, the tyrant of Corinth in the sixth century BC). Also encountered as 'unity is strength'. *See also* UNITED we stand, divided we fall.

> This union shall do more than battery can to our fast-closed gates.
> William Shakespeare, *King John*, *c.*1595

unite. *See* WOES unite foes.

united. united we stand, divided we fall (*US*) Those who stand together will remain strong, while those who quarrel among themselves will never prosper. John Dickinson, 'Liberty Song', 1768. The slogan was taken up by American troops during the War of Independence and it later became the motto of the US state of Kentucky. *See also* a HOUSE divided against itself cannot stand; UNION is strength.

> Then join Hand in Hand brave Americans all,
> By uniting we stand, by dividing we fall.
> John Dickinson, 'Liberty Song', 1768

unjust. *See* a JUST war is better than an unjust peace.

unknown. *See* no SAFE wading in an unknown water.

unlawful. an unlawful oath is better broken than kept (*English*) Oaths that threaten illegal or evil consequences are better abandoned rather than observed. John Ray, *A Collection of English Proverbs*, 1670.

unlearned. *See* PICTURES are the books of the unlearned.

unlikeliest places are often likelier than those that are likeliest (*English*) It is often in the least likeliest place that the solution is to be found. Dr Bridge, *Cheshire Proverbs*, 1917.

unlucky. *See* LUCKY at cards, unlucky in love.

unpunished. *See* no BAD deed goes unpunished.

unsent. *See* SORROW comes unsent for.

unsought. *See* it is LOST that is unsought.

untaught. *See* BETTER untaught than ill taught.

until. *See* BLESSINGS are not valued until they are gone.

untoward. an untoward boy may make a good man (*English*) An unruly youth may yet grow into a worthy man. Robert Greene, *Works*, 1592. The equivalent version for girls runs 'an untoward girl may make a good woman'.

unturned. *See* LEAVE no stone unturned.

up. what goes up must come down (*English/US*) Nature dictates that all things must in time be brought back down to earth. L.I. Wilder, *By the Shores of Silver Lake*, 1939.

upright. *See* EMPTY sacks will never stand upright.

use (noun)**. it's no use crying over spilt milk** (*English*) There is no point lamenting over some setback when there is nothing that can be done about it. J. Howell, *Paroemiographia*, 1659. Originally given as 'no weeping for shed milk'.

~ *See also* KEEP a thing seven years and you'll always find a use for it.

use (verb)**. a used key is always bright** (*English*) Constant use of something keeps it in good repair. Benjamin Franklin, *The Way to Wealth*, 1736. The proverb is sometimes quoted in condemning laziness or sloth. **use legs and have legs** (*English*) The body (and many other things beside) profits from regular use. G. Harvey, *Marginalia*, 1913.

> Use Legges, and have Legges: Use Law and have Law.
> Use nether and have nether.
> G. Harvey, *Marginalia*, 1913

~ *See also* INJURIES don't use to be written on ice; IRON not used soon rusts; an OLD cart, well used, may last out a new one abused.

V

vacuum. *See* NATURE abhors a vacuum.

vain. it is in vain to cast your net where there is no fish (*English*) There is no point speculating where there is nothing to be gained. Thomas Fuller, *Gnomologia*, 1732.

in vain the net is spread in the sight of the bird (*Hebrew*) It is futile setting a trap in sight of the proposed victim. Bible, Proverbs 1:17.

~ *See also* if APPLES bloom in March, in vain for them you'll search; if apples bloom in April, then they'll be plentiful; if apples bloom in May, you may eat them night and day; NATURE does nothing in vain.

valet. *See* no MAN is a hero to his valet.

valiant. *See* NECESSITY and opportunity may make a coward valiant.

valley. *See* he that STAYS in the valley shall never get over the hill.

valour. *See* DISCRETION is the better part of valour,

value. *See* BLESSINGS are not valued until they are gone; HEALTH is not valued till sickness comes.

variety is the spice of life (*English*) A wide range of experience or interests enriches life. William Cowper, *The Task*, 1784.

Variety's the very spice of life,
That gives it all its flavour. We have run
Through every change that fancy at the loom,
Exhausted, has had genius to supply.
William Cowper, *The Task*, 1784

varlet. *See* an APE's an ape, a varlet's a varlet, though they be clad in silk or scarlet.

veal. *See* the GREATEST calf is not the sweetest veal.

vengeance. *See* the NOBLEST vengeance is to forgive.

venison. *See* ALL flesh is not venison; GENTLEMEN and rich men are venison in heaven.

venture. venture not all in one bottom (*English*) Do not risk everything you have at once; do not put all your eggs in one basket. J. Clarke, *Paroemiologia Anglo-Latina*, 1639.

My ventures are not in one bottom trusted.
William Shakespeare, *The Merchant of Venice*, 1596–7

~ *See also* NOTHING ventured, nothing gained.

verjuice. *See* HANG a dog on a crab-tree and he'll never love verjuice.

vessel. *See* the BEST wine comes out of an old vessel; EMPTY vessels make the most sound; OLD vessels must leak.

vex. *See* he who PEEPS through a hole may see what will vex him.

vicar. the vicar of Bray will be vicar of Bray still (*English*) No matter what happens, the person spoken of will cling to his office or privilege. Thomas Fuller, *The History of the Worthies of England*, 1662. The proverb refers to a vicar of Bray who in former times famously vowed to retain his post regardless of whether the Church of his day was Protestant or Catholic in persuasion.

~ *See also* the DEVIL gets up to the belfry by the vicar's skirts; not EVERY man can be vicar of Bowden.

vice. vice is often clothed in virtue's habit (*German /English*) Evil often appears in the guise of goodness. Cornelius Agrippa, *Vanity of Arts and Sciences*, 1569. Related proverbs include 'vice makes virtue shine'.

~ *See also* what MAINTAINS one vice would bring up two children.

view (noun). *See* DISTANCE lends enchantment to the view.

view (verb). *See* ADVICE should be viewed from behind.

vigilance. *See* the PRICE of liberty is eternal vigilance.

village. *See* BETTER be first in a village than second at Rome.

vine. make the vine poor and it will make you rich (*English*) To make a vine produce a good crop of grapes it is necessary to prune it. John Ray, *A Collection of English Proverbs*, 1678.

vinegar. *See* from the SWEETEST wine, the tartest vinegar; HONEY catches more flies than vinegar.

virtue. virtue is its own reward (*Greek*) Good behaviour is an end in itself and should not be judged merely by its consequences. John Dryden, *The Assignation*, 1673 (also found in various forms in the Stoical writings of Zeno in the fourth century BC and in Ovid, Seneca and Epictetus among others). Related proverbs include 'virtue has all things in itself', 'virtue is a jewel of great price' and 'virtue is the only true nobility'. Another saying along the same lines warns that 'vice is its own punishment'. *See also* HONOUR buys no beef.

Your vertue selfe her owne reward shall breed,
Even immortall praise, and glory wyde.
Edmund Spenser, *The Faerie Queene*, 1596

~ *See also* ARTFUL speech and an ingratiating demeanour rarely accompany virtue; BEAUTY without virtue is a flower without perfume; PATIENCE is a virtue; VICE is often clothed in virtue's habit.

visit (noun). *See* SHORT visits make long friends.

visit (verb). **visit your aunt, but not every day of the year** (*Spanish*) To maintain a friendship, do not meet too often. *See also* a HEDGE between keeps friendship green.

visitor. *See* the BUSY man has few idle visitors.

voice. the voice of the people is the voice of God (*English*) The voice of the masses is as undeniable as the will of God, however mistaken it may be. Alcuin, letter, 804. Sometimes encountered in Latin, as *vox populi, vox Dei*. In the fourteenth century Archbishop of Canterbury Walter Reynolds quoted the proverb in reference to the deposition of Edward II, when preaching at the coronation of Edward III. Not everyone in history has respected the notion: in 1863 US general W.T. Sherman quipped in a letter to his wife, *vox populi, vox humbug*.

All this may be; the people's voice is odd,
It is, and it is not, the voice of God.
Alexander Pope, *Imitations of Horace*, 1738

~ *See also* APPLES, pears and nuts spoil the voice.

voluntary. *See* IGNORANCE is a voluntary misfortune.

volunteer. *See* ONE volunteer is worth two pressed men.

vomit. *See* the DOG returns to its vomit.

vote. *See* that VOYAGE never has luck where each one has a vote.

vows made in storms are forgotten in calms (*English*) Resolutions made in the face of danger are often forgotten when the danger is past. Thomas Fuller, *Holy War*, 1639. Equivalents elsewhere in the world include the Arabic 'the day obliterates the promise of the night'.

voyage. that voyage never has luck where each one has a vote (*Scottish*) Joint enterprises will not prosper where all involved have a say in the decisions to be made. Alexander Montgomerie, *Cherrie and the Slae*, 1597. Related proverbs include 'where every man is master, the world goes to wrack', 'one master in a house is enough' and 'there is no good accord, where every man would be a lord.'

vulgar. *See* THINK with the wise, but talk with the vulgar.

W

wade. *See* no SAFE wading in an unknown water.

wag. *See* 'tis MERRY in hall when beards wag all.

wages. *See* he that SERVES God for money will serve the devil for better wages; if you PAY not a servant his wages, he will pay himself.

wait. *See* ALL things come to those who wait; EVERYTHING comes to him who waits; a GIFT long waited for is sold not given; he PULLS with a long rope that waits for another's death; it's ILL waiting for dead men's shoes; MEN count up the faults of those who keep them waiting; TIME and tide wait for no man; when you don't KNOW what to do – wait.

wake. *See* when SORROW is asleep wake it not.

walk. they that walk much in the sun will be tanned at last (*English*) Those who spend much time around someone or something may acquire, or think they have acquired, expert knowledge of the subject. T. Wilson, *The Arte of Rhetoric*, 1553.

walk groundly, talk profoundly, drink roundly, sleep soundly (*English*) Traditional advice for a good life. John Heywood, *Sixth Hundred of Epigrams*, 1562.

~ *See also* AFTER dinner rest a while, after supper walk a mile; he that hath a HEAD of wax must not walk in the sun; if it LOOKS like a duck, walks like a duck and quacks like a duck, it's a duck; we must LEARN to walk before we can run.

wall. walls have ears (*English*) Be careful what you say, even to friends, as shared secrets may easily be overheard. Geoffrey Chaucer, *The Canterbury Tales*, *c.*1387. The proverb was widely heard during the years of the Second World War when it was adopted by the British government as part of the propaganda campaign to warn people to be on their guard against the German 'fifth column' (infiltrators and spies) who might be listening out for clues about troop movements and so forth. An equivalent proverb is also known in France, where Catherine de' Medici is said to have had the walls of the Louvre specially constructed so that she could hear through them the conversations of unsuspecting courtiers. A Hebrew equivalent of the proverb warns 'do not speak of secrets in a field that is full of little hills'. *See also* FIELDS have eyes, and woods have ears.

> 'She's told me. She's very particular' – he looked around to see if walls had ears.
>
> Arnold Bennett, *The Old Wives' Tale*, 1908

~ *See also* FURTHER than the wall we cannot go; HUNGER breaks through stone walls; the WEAKEST go to the wall; a WHITE wall is a fool's paper.

walnut. walnuts and pears you plant for your heirs (*Greek*) Slow-growing trees, and other projects of long gestation, must be planned with the knowledge that they will only reach fruition in subsequent generations. George Herbert, *Outlandish Proverbs*, 1640 (also found in a variant form in the writings of Cicero). The proverb is supported by the related saying 'he who plants a walnut tree expects not to eat of the fruit'.

~ *See also* a WOMAN, a dog and a walnut tree, the more you beat them the better they be.

want (noun). **for want of a nail the shoe was lost** (*English*) All might be lost if some minor flaw is not remedied in time. T. Adams, *Works*, 1629. The full version of the proverb runs, 'for want of a nail the shoe was lost; for want of a shoe the horse was lost; and for want of a horse the man was lost'. *See also* don't SPOIL the ship for a ha'porth of tar; a STITCH in time saves nine.

> For want of a nail the shoe was lost, for want of a shoe the horse was lost, an' for want of a horse the man was lost — aw, that's a darlin' proverb, a daarlin'.
>
> Sean O'Casey, *Juno and the Paycock*, 1925

want is the whetstone of wit (*English*) The wits are sharpest when one is under pressure from hunger or poverty. *Tarlton's Jests*, 1611. A variant of the proverb, however, runs 'wine is a whetstone to wit'.

want of care does us more damage than want of knowledge (*English*) Carelessness can be more harmful than ignorance. Nathan Bailey, *An Universal Etymological English Dictionary*, 1736. Related proverbs include 'want of care admits despair'.

~ *See also* ABUNDANCE, like want, ruins many; LAND was never lost for want of an heir; a MAN may lose his goods for want of demanding them; WASTE makes want; WEALTH is best known by want.

want (verb). **if you want a thing done well, do it yourself** (*English*) Others will never satisfy your own standards as well as you will yourself, so you might as well do it yourself in the first place. Miles Coverdale, *H. Bullinger's Christian State of Matrimony*, 1541. Related proverbs include 'if you want a thing done, go; if not, send.' *See also* if you would be well SERVED, serve yourself.

> That's what I always say; if you want a thing to be well done, You must do it yourself.
>
> Henry Wadsworth Longfellow, *Poems*, 1858

if you want peace, prepare for war (*Roman*) The best way to preserve peace is to maintain strong armed forces as a deterrent. David Lyndsay, *The Satyre of the Thrie Estaitis*, 1540 (also quoted by Vegetius in *Epitoma Rei Militaris*). Occasionally encountered in the original Latin, *si vis pacem, para bellum*. Also found as 'in time of peace prepare for war'. Related proverbs include ''tis safest making peace with sword in hand' and 'he that will not peace, God gives him war'.

> The Commonwealth of Venice in their Armory have this inscription, Happy is that Citty which in time of peace thinkes of warre, a fit Motto for every mans private house.
>
> Robert Burton, *Anatomy of Melancholy*, 1624

what she wants in up and down she hath in round about (*Roman*) What a person lacks in one regard (such as stature) may be compensated for in another (such as bulk). John Ray, *A Collection of English Proverbs*, 1678.

~ *See also* BRAWLING curs never want sore ears; EATING and scratching wants but a beginning; the HASTY man never wants woe; he is RICH enough that wants nothing; he that hath a WIFE and children wants not business; if the PILLS were pleasant they would not want gilding; MILLS and wives are ever wanting; the MORE you get, the more you want; an OLD man never wants a tale to tell; SEE a pin and let it lie, you'll want a pin before you die; WASTE not, want not; WOEFUL is the household that wants a woman; a WOMAN and a ship ever want mending.

wanton kittens make sober cats (*English*) Those who are wild and reckless in their youth may yet turn out sober and responsible as adults. Thomas Fuller, *Gnomologia*, 1732.

war. war makes thieves, and peace hangs them (*English*) Villains are created by war and punished when peace is restored. George Herbert, *Outlandish Proverbs*, 1640.

wars are sweet to those that know them not (*English*) To those who have never experienced it, warfare is exciting and alluring. R. Taverner, *Proverbs or Adages with New Additions, gathered out of the Chiliades of Erasmus*, 1539.

> It's a rough trade – war's sweet to them that never tried it.
>
> Walter Scott, *The Antiquary*, 1816

when war begins hell opens (*English*) Warfare brings forth horror. G. Torriano, *Select Italian Proverbs*, 1642. Related proverbs include 'war is Death's feast', 'he that preaches war is the Devil's chaplain' , and 'war, hunting, and law [or love] are as full of trouble as pleasure'.

~ *See also* ALL's fair in love and war; COUNCILS of war never fight; he that PREACHES war is the devil's chaplain; if you WANT peace, prepare for war; a JUST war is better than an unjust peace; when GREEK meets Greek, then comes the tug of war.

ware. when the wares be gone, shut up the shop windows (*English*) It is time to close the shop when there is nothing left to sell. John Webster, *The White Devil*, 1612.

~ *See also* DAUGHTERS and dead fish are no keeping wares; GLASSES and lasses are brittle ware; GOOD ware makes quick markets; PLEASING ware is half sold.

warehouse. *See* in SETTLING an island, the first building erected by a Spaniard will be a church; by a Frenchman, a fort; by a Dutchman, a warehouse; and by an Englishman, an alehouse.

warm. he that is warm thinks all so (*English*) When a person is comfortable he or she finds it hard to imagine that others are not so. George Herbert, *Outlandish Proverbs*, 1640.

~ *See also* BETTER a little fire to warm us than a great one to burn us; CLEAR autumn, windy winter; warm autumn, long winter; COLD hands, warm heart; DRY feet, warm head, bring safe to bed; if the ROBIN sings in the bush then the weather will be coarse; but if the robin sings in the barn then the weather will be warm; LOWLY sit, richly warm; of TWO disputants the warmer is generally in the wrong.

warn. be warned by others' harm (*Roman*) Learn from the mistakes of others. Rowland Hill, *Commonplace Book*, *c.*1500 (also encountered in the writings of Plautus).

~ *See also* HALF warned, half armed.

warning. *See* a RAINBOW in the morning is the shepherd's warning; a rainbow at night is the shepherd's delight; RED sky at night, shepherd's delight; red sky in the morning, shepherd's warning.

warrant. *See* WRONG has no warrant.

wash. don't wash your dirty linen in public (*French*) Do not sort out your problems under the public gaze. T.G. Fessenden, *Pills* (previously it had been quoted by Voltaire in 1720). In 1815 Napoleon quoted it – as 'people wash their dirty linen at home' – in the course of a celebrated address to the French Assembly when he reclaimed power following his escape from Elba.

> I do not like to trouble you with my private affairs; – there is nothing ... so bad as washing one's dirty linen in public.
>
> Anthony Trollope, *The Last Chronicle of Barset*, 1867

~ *See also* DRINK washes off the dawb and discovers the man; ONE hand washes the other; SALT water and absence wash away love; WISHES won't wash dishes.

waste (noun). **waste makes want** (*English*) Waste of materials or resources results in a shortage of them. James Kelly, *A Complete Collection of Scotish Proverbs*, 1721. Also encountered in the fuller form 'wilful waste makes woeful want'.

~ *See also* HASTE makes waste.

waste (verb). **waste not, want not** (*English*) Those who make the best use of what they have will never be short of what they need. John Wesley, letter, 10 August 1772.

> Helping her to vegetable she didn't want, and when it had nearly alighted on her plate, taking it across for his own use, on the plea of waste not, want not.
>
> Thomas Hardy, *Under the Greenwood Tree*, 1872

waster. *See* BUILDING and marrying of children are great wasters.

watch. a watched pot never boils (*English*) Those who wait impatiently for something to happen will find their impatience does nothing to hasten proceedings (and even seems to stretch the time of waiting). Elizabeth Gaskell, *Mary Barton*, 1848. Variants include 'a watched phone never rang'. An opposite view is expressed by the proverb 'long looked for comes at last'.

> What's the use of watching? A watched pot never boils.
>
> Elizabeth Gaskell, *Mary Barton*, 1848

~ *See also* HARM watch, harm catch.

water (noun). **water afar quencheth not fire** (*English*) Something that is potentially useful is of no actual value if it is too far away. George Herbert, *Outlandish Proverbs*, 1640.

water, fire and soldiers quickly make room (*English*) Everyone makes way for flood, fire and soldiers. George Herbert, *Outlandish Proverbs*, 1640. Also found as 'water, fire and war quickly make room'.
water is as dangerous as commodious (*English*) Water can be a threat as well as a convenience. *Politeuphuia*, 1597, attributed to J. Bodenham.

~ *See also* BEWARE of a silent dog and still water; BLOOD is thicker than water; come with the WIND, go with the water; DIRTY water will quench fire; don't go NEAR the water until you learn how to swim; don't THROW out your dirty water until you get in fresh; FIRE and water are good servants but bad masters; FOG on the hill, water to the mill; fog in the hollow, fine day to follow; he CARRIES fire in one hand and water in the other; if the LAD go to the well against his will, either the can will break or the water will spill; in the DEEPEST water is the best fishing; it is GOOD fishing in troubled waters; the MILL cannot grind with the water that is past; MIST from the hill brings water to the mill; MUCH water goes by the mill that the miller knows not of; a MONK out of his cloister is like a fish out of water; no SAFE wading in an unknown water; POUR not water on a drowned mouse; SALT water and absence wash away love; a SCALDED cat fears cold water; SHIPS fear fire more than water; SPILT wine is worse than water; STILL waters run deep; we NEVER know the worth of water till the well is dry; you can LEAD a horse to water, but you can't make him drink; you NEVER miss the water till the well runs dry.

water (verb). *See* FOLLY grows without watering.

watery. *See* if the COCK crows on going to bed, he's sure to rise with a watery head.

wave. *See* GIVE a child all he shall crave and a dog while his tail doth wave and you'll have a fair dog and a foul knave.

wax (noun). *See* he that hath a HEAD of wax must not walk in the sun; the SAME heat that melts the wax will harden the clay.

wax (verb). *See* a BOW long bent at last waxeth weak.

way. he goes not out of his way that goes to a good inn (*English*) A person does not waste his time who goes an extra distance in order to stay at a good inn. Randle Cotgrave, *A Dictionary of the French and English Tongues*, 1611.
the way to a man's heart is through his stomach (*English*) The best way to win the love of a man is to offer him a plentiful supply of appetizing food. J. Adams, letter, 15 April 1814. Also encountered as 'the way to an Englishman's heart is through his stomach'.
the way to heaven is alike in every place (*Greek*) It is no easier to get to heaven from one part of the world than it is from another. Thomas More, *Utopia*, 1516 (quoting Diogenes). Related proverbs include 'the way to heaven is as ready by water as by land'.
the way to see divine light is to put out thine own candle (*English*) Only those with humble natures can expect divine revelations. H.G. Bohn, *A Handbook of Proverbs*, 1855. Related proverbs include 'self-love is a mote in every man's eye'.

~ *See also* a BEGGAR is never out of his way; EVENING red and morning grey help the traveller on his way; he is like a CAT: fling him which way you will, he'll light on his legs; the LONGEST way round is the shortest way home; LOVE will find a way; one can go a LONG way after one is weary; the SHORT cut is often the longest way round; STRAWS tell which way the wind blows; there are MANY ways of dressing a calf's head; there are MORE ways of killing a cat than choking it with cream; there are MORE ways of killing a dog than choking it with butter; there are MORE ways of killing a dog than hanging it; where there's a WILL there's a way; a WILFUL man must have his way; you can't have it BOTH ways.

weak. the weakest go to the wall (*English*) Those who are weakest or least effective will be sacrificed first. *The Coventry Plays*, 1534. Tradition has it that the central image of 'going to the wall' derives not from the wall that a condemned man might be leaned against before execution but to the practice in former times of putting the most vulnerable in the safest beds (closest to the wall) or else to medieval churches, where seating for the elderly and infirm was arranged around the walls, while the more able stood. Variants include 'the weaker goes to the pot'.

> That shows thee a weak slave; for the weakest
> goes to the wall.
>
> William Shakespeare, *Romeo and Juliet*, *c.*1593

weak men had need be witty (*English*) Those who lack physical strength or influence must rely on their intelligence. J. Clarke, *Paroemiologia Anglo-Latina*, 1639.

~ *See also* a BOW long bent at last waxeth weak; a CHAIN is no stronger than its weakest link; the CORD breaketh at the last by the weakest pull; EVERY man hath his weak side; the SPIRIT is willing but the flesh is weak; the THREAD breaks where it is weakest; YORKSHIRE born and Yorkshire bred, strong in the arm and weak in the head.

wealth. wealth is best known by want (*English*) It is only when a person has lost their money that they begin to appreciate their former wealth. Thomas Dekker, *Penny-wise, Pound-foolish*, 1631.

wealth is enemy to health (*English*) A wealthy man lives lazily, surrounded by luxury, and thus becomes unfit and prone to illness. John Gower, *Confessio Amantis*, *c.*1390.

wealth makes worship (*English*) Wealth inspires worship in others. J. Clarke, *Paroemiologia Anglo-Latina*, 1639. Related proverbs include 'where wealth, there friends'.

~ *See also* BEAR wealth, poverty will bear itself; a GOOD wife and health is a man's best wealth; HEALTH is better than wealth; he that MARRIES for wealth sells his liberty; he who would BRING home the wealth of the Indies must carry the wealth of the Indies with him.

wealthy. *See* EARLY to bed and early to rise, makes a man healthy, wealthy and wise.

weapon. *See* a GOOD tongue is a good weapon.

wear. *See* as your WEDDING ring wears, your cares will wear away; the CHURCH is an anvil which has worn out many hammers; CONSTANT dropping wears away the stone; had I REVENGED every wrong, I had not worn my skirts so long; if the CAP fits, wear it; it is BETTER to wear out than to rust out; to GIVE a thing, and take a thing, is to wear the Devil's gold ring; WIDE will wear but narrow will tear; WINE wears no breeches.

weary. *See* one can go a LONG way after one is weary.

weather. *See* CALM weather in June sets corn in tune; CHANGE of weather is the discourse of fools; the FULL moon brings fair weather; if the COCK moult before the hen we shall have weather thick and thin, but if the hen moult before the cock we shall have weather hard as a block; if the ROBIN sings in the bush then the weather will be coarse; but if the robin sings in the barn then the weather will be warm; in FAIR weather prepare for foul; ROBIN HOOD could brave all weathers but a thaw wind; the WEST wind always brings wet weather, the east wind wet and cold together, the south wind surely brings us rain, the north wind blows it back again.

weathercock. *See* a WOMAN is a weathercock.

weather-eye. *See* KEEP your weather-eye open.

wed. he that weds before he's wise shall die before he thrive (*English*) The man who gets married young before he has had a chance to gain any experience of the world will not prosper. John Heywood, *A Dialogue containing … the Proverbs in the English Tongue*, 1546.

~ *See also* BETTER wed over the mixen than over the moor; EARLY wed, early dead.

wedding. as your wedding ring wears, your cares will wear away (*English*) Married people find their cares slowly wear away. John Ray, *A Collection of English Proverbs*, 1678.

~ *See* ONE wedding brings another.

wedge. *See* the THIN end of the wedge is to be feared.

wedlock. wedlock is a padlock (*English*) Marriage chains partners. John Ray, *A Collection of English Proverbs*, 1678.

~ *See also* AGE and wedlock bring a man to his nightcap.

Wednesday. *See* MONDAY's child is fair of face, Tuesday's child is full of grace; Wednesday's child is full of woe, Thursday's child has far to go; Friday's child is loving and giving, Saturday's child works hard for its living; and the child that's born on the Sabbath day, is fair and wise and good and gay.

weed. the weeds overgrow the corn (*English*) Those who are less worthy may prosper where their betters do not. David Fergusson, *Scottish Proverbs*, 1641.

~ *See also* ILL weeds grow apace; a MAN of words and not of deeds is like a garden full of weeds; no GARDEN without its weeds.

weeding. *See* ONE year's seeding means seven years' weeding.

week. *See* if you would be HAPPY for a week take a wife; if you would be happy for a month kill a pig; but if you would be happy all your life plant a garden.

ween. *See* they that be in HELL ween there is no other heaven.

weep. *See* LAUGH and the world laughs with you; weep and you weep alone; when TWO friends have a common purse one sings and the other weeps.

weeper. *See* FINDERS keepers, losers weepers.

weigh justly and sell dearly (*English*) Weigh your goods accurately and sell them for as high a price as you can. John Florio, *First Fruites*, 1578. A related proverb advises 'weigh not what thou givest but what is given thee.'

weight and measure take away strife (*English*) If goods are correctly weighed and measured than there can be no argument about them. George Herbert, *Outlandish Proverbs*, 1640.

welcome. welcome evil, if thou comest alone (*English*) A misfortune is more easily borne if it comes singly. George Herbert, *Outlandish Proverbs*, 1640. Sometimes found with 'mischief' rather than 'evil'.

~ *See also* a CONSTANT guest is never welcome; a HEARTY welcome is the best cheer; when ALL fruit falls, welcome haws.

well (noun). **when the well is full it will run over** (*English*) When people are subjected to too many abuses their resentment begins to show itself. James Kelly, *A Complete Collection of Scotish Proverbs*, 1721.

~ *See also* if the LAD go to the well against his will, either the can will break or the water will spill; if you LEAP into a well providence is not bound to fetch you out; the PITCHER goes so often to the well that it is broken at last; TRUTH lies at the bottom of a well; we NEVER know the worth of water till the well is dry; you NEVER miss the water till the well runs dry.

well (adv.). **he is well worth sorrow that buys it with silver** (*Scottish*) Those who have experienced some expense or inconvenience before being finally disappointed or cheated are especially to be pitied. David Fergusson, *Scottish Proverbs*, 1641.

he that would be well old must be old betimes (*Roman*) Those who hope for a lengthy old age must become old early in life. R. Taverner, *Proverbs or Adages with New Additions, gathered out of the Chiliades of Erasmus*, 1539. Quoted by Cicero in the form 'old young and old long.'

> It was prettily said, 'He that would be long an old man must begin early to be one' ... It is necessary that before the arrival of age we bid adieu to the pursuits of youth.
>
> Richard Steele, *The Spectator*, 25 August 1711

if you would be well served, serve yourself (*English*) If you want things done properly, the simplest course is to take matters into your own hands. G. Torriano, *English and Italian Dictionary*, 1659. For those who elect to be served by others comes the cautionary proverb 'he that will be served must be patient'. *See also* if you WANT a thing done well, do it yourself.

let well alone (*Roman*) If things are satisfactory as they are, then it is best not to interfere with them. *Scoggin's Jests*, *c.*1570 (also quoted by Terence). *See also* LEAVE well alone; let SLEEPING dogs lie.

> This immortal work ... will stand for centuries ...
> It is well: it works well: let well alone.
>
> Thomas Love Peacock, *The Misfortunes of Elphin*, 1829

that is well spoken that is well taken (*English*) Words that are well-received may be judged to have been well spoken. Ben Jonson, *Cynthia's Revels*, 1600.

well begun is half done (*Greek*) If you get a job off to a good start you will find half the most difficult work is already done. *Proverbs of Hendyng*, *c.*1300 (also found in the *Epistles* of Horace).

well done is twice done (*English*) A thing well done stays done for twice as long. John Day, *The Ile of Gulls*, 1606.

what is well done is done soon enough (*English*) If something is correctly completed then it is not important how long it takes. Roger Ascham, *Toxophilus*, 1545.

~ *See also* ALL's well that ends well; BACHELORS'

wives and maids' children be well taught; BORROWED garments never fit well; a CRACKED bell can never sound well; do as MOST men do and men will speak well of you; FANNED fires and forced love never did well yet; FAR folks fare well; he cannot SPEAK well that cannot hold his tongue; he LIVES long who lives well; he that DRINKETH well sleepeth well, and he that sleepeth well thinketh no harm; he that GAPETH until he be fed, well may he gape until he be dead; he that hath his HAND in the lion's mouth must take it out as well as he can; he PREACHES well that lives well; he RIDES well that never falls; he THINKS not well that thinks not again; a HOOK is well lost to catch a salmon; if a JOB's worth doing, it's worth doing well; if a THING is worth doing, it's worth doing well; if you WANT a thing done well, do it yourself; ILL will never said well; it SIGNIFIES nothing to play well if you lose; LEAVE well alone; a LITTLE house well filled, a little land well tilled, and a little wife well willed; MANY a one says well that thinks ill; an OLD cart, well used, may last out a new one abused; PAY beforehand was never well served; PAY well, command well, hang well; a PROUD heart and a beggar's purse agree not well together; RULE youth well, for age will rule itself; SOON enough, if well enough; SPARE well and have to spend; they DIE well that live well; who LIVES well dies well.

wench. *See* WINE and wenches empty men's purses.

west. the west wind always brings wet weather, the east wind wet and cold together, the south wind surely brings us rain, the north wind blows it back again (*English*) The direction in which the wind blows is a sure indication of the kind of weather shortly to be expected. Mrs Bray, *Traditions of Devon*, 1838. Of all winds, a northeasterly wind is generally agreed to promise the best prospects.

the west wind is a gentleman and goes to bed (*English*) A westerly wind is civilized enough to drop in the evening and allow men to go peacefully to sleep. M.A. Denham, *A Collection of Proverbs ... relating to the Weather*, 1846.

~ *See also* EAST, west, home's best; the west WIND always brings wet weather; when the WIND is in the west the weather is at the best.

wet. after a wet year a cold one (*English*) Wet years precede cold years. R. Inwards, *Weather Lore*, 1893.

a wet May brings plenty of hay (*English*) Rain in the month of May is a sign of a good harvest of hay to come. M.A. Denham, *A Collection of Proverbs ... relating to the Weather*, 1846.

~ *See also* ALL cats love fish, but fear to wet their paws; a GAUDY morning bodes a wet afternoon; SOW dry and set wet; TURNIPS like a dry bed but a wet head; the WEST wind always brings wet weather, the east wind wet and cold together, the south wind surely brings us rain, the north wind blows it back again.

whale. *See* however BIG the whale may be, the tiny harpoon can rob him of life.

what. it is not what is he, but what has he (*English*) A person's wealth and assets are more important than his (or her) character. Thomas Fuller, *Gnomologia*, 1732.

> It is not what is she, but has she now-a-days.
> Jonathan Swift, *Polite Conversation*, 1738

what has been, may be (*English*) Things that have happened before may well happen again. John Florio, translations from Montaigne, 1603.

what's mine's mine own (*English*) What belongs to me is mine alone. H. Parrot, *Laquei ridiculosi*, 1613.

> What's yours is mine, and what's mine is my own.
> Jonathan Swift, *Polite Conversation*, 1738

what must be, must be (*English*) What is fated to happen will happen. Geoffrey Chaucer, *The Canterbury Tales*, c.1387. Variants include 'what shall be, shall be'. The same sentiment is encountered in many other languages, including the oft-quoted Italian: *che sarà sarà*.

> I must kiss you ... What must be, must be.
> Beaumont and Fletcher, *The Scornful Lady*, 1616

wheel. there are wheels within wheels (*English*) There are complex, inner forces or other influences at work. D. Rogers, *Matrimonial Honour*, 1642.

~ *See also* the SQUEAKING wheel gets the grease; the WORLD runs on wheels.

whelp. *See* DESTROY the lion while he is yet but a whelp; the HASTY bitch brings forth blind whelps.

whetstone. *See* WANT is the whetstone of wit.

while. *See* AFTER dinner rest a while, after supper walk a mile.

whirlwind. *See* they that SOW the wind shall reap the whirlwind.

whisper. there is no whispering but there is lying (*English*) When people feel the need to whisper to one another rather than speak out loud the chances are that their conversations will give rise to lies. John Ray, *A Collection of English Proverbs*, 1678.

whistle. a whistling woman and a crowing hen is neither fit for God nor men (*English*) It is bad luck to hear a woman whistling (a reference to the unnamed woman in the Bible who is said to have stood idly by, whistling, while the nails for use at Christ's Crucifixion were made) or to hear a hen crow (an obvious offence against nature). James Kelly, *A Complete Collection of Scotish Proverbs*, 1721. In former times a woman heard whistling might be accused of witchcraft, whistling up storms to endanger ships at sea, while the crowing of a hen signified that someone nearby was close to death.

> A whistling woman, and a crowing hen, are
> two of the unluckiest things under the sun.
> *Notes & Queries*, 1855

~ *See also* a MAN cannot whistle and drink at the same time; it is a POOR dog that is not worth whistling for; a SOW may whistle, though it has an ill mouth for it.

white. a white wall is a fool's paper (*Italian*) A blank wall is an open invitation to the graffiti artist, who knows no better but to scrawl upon it. John Florio, *First Fruites*, 1578.

he that hath a white horse and a fair wife is never without trouble (*English*) Those who possess white horses and pretty wives will find themselves in constant difficulty from those who are envious of them. G. Pettie, *Guazzo's Civil Conversation*, 1581.

~ *See also* EVERY white hath its black and every sweet its sour; the FILTH under the white snow the sun discovers; no WOOL is so white that a dyer cannot blacken it; a PALE moon doth rain, a red moon doth blow; a white moon doth neither rain nor snow; TWO blacks don't make a white.

whole. *See* CATCHING fish is not the whole of fishing; a FAIR death honours the whole life; the HALF is better than the whole; HALF the truth is often a whole lie; he who REPAIRS not his gutter repairs his whole house; ONE scabbed sheep infects the whole flock.

wholly. *See* he hath a GOOD judgement that relieth not wholly on his own.

whore. *See* it is a POOR family that has neither a whore nor a thief in it; KNAVES and whores go by the clock; ONCE a whore, always a whore.

wicked. *See* the MORE wicked, the more fortunate.

wickedness. *See* DISSEMBLED sin is double wickedness.

wide. wide ears and a short tongue (*English*) It is always best for a person to keep their ears open, but say little. T. Draxe, *Bibliotheca Scholastica*, 1633.

wide will wear but narrow will tear (*English*) Clothing that is too big or too wide will serve well enough, but if it is too tight it will tear. John Ray, *A Collection of English Proverbs*, 1678.

~ *See also* CHILDREN have wide ears and long tongues; the DIFFERENCE is wide that the sheets will not decide; SOUND travelling far and wide a stormy day will betide.

widow. *See* he that MARRIES a widow and three children marries four thieves; KEEP yourself from the anger of a great man, from the tumult of a mob, from a man of ill fame, from a widow that has been thrice married, from a wind that comes in at a hole, and from a reconciled enemy.

wife. he that hath a wife and children hath given hostages to fortune (*Roman*) A man with a wife and children will find them a hindrance in his efforts to progress in the world. Francis Bacon, *Essays*, 1612.

he that has a wife has a master (*English*) A married man is always subject to the demands of his wife. James Kelly, *A Complete Collection of Scotish Proverbs*, 1721. Related proverbs include 'an obedient wife commands her husband' and 'the wife is the key of the house'

he that hath a wife and children wants not business (*English*) A man with a wife and children is never short of work to be done. George Herbert, *Outlandish Proverbs*, 1640. Related proverbs include 'he that hath a wife and children must not sit with his fingers in his mouth'.

~ *See also* BACHELORS' wives and maids' children be well taught; a BLIND man's wife needs no paint; CAESAR's wife must be above suspicion; the CALMEST husbands make the stormiest wives; CHOOSE a horse made and a wife to make; COMMEND not your wife, wine, nor house; a DEAF husband and a blind wife are always a happy couple; go down the LADDER when thou marriest a wife, go up when thou choosest a friend; a GOOD husband makes a good wife; a GOOD wife and health is a man's best wealth; he that hath a WHITE horse and a fair wife is never without trouble; he that KISSETH his wife in the market-place shall have many teachers; he that TELLS his wife news is but newly married; he that will THRIVE must first ask his wife; HUSBANDS are in heaven whose wives scold not; if you would be HAPPY for a week take a wife; if you would be happy for a month kill a pig; but if you would be happy all your life plant a garden; LEND not horse, nor wife, nor sword; a LITTLE house well filled, a little land well tilled, and a little wife well willed; MILLS and wives are ever wanting; my SON is my son till he gets him a wife, but my daughter's my daughter all the days of her life; NEXT to no wife, a good wife is best; a NICE wife and a back door will soon make a rich man poor; there's ONE good wife in the country, and every man thinks he hath her; THREE things drive a man out of his house: smoke, rain and a scolding wife; to KISS a man's wife or wipe his knife is a thankless office; TWO cats and a mouse, two wives in one house, two dogs and a bone, never agree in one; when it RAINS and the sun shines at the same time the devil is beating his wife; who hath a FAIR wife needs more than two eyes.

wild. a wild goose never lays a tame egg (*English*) It is unreasonable to expect the offspring of unruly parents to have a quiet, orderly temperament. H.G. Bohn, *A Handbook of Proverbs*, 1855.

wilful. a wilful man must have his way (*English*) A determined man cannot be denied. Walter Scott, *The Antiquary*, 1816. A related proverb cautions 'a wilful man had need be very wise' as, according to yet another ancient saying, 'a wilful man never wants woe'.

> The Hecate … ejaculated, 'A wilfu' man will hae his way.'
>
> Walter Scott, *Rob Roy*, 1818

will (noun). **where there's a will there's a way** (*English*) Those who are determined enough will always find a way to achieve what they desire. George Herbert, *Outlandish Proverbs*, 1640. Related proverbs include 'with will one can do anything'.

> Please do not suppose … that I do not know how difficult it is … But when there's a will there's a way.
>
> George Bernard Shaw, *Fanny's First Play*, preface, 1911

will will have will, though will woe win (*English*) Sometimes a person insists on having their way, even though the end result will not be to their advantage. John Heywood, *A Dialogue containing … the Proverbs in the English Tongue*, 1546.

~ *See also* he that COMPLIES against his will is of his own opinion still; if the LAD go to the well against his will, either the can will break or the water will spill; ILL will never said well.

will (verb). **he that will not when he may, when he will he shall have nay** (*English*) Those who do not seize opportunities when they are offered will find they get no second chance. AD1000, quoted in *Anglia*, 1889. *See also* make HAY while the sun shines; STRIKE while the iron is hot.

> That young lady, with whom I so much desired to be alone again, sang … 'He that will not when he may, When he will he shall have nay.'
>
> Robert Louis Stevenson, *Catriona*, 1893

he who wills the end, wills the means (*English*) Those who dictate an end result also dictate, or should dictate, how it must be achieved. R. South, *Twelve Sermons*, 1692. *See also* where there's a WILL, there's a way.

~ *See also* he that comes FIRST to the hill may sit where he will, if ONE will not, another will; a LITTLE house well filled, a little land well tilled, and a little wife well willed; PLANT the crab-tree where you will, it will never bear pippins; SPEAK fair and think what you will.

willing. a willing mind makes a light foot (*English*) Enthusiasm for some task, such as a long journey, makes its achievement much easier. Philip Massinger, *The Picture*, 1629. Variants include 'where the will is ready, the feet are light'.

~ *See also* ALL lay loads on a willing horse; a BELLY full of gluttony will never study willingly; FATE leads the willing but drives the stubborn; MEN's years and their faults are always more than they are willing to own; the SPIRIT is willing but the flesh is weak.

willow. a willow will buy a horse before an oak will pay for a saddle (*English*) The willow, which grows very quickly, will produce a crop and thereby profit faster than the slow-growing oak. Thomas Fuller, *The History of the Worthies of England*, 1662.

~ *See also* if at CHRISTMAS ice hangs on the willow, clover may be cut at Easter.

win. you can't win them all (*US*) Everyone loses sometimes. Raymond Chandler, *The Long Good-bye*, 1953.

you win a few, you lose a few (*US*) No one wins at everything, and those who win must accept that there will also be times when they lose. P. O'Donnell, *Sabre-Tooth*, 1966. Usually voiced as consolation to someone who has just been defeated at something, or else in resigned acceptance of failure. Often encountered as 'win some, lose some'.

~ *See also* FAINT heart ne'er won fair lady; he that would the DAUGHTER win, must with the mother first begin; KEEPING is harder than winning; let them LAUGH that win; SLOW but sure wins the race; the TORTOISE wins the race while the hare is sleeping; WILL will have will, though will woe win.

wind. after wind comes rain (*English*) Rain comes in the wake of a fresh wind. Edward Hall, *Hall's Chronicle*, 1542. Such predictions were regarded with particular seriousness by seafarers in the days of sail. One more specific elaboration of the proverb among seamen ran 'when the wind comes before the rain, you may hoist your topsails up again; but when the rain comes before the winds, you may reef when it begins'.

come with the wind, go with the water (*Scottish*) Riches or possessions that have been acquired dishonestly will be dissipated with no real benefit to those who possess them. James Kelly, *A Complete Collection of Scottish Proverbs*, 1721.

> Onyway, Deacon, ye'd put your ill-gotten gains to a right use: they might come by the wind but they wouldna gang wi' the water.
>
> William Henley and Robert Louis Stevenson, *Deacon Brodie*, 1880

when the wind is in the east, 'tis neither good for man nor beast (*English*) An easterly wind, which can be very cold and piercing, threatens the welfare of all living creatures. R. Cawdrey, *Treasury of Similes*, 1600. Another proverb draws a more detailed conclusion about an easterly wind that blows on Easter Day: 'if the wind is in the east on Easter Day, you'll have plenty of grass, but little good hay'. Most proverbs relating to the east wind emphasize its quality of piercing cold, among them 'a right easterly wind is very unkind' and 'an east wind is a lazy wind' (because it goes straight through people instead of taking the long way round them). Another has it that 'when the wind's in the east on Candlemas Day, there it will stick till the second of May' and another that 'if it rains when the wind is in the east, it will rain for twenty-four hours at least.' A last proverb, by way of contrast, actually welcomes an east wind, declaring that 'a dry east wind raises the spring'. *See also* if it RAINS when the wind is in the east, it will rain for twenty-four hours at least.

> When the wind's in the East, It's neither good for man nor beast ... The East-wind with us is commonly very sharp, because it comes off the Continent.
>
> John Ray, *A Collection of English Proverbs*, 1670

when the wind is in the south it blows the bait into the fish's mouth (*English*) A southerly wind brings the fish to the fishermen's lines. Izaak Walton, *The Compleat Angler*, 1653. Fishermen are less likely to prosper when the wind is in the north, however: 'when the wind is in the north the skilful fisher goes not forth'. Another proverb, furthermore, recommends fishing when the wind is in the west: 'when the wind is west the fish bite best'.

when the wind is in the west the weather is at the best (*English*) A westerly wind accompanies balmy weather. Thomas Fuller, *Gnomologia*, 1732.

~ *See also* GOD tempers the wind to the shorn lamb; HIGH winds blow on high hills; HOIST your sail when the wind is fair; if it RAINS when the wind is in the east, it will rain for twenty-four hours at least; if the RAIN comes before the wind, lower your topsails and take them in; if the wind comes before the rain, lower your topsails and hoist them again; it's an ILL wind that blows nobody any good; KEEP yourself from the anger of a great man, from the tumult of a mob, from a man of ill fame, from a widow that has been thrice married, from a wind that comes in at a hole, and from a reconciled enemy; the NORTH wind doth blow, and we shall have snow; PISS not against the wind; PUFF not against the wind; the RAIN comes south when the wind's in the south; a REED before the wind lives on, while mighty oaks do fall; ROBIN HOOD could brave all weathers but a thaw wind; STRAWS tell which way the wind blows; they that SOW the wind shall reap the whirlwind; THREE ills come from the north: a cold wind, a shrinking cloth and a dissembling man; the WEST wind always brings wet weather, the east wind wet and cold together, the south wind surely brings us rain, the north wind blows it back again; the WEST wind is a gentleman and goes to bed; WORDS are wind.

window. *See* the EYES are the window of the soul; when POVERTY comes in at the door, love flies out of the window; when the WARES be gone, shut up the shop windows.

windy. *See* CLEAR autumn, windy winter; warm autumn, long winter.

wine. when the wine is in, the wit is out (*English*) Subtle, clever humour must not be expected from those freely indulging in alcohol. John Gower, *Confessio Amantis*, *c.*1390. Also encountered in the forms 'wine in, truth out' and 'ale in, wit out'. Another variant runs 'when wine sinks, words swim'. Conversely, another proverb has it that 'wine is a whetstone to wit'. *See also* when the DRINK is in, the wit is out.

> Whan the wyne were in and the wyt out, wolde they take uppon them ... to handle holy scrypture.
>
> Thomas More, *Dialogue of Images*, 1529

wine and wenches empty men's purses (*English*) Those who indulge freely in wine and women soon find they have spent all their money. L. Evans, *Revised Withals Dictionary*, 1586.

wine and youth increase love (*English*) The thoughts of those who are drunk or young soon turn to love. Geoffrey Chaucer, *The Canterbury Tales*, *c.*1387.

wine counsels seldom prosper (*English*) Advice given by those who are drunk is rarely good. George Herbert, *Outlandish Proverbs*, 1640.

wine hath drowned more men than the sea (*English*) More men have perished through over-indulgence in wine than have died at sea. *Politeuphuia*, 1597, attributed to J. Bodenham.

wine is a turncoat (*English*) Wine brings pleasure at first but through over-indulgence can make a person ill. George Herbert, *Outlandish Proverbs*, 1640. A fuller version of the proverb runs 'wine is a turncoat, first a friend, then an enemy'.

wine savours of the cask (*English*) The origins of something may often be detected in the finished product. John Lyly, *Euphues: The Anatomy of Wit*, 1578. *See also* the CASK savours of the first fill.

> As wine savours of the cask wherein it is kept, the soul receives a tincture from the body, through which it works.
>
> Robert Burton, *Anatomy of Melancholy*, 1621

wine wears no breeches (*English*) Alcohol, by casting aside the usual social niceties, tends to expose a man's real character. Randle Cotgrave, *A Dictionary of the French and English Tongues*, 1611.

~ *See also* the BEST wine comes out of an old vessel; COMMEND not your wife, wine, nor house; DRINK wine and have the gout, drink no wine and have the gout too; from the SWEETEST wine, the tartest vinegar; GOOD wine engendereth good blood; GOOD wine needs no bush; OLD friends and old wine are best; SPILT wine is worse than water; there is TRUTH in wine; you cannot KNOW wine by the barrel; you can't put NEW wine in old bottles.

wing. *See* a BIRD never flew on one wing; do not BLAME God for having created the tiger, but thank him for not having given it wings; FEAR lends wings; make not thy TAIL broader than thy wings; MISCHIEF has swift wings; the MOTHER of mischief is no bigger than a midge's wing; no FLYING without wings; PIGS might fly, if they had wings; RICHES have wings.

wink (noun). *See* a NOD is as good as a wink to a blind horse.

wink (verb). **wink at small faults** (*English*) Ignore minor offences or flaws. William Shakespeare, *Henry V*, *c.*1598.

> If little faults, ... shall not be wink'd at, how shall we stretch our eye when capital crimes ... appear before us?
> William Shakespeare, *Henry V*, *c.*1598

~ *See also* GARLIC makes a man wink, drink and stink; let the CAT wink and let the mouse run; though the CAT winks a while, yet sure she is not blind.

winter. winter finds out what summer lays up (*English*) The stores that are laid up when the weather is fine are soon exhausted when the weather turns cold. *Good Wyfe wold a Pylgremage*, *c.*1460. Other proverbs linking winter and summer include 'winter thunder bodes summer hunger'.

> Winter draws out what summer laid in.
> Thomas Fuller, *Gnomologia*, 1732

~ *See also* CLEAR autumn, windy winter; warm autumn, long winter; EVERY mile is two in winter; a FAIR day in winter is the mother of a storm; a GOOD winter brings a good summer; a GREEN winter makes a fat churchyard; if CANDLEMAS Day be sunny and bright, winter will have another flight; if Candlemas Day be cloudy with rain, winter is gone, and won't come again; if on the TREES the leaves still hold, the coming winter will be cold; ONE woodcock does not make a winter; the RICH man has his ice in the summer and the poor man gets his in the winter; there is no SUMMER but it has a winter.

wipe. he that wipes the child's nose kisseth the mother's cheek (*English*) Mothers always look kindly upon those who show kindness to their offspring. George Herbert, *Outlandish Proverbs*, 1640.

~ *See also* to KISS a man's wife or wipe his knife is a thankless office.

wisdom. wisdom goes beyond strength (*English*) Brains will always beat brawn. T. Draxe, *Bibliotheca Scholastica*, 1616. Other proverbs extolling the virtues of wisdom include 'well goes the case when wisdom counsels', 'what is not wisdom is danger', 'wisdom is wealth to a poor man' and 'without wisdom wealth is worthless'.

~ *See also* EXPERIENCE is the mother of wisdom; SILENCE is wisdom; when an ASS climbs a ladder we may find wisdom in women; when PASSION entereth at the foregate, wisdom goeth out of the postern; with the ANCIENT is wisdom, and in the length of days understanding; WIT without wisdom is but little worth.

wise. he is not a wise man who cannot play the fool on occasion (*Roman*) A truly wise man may enjoy a little folly now and then. *Precepts of Cato*, 1553. A related proverb has it that 'if wise men play the fool, they do it with a vengeance'.

> I have reade in a booke, that to play the foole wisely, is high wisdome.
> Ben Jonson, *Poetaster*, 1601

he is not wise that is not wise for himself (*Greek*) A person is not wise who is incapable of looking after his own interests. Anthony Rivers, translation of C. de Pisa's *Moral Proverbs*, 1478. Related proverbs include 'he is wise that hath wit enough for his own affairs'.

it is a wise child that knows its own father (*Greek*) A child who claims to know who for certain who is its father is wise indeed, bearing in mind the speed with which the world (and its inhabitants) change. J. Withals, *Dictionary*, 1584 (similar sentiments are voiced by Homer in the *Odyssey*). William Shakespeare turned the proverb on its head in *The Merchant of Venice*, writing 'it is a wise father that knows his own child'.

> The children of this age must be wise children indeed if they know their fathers.
> William Wycherley, *The Gentleman Dancing Master*, 1673

some are wise and some are otherwise (*English*) Some people are wise, and some are not. Ben Jonson, *Poetaster*, 1601.

a wise head makes a still tongue (*English*) The wise man keeps his thoughts to himself. Thomas Fuller, *Gnomologia*, 1732. Also found in the form 'a wise head makes a close mouth'. Another proverb on similar lines runs 'he hath wisdom at will that with angry heart can hold his tongue still'. Much the same sentiment may be encountered rendered more succinctly in the form 'wise men silent, fools talk'.

a wise lawyer never goes to law himself (*English*) Those who practise the law and thereby know its limitations and the costs involved never make the mistake of taking their own cases to court. G. Torriano, *Select Italian Proverbs*, 1642.

a wise man changes his mind, a fool never will (*English*) A wise man is prepared to admit it when he has made a mistake. James Mabbe, *Celestina*, 1631. Related proverbs include 'a wise man ought not to be ashamed to change his purpose' and 'a wise man needs not blush for changing his purpose'.

a wise man is never less alone than when he is alone (*Roman*) A wise man is never alone when he has his thoughts to accompany him. George Pettie, *Guazzo's Civil Conversation*, 1581. The proverb is generally attributed to Scipio Africanus the Elder, though others have also ascribed it to Themistocles.

wise men learn by others' faults, fools by their own (*English*) The wise do not repeat the mistakes of others. Geoffrey Chaucer, *Troilus and Criseyde*, c.1385–90.

> Wise men, as Poor Dick says, learn by
> others' harms.
>
> Benjamin Franklin, *Poor Richard's Almanack*, 1758

a wise woman is twice a fool (*English*) A wise woman is still only the equal of two fools. Roger L'Estrange, *Select Colloquies out of Erasmus*, 1680.

~ *See also* EARLY to bed and early to rise, makes a man healthy, wealthy and wise; FAIR words and foul deeds cheat wise men as well as fools; a FOOL may give a wise man counsel; FOOLS ask questions that wise men cannot answer; FOOLS build houses and wise men live in them; a FOOL thinks himself wise; the GREATEST clerks be not the wisest men; he that is not HANDSOME at twenty, wise at forty and rich at fifty, will never be rich, wise or handsome; he that WEDS before he's wise shall die before he thrive; HONEST men marry quickly, wise men not at all; ITALIANS are wise before the deed, the Germans in the deed, the French after the deed; it is EASY to be wise after the event; it is GOOD to be merry and wise; no MAN is wise at all times; the OLDER the wiser; an OLD wise man's shadow is better than a young buzzard's sword; one cannot LOVE and be wise; PENNY wise, pound foolish; PIE-LID makes people wise; a QUIET tongue makes a wise head; REASON governs the wise man and cudgels the fool; RICHES serve a wise man but command a fool; a STILL tongue makes a wise head; SUCCESS makes a fool seem wise; THINK with the wise, but talk with the vulgar; what the FOOL does in the end, the wise man does at the beginning; a WORD to the wise is enough.

wish (noun). **if wishes were horses, beggars would ride** (*English*) If wishes came true life would be very different from what it really is. J. Carmichaell, *Proverbs in Scots*, 1628. One variant runs 'if wishes would bide, beggars would ride'. Another proverb advises 'if wishes were thrushes beggars would eat birds', while another has it that 'if wishes buttercakes, beggars might bite'.

> If wishes were horses,
> Beggars would ride;
> If turnips were watches,
> I would wear one by my side.
>
> J.O. Halliwell, *The Nursery Rhymes of England*, 1844

wishes won't wash dishes (*US*) It takes more than mere hope or good intentions to get something done. Historical variants include 'wishes never can fill a sack', which was recorded in the seventeenth century.

the wish is father to the thought (*Roman*) It is easy to believe what one wants to believe. William Shakespeare, *Henry IV, Part 2*, c.1598 (also quoted by Julius Caesar in *The Gallic Wars*).

> The wish might be father to the thought ... but the
> thought was truly there.
>
> Anthony Trollope, *Framley Parsonage*, 1860

wish (verb). **if you wish to live and thrive, let a spider run alive** (*English*) No one who kills a spider will prosper. *Notes & Queries*, 1863. Spiders have always been considered to be lucky (one legend credits a spider with spinning a web to conceal the entrance to the cave in which the Holy Family were hiding from their persecutors). Spiders are also said to have saved the lives of Mohammed and Frederick the Great in a similar manner. In medieval times spiders were encouraged to enter homes as they preyed on disease-spreading flies; it was thus very unlucky to kill one.

~ *See also* the PINE wishes herself a shrub when the axe is at her root.

wispit. *See* a BONNY bride is soon buskit and a short horse is soon wispit.

wit. wit without wisdom is but little worth (*English*) Humour without intelligence is of little value. *Proverbs of Alfred*, *c.*1270. Also encountered in the form 'wit without learning is like a tree without fruit'. Another variant warns 'wit is folly unless a wise man hath the keeping of it'. Other proverbs extolling the value of wit include 'better wit than wealth'.

~ *See also* AFTER wit comes too late; ALE in, wit out; BOUGHT wit is the best; BREVITY is the soul of wit; GREAT wits have short memories; GREAT wits jump; IDLENESS turns the edge of wit; OXFORD for learning, London for wit, Hull for women, and York for a tit; WANT is the whetstone of wit; when the DRINK is in, the wit is out; when the WINE is in, the wit is out.

witch. *See* a WOMAN is an angel at ten, a saint at fifteen, a devil at forty and a witch at fourscore.

withdraw. *See* from a CHOLERIC man withdraw a little, from him that says nothing for ever.

wither. *See* the FAIREST rose at last is withered.

witty. *See* WEAK men had need be witty.

wive. *See* FIRST thrive and then wive; HANGING and wiving go by destiny; it's HARD to wive and thrive both in a year.

wives. *See* WIFE.

woe. woes unite foes (*English*) Hardships common to all tend to bring enemies together. A. Henderson, *Scottish Proverbs*, 1832.

~ *See also* the HASTY man never wants woe; MONDAY's child is fair of face, Tuesday's child is full of grace; Wednesday's child is full of woe, Thursday's child has far to go; Friday's child is loving and giving, Saturday's child works hard for its living; and the child that's born on the Sabbath day, is fair and wise and good and gay; WILL will have will, though will woe win.

woeful. woeful is the household that wants a woman (*English*) No household that lacks women can be happy. *Towneley Mystery Play*, *c.*1460.

~ *See also* MEMORY of happiness makes misery woeful.

wolf. *See* a GROWING youth has a wolf in his belly; he that goes to LAW holds a wolf by the ears; HUNGER drives the wolf out of the wood; MAN is to man a wolf; one must HOWL with the wolves; who KEEPS company with the wolf will learn how to howl.

woman. a woman, a dog and a walnut tree, the more you beat them the better they be (*English*) Women, dogs and walnut trees benefit from harsh treatment, which will curb their natural tendency to excess. G. Pettie, *Guazzo's Civil Conversation*, 1581. It was once common practice to thrash walnut trees to shake loose the fruit and also to snap long shoots and thus encourage the growth of new fruiting spurs. It has also been suggested that beating a walnut tree encouraged the spread of the sap and thus promoted the health of the whole tree. Variants include 'a woman, a spaniel, and a walnut tree, the more you beat them the better they be'.

> Do you think that she is like a walnut-tree? Must she be cudgelled ere she bear good fruit?
> John Webster, *The White Devil*, 1612

a woman and a cherry are painted for their own harm (*English*) Women who wear make-up invite misfortune. J. Howell, *Paroemiographia*, 1659. Related proverbs include 'a woman that paints puts up a bill that she is to be let' and 'let no woman's painting breed thy heart's fainting'.

a woman and a ship ever want mending (*Roman*) Women, like ships, require constant attention and – in the case of women – regular supplies of luxuries, new clothing etc. John Florio, *First Fruites*, 1578 (also quoted by Plautus). Proverbs along similar lines include 'a woman and a glass are ever in danger'.

> Whoever wants to acquire a lot of trouble should get himself a ship and a woman. For neither of them is ever sufficiently equipped, and there is never enough means of equipping them.
> Plautus, *Poenulus*, second century BC

a woman is an angel at ten, a saint at fifteen, a devil at forty and a witch at fourscore (*English*) The character of a woman degenerates with age. *Swetnam the Woman Hater*, 1620. Related proverbs include 'a wicked woman and an evil is three halfpence worse than the devil' and 'a woman can do more than the devil'.

a woman is a weathercock (*English*) Women are easily swayed, changing their mind at the slightest persuasion (just as a weathercock responds to the wind). T. Draxe, *Bibliotheca Scholastica*, 1616. Other proverbs that support the same notion include 'a woman's mind and winter wind change oft' and 'women, wind and fortune are given to change'.

a woman's place is in the home (*English*) A woman should confine her attentions to domestic tasks about the house, looking after the welfare of her family. 'J. Slick', *High Life*, 1844. Another proverb dictates that 'a woman is to be from her house three times; when she is christened, married and buried'.

a woman's strength is in her tongue (*English*) The prime weapon of a woman is her tongue. J. Howell, *Paroemiographia*, 1659. Other equally misogynistic proverbs allege 'one tongue is enough for a woman', 'a woman's heart and her tongue are not relatives', 'women's tongues wag like lambs' tails' and 'a woman's tongue is the last thing about her that dies'. Another observes, rather dryly, 'many women many words'.

a woman's work is never done (*English*) Women face a never-ending cycle of housework, from which there is no respite. T. Tusser, *Five Hundred Points of Husbandry*, 1570.

> If you go among the Women, you will learn …
> that a Woman's Work is never done.
> Benjamin Franklin, *Papers*, 1722

women are saints in church (*English*) Women seem saintly in church, but behave quite differently in other situations. *School House of Women*, 1542. Fuller versions of the proverb vary somewhat, but one typical variant runs 'women are saints in church, angels in the street, devils in the kitchen and apes in bed'.

> God save us from wives who are angels in the
> streets, saints in the church, and devils at home.
> Charles Spurgeon, *John Ploughman*, 1869

women must have the last word (*English*) Women insist upon having the last word in any argument. *School House of Women*, 1542.

> She was like the rest of your sex, ma'am – she went
> her own way, and had the last word.
> Eden Phillpotts, *Yellow Sands*, 1926

~ *See also* ARTHUR could not tame a woman's tongue; a BAD woman is worse than a bad man; BECAUSE is a woman's reason; BEWARE of the forepart of a woman, the hind part of a mule and all sides of a priest; DALLY not with women or money; ENGLAND is the paradise of women, the hell of horses and the purgatory of servants; HELL hath no fury like a woman scorned; a MAN is as old as he feels, and a woman as old as she looks; a MAN of straw is worth a woman of gold; MANY women, many words; NEVER choose your women or your linen by candle-light; no MISCHIEF but a woman or a priest is at the bottom of it; ONE hair of a woman draws more than a team of oxen; OXFORD for learning, London for wit, Hull for women, and York for a tit; SILENCE is a woman's best garment; SIX hours' sleep for a man, seven for a woman and eight for a fool; the TAILOR must cut three sleeves to every woman's gown; TELL a woman she's a beauty and the devil will tell her so fifty times; there is no such THING as good small beer, good brown bread, or a good old woman; THREE women make a market; when an ASS climbs a ladder we may find wisdom in women; a WHISTLING woman and a crowing hen are neither fit for God nor men; a WISE woman is twice a fool; WOEFUL is the household that wants a woman.

won. *See* WIN.

wonder is the daughter of ignorance (*English*) The ignorant tend to marvel at what they do not understand. J. Florio, *First Fruites*, 1578.

wonderful. *See* he who is CONTENT in his poverty is wonderfully rich.

wonder. wonders will never cease (*English*) The unexpected and the remarkable can always happen and do so from time to time. H. Bates, 1776, quoted in T. Boaden, *The Private Correspondence of D. Garrick*, 1823.

~ *See also* TIME works wonders.

wood. wood half burnt is easily kindled (*English*) Half-forgotten resentments and arguments are quickly revived. G. Cavendish, *Life of Cardinal Wolsey*, 1557. Also encountered in the form 'wood half-coal is easily kindled'.

~ *See also* don't HALLOO till you are out of the wood; FIELDS have eyes, and woods have ears; HUNGER drives the wolf out of the wood; I have LIVED too near a wood to be frightened by owls; NEW beer, new bread and green wood will make a man's hair grow through his hood; TOUCH wood, it's sure to come good.

woodcock. *See* ONE woodcock does not make a winter.

wooing. *See* HAPPY is the wooing that is not long a-doing.

wool. no wool is so white that a dyer cannot blacken it (*English*) No person or thing is so perfect that it is entirely invulnerable to criticism. G. Pettie, *Petite Pallace*, 1576.

~ *See also* MANY go out for wool and come home shorn; MUCH cry and little wool.

word. words are wind (*English*) Words have no substance compared to actual deeds. *Ancrene Riwle*, *c.*1225. Also found as 'words and feathers the wind carries away'. Contrasting proverbs include 'words cut more than swords', 'words bind men' and 'a word spoken is an arrow let fly'. *See also* STICKS and stones may break my bones, but names will never hurt me.

> Words are wind; but deeds are mind.
>
> Samuel Richardson, *Clarissa*, 1748

a word spoken is past recalling (*Greek*) Once something has been said it is impossible to unsay it. Geoffrey Chaucer, *The Canterbury Tales*, *c.*1387 (also quoted by Horace). Equivalents in other cultures include the English 'a word and a stone let go cannot be called back'.

a word to the wise is enough (*Roman*) A wise man needs no more than a hint to do whatever is necessary. William Dunbar, *Poems*, 1513 (also quoted by Plautus).

> But what sayeth the proverb, *verbum sapienti* – a word is more to him that hath wisdom than a sermon to a fool.
>
> Walter Scott, *The Bride of Lammermoor*, 1819

~ *See also* ACTIONS speak louder than words; BARE words are no good bargain; DEEDS are fruits, words are but leaves; don't JUDGE a man by the words of his mother, listen to the comments of his neighbours; an ENGLISHMAN's word is his bond; FAIR words and foul deeds cheat wise men as well as fools; FAIR words break no bones; FEW words are best; FINE words butter no parsnips; HARD words break no bones; a MAN of words and not of deeds is like a garden full of weeds; a MAN that breaks his word bids others be false to him; MANY women, many words; ONE ill word asketh another; ONE picture is worth ten thousand words; there's MANY a true word spoken in jest; WOMEN must have the last word.

work (noun)**. it is not work that kills, but worry** (*English*) It is not overwork that is harmful to health, but stress. D.M. Mulock, *Young Mrs Jardine*, 1879. *See also* it is the PACE that kills.

work expands so as to fill the time available (*English*) Any task may be stretched to take up all the time that has been allotted to it ('Parkinson's Law'). Cyril Northcote Parkinson, in *The Economist*, 19 November 1955.

> It is a commonplace observation that work expands so as to fill the time available for its completion.
>
> Cyril Northcote Parkinson, in *The Economist*, 19 November 1955

~ *See also* ALL work and no play makes Jack a dull boy; as is the WORKMAN so is the work; CHURCH work goes on slowly; the DAY is short and the work is long; the DEVIL finds work for idle hands; the END crowns the work; EVERY man is the son of his own works; the EYE of the master does more work than both his hands; FOOLS and bairns should never see half-done work; if IFS and ands were pots and pans, there'd be no work for tinkers' hands; MANY hands make light work; NEVER trust a tailor that does not sing at his work; not a LONG day but a good heart rids work; a PROUD look makes foul work in a fine face; QUICK at meat, quick at work; a WOMAN's work is never done.

work (verb)**. if you won't work you shan't eat** (*Hebrew*) Those who do not put in some effort cannot expect any reward. Bible, 2 Thessalonians 3:10.

Variants include 'he that will not work will want'.

If you won't work you shan't eat ... You're a wild elephant, and no educated animal at all. Go back to your jungle.

Rudyard Kipling, *Life's Handicap*, 1891

work today for you know not how much you may be hindered tomorrow (*English*) Get your work done while you have the opportunity, for it may not last long. R. Codrington, *The Second Part of Youth's Behaviour*, 1664.

~ *See also* as GOOD play for nought as work for nought; BETTER sit idly than work for nothing; EAT till you sweat and work till you freeze; FORECAST is better than work hard; if PHYSIC do not work, prepare for the kirk; MONDAY's child is fair of face, Tuesday's child is full of grace; Wednesday's child is full of woe, Thursday's child has far to go; Friday's child is loving and giving, Saturday's child works hard for its living; and the child that's born on the Sabbath day, is fair and wise and good and gay; NEVER work with children or animals; they must HUNGER in frost that will not work in heat; TIME works wonders.

workhouse. *See* IDLE bairns are the devil's workhouses.

workman. as is the workman so is the work (*English*) The quality of work done depends upon the calibre of the workman doing it. Randle Cotgrave, *A Dictionary of the French and English Tongues*, 1611.
what is a workman without his tools? (*English*) Even the best workmen can do little without their tools. John Heywood, *A Dialogue containing ... the Proverbs in the English Tongue*, 1546.

~ *See also* a BAD workman blames his tools.

workshop. *See* an IDLE brain is the Devil's workshop.

world. the world runs on wheels (*English*) Things change rapidly and without pause. John Heywood, *A Dialogue containing ... the Proverbs in the English Tongue*, 1546.

~ *See also* ALL's for the best in the best of all possible worlds; BETTER be out of the world than out of fashion; the CALF, the goose, the bee: the world is ruled by these three; GOD's in his heaven; all's right with the world; HALF the world doesn't know how the other half lives; the HAND that rocks the cradle rules the world; it's a SMALL world; it takes ALL sorts to make a world; KNAVES and fools divide the world; LAUGH and the world laughs with you; weep and you weep alone; a LIE travels around the world while truth is putting on her boots; LOVE makes the world go round; the MIRTH of the world dureth but a while; MONEY makes the world go round; OPINION rules the world.

worm. even a worm will turn (*English/French*) Given sufficient cause, even the most retiring person will eventually turn on an aggressor. John Heywood, *A Dialogue containing ... the Proverbs in the English Tongue*, 1546. A worm when trodden upon will turn back on itself, as though to menace an attacker.

The smallest worm will turn, being trodden on.

William Shakespeare, *Henry VI, Part 3*, *c.*1591

~ *See also* the EARLY bird catches the worm.

worn. *See* WEAR.

worry. *See* it is not WORK that kills, but worry.

worse. worse things happen at sea (*English*) However bad things might be, there is always the consolation of knowing that they could have been even worse. Charles Spurgeon, *John Ploughman's Talk*, 1869. Other proverbs aiming to provide consolation for those who feel down on their luck include 'the worse luck now, the better another time'.

~ *See also* a BAD woman is worse than a bad man; be it for BETTER, be it for worse, do you after him that beareth the purse; the BETTER gamester the worser man; the BETTER, the worse; a GOOD tale is none the worse for being twice told; he that THINKS amiss concludes worse; he who DEPENDS on another dines ill and sups worse; ILL luck is worse than found money; it is a SHAME to steal but a worse to carry home; it is HARD to be wretched but worse to be known so; LEARNING makes a good man better and an ill man worse; a LIAR is worse than a thief; the MORE you stir, the worse it will stink; NOTHING agreeth worse than a lady's heart and a beggar's purse; NOTHING so bad but it might have been worse; PRAISE makes good men better and bad men worse; the PROPERER the man, the worse luck; the REMEDY may be worse than the disease; SPILT wine is worse than water; a TALE-TELLER is worse than a thief; when the HEAD acheth all the body is the worse.

worship. *See* WEALTH makes worship.

worst. he that worst may shall hold the candle (*English*) It often seems to happen that the least suitable person is selected to enjoy some privilege or honour. *Coventry Plays*, *c.*1534. Equivalent proverbs include 'the worst pig often gets the best pear'.

our worst misfortunes are those which never befall us (*English*) The misfortunes a person anticipates often cause them more grief than those that actually come to pass. E.P. Hood, *World of Proverbs*, 1885.

the worst spoke in a cart breaks first (*English*) The weakest point is where something usually breaks. John Ray, *A Collection of English Proverbs*, 1678. Variants include 'the worst wheel of a cart creaks most'.

~ *See also* the BEST things are worst to come by; CORRUPTION of the best becomes the worst; he who SHARES has the worst share; HOPE for the best and prepare for the worst; PROVIDE for the worst, the best will save itself; when THINGS are at the worst they soon begin to mend.

worth (noun). **the worth of a thing is what it will bring** (*French/English*) The value of something depends upon how much it can be sold for. J. Sanforde, *H.C. Agrippa's Vanity of the Arts and Sciences*, 1569. Equivalent proverbs include 'the worth of a thing is known by its want'.

> For what is Worth in any thing, But so much
> Money as 'twill bring?
> Samuel Butler, *Hudibras*, 1664

~ *See also* the COW knows not the worth of her tail till she loses it; we NEVER know the worth of water till the well is dry.

worth (adj.). *See* a BIRD in the hand is worth two in the bush; he is WELL worth sorrow that buys it with silver; it is a POOR dog that is not worth whistling for; a JANUARY spring is worth nothing; if a JOB's worth doing, it's worth doing well; if a THING is worth doing, it's worth doing well; a LAWYER's opinion is worth nothing unless paid for; a MAN of straw is worth a woman of gold; ONE acre of performance is worth twenty of the Land of Promise; ONE hour's sleep before midnight is worth two after; ONE pair of heels is often worth two pairs of hands; ONE picture is worth ten thousand words; ONE today is worth two tomorrows; ONE volunteer is worth two pressed men; an OUNCE of mirth is worth a pound of sorrow; an OUNCE of practice is worth a pound of precept; a PECK of March dust is worth a king's ransom; a PENNY at a pinch is worth a pound; a PENNYWEIGHT of love is worth a pound of law; a SPUR in the head is worth two in the heel; a SWARM of bees in May is worth a load of hay; WIT without wisdom is but little worth.

worthy. *See* he that DESIRES honour is not worthy; the LABOURER is worthy of his hire.

wound. though the wound be healed, a scar remains (*English*) Past grievances, though apparently forgotten, may not have been forgiven. William Shakespeare, *The Rape of Lucrece*, 1594. Related proverbs include 'the wound that bleedeth inwardly is most dangerous'.

~ *See also* a GREEN wound is soon healed; TIME heals all wounds.

wranglers are never in the wrong (*English*) Those who are given to argument always have an answer to those who suggest they may be mistaken. T. Draxe, *Bibliotheca Scholastica*, 1616. Also found as 'wranglers never want words'.

wrath. *See* let not the SUN go down on your wrath; a SOFT answer turneth away wrath.

wren. *See* as SORE fight wrens as cranes; the ROBIN and the wren are God's cock and hen.

wretched. *See* it is HARD to be wretched but worse to be known so.

wrinkle. *See also* an EMPTY purse fills the face with wrinkles.

wrinkled purses make wrinkled faces (*English*) Lack of money prematurely ages a person. Thomas Fuller, *Gnomologia*, 1732.

write. *See* INJURIES don't use to be written on ice; THINK much, speak little and write less.

writer. *See* TAILORS and writers must mind the fashion.

writing. by writing you learn to write (*English*) It is only by writing that an aspiring author will improve his writing technique. Quoted by Samuel Johnson in a letter to Boswell, 1763.

wrong (noun)**. no wrong without a remedy** (*English*) There is, or should be, a remedy for every offence. *Spectator*, 10 December 1910. The sentiment in the proverb has long been enshrined as a legal maxim. Related proverbs include 'all wrong comes to wrack'.

> Again and again ... English judges have invented artifices in order to give effect to the excellent legal maxim that there shall be no wrong without a remedy.
>
> *Spectator*, 10 December 1910

wrong has no warrant (*Scottish*) No person doing wrong can claim to have authority to do so. David Fergusson, *Scottish Proverbs*, 1641. Related proverbs include 'wrong never comes right'.

~ *See also* the GREATER the right, the greater the wrong; had I REVENGED every wrong, I had not worn my skirts so long; of TWO disputants the warmer is generally in the wrong; TWO wrongs don't make a right; WRANGLERS are never in the wrong.

wrong (verb)**. he wrongs not an old man that steals his supper from him** (*English*) Those who help themselves to what others no longer have much use for do no real wrong. George Herbert, *Outlandish Proverbs*, 1640.

~ *See also* KIND hearts are soonest wronged.

wrong (adj.)**.** *See* the ABSENT are always wrong; if ANYTHING can go wrong, it will; the KING can do no wrong; our COUNTRY, right or wrong; wherever there is a SECRET there must be something wrong.

wrongful. *See* he COMPLAINS wrongfully on the sea who twice suffers shipwreck.

Y-Z

year. years know more than books (*English*) More knowledge comes with experience than through academic study. George Herbert, *Outlandish Proverbs*, 1640.

~ *See also* after a WET year a cold one; BUTTER is mad twice a year; BUTTER is once a year in the cow's horn; a CHERRY year, a merry year; a plum year, a dumb year; CHRISTMAS comes but once a year; the FIRST seven years are the hardest; GIVE me a child for the first seven years, and you may do what you like with him afterwards; a GOOD hay year a bad fog year; HORNS and grey hairs do not come by years; if SAINT Paul's Day be fair and clear, it will betide a happy year; if the OLD year goes out like a lion, the new year will come in like a lamb; it CHANCETH in an hour that happeneth not in seven years; it's HARD to wive and thrive both in a year; it will ALL be one in a hundred years' time; KEEP a thing seven years and you'll always find a use for it; a LEAP YEAR is never a good sheep year; MEN's years and their faults are always more than they are willing to own; the MORE thy years, the nearer thy grave; ONE year's seeding means seven years' weeding; a PIN a day is a groat a year; SAY no ill of the year till it be past; a SERVANT and a cock should be kept but a year; a SNOW year, a rich year; there are no BIRDS in last year's nest; TURKEY, heresy, hops and beer came into England all in one year; VISIT your aunt, but not every day of the year; you should KNOW a man seven years before you stir his fire.

yellow. *See* to the JAUNDICED eye all things look yellow.

yelping curs will raise mastiffs (*Scottish*) Trivial quarrels can easily develop into serious disputes. James Kelly, *A Complete Collection of Scottish Proverbs*, 1721.

yesterday. yesterday will not be called again (*English*) There is no way to go back in time, to how things used to be. John Skelton, *Magnyfycence*, 1529.

~ *See also* JAM tomorrow and jam yesterday, but never jam today; TODAY is yesterday's pupil.

yield. *See* OLD bees yield no honey.

York. *See* OXFORD for learning, London for wit, Hull for women, and York for a tit.

Yorkshire born and Yorkshire bred, strong in the arm and weak in the head (*English*) Those born in Yorkshire are physically strong but mentally weak. *Notes & Queries*, 1852. Over the years the proverb has been applied to the inhabitants of many other counties and towns. Other insulting proverbs aimed at Yorkshiremen include 'shake a bridle over a Yorkshireman's grave, and he will arise and steal a horse'.

> Manchester bred: Long in the arms, and short in the head.
>
> W. C. Hazlitt, *English Proverbs*, 1869

you. *See* I today, you tomorrow.

young. the young cock crows as he heard the old one (*English*) The young learn how to do things by copying the example of their elders. Alexander Barclay, *Ship of Fools*, 1509. Variants upon the theme include 'the young pig grunts like the old sow.'

> As the olde cocke crowes so doeth the chick.
>
> George Puttenham, *The Arte of English Poesie*, 1589

young folks think old folks to be fools, but old folks know young folks to be fools (*English*) Those with long experience know better than the young or less experienced, even though this may not be recognized. J. Grange, *Golden Aphroditis*, 1577. Variants include 'of young men die many, of old men scape not any'.

> You *think* us old fellows are fools; but we old fellows *know* young fellows are fools.
>
> Jonathan Swift, *Polite Conversation*, 1738

a young man should not marry yet, an old man not at all (*English*) There is never a good time for a man to get married. Nicholas Udall, *Apothegms of Erasmus*, 1542.

young men may die, but old men must die (*English*) The young must accept that the threat of death is always a risk, but the elderly must expect imminent death as a certainty. Thomas More, *Dialogue of Comfort*, 1534.

> As the younge man maye happe some time to die soone, so the olde man can never live long.
>
> Thomas More, *Dialogue of Comfort*, 1534

a young physician fattens the churchyard (*English*) The mistakes of an inexperienced doctor will lead to the deaths of many of his patients. Variants include 'a young doctor makes a humpy churchyard'. Another proverb stresses the advisability of 'a young barber and an old physician'.

young saint old devil (*English*) Well-behaved children are all too apt to grow into badly behaved adults. *Harlequin MS*, *c.*1470. A variant runs 'naughty boys sometimes make good men.' By much the same token, other proverbs have it that 'royet (wild) lads make sober men' and 'wanton kittens make sober cats.'

> But soone rype, soone rotten, yong seynt olde deuill.
>
> John Heywood, *A Dialogue containing … the Proverbs in the English Tongue*, 1546

~ *See also* BETTER be an old man's darling than a young man's slave; CHILDREN suck the mother when they are young and the father when they are old; HANG a thief when he's young, and he'll no' steal when he's old; LEARN young, learn fair; the OFFSPRING of those that are very young or very old lasts not; OLD and tough, young and tender; OLD fish and young flesh feed men best; OLD men go to death, death comes to young men; an OLD physician and a young lawyer; an OLD wise man's shadow is better than a young buzzard's sword; only the GOOD die young; whom the GODS love die young; you cannot put an OLD head on young shoulders.

youth. youth and old age will never agree (*English*) The old and the young will never see things in the same way. Geoffrey Chaucer, *The Canterbury Tales*, *c.*1387. Another proverb underlying the different attitudes of the young and old runs 'young men forgive, old men never'.

> Crabbed age and youth cannot live together.
>
> William Shakespeare, *The Passionate Pilgrim*, *c.*1599

youth must be served (*English*) The young, with their natural vigour and freshness, are at a natural advantage in certain circumstances and cannot be denied. John Lyly, *Euphues: The Anatomy of Wit*, 1578. Variants include 'youth will have its day', 'youth will have its course' (in which form it was usually quoted in the sixteenth century) and 'youth will have its fling'.

> When all the world is young, lad
> And all the trees are green:
> … Young blood must have its course, lad
> And every dog his day.
>
> Charles Kingsley, *The Water Babies*, 1863

~ *See also* a GROWING youth has a wolf in his belly; an IDLE youth, a needy age; RULE youth well, for age will rule itself; where OLD age is evil, youth can learn no good; WINE and youth increase love.

Z

zeal. zeal without knowledge is the sister of folly (*English*) Lack of knowledge coupled with enthusiasm is a recipe for disaster. Davies of Hereford, *School of Folly*, 1611. Variants include 'zeal without knowledge is fire without light', 'zeal without prudence is frenzy', 'zeal is fit only for wise men, but is found mostly in fools' and 'zeal without knowledge is a runaway horse'.

THEMATIC INDEX

rich at fifty, will never be rich, wise or handsome

HORNS and grey hairs do not come by years

LIFE begins at forty

a MAN at thirty must be either a fool or a physician

a MAN is as old as he feels, and a woman as old as she looks

MEN's years and their faults are always more than they are willing to own

the MORE thy years, the nearer thy grave

where OLD age is evil, youth can learn no good

OLD and tough, young and tender

OLD fish and young flesh feed men best

OLD men go to death, death comes to young men

an OLD physician and a young lawyer

SOON ripe, soon rotten

don't TEACH your grandmother to suck eggs

you cannot have TWO forenoons in the same day

a WOMAN is an angel at ten, a saint at fifteen, a devil at forty and a witch at fourscore

YEARS know more than books

YOUNG folks think old folks to be fools, but old folks know young folks to be fools

a YOUNG man should not marry yet, an old man not at all

YOUNG saint old devil

YOUTH and old age will never agree

See also EXPERIENCE; OLD AGE; YOUTH

ALLIANCES

ADVERSITY makes strange bedfellows

AMBITION

there is ALWAYS room at the top

it is EASIER to descend than to ascend

EVERY soldier has the baton of a field-marshal in his knapsack

the HIGHER the monkey climbs the more he shows his tail

LOOK to a gown of gold and you will at least get a sleeve of it

he that NEVER climbed never fell

if you would be POPE you must think of nothing else

he will SHOOT higher who shoots at the moon than he who aims at a tree

the SPIRIT is willing but the flesh is weak

ANGER

ANGER can be an expensive luxury

ANGER without power is folly

he who has been ANGRY becomes cool again

an ANGRY man is not fit to pray

ANGRY men make themselves beds of nettles

from a CHOLERIC man withdraw a little, from him that says nothing for ever

like ICE, anger passes away

it's ILL putting a naked sword in a madman's hand

no MAN is angry that feels not himself hurt

when MEAT is in anger is out

a SOFT answer turneth away wrath

as SORE fight wrens as cranes

SHORT folk are soon angry

TWO things a man should never be angry at; what he can help and what he cannot help

APPEARANCE

an APE's an ape, a varlet's a varlet, though they be clad in silk or scarlet

APPEARANCES are deceptive

the BAIT hides the hook

BE what you would seem to be

if the BEARD were all, the goat might preach

it is not the BEARD that makes the philosopher

BEAUTY is only skin deep

the BEST things come in small packages

the COWL does not make the monk

EVERY devil has not a cloven hoof

the FAIRER the hostess, the fouler the reckoning

the FAIREST rose at last is withered

FANCY passes beauty

FINE feathers make fine birds

FIRST impressions are the most lasting

GILT spurs do not make the knight

a GOOD face is a letter of recommendation

a GOOD horse cannot be of a bad colour

a GREAT book is a great evil

HANDSOME is as handsome does

an HONEST look covereth many faults

the JOY of the heart makes the face merry

you can't JUDGE a book by its cover

a LITTLE body often harbours a great soul

LOOKS breed love

if it LOOKS like a duck, walks like a duck and quacks like a duck, it's a duck

a MAN is as old as he feels, and a woman as old as she looks

NEVER judge by appearances

NONE can guess the jewel by the casket

the PEACOCK hath fair feathers, but foul feet

if the PILLS were pleasant they would not want gilding

PLEASE your eye and plague your heart

POISON is poison though it comes in a golden cup

the STYLE is the man

a WOMAN and a cherry are painted for their own harm

APPETITE

APPETITE comes with eating

he is like a BAGPIPE; he never talks till his belly be full

the BELLY hath no ears

CHILDREN and chicken must always be pickin'

EATING and drinking takes away one's stomach

a GROWING youth has a wolf in his belly

HUNGER is the best sauce

NEW meat begets a new appetite

ONE shoulder of mutton draws down another

POOR men seek meat for their stomach; rich men stomach for their meat

ARGUMENT AND DISPUTE

it is a DANGEROUS fire begins in the bed straw

the DIFFERENCE is wide that the sheets will not decide

DOGS begin in jest and end in earnest

put not thy HAND between the bark and the tree

in too MUCH dispute truth is lost

WRANGLERS are never in the wrong

YELPING curs will raise mastiffs

See also QUARRELLING

ART AND ARTISTS

ART consists in concealing art

ART has no enemy but ignorance

ART helps nature, and experience art

ART is long, life is short

an ARTIST lives everywhere

a NIGHTINGALE cannot sing in a cage

PAINTERS and poets have leave to lie

on PAINTING and fighting look aloof

ATHEISM

an ATHEIST is one point beyond the Devil

there are no ATHEISTS in foxholes

ATTRACTION

BEAUTY draws more than oxen

LIKE will to like

AVOIDANCE

let ANOTHER's shipwreck be your sea-mark

BEHIND the horseman sits black care

the BEST remedy against an ill man is much ground between

HALF warned, half armed

BABIES

the BABY comes out of the parsley-bed

BARGAINS

a BARGAIN is a bargain

the BARGAIN is ill made where neither party gains

at a GOOD bargain, make a pause

on a GOOD bargain, think twice

GOOD cheap is dear

it takes TWO to make a bargain

BEAUTY

BEAUTY and honesty seldom agree

BEAUTY draws more than oxen

BEAUTY is but a blossom

BEAUTY is in the eye of the beholder

BEAUTY is no inheritance

BEAUTY is only skin deep

BEAUTY is potent, but money is omnipotent

BEAUTY provoketh thieves sooner than gold

BEAUTY without virtue is a flower without perfume

the CROW thinks her own birds fairest

the FAIREST rose at last is withered

FAIR face and a foul heart

who hath a FAIR wife needs more than two eyes

the FAIREST silk is soonest stained

FANCY passes beauty

GRACE will last, beauty will blast

LOOKS breed love

PLEASE your eye and plague your heart

PRETTINESS dies first

BEGINNINGS AND ENDINGS

AFTER drought cometh rain

such BEGINNING, such end

the BEST of friends must part

if you BUY the cow, take the tail into the bargain

CALL no man happy till he dies

the CASK savours of the first fill

CE n'est que le premier pas qui coûte

be the DAY never so long, at length cometh evensong

the EVENING brings all home

the EVENING crowns the day

EVERYTHING has an end

the FIRST blow is half the battle

it is the FIRST step that is difficult

GIVE a cob a hat and a pair of shoes and he'll last for ever

a GOOD beginning makes a good ending

no GOOD building without a good foundation

GREAT oaks from little acorns grow

a HIGH building, a low foundation

LEAVE off while the play is good

LOOK to the end

it is NEVER a bad day that hath a good night

the OPERA isn't over till the fat lady sings

PLANT the crab-tree where you will, it will never bear pippins

QUIT while you are ahead

a SMALL spark makes a great fire

THINK on the end before you begin

WELL begun is half done

he who WILLS the end, wills the means

BEHAVIOUR

BASHFULNESS is an enemy to poverty

BE what you would seem to be

BEAUTY and honesty seldom agree

BOYS will be boys

CHILDREN should be seen and not heard

DO as you would be done by

what can you EXPECT from a pig but a grunt?

FAIR and soft goes far in a day

if you can't be GOOD, be careful

a GOOD dog deserves a good bone

he is a GOOD dog who goes to church

GRACE will last, beauty will blast

HANDSOME is as handsome does

do on the HILL as you would do in the hall

KEEP bad men company and you'll soon be of their number

who KEEPS company with the wolf will learn how to howl

if the LAIRD slight the lady, so will all the kitchen boys

LEAST said, soonest mended

if you LIE down with dogs, you will get up with fleas

LIVE in the shade

he LIVES long who lives well

as a MAN lives so shall he die

do as MOST men do and men will speak well of you

there's NOWT so queer as folk

OTHER times, other manners

do RIGHT and fear no man

when in ROME, do as the Romans do

SOFT and fair goes far

a SOFT answer turneth away wrath

WALK groundly, talk profoundly, drink roundly, sleep soundly

See also CHARACTER; HUMAN NATURE

BIRDS

a CROW on the thatch, soon death lifts the latch

when the CUCKOO comes he eats up all the dirt

the CUCKOO comes in April, and stays the month of May; sings a song at midsummer, and then goes away

on the FIRST of March, the crows begin to search

the LAPWING cries farthest from her nest

ONE for sorrow, two for joy; three for a girl, four for a boy; five for silver, six for gold; seven for a secret, never to be told; eight for heaven, nine for hell; and ten for the devil's own self

ONE woodcock does not make a winter

the ROBIN and the wren are God's cock and hen

if the ROBIN sings in the bush then the weather will be coarse; but if the robin sings in the barn then the weather will be warm

BLESSINGS

I was ANGERED, for I had no shoes – then I met a man who had no feet

BLESSINGS are not valued until they are gone

BLESSINGS brighten as they take their flight

BLINDNESS

if the BLIND lead the blind, both shall fall into the ditch

a BLIND man cannot judge colours

a BLIND man's wife needs no paint

BOASTFULNESS

ANYONE can kill a trussed foe

how we APPLES swim

BATE me an ace, quoth Bolton

a BOASTER and a liar are all one

they BRAG most that can do least

COMMEND not your wife, wine, nor house

CRACK was a good dog but he got hung for barking

EMPTY vessels make the most sound

EVERY cock crows on his own dunghill

EVERY cook praises his own broth

EVERY dog is a lion at home

FAR folks fare well

if you've GOT it, flaunt it

MANY talk of Robin Hood who never shot with his bow

MUCH cry and little wool

the PRIEST forgets that he was clerk

BOLDNESS

ADVENTURES are to the adventurous

BASHFULNESS is an enemy to poverty

BOLDNESS in business is the first, second and third thing

FORTUNE favours the bold

if you GENTLY touch a nettle it'll sting you for your pains

he who HESITATES is lost

NICE guys finish last

BOOKS

a BOOK that is shut is but a block

BOOKS and friends should be few and good

a GREAT book is a great evil

PICTURES are the books of the unlearned

BORROWING AND LENDING

he that goes A-BORROWING, goes a-sorrowing

who would BORROW when he hath not, let him borrow when he hath

BORROWED garments never fit well

he that BORROWS must pay again with shame or loss

CREDITORS have better memories than debtors

have a HORSE of your own and then you may borrow another's

he that doth LEND doth lose his money and friend

LEND not horse, nor wife, nor sword

LEND only that which you can afford to lose

LEND your money and lose your friend

NEITHER a borrower nor a lender be

he who has but ONE coat cannot lend it

SELDOM comes a loan laughing home

BOYS

BOYS will be boys

if you PLAY with boys you must take boys' play

TWO boys are half a boy, and three boys are no boy at all

BUILDING

you can't make BRICKS without straw

GIVE a cob a hat and a pair of shoes and he'll last for ever

no GOOD building without a good foundation

a HIGH building, a low foundation

it is the MEN who make a city

BURDENS

it is the LAST straw that breaks the camel's back

LIGHT burdens far heavy

BUSINESS AND COMMERCE

BOLDNESS in business is the first, second and third thing

BUSINESS before pleasure

BUSINESS is business

BUSINESS makes a man as well as tries him

CORPORATIONS have neither bodies to be punished nor souls to be damned

the CUSTOMER is always right

DRIVE your business, do not let it drive you

the ENGLISH are a nation of shopkeepers

EVERY honest miller has a thumb of gold

EVERY man to his trade

EVERYONE has a penny to spend at a new alehouse

the FAIRER the hostess, the fouler the reckoning

GOOD ware makes quick markets

JACK of all trades is master of none

KEEP your shop and your shop will keep you

there is KNAVERY in all trades

KNAVES and whores go by the clock

who LIKES not his business, his business likes not him

no MAN cries stinking fish

a MAN of many trades begs his bread on Sunday

MANY irons in the fire, some must cool

NEVER work with children or animals

ONE business begets another

it PAYS to advertise

PROFFERED service stinks

QUICK returns make rich merchants

SEND a fool to market and a fool he'll return

THREE women make a market

TRADE follows the flag

TRADE is the mother of money

there are TRICKS in every trade

when the WARES be gone, shut up the shop windows

WEIGH justly and sell dearly

BUTTER

BUTTER is mad twice a year

BUTTER is once a year in the cow's horn

BUYING AND SELLING

BUY in the cheapest market and sell in the dearest

you BUY land you buy stones, you buy meat you buy bones

let the BUYER beware

the BUYER has need of a hundred eyes, the seller of but one

while the DUST is on your feet, sell what you have bought

EVERYONE has a penny to spend at a new alehouse

GOOD ware makes quick markets

a MERCHANT that gains not, loseth

a MONEYLESS man goes fast through the market

NEVER offer your hen for sale on a rainy day

PLEASING ware is half sold

WEIGHT and measure take away strife

CARELESSNESS

it is EASY to rob an orchard when none keeps it

PROSPERITY lets go the bridle

he that RUNS in the night stumbles

he that SHOWS his purse bribes the thief

for WANT of a nail the shoe was lost

WANT of care does us more damage than want of knowledge

CAUSE AND EFFECT

an ANT hole may collapse an embankment

take away the CAUSE and the effect must cease

COMING events cast their shadows before

EVERY why hath its wherefore

take away FUEL, take away flame

ITCH and ease can no man please

a LITTLE leak will sink a great ship

a PENNY soul never came to twopence

PLANT the crab-tree where you will, it will never bear pippins

if you PLAY with boys you must take boys' play

REVOLUTIONS are not made with rose-water

RIGHT mixture makes good mortar

the SAME heat that melts the wax will harden the clay

the SAME knife cuts bread and fingers

there's no SMOKE without fire

See also RESULTS

CAUSES

it is a BAD cause that none dare speak in

CAUTIOUSNESS

ACT quickly, think slowly

don't put ALL your eggs in one basket

be not a BAKER if your head be of butter

BATE me an ace, quoth Bolton

it is BEST to be on the safe side

BETTER safe than sorry

BEWARE of Greeks bearing gifts

be not too BOLD with your biggers or betters

let the BUYER beware

the BUYER has need of a hundred eyes, the seller of but one

CALL the bear 'uncle' till you are safe across the bridge

CARE and diligence bring luck

a CAT in gloves catches no mice

CHILDREN and fools must not play with edged tools

from a CHOLERIC man withdraw a little, from him that says nothing for ever

CHOOSE not a house near an inn or in a corner

he that COUNTS all costs will never put plough in the earth

when you go to DANCE take heed whom you take by the hand

when in DOUBT, do nowt

DRIVE gently over the stones

the EARTHEN pot must keep clear of the brass kettle

let EVERY man praise the bridge he goes over

FIRST try and then trust

the FISH will soon be caught that nibbles at every bait

FULL cup, steady hand

GIVE a loaf and beg a slice

if you can't be GOOD, be careful

put not thy HAND between the bark and the tree

do not HANG all your bells upon one horse

take HEED is a fair thing

take HEED of an ox before, of a horse behind, of a monk on all sides

take HEED of reconciled enemies and of meat twice boiled

he who HESITATES is lost

the HORSES of hope gallop, but the asses of experience go slowly

KINDLE not a fire that you cannot extinguish

JOUK and let the jaw go by

LEAVE well alone

LOOK before you leap

MEASURE thrice and cut once

do not MEET troubles halfway

don't go NEAR the water until you learn how to swim

NEVER catch at a falling knife or friend

he that NEVER climbed never fell

NEVER praise a ford till you get over

ONCE bitten, twice shy

PISS not against the wind

PROSPERITY lets go the bridle

RECULER pour mieux sauter

no ROSE without a thorn

he that RUNS in the night stumbles

he who SAYS what he likes shall hear what he does not like

SECOND thoughts are best

SEEING is believing

let SLEEPING dogs lie

SOFTLY, softly, catchee monkey

the THIN end of the wedge is to be feared

don't THROW out your dirty water until you get in fresh

don't THROW the baby out with the bathwater

let not your TONGUE cut your throat

put your TRUST in God and keep your powder dry

TRY your skill in gilt first and then in gold

VENTURE not all in one bottom

See also COMMITMENT; DANGER; DILIGENCE; DISCRETION; EFFICIENCY; HASTE; RISK; WARNING; WATCHFULNESS

CERTAINTY

BELIEVE nothing of what you hear, and only half of what you see

NEVER quit certainty for hope

NOTHING is certain but death and taxes

SEEING is believing

a THOUSAND probabilities do not make one truth

CHANCE

it CHANCETH in an hour that happeneth not in seven years

LIGHTNING never strikes the same place twice

NEVER quit certainty for hope

CHANGE

there are no BIRDS in last year's nest

the CASE is altered

a CHANGE is as good as a rest

CHANGE of pasture makes fat calves

CIRCUMSTANCES alter cases

COMING events cast their shadows before

NAIL drives out nail

NEW lords, new laws

you can't put NEW wine in old bottles

PLUS ça change, plus c'est la même chose

when THINGS are at the worst they soon begin to mend

TIMES change and we with time

here TODAY, gone tomorrow

CHARACTER

ADVENTURES are to the adventurous

APPEARANCES are deceptive

you ARE what you eat

the BAIT hides the hook

BE what you would seem to be

it is not the BEARD that makes the philosopher

if the BEARD were all, the goat might preach

BEAUTY is only skin deep

BEAUTY without virtue is a flower without perfume

the BEST go first, the bad remain to mend

the COWL does not make the monk

it EARLY pricks that will be a thorn

EVERY man is the son of his own works

EVERY shoe fits not every foot

EVERYONE to his taste

FAIR face and a foul heart

FIRST impressions are the most lasting

GENTLE is that gentle does

GILT spurs do not make the knight

GOD is better pleased with adverbs than with nouns

a GOOD face is a letter of recommendation

GREAT men have great faults

HANDSOME is as handsome does

HORSES for courses

the HOUSE shows the owner

you can't JUDGE a book by its cover

a LAMB in the house, a lion in the field

a LEOPARD can't change its spots

the LION is not so fierce as he is painted

a LITTLE body often harbours a great soul

LONGEST at the fire soonest finds cold

a MAN is known by the company he keeps

NAMES and natures do often agree

NATURE passes nurture

NEVER judge by appearances

NICE guys finish last

ONCE a whore, always a whore

ONE man's meat is another man's poison

the OWL was a baker's daughter

the PEACOCK hath fair feathers, but foul feet

he that would make a PUN would pick a pocket

a ROSE by any other name would smell as sweet

SEEM not greater than thou art

SOFT and fair goes far

a SOFT answer turneth away wrath

you can't make a SPARROW-HAWK of a buzzard

in SPORTS and journeys men are known

the STYLE is the man

TASTES differ

See also BEHAVIOUR; HUMAN NATURE

CHARITY

ALMS quencheth sin

CHARITY and pride do both feed the poor

CHARITY begins at home

CHARITY covers a multitude of sins

CHEATS AND CHEATING

where the CARCASS is, there shall the eagles be gathered together

he that will CHEAT at play, will cheat you anyway

CHEATS never prosper

EVERY honest miller has a thumb of gold

there is KNAVERY in all trades

the TAILOR must cut three sleeves to every woman's gown

there are TRICKS in every trade

CHEERFULNESS

when GOOD cheer is lacking, our friends will be packing

it is GOOD to be merry at meat

a MAN of gladness seldom falls into madness

CHILDREN

BUILDING and marrying of children are great wasters

the CHILD is the father of the man

a CHILD may have too much of his mother's blessing

CHILDREN and chicken must always be pickin'

CHILDREN and fools must not play with edged tools

CHILDREN and fools have merry lives

CHILDREN and fools tell the truth

CHILDREN are certain cares, but uncertain comforts

CHILDREN are poor men's riches

CHILDREN have wide ears and long tongues

what CHILDREN hear at home soon flies abroad

he that has no CHILDREN knows not what is love

there are no CHILDREN nowadays

CHILDREN should be seen and not heard

when CHILDREN stand still they have done some ill

CHILDREN suck the mother when they are young, and the father when they are old

CLERGYMEN's sons always turn out badly

the CROW thinks her own birds fairest

it EARLY pricks that will be a thorn

FIRST born, first fed

FOOLS and bairns should never see half-done work

GIVE a child all he shall crave and a dog while his tail doth wave and you'll have a fair dog and a foul knave

HAPPY is he that is happy in his children

LATE children, early orphans

LITTLE pitchers have big ears

MAY chickens come cheeping

MONDAY's child is fair of face, Tuesday's child is full of grace; Wednesday's child is full of woe, Thursday's child has far to go; Friday's child is loving and giving, Saturday's child works hard for its living; and the child that's born on the Sabbath day, is fair and wise and good and gay

out of the MOUTHS of babes and sucklings

NEVER work with children or animals

the OFFSPRING of those that are very young or very old lasts not

PRAISE the child and you make love to the mother

SMALL birds must have meat

SPARE the rod and spoil the child

an UNTOWARD boy may make a good man

WANTON kittens make sober cats

he that WIPES the child's nose kisseth the mother's cheek

it is a WISE child that knows its own father

See also FAMILIES

CHOICE

BEGGARS can't be choosers

you can't have it BOTH ways

the BOUND must obey

you can't have your CAKE and eat it

when you go to DANCE take heed whom you take by the hand

a DOOR must either be shut or open

out of the FRYING-PAN into the fire

NEVER choose your women or your linen by candlelight

you PAYS your money and you takes your choice

you cannot SELL the cow and sup the milk

there is SMALL choice in rotten apples

there are MORE ways of killing a cat than choking it with cream

there are MORE ways of killing a dog than choking it with butter

there are MORE ways of killing a dog than hanging it

of TWO evils choose the lesser

there are TWO sides to every question

CHRISTMAS

CHRISTMAS comes but once a year

if at CHRISTMAS ice hangs on the willow, clover may be cut at Easter

EASTER in snow, Christmas in mud; Christmas in snow, Easter in mud

See also FARMING AND COUNTRY SAYINGS; SEASONS; WEATHER

CHURCH AND CHRISTIANITY

the BLOOD of the martyrs is the seed of the Church

the CHURCH is an anvil which has worn out many hammers

let the CHURCH stand in the churchyard

CHURCH work goes on slowly

where GOD builds a church, the Devil will build a chapel

the NEARER the church, the further from God

NEW church, old steeple, poor town and proud people

PINCH on the parson's side

the POORER the church, the purer the church

SALMON and sermon have both their season in Lent

TURKEY, heresy, hops and beer came into England all in one year

See also CLERGY; RELIGION

CLASS

when ADAM delved and Eve span, who was then the gentleman?

BRING a cow to the hall and she'll run to the byre

EVERYBODY loves a lord

it is not the GAY coat that makes the gentleman

JOAN is as good as my lady in the dark

a NOD from a lord is a breakfast for a fool

See also GENTLEMEN; HEREDITY; STATUS; UPBRINGING

CLEANLINESS

the CLARTIER the cosier

CLEANLINESS is next to godliness

if EVERY man would sweep his own doorstep the city would soon be clean

CLERGY

BEWARE of the forepart of a woman, the hind part of a mule, and all sides of a priest

CLERGYMEN's sons always turn out badly

take HEED of an ox before, of a horse behind, of a monk on all sides

a HOUSE-GOING parson makes a church-going people

a MONK out of his cloister is like a fish out of water

ONCE a priest, always a priest

like PEOPLE, like priest

the PRIEST forgets that he was clerk

a RUNAWAY monk never praises his convent

THREE things are insatiable, priests, monks, and the sea

See also CHURCH AND CHRISTIANITY; RELIGION

CLOTHES

an APE's an ape, a varlet's a varlet, though they be clad in silk or scarlet

APPAREL makes the man

BORROWED garments never fit well

at EASTER let your clothes be new, or else be sure you will it rue

FINE feathers make fine birds

it is not the GAY coat that makes the gentleman

GOOD clothes open all doors

our LAST garment is made without pockets

the TAILOR makes the man

WIDE will wear but narrow will tear

COERCION

the BOUND must obey

he that COMPLIES against his will is of his own opinion still

FANNED fires and forced love never did well yet

a FORCED kindness deserves no thanks

GIFTS enter without knocking

if the LAD go to the well against his will, either the can will break or the water will spill

you can LEAD a horse to water, but you can't make him drink

LITTLE birds that can sing and won't sing must be made to sing

LOVE cannot be compelled

MUST is for the king

ONE volunteer is worth two pressed men

SOFT and fair goes far

a SOFT answer turneth away wrath

COINCIDENCE

EVERY cake hath its make

GREAT minds think alike

it's a SMALL world

TALK of the Devil and he is bound to appear

COLLABORATION

CAT will to kind

EVERY cake hath its make

FOUR eyes see more than two

GREAT minds think alike

LIKE will to like

too MANY boatmen will run the boat up to the top of the mountain

too MANY cooks spoil the broth

MANY hands make light work

ONE bad general is better than two good ones

ONE hand washes the other

ONE mule doth scrub another

THREE helping one another bear the burthen of six

while the THUNDER lasted two bad men were friends

TWO boys are half a boy, and three boys are no boy at all

TWO heads are better than one

it takes TWO to tango

UNION is strength

UNITED we stand, divided we fall

See also HELP

COMMITMENT

it is a BAD cause that none dare speak in

COUNCILS of war never fight

whosoever DRAWS his sword against the prince must throw the scabbard away

you might as well be HANGED for a sheep as for a lamb

in for a PENNY, in for a pound

you cannot RUN with the hare and hunt with the hounds

See also CAUTIOUSNESS; INDECISION; RISK

COMMITTEES

COUNCILS of war never fight

too MANY boatmen will run the boat up to the top of the mountain

too MANY cooks spoil the broth

TWO boys are half a boy, and three boys are no boy at all

that VOYAGE never has luck where each one has a vote

COMPANIONSHIP

BIRDS of a feather flock together

the COMPANY makes the feast

GOOD company is the shortest cut

it is GOOD to have company in misery

KEEP bad men company and you'll soon be of their number

who KEEPS company with the wolf will learn how to howl

if you LIE down with dogs, you will get up with fleas

a MAN is known by the company he keeps

a MAN knows his companion in a long journey and a little inn

the MORE the merrier

SEVEN may be company but nine are confusion

TELL me with whom thou goest, and I'll tell thee what thou doest

TWO's company, three's a crowd

See also FRIENDS AND FRIENDSHIP

COMPARISON

in the ANTS' house the dew is a flood

a BARLEY-CORN is better than a diamond to a cock

there may be BLUE and better blue

COMPARISONS are odious

in the COUNTRY of the blind, the one-eyed man is king

the FAIRER the paper, the fouler the blot

they that be in HELL ween there is no other heaven

an HOUR of pain is as long as a day of pleasure

a HUMBLE-BEE in a cow-turd thinks himself a king

don't MEASURE other people's corn by one's own bushel

THINGS present are judged by things past

COMPENSATION

there's no GREAT loss without some gain

what you LOSE on the swings you gain on the roundabouts

out of OFFICE, out of danger

See also CONSOLATION

COMPLAINTS

a BLEATING sheep loses a bite

LIGHT cares speak, great ones are dumb

the SQUEAKING wheel gets the grease

the TONGUE ever turns to the aching tooth

COMPLIMENTS

COMPLIMENTING is lying

COMPROMISE

AGREE, for the law is costly

a BAD bush is better than an open field

BAD is the best

make the BEST of a bad bargain

BETTER a louse in the pot than no flesh at all

BETTER bend than break

CUT your coat according to your cloth

we must DO as we may, if we can't do as we would

EVERYONE stretches his legs according to the length of his coverlet

take what you FIND or what you bring

when all FRUIT falls, welcome haws

GNAW the bone which is fallen to thy lot

the GOAT must browse where she is tied

HALF a loaf is better than no bread

the HALF is better than the whole

one must HOWL with the wolves

we must not LOOK for a golden life in an iron cage

LOSE a leg rather than a life

a MAN must take such as he finds, or such as he brings

if the MOUNTAIN will not go to Mahomet, Mahomet must go to the mountain

you must PLOUGH with such oxen as you have

PUFF not against the wind

CONCEALMENT

CATS hide their claws

he that would HANG his dog gives out first that he is mad

those who HIDE can find

HIDE nothing from thy minister, physician and lawyer

NONE can guess the jewel by the casket

POISON is poison though it comes in a golden cup

one is not SMELT where all stink

See also DISCRETION; SECRETS; SILENCE

CONDITIONS

'IF' and 'an' spoils many a good charter

CONFESSION

CONFESS and be hanged

DRUNKENNESS reveals what soberness conceals

a FAULT confessed is half redressed

a GENEROUS confession disarms slander

OPEN confession is good for the soul

See also SLANDER

CONFIDENCE

in a CALM sea every man is a pilot

CONFIDENCE is a plant of slow growth

SKILL and confidence are an unconquered army

CONFIDENTIALITY

ANYTHING may be spoken if it be under the rose

CONFORMITY

one must HOWL with the wolves

do as MOST men do and men will speak well of you

if you PLAY with boys you must take boys' play

when in ROME, do as the Romans do

CONSCIENCE

a CLEAR conscience can bear any trouble

CONSCIENCE is a cut-throat

CONSCIENCE makes cowards of us all

a GOOD conscience is a continual feast

a GUILTY conscience needs no accuser

a QUIET conscience sleeps in thunder

CONSEQUENCES

the CASK savours of the first fill

the END justifies the means

FROST and fraud both end in foul

if the LAIRD slight the lady, so will all the kitchen boys

a LITTLE fire burns up a great deal of corn

ONE year's seeding means seven years' weeding

if you PLAY with boys you must take boys' play

the THIN end of the wedge is to be feared

CONSOLATION

I was ANGERED, for I had no shoes – then I met a man who had no feet

EVERY cloud has a silver lining

it's an ILL wind that blows nobody any good

what you LOSE on the swings you gain on the roundabouts

NOTHING so bad but it might have been worse

out of OFFICE, out of danger

there are PLENTY more fish in the sea

when THINGS are at the worst they soon begin to mend

TOMORROW is another day

what she WANTS in up and down she hath in round about

WORSE things happen at sea

See also COMPENSATION

CONTEMPT
CONTEMPT will sooner kill an injury than revenge

MOCKING is catching

SCORN at first makes after-love the more

CONTENTMENT
he who is CONTENT in his poverty is wonderfully rich

CONTENT is more than a kingdom

a CONTENTED mind is a continual feast

GOD's in his heaven; all's right with the world

COOKS AND COOKING
BOIL stones in butter and you may sup the broth

a COOK is known by his knife

EVERY cook praises his own broth

FISH must swim thrice

See also FOOD AND DRINK

CORRUPTION AND INCORRUPTIBILITY
he who has no BREAD has no authority

a BRIBE will enter without knocking

CORRUPTION of the best becomes the worst

EVERY man has his price

EVIL communications corrupt good manners

the FILTH under the white snow the sun discovers

the FISH always stinks from the head downwards

KEEP bad men company and you'll soon be of their number

a LITTLE poison embitters much sweetness

ONE scabbed sheep infects the whole flock

POWER corrupts

do RIGHT and fear no man

the ROTTEN apple injures its neighbours

he that TOUCHES pitch shall be defiled

TRUE blue will never stain

See also INFLUENCE; POWER

COST
HONEY is dear bought if licked off thorns

the MORE cost, the more honour

NOTHING costs so much as what is given us

See also VALUE

COURAGE
a BULLY is always a coward

he was a BOLD man that first ate an oyster

it is a BOLD mouse that breeds in the cat's ear

DESPAIR gives courage to a coward

DISCRETION is the better part of valour

EVERY dog is a lion at home

HARES may pull dead lions by the beard

a LAMB in the house, a lion in the field

NECESSITY and opportunity may make a coward valiant

NONE but the brave deserve the fair

ONE butcher does not fear many sheep

put a STOUT heart to a stey brae

COWARDICE
a BULLY is always a coward

put a COWARD to his mettle and he'll fight the devil

COWARDS are cruel

COWARDS die many times before their death

NECESSITY and opportunity may make a coward valiant

CREDITORS
CREDITORS have better memories than debtors

CRIME AND CRIMINALS
a BEGGAR may sing before a pickpocket

the DOG returns to its vomit

it is EASY to rob an orchard when none keeps it

the FOX preys furthest from his hole

it's an ILL bird that fouls its own nest

KILLING no murder

KNAVES and fools divide the world

the JAY bird don't rob his own nest

LITTLE thieves are hanged, but great ones escape

there is no PACK of cards without a knave

if there were no RECEIVERS, there would be no thieves

he that will be RICH before night may be hanged before noon

it is a SHAME to steal but a worse to carry home

he that SHOWS his purse bribes the thief

TWO blacks don't make a white

See also THIEVES; VICE

CRITICISM
ADMONISH your friends in private, praise them in public

he that BLAMES would buy

FAULTS are thick where love is thin

HARD words break no bones

NEVER speak ill of the dead

the STING of a reproach is the truth of it

no WOOL is so white that a dyer cannot blacken it

See also PRAISE

CRUELTY

who is BAD to his own is bad to himself

you've got to be CRUEL to be kind

CUNNING

ARTFUL speech and an ingratiating demeanour rarely accompany virtue

it is a BOLD mouse that breeds in the cat's ear

a CRAFTY fellow never has any peace

a CRAFTY knave needs no broker

CUNNING is no burden

he that would HANG his dog gives out first that he is mad

if the LION's skin cannot, the fox's shall

an OLD fox is not easily snared

SUBTLETY is better than force

CURIOSITY

CURIOSITY killed the cat

CURSES

CURSES, like chickens, come home to roost

he was CURSED in his mother's belly that was killed by a cannon

See also INSULTS; MALICE; REVENGE

CUSTOM

a BAD custom is like a good cake, better broken than kept

the COMMAND of custom is great

CUSTOM is a second nature

CUSTOM without reason is but ancient error

so MANY countries, so many customs

CUSTOMERS

the CUSTOMER is always right

CYNICISM

to the JAUNDICED eye all things look yellow

DANCING

when you go to DANCE take heed whom you take by the hand

it takes TWO to tango

DANGER

BEES that have honey in their mouths have stings in their tails

BEWARE of a silent dog and still water

BEWARE of Greeks bearing gifts

it is a BOLD mouse that breeds in the cat's ear

a DANGER foreseen is half avoided

DANGER is next neighbour to security

DANGERS are overcome by dangers

the DANGER past and God forgotten

out of the FRYING-PAN into the fire

don't HALLOO till you are out of the wood

he that HANDLES thorns shall prick his fingers

he that HATH his hand in the lion's mouth must take it out as well as he can

HARM watch, harm catch

HEAVEN protects children, sailors and drunken men

the MORE danger, the more honour

NOUGHT is never in danger

we PERISH by permitted things

if you PLAY with boys you must take boys' play

if you PLAY with fire you get burnt

he that PLAYS with cats must expect to be scratched

the POST of honour is the post of danger

he who RIDES a tiger is afraid to dismount

the RIVER passed and God forgotten

no ROSE without a thorn

no SAFE wading in an unknown water

there is a SCORPION under every stone

THREE things are not to be trusted: a cow's horn, a dog's tooth and a horse's hoof

while the THUNDER lasted two bad men were friends

WATER, fire and soldiers quickly make room

WATER is as dangerous as commodious

See also CAUTIOUSNESS; WARNING

DAUGHTERS

he that would the DAUGHTER win, must with the mother first begin

DAUGHTERS and dead fish are no keeping wares

like MOTHER, like daughter

my SON is my son till he gets him a wife, but my daughter's my daughter all the days of her life

TWO daughters and a back door are three arrant thieves

See also FAMILIES

DAYS

BARNABY bright, Barnaby bright, the longest day and the shortest night

the BETTER the day, the better the deed

CANDLEMAS Day, put beans in the clay, put candles and candlesticks away

the DAY is short and the work is long

what a DAY may bring a day may take away

be the DAY never so long, at length cometh evensong

no DAY passeth without some grief

no DAY so clear but hath dark clouds

no DAY without a line

the EVENING crowns the day

FRIDAY night's dream on the Saturday told, is sure to come true be it never so old

as the FRIDAY, so the Sunday

FRIDAY's hair and Sunday's horn go to the Devil on Monday morn

when our LADY falls in our Lord's lap, then let England beware a sad clap

the LONGEST day must have an end

MONDAY's child is fair of face, Tuesday's child is full of grace; Wednesday's child is full of woe, Thursday's child has far to go; Friday's child is loving and giving, Saturday's child works hard for its living; and the child that's born on the Sabbath day, is fair and wise and good and gay

there is NEVER a Saturday without some sunshine

if SAINT Paul's Day be fair and clear, it will betide a happy year

SAINT Swithin's Day, if thou dost rain, for forty days it will remain; Saint Swithin's Day, if thou be fair, for forty days 'twill rain no more

on SAINT Thomas the Divine kill all turkeys, geese and swine

SATURDAY's flit will never sit

TOMORROW is another day

there are only TWENTY-FOUR hours in the day

See also SUPERSTITIONS AND SAYINGS

DEATH

the BEST go first, the bad remain to mend

CALL no man happy till he dies

a CROW on the thatch, soon death lifts the latch

let the DEAD bury the dead

DEAD folks are past fooling

the DEAD have few friends

DEAD men don't bite

DEAD men tell no tales

DEATH defies the doctor

DEATH devours lambs as well as sheep

DEATH is the great leveller

DEATH keeps no calendar

DEATH pays all debts

they DIE well that live well

if the DOCTOR cures, the sun sees it, but if he kills, the earth hides it

DREAM of a funeral and you hear of a marriage

a DRY cough is the trumpeter of death

EARLY wed, early dead

a FAIR death honours the whole life

whom the GODS love die young

only the GOOD die young

our LAST garment is made without pockets

we shall LIE all alike in our graves

a MAN can die but once

there is no MEDICINE against death

the MORE thy years, the nearer thy grave

it is as NATURAL to die as to be born

NEVER speak ill of the dead

NOTHING is certain but death and taxes

OLD men go to death, death comes to young men

OLD men will die and children soon forget

a PIECE of churchyard fits everybody

he PULLS with a long rope that waits for another's death

there is a REMEDY for everything except death

SIX feet of earth make all men equal

STONE-DEAD hath no fellow

SOON todd, soon with God

a THOUSAND pounds and a bottle of hay is all one thing at doomsday as a TREE falls, so shall it lie

YOUNG men may die, but old men must die

See also LIFE AND DEATH; MORTALITY

DEBT

DEATH pays all debts

out of DEBT, out of danger

DEBTORS are liars

a HUNDRED pounds of sorrow pays not one ounce of debt

NOTHING costs so much as what is given us

a POUND of care will not pay an ounce of debt

SHORT reckonings make long friends

SPEAK not of my debts unless you mean to pay them

See also MONEY; SAVING AND SPENDING

DECEPTION

an APE's an ape, a varlet's a varlet, though they be clad in silk or scarlet

APPEARANCES are deceptive

ARTFUL speech and an ingratiating demeanour rarely accompany virtue

the BAIT hides the hook

BEES that have honey in their mouths have stings in their tails

a BLIND man's wife needs no paint

he CARRIES fire in one hand and water in the other

you cannot CATCH old birds with chaff

CATS hide their claws

CHILDREN are to be deceived with comfits and men with oaths

the COWL does not make the monk

CRAFT must have clothes but truth loves to go naked

DEAD folks are past fooling

to DECEIVE a deceiver is no deceit

he that will DECEIVE the fox must rise betimes

EVERY devil has not a cloven hoof

EVERYTHING tastes of porridge

FAIR words and foul deeds cheat wise men as well as fools

a FALSE tongue hardly speaks truth

you may FOOL all of the people some of the time, some of the people all of the time, but not all of the people all of the time

GILT spurs do not make the knight

he that would HANG his dog gives out first that he is mad

an HONEST look covereth many faults

you can't JUDGE a book by its cover

no MAN cries stinking fish

if a MAN deceive me once, shame on him, but if he deceive me twice, shame on me

if the PILLS were pleasant they would not want gilding

POISON is poison though it comes in a golden cup

PROFFERED service stinks

TRUST is the mother of deceit

DEEDS

ACTIONS speak louder than words

DEEDS are fruits, words are but leaves

what's DONE cannot be undone

ONE acre of performance is worth twenty of the Land of Promise

ONE today is worth two tomorrows

it is not with SAYING honey, honey, that sweetness will come into the mouth

SAYING is one thing, and doing another

the SHORTEST answer is doing

THINGS done cannot be undone

THINGS past cannot be recalled

DEFEAT

the BIGGER they are, the harder they fall

GIVE losers leave to speak

if a MAN once fall, all will tread on him

it SIGNIFIES nothing to play well if you lose

DEFENCE

ATTACK is the best form of defence

it is EASY to keep a castle that was never assaulted

TWO wrongs don't make a right

DELAYING

AFTER wit comes too late

CABBAGE twice cooked is death

DELAYS are dangerous

DELAYS are not denials

DESIRES are nourished by delays

HOPE deferred makes the heart sick

it's ILL waiting for dead men's shoes

MEN count up the faults of those who keep them waiting

PROCRASTINATION is the thief of time

TIME and tide wait for no man

no TIME like the present

DEMANDS

ASK much to have a little

when the DEMAND is a jest, the answer is a scoff

DENIAL

DENYING a fault doubles it

DESIRES are nourished by delays

DISSEMBLED sin is double wickedness

HOPE deferred makes the heart sick

DEPENDENCE

he who DEPENDS on another dines ill and sups worse

DESIRE

he BEGINS to die that quits his desires

DESIRE hath no rest

DESIRES are nourished by delays

he that DESIRES honour is not worthy

DIRTY water will quench fire

HUMBLE hearts have humble desires

DESPAIR

the DARKEST hour is just before the dawn

DESPAIR gives courage to a coward

HARE is melancholy meat

DESPERATION

a DROWNING man will clutch at a straw

DESTINY

ACCIDENTS will happen in the best regulated families

the BEST cart may overthrow

if you're BORN to be hanged then you'll never be drowned

he was CURSED in his mother's belly that was killed by a cannon

there are no FANS in hell

FORTUNE favours the bold

HANGING and wiving go by destiny

a MAN's destiny is always dark

there are MORE old drunkards than old doctors

SOON todd, soon with God

he that WORST may shall hold the candle

See also FATE; FORTUNE

DETERMINATION

one can go a LONG way after one is weary

SET hard heart against hard hap

put a STOUT heart to a stey brae

where there's a WILL there's a way

See also ENDURANCE

DEVIL

AWAY goes the devil when he finds the door shut against him

BETTER the devil you know than the devil you don't know

they that DEAL with the devil get a dear pennyworth

the DEVIL always leaves a stink behind him

the DEVIL bides his day

where the DEVIL cannot come, he will send

the DEVIL can quote scripture for his own purpose

the DEVIL dances in an empty pocket

the DEVIL finds work for idle hands

the DEVIL gets up to the belfry by the vicar's skirts

the DEVIL goes shares in gaming

why should the DEVIL have all the best tunes?

there is a DEVIL in every berry of the grape

the DEVIL is a busy bishop in his own diocese

the DEVIL is an ass

the DEVIL is at home

when the DEVIL is dead, he never lacks a chief mourner

the DEVIL is not as black as he is painted

the DEVIL looks after his own

the DEVIL lurks behind the cross

the DEVIL makes his Christmas-pies of lawyers' tongues and clerks' fingers

where no one else will, the DEVIL must bear the cross

the DEVIL rides upon a fiddlestick

the DEVIL to pay and no pitch hot

the DEVIL's behind the glass

the DEVIL's children have the Devil's luck

the DEVIL's mouth is a miser's purse

it is EASIER to raise the devil than to lay him

those that EAT black pudding will dream of the devil

EVERY devil has not a cloven hoof

GIVE the Devil his due

where GOD builds a church, the Devil will build a chapel

what is GOT over the devil's back is spent under his belly

SATAN reproves sin

he who SUPS with the Devil should have a long spoon

TALK of the Devil and he is bound to appear

See also EVIL

DIFFICULTY

the BEST fish swim near the bottom

the BEST things are worst to come by

in a CALM sea every man is a pilot

no DAY passeth without some grief

no DAY so clear but hath dark clouds

the DIFFICULT we do at once, the impossible takes a little longer

EASIER said than done

EVERY path hath a puddle

the FIRST seven years are the hardest

GOD makes the back to the burden

GOD tempers the wind to the shorn lamb

when the GOING gets tough, the tough get going

GOOD things are hard

HONOUR and ease are seldom bedfellows

MAN's extremity is God's opportunity

those who PLAY at bowls must look out for rubbers

there will be RUBS in the smoothest road

THINGS that are hard to come by are much set by

See also EASINESS

DIFFIDENCE

BASHFULNESS is an enemy to poverty

COLD hands, warm heart

in the COLDEST flint there is hot fire

the DUMB man gets no land

FAINT heart ne'er won fair lady

a GENTLE heart is tied with an easy thread

don't HIDE your light under a bushel

HUMBLE hearts have humble desires

a MAN may lose his goods for want of demanding them

he that STAYS in the valley shall never get over the hill

DILIGENCE

CARE and diligence bring luck

the DOG that trots about finds a bone

the EARLY bird catches the worm

GENIUS is an infinite capacity for taking pains

there is but an HOUR in a day between a good housewife and a bad

NINETY per cent of inspiration is perspiration

SOON enough, if well enough

See also CAUTIOUSNESS; EFFICIENCY

DISAPPOINTMENT

the BEST laid schemes of mice and men gang oft agley

he who DEPENDS on another dines ill and sups worse

you've got to EAT a peck of dirt before you die

the FAIRER the paper, the fouler the blot

they that be in HELL ween there is no other heaven

MANY go out for wool and come home shorn

but ONE egg and that addled too

PLEASE your eye and plague your heart

the ROAD to Hell is paved with good intentions

the SPIRIT is willing but the flesh is weak

DISCIPLINE

a BOISTEROUS horse must have a rough bridle

you may BREAK a horse's back, be he never so strong

a COLT you may break, but an old horse you never can

GIVE a child all he shall crave and a dog while his tail doth wave and you'll have a fair dog and a foul knave

SPARE the rod and spoil the child

DISCRETION

ALE-SELLERS should not be tale-tellers

don't put the CART before the horse

DISCRETION is the better part of valour

whosoever DRAWS his sword against the prince must throw the scabbard away

you might as well be HANGED for a sheep as for a lamb

not even HERCULES could contend against two

one must HOWL with the wolves

he KNOWS how many beans make five

in for a PENNY, in for a pound

you cannot RUN with the hare and hunt with the hounds

there is a TIME to speak, and a time to be silent

See also CAUTIOUSNESS; CONCEALMENT; SECRETS; SILENCE

DISEASE

AGUES come on horseback, but go away on foot

a DISEASE known is half cured

DISEASE will have its course

DISEASES are the price for ill pleasures

you should NEVER touch your eye but with your elbow

ONE scabbed sheep infects the whole flock

See also HEALTH AND ILLNESS; INFIRMITY; MEDICAL TREATMENT; REMEDIES

DISGRACE

there's a BLACK sheep in every family

DISHONESTY

he is a GOOD dog who goes to church

he that would HANG his dog gives out first that he is mad

ILL-GOTTEN gains seldom prosper

a MAN that breaks his word bids others be false to him

he that would make a PUN would pick a pocket

a SLICE off a cut loaf isn't missed

DISTANCE

BLUE are the hills that are far away

DISTANCE lends enchantment to the view

a STRANGER's eye sees clearest

DISTRACTION

CARE not would have it

CAST a bone in the devil's teeth

CATCH not at the shadow and lose the substance

the DEVIL rides upon a fiddlestick

the DOG that is idle barks at his fleas, but he that is hunting feels them not

LOOKERS-ON see most of the game

NEAREST the heart, nearest the mouth

NEVER let the plough stand to catch a mouse

the TONGUE ever turns to the aching tooth

TWO dogs fight for a bone, and a third runs away with it

DOCTORS

AFTER death the doctor

the BEST doctors are Dr Diet, Dr Quiet and Dr Merryman

if the DOCTOR cures, the sun sees it, but if he kills, the earth hides it

the DOCTOR is often more to be feared than the disease

GOD heals and the physician hath the thanks

he is a GOOD physician who cures himself

a GOOD surgeon must have an eagle's eye, a lion's heart and a lady's hand

there are MORE old drunkards than old doctors

an OLD physician and a young lawyer

PHYSICIAN, heal thyself

a PHYSICIAN is an angel when employed but a devil when one must pay him

a YOUNG physician fattens the churchyard

See also HEALTH AND ILLNESS

DOGS

a BARKING dog never bites

a DOG's nose and a maid's knees are always cold

a DOG will bark ere he bite

a GOOD dog deserves a good bone

he is a GOOD dog who goes to church

a MAN's best friend is his dog

it is a POOR dog that is not worth whistling for

DOWRIES

a GREAT dowry is a bed full of brambles

the LASS in the red petticoat shall pay for all

he that MARRIES for wealth sells his liberty

DREAMS

DREAM of a funeral and you hear of a marriage

DREAMS go by contraries

those that EAT black pudding will dream of the devil

FRIDAY night's dream on the Saturday told, is sure to come true be it never so old

MORNING dreams come true

DROUGHT

DROUGHT never bred dearth in England

DRUNKENESS

BACCHUS hath drowned more men than Neptune

you had BETTER be drunk than drowned

CIDER is treacherous because it smiles in the face and then cuts the throat

DRINK washes off the dawb and discovers the man

when the DRINK is in, the wit is out

he that DRINKETH well sleepeth well, and he that sleepeth well thinketh no harm

ever DRUNK, ever dry

he that is DRUNK is as great as a king

DRUNKEN days have all their tomorrows

DRUNKENNESS reveals what soberness conceals

EAT at pleasure, drink by measure

the FIRST glass for thirst, the second for nourishment, the third for pleasure, and the fourth for madness

he that KILLETH a man when he is drunk shall be hanged when he is sober

there are MORE old drunkards than old doctors

the MORE one drinks the more one may

a SPUR in the head is worth two in the heel

there is TRUTH in wine

WINE counsels seldom prosper

EARLY RISING

go to BED with the lamb and rise with the lark

the COW that's first up gets the first of the dew

the EARLY bird catches the worm

EARLY to bed and early to rise, makes a man healthy, wealthy and wise

he that comes FIRST to the hill, may sit where he will

he that RISETH late must trot all day

he that will THRIVE must rise at five

EASINESS

ANYONE can kill a trussed foe

a BALD head is soon shaven

a BONNY bride is soon buskit and a short horse is soon wispit

CROSS the stream where it is ebbest

it is EASIER to descend than to ascend

it is EASIER to pull down than to build up

EASY come, easy go

EASY does it

it is EASY to fall into a trap but hard to get out again

it is EASY to find a stick to beat a dog

it is EASY to keep a castle that was never assaulted

it is EASY to rob an orchard when none keeps it

LIGHT come, light go

MEN leap over where the hedge is lowest

a SHORT horse is soon curried

SOON gotten, soon spent

a THIN meadow is soon mowed

See also DIFFICULTY

EASTER

when EASTER falls in Our Lady's lap, then let England beware of a rap

EASTER in snow, Christmas in mud; Christmas in snow, Easter in mud

at EASTER let your clothes be new, or else be sure you will it rue

EASTER so longed for is gone in a day

SALMON and sermon have both their season in Lent

EATING

AFTER dinner rest a while, after supper walk a mile

a CHEERFUL look makes a dish a feast

EAT at pleasure, drink by measure

EAT till you sweat and work till you freeze

EATING and drinking takes away one's stomach

EATING and scratching wants but a beginning

HALF an hour is soon lost at dinner

QUICK at meat, quick at work

See also FOOD AND DRINK

EAVESDROPPING

LISTENERS never hear any good of themselves

WALLS have ears

EDUCATION

See LEARNING; TEACHERS

EFFICIENCY

the BUSIEST men have the most leisure

the EARLY bird catches the worm

the EARLY man never borrows from the late man

FIRST come, first served

he GIVES twice who gives quickly

PUNCTUALITY is the politeness of princes

PUNCTUALITY is the soul of business

SOON enough, if well enough

what is WELL done is done soon enough

See also CAUTIOUSNESS; DILIGENCE

EFFORT

ANYONE can kill a trussed foe

the BEST fish swim near the bottom

the BEST things are worst to come by

the DOG that trots about finds a bone

he that would EAT the fruit must climb the tree

ELBOW-GREASE gives the best polish

the END crowns the work

EVERY little helps

FAR behind must follow the faster

the FURTHER you go, the further behind

no GAINS without pains

GOD gives the milk but not the pail

GOD makes the back to the burden

GREAT bodies move slowly

the HIGHER the tree, the sweeter the plum

INDUSTRY is fortune's right hand, and frugality her left

it is the PACE that kills

SEEK and ye shall find

no SWEET without sweat

ELOQUENCE

a GOOD tongue is a good weapon

he that has not SILVER in his purse should have silk on his tongue

the TONGUE is the rudder of our ship

that is WELL spoken that is well taken

ENDINGS

See BEGINNINGS AND ENDINGS

ENDURANCE

BEAR and forbear

BEAR with evil and expect good

you may BREAK a horse's back, be he never so strong

the BOUGHS that bear most hang lowest

no CROSS, no crown

CROSSES are ladders that lead to heaven

what can't be CURED must be endured

he that would have EGGS must endure the cackling of hens

he that ENDURES is not overcome

an HOUR of pain is as long as a day of pleasure

it is the LAST straw that breaks the camel's back

SIT awhile and go a mile

SOFT pace goes far

SOON hot, soon cold

he that can STAY obtains

See also DETERMINATION

ENEMIES

the CAT and dog may kiss, yet are none the better friends

GOD defend me from my friends; from my enemies I can defend myself

the only GOOD Indian is a dead one

take HEED of reconciled enemies and of meat twice boiled

there is no LITTLE enemy

ONE enemy is too much

ENGLAND AND THE ENGLISH

ENGLAND is the paradise of women, the hell of horses and the purgatory of servants

ENGLAND's difficulty is Ireland's opportunity

the ENGLISH are a nation of shopkeepers

the ENGLISH never know when they are beaten

an ENGLISHMAN's word is his bond

when HEMPE is spun, England is done

when our LADY falls in our Lord's lap, then let England beware a sad clap

out of the NORTH all ill comes forth

ONE Englishman can beat three Frenchmen

THREE ills come from the north, a cold wind, a shrinking cloth, and a dissembling man

YORKSHIRE born and Yorkshire bred, strong in the arm and weak in the head

ENJOYMENT

FORBIDDEN fruit tastes sweetest

'tis MERRY in hall when beards wag all

it is a POOR heart that never rejoices

ENTHUSIASM

a NEW broom sweeps clean

ONE volunteer is worth two pressed men

a WILLING mind makes a light foot

ZEAL without knowledge is the sister of folly

ENVY

ENVY never dies

ENVY never enriched any man

the GRASS is always greener on the other side of the fence

MONEY makes friends enemies

your NEIGHBOUR's apples are the sweetest

ONE potter envies another

the SMOKE follows the fairest

he that hath a WHITE horse and a fair wife is never without trouble

EQUALITY

one BEATS the bush, another takes the bird

DEATH is the great leveller

DIAMOND cuts diamond

DOG does not eat dog

a FOOL may give a wise man counsel

MEDDLE with your match

EUTHANASIA

BETTER to hang than to hold

EVIDENCE

where the DEER is slain, some of her blood will lie

the SACK is known by the sample

STRAWS tell which way the wind blows

EVIL

when BALE is highest, boot is nighest

the DEVIL makes his Christmas-pies of lawyers' tongues and clerks' fingers

EVIL be to him who thinks it

EVIL communications corrupt good manners

EVIL doers are evil dreaders

an EVIL lesson is soon learned

GOD made man, man made money

GOD sends meat, but the Devil sends cooks

IDLENESS is the root of all evil

an ILL bird lays an ill egg

ILL doers are ill dreaders

an ILL turn is soon done

ILL weeds grow apace

the LOVE of money is the root of all evil

where OLD age is evil, youth can learn no good

he that PREACHES war is the Devil's chaplain

of TWO evils choose the lesser

the WEEDS overgrow the corn

See also DEVIL; GOOD AND GOODNESS; HEAVEN

EXAGGERATION

the LION is not so fierce as he is painted

no MAN cries stinking fish

don't make a MOUNTAIN out of a molehill

MUCH smoke, little fire

PROFFERED service stinks

a TALE never loses in the telling

EXAMPLE

BEAT the dog before the lion

he that CHASTENS one chastens twenty

where the DAM leaps over, the kid follows

DO as I say, not as I do

DO as you would be done by

EXAMPLE is better than precept

a GOOD example is the best sermon

where OLD age is evil, youth can learn no good

if ONE sheep leap o'er the dyke, all the rest will follow

he PREACHES well that lives well

he THREATENS many that hurts any

be WARNED by others' harm

the YOUNG cock crows as he heard the old one

EXCELLENCE

the BEST fish swim near the bottom

he is the BEST general who makes the fewest mistakes

the BEST go first, the bad remain to mend

the BEST is the enemy of the good

the BEST of men are but men at best

the BEST smell is bread, the best savour salt, the best love that of children

the BEST things are worst to come by

the BEST things come in small packages

the BEST things in life are free

the BEST things may be abused

if not BRAN, it is Bran's brother

the GOOD is the enemy of the best

EXCEPTIONS

there is an EXCEPTION to every rule

WONDERS will never cease

EXCESS

ABUNDANCE, like want, ruins many

you cannot BURN the candle at both ends

the LAST drop makes the cup run over

it is the LAST straw that breaks the camel's back

LIGHT burdens far heavy

MORE than enough is too much

you can have too MUCH of a good thing

it NEVER rains but it pours

it is the PACE that kills

PLENTY makes poor

SYMPATHY without relief is like mustard without beef

EXCUSES

ACCUSING the times is but excusing ourselves

a BAD excuse is better than none

he who EXCUSES himself, accuses himself

IDLE people lack no excuses

he that KILLETH a man when he is drunk shall be hanged when he is sober

See also GUILT

EXPECTATION

the BEST of men are but men at best

it is BETTER to travel hopefully than to arrive

BLESSED is he who expects nothing, for he shall never be disappointed

don't CROSS the bridge until you get to it

the DIFFICULT we do at once, the impossible takes a little longer

he that GAPETH until he be fed, well may he gape until he be dead

it is ILL fishing before the net

JAM tomorrow and jam yesterday, but never jam today

LONG looked for comes at last

MANY go out for wool and come home shorn

that which one MOST anticipates soonest comes to pass

the SACK is known by the sample

WONDERS will never cease

EXPERIENCE

he who has been BITTEN by a snake fears a piece of string

BITTER pills may have blessed effects

a BURNT child dreads the fire

you cannot CATCH old birds with chaff

a COLT you may break, but an old horse you never can

EXPERIENCE is a comb which nature gives us when we are bald

EXPERIENCE is the best teacher

EXPERIENCE is the mother of wisdom

EXPERIENCE is the teacher of fools

EXPERIENCE keeps a dear school

it is GOOD to learn at other men's cost

HANG a dog on a crab-tree and he'll never love verjuice

the HORSES of hope gallop, but the asses of experience go slowly

LIVE and learn

they that LIVE longest, see most

a MAN at thirty must be either a fool or a physician

MEN's years and their faults are always more than they are willing to own

an OLD cat sports not with her prey

you cannot put an OLD head on young shoulders

an OLD ox makes a straight furrow

an OLD physician and a young lawyer

an OLD wise man's shadow is better than a young buzzard's sword

ONCE bitten, twice shy

he who has ONCE burnt his mouth always blows his soup

an OUNCE of practice is worth a pound of precept

the PROOF of the pudding is in the eating

he who will not be RULED by the rudder must be ruled by the rock

a SCALDED cat fears cold water

whom a SERPENT has bitten, a lizard alarms

from the SWEETEST wine, the tartest vinegar

don't TEACH your grandmother to suck eggs

VARIETY is the spice of life

they that WALK much in the sun will be tanned at last

YEARS know more than books

See also AGE; LEARNING; OLD AGE; WISDOM

EXTRAVAGANCE

who DAINTIES love, shall beggars prove

FAR-FETCHED and dear-bought is good for ladies

MEN cut large thongs of other men's leather

who hath no MORE bread than need must not keep a dog

NOTHING agreeth worse than a lady's heart and a beggar's purse

SILKS and satins put out the fire in the chimney

TRASH and trumpery is the highway to beggary

WINE and wenches empty men's purses

EXTREMES

DESPERATE diseases call for desperate remedies

EXTREMES meet

it is the LAST straw that breaks the camel's back

LIGHT burdens far heavy

you can have too MUCH of a good thing

EYES

the EYES are the window of the soul

you should NEVER touch your eye but with your elbow

FACTS

FACT is stranger than fiction

FACTS are stubborn things

FAILURE

if ANYTHING can go wrong, it will

if the BLIND lead the blind, both shall fall into the ditch

no BUTTER will stick to his bread

he who CAN does, he who cannot teaches

it is EASIER to descend than to ascend

a MISS is as good as a mile

he who NEVER fails will never grow rich

you WIN a few, you lose a few

you can't WIN them all

FAIRNESS AND UNFAIRNESS

one BEATS the bush, another takes the bird

EVEN reckoning makes long friends

FAIR exchange is no robbery

FAIR play is a jewel

GIVE and take is fair play

be JUST before you're generous

the LEAST boy always carries the greatest fiddle

PLAY the game

it SIGNIFIES nothing to play well if you lose

TURN about is fair play

WEIGH justly and sell dearly

WEIGHT and measure take away strife

FAITH

the CHAMBER of sickness is the chapel of devotion

the DANGER past and God forgotten

FAITH will move mountains

IGNORANCE is the mother of devotion

MAN's extremity is God's opportunity

a MAN without religion is like a horse without a bridle

the NEARER the church, the further from God

the RIVER passed and God forgotten

put your TRUST in God and keep your powder dry

FAME

FAME is a magnifying glass

FAME is but the breath of the people

MORE people know Tom Fool than Tom Fool knows

FAMILIARITY

BETTER the devil you know than the devil you don't know

BETTER wed over the mixen than over the moor

CAT will to kind

let the COBBLER stick to his last

FAMILIARITY breeds contempt

come LIVE with me and you'll know me

I have LIVED too near a wood to be frightened by owls

no MAN is a hero to his valet

when a NEW book appears, read an old one

FAMILIES

there's a BLACK sheep in every family

BLOOD is thicker than water

EVERY family has a skeleton in the cupboard

the FAMILY that prays together stays together

it is a POOR family that has neither a whore nor a thief in it

the SHOEMAKER's son always goes barefoot

he that hath a WIFE and children hath given hostages to fortune

he that hath a WIFE and children wants not business

See also CHILDREN; DAUGHTERS; MOTHERS; MOTHERS-IN-LAW

FARMING AND COUNTRY SAYINGS

AFTER a famine in the stall comes a famine in the hall

BUTTER is once a year in the cow's horn

CALM weather in June sets corn in tune

if CANDLEMAS Day be sunny and bright, winter will have another flight; if Candlemas Day be cloudy with rain, winter is gone, and won't come again

CANDLEMAS Day, put beans in the clay, put candles and candlesticks away

a CHERRY year, a merry year; a plum year, a dumb year

if at CHRISTMAS ice hangs on the willow, clover may be cut at Easter

CLEAN heels, light meals

a COLD April the barn will fill

there is CORN in Egypt

a DRIPPING June sets all in tune

DUNDER do gally the beans

EARLY sow, early mow

he that would EAT the fruit must climb the tree

if you would ENJOY the fruit, pluck not the flower

if in FEBRUARY there be no rain, 'tis neither good for hay nor grain

FRUIT out of season, sorrow out of reason

if you would have FRUIT, you must bring the leaf to the grave

when all FRUIT falls, welcome haws

he that hath a GOOD harvest may be content with some thistles

a GOOD hay year a bad fog year

GOOD seed makes a good crop

a GOOD tree brings forth good fruit

the HIGHER the tree, the sweeter the plum

a LEAP YEAR is never a good sheep year

ONE for the mouse, one for the crow, one to rot, one to grow

PARSLEY seed goes nine times to the devil

PLAY in summer starve in winter

PLENTY of ladybirds, plenty of hops

SEPTEMBER blow soft, till the fruit's in the loft

SOW dry and set wet

as you SOW, so shall you reap

SOW with the hand and not with the sack

a SWARM of bees in May is worth a load of hay

like TREE, like fruit

TURNIPS like a dry bed but a wet head

UP corn, down horn

a WET May brings plenty of hay

See also GARDENING AND GROWING; TREES; WEATHER

FASHION

BETTER be out of the world than out of fashion

TAILORS and writers must mind the fashion

FATE

BE as be may

EACH cross hath its inscription

EVERY bullet has its billet

EVERY elm has its man

FATE leads the willing but drives the stubborn

FORTUNE is blind

See also DESTINY; FORTUNE

FAULTS

the FIRST faults are theirs that commit them, the second theirs that permit them

no GARDEN without its weeds

GREAT men have great faults

MEN's years and their faults are always more than they are willing to own

MOCKING is catching

FAVOURS

ASK no favour during the solano

he that EATS the king's goose shall be choked with his feathers

there is no such THING as a free lunch

FEAR

there are no ATHEISTS in foxholes

FEAR lends wings

he that has NOTHING is frightened of nothing

FERTILITY

the MORE hazelnuts, the more bastard children

FICKLENESS

ABSENCE makes the heart grow fonder

the DANGER past and God forgotten

the DEVIL sick would be a monk

LONG absent, soon forgotten

a ROLLING stone gathers no moss

SALT water and absence wash away love

out of SIGHT, out of mind

FIGHTING

CLUBS are trumps

where DRUMS beat, laws are silent

FAR shooting never killed bird

the SECOND blow makes the fray

as SORE fight wrens as cranes

the STICK is the surest peacemaker

FISHING

he that will CATCH eels must disturb the flood

CATCHING fish is not the whole of fishing

in the DEEPEST water is the best fishing

it is GOOD fishing in troubled waters

a HOOK is well lost to catch a salmon

SALMON and sermon have both their season in Lent

if you SWEAR you will catch no fish

FLATTERY

there is no such FLATTERER as a man's self

ILL egging makes ill begging

IMITATION is the sincerest form of flattery

'tis an OLD rat that won't eat cheese

FLEXIBILITY

BETTER bend than break

a BEGGAR is never out of his way

a REED before the wind lives on, while mighty oaks do fall

the VICAR of Bray will be vicar of Bray still

FOOD AND DRINK

ADAM's ale is the best brew

that is not ALWAYS good in the maw that is sweet in the mouth

an APPLE a day keeps the doctor away

APPLES, pears and nuts spoil the voice

APPLES taste sweetest when they are going

you ARE what you eat

an ARMY marches on its stomach

the BELLY carries the legs and not the legs the belly

he whose BELLY is full believes not him who is fasting

when the BELLY is full the mind is among the maids

BOIL stones in butter and you may sup the broth

BREAD and cheese be two targets against death

BREAD is the staff of life

BUTTER is mad twice a year

BUTTER is once a year in the cow's horn

CABBAGE twice cooked is death

CHEESE digests all things but itself

COLD pudding will settle your love

DIET cures more than doctors

if you DRINK in your pottage, you'll cough in your grave

DRY bread at home is better than roast meat abroad

you've got to EAT a peck of dirt before you die

EAT at pleasure, drink by measure

those that EAT black pudding will dream of the devil

EAT peas with the king and cherries with the beggar

we must EAT to live and not live to eat

EATEN bread is soon forgotten

EATING and drinking takes away one's stomach

EMPTY sacks will never stand upright

EVERYTHING tastes of porridge

FEED by measure and defy the physician

the FIRST dish pleaseth all

FISH must swim thrice

FULL bellies make empty skulls

GARLIC makes a man wink, drink and stink

GOD never sends mouths but He sends meat

GOOD ale is meat, drink and cloth

GOOD broth may be made in an old pot

a GOOD salad may be the prologue to a bad supper

it is a GOOD thing to eat your brown bread first

it is GOOD to be merry at meat

HALF a loaf is better than no bread

he was HANGED that left his drink behind

HARE is melancholy meat

HOT sup, hot swallow

HUNGER is the best sauce

a LEG of a lark is better than the body of a kite

he that would LIVE for aye must eat sage in May

MAN cannot live by bread alone

MEAT and mass never hindered man

when MEAT is in anger is out

'tis MERRY in hall when beards wag all

the MORE one drinks the more one may

NEVER eat an oyster unless there is an R in the month

NEW meat begets a new appetite

OLD fish and young flesh feed men best

ONE shoulder of mutton draws down another

POOR men seek meat for their stomach; rich men stomach for their meat

PUDDINGS and paramours should be hotly handled

SCORNFUL dogs will eat dirty puddings

of SOUP and love the first is the best

a SPUR in the head is worth two in the heel

TEMPERANCE is the best physic

a THISTLE is a fat salad for an ass's mouth

the WAY to a man's heart is through his stomach

See also COOKS AND COOKING; EATING

FOOLS AND FOOLISHNESS

ANOTHER course would have done it

he that makes himself an ASS must not take it ill if men ride him

a BARLEY-CORN is better than a diamond to a cock

go to BATTERSEA to get your simples cut

BETTER be a fool than a knave

it is BETTER to be born a beggar than a fool

CHANGE of weather is the discourse of fools

CHILDREN and fools have merry lives

CHILDREN and fools tell the truth

he COMPLAINS wrongfully on the sea who twice suffers shipwreck

the COW gives good milk but kicks over the pail

the DOG returns to its vomit

EVERY ass loves to hear himself bray

FOLLY grows without watering

a FOOL and his money are soon parted

a FOOL at forty is a fool indeed

a FOOL's bolt is soon shot

what the FOOL does in the end, the wise man does at the beginning

there's no FOOL like an old fool

a FOOL may give a wise man counsel

he is a FOOL that is not melancholy once a day

a FOOL thinks himself wise

a FOOL's tongue is long enough to cut his own throat

a FOOL will laugh when he is drowning

FOOLS and bairns should never see half-done work

FOOLS and madmen speak the truth

FOOLS ask questions that wise men cannot answer

FOOLS build houses, and wise men live in them

only FOOLS exult when governments change

FOOLS for luck

FOOLS rush in where angels fear to tread

FORTUNE favours fools

GIVE a clown a finger and he will take your hand

it is ILL sitting at Rome and striving with the Pope

there is no JOLLITY but hath a smack of folly

KNAVES and fools divide the world

no MAN is wise at all times

there are MANY ways of dressing a calf's head

'tis an OLD rat that won't eat cheese

SEND a fool to market and a fool he'll return

he that TALKS to himself talks to a fool

TWO fools in a house are too many

See also GULLIBILITY

FORCE

CLUBS are trumps

where DRUMS beat, laws are silent

MIGHT is right

the PEN is mightier than the sword

the STICK is the surest peacemaker

FORESIGHT

let ANOTHER's shipwreck be your sea-mark

a DANGER foreseen is half avoided

if you would ENJOY the fruit, pluck not the flower

FORECAST is better than work hard

FOREWARNED is forearmed

HALF warned, half armed

LOOK to the end

SUFFICIENT unto the day is the evil thereof

THINK on the end before you begin

the UNEXPECTED always happens

for WANT of a nail the shoe was lost

FORGIVENESS

to ERR is human, to forgive divine

FORGIVE and forget

he that does you an ILL turn will never forgive you

the NOBLEST vengeance is to forgive

OFFENDERS never pardon

ONCE nought, twice somewhat

PARDON all but thyself

though the WOUND be healed, a scar remains

FORTUNE

from CLOGS to clogs is only three generations

EVERY flow hath its ebb

FORTUNE favours fools

FORTUNE favours the bold

FORTUNE helps those who help themselves

FORTUNE is blind

FORTUNE knocks once at least at every man's gate

when FORTUNE smiles, embrace her

I today, you tomorrow

it is a LONG lane that has no turning

what you LOSE on the swings you gain on the roundabouts

what ONE day gives us, another takes away from us

the RISING of one man is the falling of another

from SHIRTSLEEVES to shirtsleeves in three generations

a SUDDEN rising hath a sudden fall

the TIDE never goes out so far but it always comes in again

TODAY you, tomorrow me

an UNHAPPY man's cart is eith to tumble

what goes UP must come down

whom GOD loves, his bitch brings forth pigs

See also DESTINY; FATE

FRANKNESS

CALL a spade a spade

PLAIN dealing is a jewel

FREEDOM

LEAN liberty is better than fat slavery

LIBERTY is not licence

as LONG as I live I'll spit in my parlour

the PRICE of liberty is eternal vigilance

a ROLLING stone gathers no moss

FRIENDS AND FRIENDSHIP

ADVERSITY makes strange bedfellows

a BAD penny always turns up

the BEST of friends must part

BIRDS of a feather flock together

BOOKS and friends should be few and good

the COMPANY makes the feast

a CROWD is not company

when DISTRUST enters in at the foregate, love goes out at the postern

the FALLING out of friends is the renewal of love

FANCY passes beauty

a FRIEND in need is a friend indeed

a FRIEND is not so soon gotten as lost

a FRIEND to all is a friend to none

FRIENDSHIP cannot stand always on one side

GOD defend me from my friends; from my enemies I can defend myself

when GOOD cheer is lacking, our friends will be packing

GOOD company is the shortest cut

it is GOOD to have company in misery

a HEDGE between keeps friendship green

take HEED of reconciled enemies and of meat twice boiled

one must HOWL with the wolves

he is an ILL companion that has a good memory

KEEP bad men company and you'll soon be of their number

who KEEPS company with the wolf will learn how to howl

you should KNOW a man seven years before you stir his fire

go down the LADDER when thou marriest a wife, go up when thou choosest a friend

LEAST said, soonest mended

he that doth LEND doth lose his money and friend

LEND your money and lose your friend

if you LIE down with dogs, you will get up with fleas

when LOVE puts in, friendship is gone

LOVE your friend with his fault

a MAN is known by the company he keeps

a MAN knows his companion in a long journey and a little inn

a MAN's best friend is his dog

it is MERRY when friends meet

MONEY makes friends enemies

the MORE the merrier

a NEAR friend is better than a far-dwelling kinsman

OLD friends and old wine are best

PROVE thy friend ere thou have need

SEVEN may be company but nine are confusion

SUDDEN friendship, sure repentance

TELL me with whom thou goest, and I'll tell thee what thou doest

while the THUNDER lasted two bad men were friends

TWO's company, three's a crowd

VISIT your aunt, but not every day of the year

See also COMPANIONSHIP

FRUIT

if you would ENJOY the fruit, pluck not the flower

when all FRUIT falls, welcome haws

FRUIT out of season, sorrow out of reason

if you would have FRUIT, you must bring the leaf to the grave

the HIGHER the tree, the sweeter the plum

SEPTEMBER blow soft, till the fruit's in the loft

like TREE, like fruit

FULFILMENT

NEVER sigh but send

FUNERALS

BLESSED are the dead that the rain rains on

DREAM of a funeral and you hear of a marriage

ONE funeral makes many

FUTILITY

ANGER without power is folly

BEG from beggars and you'll never be rich

it is ILL sitting at Rome and striving with the Pope

it is too LATE to shut the stable-door after the horse has bolted

the MOON does not heed the barking of dogs

the MORE you tramp on a turd the broader it grows

TWO things a man should never be angry at: what he can help and what he cannot help

it's no USE crying over spilt milk

it is in VAIN to cast your net where there is no fish

GAMBLING

the BEST throw of the dice is to throw them away

the BETTER gamester the worser man

CARDS are the Devil's books

the DEVIL goes shares in gaming

LOOK for your money where you lost it

LUCKY at cards, unlucky in love

on the TURF all men are equal, and under it

GARDENING AND GROWING

AFTER a famine in the stall comes a famine in the hall

if APPLES bloom in March, in vain for them you'll search; if apples bloom in April, then they'll be plentiful; if apples bloom in May, you may eat them night and day

CANDLEMAS Day, put beans in the clay, put candles and candlesticks away

CLEAN heels, light meals

DUNDER do gally the beans

as is the GARDENER, so is the garden

if you would be HAPPY for a week take a wife; if you would be happy for a month kill a pig; but if you would be happy all your life plant a garden

the MORE camomile is trodden on, the faster it grows

ONE year's seeding means seven years' weeding

See also FARMING AND COUNTRY SAYINGS; TREES

GENEROSITY

GIVE a clown a finger and he will take your hand

GIVE a loaf and beg a slice

GIVE and be blessed

GIVE and spend and God will send

who GIVES to all denies all

he that GIVES to be seen will relieve none in the dark

GIVING is dead and restoring very sick

the HAND that gives, gathers

be JUST before you're generous

GENIUS

GENIUS is an infinite capacity for taking pains

GENTLEMEN

it is not the GAY coat that makes the gentleman

a GENTLEMAN without an estate is a pudding without suet

GENTLEMEN and rich men are venison in heaven

GENTRY sent to market will not buy one bushel of corn

the KING can make a knight, but not a gentleman

NINE tailors make a man

it takes THREE generations to make a gentleman

See also CLASS; HEREDITY

GENTLENESS

GENTLE is that gentle does

if you GENTLY touch a nettle it'll sting you for your pains

NICE guys finish last

SOFT and fair

a SOFT answer turneth away wrath

GIFTS

the BEST things come in small packages

BEWARE of Greeks bearing gifts

a GIFT long waited for is sold not given

GIFTS enter without knocking

to GIVE a thing, and take a thing, is to wear the Devil's gold ring

he GIVES twice who gives quickly

NOTHING costs so much as what is given us

GOD

where GOD builds a church, the Devil will build a chapel

GOD comes at last when we think he is furthest off

GOD gives the milk but not the pail

GOD heals and the physician hath the thanks

GOD help the poor, for the rich can help themselves

GOD helps those who help themselves

GOD is always on the side of the big battalions

GOD is better pleased with adverbs than with nouns

GOD is where He was

whom GOD loves, his bitch brings forth pigs

GOD made man, man made money

GOD makes the back to the burden

GOD never sends mouths but He sends meat

GOD sends meat, but the Devil sends cooks

GOD send you joy, for sorrow will come fast enough

GOD's in his heaven; all's right with the world

there are GOD's poor and the devil's poor

GOD tempers the wind to the shorn lamb

where GOD will help, nothing does harm

the GODS send nuts to those who have no teeth

MAN proposes, but God disposes

you cannot SERVE God and Mammon

put your TRUST in God and keep your powder dry

the VOICE of the people is the voice of God

GOOD AND GOODNESS

where the BEE sucks honey the spider sucks poison

the BETROTHED of good is evil, the betrothed of life is death, the betrothed of love is divorce

CLEANLINESS is next to godliness

GOD is better pleased with adverbs than with nouns

GOOD and quickly seldom meet

GOOD finds good

a GOOD heart cannot lie

a GOOD horse cannot be of a bad colour

GOOD men are scarce

GOODNESS is not tied to greatness

he KNOWS best what good is that has endured evil

PLANT the crab-tree where you will, it will never bear pippins

do RIGHT and fear no man

See also EVIL; HEAVEN

GOSSIP

a DOG that will fetch a bone will carry a bone

See also RUMOUR

GRAFFITI

a WHITE wall is a fool's paper

GREED

a BEGGAR's purse is bottomless

a BELLY full of gluttony will never study willingly

where the CARCASS is, there shall the eagles be gathered together

EATING and scratching wants but a beginning

the EYE is bigger than the belly

GLUTTONY kills more than the sword

GREEDY folks have long arms

MANY dishes make many diseases

MUCH meat, much malady

you can have too MUCH of a good thing

MUCH would have more

NEED makes greed

PLENTY makes poor

GRIEF

EVERY heart hath its own ache

ONE grief drives out another

GUESTS

a CONSTANT guest is never welcome

he that DINES and leaves lays the cloth twice

FISH and guests stink after three days

SHORT visits make long friends

an UNBIDDEN guest knoweth not where to sit

VISIT your aunt, but not every day of the year

See also HOSPITALITY

GUILT

ALMOST was never hanged

if the CAP fits, wear it

when CHILDREN stand still they have done some ill

a CRAFTY fellow never has any peace

EVERYONE is innocent until proved guilty

a GUILTY conscience needs no accuser

it's an ILL bird that fouls its own nest

he that does you an ILL turn will never forgive you

he that KILLETH a man when he is drunk shall be hanged when he is sober

no NAMES, no pack drill

there is no REDEMPTION from hell

SET the saddle on the right horse

one is not SMELT where all stink

See also EXCUSES; HELL AND DAMNATION

GULLIBILITY

ADMIRATION is the daughter of ignorance

if a MAN deceive me once, shame on him, but if he deceive me twice, shame on me

it is a SILLY fish that is caught twice with the same bait

they that THINK none ill are soonest beguiled

See also FOOLS AND FOOLISHNESS

HABIT

the ASS loaded with gold still eats thistles

a BAD custom is like a good cake, better broken than kept

the COMMAND of custom is great

OLD habits die hard

HAPPINESS

BETTER be happy than wise

CALL no man happy till he dies

he is a FOOL that is not melancholy once a day

HAPPINESS takes no account of time

if you would be HAPPY for a week take a wife; if you would be happy for a month kill a pig; but if you would be happy all your life plant a garden

HAPPY is he that is happy in his children

HAPPY is the bride the sun shines on

HAPPY is the country which has no history

HAPPY is the wooing that is not long a-doing

a LITTLE house well filled, a little land well tilled, and a little wife well willed

MEMORY of happiness makes misery woeful

the MIRTH of the world dureth but a while

he that TALKS much of his happiness, summons grief

HARMONY

AGREE, for the law is costly

BIRDS in their little nests agree

there is no GOOD accord where every man would be a lord

a HOUSE divided against itself cannot stand

an ILL agreement is better than a good judgement

ORDER is heaven's first law

it takes TWO to make a bargain

HASTE

HASTE is from the Devil

HASTE makes waste

make HASTE slowly

the HASTY bitch bringeth forth blind whelps

HASTY climbers have sudden falls

HASTY love is soon hot and soon cold

the HASTY man never wants woe

MARRY in haste and repent at leisure

MORE haste, less speed

NOTHING should be done in haste but gripping a flea

he that will be RICH before night may be hanged before noon

a SOFT fire makes a sweet malt

See also CAUTIOUSNESS

HEALTH AND ILLNESS

AFTER dinner rest a while, after supper walk a mile

AGUES come on horseback, but go away on foot

an APPLE a day keeps the doctor away

APPLES, pears and nuts spoil the voice

he who BATHES in May will soon be laid in clay; he who bathes in June, will sing a merry tune; he who bathes in July, will dance like a fly

he that goes to BED thirsty riseth healthy

the BEST doctors are Dr Diet, Dr Quiet and Dr Merryman

BETTER to hang than to hold

BREAD and cheese be two targets against death

you cannot BURN the candle at both ends

the CHAMBER of sickness is the chapel of devotion

CREAKING doors hang the longest

DIET cures more than doctors

if you DRINK in your pottage, you'll cough in your grave

a DRY cough is the trumpeter of death

FEED a cold and starve a fever

GLUTTONY kills more than the sword

when the HEAD acheth all the body is the worse

HEALTH is better than wealth

HEALTH is not valued till sickness comes

a LEAN dog to get through the hedge

MANY dishes make many diseases

MUCH meat, much malady

you should NEVER touch your eye but with your elbow

it is the PACE that kills

POVERTY is the mother of health

SICKNESS comes on horseback, but goeth away on foot

SICKNESS shows us what we are

SIT awhile and go a mile

where the SUN enters the doctor does not

TEMPERANCE is the best physic

WEALTH is enemy to health

he that would be WELL old must be old betimes

See also DISEASE; DOCTORS; INFIRMITY; MEDICAL TREATMENT; REMEDIES

HEAVEN

BLESSED are the dead that the rain rains on

CROSSES are ladders that lead to heaven

it is EASIER for a camel to go through the eye of a needle than it is for a rich man to enter into the kingdom of heaven

GOD's in his heaven; all's right with the world

GOLD goes in at any gate except heaven's

HEAVEN protects children, sailors and drunken men

no coming to HEAVEN with dry eyes

ORDER is heaven's first law

who SPITS against heaven it falls in his face

See also EVIL; GOOD AND GOODNESS

HELL AND DAMNATION

there are no FANS in hell

from HELL, Hull and Halifax, Good Lord deliver us

HELL and Chancery are always open

HELL hath no fury like a woman scorned

they that be in HELL ween there is no other heaven

there is no REDEMPTION from hell

See also GUILT; MERCY; WICKEDNESS

HELP

when BALE is highest, boot is nighest

he HELPS little that helps not himself

a MOUSE may help a lion

SLOW help is no help

THREE helping one another bear the burthen of six

too MANY cooks spoil the broth

See also COLLABORATION

HEREDITY

BEGGARS breed and rich men feed

BIRTH is much but breeding more

BREEDING rather than birth

there is no DIFFERENCE of bloods in a basin

DOGS bark as they are bred

what can you EXPECT from a pig but a grunt?

like FATHER, like son

it is not the GAY coat that makes the gentleman

no GOOD apple on a sour stock

a GOOD tree brings forth good fruit

the KING can make a knight, but not a gentleman

MANY a good cow hath an evil calf

like MOTHER, like daughter

you can't make a SILK purse out of a sow's ear

a STREAM cannot rise above its source

like TREE, like fruit

a WILD goose never lays a tame egg

See also CLASS; GENTLEMEN; UPBRINGING

HERESY

TURKEY, heresy, hops and beer came into England all in one year

HINDSIGHT

ADVICE should be viewed from behind

BLESSINGS are not valued until they are gone

it is EASY to be wise after the event

HINTS

a NOD is as good as a wink to a blind horse

a WORD to the wise is enough

HISTORY AND THE PAST

BRAVE men lived before Agamemnon

HAPPY is the country which has no history

HISTORY repeats itself

THINGS present are judged by things past

TIMES past cannot be recalled

TODAY is yesterday's pupil

YESTERDAY will not be called again

See also NOSTALGIA

HOME

CHOOSE not a house near an inn or in a corner

EAST, west, home's best

an ENGLISHMAN's home is his castle

HOME is home, though it be never so homely

HOME is where the heart is

HOME, sweet home

the HOUSE shows the owner

it's an ILL bird that fouls its own nest

there's no PLACE like home

HONESTY

BE what you would seem to be

BEAUTY and honesty seldom agree

CALL a spade a spade

CHILDREN and fools tell the truth

DRINK washes off the dawb and discovers the man

DRUNKENNESS reveals what soberness conceals

FAR folks fare well

a GOOD face is a letter of recommendation

a GOOD heart cannot lie

HONESTY is the best policy

a MAN that breaks his word bids others be false to him

you cannot make PEOPLE honest by Act of Parliament

PLAIN dealing is a jewel

PLAY the game

he PREACHES well that lives well

do RIGHT and fear no man

SEEM not greater than thou art

TRUE blue will never stain

See also INSINCERITY

HONOUR

he that DESIRES honour is not worthy

an ENGLISHMAN's word is his bond

GIVE credit where credit is due

there is HONOUR among thieves

HONOUR and ease are seldom bedfellows

HONOUR buys no beef

HONOURS change manners

the POST of honour is the post of danger

HOPE
AFTER drought cometh rain

he BEGINS to die that quits his desires

HOPE and have

HOPE deferred makes the heart sick

HOPE for the best and prepare for the worst

HOPE is a good breakfast but a bad supper

HOPE springs eternal in the human breast

if it were not for HOPE, the heart would break

the HORSES of hope gallop, but the asses of experience go slowly

where there's LIFE there's hope

he that LIVES in hope dances to an ill tune

NEVER quit certainty for hope

when THINGS are at the worst they soon begin to mend

HORSES
CHOOSE a horse made and a wife to make

there is NOTHING so good for the inside of a man as the outside of a horse

HOSPITALITY
a HEARTY welcome is the best cheer

See also GUESTS

HOUSEKEEPING
a CARELESS hussy makes many thieves

where COBWEBS are plenty, kisses are scarce

FAT housekeepers make lean executors

a GENTLE housewife mars the household

there is but an HOUR in a day between a good housewife and a bad

HUMAN NATURE
the BEST of men are but men at best

BLACK will take no other hue

BOYS will be boys

if the BRAIN sows not corn, it plants thistles

CAT will to kind

EACH bird loves to hear himself sing

EAGLES don't catch flies

EAGLES fly alone

LIKE will to like

LONGEST at the fire soonest finds cold

there's NOWT so queer as folk

See also CHARACTER; BEHAVIOUR

HUMILITY
it is EASIER for a camel to go through the eye of a needle than it is for a rich man to enter into the kingdom of heaven

HUMBLE hearts have humble desires

the WAY to see divine light is to put out thine own candle

HUNGER
a BELLY full of gluttony will never study willingly

HUNGER and cold deliver a man up to his enemy

HUNGER breaks through stone walls

HUNGER drives the wolf out of the wood

they must HUNGER in frost that will not work in heat

HUNGER is the best sauce

HUNGRY bellies have no ears

HUNGRY flies bite sore

a HUNGRY man is an angry man

it's ILL speaking between a full man and a fasting

a SHARP stomach makes short devotion

HUSBANDS AND WIVES
it is BETTER to marry a shrew than a sheep

the CALMEST husbands make the stormiest wives

CHOOSE a horse made and a wife to make

when a COUPLE are newly married the first month is honeymoon, or smick smack; the second is hither and thither; the third is thwick thwack; the fourth the Devil take them that brought thee and I together

a DEAF husband and a blind wife are always a happy couple

EVERY Jack has his Jill

EVERY man can rule a shrew but he who has her

who hath a FAIR wife needs more than two eyes

a GOOD husband makes a good wife

a GOOD Jack makes a good Jill

a GOOD wife and health is a man's best wealth

the GREY mare is the better horse

the HUSBAND is always the last to know

HUSBANDS are in heaven whose wives scold not

if the LAIRD slight the lady, so will all the kitchen boys

a LEWD bachelor makes a jealous husband

MILLS and wives are ever wanting

NEXT to no wife, a good wife is best

a NICE wife and a back door will soon make a rich man poor

it is a SAD house where the hen crows louder than the cock

he that TELLS his wife news is but newly married

THREE things drive a man out of his house: smoke, rain, and a scolding wife

he that will THRIVE must first ask his wife

he that has a WIFE has a master

See also MARRIAGE

HYPOCRISY

one has ALWAYS strength enough to bear the misfortunes of one's friends

CARRION crows bewail the dead sheep, and then eat them

DO as I say, not as I do

he that GIVES to be seen will relieve none in the dark

HYPOCRISY can find out a cloak for every rain

MANY a one says well that thinks ill

PHYSICIAN, heal thyself

the POT calls the kettle black

PRACTISE what you preach

he PREACHES well that lives well

the VICAR of Bray will be vicar of Bray still

IDLENESS

without BUSINESS, debauchery

the DEVIL finds work for idle hands

the DOG that is idle barks at his fleas, but he that is hunting feels them not

IDLE bairns are the devil's workhouses

an IDLE brain is the Devil's workshop

IDLE people have the least leisure

IDLE people lack no excuses

it is IDLE to swallow the cow and choke on the tail

an IDLE youth a needy age

IDLENESS is the root of all evil

IDLENESS turns the edge of wit

IRON not used soon rusts

by doing NOTHING we learn to do ill

IGNORANCE

ADMIRATION is the daughter of ignorance

if the BLIND lead the blind, both shall fall into the ditch

a BLIND man cannot judge colours

in the COUNTRY of the blind, the one-eyed man is king

a DEAF husband and a blind wife are always a happy couple

what the EYE does not see, the heart does not grieve over

he that GROPES in the dark finds that he would not

HALF the world doesn't know how the other half lives

IGNORANCE is bliss

IGNORANCE is the mother of devotion

IGNORANCE is the mother of impudence

IGNORANCE of the law is no excuse

it is ILL to drive black hogs in the dark

what you don't KNOW can't hurt you

he that KNOWS nothing, doubts nothing

there are NONE so blind as those who will not see

there are NONE so deaf as those who will not hear

NOTHING so bold as a blind mare

he that RUNS in the night stumbles

he that is WARM thinks all so

WONDER is the daughter of ignorance

ZEAL without knowledge is the sister of folly

IMITATION

IMITATION is the sincerest form of flattery

what MANCHESTER says today, the rest of England says tomorrow

IMPARTIALITY

on PAINTING and fighting look aloof

SHOW me the man and I'll show you the law

a STRANGER's eye sees clearest

there are TWO sides to every question

IMPERFECTION

a CRACKED bell can never sound well

CROOKED logs make straight fires

no GARDEN without its weeds

the PEACOCK hath fair feathers, but foul feet

IMPOSSIBILITY

you cannot get BLOOD from a stone

you can't make BRICKS without straw

the DIFFICULT we do at once, the impossible takes a little longer

you can't FIT a quart into a pint pot

FURTHER than the wall we cannot go

no LIVING man all things can

a MAN can do no more than he can

a MAN cannot give what he hasn't got

a MAN cannot spin and reel at the same time

a MAN cannot whistle and drink at the same time

the MOON does not heed the barking of dogs

NOTHING is impossible

there comes NOUGHT out of the sack but what was there

PLANT the crab-tree where you will, it will never bear pippins

you can't PLEASE everyone

you can't make a SILK purse out of a sow's ear

a STREAM cannot rise above its source

IMPUDENCE

IGNORANCE is the mother of impudence

don't TEACH your grandmother to suck eggs

INCOMPETENCE

a BAD workman blames his tools

as the BLIND man catches the hare

INDECISION

BETWEEN two stools you fall to the ground

when in DOUBT, do nowt

when you don't KNOW what to do – wait

See also COMMITMENT

INDEPENDENCE

EAGLES fly alone

PADDLE your own canoe

INDIFFERENCE

the DOGS bark but the caravan goes on

THINGS that are above us are nothing to us

INDIVIDUALITY

EVERY cake hath its make

EVERY heart hath its own ache

EVERY shoe fits not every foot

EVERYONE to his taste

no HAIR so small but hath his shadow

HORSES for courses

ONE man's meat is another man's poison

TASTES differ

INDULGENCE

See TOLERANCE

INEVITABILITY

if ANYTHING can go wrong, it will

the FAIREST rose at last is withered

the MOON does not heed the barking of dogs

TIME devours all things

TIME will tell

WHAT must be, must be

See also TIME

INEXPERIENCE

a BARBER learns to shave by shaving fools

EARLY master, long knave

HEAVEN protects children, sailors and drunken men

a YOUNG physician fattens the churchyard

INFIDELITY

it is BETTER to be a cuckold and not know it, than be none and everybody say so

HORNS and grey hairs do not come by years

the HUSBAND is always the last to know

who hath a FAIR wife needs more than two eyes

INFIRMITY

CREAKING doors hang the longest

it is HARD halting before a cripple

he can ILL pipe that lacketh his upper lip

he may ILL run that cannot go

See also DISEASE; HEALTH AND ILLNESS; MEDICAL TREATMENT; REMEDIES

INFLUENCE

he who has no BREAD has no authority

he whose FATHER is judge goes safe to his trial

a FRIEND in court is better than a penny in purse

the HAND that rocks the cradle rules the world

KINGS have long arms

where MACGREGOR sits is the head of the table

TELL me with whom thou goest, and I'll tell thee what thou doest

as the TWIG is bent, so is the tree inclined

there are WHEELS within wheels

See also CORRUPTION AND INCORRUPTIBILITY; POWER

INGRATITUDE

put ANOTHER man's child in your bosom and he'll creep out at your elbow

don't BITE the hand that feeds you

KILL not the goose that lays the golden egg

SAVE a thief from the gallows and he shall cut your throat

SIT a beggar at your table, and he will soon put his feet on it

INGREDIENTS

you can't make BRICKS without straw

REVOLUTIONS are not made with rose-water

RIGHT mixture makes good mortar

you can't make a SILK purse out of a sow's ear

INHERITANCE

the APPLE never falls far from the tree

as a BEAR has no tail, for a lion he'll fail

BLOOD will tell

what's BRED in the bone will come out in the flesh

LAND was never lost for want of an heir

LIKE breeds like

INNOCENCE

the BRIDE goes to her marriage-bed but knows not what shall happen to her

a CLEAR conscience can bear any trouble

EVERYONE is innocent until proved guilty

a QUIET conscience sleeps in thunder

they that THINK none ill are soonest beguiled

a TRULY great man never puts away the simplicity of a child

INSINCERITY

the ACOLYTE at the gate reads scriptures he has never learnt

a BELLOWING cow soon forgets her calf

CARE not would have it

he CARRIES fire in one hand and water in the other

CARRION crows bewail the dead sheep, and then eat them

the CAT and dog may kiss, yet are none the better friends

MANY a one says well that thinks ill

NOTHING dries sooner than a tear

See also HONESTY

INSTINCT

FEELING hath no fellow

INSULTS

CURSES, like chickens, come home to roost

FLING enough dirt and some will stick

HARD words break no bones

there were no ILL language if it were not ill taken

INJURIES don't use to be written on ice

if the LAIRD slight the lady, so will all the kitchen boys

ONE ill word asketh another

STICKS and stones may break my bones, but names will never hurt me

the TONGUE is not steel yet it cuts

See also CURSES

INTELLIGENCE

FAT paunches make lean pates

FULL bellies make empty skulls

GLOWING coals sparkle oft

GREAT wits jump

IDLENESS turns the edge of wit

he KNOWS how many beans make five

a MAN will never change his mind if he has no mind to change

the MIND is the man

my MIND to me a kingdom is

the MOB has many heads but no brains

INTENTION

the BEST laid schemes of mice and men gang oft agley

the ROAD to Hell is paved with good intentions

INVITATIONS

it is as CHEAP sitting as standing

come not to COUNSEL uncalled

IRRITATION

FISH and guests stink after three days

ITCH and ease can no man please

the TONGUE ever turns to the aching tooth

JEALOUSY

JEALOUSY shuts one door and opens two

LOVE is never without jealousy

JOKES

if you GIVE a jest, you must take a jest

a JOKE breaks no bones

a JOKE never gains over an enemy, but often loseth a friend

LEAVE a jest when it pleases you best

there's MANY a true word spoken in jest

JOY

there is no JOLLITY but hath a smack of folly

JOY and sorrow are next door neighbours

the MIRTH of the world dureth but a while

an OUNCE of mirth is worth a pound of sorrow

SADNESS and gladness succeed each other

JUDGEMENT

he is the BEST general who makes the fewest mistakes

CIRCUMSTANCES alter cases

he hath a GOOD judgement that relieth not wholly on his own

JUDGE not, that ye be not judged

NEVER judge by appearances

See also LAW

JUDGES

a GOOD judge conceives quickly, judges slowly

a JUDGE knows nothing unless it has been explained to him three times

no one should be JUDGE in his own cause

SHOW me the man and I'll show you the law

KINDNESS

CARE is no cure

a KIND heart loseth nought at last

KIND hearts are soonest wronged

KINDNESS is lost that is bestowed on children and old folks

one NEVER loses by doing a good turn

SIT a beggar at your table, and he will soon put his feet on it

KINGS AND RULERS

the CAT, the Rat, and Lovell our Dog rule all England under an Hog

a CROWN is no cure for the headache

the KING can do no wrong

the KING can make a knight, but not a gentleman

a KING without learning is but a crowned ass

KINGS have long arms

no MAN can be a good ruler unless he hath first been ruled

the PEOPLE's love is the king's lifeguard

like PRINCE, like people

SPIES are the ears and eyes of princes

put not your TRUST in princes

KISSING

when the GORSE is out of bloom, kissing's out of fashion

he that KISSETH his wife in the market-place shall have many teachers

KISSES are keys

KISSING goes by favour

to KISS a man's wife or wipe his knife is a thankless office

a LISPING lass is good to kiss

MANY kiss the child for the nurse's sake

KNOWLEDGE

a BLIND man cannot judge colours

BOUGHT wit is the best

you can't make BRICKS without straw

a DWARF on a giant's shoulders sees further of the two

KNOWLEDGE is power

he that KNOWS little, often repeats it

an OLD poacher makes the best gamekeeper

THINKING is very far from knowing

YEARS know more than books

LANGUAGE

that is not GOOD language which all understand not

THINK with the wise, but talk with the vulgar

LATENESS

AFTER death the doctor

the EARLY man never borrows from the late man

a GIFT long waited for is sold not given

while the GRASS grows, the steed starves

who cometh LATE lodgeth ill

it is too LATE to shut the stable-door after the horse has bolted

LOSE an hour in the morning, chase it all day

MEN count up the faults of those who keep them waiting

he that RISETH late must trot all day

SLOW help is no help

when a THING is done, advice comes too late

See also PUNCTUALITY

LAUGHTER

LAUGH and grow fat

LAUGH and the world laughs with you; weep and you weep alone

LAUGH before breakfast, you'll cry before supper

let them LAUGH that win

he is not LAUGHED at that laughs at himself first

he who LAUGHS last laughs longest

LAUGHTER is the best medicine

LAW

AGREE, for the law is costly

where DRUMS beat, laws are silent

EVERY land has its own law

he whose FATHER is judge goes safe to his trial

HARD cases make bad law

HELL and Chancery are always open

HOME is home, as the Devil said when he found himself in the Court of Session

IGNORANCE of the law is no excuse

an ILL agreement is better than a good judgement

the JEWS spend at Easter, the Moors at marriages, the Christians in suits

LAW governs man, and reason the law

he that goes to LAW holds a wolf by the ears

the LAW is a bottomless pit

the LAW is an ass

LAW makers should not be law breakers

that may be LAWFULLY done which cannot be forborne

the MORE laws, the more offenders

NEW lords, new laws

there's ONE law for the rich and another for the poor

a PENNYWEIGHT of love is worth a pound of law

SUE a beggar and get a louse

in a THOUSAND pounds of law there's not an ounce of love

See also JUDGEMENT

LAWYERS

the DEVIL makes his Christmas-pies of lawyers' tongues and clerks' fingers

a GOOD lawyer makes a bad neighbour

a GOOD lawyer must be a great liar

a LAWYER's opinion is worth nothing unless paid for

LAWYERS' houses are built on the heads of fools

a MAN who is his own lawyer has a fool for a client

an OLD physician and a young lawyer

a WISE lawyer never goes to law himself

LAZINESS

an ANGLER eats more than he gets

what may be done at ANY time will be done at no time

BELLS call others but themselves enter not into the church

where COBWEBS are plenty, kisses are scarce

the DOG that is idle barks at his fleas, but he that is hunting feels them not

EAT till you sweat and work till you freeze

no GAINS without pains

they must HUNGER in frost that will not work in heat

LAZY folk take the most pains

a LEAN fee is a fit reward for a lazy clerk

that SICK man is not to be pitied who hath his cure in his sleeve

SLOTH is the key to poverty

the SLUGGARD must be clad in rags

LEADERSHIP

BELLS call others but themselves enter not into the church

he is the BEST general who makes the fewest mistakes

if the BLIND lead the blind, both shall fall into the ditch

in the COUNTRY of the blind, the one-eyed man is king

he is not FIT to command others that cannot command himself

a GENTLE heart is tied with an easy thread

he'll be QUARTER-MASTER wherever he comes

that VOYAGE never has luck where each one has a vote

LEAP YEARS

a LEAP YEAR is never a good sheep year

LEARNING

BACHELORS' wives and maids' children be well taught

a BELLY full of gluttony will never study willingly

BETTER untaught than ill taught

a COLT you may break, but an old horse you never can

GIVE me a child for the first seven years, and you may do what you like with him afterwards

it is GOOD to learn at other men's cost

a KING without learning is but a crowned ass

we must LEARN to walk before we can run

LEARN young, learn fair

LEARNING is better than house and land

LEARNING makes a good man better and an ill man worse

a LITTLE learning is a dangerous thing

LIVE and learn

a MAN's studies pass into his character

it is NEVER too late to learn

you're NEVER too old to learn

ONE father is more than a hundred schoolmasters

there is no ROYAL road to learning

the SCHOLAR teacheth the master

SOON learnt, soon forgotten

he that TEACHES himself has a fool for his master

TODAY is yesterday's pupil

See also EXPERIENCE; TEACHERS; WISDOM

LEISURE

the BUSIEST men have the most leisure

IDLE people have the least leisure

there is LUCK in leisure

LIBEL

FLING enough dirt and some will stick

the GREATER the truth, the greater the libel

LIES AND LYING

a BLISTER will rise upon one's tongue that tells a lie

a BOASTER and a liar are all one

a FALSE tongue hardly speaks truth

a FOE is better than a dissembling friend

FROST and fraud both end in foul

a GOOD heart cannot lie

HALF the truth is often a whole lie

JOVE but laughs at lovers' perjury

a LIAR is not believed when he speaks the truth

a LIAR is worse than a thief

a LIAR ought to have a good memory

a LIE travels around the world while truth is putting on her boots

LIES have short legs

MUCH cry and little wool

ONE lie makes many

they SAY so is half a lie

SHOW me a liar and I will show you a thief

a TALE-TELLER is worse than a thief

there is no WHISPERING but there is lying

LIFE

we are BORN crying, live complaining and die disappointed

LIFE begins at forty

LIFE is just a bowl of cherries

LIFE isn't all beer and skittles

LIFE is sweet

he LIVES long who lives well

MAN is a bubble

he that hath TIME hath life

LIFE AND DEATH

the BETROTHED of good is evil, the betrothed of life is death, the betrothed of love is divorce

the COFFIN is the brother of the cradle

they DIE well that live well

a FAIR death honours the whole life

the FIRST breath is the beginning of death

GIVE a man an annuity and he'll live for ever

a LIVE dog is better than a dead lion

he who LIVES by the sword dies by the sword

who LIVES well dies well

as a MAN lives so shall he die

as SOON as man is born he begins to die

TODAY a man, tomorrow none

See also DEATH

LIGHTNING

BEWARE of the oak, it draws the stroke; avoid the ash, it courts the flash

LIGHTNING never strikes the same place twice

LITERATURE

LITERATURE is a good staff but a bad crutch

LOGIC

BECAUSE is a woman's reason

why BUY a cow when milk is so cheap?

FOLLOW the river and you'll get to the sea

LAW governs man, and reason the law

if it LOOKS like a duck, walks like a duck and quacks like a duck, it's a duck

TWO and two make four

TWO negatives make an affirmative

LOQUACIOUSNESS

a BRIDLE for the tongue is a necessary piece of furniture

the GREATEST talkers are the least doers

MANY women, many words

the MILL that is always going grinds coarse and fine

MORE have repented speech than silence

he who SAYS what he likes shall hear what he does not like

let not your TONGUE cut your throat

See also TALK

LOSS

BETTER lost than found

there's no GREAT loss without some gain

it is not LOST that comes at last

it is LOST that is unsought

MUCH water goes by the mill that the miller knows not of

you NEVER miss the water till the well runs dry

ONE man's loss is another man's gain

LOVE

ABSENCE makes the heart grow fonder

'tis BETTER to have loved and lost than never to have loved at all

CALF love, half love; old love, cold love

COLD pudding will settle your love

the COURSE of true love never did run smooth

the DIFFERENCE is wide that the sheets will not decide

when DISTRUST enters in at the foregate, love goes out at the postern

EVERY Jack has his Jill

FAINT heart ne'er won fair lady

FANCY passes beauty

FANNED fires and forced love never did well yet

FOLLOW love and it will flee thee; flee love and it will follow thee

when the FURZE is in bloom, my love's in tune

HAPPY is the wooing that is not long a-doing

HASTY love is soon hot and soon cold

no HERB will cure love

HOT love is soon cold

JOVE but laughs at lovers' perjury

LABOUR is light where love doth pay

LAD's love's a busk of broom, hot awhile and soon done

LOOKS breed love

LOVE and a cough cannot be hid

one cannot LOVE and be wise

LOVE as in time to come thou shouldest hate and hate as thou shouldest in time to come, love

LOVE begets love

whom we LOVE best, to them we can say least

LOVE cannot be compelled

LOVE conquers all

LOVE does much, money does everything

LOVE is blind

LOVE is free

LOVE is full of fear

LOVE is love's reward

LOVE is never without jealousy

in LOVE is no lack

LOVE laughs at locksmiths

LOVE lives in cottages as well as in courts

LOVE makes the world go round

LOVE me little, love me long

LOVE me, love my dog

when LOVE puts in, friendship is gone

LOVE will creep where it can not go

LOVE will find a way

LOVE your friend with his fault

LOVE your neighbour, yet pull not down your hedge

LUCKY at cards, unlucky in love

a MAN has choice to begin love but not to end it

NEVER sigh but send

be off with the OLD love before you are on with the new

OLD love will not be forgotten

ONE love expels another

a PENNYWEIGHT of love is worth a pound of law

PLEASE your eye and plague your heart

when POVERTY comes in at the door, love flies out of the window

PRAISE the child and you make love to the mother

PUDDINGS and paramours should be hotly handled

the QUARREL of lovers is the renewal of love

SALT water and absence wash away love

SCORN at first makes after-love the more

out of SIGHT, out of mind

SOUND love is not soon forgotten

of SOUP and love the first is the best

from the SWEETEST wine, the tartest vinegar

in a THOUSAND pounds of law there's not an ounce of love

the WAY to a man's heart is through his stomach

WINE and youth increase love

LOYALTY

no MAN can serve two masters

a MAN's best friend is his dog

you cannot RUN with the hare and hunt with the hounds

LUCK

BAD luck is fertile

it is BETTER to be born lucky than rich

the BREAD never falls but on the buttered side

CARE and diligence bring luck

a CAT has nine lives

to CHANGE the name and not the letter, is a change for the worse, and not for the better

the DEVIL's children have the Devil's luck

EVIL be to him who thinks it

FOOLS for luck

GOD is always on the side of the big battalions

GOOD luck never comes too late

he was HANGED that left his drink behind

HAP and halfpenny goods enough

HELP you to salt, help you to sorrow

ILL luck is worse than found money

it is a LONG lane that has no turning

there is LUCK in leisure

there is LUCK in odd numbers

LUCKY at cards, unlucky in love

MEET on the stairs and you won't meet in heaven

the MORE knave, the better luck

the MORE wicked, the more fortunate

the PROPERER the man the worse luck

RICHES are but the baggage of fortune

SEE a pin and pick it up, all the day you'll have good luck

THIRD time lucky

TOUCH wood, it's sure to come good

a WHISTLING woman and a crowing hen are neither fit for God nor men

if you WISH to live and thrive, let a spider run alive

See also MISFORTUNE

MADNESS

whom the GODS would destroy, they first make mad

a MAN of gladness seldom falls into madness

ONE mad action is not enough to prove a man mad

he that TALKS to himself talks to a fool

MAINTENANCE

BETTER a clout than a hole out

if it ain't BROKE, don't fix it

BROKEN bones well set become stronger

it is EASIER to build two chimneys than to maintain one

either MEND or end

an OLD cart, well used, may last out a new one abused

an OLD sack asketh much patching

he who REPAIRS not his gutter repairs his whole house

don't SPOIL the ship for a ha'porth of tar

a STITCH in time saves nine

for WANT of a nail the shoe was lost

a WOMAN and a ship ever want mending

See also THOROUGHNESS

MALICE

a LITTLE poison embitters much sweetness

MALICE hurts itself most

See also CURSES; REVENGE

MAN

MAN is a bubble

MAN is the measure of all things

MAN proposes, but God disposes

MANAGEMENT

the EYE of the master does more work than both his hands

a GENTLE heart is tied with an easy thread

MANNERS

CHILDREN should be seen and not heard

what can you EXPECT from a pig but a grunt?

FINGERS were made before forks and hands before knives

FULL of courtesy, full of craft

HONOURS change manners

LEAST said, soonest mended

LEAVE is light

MANNERS maketh man

MEAT is much, but manners is more

MIND your own business

there is NOTHING lost by civility

OTHER times, other manners

when in ROME, do as the Romans do

SOFT and fair goes far

SPEAK when you are spoken to

See also POLITENESS

MARRIAGE

BETTER no ring than a ring of rush

BETTER one house spoiled than two

it is BETTER to marry a shrew than a sheep

BETTER wed over the mixen than over the moor

the BRIDE goes to her marriage-bed but knows not what shall happen to her

why BUY a cow when milk is so cheap?

to CHANGE the name and not the letter, is a change for the worse, and not for the better

it is a DANGEROUS fire begins in the bed straw

a DEAF husband and a blind wife are always a happy couple

the DIFFERENCE is wide that the sheets will not decide

EARLY wed, early dead

who hath a FAIR wife needs more than two eyes

the FIRST seven years are the hardest

FIRST thrive and then wive

a GREAT dowry is a bed full of brambles

HANGING and wiving go by destiny

it's HARD to wive and thrive both in a year

HONEST men marry quickly, wise men not at all

go down the LADDER when thou marriest a wife, go up when thou choosest a friend

the LASS in the red petticoat shall pay for all

MARRIAGE halves our griefs, doubles our joys, and quadruples our expenses

MARRIAGE is a lottery

MARRIAGE makes or mars a man

MARRIAGES are made in heaven

he that MARRIES a widow and three children marries four thieves

he that MARRIES for wealth sells his liberty

he that MARRIES late marries ill

MARRY in haste and repent at leisure

MARRY in Lent, and you'll live to repent

MARRY in May and rue the day

MARRY with your match

there goes MORE to marriage than four bare legs in a bed

NEEDLES and pins, needles and pins, when a man marries his trouble begins

he that TELLS his wife news is but newly married

as your WEDDING ring wears, your cares will wear away

WEDLOCK is a padlock

he that WEDS before he's wise shall die before he thrive

a YOUNG man should not marry yet, an old man not at all

See also HUSBANDS AND WIVES

MASTERS AND SERVANTS

a FALLING master makes a standing servant

FIRE and water are good servants, but bad masters

GIVE a slave a rod and he'll beat his master

an ILL master makes an ill servant

JACK is as good as his master

MASTERS should be sometimes blind, and sometimes deaf

no MAN is a hero to his valet

like MASTER, like man

ONE thing thinketh the horse, and another he that saddles him

TRIM tram, like master like man

MEANNESS

a PENNY soul never came to twopence

MEDDLING

BUSY folks are always meddling

the MORE you stir, the worse it will stink

SCALD not your lips in another man's pottage

let WELL alone

MEDICAL TREATMENT

the BEST doctors are Dr Diet, Dr Quiet and Dr Merryman

that which is GOOD for the head is evil for the neck and the shoulders

a GREEN wound is soon healed

KITCHEN physic is the best physic

LAUGHTER is the best medicine

there is no MEDICINE against death

NATURE, time, and patience are the three great physicians

you should NEVER touch your eye but with your elbow

if PHYSIC do not work, prepare for the kirk

QUININE is made of the sweat of ship carpenters

there's a SALVE for every sore

TEMPERANCE is the best physic

See also DISEASE; HEALTH AND ILLNESS; INFIRMITY; REMEDIES

MEN

GARLIC makes a man wink, drink and stink

a MAN is as old as he feels, and a woman as old as she looks

MEN's years and their faults are always more than they are willing to own

OLD fish and young flesh feed men best

MEMORY

ABSENCE makes the heart grow fonder

an ELEPHANT never forgets

GREAT wits have short memories

he is an ILL companion that has a good memory

a LIAR ought to have a good memory

LONG absent, soon forgotten

MEMORY is the treasure of the mind

MEMORY of happiness makes misery woeful

SALT water and absence wash away love

out of SIGHT, out of mind

MERCY

there are no FANS in hell

MERCY surpasses justice

MERCY to the criminal may be cruelty to the people

POUR not water on a drowned mouse

if you WISH to live and thrive, let a spider run alive

See also HELL AND DAMNATION

MISCHIEF

when the CAT's away, the mice will play

no MISCHIEF but a woman or a priest is at the bottom of it

he that MISCHIEF hatcheth, mischief catcheth

MISCHIEF comes by the pound and goes away by the ounce

MISCHIEF has swift wings

the MOTHER of mischief is no bigger than a midge's wing

MISERY

it is GOOD to have company in misery

it is MISERY enough to have been once happy

MISERY loves company

MISFORTUNE

ACCIDENTS will happen in the best regulated families

ADVERSITY makes strange bedfellows

a BAD penny always turns up

the BEST cart may overthrow

the BLACK ox treads on one's foot

the BREAD never falls but on the buttered side

he that is DOWN, down with him

he that is FALLEN cannot help him that is down

he that FALLS today may rise tomorrow

no FENCE against ill fortune

out of the FRYING-PAN into the fire

it is a GOOD thing to eat your brown bread first

it is GOOD to have company in misery

it is HARD to be wretched but worse to be known so

ILL comes in by ells and goes out by inches

ILL luck is worse than found money

it's an ILL wind that blows nobody any good

MISFORTUNES never come singly

it NEVER rains but it pours

NOTHING so bad but it might have been worse

ONE cloud is enough to eclipse all the sun

take the ROUGH with the smooth

WELCOME evil, if thou comest alone

WOES unite foes

See also LUCK

MISTAKES

if the DOCTOR cures, the sun sees it, but if he kills, the earth hides it

it is EASY to fall into a trap but hard to get out again

to ERR is human, to forgive divine

EVERY dog is allowed one bite

it is a GOOD horse that never stumbles

even HOMER sometimes nods

no MAN is infallible

if you don't make MISTAKES you don't make anything

NEAREST the heart, nearest the mouth

he RIDES well that never falls

he STANDS not surely that never slips

a STUMBLE may prevent a fall

he that THINKS amiss concludes worse

MISUNDERSTANDING

LITTLE knoweth the fat man what the lean man thinketh

MISUNDERSTANDING brings lies to town

he that THINKS amiss concludes worse

who UNDERSTANDS ill answers ill

MODERATION

you had BETTER be drunk than drowned

BIND the sack before it be full

EAT at pleasure, drink by measure

EATING and scratching wants but a beginning

LITTLE fish are sweet

there is a MEASURE in all things

MODERATION in all things

MONEY

ABUNDANCE, like want, ruins many

BAD money drives out good

BEAUTY is potent, but money is omnipotent

BEG from beggars and you'll never be rich

a BEGGAR's purse is bottomless

the BEST things in life are free

be it for BETTER, be it for worse, do you after him that beareth the purse

he that BORROWS must pay again with shame or loss

BUILDING and marrying of children are great wasters

CREDITORS have better memories than debtors

DALLY not with women or money

DIRTY hands make clean money

EVERYONE has a penny to spend at a new alehouse

a FOOL and his money are soon parted

GOD made man, man made money

GOLD is an orator

a GOLDEN key can open any door

no LOCK will hold against the power of gold

LOOK for your money where you lost it

a JADE eats as much as a good horse

don't let your JAWS outrun your claws

he that doth LEND doth lose his money and friend

LEND only that which you can afford to lose

LEND your money and lose your friend

LOOK after the pennies and the pounds will look after themselves

LOOK for your money where you lost it

LOVE does much, money does everything

the LOVE of money is the root of all evil

if MONEY be not thy servant, it will be thy master

MONEY begets money

MONEY has no smell

MONEY isn't everything

MONEY is power

MONEY makes a man

MONEY makes friends enemies

MONEY makes money

MONEY makes the mare to go

MONEY makes the world go round

MONEY never comes out of season

MONEY talks

MUCH coin, much care

where there's MUCK, there's money

a NIMBLE ninepence is better than a slow shilling

a PENNY at a pinch is worth a pound

a PENNY in purse will bid me drink when all the friends I have will not

a PENNY saved is a penny earned

PENNY wise, pound foolish

PINCH on the parson's side

PLENTY makes poor

a POUND of care will not pay an ounce of debt

let your PURSE be your master

READY money is a ready medicine

READY money will away

SAMSON was a strong man yet he could not pay money before he had it

SELDOM comes a loan laughing home

you cannot SERVE God and Mammon

he that SERVES God for money will serve the Devil for better wages

SOON gotten, soon spent

you can't TAKE it with you

TELL money after your own father

a THOUSAND pounds and a bottle of hay is all one thing at doomsday

when TWO friends have a common purse one sings and the other weeps

See also DEBT; PAYMENT; SAVING AND SPENDING; WORK AND WORKERS

MOON

the FULL moon brings fair weather

the MOON does not heed the barking of dogs

no MOON, no man

a PALE moon doth rain, a red moon doth blow; a white moon doth neither rain nor snow

MORTALITY

ARTHUR was not but whilst he was

DEATH devours lambs as well as sheep

EARTH must to earth

an INCH of gold will not buy an inch of time

THREATENED men live long

See also DEATH

MOTHERS

a CHILD may have too much of his mother's blessing

the CROW thinks her own birds fairest

he that would the DAUGHTER win, must with the mother first begin

a LIGHT heeled mother makes a heavy heeled daughter

like MOTHER, like daughter

PRAISE the child and you make love to the mother

See also FAMILIES

MOTHERS-IN-LAW

NEVER rely on the glory of the morning or on the smile of your mother-in-law

there is but ONE good mother-in-law, and she is dead

See also FAMILIES

MOVING HOUSE

THREE removals are as bad as a fire

MURDER

KILLING no murder

MURDER will out

MUSIC

why should the DEVIL have all the best tunes?

MUSIC hath charms

MUSIC helps not the toothache

the OPERA isn't over till the fat lady sings

NAMES

to CHANGE the name and not the letter, is a change for the worse, and not for the better

NAMES and natures do often agree

no NAMES, no pack drill

a ROSE by any other name would smell as sweet

NATIONALITIES

ALWAYS something new out of Africa

ENGLAND is the paradise of women, the hell of horses and the purgatory of servants

ENGLAND's difficulty is Ireland's opportunity

the ENGLISH are a nation of shopkeepers

the ENGLISH never know when they are beaten

when HEMPE is spun, England is done

put an IRISHMAN on the spit and you can always get another Irishman to baste him

ITALIANS are wise before the deed, the Germans in the deed, the French after the deed

the JEWS spend at Easter, the Moors at marriages, the Christians in suits

when our LADY falls in our Lord's lap, then let England beware a sad clap

so MANY countries, so many customs

out of the NORTH all ill comes forth

ONE Englishman can beat three Frenchmen

in SETTLING an island, the first building erected by a Spaniard will be a church; by a Frenchman, a fort; by a Dutchman, a warehouse; and by an Englishman, an alehouse

SCRATCH a Russian and you find a Tartar

THREE ills come from the north, a cold wind, a shrinking cloth, and a dissembling man

YORKSHIRE born and Yorkshire bred, strong in the arm and weak in the head

NATURE

though you CAST out nature with a fork, it will still return

NATURE abhors a vacuum

NATURE does nothing in vain

NATURE will have its course

NECESSITY

that may be LAWFULLY done which cannot be forborne

NECESSITY and opportunity may make a coward valiant

you cannot make an OMELETTE without breaking eggs

NEED

ANYTHING will fit a naked man

BASHFULNESS is an enemy to poverty

BEGGARS can't be choosers

NECESSITY is the mother of invention

NECESSITY knows no law

NEED makes greed

NEEDS must when the Devil drives

WANT is the whetstone of wit

NEGOTIATION

a CASTLE that speaketh is near a surrender

NEIGHBOURS

a GOOD example is the best sermon

a GOOD lawyer makes a bad neighbour

LOVE your neighbour, yet pull not down your hedge

what a NEIGHBOUR gets is not lost

NEWS

go ABROAD and you'll hear news of home

BAD news travels fast

he that BRINGS good news knocks hard

no NEWS is good news

QUEEN Anne is dead

NIGHT

the DARKEST hour is just before the dawn

the NIGHT is no man's friend

NIGHT is the mother of counsel

NOBILITY

BLUSHING is a sign of grace

NOBLESSE oblige

NOSTALGIA

the GOLDEN age never was the present age

JAM tomorrow and jam yesterday, but never jam today

THINGS present are judged by things past

YESTERDAY will not be called again

See also HISTORY AND THE PAST

NOTHING

NATURE abhors a vacuum

NOTHING for nothing

NOTHING comes of nothing

by doing NOTHING we learn to do ill

SOMETHING is better than nothing

NOVELTY

ALWAYS something new out of Africa

when a NEW book appears, read an old one

what is NEW cannot be true

NEW things are fair

you can't put NEW wine in old bottles

there is NOTHING new under the sun

NUMBERS

there is LUCK in odd numbers

OBSESSION

GOD keep me from the man that has but one thing to mind

OBSTACLES

EVERY path hath a puddle

a LOW hedge is easily leaped over

MEN leap over where the hedge is lowest

those who PLAY at bowls must look out for rubbers

OBSTINACY

he that will to CUPAR maun to Cupar

there is no GOOD accord where every man would be a lord

SUSSEX won't be druv

the VICAR of Bray will be vicar of Bray still

WRANGLERS are never in the wrong

OLD AGE

AGE and wedlock bring a man to his nightcap

AGE can be a bad travelling companion

AGE does not give sense – it only makes one go slowly

with the ANCIENT is wisdom; and in the length of days understanding

the BEST wine comes out of an old vessel

BETTER to hang than to hold

there's no FOOL like an old fool

he that LIVES long suffers much

it is NEVER too late to learn

it is NEVER too late to mend

you're NEVER too old to learn

OLD bees yield no honey

an OLD fox is not easily snared

OLD maids lead apes in hell

an OLD man in a house is a good sign

an OLD man never wants a tale to tell

OLD men are twice children

OLD men go to death, death comes to young men

OLD men will die and children soon forget

an OLD ox makes a straight furrow

an OLD poacher makes the best gamekeeper

'tis an OLD rat that won't eat cheese

OLD soldiers never die, they simply fade away

OLD vessels must leak

an OLD wise man's shadow is better than a young buzzard's sword

the OLDER the crab-tree the more crabs it bears

the OLDER the wiser

you can't TEACH an old dog new tricks

YEARS know more than books

See also AGE; EXPERIENCE

OMENS

to CHANGE the name and not the letter, is a change for the worse, and not for the better

a CHERRY year, a merry year; a plum year, a dumb year

if your EAR burns someone is thinking about you

if you would ENJOY the fruit, pluck not the flower

when all FRUIT falls, welcome haws

FRUIT out of season, sorrow out of reason

if you would have FRUIT, you must bring the leaf to the grave

a GOOD tree brings forth good fruit

GREY hairs are death's blossoms

the HIGHER the tree, the sweeter the plum

MEET on the stairs and you won't meet in heaven

RATS desert a sinking ship

RED sky at night, shepherd's delight; red sky in the morning, shepherd's warning

SEPTEMBER blow soft, till the fruit's in the loft

SOON todd, soon with God

like TREE, like fruit

See also PROPHETS AND PROPHECY; SUPERSTITIONS AND SAYINGS

OPINION

BETTER say nothing than nothing to the purpose

one must HOWL with the wolves

a MAN will never change his mind if he has no mind to change

MANY men have many minds

so MANY men, so many opinions

OPINION rules the world

one may THINK that dares not speak

the VOICE of the people is the voice of God

OPPORTUNITY

there is ALWAYS room at the top

where the CARCASS is, there shall the eagles be gathered together

when the CAT's away, the mice will play

in the COUNTRY of the blind, the one-eyed man is king

a DOOR must either be shut or open

EVERY dog has his day

FLIES come to feasts unasked

GATHER ye rosebuds while ye may

GIVE a man enough rope and he will hang himself

it is not GIVEN to every man to go to Corinth

the GOAT must browse where she is tied

GOOD clothes open all doors

it is GOOD fishing in troubled waters

take the GOODS the gods provide

make HAY while the sun shines

HOIST your sail when the wind is fair

the HOLE calls the thief

no LARDER but hath its mice

LIFE begins at forty

LOOK to the main chance

he has not LOST all who has one cast left

the MILL cannot grind with the water that is past

NECESSITY and opportunity may make a coward valiant

NEVER give a sucker an even break

NEVER look a gift horse in the mouth

an OCCASION lost cannot be redeemed

when ONE door shuts, another opens

ONE man may steal a horse, while another may not look over a hedge

if ONE will not another will

an OPEN door may tempt a saint

OPPORTUNITY makes a thief

OPPORTUNITY seldom knocks twice at any man's door

there are PLENTY more fish in the sea

a POSTERN door makes a thief

SET a beggar on horseback, and he'll ride to the devil

the STREETS of London are paved with gold

STRIKE while the iron is hot

take TIME by the forelock

there is a TIME for everything

TOMORROW is another day

when the TREE is fallen, all go with their hatchet

there are only TWENTY-FOUR hours in the day

TWO dogs fight for a bone, and a third runs away with it

he that WILL not when he may, when he will he shall have nay

See also POSSIBILITY AND POTENTIAL

OPPOSITES

AFTER a storm comes a calm

the BETROTHED of good is evil, the betrothed of life is death, the betrothed of love is divorce

you cannot BURN the candle at both ends

COLD hands, warm heart

in the COLDEST flint there is hot fire

EVERY medal hath its reverse

EVERY white hath its black and every sweet its sour

the NEARER the bone, the sweeter the flesh

no ROSE without a thorn

from the SUBLIME to the ridiculous is but a step

TWO blacks don't make a white

TWO negatives make an affirmative

OPTIMISM
ALWAYS look on the bright side

where the BEE sucks honey the spider sucks poison

DEEM the best till the truth be tried

there is a GOOD time coming

HOPE springs eternal in the human breast

LIFE begins at forty

a MAN of gladness seldom falls into madness

NEVER say die

to the PURE all things are pure

the STREETS of London are paved with gold

when THINGS are at the worst they soon begin to mend

TOMORROW is another day

ORDERLINESS
a PLACE for everything and everything in its place

ORGANIZATIONS
CORPORATIONS have neither bodies to be punished nor souls to be damned

OVER-AMBITION
he who BEGINS too much accomplishes little

GRASP all, lose all

he that HEWS too high may get a chip in his eye

don't let your JAWS outrun your claws

we must LEARN to walk before we can run

LOOK high and fall low

METTLE is dangerous in a blind horse

if you RUN after two hares you will catch neither

STRETCH your arm no further than your sleeve will reach

a SHOE too large trips you up

make not thy TAIL broader than thy wings

OVER-CONFIDENCE
it is the BEST swimmers who drown

they BRAG most that can do least

he that is DRUNK is as great as a king

METTLE is dangerous in a blind horse

he that is too SECURE is not safe

OVERWORK
it is not the BURDEN but the overburden that kills the beast

DOUBLE charge will rive a cannon

it is the PACE that kills

it is not WORK that kills, but worry

See also WORK AND WORKERS

OWNERSHIP
what BELONGS to everybody belongs to nobody

CHILD's pig but father's bacon

FINDERS keepers, losers weepers

he KENS his groats among other folk's kail

you cannot LOSE what you never had

WHAT's mine's mine own

See also SELFISHNESS

PAIN
See SUFFERING

PASSION
COLD hands, warm heart

in the COLDEST flint there is hot fire

EVERY man has his hobby-horse

when the HEART is a fire some sparks will fly out of the mouth

when PASSION entereth at the foregate, wisdom goeth out of the postern

SOON hot, soon cold

STILL waters run deep

PATIENCE AND IMPATIENCE
BETTER a mischief than an inconvenience

don't CROSS the bridge until you get to it

he that would have EGGS must endure the cackling of hens

EVERYTHING comes to him who waits

he was HANGED that left his drink behind

who HOLDS his peace and gathers stones will find a time to throw them

it's ILL waiting for dead men's shoes

he that hath no PATIENCE hath nothing

PATIENCE is a virtue

PATIENCE perforce

no REMEDY but patience

ROME was not built in a day

a WATCHED pot never boils

he goes not out of his WAY that goes to a good inn

PATRIOTISM

our COUNTRY, right or wrong

PATIOTISM is the last refuge of a scoundrel

the SMOKE of a man's own country is better than the fire of another's

PAYMENT

BETTER sit idly than work for nothing

no CHINK, no drink

so we get the CHINK, we'll bear with the stink

they that DANCE must pay the fiddler

as GOOD play for nought as work for nought

it is HARD to pay for bread that has been eaten

KNAVES and whores go by the clock

a LEAN fee is a fit reward for a lazy clerk

MERRY is the company till the reckoning comes

MISRECKONING is no payment

NOTHING for nothing

PAY beforehand was never well served

if you PAY not a servant his wages, he will pay himself

if you PAY peanuts, you get monkeys

PAY well, command well, hang well

he who PAYS the piper calls the tune

you PAYS your money and you takes your choice

no PENNY, no paternoster

PITCH and pay

SERVICE without reward is punishment

you don't get SOMETHING for nothing

no SONG, no supper

See also MONEY; WORK AND WORKERS

PEACE

AFTER a storm comes a calm

PEACE makes plenty

the STICK is the surest peacemaker

See also WAR AND PEACE

PEOPLE

CITIES are taken by the ears

it is the MEN who make a city

the MOB has many heads but no brains

there's NOWT so queer as folk

the VOICE of the people is the voice of God

PERFECTION

the BEST is the enemy of the good

the BEST smell is bread, the best savour salt, the best love that of children

when all FRUIT falls, welcome haws

he is LIFELESS that is faultless

no WOOL is so white that a dyer cannot blacken it

PERFUME

she SMELLS best that smells of nothing

PERSEVERANCE

BRAG is a good dog, but Holdfast is better

he who COMMENCES many things finishes but a few

CONSTANT dropping wears away the stone

it's DOGGED as does it

he that would EAT the fruit must climb the tree

FEATHER by feather the goose is plucked

if at FIRST you don't succeed, try, try, try again

HAIR and hair makes the carle's head bare

JACK of all trades is master of none

the LAME foot overtakes the swift one in the end

LITTLE and good fills the trencher

by LITTLE and little the bird makes his nest

LITTLE strokes fell great oaks

one can go a LONG way after one is weary

a MAN of many trades begs his bread on Sunday

MANY a mickle makes a muckle

MANY irons in the fire, some must cool

a MOUSE in time may bite in two a cable

an OAK is not felled at one stroke

if you would be POPE you must think of nothing else

the RACE is not to the swift, nor the battle to the strong

ROME was not built in a day

he that SHOOTS oft shall at last hit the mark

SLOW but sure wins the race

SOFT pace goes far

he that can STAY obtains

the THIRD time pays for all

the TORTOISE wins the race while the hare is sleeping

the TREE falls not at the first blow

PERSUASION

CHILDREN are to be deceived with comfits and men with oaths

he that COMPLIES against his will is of his own opinion still

HONEY catches more flies than vinegar

there are NONE so deaf as those who will not hear

the PERSUASION of the fortunate sways the doubtful

SOFT and fair goes far

SPEAK softly and carry a big stick

PESSIMISM

where the BEE sucks honey the spider sucks poison

they that be in HELL ween there is no other heaven

it NEVER rains but it pours

our WORST misfortunes are those which never befall us

PICTURES

EVERY picture tells a story

ONE picture is worth ten thousand words

PICTURES are the books of the unlearned

PITY

PITY cureth envy

PITY is akin to love

that SICK man is not to be pitied who hath his cure in his sleeve

PLEASURE

FLY the pleasure which paineth afterward

a LITTLE of what you fancy does you good

LITTLE things please little minds

the MIRTH of the world dureth but a while

the PLEASURES of the rich are bought with the tears of the poor

no PLEASURE without pain

SHORT pleasure, long lament

POETS

PAINTERS and poets have leave to lie

a POET is born not made

POLITENESS

CIVILITY costs nothing

COURTESY on one side never lasts long

FULL of courtesy, full of craft

there is NOTHING lost by civility

SPEAK fair and think what you will

See also MANNERS

POLITICS

ADVERSITY makes strange bedfellows

the DOGS bark but the caravan goes on

the FISH always stinks from the head downwards

only FOOLS exult when governments change

POLITICS makes strange bedfellows

POSSESSION

what BELONGS to everybody belongs to nobody

a BIRD in the hand is worth two in the bush

FINDERS keepers, losers weepers

he who GETS doth much, but he who keeps doth more

GUT no fish till you get them

what you have, HOLD

KEEPING is harder than winning

you cannot LOSE what you never had

the MORE you get, the more you want

POSSESSION is nine points of the law

PROSPECT is often better than possession

THREE removals are as bad as a fire

it is not WHAT is he, but what has he

POSSIBILITY AND POTENTIAL

BETTER an egg today than a chicken tomorrow

a BLOT is not blot unless it be hit

whatever MAN has done, man may do

a MOUSE may help a lion

it is a POOR dog that is not worth whistling for

PROSPECT is often better than possession

WHAT has been, may be

See also OPPORTUNITY

POSTPONEMENT

what may be done at ANY time will be done at no time

ONE of these days is none of these days

PUT off the evil hour as long as you can

by the STREET of by and by one arrives at the house of never

POVERTY
BASHFULNESS is an enemy to poverty
BETTER no ring than a ring of rush
he who is CONTENT in his poverty is wonderfully rich
who DAINTIES love, shall beggars prove
the DEVIL dances in an empty pocket
an EMPTY purse fills the face with wrinkles
GIVE a man an annuity and he'll live for ever
GOD help the poor, for the rich can help themselves
there are GOD's poor and the devil's poor
a LIGHT purse makes a heavy heart
he that has NOTHING is frightened of nothing
he that hath NOUGHT shall have nought
a POOR man's table is soon spread
POOR men seek meat for their stomach; rich men stomach for their meat
he is not POOR that hath little, but he that desireth much
POVERTY breeds strife
when POVERTY comes in at the door, love flies out of the window
POVERTY is no disgrace, but it is a great inconvenience
POVERTY is not a crime
POVERTY is the mother of health
he that has not SILVER in his purse should have silk on his tongue
no SILVER, no servant
WRINKLED purses make wrinkled faces

POWER
BEAUTY is potent, but money is omnipotent
BIG fish eat little fish
the CLOCK goes as it pleases the clerk
EAGLES don't catch flies
EAGLES fly alone
GOD is always on the side of the big battalions
not even HERCULES could contend against two
KNOWLEDGE is power
where MACGREGOR sits is the head of the table
MAN is the measure of all things
MIGHT is right
MONEY is power
the PEN is mightier than the sword
POWER corrupts
there are WHEELS within wheels
See also CORRUPTION AND INCORRUPTIBILITY; INFLUENCE

PRACTICALITY
ADVERSITY makes strange bedfellows
not even HERCULES could contend against two
one must HOWL with the wolves
it's no USE crying over spilt milk
the WORTH of a thing is what it will bring

PRACTICE
PRACTICE makes perfect
TRY your skill in gilt first and then in gold
they that WALK much in the sun will be tanned at last
by WRITING you learn to write

PRAISE
let EVERY man praise the bridge he goes over
NEVER praise a ford till you get over
OLD praise dies unless you feed it
PRAISE is not pudding
PRAISE makes good men better and bad men worse
PRAISE no man till he is dead
PRAISE the child and you make love to the mother
PRAISE the sea but keep on land
See also CRITICISM

PRAYER
an ANGRY man is not fit to pray
the FAMILY that prays together stays together
he that would LEARN to pray, let him go to sea
he PREACHES well that lives well
a SHORT prayer reaches heaven

PRECAUTIONS
ACCIDENTS will happen in the best regulated families
the BEST cart may overthrow
DRAW not your bow till your arrow is fixed
FIRST catch your hare
no FLYING without wings
no GOOD building without a good foundation
it is too LATE to shut the stable-door after the horse has bolted

he that LOOKS not before finds himself behind

PROVIDE for the worst, the best will save itself

SCORE twice before you cut once

put your TRUST in God and keep your powder dry

PRECEDENCE

FIRST born, first fed

FIRST come, first served

he who HIRES the horse must ride before

PREJUDICE

do not make FISH of one and flesh of another

to the JAUNDICED eye all things look yellow

don't JUDGE a man by the words of his mother, listen to the comments of his neighbours

the MASTER's eye maketh the horse fat

it is not as thy MOTHER says but as thy neighbours say

when a NEW book appears, read an old one

there is NOTHING like leather

PRESUMPTION

BETTER an egg today than a chicken tomorrow

the BRIDE goes to her marriage-bed but knows not what shall happen to her

don't put the CART before the horse

don't COUNT your chickens before they are hatched

GUT no fish till you get them

don't HALLOO till you are out of the wood

it is ILL fishing before the net

there's MANY a slip 'twixt cup and lip

NEVER praise a ford till you get over

SAY no ill of the year till it be past

PREVENTION

HANG a thief when he's young and he'll no' steal when he's old

PREVENTION is better than cure

PRIDE

CHARITY and pride do both feed the poor

EVERY cock crows on his own dunghill

a HUMBLE-BEE in a cow-turd thinks himself a king

PRIDE and grace dwell never in one place

PRIDE feels no pain

PRIDE goes before a fall

PRIDE may lurk under a threadbare cloak

PRIDE must abide

the PRIEST forgets that he was clerk

a PROUD heart and a beggar's purse agree not well together

it is a PROUD horse that will not bear his own provender

a PROUD look makes foul work in a fine face

SET a beggar on horseback, and he'll ride to the devil

PRIORITY

don't put the CART before the horse

FIRST things first

it is a GOOD thing to eat your brown bread first

LAST but not least

MESSMATE before a shipmate, shipmate before a stranger, stranger before a dog

PRIVACY

he that KISSETH his wife in the market-place shall have many teachers

MIND your own business

don't WASH your dirty linen in public

PROCRASTINATION

what may be done at ANY time will be done at no time

NEVER put off till tomorrow what you can do today

ONE of these days is none of these days

PROCRASTINATION is the thief of time

PUT off the evil hour as long as you can

by the STREET of by and by one arrives at the house of never

no TIME like the present

TOMORROW never comes

PRODUCTIVITY

CLEAN heels, light meals

a DEAD bee will make no honey

OLD bees yield no honey

PROFIT AND LOSS

what you LOSE on the swings you gain on the roundabouts

ONE man's loss is another man's gain

QUICK returns make rich merchants

a WILLOW will buy a horse before an oak will pay for a saddle

See also REWARD

PROGRESS

go FORWARD and fall, go backward and mar all

ONE step at a time

STEP after step the ladder is ascended

the WORLD runs on wheels

PROMISES

BETTER an egg today than a chicken tomorrow

an ENGLISHMAN's word is his bond

a LONG tongue is a sign of a short hand

a MAN apt to promise is apt to forget

a MAN that breaks his word bids others be false to him

PROMISE is debt

PROMISES, like pie-crust, are made to be broken

he that will SWEAR will lie

an UNLAWFUL oath is better broken than kept

VOWS made in storms are forgotten in calms

PROPAGANDA

CITIES are taken by the ears

PROPERTY

he that hath LAND hath quarrels

LAND was never lost for want of an heir

PROPERTY has its duties as well as its rights

PROPHETS AND PROPHECY

DREAM of a funeral and you hear of a marriage

DREAMS go by contraries

FRIDAY night's dream on the Saturday told, is sure to come true be it never so old

MORNING dreams come true

a PROPHET is not without honour save in his own country

See also OMENS

PUBLICANS

ALE-SELLERS should not be tale-tellers

PUNCTUALITY

the EARLY bird catches the worm

the EARLY man never borrows from the late man

FIRST come, first served

he GIVES twice who gives quickly

PUNCTUALITY is the politeness of princes

PUNCTUALITY is the soul of business

SOON enough, if well enough

what is WELL done is done soon enough

See also LATENESS

PUNISHMENT

EVERY sin brings its punishment with it

HANG a thief when he's young and he'll no' steal when he's old

LAY-OVERS for meddlers

ONCE nought, twice somewhat

PUNISHMENT is lame but it comes

the STICK is the surest peacemaker

PUNS

he that would make a PUN would pick a pocket

QUALITY

the BEST fish swim near the bottom

the BEST is the enemy of the good

you had BETTER be drunk than drowned

the DEEPER the sweeter

EVERYTHING is good in its season

the GOOD is the enemy of the best

the GREATEST calf is not the sweetest veal

the GREATEST crabs be not all the best meat

you cannot KNOW wine by the barrel

LITTLE fish are sweet

there's MANY a good cock come out of a tattered bag

there's MANY a good tune played on an old fiddle

the NEARER the bone, the sweeter the flesh

OLD and tough, young and tender

the SACK is known by the sample

he goes not out of his WAY that goes to a good inn

QUARRELLING

BRAWLING curs never want sore ears

it is a DANGEROUS fire begins in the bed straw

DOGS begin in jest and end in earnest

there is no GOOD accord where every man would be a lord

OLD reckonings make new quarrels

the QUARREL of lovers is the renewal of love

QUARRELSOME dogs get dirty coats

TWO cats and a mouse, two wives in one house, two dogs and a bone, never agree in one

of TWO disputants the warmer is generally in the wrong

it takes TWO to make a quarrel

WOOD half burnt is easily kindled

See also ARGUMENT AND DISPUTE

QUESTIONS AND ANSWERS

AFTER wit comes too late

ASK a silly question and you'll get a silly answer

ASK no questions and hear no lies

FOOLS ask questions that wise men cannot answer

LOSE nothing for asking

QUESTION for question is all fair

he that QUESTIONETH nothing, nothing learneth

there are TWO sides to every question

RAIN

AFTER drought cometh rain

AFTER rain comes sunshine

AFTER wind comes rain

APRIL showers bring forth May flowers

BLESSED are the dead that the rain rains on

BRIGHT rain makes fools fain

DROUGHT never bred dearth in England

DRY feet, warm head, bring safe to bed

if in FEBRUARY there be no rain, 'tis neither good for hay nor grain

FOG on the hill, water to the mill; fog in the hollow, fine day to follow

it is GOOD to have a cloak for the rain

MANY drops make a shower

it NEVER rains but it pours

when it RAINS and the sun shines at the same time the devil is beating his wife

in RAIN and sunshine cuckolds go to heaven

RAIN before seven, fine before eleven

it RAINS by planets

if the RAIN comes before the wind, lower your top-sails and take them in; if the wind comes before the rain, lower your topsails and hoist them again

the RAIN comes south when the wind's in the south

RAIN on the green grass, and rain on the tree, and rain on the house-top, but not upon me

RAIN, rain, go away, come again on Saturday

if it RAINS when the wind is in the east, it will rain for twenty-four hours at least

See also WEATHER

REASON

ONE reason is as good as fifty

REASON governs the wise man and cudgels the fool

there is REASON in the roasting of eggs

RECIPROCITY

BIG fleas have little fleas upon their backs to bite them, and little fleas have lesser fleas, and so *ad infinitum*

he that EATS the king's goose shall be choked with his feathers

KA me, ka thee

ONE good turn deserves another

you SCRATCH my back and I'll scratch yours

there is no such THING as a free lunch

RECKLESSNESS

he that BRINGETH himself into needless dangers dieth the devil's martyr

the FISH will soon be caught that nibbles at every bait

FOOLS rush in where angels fear to tread

it is ILL jesting with edged tools

it's ILL putting a naked sword in a madman's hand

if you LEAP into a well Providence is not bound to fetch you out

NOTHING so bold as a blind mare

PEOPLE who live in glass houses shouldn't throw stones

they that SOW the wind shall reap the whirlwind

RECOGNITION

GIVE credit where credit is due

a PROPHET is not without honour save in his own country

RECONCILIATION

AGREE, for the law is costly

let BYGONES be bygones

the DIFFERENCE is wide that the sheets will not decide

it's ILL healing of an old sore

NEGLECT will kill an injury sooner than revenge

OLD pottage is sooner heated than new made

let not the SUN go down on your wrath

though the WOUND be healed, a scar remains

REGRET

he that goes A-BORROWING, goes a-sorrowing

BLESSINGS are not valued until they are gone

BLESSINGS brighten as they take their flight

THINGS done cannot be undone

THINGS past cannot be recalled

TIME and tide wait for no man

TIME lost cannot be recalled

it's no USE crying over spilt milk

a WORD spoken is past recalling

RELIABILITY

a NEAR friend is better than a far-dwelling kinsman

RELIGION

there are no ATHEISTS in foxholes

the JEWS spend at Easter, the Moors at marriages, the Christians in suits

a MAN without religion is like a horse without a bridle

MEAT and mass never hindered man

PRESBYTERIANISM is no religion for a gentleman

See also CHURCH AND CHRISTIANITY; CLERGY

REMEDIES

is there no BALM in Gilead?

a BROKEN leg is not healed by a silk stocking

CARE is no cure

what can't be CURED must be endured

DANGERS are overcome by dangers

DESPERATE diseases call for desperate remedies

DIET cures more than doctors

a DISEASE known is half cured

in DOCK, out nettle

FEED a cold and starve a fever

FEED by measure and defy the physician

FIRE drives out fire

take away FUEL, take away flame

that which is GOOD for the head is evil for the neck and the shoulders

take the HAIR of the dog that bit you

no HERB will cure love

KITCHEN physic is the best physic

LIKE cures like

NATURE, time, and patience are the three great physicians

no REMEDY but patience

there is a REMEDY for everything except death

the REMEDY may be worse than the disease

there's a SALVE for every sore

TEMPERANCE is the best physic

TIME heals all wounds

no WRONG without a remedy

See also DISEASE; HEALTH AND ILLNESS; INFIRMITY; MEDICAL TREATMENT

REMORSE

THINGS done cannot be undone

THINGS past cannot be recalled

it's no USE crying over spilt milk

a WORD spoken is past recalling

REPAIRS

See MAINTENANCE

REPENTANCE

who ERRS and mends to God himself commends

the GREATER the sinner, the greater the saint

LATE repentance is seldom true

there's no LEAPING from Delilah's lap into Abraham's bosom

MERRY nights make sorry days

it is NEVER too late to mend

REPENTANCE comes too late

SHORT pleasure, long lament

REPETITION

a GOOD tale is none the worse for being twice told

he that KNOWS little, often repeats it

LENGTH begets loathing

REPUTATION

BETTER a good cow than a cow of a good kind

it is BETTER to be a cuckold and not know it, than be none and everybody say so

CAESAR's wife must be above suspicion

CALL a man a thief and he will steal

the DEAD have few friends

GIVE a dog a bad name and hang him

a GOOD name is better than a good girdle

a HOG that's bemired endeavours to bemire others

he that has an ILL name is half hanged

the MORE the fox is cursed, the better he fares

get a NAME to rise early, and you may lie all day

RESENTMENT

it's ILL healing of an old sore

ILL will never said well

INJURIES don't use to be written on ice

LENGTH begets loathing

OLD reckonings make new quarrels

TRAMP on a snail and she'll shoot out her horns

when the WELL is full it will run over

WOOD half burnt is easily kindled

RESIGNATION

that which cometh from ABOVE let no man question

BE as be may

as you make your BED, so you must lie in it

BONES bring meat to town

EVERYONE stretches his legs according to the length of his coverlet

when all FRUIT falls, welcome haws

GNAW the bone which is fallen to thy lot

the GOAT must browse where she is tied

the HALF is better than the whole

we must not LIE down and cry God help us

LIKE it or lump it

the NIGHTINGALE and cuckoo sing both in one month

take the ROUGH with the smooth

take the SWEET with the sour

take THINGS as they come

you WIN a few, you lose a few

you can't WIN them all

RESOURCES

you cannot BURN the candle at both ends

EVERYONE stretches his legs according to the length of his coverlet

the GOAT must browse where she is tied

GOOD riding at two anchors

HUNGER and cold deliver a man up to his enemy

don't let your JAWS outrun your claws

who hath no MORE bread than need must not keep a dog

SIT awhile and go a mile

SOFT pace goes far

RESPECT

FAMILIARITY breeds contempt

LEAVE is light

NEVER speak ill of the dead

RESPECT a man, he will do the more

RESPONSIBILITY

EVERY herring must hang by its own gill

if EVERY man would sweep his own doorstep the city would soon be clean

EVERYBODY'S business is nobody's business

that which a MAN causes to be done, he does himself

MUCH coin, much care

NOBLESSE oblige

make a PAGE of your own age

SET the saddle on the right horse

RESTRAINT

BETTER say nothing than nothing to the purpose

BURN not your house to fright away the mice

GIVE neither counsel nor salt till you are asked for it

don't let your JAWS outrun your claws

do not REMOVE a fly from your friend's forehead with a hatchet

RESERVE the master-blow

SIT awhile and go a mile

SOFT pace goes far

TEMPERANCE is the best physic

don't THROW the baby out with the bathwater

let WELL alone

RESULTS

the EFFECT speaks, the tongue needs not

the END crowns the work

the END justifies the means

GARBAGE in, garbage out

as is the GARDENER, so is the garden

GRAIN by grain the hen fills her belly

GREAT oaks from little acorns grow

an INCH is as good as a mile

MANY sands will sink a ship

the RACE is not to the swift, nor the battle to the strong

the TREE is known by its fruit

he who WILLS the end, wills the means

See also CAUSE AND EFFECT

RETALIATION

AFTER wit comes too late

in the COLDEST flint there is hot fire

ONE ill word asketh another

the SECOND blow makes the fray

TRAMP on a snail and she'll shoot out her horns

even a WORM will turn

RETREAT

he who FIGHTS and runs away, lives to fight another day

go FORWARD and fall, go backward and mar all

ONE pair of heels is often worth two pairs of hands

RETRIBUTION

no BAD deed goes unpunished

the BITER is sometimes bit

BLOOD will have blood

CLAW me and I'll claw thee

CURSES, like chickens, come home to roost

a CURST cow has short horns

EVERY dog is allowed one bite

an EYE for eye, and a tooth for a tooth

he that KILLETH a man when he is drunk shall be hanged when he is sober

what's done by NIGHT appears by day

who SPITS against heaven it falls in his face

REVENGE

CONTEMPT will sooner kill an injury than revenge

a CURST cow has short horns

EVERY dog has his day

an EYE for eye, and a tooth for a tooth

the MILLS of God grind slowly, yet they grind exceeding small

the NOBLEST vengeance is to forgive

REVENGE is a dish that is best eaten cold

REVENGE is sweet

had I REVENGED every wrong, I had not worn my skirts so long

See also CURSES; MALICE

REWARD

as you make your BED, so you must lie in it

the BEST fish swim near the bottom

he that BLOWS best bears away the horn

as you BREW, so shall you bake

CROSSES are ladders that lead to heaven

CURSES, like chickens, come home to roost

DESERT and reward seldom keep company

he DESERVES not the sweet that will not taste the sour

the DOG that trots about finds a bone

it is EASIER for a camel to go through the eye of a needle than it is for a rich man to enter into the kingdom of heaven

he that would EAT the fruit must climb the tree

if you would ENJOY the fruit, pluck not the flower

EVERY dog has his day

no GAINS without pains

the GODS send nuts to those who have no teeth

a GOOD dog deserves a good bone

it's an ILL dog that deserves not a crust

it's ILL waiting for dead men's shoes

INDUSTRY is fortune's right hand, and frugality her left

the LAST benefit is most remembered

you can have no MORE of a cat than her skin

you can have no MORE of a fox than the skin

the NET fills though the fisherman sleeps

PAIN is forgotten where gain follows

PAIN is gain

it is a POOR heart that never rejoices

SEEK and ye shall find

no SONG, no supper

as you SOW, so shall you reap

they that SOW the wind shall reap the whirlwind

there is no such THING as a free lunch

you WIN a few, you lose a few

the WORTH of a thing is what it will bring

See also PROFIT AND LOSS

RIGHT AND WRONG

EVERY dog has his day

the GREATER the right, the greater the wrong

LOSERS are always in the wrong

MIGHT is right

do RIGHT and fear no man

TWO blacks don't make a white

TWO wrongs don't make a right

RIPENESS

APPLES taste sweetest when they are going

SOON ripe, soon rotten

RISK

don't put ALL your eggs in one basket

CURIOSITY killed the cat

HIGH places have their precipices

no one LIKES to be the first to step on the ice

he that NEVER climbed never fell

NOTHING ventured, nothing gained

if you PLAY with fire you get burnt

he that PLAYS with cats must expect to be scratched

he who RIDES a tiger is afraid to dismount

VENTURE not all in one bottom

See also CAUTIOUSNESS; COMMITMENT

RIVALRY

DIAMOND cuts diamond

not EVERY man can be vicar of Bowden

there is no GOOD accord where every man would be a lord

when GREEK meets Greek, then comes the tug of war

HAWKS will not pick out hawks' eyes

the JAY bird don't rob his own nest

MAN is to man a wolf

ONE beggar does not hate another as much as one doctor hates another

if you PLAY with boys you must take boys' play

PULL Devil, pull baker

a STERN chase is a long chase

TWO of a trade never agree

RULES

that which cometh from ABOVE let no man question

there is an EXCEPTION to every rule

PLAY the game

RUMOUR

COMMON fame is a common liar

a DOG that will fetch a bone will carry a bone

what EVERYBODY says must be true

he that FALLS in the dirt, the longer he stays there the fouler he is

the MORE you tramp on a turd the broader it grows

NEVER tell tales out of school

they SAY so is half a lie

there's no SMOKE without fire

there is no WHISPERING but there is lying

See also GOSSIP

SACRIFICE

a CANDLE lights others and consumes itself

the MORE cost, the more honour

you cannot make an OMELETTE without breaking eggs

THROW out a sprat to catch a mackerel

SAFETY

SAFETY first

there is SAFETY in numbers

SALVATION

ONCE a whore, always a whore

he that will not be SAVED needs no preacher

the WAY to heaven is alike in every place

SAVING AND SPENDING

KEEP something for the sore foot

it is too LATE to spare when the bottom is bare

LOOK after the pennies and the pounds will look after themselves

a PENNY saved is a penny earned

a PIN a day is a groat a year

what the RAKE gathers, the fork scatters

SAVE something for a rainy day

SAVING is getting

SPARE at the spigot, and let out at the bung-hole

SPARE well and have to spend

SPEND and God will send

SPEND not where you may save, spare not where you must spend

what you SPEND, you have

STORE is no sore

See also DEBT; MONEY

SCEPTICISM

BELIEVE nothing of what you hear, and only half of what you see

SEEING is believing

SEA AND SAILING

he that would LEARN to pray, let him go to sea

MESSMATE before a shipmate, shipmate before a stranger, stranger before a dog

PRAISE the sea but keep on land

if the RAIN comes before the wind, lower your topsails and take them in; if the wind comes before the rain, lower your topsails and hoist them again

the SEA and the gallows refuse none

he that would go to SEA for pleasure, would go to hell for a pastime

SHIPS fear fire more than water

THREE things are insatiable, priests, monks, and the sea

WORSE things happen at sea

See also TIDES

SEASONS

the CUCKOO comes in April, and stays the month of May; sings a song at midsummer, and then goes away

EARLY thunder, early spring

EVERY mile is two in winter

EVERYTHING is good in its season

a FAIR day in winter is the mother of a storm

a GOOD winter brings a good summer

a GREEN winter makes a fat churchyard

ONE woodcock does not make a winter

SALMON and sermon have both their season in Lent

it is not SPRING until you can plant your foot upon twelve daisies

there is no SUMMER but it has a winter

if on the TREES the leaves still hold, the coming winter will be cold

WINTER finds out what summer lays up

See also CHRISTMAS; FARMING AND COUNTRY SAYINGS; WEATHER

SECRETS

ANYTHING may be spoken if it be under the rose

a DOG that will fetch a bone will carry a bone

EVERY family has a skeleton in the cupboard

FIELDS have eyes, and woods have ears

no NAMES, no pack drill

NEVER tell tales out of school

what's done by NIGHT appears by day

NOTHING is burdensome as a secret

wherever there is a SECRET there must be something wrong

he that TELLS a secret is another's servant

TELL it not in Gath

TELL not all you know, nor do all you can

THREE may keep a secret, if two of them are dead

TRUTH should not always be revealed

WALLS have ears

See also CONCEALMENT; DISCRETION; SILENCE

SECURITY

a BAD padlock invites a picklock

FAST bind, fast find

LAST make fast

it is too LATE to shut the stable-door after the horse has bolted

no LOCK will hold against the power of gold

an OLD poacher makes the best gamekeeper

SAFE bind, safe find

SELF-DECEPTION

how we APPLES swim

an ARGUS abroad but a mole at home

the CAT shuts its eyes while it steals cream

he that is DRUNK is as great as a king

the FLY sat upon the axletree of the chariot-wheel and said, what a dust do I raise!

the HUNCHBACK does not see his own hump, but sees his companion's

there are NONE so blind as those who will not see

there are NONE so deaf as those who will not hear

SELF-INTEREST

the BEST manure is under the farmer's foot

where the CARCASS is, there shall the eagles be gathered together

the CAT knows whose lips she licks

COMMAND your man and do it yourself

don't CUT off your nose to spite your face

the DUMB man gets no land

EACH bird loves to hear himself sing

EAGLES don't catch flies

EAGLES fly alone

HAWKS will not pick out hawks' eyes

INTEREST will not lie

the JAY bird don't rob his own nest

no one should be JUDGE in his own cause

KILL not the goose that lays the golden egg

a MAN is a lion in his own cause

MEN are blind in their own cause

NEAR is my coat but nearer my skin

there is NOTHING like leather

ONE hand for oneself and one for the ship

PEOPLE who live in glass houses shouldn't throw stones

he is a POOR cook that cannot lick his own fingers

the SHOEMAKER's son always goes barefoot

SPARE to speak and spare to speed

don't THROW the baby out with the bathwater

the VICAR of Bray will be vicar of Bray still

he is not WISE that is not wise for himself

SELFISHNESS

the BEST manure is under the farmer's foot

he CARES not whose child cry so his laugh

EACH bird loves to hear himself sing

a WILFUL man must have his way

See also OWNERSHIP

SELF-JUSTIFICATION

a BIRD never flew on one wing

he who EXCUSES himself, accuses himself

SELF-KNOWLEDGE

he that DESPISES his own life is soon master of another's

KNOW thyself

he is not LAUGHED at that laughs at himself first

you NEVER know what you can do till you try

the OWL was a baker's daughter

the PEACOCK hath fair feathers, but foul feet

SICKNESS shows us what we are

SELF-PRESERVATION

he that goes BAREFOOT must not plant thorns

CALL the bear 'uncle' till you are safe across the bridge

CAST a bone in the devil's teeth

he is like a CAT; fling him which way you will, he'll light on his legs

take the CHESTNUTS out of the fire with the cat's paw

CUT not the bough that thou standest upon

no FENCE against ill fortune

he who FIGHTS and runs away, lives to fight another day

if you can't be GOOD, be careful

he that HATH his hand in the lion's mouth must take it out as well as he can

he must have IRON nails that scratches a bear

KEEP yourself from the anger of a great man, from the tumult of a mob, from a man of ill fame, from a widow that has been thrice married, from a wind that comes in at a hole, and from a reconciled enemy

LEAN not on a reed

LOOK to thyself when thy neighbour's house is on fire

don't go NEAR the water until you learn how to swim

ONE pair of heels is often worth two pairs of hands

on PAINTING and fighting look aloof

SAFETY first

SELF-PRESERVATION is the first law of nature

if you can't STAND the heat, get out of the kitchen

the VICAR of Bray will be vicar of Bray still

SELF-RELIANCE

COMMAND your man and do it yourself

EAGLES fly alone

EVERY herring must hang by its own gill

EVERY man for himself and the devil take the hindmost

EVERY man is the architect of his own fortune

EVERY man is the son of his own works

let EVERY man sweep the ice with his own broom

EVERY tub must stand on its own bottom

FORTUNE helps those who help themselves

GOD helps those who help themselves

he HELPS little that helps not himself

we must not LIE down and cry God help us

PADDLE your own canoe

make a PAGE of your own age

SELF do, self have

if you WANT a thing done well, do it yourself

if you would be WELL served, serve yourself

SELF-RESPECT

NOBODY calls himself rogue

SCORNFUL dogs will eat dirty puddings

don't WASH your dirty linen in public

SELF-RESTRAINT

DALLY not with women or money

FAIR and soft goes far in a day

he is not FIT to command others that cannot command himself

it is GOOD to be merry and wise

LEAVE off while the play is good

LEAVE well alone

LIVE in the shade

METTLE is dangerous in a blind horse

ORDER is heaven's first law

SAVE your breath to cool your porridge

TEMPERANCE is the best physic

SENSITIVITY

BLUSHING is a sign of grace

if your EAR burns someone is thinking about you

he that has a GREAT nose thinks everybody is speaking of it

no MAN is angry that feels not himself hurt

NEVER tread on a sore toe

a WORD to the wise is enough

SERVANTS

BEGGARS breed and rich men feed

a COMMON servant is no man's servant

why KEEP a dog and bark yourself?

SATURDAY's flit will never sit

a SERVANT and a cock should be kept but a year

he who SERVES is preserved

SERVICE is no inheritance

no SILVER, no servant

a SMILING boy seldom proves a good servant

SEX

BED is the poor man's opera

when the BELLY is full the mind is among the maids

why BUY a cow when milk is so cheap?

DALLY not with women or money

the DIFFERENCE is wide that the sheets will not decide

DIRTY water will quench fire

the MORE hazelnuts, the more bastard children

SHAME

he that BORROWS must pay again with shame or loss

he that has no SHAME has no conscience

it is a SHAME to steal but a worse to carry home

SHARING

a COMMON servant is no man's servant

EVERYBODY's business is nobody's business

SHARE and share alike

he who SHARES has the worst share

a TROUBLE shared is a trouble halved

THREE helping one another bear the burthen of six

if TWO ride on a horse, one must ride behind

TWO in distress makes sorrow less

when TWO friends have a common purse one sings and the other weeps

SHORTCUTS

the HIGHWAY is never about

the LONGEST way round is the shortest way home

the SHORT cut is often the longest way round

SHYNESS

FAINT heart ne'er won fair lady

the LAME tongue gets nothing

SIGNIFICANCE

CATCH not at the shadow and lose the substance

the DEVIL rides upon a fiddlestick

EVERY picture tells a story

no HAIR so small but hath his shadow

SILENCE

BETTER say nothing than nothing to the purpose

from a CHOLERIC man withdraw a little, from him that says nothing for ever

a CLOSE mouth catches no flies

HEAR all, see all, say nowt

HEAR much, speak little

KEEP your mouth shut and your eyes open

he that KNOWS not how to hold his tongue, knows not how to talk

the LAME tongue gets nothing

NEVER tell tales out of school

a QUIET tongue makes a wise head

QUIETNESS is best

a SHUT mouth never fills a black coffin

SILENCE catches a mouse

SILENCE is a woman's best garment

SILENCE is golden

SILENCE is wisdom

SILENCE means consent

he cannot SPEAK well that cannot hold his tongue

SPEECH is silver, silence is golden

a STILL tongue makes a wise head

TACE is Latin for candle

one may THINK that dares not speak

there is a TIME to speak, and a time to be silent

WIDE ears and a short tongue

See also CONCEALMENT; DISCRETION; SECRETS

SIN

CHARITY covers a multitude of sins

DISSEMBLED sin is double wickedness

EVERY sin brings its punishment with it

the GREATER the sinner, the greater the saint

there's no LEAPING from Delilah's lap into Abraham's bosom

OLD sins cast long shadows

SATAN reproves sin

it is a SIN to lie against the devil

it is a SIN to steal a pin

SINCERITY

what comes from the HEART goes to the heart

the NEARER the church, the further from God

PRACTISE what you preach

SIZE

the BEST things come in small packages

BIG fleas have little fleas upon their backs to bite them, and little fleas have lesser fleas, and so *ad infinitum*

BIG is beautiful

however BIG the whale may be, the tiny harpoon can rob him of life

the BIGGER they are, the harder they fall

GREAT bodies move slowly

the GREATEST crabs be not all the best meat

a LITTLE body often harbours a great soul

LITTLE fishes slip through nets but great fishes are taken

LITTLE knoweth the fat man what the lean man thinketh

a LITTLE pot is soon hot

LONG and lazy, little and loud

MEN are not to be measured by inches

SHORT folk are soon angry

SMALL is beautiful

as SORE fight wrens as cranes

what she WANTS in up and down she hath in round about

SKILL

the BETTER, the worse

a CARPENTER is known by his chips

CUNNING is no burden

EVERY man to his trade

JACK of all trades is master of none

a MAN of many trades begs his bread on Sunday

if you can't RIDE two horses at once, you shouldn't be in the circus

SKILL and confidence are an unconquered army

a SOW may whistle, though it has an ill mouth for it

SLANDER

FLING enough dirt and some will stick

GIVE a dog a bad name and hang him

SLANDER leaves a scar behind it

TRUTH is no slander

See also CONFESSION

SLEEP

go to BED with the lamb and rise with the lark

let not a CHILD sleep upon bones

he that DRINKETH well sleepeth well, and he that sleepeth well thinketh no harm

ONE hour's sleep before midnight is worth two after

SIX hours' sleep for a man, seven for a woman and eight for a fool

SLEEP is the brother of death

let SLEEPING dogs lie

there will be SLEEPING enough in the grave

the SLEEPING fox catches no poultry

he that SLEEPS bites no body

SNEEZING

SNEEZE on a Monday, you sneeze for danger

SOLDIERS

an ARMY marches on its stomach

he is the BEST general who makes the fewest mistakes

EVERY soldier has the baton of a field-marshal in his knapsack

the FIRST duty of a soldier is obedience

OLD soldiers never die, they simply fade away

SOLDIERS and travellers may lie by authority

SOLDIERS in peace are like chimneys in summer

SOLITUDE

a CROWD is not company

a WISE man is never less alone than when he is alone

SOLUTIONS

AVOIDANCE is the only remedy

DESPERATE diseases call for desperate remedies

it is GOOD to have a cloak for the rain

if you're not PART of the solution, you're part of the problem

UNLIKELIEST places are often likelier than those that are likeliest

SORROW

EVERY heart hath its own ache

GOD send you joy, for sorrow will come fast enough

JOY and sorrow are next door neighbours

REMEMBRANCE of past sorrow is joyful

SADNESS and gladness succeed each other

SORROW comes unsent for

SORROW is always dry

when SORROW is asleep wake it not

SORROW is good for nothing but sin

SMALL sorrows speak; great ones are silent

TWO in distress makes sorrow less

he is WELL worth sorrow that buys it with silver

SPECIALIZATION

he who COMMENCES many things finishes but a few

EVERY man to his trade

JACK of all trades is master of none

a MAN of many trades begs his bread on Sunday

MANY irons in the fire, some must cool

SPORTS

in SPORTS and journeys men are known

SPORTSMANSHIP

PLAY the game

STATUS

a CAT may look at a king

there is no DIFFERENCE of bloods in a basin

EAT peas with the king and cherries with the beggar

he that EATS the king's goose shall be choked with his feathers

EVERYBODY loves a lord

HALL benches are slippery

HIGH winds blow on high hills

he that LIES upon the ground can fall no lower

LOWLY sit, richly warm

See also CLASS

STORY-TELLING

a TALE never loses in the telling

the TALE runs as it pleases the teller

STRATEGY

ATTACK is the best form of defence

if you can't BEAT 'em, join 'em

BETWEEN two stools you fall to the ground

a CASTLE that speaketh is near a surrender

he that will CATCH eels must disturb the flood

don't CHANGE horses in midstream

DESTROY the lion while he is yet but a whelp

DESTROY the nests and the birds will fly away

DIVIDE and rule

when in DOUBT, do nowt

he that would have EGGS must endure the cackling of hens

if you would ENJOY the fruit, pluck not the flower

FIGHT fire with fire

when all FRUIT falls, welcome haws

FRUIT out of season, sorrow out of reason

if you would have FRUIT, you must bring the leaf to the grave

it is GOOD to make a bridge of gold to a flying enemy

it is HARD to turn tack upon a narrow bridge

he who HESITATES is lost

the HIGHER the tree, the sweeter the plum

when you don't KNOW what to do – wait

the LAPWING cries farthest from her nest

LEAVE off while the play is good

a MAN surprised is half beaten

if the MOUNTAIN will not go to Mahomet, Mahomet must go to the mountain

NEVER give a sucker an even break

NEVER tell thy foe that thy foot acheth

ONE step at a time

ONE sword keeps another in the scabbard

POLICY goes beyond strength

QUIT while you are ahead

RESERVE the master-blow

the ROUGH net is not the best catcher of birds

SAY before they say

SEPTEMBER blow soft, till the fruit's in the loft

SOFTLY, softly, catchee monkey

SPEAK softly and carry a big stick

TELL it not in Gath

like TREE, like fruit

in VAIN the net is spread in the sight of the bird

STRENGTH

he may BEAR a bull that hath borne a calf

a CHAIN is no stronger than its weakest link

only an ELEPHANT can bear an elephant's load

GOD makes the back to the burden

not even HERCULES could contend against two

SUCCESS

FAR shooting never killed bird

NICE guys finish last

NINETY per cent of inspiration is perspiration

NOTHING succeeds like success

he that ONCE hits will be ever shooting

SUCCESS makes a fool seem wise

he that will THRIVE must rise at five

SUFFERING

the COMFORTER's head never aches

CROSSES are ladders that lead to heaven

EACH cross hath its inscription

no CROSS, no crown

what can't be CURED must be endured

no coming to HEAVEN with dry eyes

an HOUR of pain is as long as a day of pleasure

he that LIVES long suffers much

PAIN is forgotten where gain follows

PAIN is gain

PAIN past is pleasure

the PLEASURES of the rich are bought with the tears of the poor

of SUFFERANCE cometh ease

it is not the SUFFERING but the cause which makes a martyr

SUFFICIENCY

he is at EASE who has enough

ENOUGH is as good as a feast

ENOUGH is enough

SUITABILITY

BORROWED garments never fit well

if the CAP fits, wear it

GOD makes the back to the burden

GOD tempers the wind to the shorn lamb

what's SAUCE for the goose is sauce for the gander

WIDE will wear but narrow will tear

SUPERFICIALITY

APPEARANCES are deceptive

the BAIT hides the hook

BE what you would seem to be

if the BEARD were all, the goat might preach

it is not the BEARD that makes the philosopher

BEAUTY is but a blossom

BEAUTY is in the eye of the beholder

BEAUTY is no inheritance

BEAUTY is only skin deep

the COWL does not make the monk

EMPTY vessels make the most sound

EVERY devil has not a cloven hoof

EVERY picture tells a story

GILT spurs do not make the knight

he is a GOOD dog who goes to church

a GREAT book is a great evil

PLEASE your eye and plague your heart

SHALLOW streams make most din

STILL waters run deep

SUPERSTITIONS AND SAYINGS

a CHERRY year, a merry year; a plum year, a dumb year

if at CHRISTMAS ice hangs on the willow, clover may be cut at Easter

a CROW on the thatch, soon death lifts the latch

EASTER in snow, Christmas in mud; Christmas in snow, Easter in mud

on the FIRST of March, the crows begin to search

at EASTER let your clothes be new, or else be sure you will it rue

HELP you to salt, help you to sorrow

ONE for sorrow, two for joy; three for a girl, four for a boy; five for silver, six for gold; seven for a secret, never to be told; eight for heaven, nine for hell; and ten for the devil's own self

it RAINS by planets

if the ROBIN sings in the bush then the weather will be coarse; but if the robin sings in the barn then the weather will be warm

See also DAYS; OMENS

SURPRISE

a MAN surprised is half beaten

the STING is in the tail

UNLIKELIEST places are often likelier than those that are likeliest

SUSPICION

CHARITY covers a multitude of sins

JEALOUSY shuts one door and opens two

SUSPICION has double eyes

SYMPATHY

one has ALWAYS strength enough to bear the misfortunes of one's friends

the COMFORTER's head never aches

SYMPATHY without relief is like mustard without beef

he that is WARM thinks all so

TACT

ADMONISH your friends in private, praise them in public

although there EXIST many thousand subjects for elegant conversation, there are persons who cannot meet a cripple without talking about feet

it is ILL talking of a halter in the house of a man that was hanged

NEVER tread on a sore toe

TALK

FINE words butter no parsnips

GIVE losers leave to speak

SPEECH is the index of the mind

TALK is but talk

TALKING pays no toll

he that TALKS much of his happiness, summons grief

he that TALKS to himself talks to a fool

See also LOQUACIOUSNESS

TASTE

EVERY man after his fashion

EVERYONE to his taste

HORSES for courses

TASTES differ

TAXES

NOTHING is certain but death and taxes

PINCH on the parson's side

RENDER unto Caesar that which is Caesar's

TEACHERS

he who CAN does, he who cannot teaches

See also LEARNING

TEMPTATION

AWAY goes the devil when he finds the door shut against him

without BUSINESS, debauchery

the DEVIL dances in an empty pocket

the DEVIL finds work for idle hands

the FAIREST silk is soonest stained

GIVE a man enough rope and he will hang himself

an IDLE brain is the Devil's workshop

an OPEN door may tempt a saint

THIEVES

a BEGGAR may sing before a pickpocket

CALL a man a thief and he will steal

the HOLE calls the thief

there is HONOUR among thieves

the JAY bird don't rob his own nest

no LARDER but hath its mice

ONCE a thief, always a thief

ONE thief robs another

if there were no RECEIVERS, there would be no thieves

SET a thief to catch a thief

he that SHOWS his purse bribes the thief

the THIEF doth fear each bush an officer

when THIEVES fall out honest men come by their own

See also CRIME AND CRIMINALS

THINKING

THINK first and speak afterwards

THINK much, speak little and write less

they that THINK none ill are soonest beguiled

THINK on the end before you begin

one may THINK that dares not speak

THINKING is very far from knowing

he that THINKS amiss concludes worse

he THINKS not well that thinks not again

THOUGHT is free

THOROUGHNESS

GIVE a cob a hat and a pair of shoes and he'll last for ever

no GOOD building without a good foundation

a HIGH building, a low foundation

if a JOB's worth doing, it's worth doing well

LEAVE no stone unturned

the MILLS of God grind slowly, yet they grind exceeding small

NEVER do things by halves

a NEW broom sweeps clean

SOON enough, if well enough

don't SPOIL the ship for a ha'porth of tar

if a THING is worth doing, it's worth doing well

if you WANT a thing done well, do it yourself

WELL done is twice done

what is WELL done is done soon enough

See also MAINTENANCE

THREATS

the BAIT hides the hook

a BARKING dog never bites

if you cannot BITE, never show your teeth

out of OFFICE, out of danger

ONE sword keeps another in the scabbard

THREATENED men live long

THRIFT

CUT your coat according to your cloth

INDUSTRY is fortune's right hand, and frugality her left

THRIFT is a great revenue

TIDES

EVERY flow hath its ebb

the HIGHEST flood has the lowest ebb

the TIDE never goes out so far but it always comes in again

See also SEA AND SAILING

TIME

the CLOCK goes as it pleases the clerk

he that GAINS time gains all things

HALF an hour is soon lost at dinner

LOSE an hour in the morning, chase it all day

if you LOSE your time you cannot get money or gain

NEVER is a long time

TIME devours all things

TIME flies

there is a TIME for everything

he that hath TIME hath life

TIME heals all wounds

TIME is money

TIME lost cannot be recalled

TIME tries all things

TIME will tell

TIME works wonders

TIMES change and we with time

TIMES past cannot be recalled

See also INEVITABILITY

TOLERANCE

let the CAT wink and let the mouse run

though the CAT winks a while, yet sure she is not blind

EVERY dog is allowed one bite

LIVE and let live

MASTERS should be sometimes blind, and sometimes deaf

ONCE nought, twice somewhat

WINK at small faults

TOWNS

GOD made the country, and man made the town

what MANCHESTER says today, the rest of England says tomorrow

there was NEVER a good town but had a mire at one end of it

OXFORD for learning, London for wit, Hull for women, and York for a tit

TRANSIENCE

what a DAY may bring a day may take away

the DOGS bark but the caravan goes on

the FAIREST rose at last is withered

an HOUR may destroy what an age was a building

like ICE, anger passes away

MAN is a bubble

the MIRTH of the world dureth but a while

what ONE day gives us, another takes away from us

PAUL's will not always stand

QUICKLY come, quickly go

the SHARPER the storm, the sooner it's over

a THOUSAND pounds and a bottle of hay is all one thing at doomsday

TODAY a man, tomorrow none

here TODAY, gone tomorrow

TRAVEL

go ABROAD and you'll hear news of home

it is BETTER to travel hopefully than to arrive

EVERY mile is two in winter

he goes FAR that never returns

GOOD company is the shortest cut

a MAN knows his companion in a long journey and a little inn

when in ROME, do as the Romans do

SEE Naples and die

SOLDIERS and travellers may lie by authority

in SPORTS and journeys men are known

TRAVEL broadens the mind

a TRAVELLER may lie with authority

TRAVELLERS change climates not conditions

he TRAVELS fastest who travels alone

TREASON

the TREASON is loved but the traitor is hated

TREES

BEWARE of the oak, it draws the stroke; avoid the ash, it courts the flash

EVERY elm has its man

GREAT trees keep down little ones

the HIGHER the tree, the sweeter the plum

the PINE wishes herself a shrub when the axe is at her root

PLANT the crab-tree where you will, it will never bear pippins

REMOVE an old tree and it will die

you cannot SHIFT an old tree without it dying

as a TREE falls, so shall it lie

when the TREE is fallen, all go with their hatchet

the TREE is known by its fruit

like TREE, like fruit

if on the TREES the leaves still hold, the coming winter will be cold

as the TWIG is bent, so is the tree inclined

WALNUTS and pears you plant for your heirs

a WILLOW will buy a horse before an oak will pay for a saddle

See also FARMING AND COUNTRY SAYINGS; GARDENING AND GROWING

TROUBLE

AFTER a storm comes a calm

let SLEEPING dogs lie

NEVER trouble trouble till trouble troubles you

STIR with a knife, stir up strife

a TROUBLE shared is a trouble halved

TRUST

ANYTHING may be spoken if it be under the rose

ARTFUL speech and an ingratiating demeanour rarely accompany virtue

BELIEVE nothing of what you hear, and only half of what you see

when DISTRUST enters in at the foregate, love goes out at the postern

EVERYTHING tastes of porridge

take HEED of reconciled enemies and of meat twice boiled

NEVER trust a tailor that does not sing at his work

SEEING is believing

THREE things are not to be credited

if you TRUST before you try, you may repent before you die

TRUST is the mother of deceit

TRUST not a new friend nor an old enemy

TRUST not one night's ice

TRUTH

CRAFT must have clothes but truth loves to go naked

FACE to face the truth comes out

FOLLOW not truth too near the heels, lest it dash out they teeth

FOOLS and madmen speak the truth

it takes a GOOD many shovelfuls of earth to bury the truth

the GREATER the truth, the greater the libel

HALF the truth is often a whole lie

there's MANY a true word spoken in jest

out of the MOUTHS of babes and sucklings

in too MUCH dispute truth is lost

there are NONE so blind as those who will not see

there are NONE so deaf as those who will not hear

TELL the truth and shame the Devil

a THOUSAND probabilities do not make one truth

TRUTH and sweet oil always come to the top

TRUTH fears no trial

TRUTH has a scratched face

there is TRUTH in wine

TRUTH is no slander

TRUTH is stranger than fiction

TRUTH lies at the bottom of a well

TRUTH's best ornament is nakedness

TRUTH should not always be revealed

TRUTH will out

TYRANNY

'tis TIME to fear when tyrants seem to kiss

UNHAPPINESS

EVERY heart hath its own ache

he is a FOOL that is not melancholy once a day

it is GOOD to have company in misery

NOTHING dries sooner than a tear

UPBRINGING

BIRTH is much but breeding more

BREEDING rather than birth

DOGS bark as they are bred

the MAN who is born in a stable is a horse

NATURE passes nurture

NURTURE passes nature

See also CLASS; HEREDITY

USE

it is BETTER to wear out than to rust out

a BOW long bent at last waxeth weak

IRON not used soon rusts

the PITCHER goes so often to the well that it is broken at last

STANDING pools gather filth

USE legs and have legs

a USED key is always bright

USEFULNESS

AFTER death the doctor

it is a BAD cause that none dare speak in

EMPTY hands no hawks allure

FAR shooting never killed bird

why KEEP a dog and bark yourself?

KEEP a thing seven years and you'll always find a use for it

KEEP no more cats than will catch mice

it is a POOR dog that is not worth whistling for

the PROOF of the pudding is in the eating

WATER afar quencheth not fire

VALUE

BLESSINGS are not valued until they are gone

BLESSINGS brighten as they take their flight

the COW knows not the worth of her tail till she loses it

the DEEPER the sweeter

no MAN is indispensable

a MAN of straw is worth a woman of gold

we NEVER know the worth of water till the well is dry

you NEVER miss the water till the well runs dry

NONE can guess the jewel by the casket

NOUGHT is never in danger

it is a POOR dog that is not worth whistling for

the PROOF of the pudding is in the eating

THINGS that are hard to come by are much set by

the WORTH of a thing is what it will bring

VANITY

EACH bird loves to hear himself sing

EVERY ass loves to hear himself bray

there is no such FLATTERER as a man's self

MEN's years and their faults are always more than they are willing to own

SELF-PRAISE is no recommendation

TELL a woman she's a beauty and the devil will tell her so fifty times

VARIETY

VARIETY is the spice of life

VICE

DISEASES are the price for ill pleasures

FORBIDDEN fruit tastes sweetest

what MAINTAINS one vice would bring up two children

VICE is often clothed in virtue's habit

See also CRIME AND CRIMINALS

VIOLENCE

he that HURTS another hurts himself

he who LIVES by the sword dies by the sword

REVOLUTIONS are not made with rose-water

VIRTUE

BEAUTY without virtue is a flower without perfume

GOOD men are scarce

the SUN loses nothing by shining into a puddle

VICE is often clothed in virtue's habit

VIRTUE is its own reward

VOLUNTEERS

See COERCION

VULNERABILITY

he that hath a HEAD of wax must not walk in the sun

the HIGHER the monkey climbs the more he shows his tail

the MOUSE that has only one hole is easily taken

who hath SKIRTS of straw needs fear the fire

WAR AND PEACE

there are no ATHEISTS in foxholes

where DRUMS beat, laws are silent

FAR shooting never killed bird

a JUST war is better than an unjust peace

he that PREACHES war is the Devil's chaplain

if you WANT peace, prepare for war

WAR makes thieves, and peace hangs them

when WAR begins Hell opens

WARS are sweet to those that know them not

See also PEACE

WARNING

let ANOTHER's shipwreck be your sea-mark

a DOG will bark ere he bite

FOREWARNED is forearmed

HALF warned, half armed

See also CAUTIOUSNESS; DANGER

WASTE
the BEST things may be abused
a CARPENTER is known by his chips
don't CAST your pearls before swine
CATS eat what hussies spare
HASTE makes waste
MEN cut large thongs of other men's leather
SEE a pin and let it lie, you'll want a pin before you die
SPARE at the spigot, and let out at the bung-hole
SPILT wine is worse than water
WASTE makes want
WASTE not, want not

WATCHFULNESS
the GOOD Bernard does not see everything
KEEP your mouth shut and your eyes open
KEEP your weather-eye open
LOOKERS-ON see most of the game
NEVER praise a ford till you get over
PROSPERITY lets go the bridle
See also CAUTIOUSNESS

WEAK LINKS
a CHAIN is no stronger than its weakest link
the THREAD breaks where it is weakest
the WORST spoke in a cart breaks first

WEAKNESS
ANGER without power is folly
the CORD breaketh at the last by the weakest pull
EVERY man hath his weak side
the HIGHER the monkey climbs the more he shows his tail
it is ILL sitting at Rome and striving with the Pope
the LEAST boy always carries the greatest fiddle
the MOUSE that has only one hole is easily taken
ONE butcher does not fear many sheep
the SPIRIT is willing but the flesh is weak
WEAK men had need be witty
the WEAKEST go to the wall

WEALTH
ABUNDANCE, like want, ruins many
a BARLEY-CORN is better than a diamond to a cock
BEAR wealth, poverty will bear itself
he who would BRING home the wealth of the Indies, must carry the wealth of the Indies with him
CUT your coat according to your cloth
EVERYONE stretches his legs according to the length of his coverlet
GEAR is easier gained than guided
GENTLEMEN and rich men are venison in heaven
GIVE a man an annuity and he'll live for ever
the GOAT must browse where she is tied
GOD help the poor, for the rich can help themselves
GOLD goes in at any gate except heaven's
GOLD may be bought too dear
when we have GOLD we are in fear; when we have none we are in danger
a GREAT fortune is a great slavery
a HEAVY purse makes a light heart
an INCH of gold will not buy an inch of time
ITCH and ease can no man please
LIGHT gains make heavy purses
LITTLE gear, less care
LONGEST at the fire soonest finds cold
don't let your JAWS outrun your claws
MANY haws, many snows
the MORE you get, the more you want
MUCH coin, much care
MUCH would have more
NINE tailors make a man
PAINS to get, care to keep, fear to lose
PEACE makes plenty
the PLEASURES of the rich are bought with the tears of the poor
PLENTY makes poor
he is RICH enough that wants nothing
RICH folk have many friends
the RICH man has his ice in the summer and the poor man gets his in the winter
a RICH man's money hangs him oftentimes
RICHES are but the baggage of fortune
RICHES are like muck, which stink in a heap, but spread abroad make the earth fruitful
RICHES have wings
RICHES serve a wise man but command a fool

SHROUDS have no pockets

WEALTH is best known by want

WEALTH is enemy to health

WEALTH makes worship

come with the WIND, go with the water

WEATHER

AFTER a storm comes a calm

AFTER a wet year a cold one

AFTER rain comes sunshine

AFTER wind comes rain

ALTHOUGH the sun shine, leave not thy cloak at home

as AUGUST so the next February

BEWARE of the oak, it draws the stroke; avoid the ash, it courts the flash

a BLUSTERING night, a fair day follows

BUTTON up to the chin till May comes in

CALM weather in June sets corn in tune

if CANDLEMAS Day be sunny and bright, winter will have another flight; if Candlemas Day be cloudy with rain, winter is gone, and won't come again

ne'er CAST a clout till May be out

CHANGE of weather is the discourse of fools

if at CHRISTMAS ice hangs on the willow, clover may be cut at Easter

CLEAR autumn, windy winter; warm autumn, long winter

when the CLOUDS go up the hills, they'll come down by the mills

if the COCK crows on going to bed, he's sure to rise with a watery head

if the COCK moult before the hen we shall have weather thick and thin, but if the hen moult before the cock we shall have weather hard as a block

a COLD April the barn will fill

when the CUCKOO comes he eats up all the dirt

as the DAY lengthens, so the cold strengthens

a DRIPPING June sets all in tune

DUNDER do gally the beans

EARLY thunder, early spring

EASTER in snow, Christmas in mud; Christmas in snow, Easter in mud

an ENGLISH summer, three hot days and a thunderstorm

EVENING red and morning grey help the traveller on his way

a FAIR day in winter is the mother of a storm

in FAIR weather prepare for foul

if in FEBRUARY there be no rain, 'tis neither good for hay nor grain

FOG on the hill, water to the mill; fog in the hollow, fine day to follow

a FOUL morning may turn to a fair day

as the FRIDAY, so the Sunday

FROST and fraud both end in foul

the FULL moon brings fair weather

a GAUDY morning bodes a wet afternoon

a GOOD hay year a bad fog year

a GOOD winter brings a good summer

a GREEN winter makes a fat churchyard

HAIL brings frost in the tail

HAPPY is the bride the sun shines on

if the ICE will bear a man before Christmas, it will not bear a duck after

a JANUARY spring is worth nothing

LONG foretold long last, short notice soon past

MACKEREL sky and mares' tails make lofty ships carry low sails

MANY hips and haws, many frosts and snaws

so MANY mists in March, so many frosts in May

MARCH comes in like a lion and goes out like a lamb

MIST from the hill brings water to the mill

a MISTY morning may have a fine day

the MONTH that comes in good will go out bad

it NEVER rains but it pours

the NORTH wind doth blow and we shall have snow

as NOVEMBER so the following March

when the OAK is before the ash, then you will get only a splash

if the OLD year goes out like a lion, the new year will come in like a lamb

a PALE moon doth rain, a red moon doth blow; a white moon doth neither rain nor snow

the PALENESS of the pilot is a sign of a storm

a PECK of March dust is worth a king's ransom

the PORPOISE plays before a storm

in RAIN and sunshine cuckolds go to heaven

RAIN before seven, fine before eleven

if the RAIN comes before the wind, lower your topsails and take them in; if the wind comes before the rain, lower your topsails and hoist them again

RAIN on the green grass, and rain on the tree, and rain on the house-top, but not upon me

RAIN, rain, go away, come again on Saturday

a RAINBOW in the morning is the shepherd's warning; a rainbow at night is the shepherd's delight

when it RAINS and the sun shines at the same time the devil is beating his wife

it RAINS by planets

if it RAINS when the wind is in the east, it will rain for twenty-four hours at least

RED sky at night, shepherd's delight; red sky in the morning, shepherd's warning

if the ROBIN sings in the bush then the weather will be coarse; but if the robin sings in the barn then the weather will be warm

ROBIN HOOD could brave all weathers but a thaw wind

SAINT Swithin's Day, if thou dost rain, for forty days it will remain; Saint Swithin's Day, if thou be fair, for forty days 'twill rain no more

SEPTEMBER blow soft, till the fruit's in the loft

the SHARPER the storm, the sooner it's over

a SNOW year, a rich year

SOUND travelling far and wide a stormy day will betide

TRUST not one night's ice

the WEST wind always brings wet weather, the east wind wet and cold together, the south wind surely brings us rain, the north wind blows it back again

the WEST wind is a gentleman and goes to bed

a WET May brings plenty of hay

when the WIND is in the east, 'tis neither good for man nor beast

when the WIND is in the south it blows the bait into the fish's mouth

when the WIND is in the west the weather is at the best

See also FARMING AND COUNTRY SAYINGS; RAIN; SEASONS

WEDDINGS

HAPPY is the bride the sun shines on

ONE wedding brings another

WHISTLING

a WHISTLING woman and a crowing hen are neither fit for God nor men

WICKEDNESS

BETTER be a fool than a knave

BETTER to hang than to hold

BLACK will take no other hue

he that hath done ILL once will do it again

KNAVES and fools divide the world

KNAVES and whores go by the clock

MAN is to man a wolf

the MORE knave, the better luck

the MORE wicked, the more fortunate

there is no PACK of cards without a knave

See also GUILT; HELL AND DAMNATION

WIDOWS

he that MARRIES a widow and three children marries four thieves

WILFULNESS

there are NONE so blind as those who will not see

there are NONE so deaf as those who will not hear

a WILFUL man must have his way

WILL will have will, though will woe win

WINE

the BEST wine comes out of an old vessel

there is a DEVIL in every berry of the grape

DRINK wine and have the gout, drink no wine and have the gout too

GOOD wine engendreth good blood

GOOD wine needs no bush

OLD friends and old wine are best

SPILT wine is worse than water

from the SWEETEST wine, the tartest vinegar

there is TRUTH in wine

make the VINE poor and it will make you rich

WINE and wenches empty men's purses

WINE and youth increase love

WINE counsels seldom prosper

WINE hath drowned more men than the sea

WINE is a turncoat

when the WINE is in, the wit is out

WINE savours of the cask

WINE wears no breeches

WISDOM

BETTER be happy than wise

don't put the CART before the horse

it is EASY to be wise after the event

EXPERIENCE is the mother of wisdom

what the FOOL does in the end, the wise man does at the beginning

a FOOL thinks himself wise

it is GOOD to be merry and wise

one must HOWL with the wolves

one cannot LOVE and be wise

no MAN is wise at all times

the OLDER the wiser

when PASSION entereth at the foregate, wisdom goeth out of the postern

PIE-LID makes people wise

a TRULY great man never puts away the simplicity of a child

WISDOM goes beyond strength

some are WISE and some are otherwise

it is a WISE child that knows its own father

a WISE head makes a still tongue

a WISE lawyer never goes to law himself

a WISE man changes his mind, a fool never will

a WISE man is never less alone than when he is alone

he is not a WISE man who cannot play the fool on occasion

WISE men learn by others' faults, fools by their own

he is not WISE that is not wise for himself

a WISE woman is twice a fool

a WORD to the wise is enough

See also EXPERIENCE; LEARNING

WISHFUL THINKING

if the ADDER could hear and the blindworm could see, neither man nor beast would ever go free

if my AUNT had been a man, she'd have been my uncle

BEWARE of 'had I wist'

I wouldn't CALL the king my cousin

he that hath no CHILDREN feedeth them fat

don't COUNT your chickens before they are hatched

if IFS and ands were pots and pans, there'd be no work for tinkers' hands

JACK would be a gentleman if he could speak French

PIGS might fly, if they had wings

if the SKY falls we shall catch larks

we SOON believe what we desire

the WISH is father to the thought

if WISHES were horses, beggars would ride

WISHES won't wash dishes

WIT

AFTER wit comes too late

BREVITY is the soul of wit

when the DRINK is in, the wit is out

GLOWING coals sparkle oft

WANT is the whetstone of wit

when the WINE is in, the wit is out

WIT without wisdom is but little worth

WIVES

See HUSBANDS AND WIVES

WOMEN

ARTHUR could not tame a woman's tongue

when an ASS climbs a ladder we may find wisdom in women

a BAD woman is worse than a bad man

BECAUSE is a woman's reason

BEWARE of the forepart of a woman, the hind part of a mule, and all sides of a priest

a DOG's nose and a maid's knees are always cold

the FAIREST silk is soonest stained

the FEMALE of the species is more deadly than the male

the GIST of a lady's letter is in the postscript

GLASSES and lasses are brittle ware

HELL hath no fury like a woman scorned

if the HEN does not prate, she will not lay

MAIDS say nay and take

a MAN is as old as he feels, and a woman as old as she looks

MANY women, many words

when the MISTRESS is the master, parsley grows the faster

OLD maids lead apes in hell

ONE hair of a woman draws more than a team of oxen

where ROSEMARY flourishes the lady rules

she SMELLS best that smells of nothing

there is no such THING as good small beer, good brown bread, or a good old woman

THREE women make a market

a WHISTLING woman and a crowing hen are neither fit for God nor men

WOEFUL is the household that wants a woman

a WOMAN, a dog and a walnut tree, the more you beat them the better they be

a WOMAN and a cherry are painted for their own harm

a WOMAN and a ship ever want mending

a WOMAN is an angel at ten, a saint at fifteen, a devil at forty and a witch at fourscore

a WOMAN is a weathercock

a WOMAN's place is in the home

a WOMAN's strength is in her tongue

a WOMAN's work is never done

WOMEN are saints in church

WOMEN must have the last word

WORDS

BARE words are no good bargain

FAIR words break no bones

FEW words are best

FINE words butter no parsnips

GOD is better pleased with adverbs than with nouns

that is not GOOD language which all understand not

HARD words break no bones

a MAN of words and not of deeds is like a garden full of weeds

the MORE said, the less done

it is not with SAYING honey, honey, that sweetness will come into the mouth

a WORD spoken is past recalling

a WORD to the wise is enough

WORDS are wind

WORK AND WORKERS

one BEATS the bush, another takes the bird

a BEGGAR is never out of his way

BELLS call others but themselves enter not into the church

BETTER sit idly than work for nothing

you cannot BURN the candle at both ends

a CARPENTER is known by his chips

so we get the CHINK, we'll bear with the stink

the CLERK makes the justice

the CLOCK goes as it pleases the clerk

let the COBBLER stick to his last

come DAY, go day, God send Sunday

the DAY is short and the work is long

no DAY without a line

DIRTY hands make clean money

EAT till you sweat and work till you freeze

EVERY cook praises his own broth

EVERY man to his trade

FORECAST is better than work hard

as is the GARDENER, so is the garden

as GOOD play for nought as work for nought

the GREATEST clerks be not the wisest men

an HOUR in the morning is worth two in the evening

it is IDLE to swallow the cow and choke on the tail

it's ILL waiting for dead men's shoes

INDUSTRY is fortune's right hand, and frugality her left

there is KNAVERY in all trades

KNAVES and whores go by the clock

LABOUR is light where love doth pay

the LABOURER is worthy of his hire

a LEAN fee is a fit reward for a lazy clerk

LITERATURE is a good staff but a bad crutch

not a LONG day but a good heart rids work

MANY hands make light work

NEVER work with children or animals

NINE tailors make a man

NINETY per cent of inspiration is perspiration

if you PAY peanuts, you get monkeys

QUICK at meat, quick at work

SATURDAY's flit will never sit

THREE helping one another bear the burthen of six

there are TRICKS in every trade

TWO of a trade never agree

a WOMAN's work is never done

WORK expands so as to fill the time available

it is not WORK that kills, but worry

WORK today for you know not how much you may be hindered tomorrow

if you won't WORK you shan't eat

as is the WORKMAN so is the work

what is a WORKMAN without his tools?

See also OVERWORK; PAYMENT

WORRY

BEHIND the horseman sits black care

the BLACK ox treads on one's foot

CARE killed the cat

he that COUNTS all costs will never put plough in the earth

HORNS and grey hairs do not come by years

LIGHT cares speak, great ones are dumb

MUCH coin, much care

PAST cure, past care

a POUND of care will not pay an ounce of debt

SUFFICIENT unto the day is the evil thereof

WRITING

the CALF, the goose, the bee: the world is ruled by these three

the GIST of a lady's letter is in the postscript

a GOOSE-QUILL is more dangerous than a lion's claw

the PEN is mightier than the sword

PENS may blot but they cannot blush

THINK much, speak little and write less

THINK with the wise, but talk with the vulgar

by WRITING you learn to write

WRONGDOING

WRONG has no warrant

no WRONG without a remedy

he WRONGS not an old man that steals his supper from him

YOUTH

EARLY master, long knave

a GROWING youth has a wolf in his belly

where OLD age is evil, youth can learn no good

you cannot put an OLD head on young shoulders

a RAGGED colt may make a good horse

RULE youth well, for age will rule itself

the YOUNG cock crows as he heard the old one

YOUNG folks think old folks to be fools, but old folks know young folks to be fools

a YOUNG man should not marry yet, an old man not at all

YOUNG men may die, but old men must die

a YOUNG physician fattens the churchyard

YOUNG saint old devil

YOUTH and old age will never agree

YOUTH must be served

See also AGE